The Middle East

A History

Volume I

Population Density of the Middle East

250+	60–125	2–25
125–250	25–60	0–2

Uninhabited

Persons per sq. mile

Major Occupations of the Middle East

Manufacturing	Grazing	Fishing
Agriculture	Non-production	

POLAND

LUX. GERMANY
Prague
CZECH. REP.

Paris

Danube

SLOVAKIA
Bratislava

Orleans

Munich

Vienna

Budapest

Tours

AUSTRIA

HUNGARY

Nantes

Rhine

Graz

Poitiers

LIECH.

SWITZ.

Bern

Lyon

ATLANTIC OCEAN

FRANCE

Loire

SLO. Ljubljana
Zagreb

Turin

Milan

Verona

Trieste
Venice

CROATIA

Bordeaux

Garonne

Avignon

Genoa

Bologna
SAN
MARINO

BOSNIA
AND
HERZEGOVINA

Belgrade

Toulouse

Nice

Florence

Sarajevo

YUGOSLAVIA

Nish

A Coruña

Bilbao

Marseille

Toulon

ITALY

ADRIATIC SEA

Burgos

Ebro

ANDORRA

Zaragoza

CORSICA
(FR.)

Rome

Skopje

MACEDONIA

Oporto

Duero

Valladolid

Barcelona

*TYRRHENIAN
SEA*

Naples

Tirana

ALBANIA

PORTUGAL

Salamanca

Madrid

Tagus

Brindisi

IONIAN IS.

Toledo

Caceres

Tagus

Valencia

BALEARIC IS.

MAJORCA

SARDINIA
(IT.)

Lisbon

SPAIN

Alicante

Palermo

Córdoba

Granada

Cartagena

Annaba

Bizerte

SICILY

Seville

Malaga

Almeria

Algiers

Constantine

Tunis

Cadiz

Gibraltar (BR.)

Tangier

Ceuta
(SP.)

Melilla
(SP.)

Oran

Kasserine

MEDITERRANEAN

MALTA

Rabat

Fez

TUNISIA

Casablanca

Gabes

MOROCCO

ATLAS MOUNTAINS

Tripoli

Misratah

Béchar

Touggourt

Benghazi

Ouargla

Surt

TRIPOLITANIA

Al Ugaylah

Ghadamis

CYRENAICA

ALGERIA

LIBYA

In Salah

Reggane

Ghat

Marzuq

FEZZAN

MAURITANIA

S A H A R A

MALI

0	250	500 mi
0	400	800 km

NIGER

CHAD

10°

0°

10°

20°

Climate of the Middle East

- Highland
- Mediterranean
- Steppe
- Desert

Physical Contour of the Middle East

- Over 10,000 ft.
- 5,000–10,000 ft.
- 2,000–5,000 ft.
- 1,000–2,000 ft.
- 0–1,000 ft.
- Below Sea Level

The Mediterranean and the Middle East

50°

UKRAINE
Dnipropetrovsk
MOLDOVA
Chisinau
Odessa
Dnieper
Rostov
Don
Volga
KAZAKHSTAN
RUSSIA
Astrakan

ROMANIA
SEA OF AZOV
CRIMEA

Bucharest
Sevastopol
Danube

Sofia
BULGARIA
Varna
BLACK SEA
CAUCASUS MTS.
CASPIAN SEA

Istanbul
Bosphorus
Sinop
Batumi
GEORGIA
Tbilisi
Trabzon
Ardahan
Kars
ARMENIA
AZERBAIJAN
Baku
40°

GREECE
Dardanelles
Ankara
Yerevan
AEGEAN SEA
Izmir
TURKEY
Murat
Lake Van
Tabriz
Lake Urmia
SPORADES
Athens
Konya
Adana
Antalya
TAURUS MTS.
Iskenderun
Aleppo
Mosul
Tehran

RHODES
CYPRUS
Nicosia
SYRIA
Kirkuk
Hamadan
IRAN

CRETE
SEA
Beirut
LEBANON
Damascus
Isfahan

Darnah
Haifa
ISRAEL
Tel Aviv-Yafo
Port Said
Amman
SYRIAN
DESERT
IRAQ
Baghdad
MESOPOTAMIA
Euphrates
Tigris

Tobruq
Alexandria
Matruh
Jerusalem
JORDAN
Basrah
Abadan
30°

El Alamein
QATTARA DEPRESSION
Cairo
Suez Canal
Suez
NAFUD DESERT
KUWAIT
Kuwait
Shiraz
Siwa Oasis
SINAI PEN.

EGYPT
Farafra Oasis
Asyut
Nile
EASTERN DESERT
HIJAZ
BAHRAIN
Manama
Dhahran
QATAR
Doha
Persian Gulf

LIBYAN
Kufra Oasis
Kharga Oasis
Aswan High Dam
Aswan
Lake Nasser
NUBIAN
Medina
NAJD
Riyadh
U.A.E.

DESERT
SAUDI ARABIA

Wadi Halfa
DESERT
Red Sea
Mecca

Dongola
Port Sudan
ASIR
20°

SUDAN
30°
ERITREA 40°
YEMEN
OMAN
50°

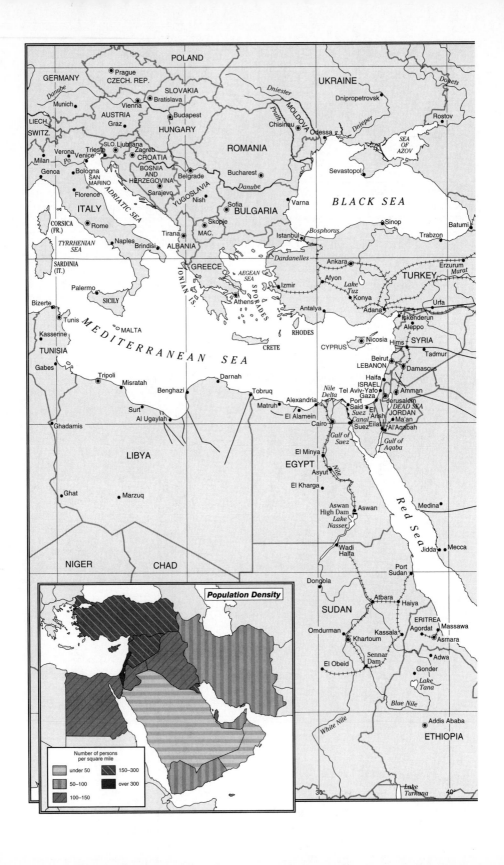

POLAND

GERMANY
Prague
CZECH. REP.
SLOVAKIA
Munich
Vienna
Bratislava
AUSTRIA
Graz
Budapest
LIECH.
SWITZ.
HUNGARY
SLO. Ljubljana
Verona
Trieste
Zagreb
Venice
CROATIA
Milan
Po
Genoa
Bologna
SAN
MARINO
BOSNIA
AND
HERZEGOVINA
Belgrade
Florence
Sarajevo
YUGOSLAVIA
Nish
ITALY
Rome
Tirana
Skopje
MAC.
Naples
ALBANIA
Brindisi
CORSICA
(FR.)
TYRRHENIAN
SEA
SARDINIA
(IT.)
GREECE

Danube
Dniester
Prut
MOLDOVA
Chisinau
Odessa

UKRAINE
Donets
Dnipropetrovsk
Dnieper
Rostov
SEA
OF
AZOV
Sevastopol

ROMANIA
Bucharest
Danube
Sofia
BULGARIA
Varna
BLACK SEA
Sinop
Batumi
Trabzon
Istanbul
Bosphorus
Dardanelles
Ankara
Erzurum
Murat
AEGEAN
SEA
Izmir
Afyon
Lake
Tuz
Konya
TURKEY
Urfa
SPORDES
Athens
Antalya
Adana
Iskenderun
Aleppo
RHODES
Hims
SYRIA
CRETE
CYPRUS
Nicosia
Tadmur
Beirut
LEBANON
Damascus

Palermo
SICILY
Bizerte
Tunis
MALTA
Kasserine
TUNISIA
Gabes
Tripoli
Misratah
Darnah
Benghazi
Tobruq
Surt
Al Ugaylah
Ghadamis

M E D I T E R R A N E A N   S E A

Nile
Delta
Haifa
ISRAEL
Tel Aviv-Yafo
Gaza
Amman
Alexandria
Port
Said
Jerusalem
DEAD SEA
JORDAN
Matruh
Suez
Canal
Arish
Ma'an
El Alamein
Cairo
Suez
Eilat
Al'Aqabah
Gulf of
Suez
Gulf of
Aqaba

LIBYA

EGYPT
El Minya
Asyut
Nile
El Kharga
Ghat
Marzuq
Aswan
High Dam
Aswan
Lake
Nasser
Medina
Red Sea
Wadi
Halfa
Jidda
Mecca
Port
Sudan

NIGER
CHAD
Dongola
Atbara
Haiya
SUDAN
ERITREA
Omdurman
Kassala
Agordat
Massawa
Khartoum
Asmara
Sennar
Dam
Adwa
El Obeid
Gonder
Lake
Tana
Blue Nile
White Nile
Addis Ababa
ETHIOPIA
30°
40°
Lake
Turkana

Population Density

Number of persons
per square mile

under 50
50–100
100–150
150–300
over 300

The Middle East

RUSSIA

Don
Volga

Astrakan

Atyrau

KAZAKHSTAN

Lake Balkhash

ARAL SEA

Syr Darya

Bishkek

GEORGIA
Tbilisi

UZBEKISTAN

Tashkent

KYRGYZISTAN

Ardahan
ARMENIA
Kars
Yevlax
Yerevan
AZERBAIJAN
Baku

Turkmenbashi

Amu Darya

Bukhara
Samarkand

40°

CASPIAN SEA

TURKMENISTAN

Charjew

Dushanbe
TAJIKISTAN

CHINA

Lake Van

Tabriz

Ashkabad

Kerki

Khorugh

Lake Urmia

Meshhed

Mosul

Tehran

Kirkuk

Hamadan

Qumm

Herat

AFGHANISTAN
Kabul

Peshawar
Bannu
Srinagar
Islamabad

Al Hadithah

Kermanshah

IRAN

Baghdad

Isfahan

Yazd

Farah

Qandahar

Indus

Lahore

IRAQ

Euphrates

Tigris

Karun

Abadan

Kerman

Zahedan

Quetta

PAKISTAN

Multan

30°

Ad Duwayd
As Salman
Basrah

Shiraz

Mirjaveh

Nushki
Dalbandin

Rafha

KUWAIT
Kuwait
Wafra

Strait of Hormuz

Turbat

Sukkur
Larkana

Jaisalmer

Jodhpur

Persian Gulf

BAHRAIN
Manama

Dubai

Hyderabad

INDIA

Dhahran
Al Hufuf
QATAR
Doha

Abu Dhabi

Gulf of Oman

Karachi

Riyadh

UNITED ARAB EMIRATES

Muscat

Mandvi

SAUDI ARABIA

Khaluf

MASIRAH

OMAN

20°

Jizan

Salalah

ARABIAN SEA

Sana

YEMEN

Bab al-Mandeb

Assab

Aden

Gulf of Aden

SOCOTRA (YEMEN)

DJIBOUTI
Djibouti

Berbera

10°

Qardho

INDIAN OCEAN

SOMALIA

| 0 | 250 | 500 mi |
| 0 | 400 | 800 km |

Oil pipline

Railroad

50°

60°

70°

The Middle East

A History

Volume I

FIFTH EDITION

Sydney Nettleton Fisher

Late Professor of History
The Ohio State University

William Ochsenwald

Professor of History
Virginia Polytechnic Institute and State University

The McGraw-Hill Companies, Inc.

New York   St. Louis   San Francisco   Auckland   Bogotá   Caracas
Lisbon   London   Madrid   Mexico City   Milan   Montreal   New Delhi
San Juan   Singapore   Sydney   Tokyo   Toronto

McGraw-Hill

A Division of The **McGraw·Hill** Companies

THE MIDDLE EAST: A HISTORY
Volume I

This book is printed on acid-free paper.

1 2 3 4 5 6 7 9 0   FGRFGR   9 0 9 8 7 6

ISBN 0-07-021231-7

This book was set in Times Roman by Ruttle, Shaw & Wetherill, Inc.
The editor was Leslye Jackson;
the design manager was Christopher Brady;
the production supervisor was Kathryn Porzio.
Cover photo: Tony Stone/David Reynolds
Project supervision was done by Editorial Services of New England, Inc.
Quebecor Printing, Fairfield, was printer and binder.

Library of Congress Cataloging-in-Publication Data

Fisher, Sydney Nettleton,
    The Middle East: a history / Sydney Nettleton Fisher, William
Ochsenwald. — 5th ed.
        p.   cm.
    Includes bibliographical references and index.
    ISBN 0–07–021231–7 (v. 1). — ISBN 0–07–021719–X (v.
2)
    1. Middle East—History.   2. Middle East—History—20th century.
I. Ochsenwald, William.   II. Title.
DS62.F5   1996   96–42103
956—dc20

http://www.mhcollege.com

About the Authors

SYDNEY NETTLETON FISHER was born in Warsaw, New York, in 1906 and attended Oberlin College (A.B., M.A.) and the University of Illinois (Ph.D., 1935). He was a member of the faculty of the Ohio State University from 1937 to 1972, except for leaves of absence to accept visiting professorships and grants for foreign travel and study. In addition, Professor Fisher worked with various branches of the U.S. government as a specialist in Middle Eastern problems. He was a member of Phi Beta Kappa, a Fellow of the Royal Historical Society, and a member of the Accadèmia del Mediterràneo. He served as Director of Publications of the Middle East Institute and as editor of *The Middle East Journal* and contributed articles to numerous journals and encyclopedias. He was the author or editor of several books, among them *Foreign Relations of Turkey, 1481–1512* (1948), *Social Forces in the Middle East* (1955), and *The Military in the Middle East* (1963). He died on December 10, 1987.

WILLIAM OCHSENWALD attended the Ohio State University (B.A., M.A.) and the University of Chicago (Ph.D., 1971). He has been a member of the faculty of Virginia Polytechnic Institute and State University since 1971, with occasional leaves for research in Lebanon, Syria, Jordan, Israel, Egypt, Turkey, Britain, and France. He has received grants from the Fulbright-Hays program; the American Research Institute in Turkey; the former United States Department of Health, Education, and Welfare; and the Social Science Research Council and American Council of Learned Societies. In 1979–1980 and 1991 he was an Associate Fellow of the Middle East Centre, University of Cambridge. He is the author of two books, *The Hijaz Railroad* (1980) and *Religion, Society, and the State in Arabia* (1984), and the co-editor of *Nationalism in a Non-National State: The Dissolution of the Ottoman Empire* (1977); and has published many articles, among them essays appearing in *The Middle East Journal, International Journal of Middle East Studies, Die Welt des Islams, The Muslim World, Arabian Studies,* and the *Encyclopaedia Britannica.*

Contents

Part Two
THE OTTOMAN AND SAFAVID EMPIRES

Part Three
THE NINETEENTH-CENTURY MIDDLE EAST

VOLUME II BRIEF CONTENTS

List of Maps

List of Charts and Genealogies

Preface to the Fifth Edition

Sydney Nettleton Fisher's *The Middle East: A History* has been for many years the most important work in its field. Since it first appeared in 1959 it has gone through two later editions published in 1969 and 1979. After Professor Fisher's death in 1987, I completed work on the fourth edition, which was published in early 1990.

For the fifth edition of this work I have made numerous changes affecting almost every chapter. Many significant events have taken place in the Middle East and discussion of these matters has been added. In addition, much new research dealing with earlier times has been incorporated into appropriate chapters. Since general studies, monographs, and journal articles of high quality dealing with the history of the Middle East continue to appear in great abundance, I have made changes in the bibliographic references found at the end of each chapter. Despite these additions and changes, the total length of the work is about the same as the previous edition. I have divided the book into two volumes so as to make it easier to use in the two or three term course sequence. Each volume includes a brief table of contents for the other volume, as part of the frontmatter.

On a more substantial level, I have expanded the geographic scope of the book, thereby including more discussion of central Asia, the Caucasus, and Afghanistan, as well as Libya, both for earlier periods and for the nineteenth and twentieth centuries. And while maintaining the basic approach of earlier editions, I have placed greater emphasis upon cultural, religious, gender, and social history. Other changes to this edition include a revised and expanded map program, the addition of a glossary, and the elimination of much detail, so as to permit attention to broader themes.

Throughout the book I have attempted to help the reader more easily understand periodization in the history of the Islamic Middle East. To this end, I have reorganized, expanded, and clarified the treatment of medieval history presented in Chapters 6, 11, and 12. Discussion of Islamic civilization in the Middle East has also been reorganized, with a separate chapter on social patterns. Chapter 19 now contains all the discussion of the Safavids, thereby making it easier to follow their story. Chapter 20 represents a new interpretation of the seventeenth century Ottoman Empire, while a more traditional view is still maintained for the eighteenth century in Chapter 21. To encourage comparisons, I have combined analysis of Turkish and Arab nationalism with late Ottoman political history in Chapter 27. Similarly, the discussions of combat during World War I and its diplomatic consequences have been placed together in Chapter 31.

Expansion of the scope of the text to include Afghanistan, central Asia, the Caucasus, and Libya is particularly noticeable in Part IV on the twentieth century. Chapters dealing with the period since 1945 for Iran and for Egypt, Sudan, and Libya have been subdivided chronologically so as to provide better treatment of the main themes of their history. I have placed the discussion of Iraq in a separate chapter from that devoted to Lebanon and Syria, just as I created a separate chapter about Yemen to indicate its historical differences from the other Arabian Peninsula states. The history of Jordan has been integrated into Chapters 48 and 49. While retaining the basic plan of Chapter 50 from the fourth edition, its length has been almost doubled so as to provide a fuller treatment of general trends since 1945.

I have attempted to provide a somewhat more systematic transliteration system for the fifth edition than was previously employed, but I have not attempted, nor achieved, complete consistency. As Sydney Fisher pointed out in his preface to the first edition, words from Middle Eastern languages have been written in English in different ways, thereby causing much confusion. While most specialists have strongly held but divergent views on proper transliteration, I have usually opted for what seem the simplest and most widely employed methods and spellings. Thus, I have shown 'ains in Arabic words in only one case (the Ba'th political party), and only in a few cases have I employed the symbols needed to represent modern Turkish spelling. In some instances, however, I have opted for a spelling that is closer to the original, as in the words Quran and ulama, instead of Koran and ulema.

Many people have helped me in various ways as I worked on this new edition. Students in my classes critically read and discussed the fourth edition of this work and offered useful suggestions for improvements. Dr. Jean Braden reminded me of the need to retain the basic approaches in earlier editions. Once again, professional colleagues who have written other general studies of the history of the Middle East provided important new ideas, data, and interpretations which challenged me to rethink my own earlier work. I found especially useful and stimulating works by Albert Hourani, William L. Cleveland, Arthur Goldschmidt, Jr., and Ira M. Lapidus. Karl Barbir, Justin McCarthy, Donald Reid, and John Voll offered valuable suggestions for improvements. I greatly appreciated the comments of Linda Darling which made me reexamine the paradigm of Ottoman decline. And finally, I would like to thank all the manuscript reviewers whose valuable comments helped to shape this text: Karl Barbir, Siena College; Justin McCarthy, University of Louisville; Ronald Davis, Western Michigan University; Donald Reid, Georgia State University; and Ezel Kural Shaw, California State University, Northridge. Of course, I alone am responsible for those faults still remaining in this new edition.

My general approach to the history of the Middle East rests upon foundations established with the help of dedicated teachers and scholars with whom I have studied. They are Sydney Fisher, William McNeill, Marshall Hodgson, William Polk, Richard Chambers, Reuben Smith, Leonard Binder, and Marvin Zonis. I have also gained many insights about general surveys of the history of the Middle East from discussions with Jere Bacharach, Herbert Bodman, Lynne Rienner, and Marilyn Waldman.

The members of the Virginia Tech Middle East Studies Society have been of considerable assistance through their stimulating and provocative discussions. I wish to thank David Barzilai, Burton Kaufman, Charles Kennedy, Robert Landen, Dean O'Donnell, Djavad Salehi Isfahani, and Peter Schmitthenner. I am especially grateful to Glenn Bugh, whose tactful help on ancient history was invaluable. I highly appreciate the help of Andrea Kavanaugh, who provided exciting insights into communications technology in the Middle East and North Africa. I acknowledge with gratitude the support of the Department of History at Virginia Tech under the leadership of Burton Kaufman and Albert Moyer. The three departmental secretaries—Linda Fountaine, Jan Francis, and Rhonda Wells—assisted me patiently and efficiently. Janet Bland and others on the staff of the Interlibrary Loan office of Newman Library worked diligently in providing access to many books and articles.

I am very grateful to my friends and family who have provided encouragement and support during the long time needed to complete this project. My thanks go in particular to Stewart A. Dean, Elizabeth Fisher, Donald Miller, Ronald and Joyce Ochsenwald, and Charles and Barbara Kaiser.

I can only hope that this fifth edition will be as useful to students and the general public as preceding versions have been. In this way the memory of Sydney Fisher, an inspiring teacher, writer, and friend, will be commemorated.

William Ochsenwald

Preface to the First Edition

For the last two thousand years and more the West has been drawn to, involved in, and fascinated by the culture, religion, resources, and politics of the Middle East. First the Greeks, then the Romans, later the Western Europeans, and now the Americans are discovering the Middle East and its peoples. Historically, the area has been labeled the Orient, the East, and Levant, or the Near East; at present the most widely used term is the Middle East.

The United States, because of her great power and world position since the end of World War II, finds herself concerned with the contemporary problems of the Middle East. In general, Americans of today, many of whom have just become cognizant of the existence of the Middle East, find numerous aspects of its life and affairs quite unintelligible. This is particularly true when these complexities are expressed in the various and often conflicting pronouncements of propagandists for the Arabs, the Israelis and Zionism, the imperialists, the oil companies, the internationalists, the isolationists, the various nationalisms of the Middle East, and all sundry interests.

The attempt of this volume has been to present a brief account of the contemporary Middle Eastern scene so that the beginning college student or general reader can place the area in its proper setting and perspective. Many of the present situations and problems cannot be appreciated or evaluated properly without a knowledge and comprehension of the past, since the contemporary civilization of the Middle East probably has deeper and more significant roots in its past culture and experience than many other civilizations.

With this in mind, it was deemed advisable to begin the story, after a short introduction, with the life of the prophet Muhammad and the revolutionary changes that he made upon the society of his time. From this point the narrative has been carried forward, changing the central locus of the scene from Medina to Damascus to Baghdad to Asia Minor to Istanbul and back to the Arab lands as the fortunes of the area have developed, and at the same time examining each era more in detail as the present is approached.

Certain technicalities have been simplified for the beginner. The titles of many positions, past and present, have been translated into English equivalents in order not to confuse the reader with strange words or tire his eyes with unfamiliar combinations of letters and words. The transliteration of Middle Eastern proper names has always presented difficulties. In Western literature pertaining to the Middle East, one can find the name of the Prophet rendered as Muhammad, Mohammed, Mohammad, Mohamed, Mahomet, Mehmed, Mehmet, Mehemet, and several other ways. In this book, Muhammad has been used for Arabs, Mehmed for Turks, and Mohammed for some others when individuals spelled the name in that fashion. For most words a spelling has been employed that would render them and their pronunciation most easily adopted by American readers. Where names of places or people have acquired a widely accepted Western spelling, those forms have been used.

Since almost every volume concerning detailed or specialized aspects of Middle Eastern life and affairs contains considerable bibliographical material, and because of the excellent and wide coverage provided in Richard Ettinghausen's *A Selected and Annotated Bibliography of Books and Periodicals in Western Languages dealing with the Near and Middle East with Special Emphasis on Mediaeval and Modern Times* (The Middle East Institute, Washington, D.C., 1952 and 1954), the inclusion of an extensive bibliography has not been felt necessary. The bibliographical entries at the end of the chapters have been supplied to indicate to the beginning student where easily accessible additional material on particular subjects may be obtained. These titles are suggested to serve as second steps for inquiring students who wish to dig more deeply into the many topics discussed only summarily in this text.

In gathering material for this volume it has been necessary to refer to a wide range of books, produced after years of diligent research and study by several generations of scholars in various lands. All will recognize my debt to these; students familiar with the literature of the diverse aspects of Middle Eastern history will appreciate my indebtedness to scholars of other years. This text could not have been written without their labors.

Through the years it has been my good fortune to obtain a closer knowledge of many aspects of Middle Eastern affairs and society through personal conversations and correspondence with many individuals concerned with that area of the world. Without mentioning names, I wish to thank them for the contributions they have made, sometimes unknowingly, to this text. Specifically I desire to pay tribute to inspiring teachers and mentors who have given me a better understanding of general and detailed problems and periods of Middle Eastern history. They are Frederick B. Artz of Oberlin College; Dr. Edgar J. Fisher of Amherst, Virginia; the late Albert Howe Lybyer of the University of Illinois; Philip K. Hitti and the late Walter Livingston Wright, Jr., of Princeton University; and Paul Wittek of the University of London.

In addition to these I am under deep obligation to my colleagues Professors William F. McDonald and John R. Randall for their criticism and aid in regard to certain chapters. Also, Dr. Halford L. Hoskins of the Library of Congress and Professor George G. Arnakis of the University of Texas read the entire volume, offered valuable suggestions, and caught numerous errors and slips. Dr. J. Merle Rife, State University, Indiana, Pennsylvania, was most helpful in assisting in the compilation of the bibliographical references.

However, any faults in fact or judgment which remain are my sole responsibility. Further recognition is due The Ohio State University Graduate School for assistance in the preparation of the manuscript.

This text could not have been prepared without the tolerance and cooperation of my entire family, which has lived with the manuscript for several years.

Sydney Nettleton Fisher

The Middle East

A History

Volume I

Geographic Prologue

GEOGRAPHY

Since the end of World War II the term Middle East has referred to that area of the world comprising the present political states of Egypt, Sudan, Lebanon, Syria, Israel and the Occupied Territories, Jordan, Iraq, Saudi Arabia, Kuwait, Bahrain, Qatar, the United Arab Emirates, Oman, Yemen, Turkey, and Iran. In addition to this central core region of the Middle East, other nearby localities are now or have been in the past associated culturally and politically with it, including Afghanistan, Pakistan, central Asia, the Caucasus, the Balkan Peninsula, Cyprus, Libya, Tunisia, Algeria, Morocco, and Spain. Many people in the modern Middle East use this term to designate their region even though it originated in Britain and the United States and therefore reflects a geographic definition of world regions as seen from London and Washington. In earlier times, the peoples of the Middle East viewed their region as the center of the world, while the lands to the east and west, including Europe and later the Americas, were seen as the peripheries.

Two geographic features of the Middle East have been significant in all periods of history. Its location has given it an important, sometimes strategic, central position between Africa and Eurasia, and between the Mediterranean world and the Asia of India and China. Nations, tribes, traders, armies, and pilgrims—peoples on the move—have traversed the Middle East, finding the land bridge convenient and along the way discovering the wealth of the area and the civilizations of its peoples.

The second important geographic feature is the relative magnitude of the Middle East. Arabia, the central land mass of the Middle East, embraces an area about the same size as that of the United States east of the Mississippi River plus Texas and California. The southern shore facing the Indian Ocean from Aden to Muscat spans the same distance as that between Boston and New Orleans; on the west, the Red Sea is as wide as Lake Erie is long, and the distance from Aden to Port Said is nearly the same as that from New York to Denver. Northward from Arabia proper to the Turkish frontier is another 400 miles, or 644 kilometers. When Egypt, Iran, and Turkey are added, the area becomes equivalent to that of the continental United States or about thirty times the size of Britain.

Stretching out 2000 miles (3218 km.) westward from the mouth of the Nile River to the Atlantic Ocean lies North Africa, culturally a part of the Middle East since the end of the seventh century. Moreover, the delimitation of the Middle East could include the central Asian republics, Afghanistan, and Pakistan, with such historic cities as Bukhara, Samarkand, Kabul, and Lahore. Thus, the physical size of the Middle East becomes impressive to Europeans and Americans who are accustomed to seeing these areas in the framework of maps of Asia and Africa.

PHYSIOGRAPHY

The geologic characteristics of the Middle East show a wide variety of land features, ranging from great bodies of water to low-lying land and swampy regions to rough mountain areas. Over the past 7000 years or so there seems to have been no important physiographic change except that the deltas of most of the rivers have grown and extended the land seaward. In western Turkey, for example, animals now graze on the floodplain of the Meander River in the exact spot where the Persian fleet vanquished the Greeks in antiquity.

Arabia, in general, is a tilted plateau, slanting upward from the northeast to the southwest with a sharp drop in Yemen from 12,000 feet (3657 m.) down to the Red Sea. Central Turkey and central Iran are elevated plateaus, in places reaching an altitude of 8000 feet (2438 m.). Rugged mountains dominate Middle Eastern geography. From a high center in northwestern Iran in the neighborhood of Mount Ararat, mountain ranges up to 18,000 feet (5486 m.) in altitude branch out in several chains: the Elburz group, running eastward south of the Caspian Sea; the Zagros system, a wide series of ranges protruding in a southeasterly direction to Afghanistan and India; and the famed Taurus Mountains, pushing southwestward to the Mediterranean and separating the Anatolian plateau from Syria. The numerous mountains have tended to divide and separate the residents of the Middle East, while allowing relatively small groups of mountaineers to defend themselves easily against armies coming from the plains. Earthquakes in the mountainous zones have often caused great damage, as in 1990, when at least 25,000 people were killed in northern Iran.

Rivers have played an important role in fostering political unity and settled agriculture, and they have deeply influenced the development of civilization in the Middle East. Two river systems are basic to the history of the area: the Nile and the Tigris-Euphrates. Flowing from central Africa and Ethiopia, the Nile passes through a relatively flat region in the Sudan, where an enormous swamp impedes transportation in the south; the Nile, the world's longest river, then reaches the cataract zone north of Khartoum, where a gorge has been cut. Below Aswan, the Nile flows through a well-developed valley about 6 miles (10 km.) wide to Cairo, where the delta begins. Before the construction of the Aswan High Dam in 1970, the river started to rise in Egypt in August, reaching its peak in September, 18 feet above the low of April and May. Each year some 110 million tons of sediment, rich in mineral substances, are carried into Egypt, and more than half of this silt formerly reached the delta.

The other great river system, the Tigris-Euphrates, rises in the highlands of eastern Turkey. Winter snowfall feeds both streams, which turn and twist through narrow defiles, emptying out upon the plateau plains of Syria and Kurdistan. Rushing southward, the rivers converge upon Baghdad but meet only about 230 miles (370 km.) farther on where they form the Shatt al-Arab, which flows gently for about 75 miles (121 km.) to the Persian (or Arabian) Gulf. The rivers are at their lowest in September and October but then begin to rise, reaching a flood stage in April for the Tigris and, until recently, in May for the Euphrates. The Tabqa Dam in Syria, completed in 1973, and the Turkish Keban Dam on the Euphrates control much of the flooding, generate electric power, and extend the arable lands in both countries. Within historic times silt from the Tigris and the Euphrates and two Iranian tributaries of the former filled in the Persian Gulf from near the site of Baghdad to the present shoreline.

Three straits play a major role in Middle Eastern commerce and strategy: the Bab al-Mandeb and the Strait of Hormuz at the entrances from the Indian Ocean to the Red Sea and the Persian Gulf, and the famous straits that form the waterway from the Black Sea to the Aegean Sea. The last of these has historically been the most important. From the Black Sea extends the narrow Bosphorus, a 17-mile (28-km.) waterway. Everywhere the channel is deep, and the drop-off at the edge is so sharp that vessels requiring considerable draft may tie up at many places along the shore. On a point of land in Europe where the Bosphorus empties into the Sea of Marmara stands one of the great cities of the Middle East—variously known as Byzantium, Constantinople, or Istanbul. The Sea of Marmara extends some 125 miles southwestward to the Dardanelles. This historic passage, often called the Hellespont, is 36 miles (57 km.) long and empties into the Aegean. The Bosphorus, Marmara, and Dardanelles separate Europe from Asia yet serve as a strong connecting link between east and west. Economically, politically, and strategically, the straits have been important in controlling passage between the Mediterranean and the Black seas.

CLIMATE

During the fourth glacial period, some 25,000 years ago, when much of Europe and northern Asia was covered with an ice sheet, the southern Middle East and the Sahara regions were moist and dotted with lakes and seas, a well-watered wooded land abounding with animals. As the ice receded, the desert area between the tropical and the temperate zones appeared and gradually grew. Compared with these major events, however, little change has occurred in the climate of the Middle East in the last 5000 years.

Rainfall along the shores of the Mediterranean, Black, and Caspian seas and the southern part of the Red Sea is relatively abundant. Many areas receive an average annual fall of 30 inches (762 mm.) or more. (As one progresses inland, however, the average drops appreciably; most of Egypt and the plateaus of Arabia, Iran, and eastern Turkey have a desert climate.) Moreover, the rains are not only seasonal but almost capricious. Damascus has an average annual rainfall of about 10

The Geography of the Middle East

THE STEPPES

Don

Volga

CASPIAN DEPRESSION

Lake Balkhash

ARAL SEA

CAUCASUS MTS

▲ Mount Ararat

Lake Van

Lake Urmia

CASPIAN SEA

TURAN LOWLAND

Syr Darya

TURAN DESERT

Amu Darya

TIAN SHAN

KARA KUM

KOPET MTS

PAMIRS

ELBURZ MTS

Mount Damavand

KURDISTAN

ZAGROS MOUNTAINS

MESOPOTAMIA

Euphrates

Tigris

Karun

KHURASAN

KAVIR DESERT

IRANIAN PLATEAU

LUT DESERT

KHASH DESERT

HINDU KUSH

Khyber Pass

KASHMIR

Indus

Persian Gulf

FARS

Strait of Hormuz

GREAT INDIAN DESERT

AL DAHNA DESERT

Gulf of Oman

Rann of Kutch

TUWAIQ MTS

ARABIAN PENINSULA

ASIR

RUB' AL KHALI

ℐ MASIRAH

ARABIAN SEA

HADHRAMAUT

Bab al-Mandeb

Gulf of Aden

SOCOTRA

SOMALI PENINSULA

INDIAN OCEAN

0	250	500 mi
0	400	800 km

50°   40°   30°   20°   10°

50°   60°   70°

inches (254 mm.), but four inches have been known to fall in one morning. The mountainous areas of eastern Turkey and Iran receive more moisture, but here, too, winter is the wet season, with much of the precipitation occurring in the form of snow. The one exception to the winter rain pattern is the monsoon region of southern and southwestern Arabia, which gets most of its rainfall in the months of July, August, and September.

Temperatures depend upon latitude and altitude, and winter in the mountains of Arabia, Iran, and eastern Anatolia can be quite bitter. Summer temperatures in Egypt, Arabia, and Iraq are hot, sometimes over 100°F. (38°C.) during the day, but nights are cool everywhere except in some of the lower valleys and along some coasts where the humidity is high.

FLORA AND FAUNA

Wood has been a prized building material and, along with animal dung, the principal fuel in the Middle East from the beginning of history until the advent of coal and oil. Over the last 5000 years a process of deforestation has denuded most of the land. Some stands of trees remain on the slopes of the Zagros and Elburz mountains, in coastal Anatolia, and on the Lebanon Mountains, while the systematic planting of trees has restored some of the earlier landscape in Israel. Elsewhere the land would be bare but for cypresses in cemeteries and gardens and poplars along streams and irrigation ditches.

It has been estimated that unconcern about land conservation over the last 5000 years has resulted in the destruction of 90 percent of the forest and topsoil resources of the Middle East, and pollution of water sources is also now a major problem. But absence of concern cannot be said to have existed with respect to the cultivation of edible flora of the area. Wheat, barley, rye, broad beans, lentils, onions, garlic, figs, grapes, melons, pomegranates, plums, apples, peaches, apricots, olives, and dates are the principal foods developed from the vegetation of the area. Industrial crops include cotton, tobacco, and sugar beets.

Domestication of native animals of the Middle East probably began about 8000 B.C. It is difficult to tell in what order, but at some very early time the dog (probably first), sheep, goat, pig, ox, and donkey were tamed and used for work or to provide food and clothing. Domesticated horses and camels were introduced into the area from farther east in Asia in the second millennium B.C. As the forests became scarcer, the pig was replaced by more economical all-purpose animals like the ox, goat, and sheep; and the arrival of the camel made habitation in the desert possible and facilitated Middle Eastern nomadism in Arabia proper.

Middle Eastern waters teem with fish. The Caspian Sea has long been noted for its sturgeon and caviar. The Black Sea and the Arabian Sea have numerous varieties of fish. And the eastern Mediterranean, fed by the vegetable matter of the Nile, has been for centuries an attractive and productive spot for fish of all kinds, though the Aswan High Dam and recent environmental pollution have presented new challenges to fishers.

RESOURCES

The significant natural resources of the Middle East have been, and still are, the availability and interrelationship of water, soil, sun, plants, and animals, allowing for a productive agriculture. Other natural resources are the excellent clays with which the bricks, pots, and finer ceramics of many cultures have been fashioned. Mountains, lava coming from geologic faults, and rock formations laid bare by river erosion have provided extensive quarries for basalt, granite, marble, sandstone, and limestone.

Gold, silver, copper, and iron are extracted in easily workable ores, and their ready utilization marked the end of the Neolithic age. The presence of other metals such as tin, nickel, and copper led the way to the development of bronze and brass. Deposits of these metals have been worked almost continuously up to the present, and the output has been of considerable value in the economy and life of the area. In the twentieth century other metals have come to the fore. Chromium and manganese are found in sizable deposits, and phosphate rock can be used in making chemical fertilizers. Coal, lignite, and iron ore exist in considerable amounts in Turkey and Iran, and to a lesser extent in Egypt.

The greatest of the natural resources of the Middle East of the twentieth century, beyond land and water, are oil and natural gas. Small oil fields have been located in Turkey, Syria, Yemen, and Israel, but the large ones are those of Iran; Iraq; along the Persian Gulf in Saudi Arabia, Kuwait, Bahrain, Qatar, the United Arab Emirates, and Oman; and in Egypt, Libya, and Algeria. No one yet knows the full extent of the oil and natural gas of the Middle East, but the area's known reserves alone far outstrip those of any other oil-producing region, and the presence of this natural resource has changed the world importance of the Middle East.

PEOPLE

While the Middle East is drier than many other regions of the world, the stereotypical view that it is mostly desert is incorrect. The Middle East, despite its large deserts, was blessed with a warm climate, a fertile soil, animals and plants suitable for food, some waters available for irrigation, and varied mineral resources; it thus was a favorable area for the development of settled life, for the increase in standards of living, and for the growth of organized and complex societies. Most people have tended to live in the well-watered areas, and settlement patterns have been complicated, with many different groups who live close to each other or even together in the same communities.

The earliest known human inhabitants in the Middle East lived at least 600,000 years ago. Although scientists have yet to unravel the wanderings of prehistoric Homo sapiens in the Middle East, it seems certain that around 15,000 B.C., as the fourth glacial period terminated, the well-watered regions of Arabia and the Sahara were inhabited by widely dispersed groups of people, most of whom gathered food rather than raised crops. Then, through ten millennia, as the ice cap was retreating to Scandinavia, Arabia and the Sahara became drier and hotter, and their inhabitants moved northward and seaward.

Much domestication of plants and animals took place in the highlands, with the plow and the wheel being developed in the fourth millennium. With the advent of settled agriculture into the chief river valleys, Middle Eastern civilization had its beginnings. Because rivers flooded annually, renewing the soil with the silt they deposited, Neolithic agriculturalists could continue to cultivate the same fields year after year, generation after generation. Eventually this development permitted the growth of settled, complex communities, leading to a crucial and long-lasting triple division of social and economic activity that came to influence the way most people lived.

The three economic groups were nomads, who gained their livelihood by herding animals; farmers or peasants, who constituted the bulk of the population in most parts of the Middle East and who raised crops as they resided in villages; and townspeople, who provided services and goods of diverse types. All three groups interacted with each other and were often mutually interdependent. In this context, records accumulated and history in the Middle East began.

References

BACHARACH, JERE L.: *A Middle East Studies Handbook.* Seattle: University of Washington Press, 1984. Invaluable not only for its maps but also for its chronology, dynastic tables, and lists of heads of state. Excellent for the beginning student and also highly useful for specialists.

BEAUMONT, PETER, et al.: *The Middle East: A Geographical Study.* 2d ed. New York: Halsted Press, 1988. Covers physical and social geography for the whole region and country by country.

BLAKE, GERALD, et al.: *The Cambridge Atlas of the Middle East and North Africa.* Cambridge, England: Cambridge University Press, 1987. Many clear maps show physical, cultural, economic, and political aspects of modern geography.

BRICE, WILLIAM C.: *An Historical Atlas of Islam.* Leiden: Brill, 1981. Valuable for its extensive coverage.

COON, CARLETON S.: *Caravan: The Story of the Middle East.* New York: Holt, 1951. An excellent anthropological introduction to the Middle East, written in a style easily understood by the beginning student.

DRYSDALE, ALASDAIR, AND GERALD H. BLAKE: *The Middle East and North Africa: A Political Geography.* New York: Oxford University Press, 1985. Shows the relationship between political and diplomatic issues and geographic factors.

FISHER, W. B.: *The Middle East: A Physical, Social and Regional Geography.* 7th ed. London: Methuen, 1978. Authoritative; a classic.

HELD, COLBERT C.: *Middle East Patterns: Places, Peoples, and Politics.* 2d ed. Boulder, Colo.: Westview, 1994. In addition to country-by-country coverage there is thorough treatment of historical and general factors. The best introductory work available.

ROBINSON, FRANCIS: *Atlas of the Islamic World since 1500.* New York: Facts on File, 1982. Filled with beautiful illustrations, maps, and a historical narrative that is comparative and informative.

WAGSTAFF, J. M.: *The Evolution of Middle Eastern Landscapes: An Outline to A.D. 1840.* London: Croom Helm, 1985. A thoughtful and elegant study of the impact of society on the environment, with an emphasis on the period up to the rise of Islam.

Pre-Islamic Politics and Society in the Middle East

THE RISE OF CIVILIZATION

The history of the Middle East may be usefully divided into several units: the period of antiquity, stretching from the rise of civilization to the coming of Islam; the classical Islamic period, which extended from the life of Muhammad to the middle of the tenth century; the two parts of medieval Middle Eastern history—from about A.D. 950 to about 1250, and a second part to about 1500; and then the two phases of the history of the modern Middle East—a time dominated by great empires (1500 to 1800) and then recent centuries that saw the integration of the Middle East into world systems.

The first of these historical units began when the civilization of the Middle East started either in the Nile valley or in Mesopotamia along the Tigris and Euphrates rivers (located in modern-day Iraq). Archaeologists are also now discovering that significant cultures were independently developed in northern Syria and in Palestine, especially at Jericho after 9000 B.C.; in northern Mesopotamia around 8900 B.C.; and in the south-central plateau of Anatolia some time before 7000 B.C. Botanists and geneticists have shown that in the foothills of western Asia between the Mediterranean and the Himalayas, edible grasses, like wheat and barley, and herd animals, such as sheep, goats, and cattle, had their natural habitats. Small, sheltered groups of people learned to cultivate and domesticate these natural resources and established settled societies. Eventually, large walled towns were built and defended, although the residents of the towns depended ultimately on peasants, nomads, and merchants for food and goods. Civilizations with writing, art forms, religious practices, foreign trade, and social and political norms appeared.

Only when agricultural skills and social techniques had been developed adequately could the complex problems of living on the plains of rivers be solved. Just how and where the transitions occurred has not yet been determined, but they undoubtedly took place slowly over several millennia. In any case, in two centers of highly evolved urban civilizations along the Tigris-Euphrates and the Nile it can be

PERIODIZATION IN THE HISTORY OF THE ISLAMIC MIDDLE EAST

Antiquity: from the rise of civilization to the coming of Islam

Classical Islamic period: from the life of the prophet Muhammad to the middle of the tenth century A.D.

The early medieval era in the Middle East: from about 950 to about 1250

The late medieval era in the Middle East: from about 1250 to about 1500

The early modern Middle East: from about 1500 to about 1800

The modern Middle East: from about 1800 to the present

shown that each culture arrived in the area already in a transitional stage, that each brought with it domesticated plants and animals (many of which were of common origin), but that each in its new habitat independently developed an urban civilization.

Somewhat after the year 4000 B.C. the Sumerian people arrived in the Tigris-Euphrates valley, where Sumerian city-states evolved around 3400 B.C. with society divided into technological-social classes—bureaucrats, priests, traders, farmers, and artisans—divisions that have remained significant in Middle Eastern civilizations. Writing was invented. As early as 5000 B.C. the peoples of Mesopotamia began to use irrigation techniques to provide water for crops. Other peoples from Arabia were drawn to the prosperous Sumerian cities and to the densely settled countryside. They spoke a language belonging to the Semitic family, which predominated in central Arabia. Thus, very early in history, a mixture of people with different languages and origins influenced events.

Farther north along the middle Euphrates about 3000 B.C., Semitic-language speakers, probably seminomads from the steppes or desert, began to become sedentary in the cities of the region. For a thousand years the ruling families of Sumerian and northern states were ardent rivals, although conflict among the cities in each group was the norm. Cities such as Ur, Lagash, and Akkad each had its day and then passed overlordship to another. A larger unit was created about the year 1700 B.C. by the union of all of Mesopotamia under Hammurabi of Babylon.

With the rise of warring states, patriarchal values probably became predominant, while the authority of women and female deities decreased. Kingship was usually hereditary within the males belonging to a family, and the dynastic principle dominated political structures. Women could become scribes, and at least some upper-class women were literate; however, most aspects of public life were usually controlled by men.

At approximately the same time that the Sumerians appeared in Mesopotamia, a civilization with its own distinctive language slowly began to develop along the Nile. The nature of the land, the annual flooding of the Nile, the local presence of copper, and the relative isolation of the Nile valley by the surrounding deserts were conducive to the establishment of an absolute monarchy and a flourishing culture. Shortly after 3000 B.C. a series of dynasties headed by pharaohs who were considered divine ruled a united Egypt, developed hieroglyphic writing, and constructed enormous pyramids that served as royal tombs. Ruling first from Memphis and then from Thebes, the pharaohs supervised a highly efficient and centralized state. Irrigation projects, preparation for a life after death, and the worship of the gods preoccupied the rulers. Egypt often dominated nearby areas, while its art, commerce, and religions had a wide influence.

Other areas beyond the two great river valleys developed aspects of civilization somewhat later. Yemen experienced settled agriculture about 2000 B.C., while Oman saw long-distance trade, cultivation of animals, and sophisticated use of metals by about 2500 B.C. Ebla in northern Syria employed cuneiform writing by 2400 B.C., and its widespread commerce and diverse gods reflected the open horizons of its population. The changes that affected southern Mesopotamia so greatly also influenced nearby southwestern Persia.

Early in the second millennium B.C. peoples from eastern Europe and western Asia began a southward movement, exerting population pressures upon the whole of the Middle East. In a succession of thrusts, these intruders, first equipped with bronze weapons and then with iron weapons, and accompanied by horses and camels, pushed ahead into the Middle East. The Kassites came down with horses from the Zagros Mountains to rule Mesopotamia through much of the second millennium B.C.; and the Hyksos came with their horse-drawn chariots to rule Egypt for two centuries beginning about 1800 B.C. Later waves brought Hittites, Armenians, Greeks, Philistines, Medes, and Persians. Between these invasions and conquests of the northmen, pharaonic Egypt was independent and flourishing, and Semitic-language tribes such as Assyrians, Aramaeans, Phoenicians, Nabataeans, and Hebrews established states in Mesopotamia, Syria, or Palestine.

Around 1000 B.C. King David made Jerusalem the capital of the expanding Jewish state; prophets, who built on the experiences of earlier leaders such as Moses, established the foundations of monotheistic faith and a religious-moral code for living. Eventually, the Torah, the books of the prophets, and later scriptures became the basis of what Christians call the Old Testament. Ruled sometimes by judges, then by kings, and often in later centuries controlled by foreign dynasties, the Jewish Israelites strove to preserve their covenant with God by rejecting polytheism.

Each group of invaders, at the time of its arrival upon the Middle Eastern scene and in its first contact with Middle Eastern civilization, was leading a nomadic or pastoral life. The change to an organized life with greater specialization and division of labor produced turmoil and strains, but the transition was usually made successfully. Each group added something in religion, the art of writing, metallurgical skills, political organization, transportation, irrigation, or astronomy, and within a brief period the knowledge was disseminated over the entire area.

The Middle East in Antiquity

Alexander's Hellenistic Empire
B.C. 323

Roman Empire
A.D. 117

Byzantine Empire
A.D. 486

The Middle East in Antiquity

MEDITERRANEAN SEA
BLACK SEA
CASPIAN SEA
ARAL SEA
Persian Gulf
RED SEA
ARABIAN SEA

Egyptian Empire B.C. 1450	
Hittite Empire B.C. 1700	
Old Babylonian Empire B.C. 1700	

0   200   400 mi
0   300   600 km

MEDITERRANEAN SEA
BLACK SEA
CASPIAN SEA
ARAL SEA
Persian Gulf
RED SEA
ARABIAN SEA

Empires in B.C. 600

Egyptian	Median
Chaldean	Lydian

0   200   400 mi
0   300   600 km

MEDITERRANEAN SEA
BLACK SEA
CASPIAN SEA
ARAL SEA
Persian Gulf
RED SEA
ARABIAN SEA

Persian Empire B.C. 500

0   200   400 mi
0   300   600 km

13

ANCIENT EMPIRES

By the beginning of the first millennium B.C. the Middle East was rapidly becoming one cultural region, the use of iron started to spread, and a number of efforts were made to unite the area politically. Throughout the second millennium B.C. the Egyptian pharaohs sought and from time to time held control of Syria, Palestine, and parts of the Sudan. Anatolian kings such as the Hittites, however, vied with the pharaohs for these provinces; and from that age until the present the Syrian coast has been able to maintain its independence only when both Egypt and Anatolia/Mesopotamia have been weak or evenly matched.

One of the great empires controlling a major part of the Middle East was that of the Assyrians, whose last capital was at Nineveh on the upper Tigris in Mesopotamia. Iron weapons, a disciplined army, a well-organized bureaucracy, and battering rams on wheels gave the Assyrians such an advantage in the seventh century B.C. that Nineveh held sway from Sinai to the Caspian Sea and from southern Mesopotamia to the plains of central Anatolia. Assyrian rulers believed they were entitled by the gods to rule all peoples, and the tactics the kings used were often extremely brutal, including the forcible relocation of whole populations. Ultimately, overextension of the empire, exhausting battles, and civil strife, coupled with hatred and resistance among their subjects, weakened the army and the government, with the result that Nineveh was sacked.

The unity of the Middle East was restored by the Persians, a group of Zoroastrian Iranians from the Zagros range, who reunited the areas of the previous Assyrian Empire and added Greek Anatolia, Thrace, the Nile valley to the Sudan, Afghanistan, Baluchistan, the Punjab, coastal Oman, and parts of central Asia. The heart of their empire was Persia (later known as Iran) and Mesopotamia (modern Iraq). With the establishment of the Persian Empire in the sixth century B.C. Semitic speakers lost rule in the Middle East for over a thousand years. It was not until the rise of the Arabs under the banners of Islam that they regained their hegemony.

Despite being checked by Greeks around 490 B.C., the Persians maintained their power in the Middle East by an imperial system of government that skillfully combined local autonomy with centralized authority and responsibility. This form of government fashioned by the Persians was adopted in most essentials by succeeding rulers for over 2000 years and established a governmental pattern that often was accepted as a part of Middle Eastern civilization. The twenty-three provinces, or satrapies, of the Persian Empire were organized along ethnic lines, and toleration of local differences was considerable. Taxes and loyalty were the important requirements; a governor (satrap), a general, and a tax authority, each reporting independently to the royal residence (Susa, Babylon, or Persepolis), preserved Persian rule.

Another secret of Persian success was the advancement of communications and transportation. Good roads from the frontier to the heart of the empire were kept open under constant repair and surveillance. The old canals between the Nile and the Red Sea were repaired so that the Phoenicians, the stalwarts of the Persian fleet, could sail directly from the Persian Gulf to the Mediterranean. In the end, however, the old story was repeated: the empire changed as central political power decreased and new peoples on the periphery of control challenged Persian dominance.

The history of the great empires of antiquity would be employed much later, in the twentieth century, to inspire pride and foster national unity, as Persians, Turks, Arabs, and Israelis used examples of earlier accomplishments from the historical record, while often altering it to show a greater continuity between the ancient past and the present than actually existed.

ALEXANDER AND THE GREEKS

In the fourth century B.C. a new people in the Balkans who were related to the Greeks began their ascent to power under Philip of Macedon. By the use of heavier armor and the integration of cavalry and the Macedonian phalanx, Greece was subjected to his rule. But Greece captured the mind and spirit of Philip's son, Alexander. The campaigns and conquests of Alexander the Great and the creation of his vast Greek empire have been retold through the ages by countless poets, romantics, and historians of many lands.

After defeating the Persian army in 334 B.C., the young Alexander, only twenty-two years old, swept all before him. Anatolia, Syria, Palestine, Egypt, Mesopotamia, Persia, and India to the Indus River had been conquered before his death in 323. Alexander had hoped to unify the entire Middle East into one lasting empire. He married a Persian princess. But his untimely death left only his chief generals to battle for the empire, which they eventually divided: Ptolemy in Egypt, Antigonus initially in Anatolia and then his successors in Macedonia and Greece, and Seleucus in Syria and Asia.

Following the breakup of Alexander's empire, the Middle East fell heir to a century of international political anarchy and intermittent wars; yet it enjoyed a period of vast trade and wealth as well as many decades of important intellectual and artistic activity. It was the apogee of the brilliant Hellenistic age, which persisted for two centuries more until the last vestige of Ptolemaic rule in Egypt ended with Cleopatra's suicide and the Nile valley became a Roman province.

THE ROMAN EMPIRE AND ITS SUCCESSORS

Rome became the arbiter of Middle Eastern affairs, as the Mediterranean was turned into a vast Roman lake. Except for the Tigris-Euphrates, the plateaus of Persia, and most of Arabia, the Middle East was transformed into Roman provinces and was ruled from Rome until the emperor Constantine transferred his capital eastward to Constantinople, on the shores of the Bosphorus. (The Greek city of Byzantium was traditionally said to have been founded in 667 B.C.; renamed Constantinople, it kept that designation until the Ottoman Muslim conquest in 1453, after which it generally became known as Istanbul.) From the establishment of Constantinople in A.D. 330 to the defeat of the emperor Heraclius by the Arab Muslim armies in 638, the provinces of the Middle East were important parts of the Byzantine or Eastern Roman Empire, whose history will be more fully discussed in Chapter 13.

In Mesopotamia and Persia in the second century B.C. the great Parthian Empire was established by Mithridates I. All territory east of the Euphrates was seized by the Parthian king of kings, who built his royal palace at Ctesiphon on the Tigris. The Parthian power rested on its nomadic cavalry, Zoroastrianism, and on a cultural reaction against Hellenism, even though the kings knew Greek and had Greek tragedies performed at their court. The Parthians defeated the Romans, who recognized Parthian dominion over all of Mesopotamia.

Early in the third century A.D. internal weakness brought the downfall of the Parthian kings at the hands of a new Persian family, the Sasanians, who used extensive irrigation and international commerce to create a wealthy empire. The founder of the dynasty was a Zoroastrian, and that dualistic faith was vigorously advanced as the official religion of the empire. Wars with the Romans and Byzantines found the religious differences to be as important as the political ones.

From their main residence at Ctesiphon the Sasanians time and again harried the Byzantine provinces of Syria and Anatolia. After the fifth century, when Christianity was tolerated and the Nestorian church had become widespread in the Sasanian Empire, particularly in Mesopotamia, the conflicts with Constantinople were more imperial in nature. The Byzantine emperor Justinian checked the Sasanians temporarily, but they sacked Aleppo and Antioch. Exhausting campaigns were resumed under Justinian's successors. Bubonic plague and the decline of urban life further weakened the Byzantine lands.

A powerful Sasanian army erupted into Syria in 613, destroying the Church of the Holy Sepulcher in Jerusalem and pillaging Damascus. A Sasanian army conquered Egypt in 619, and another captured the cities across from Constantinople. Evil days appeared for the Byzantines, but the tide turned. Between 622 and 628 Heraclius, the new Byzantine emperor, succeeded in driving the Sasanians from Egypt and Syria, and looted Ctesiphon. But the wars, ensuing destruction, and internal changes left both empires weakened. Syria, Egypt, and Mesopotamia were ripe for picking by the new armies of the Muslim Arabs in the next decade.

PRE-ISLAMIC CIVILIZATION IN THE MIDDLE EAST

For nearly a thousand years much of the Middle East had been subjected to the influence and the forced cultivation of Greek, Hellenistic, Roman, and Byzantine civilizations. Although it would be possible to point out distinguishing characteristics of each of these four civilizations and to show how each evolved from its predecessor, they form one continuous cultural experience and development for the history of the later Middle East.

First and foremost among the changes was the adoption of Greek by the educated and by the leaders of society as the language of government, philosophy, literature, and sophisticated communication. Greek colonists—merchants, soldiers, and government officials—settled in most of the Middle Eastern cities and founded many new Greek cities like Antioch in Syria and Alexandria in Egypt. Intellectually and artistically, much of the Middle East appeared as one world. Greek philosophies and science became universal throughout the area, although many leaders were not originally Greek speakers.

Roman and Sasanian rule ended the internecine warfare of the Alexandrian successor states and brought a more bountiful material life to the cities of the Middle East. The remains of the almost countless theaters, temples, baths, gymnasiums, and public buildings that dot the Middle East today are silent witnesses of the populous, thriving, and wealthy cities of that age and of the public life that was dominated by men. Urban upper-class women were often veiled in areas influenced by the Greeks and Persians; while rulers frequently had harems, most men were monogamous.

Even Roman military might, genius for efficiency, and administrative skill could not always control the Middle East. Many people did not adopt Greek and Roman ways in speech, dress, food, religion, and manners. As the years passed, the Hellenistic states became less and less Greek, conforming more faithfully to earlier patterns of life in the Middle East. The Ptolemies appeared as pharaohs, and the Seleucids lived as Assyrian and Persian monarchs. Jesus of Nazareth spoke Aramaic, not Greek.

Greek and Roman civilization pervaded many of the cities of Syria and Egypt, but not the villages or nomadic areas of the Middle East. Under the rule of the Byzantine emperors the reassertion of Middle Eastern patterns was accelerated in Syria and Egypt. Since western Anatolia had participated in Greek cultural development long before the age of Alexander, it exhibited a greater Hellenization than did Syria or Egypt.

CHRISTIANITY

The new contribution that came to the cultural stream of the Middle East with Byzantine dominion was Christianity, which received recognition as the official religion of the empire. In Hellenistic and Roman periods people were groping for a philosophy of life and a religion that would answer some of the problems of those rapidly changing and turbulent days. Faith in the power or protection of the Greek gods had largely disappeared by the time of Alexander. The educated neglected the gods and pursued philosophical systems that served as intellectual shelters where sensitive and distressed souls might take refuge from a materialistic and heartless society.

To the masses these philosophies were meaningless. The formation of large empires deprived the individual of a sense of identity with a city-state and its protecting god. As helpless individuals, people needed a personal savior. They therefore turned to the mystery cults of Asia, which had a devoted following. Here the individual, by witnessing and participating in an esoteric ritual, was initiated into the mysteries of life and death, god and immortality. As the savior-god had lived and died and risen again, so the lonely and helpless individual, living in a tumultuous world, might win eternal salvation by personal union with the god.

In the second century A.D. the greatest change in the Middle East, under Roman rule, came with the rise and spread of Christianity. Taking many of the positive and uplifting tenets of monotheistic Judaism, of the Greek philosophies, and of the Asian cults, Christianity added two vital factors that were largely absent in Hellenism and Romanism: Christ offered immortality to all, and his creed was based on love of humanity.

Early Christianity appealed almost solely to urban Hellenistic society, the language of the church being Greek. After Christianity obtained official status, the Byzantine state rapidly developed into a synthesis of Hellenism and Christianity with earlier influences, and a blending of the political power of the state and the religious authority of the church.

The union of autocracy and theocracy in the Byzantine state—the so-called Caesaro-papism of Constantinople—ensured the alienation of some of the masses in the Middle Eastern provinces. As new Christian doctrines from the Middle East were branded heresies by the state-dominated church councils—Nicaea (325), Ephesus (431), and Chalcedon (451)—separate native Christian churches evolved. Aramaic, its Syriac dialect, and Ethiopic became liturgical languages. Byzantine Constantinople could not force its type of Christianity upon all the Middle Eastern peoples.

The Nestorian church presented a dualism of good and evil not far distant from Zoroastrian doctrines, a fact that may explain its acceptance in Mesopotamia and Persia. Monophysite Christianity certainly embodied some of the Egyptian ideas of human divinity. Heresies flourished in non-Greek areas of the Byzantine Empire and served as basic factors in the almost complete lack of resistance and even passive cooperation of the Middle Eastern provinces at the time of the conquests by the Muslim Arabs.

THE ARABS

In the first half of the seventh century, the Arabs, under the banners of Islam, descended upon Syria, Egypt, Mesopotamia, and Persia. Coming from an area on the edges of the great empires, the Muslim Arabs seemed to be a new and different force to the peoples of that age.

The Arabs mostly lived along the shores of Arabia, in the southern highlands where there was some rainfall, and in scattered oases; they spoke an Arabic language whose form emerged between 500 B.C. and A.D. 500 in central and western Arabia. These desert inhabitants—farmers and nomadic shepherds—were few and insignificant until the advent of a new saddle for riding camels. The peculiar characteristics of this animal made nomadic life in the desert profitable; indeed, the one-humped dromedary was as revolutionary to life in Arabia at that time as oil and the motor vehicle have been in the twentieth century. The camel people became lords of the desert. Above all, the camel welded town and desert life in Arabia into one integrated society, each dependent upon the other.

The use of the camel, moreover, eased many difficulties of the transit trade between India and the Mediterranean. Camel caravans began to carry spices and incense from Yemen to Mecca (Makkah), the Hijaz, Damascus, and the Mediterranean. Other trade routes connected western Arabia with towns on the Euphrates and the Persian Gulf. Cities prospered and small kingdoms were established as the commerce of the Hellenistic, Roman, and Sasanian worlds expanded. Many Arabs moved northward, where they settled in Byzantine-controlled provinces and became Christians; at the same time other Arabs also settled in the Sasanian-dominated northeastern parts of the peninsula. Arabia in the sixth century, the time of the birth of Muhammad the Prophet, was being affected increasingly by events in surrounding states.

WESTERN ARABIAN SOCIETY

In order to understand Muhammad and the people's response to his preaching, it is useful to examine briefly the economic, political, social, and religious forces current in his day in the Hijaz and in Mecca. Mecca, Muhammad's birthplace, was near the caravan routes from Yemen to Syria. Possessing a permanent spring and an ancient sacred shrine, Mecca dominated the Hijaz. It was a religious and commercial town and a growing financial center. Mecca had originated as an entrepôt, but by the end of the sixth century Meccan merchants were buying and selling wares (especially leather) in markets from Yemen to southern Syria. Mercantile wealth was turning to financial speculation and investment. There is little evidence of local agriculture in Mecca, although there were orchards and cereal production at al-Taif, and dates grew at the oasis of Medina. Mecca itself had a spring, but the unwalled town was set in the midst of a barren, narrow valley.

Nomads—Bedouins, or desert Arabs—dwelled with their herds in the neighborhood of Mecca. Moving about in search of pasturage, they enjoyed a free, open, precarious existence; yet they were exceedingly jealous of their rights in the desert where they roamed. Brigandage to them was perfectly legitimate, whether upon oases or caravans. The Bedouins were good fighters, and when the advent of the north Arabian saddle greatly enhanced their raiding abilities, merchants, towns, and peasants often bought protection by paying tribute. Between the nomads and Mecca an interdependence developed, and the situation of the Bedouins in the Hijaz improved with the growing prosperity of Mecca.

In Muhammad's time the Quraish tribe of Arabs had dominated life in Mecca for more than a century, although families from the older inhabitants still lived in the city. The tribe had split into a dozen or more clans, which were grouped into two federations. Muhammad's clan was the Hashim, so named for his great-grandfather. Membership in a clan was based on kinship through the male line. Security of person and property was a clan responsibility; violation of either was a cause for reprisal by the clan. An irresponsible member was usually disowned by the clan and consequently became a kind of social, political, and economic outcast.

The clans prized the virtues related to desert nomadism—"bravery in battle, patience in misfortune, persistence in revenge, protection of the weak, defiance of the strong." Other values that were expressed in poetry were generosity, hospitality, loyalty, and fidelity. A man with honor and moral excellence exhibited the possession of these characteristics and demonstrated his capacity to govern his life by wise judgment.

Government in Mecca was simple, direct, unorganized, and exceedingly democratic. An assembly of chiefs and leading men of the clans met as a council, but each clan was independent and could go its own way. Individuals within a clan might differ with the majority and act accordingly, but they were sure to find such action difficult and the results uncomfortable. Unanimity of clan action had to be achieved by personal negotiation among the leaders, who commanded respect because of wealth, wisdom, and strength of character. A few religious offices possessed privileges, sometimes with opportunities for profit, such as control over the water of the sacred well or supplying food to pilgrims.

Political affairs in the foreign field taxed the skill and ingenuity of the Meccan leaders, for the Arabs were buffeted by the contest between the Byzantine and Sasanian empires. Eastern Arabs were satellites of Persia, and such Arabs as the Ghassanids east of the Jordan were on the Byzantine side. Upon the development of a Persian-sponsored rule in Yemen and with frequent battles between Persia and the Byzantines, Meccan regional commerce northward to Byzantine Syria became a touchy enterprise. But Meccan neutrality, religious prestige, and diplomatic and economic shrewdness kept caravan trade going.

Previously, the Hashim clan had operated caravans north to Syria, but in Muhammad's time it began to lose that monopoly. Hashim, Muhammad's great-grandfather, had obtained from the Byzantines protection for Meccan merchants and their goods in Syria and Palestine. To complement this arrangement, Hashim organized what some have labeled the "Commonwealth of Mecca." He and his successors secured a novel partnership with hitherto hostile Bedouin tribes in the northern area of Arabia whereby Meccan commerce prospered through a sharing of the profits between Meccan merchants and leaders of the tribes, as well as the hiring of the tribes to escort the caravans. Other factors in strengthening the Meccan trade position were the innovations of joining investments from poor members of Meccan families to those of their rich brethren and of including some Bedouin goods in merchandise marketed in Mecca and in Syria. Furthermore, many Meccan leaders married daughters of prominent Bedouin leaders. Thus, beginning with Hashim many groups developed a common interest in the Meccan trade enterprise.

Society in Mecca was reeling from the strains of a swift transition. Not only had the emphasis among the Quraish shifted from tribe to clan membership, with intense rivalry developing among clans, but individualism within a clan was growing at a quickening tempo. Business partnerships were being formed across clan lines. And the leaders and powerful men of Mecca were successful businessmen and merchants, who did not always live by the long-accepted Arab standards. Common material interests seemed to be replacing common blood in the determination of kinship in the new Mecca. Social maladjustment resulted from the failure of the new economic life to accommodate itself to the old moral values of Arab life. At the same time, the economic disruptions caused in southern Syria by the Byzantine-Sasanian wars of the early seventh century limited trading opportunities.

Pagan Mecca had numerous gods and goddesses, most of whom possessed abstract characteristics. Stones, trees, and other objects were venerated as places in which these deities were thought to reside. Magic and superstition were inextricably interwoven in this paganism, but belief in the gods had begun to fade in

Muhammad's time, though brutal social customs like female infanticide were still practiced.

A more forceful religion was one that was bound up with the belief in the immortality of the tribe and clan. Honor, bravery, generosity, and other virtues were possessions that ensured the survival of the tribe. Fate was believed to govern life in only a few ways, determining, for instance, the length of life, gender, and happiness. Otherwise individuals controlled their own destiny. It was not quite the same for the desert Arab, however, for life in the desert was so precarious that it seemed to be governed by some unfathomable law or whim of a force beyond one's control or responsibility. As everything in one's life was considered transient, the fate of the individual was unimportant. There was no belief in personal immortality; immortality rested with the tribe.

Finally, in Mecca a conception of monotheism was evolving. The Arab word Allah was derived from the word al-ilah, meaning "the god." Allah, then, was the supreme God, and Muhammad, in using this word, did not have to give his audiences any explanation. The idea, evidently, was in the air at Mecca, though undoubtedly the understanding of monotheism was vague and ill defined in Meccan minds.

The source of the concept of monotheism in Mecca is a hotly debated issue. Judaism and Christianity have had their champions, and certainly the Meccans had had ample opportunities to become acquainted with each of these religions. Later, Muslims argued that their faith was a continuation of a religious tradition that included Judaism and Christianity, whose original revelations had become obscured and needed to be reformed and purified. From that point of view there was no "borrowing" from Judaism or Christianity; rather, Islam was a renewal and a completion of divine inspirations that were the original bases of various monotheistic beliefs.

It is important to note that Muhammad and Meccan society were familiar with monotheistic concepts. As is obvious from the events that followed, they were ready to have these thoughts organized and marshaled into a systematic religion—a religion that was originally distinctly Arab in character. That was the great work and accomplishment of Muhammad.

References

BOWERSOCK, G. W.: *Roman Arabia.* Cambridge, Mass.: Harvard University Press, 1983. Particularly useful for early Arab-Roman contacts.

BULLIET, RICHARD W.: *The Camel and the Wheel.* Cambridge, Mass.: Harvard University Press, 1975. Discusses the domestication of the camel and how the camel displaced the wheel in transportation in the Middle East.

CRONE, PATRICIA: *Meccan Trade and the Rise of Islam.* Princeton, N.J.: Princeton University Press, 1987. A controversial revision of earlier works on Mecca before Islam; asserts that trade was local and regional and that there was little social upheaval in Mecca at this time.

HALLO, WILLIAM W., AND WILLIAM KELLY SIMPSON: *The Ancient Near East: A History.* New York: Harcourt Brace Jovanovich, 1971. Concentrates on Mesopotamia and Egypt, and is the best introductory account of their histories in antiquity.

HOURANI, ALBERT: *A History of the Arab Peoples.* Cambridge, Mass.: Harvard University Press,

1991. This beautifully written and truly outstanding work is a magisterial summary of existing knowledge combined with extraordinary insights by the author.

KNAPP, A. BERNARD: *The History and Culture of Ancient Western Asia and Egypt.* Belmont, Calif.: Wadsworth, 1988. A short and useful survey with special emphasis on social and cultural matters.

LEWIS, NAPHTALI: *Life in Egypt under Roman Rule.* Oxford, England: Oxford University Press, 1983. A witty look at social history and the life of those outside the ruling circles.

MILLAR, FERGUS: *The Roman Near East, 31 BC—AD 337.* Cambridge, Mass.: Harvard University Press, 1993. Carefully based on available evidence, this important book examines linguistic, religious, and ethnic factors.

PETERS, FRANK E.: *The Harvest of Hellenism.* New York: Simon and Schuster, 1971. Broad view of late antiquity, concentrating on intellectual and philosophical approaches and issues.

ROUX, GEORGES: *Ancient Iraq.* 2d ed. New York: Penguin Books, 1980. Introduction to Iraq, or Mesopotamia, from earliest times to the Parthians; includes intellectual, economic, and religious trends.

SAGGS, H. W. F.: *Civilization before Greece and Rome.* New Haven, Conn.: Yale University Press, 1989. Useful discussions of writing, cities, the sciences, law, religion, and politics.

SELLS, MICHAEL: *Desert Tracings: Six Classical Arabian Odes.* Middletown, Conn.: Wesleyan University Press, 1989. A valuable short introduction to early Arab poetry beautifully translated into English.

SHAHID, IRFAN: "Pre-Islamic Arabia." In P. M. Holt et al. (eds.), *The Cambridge History of Islam.* Vol. 1A: *The Central Islamic Lands from Pre-Islamic Times to the First World War.* New York: Cambridge University Press, 1970. An important survey of the subject by an expert on early Arabian history.

YARSHATER, EHSAN, ED.: *The Cambridge History of Iran.* Vol. 3: *The Seleucid, Parthian and Sasanian Periods.* New York: Cambridge University Press, 1983. Scholarly essays on political, social, religious, and cultural aspects of Iranian history before the rise of Islam.

The Rise and Spread of Islam

CHAPTER 3

Muhammad: His Life and Leadership

"There is no god but God, Muhammad is the messenger of God." The acceptance of this statement as the fundamental truth of life identifies all who follow the teachings of Muhammad. Allah is the God worshiped by Jews and Christians. But who was this man Muhammad?

It has been said that Muhammad was the only great prophet born in the full light of history. However, the first biography of Muhammad was not written until he had been dead for 100 years; others were compiled during the second century after his passing. We have no original sources about the life of Muhammad from non-Muslims. It is from the Quran (Koran), biographies, the oral stories of the early conquests, and the non-Quranic sayings of or about Muhammad (the hadith) that the traditional accounts of Muhammad's life have come. Modern scholars, both Muslims and non-Muslims, have been able to establish many points of mutual agreement. By analyzing words and phrases of various early accounts of Muhammad's life and the lives of his contemporaries, and by studying social, economic, political, and religious aspects of the society in which he moved, they have been able to reconstruct the history of this time so as to make it reasonable and understandable.

Muhammad was a mortal human being; he never professed otherwise and always emphasized this point to his followers, indicating that he would die like any other man. Nevertheless, as the founder of a great religion, he was revered as a most holy man even within his own lifetime. It is not strange, then, to find his biographies, written five or six generations later, full of unlikely incidents designed to exalt him. Perhaps this traditional figure has been more important than the real one in fashioning the culture and civilization of the Middle East and the Islamic world from his day to our own.

MUHAMMAD'S EARLY LIFE

In the year A.D. 570 (or perhaps somewhat later in the 570s), a male child was born in Mecca to the Hashim clan of the Quraish tribe. He was given the name Muham-

> ## PERIODIZATION IN THE HISTORY OF THE ISLAMIC MIDDLE EAST
>
> **Antiquity:** from the rise of civilization to the coming of Islam
>
> **Classical Islamic period:** from the life of the prophet Muhammad to the middle of the tenth century A.D.
>
> **The early medieval era in the Middle East:** from about 950 to about 1250
>
> **The late medieval era in the Middle East:** from about 1250 to about 1500
>
> **The early modern Middle East:** from about 1500 to about 1800
>
> **The modern Middle East:** from about 1800 to the present

mad, meaning "highly praised." His immediate family was not one of the wealthier or more powerful of the city, nor was it of the poorest groups. His father, Abd Allah, died before the child was born, and his mother died when Muhammad was about six years old. First as a fatherless boy, and then as an orphan, his lot was not easy. His paternal grandfather, Abd al-Muttalib, cared for and protected him. Upon his grandfather's death Muhammad became the ward of his uncle Abu Talib.

From many of Muhammad's statements it is apparent that his uncle was not a prosperous man and that they lived in modest circumstances. Evidently there was no opportunity for Muhammad in any of the businesses of his uncles; without any capital from his father, a job had to be found for him outside the family circle. Such a post was located with a rich widow, Khadijah, who had been married twice and had children from each marriage.

Khadijah was older than Muhammad, some say as much as fifteen years, and certainly her social position in Mecca was far superior to his. She was an astute businesswoman and continued her husbands' commercial activities. It is uncertain at what age Muhammad began working for her, exactly what he did, and how old he was when she asked him to marry her. The story of her proposal is probably factual. In Mecca it was not the usual custom for a woman to propose; in this instance, however, because of Khadijah's wealth, her better social class, and her position as employer, it would not have been unlikely. This step altered Muhammad's life greatly, and at this point he becomes a clearer historical personage.

Muhammad had already gained recognition as a successful trader and skilled administrator, and this marriage reinforced his reputation. He and Khadijah had four daughters who grew to maturity and several sons, all of whom died in infancy. Khadijah died about A.D. 619, but as long as she lived Muhammad had no other wife. Since he continued to act as Khadijah's commercial agent after their marriage, giving him security, Muhammad now had means and a definite position in the society of Mecca.

The Eastern Mediterranean and the Middle East, A.D. 600

INDIA

ARABIAN SEA

Hephthalite

Samarkand
Bukhara
Balkh
BACTRIA

Jaxartes

ARAL SEA

Oxus

SISTAN

Nishapur
KHURASAN

PERSIA

Damghan

CASPIAN SEA

CARMANIA

PARS

Persian Gulf

AZERBAIJAN
ARMENIA
Araxes
Ardabil
MEDIA
Hamadan
Nihavend
Ctesiphon

KHUZISTAN

CAUCASUS
LAZICA

Tigris

Seleucia

MESOPOTAMIA

ARABIA

Euphrates

Trebizond

Antakya

Damascus

Ghassanids

RED SEA

Yathrib
(Medina)

Mecca

Sinope

BLACK SEA

ANATOLIA

Nile

CYPRUS

EGYPT

Dnieper

Dniester

Alexandria

Constantinople

LIBYA

Avars

Danube

CRETE

MEDITERRANEAN SEA

KINGDOM OF THE LOMBARDS

SICILY

Po

CORSICA

SARDINIA

0   200   400 mi
0   300   600 km

Kingdom of
the Sasanids

Byzantine Empire

HIS CALL

In the Middle East, it has been the custom for people who have some means and who are troubled intellectually and emotionally by the cares and ills of society to retreat to a lonely spot to think and to seek answers for problems of the day. A number of people in Arabia in the sixth and early seventh centuries were searching for such greater insight. Muhammad, after his marriage, began to follow this practice.

Perhaps it was in the year 610 that Muhammad had a sudden and unusual experience in the form of thoughts flooding upon him. In the language and understanding of his time it was a revelation, and he readily accepted it as such. (This occasion is celebrated each year by Muslims as the "night of power.") Probably occurring in a cave on one of the hillsides outside Mecca, the message commanded Muhammad to preach the Truth to his fellow Meccans. This was his call.

Beginning with this first revelation, Muhammad on frequent occasions heard voices. Certainly he fully believed in the voices; he was his first convert. The revelations often concerned ideas that were being widely discussed in Arabia and that he had contemplated earlier. There can be no real doubt of his own sincerity and conviction that the messages were from God.

With respect to religion, Muhammad had grown up in the pagan society of Mecca. One of his sons, Abd Manaf, bore a pagan name. Mecca was a holy place, famed for the Kaba, the earthly abode of many gods and the only stone building in the town. The Quraish had a special relationship and certain responsibilities to this temple.

At this time, however, Mecca and the Hijaz were experiencing a gradual trend toward a more intellectual religion. Moreover, the ideas and teachings of Judaism and Christianity had spread and become known in Mecca through slaves, pilgrims, and traders as the small town grew somewhat more prosperous and its life more settled. Repeatedly, Muhammad referred to Judaism and Christianity, and to help demonstrate the truth of the revelations he showed a congruity between Islam and those older faiths. Although Muhammad apparently could not read anything other than the most simple writing, he was familiar with many of the ideas of the Monophysite sect of Christians in Syria.

PREACHING AND CONVERTS

The first revelations presented quite a simple religion. God was represented as all-powerful, good, and loving. Created existence was transitory; the creator was permanent. But God, in creating humans, implanted in them moral responsibility for themselves and, particularly, for their fellows. There would be a final judgment on the day of resurrection. Pure individuals were those who were grateful to God, worshiped him, appealed to him for the forgiveness of sin, offered frequent prayers, helped other people, avoided all forms of cheating, led chaste lives, and had cleansed themselves from love of wealth. Such persons, then, would recognize the goodness and power of God and their dependence upon God. This was Islam—the surrender to God—and the pious who thus purified themselves became Muslims.

At first, Muhammad was reluctant to tell many people about the revelations. However, the heavenly truths had been revealed to him and duty compelled him to remind the Arabs of Mecca of these truths in order to save them from divine wrath on the approaching day of judgment. In the beginning his preaching brought no firm opposition. His first converts were members of his own family: his wife Khadijah, his young cousin Ali, and Zaid, a former slave. The most important of the others were Abu Bakr, Umar, Uthman, and Zubair. Some of the early converts were younger sons of influential men of the leading families and clans of Mecca. The father of one was the most prominent financier in Mecca; another's father had been a religious leader prior to Muhammad's time; two others were nephews of the head of the Makhzum clan, the wealthiest and dominant family among the Quraish. The majority, however, were men of no great social standing. Some had neither family nor clan ties, and the families of others had ceased for one reason or another to afford them protection.

Early Islam was a movement of people mostly well under forty years old and from the middle socioeconomic groups of Mecca. They were individuals who felt their positions to be inferior when they compared their wealth and influence with the fortunes and power of those at the top. Such a generalization certainly implies that economic, social, and political conditions in Mecca had a hand in fostering the development and growth of Islam. In the century before Muhammad's call, life in Mecca had been changing. The rapid growth of commerce had widened the gap between rich and poor and between the influential and their dependents. Wealth and the life of a merchant promoted individualism as contrasted to family and clan solidarity. Kinship based on money was supplanting that of blood, a substitution that did not satisfy the less successful. Nomadic virtues were hardly those valued in a mercantile society. Old ideals of generosity, honor, the moral responsibilities of family and clan, and the group's accountability for crimes against its members were seriously challenged in the evolving individualistic society. Seemingly, anything could be obtained through money and power. Also, in the last few decades before Muhammad's call, military conflict between Byzantines and Sasanians had decreased commercial opportunities while increasing the risks involved in long-distance trading.

Muhammad and his early converts, however, were not consciously frustrated men seeking solace in religion. In these first days, they were conservatives preaching against the abandonment of the old virtues. Nevertheless, Islam did recognize individualism as a permanent aspect of society. The last judgment concerned individuals; for it was said that on the day of the last judgment "one shall have no influence on behalf of another." Salvation came from the mercy of God, but one should take care of poor relatives, make sure of the well-being of orphans, and be generous to the poor. For the rich the new faith meant sacrificing and cooperating with the poor.

PERSECUTION

Muhammad and Islam entered a new period of development in 615. Monotheism was plainly recognized, and opposition and persecution began. Muslims were subjected to all manner of verbal insults. Garbage was dumped at their doors. Unprotected individuals were beaten, as were Quraish Muslims by their fellow clansmen. Some Muslims went to Ethiopia, seeking refuge from the persecution. Economic pressure was exerted by refusal to pay debts and by a severe boycott that harmed many, including Muhammad's closest friend, Abu Bakr. Muhammad warned his opponents that God had sent earlier messengers and warners, that they, too, had been persecuted, and that God had then punished the people who had ignored the divine revelations.

Abu Jahl, the head of the Makhzum clan, declared economic war upon the Muslims and asserted that every one of them would be ruined financially. He coaxed and threatened Abu Talib, Muhammad's uncle and the leader of the Hashim clan, to abandon Muhammad. Failure in this approach led to the formation of an alliance of all the Quraish clans to pursue an economic boycott of the Hashim clan and its closest ally, the al-Muttalib clan. There were to be no business dealings and no intermarriage with any member of either clan. Apparently during this break the Hashim maintained their own caravans to Syria and withstood the pressure. After two years the grand alliance was dissolved and the economic sanctions lapsed, since they had proved unsuccessful in destroying Muhammad.

More significant was the verbal assault, which indicated the opinions held by those in opposition. They scoffed at the idea of the day of last judgment and ridiculed Muhammad's preaching of the resurrection of the body after it had moldered in the grave. They kept asking scornfully: "When is the Hour?" Muhammad's conviction that God was one and only one and that all idolatry was evil disturbed Meccan society because, to a considerable degree, this meant forsaking the religion of the forefathers. Muhammad tried to counter this with the contention that he was following in the footsteps of the religion of Abraham and the prophets of old, and thus, that Muslims were only regaining the old Arab religion.

The opposition jeered at Muhammad's claim to prophethood, calling him a magician, a poet possessed by spirits, and even a madman. If God had desired to reveal the truth, they asserted sarcastically, he would have selected someone more important than Muhammad for this role. And why was not the full revelation made all at one time? How else could Muhammad explain the driblets of revelation except that he and some assistants were busy making up the verses!

Traditionally, the opposition to Muhammad by the leaders of Mecca centered around his preaching of the unity of God and his rejection of the use of idols. Some rich Meccans objected to his message that the rich should help the poor among them. They also feared that the adoption and practice of these beliefs would ruin Mecca as a modest commercial center if it lost its shrine and thereby its role in drawing Bedouins to the town. Abu Jahl, the most ambitious financier of Mecca, recognized the threat of Islam and its philosophy to his way of life and realized that widespread acceptance would give the leadership of the city to Muhammad. Other leaders opposed Muhammad as an innovator who was disrupting the social order of Mecca.

It was at about this time that Muhammad, according to Muslim belief, underwent a mystical experience—he was transported during a night journey to Jerusalem, and from there he visited heaven, before returning once again to

Mecca. Jerusalem thus would eventually become one of the holiest places in the world for Muslims.

Possibly this experience and the ending of the economic boycott in 619 were interpreted as indications that success was at hand. But one incident after another quickly dashed such optimism and brought Muhammad close to the breaking point. Khadijah died, and then his uncle and protector, Abu Talib, followed her. Abu Lahab, another uncle, who now became the leader of the Hashim, refused to continue protection. Several years had elapsed since any important person had accepted Islam. There was no Muslim in Mecca with sufficient stature to offer Muhammad protection. How easily Islam could have perished! The only alternative was to leave the city.

FLIGHT TO MEDINA

Muhammad first visited the neighboring town of al-Taif to explore the possibilities of establishing residence and the headquarters of Islam there. He was met with a quick rebuff and upon leaving was stoned.

Some 200 miles (about 320 km.) to the north and east lay the town of Yathrib—later called Medina (the city, i.e., the city of the Prophet) by the Muslims. Yathrib comprised an area of 20 square miles of date oases, fertile lands, and scattered settlements. Numerous tribes occupied quarters of the town and had been engaged in bloody and exhausting civil war, in part over the limited cultivated lands of Yathrib. The most important clans were Aws, Khazraj, Nadir, Quraizah, and Qainuqa, of which the last three adhered to Judaism.

During the pilgrimage of 620 and following the rebuff at al-Taif, Muhammad discussed Islam with several pilgrims of the Khazraj tribe of Yathrib and raised the question of asylum. The following year additional people from Yathrib participated in the pilgrimage and more discussions occurred. One of Muhammad's trusted supporters returned with them, and converts were obtained from every important family except one. In 622, a number of Medinans made the famous Pledge of al-Aqabah to protect Muhammad. Furthermore, there was some agreement concerning the migration of the Muslims, including Muhammad, from Mecca to Yathrib and the establishment of an alliance between Muslims and the people of Yathrib. Later additions to the pledge in the so-called constitution of Medina granted Muhammad sufficient authority to form the commonwealth of Medina. Pagan Arabs from Yathrib saw Muhammad as an arbitrator who might end the continual feuding of the clans.

As soon as agreement had been reached, Muhammad urged all Muslims to go to Yathrib. Over a period of weeks they left secretly in small groups until only Muhammad, Abu Bakr, Ali, and a handful of Muslims remained in Mecca. After all who planned to migrate had gone, Muhammad and Abu Bakr slipped away at night, hid in a nearby cave for a couple of days until the search for them had relaxed, and then proceeded to Yathrib (Medina). On September 24, 622, they were joyously greeted at the outskirts of the city.

This migration, or hijrah (hegira), was a dangerous move on the part of the

Muslims, for they were abandoning the protection of their families and their town for the untested protection of strangers. Almost overnight their position was so changed that the hijrah came to mark the new era. The lunar Muslim religious calendar A.H. 1 begins on July 16, 622, the first day of the year in which the hijrah occurred and the year in which the new Muslim community of believers was founded. In Mecca, Muhammad and the preaching of Islam had failed to win a majority of the population. In Medina, Muhammad immediately became the acknowledged political and social leader of the whole town, as well as the religious head of the small community of Muslims.

Residence in Medina placed new demands on Muhammad's diplomatic and executive talents. He could count definitely on the full support of the Muhajirun— the "emigrants" from Mecca—and the converts of Medina, called Ansar, or "helpers." For protection and sustenance, as well as for religious reasons, Muhammad created a new kind of community, which emphasized the mutual obligations of Muslims to each other. The problems and the affairs of the Muslim community were to be brought before God and Muhammad, whose judgments had to be obeyed. Herein lay the basis for the establishment of Muslim theocracy. God was Muhammad's guide and protector, and the disobedient would suffer the agonies of hell. The revelations received in Medina turned more to social and political matters and stressed, to a much lesser degree, forms of worship and religious ideas that had been revealed in the Meccan prophecies.

To help the Muhajirun and to establish rules for economic development, Muhammad encouraged regulations for sharecropping, hiring farm labor, new ways of allocating water, land reclamation, and the creation of a central market to replace several small markets.

Feuds among the disparate groups in Medina were rekindled quickly. The Jews soon began to quiz and mock Muhammad because of their knowledge of the Torah. He had expected that they would testify to the validity of his message, but they could not accept an Arab as the Messiah, even though Islam accepted Abraham and Moses as prophets. Islam had a distinctly Arab cultural flavor. This aspect came to be emphasized with the beginning of Muhammad's Medina residence.

In the first days following the hijrah the Muslims had adopted several of the Jewish rites. They prayed facing Jerusalem; they observed midday prayers and Jewish fast days; and Friday, market day as well as the Jewish day of preparation for the Sabbath, became the most important Muslim day of public prayer. Later, when relations with the Medina Jews became tense, Muslims, in accordance with new revelations, turned away from some of the Jewish forms. In worship the faithful now faced the Kaba sanctuary in Mecca; an annual pilgrimage to Mecca (the hajj) was prescribed for Muslims and a period of fasting (the month of Ramadan) was ordered.

CONFLICT WITH MECCA

During the winter of the first year in Medina, Muhammad and his followers were busy establishing their new homes. When spring and summer came and the Meccan caravans began to pass northward toward Syria, armed Muslim bands from Medina menaced the merchants. No booty was taken, and the caravans were so well protected that these incidents served only as reconnaissance missions. However, the need to provide a livelihood for the expatriates of Mecca forced Muhammad to direct attacks upon the passing caravans. It was a normal expediency in Arabia.

Late in 623 a handful of Muslims under orders from Muhammad surprised a small Meccan caravan on the road between Mecca and al-Taif. One Meccan was killed and much booty was captured. Nevertheless, sentiment in Medina was divided. The Medinans had promised the emigrants from Mecca protection from attack but had not agreed to let their city serve as a base of operations against Mecca. The success of the venture, however, invited other and larger expeditions.

Muhammad decided to ambush the main caravan of the Quraish upon its return from Syria. Muhammad himself led a group of about 300 to waylay the caravan under Abu Sufyan, the head of the powerful Umayyad family. At Badr, 20 miles (32 km.) southwest of Medina, Muhammad was challenged by a force of some 800 or 900 armed Meccans. The fighting was fierce and bloody, but the smaller force of Muslims was victorious. Although the battle of Badr was hardly more than a minor fracas (Muhammad lost fourteen men; the Meccans lost fifty), some have called it one of the decisive battles of history. To the Muslims it was a miracle, positive proof that God was supreme.

Henceforth Muhammad was a marked man, for the news of this victory traveled quickly to many parts of Arabia. Moreover, the battle set the stage and the pattern of the future: a fifth of all booty was assigned to Muhammad to be allotted to the needy or used by the state. The commonwealth of Medina now became a real possibility. From the moment of victory there could be no peace until the supremacy between pagans and Muslims was decided. Within two decades Muslims came to appreciate the importance of this battle; those who had participated in it were the "nobility of Islam"; and a cloak that had been worn at the battle of Badr was a most distinguished robe of honor.

This victory by no means guaranteed to Muhammad an easy path to his now clearly recognizable goal: control over Mecca and the incorporation of all its inhabitants into his Muslim community. Indeed, although the battle showed the Muslims that such a goal was attainable, it also goaded the leaders of Mecca into a real effort to annihilate the Muslim community.

Muhammad, taking advantage of his success, moved to consolidate his position. Alliances were made with a number of neighboring Bedouin tribes. The Qainuqa tribe, the weakest of those adhering to the Jewish faith, was driven from Medina. In 625, however, Abu Sufyan, the new leader of Mecca since the death of Abu Jahl on the battlefield of Badr, set forth with an army of 3000 for revenge. Electing to meet the enemy outside the town at the foot of the hill of Uhud, the Muslims appeared at first to be winning but were subsequently overrun by the Meccan cavalry. In the melee Muhammad was wounded but managed to escape. Torn by dissension as usual, the Meccan army neither pursued the Muslims nor pressed on to Medina. Two years later, Abu Sufyan returned again with an even larger Bedouin and Meccan army. Forewarned, Muhammad ordered a wide ditch dug in front of the less protected sides of Medina. After a two-week siege, the withdrawal of the Meccans was prompted by bad weather, persistent quarrels, and the disaffection of some of the nomad allies. In addition, the Meccans claimed that the Muslim trench was a dishonorable trick to which no Arab would resort. The "battle of the ditch" joined with Badr and Uhud to make the three battles where lines were drawn between the pagans and Muslims. The battles were in some measure part of a civil war. Participants on each side were well known to each other. Old slights and grudges were remembered, and emotions and the spirit of vengeance ran high.

Following each of these failures by pagan Mecca, Muhammad moved quickly to solidify the Medina community. When the Medina Jews had failed to hide their delight over the Uhud misadventure, the Muslims attacked the Jewish Nadir clan and drove them from Medina to Khaibar. After the third battle the men in the Jewish tribe of the Quraizah were killed, and the women and children were sold as slaves, because the Muslims felt the Quraizah had betrayed them. Citizens of Medina who, until now, had neither accepted Islam nor recognized Muhammad as their leader joined the Muslim band. This meant that by the end of 627 Muhammad had established Medina as a united community with one religion as its cohesive force.

The next spring Muhammad was advised that some of the men of Mecca wished to arrange peace with the Muslims. With this information Muhammad called for an advance upon Mecca during the month of a minor pilgrimage. His Bedouin allies would not join him, and Mecca sent forth an armed force to contest his entry. A compromise was reached stipulating that the Muslims might participate freely in the lesser pilgrimage the following year, and marking Muhammad's first success in his peaceful conquest of Mecca. Later that year, the Muslims captured the fertile oasis of Khaibar, largely inhabited by Jews. This acquisition made the Muslims wealthy, since the lands were most productive. The inhabitants were not exiled but remained on their lands, paying yearly taxes to the conquerors and establishing a precedent for the years and centuries to come—when other monotheists paid tribute and accepted Muslim supremacy, they could live in peace and practice their faiths.

VICTORY

In March 629 Muhammad led more than a thousand of his men into Mecca to perform the rites of the lesser pilgrimage as agreed upon the previous year. A number of Meccans joined him, recognizing Muhammad as the coming leader. Two of the most redoubtable military figures of Islam were among those who joined: Amr ibn al-As and Khalid ibn al-Walid. Even Abu Sufyan, in secret negotiations, tried to adjust to the inevitable.

As more Bedouin tribes joined the Muslims, Muhammad began to insist that they accept Islam and become an integral part of the community rather than serve merely as military allies. However, the sense of completeness and fulfillment of the Muslim community was lacking so long as Mecca did not recognize Muhammad as the leader and refused to accept Islam. Mecca was the site of the Kaba, the religious sanctuary and holy shrine. It had also been the home of the leaders of the Muslim community.

An insignificant incident brought Muhammad and the Muslims to Mecca to do battle in 630. Hardly anyone in Mecca was disposed to fight, however. Abu Sufyan came out from the city to pay homage to Muhammad, and Muhammad granted amnesty to him and most of the Meccans. Upon entering the city Muhammad demanded the destruction of all idols; he then prayed at the Kaba. He had merged his commonwealth with that of Mecca.

Muhammad's astuteness in politics and diplomacy was revealed by his decision not to settle again in Mecca but to return to his adopted city of Medina. The Quraish were a proud people, and it had not been easy for them to acknowledge Muhammad as the leader. He did not tarry to remind them too plainly of their new position. Moreover, the rapid spread of Islam and the increasing numbers of Muslims were presenting a multitude of problems. A rather unsuccessful campaign occurred in Transjordan, and missions went as far as Yemen, Bahrain, and Oman. There were small Muslim groups to be found in most parts of Arabia, but many still denied that Muhammad was God's messenger. (In areas where Muslim political authority had penetrated, Christians, Jews, and Zoroastrians were tolerated on the condition that they concede political rule to the Muslims.)

Muhammad could now see that Arabia was rapidly becoming one great united religious community (in Arabic, ummah). In this community religion rather than blood, language, customs, or economics held the people together; there were no distinctions among the believers except their degree of piety. It is probable, however, that some professed Islam not because they submitted to the will of God but because they feared not being a Muslim or because they wanted the political, social, and economic advantages of being one.

Although Mecca acknowledged Muhammad as its leader, many in the host of visitors to the Kaba in the month of the great pilgrimage were still pagan Arabs. Muhammad declined to go on the great pilgrimage in 631 and sent Abu Bakr at the head of the Muslims. Ali, Muhammad's cousin and son-in-law, was deputized to announce that after four months no pagan would be permitted to participate in a pilgrimage to Mecca and that all political alliances between Muslims and Arab tribes would be revoked if Islam were not accepted. Muhammad's authority and Muslim power were such that no trouble arose immediately from these pronouncements.

Thus, the stage was set for Muhammad to lead the reformed pilgrimage in March 632. Only Muslims would be present, and the veneration for the one God would be complete. Since Muhammad died soon after this pilgrimage, it has been called the farewell pilgrimage; and the events of the occasion are steeped in tradition. Muhammad eliminated many of the pagan aspects from the ceremonial rites that had been performed at the Meccan sanctuary in earlier days. His every move and act have been described and followed by devout pilgrims. He knew the significance of this first solidly Muslim pilgrimage; in his address, as leader, he must have said something like, "Today I have perfected your religion and completed my favors for you and chosen Islam as a religion for you."

Three days later, he departed for Medina and in less than three months (on June 8, 632) he died from fever. He had no sons still living, and, according to most Muslims, no provision had been made for a successor as leader of the Muslim community-state. Genuine bewilderment reigned in Medina. For a whole day Muhammad's body lay disregarded. He was finally buried under the floor of the hut of his wife Aishah.

The personality and private life of Muhammad remain to be considered. In general his tastes were quite simple. There is no evidence that his standard of living changed greatly upon the successes and the growth of the Muslim community. Perhaps the only significant change was his practice regarding marriage. After Khadijah died, Muhammad married several times. At one time he had nine wives. Without question, his favorite was the daughter of Abu Bakr, Aishah, whom he married soon after the hijrah while she was still a child. His disposition was usually kindly and gentle, and he made no distinction in his treatment of people. The frailties of human nature were well appreciated, and Muhammad never expected too much from his converts. When he found wrongdoing, he upbraided the culprits for their actions but was lenient and cautious in his condemnations.

Most outstanding, however, were Muhammad's personality and character. The loyalty and compliance rendered naturally and generously to Muhammad by his companions in Mecca and Medina stemmed from the charisma of his being. His great intelligence, his display of a sense of justice, and his revelation of religious truth centered the attention of the citizens of Medina upon him. His converts, from first to last, testified to something special and irresistible in his nature. Lacking this quality, Muhammad's stand as a prophet of God would surely have been ignored by the worldly townspeople of Mecca.

References

BUHL, F., AND A. T. WELCH: "Muhammad." *Encyclopaedia of Islam.* New ed. Vol. 7, pp. 360–376. Leiden: Brill, 1993. In this first part of the article on Muhammad the authors deal with his life; later sections by other writers discuss Muslim popular piety and European critics. Indispensable.

COOK, MICHAEL: *Muhammad.* Oxford, England: Oxford University Press, 1983. A short and simply written account of the life of Muhammad; it includes new views that are critical of the sources often used.

HAYKAL, MUHAMMAD HUSAYN: *The Life of Muhammad.* Translated by Ismail al Faruqi. Philadelphia: North American Trust Publications, 1976. The first Arabic edition of the book appeared in 1935; it is perhaps the most influential of the modern biographies of the Prophet written by a Muslim.

HODGSON, MARSHALL G. S.: *The Venture of Islam: Conscience and History in a World Civilization.* Vol. 1: *The Classical Age of Islam.* Chicago: University of Chicago Press, 1974. Written in a difficult style, this, the first of three volumes, brilliantly covers pre-Islamic and early Islamic history, with an emphasis on religious thought, philosophy, and literary developments.

IBN ISHAQ, MUHAMMAD: *The Life of Muhammad.* Edited by Abd al-Malik ibn Hisham. Translated by Alfred Guillaume. New York: Oxford University Press, 1955. Ibn Ishaq was born about 705 and died in 768 in Baghdad. His work is the earliest known biography of the Prophet. The original is lost but remains in the edited version by ibn Hisham, who died in 833. This is the source of most traditional accounts of Muhammad's life.

PETERS, F. E.: *Muhammad and the Origins of Islam.* Albany: State University of New York Press, 1994. Contains extensive excerpts from early materials dealing with Mecca, the life of Muhammad, and the religion of Islam.

RODINSON, MAXIME: *Mohammed.* Translated by Anne Carter. New York: Pantheon, 1971. The author uses a psychological approach in analyzing stories and events to explain and interpret the Prophet's life.

SCHIMMEL, ANNEMARIE: *And Muhammad Is His Messenger: The Veneration of the Prophet in Islamic Piety.* Chapel Hill: University of North Carolina Press, 1985. The views of later generations of Muslims in regard to Muhammad are shown through developments in philosophy, poetry, and theology.

SHABAN, M. A.: *Islamic History, A.D. 600–750 (A.H. 132): A New Interpretation.* Cambridge, England: Cambridge University Press, 1971. This is a most significant volume, giving many ideas about developments during this formative period in the Middle East.

WATT, W. MONTGOMERY: *Muhammad: Prophet and Statesman.* London: Oxford University Press, 1961. A thorough and scholarly study of the life of the Prophet and his social setting.

The Establishment of the Muslim State

The leadership or caliphate of the Muslim community in the nearly thirty years after the death of Muhammad went in turn to Abu Bakr, Umar, Uthman, and Ali. Even though all four of these figures faced considerable administrative difficulties, the Muslim state expanded enormously and enjoyed a tremendous period of success. A number of crucial decisions were made about basic matters of faith and government even as differences of opinion among certain Muslim groups began to threaten the unity of the community.

THE CALIPHATE

Muhammad's position as a prophet of God precluded the nomination of a successor, even though his other roles as head of state, chief judge, and commander of the army did warrant some provisions for his replacement. Muhammad had sought counsel and taken advice from his companions as situations demanded. After his death, his three most frequent and trusted counselors agreed that Abu Bakr should be the leader of the Muslims. Muhammad's closest friend, Abu Bakr had led the prayers in the mosque and presided over the gatherings of Muslims in the last days when the Prophet had been too ill to perform these functions of leadership. When news of Muhammad's death spread through the city, the native Medinans nominated one of their own as head of the community, but the Meccan Quraish prevailed upon all to accept Abu Bakr as their commander. The following day in the mosque, even before Muhammad was laid to rest, the assembled Muslims swore allegiance to Abu Bakr as the successor of Muhammad.

This outcome was neither unusual nor startling. Chiefs in Mecca and Medina, as well as in Arab tribes, were chosen on the basis of consensus by the heads of families. Leadership often passed to another within the same family but without any idea of inheritance or of legal claim; the power and prestige of a family influenced the decision in its favor. In this instance Abu Bakr commanded the support of the Muslims who had emigrated to Medina, and that fact won his election. Other aspirants would have been from the Makhzum or Umayyad families of Mecca, from a prominent family of Medina, or perhaps from Muhammad's immediate family, but the election of one of these would not have been based on religious considerations. Authority passing into the hands of Abu Bakr, one of Muhammad's close companions, meant the survival of the Muslim community. The consensus of the community became a key ingredient in the political and religious realm.

Khalifah Rasul Allah ("Successor of the Messenger of God") was the name frequently used to describe Abu Bakr and his position. Abu Bakr probably used it himself, although not as a title. From this appellation came the title and institution of the khalifah (caliph), present for centuries in the Muslim world. It implied the assumption of all the duties and prerogatives exercised by Muhammad except those connected with his role as prophet. The caliph was head of the state, supreme judge, leader in public worship, and commander of the army. If he did not actually occupy the pulpit in the mosque, the sermon was delivered in his name and he issued authoritative rulings on law. His name appeared on coins. And it was he whom Muslims revered.

ABU BAKR

Abu Bakr, about three years younger than Muhammad, had probably been the first convert outside Muhammad's immediate family. A prosperous merchant from one of the lesser Quraish families and totally devoted to Muhammad and Islam, Abu Bakr maintained his position of great respect because of a gentle and genial personality coupled with a clear head in matters of judgment and advice. It was a wise selection in that Abu Bakr pursued Muhammad's ways and thoughts. No innovator, he succeeded in holding together the remarkable and talented people who had risen to prominence in this new community.

The first significant task facing the new leadership was to maintain the degree of centralization in Arabia already established by Muhammad. Except in Medina, Mecca, and a few other nearby places, most Arabs questioned the political and taxation authority of Medina. Some even denounced Islam, seizing the end of personal allegiance to Muhammad as an opportunity to cast off the yoke of submission.

Abu Bakr viewed these actions as apostasy, and he met their challenge with the vigor and fire of the Prophet. Khalid ibn al-Walid, a general and a fortunate choice, subdued the tribes of central Arabia, many of which had not given their allegiance to Muhammad. Encouraged, other Muslim generals suppressed revolts and more thoroughly established Islam throughout Arabia, including Bahrain, Oman, and Yemen. Usually treating the vanquished and renegade with mercy, Abu Bakr subjugated most of Arabia in less than a year. The riddah (apostasy) wars were quickly and decisively won.

Indirectly, the Islamization of the Hijaz and the domination of the Arabian peninsula by the Muslims led, in the year 633, to military expeditions into Syria and Mesopotamia (Iraq). Although fighting among Muslims was contrary to the principles of the new society, raiding was an economic necessity in Arabia as well as a frequent activity of most Arab tribes; thus, ventures into adjacent lands were to be expected. Muslims also wished to expand the faith through jihad (holy war; also, internal and spiritual struggling for Islam). With little direct encouragement from Medina, Khalid finished the conquest of northeastern Arabia and then, joining some Arab Muslim tribes, spilled over into the Sasanian lands.

For the ex-merchants of Mecca and Medina who directed the Arab Muslim armies, Syria was more important than Mesopotamia. Their caravans went there; it was more accessible; and to them it was a land flowing with milk and honey. The Syrian expedition was thus a calculated raiding campaign. Three forces of 3000 men each, led by Amr ibn al-As and Yazid ibn Abu Sufyan, defeated the Byzantine governor of Palestine near the Dead Sea and destroyed his fleeing troops near Gaza early in 634. To oppose the fresh Byzantine levies Abu Bakr ordered Khalid to cross the desert from Mesopotamia to Syria. Appearing almost miraculously, Khalid, as the supreme commander of the united Arab forces, defeated the Byzantine army in 634, in the historic battle at Ajnadain, near Jerusalem, thus opening all of Palestine to the Muslims.

The news of this victory reached Medina after the death of Abu Bakr. His passing, however, hardly caused a ripple across Arabia, for Umar immediately assumed the power of leadership that he had been exercising behind the scenes. Recognition and fealty were given to Umar publicly and voluntarily by all. But the two-year caliphate of Abu Bakr must not be considered as a brief empty interlude between two glorious periods, nor should Abu Bakr be seen as a shallow, colorless figure. He made the important distinction between state property and the privy purse of the ruler, even though this action irreconcilably alienated Muhammad's daughter Fatimah. Perhaps most important, when war booty was first coming to Medina from outside of Arabia, Abu Bakr held fast to Muhammad's rule on the spoils of war—all true believers, whether at the front or at home in Arabia, had equal rights.

UMAR

Umar's accession to the caliphate by consensus marked the opening of a ten-year administration of an energetic and brilliant man, then only forty-three years old, whom Muslims consider the second founder of Islam. An early convert, Umar, like Abu Bakr, belonged to one of the less important families of Mecca. Leadership in the hands of Umar signified that Muslim aspects of the community continued.

The affairs most pressing upon Umar at his accession were the military campaigns in Syria and Mesopotamia. Umar's accession to the caliphate did not change Muslim activities in Palestine or Syria. Several Arab forces converged on Damascus in 635, which surrendered on terms to Khalid. The emperor Heraclius (r. 610–641), not willing to cede Syria to the invader, gathered a large army, but it, too, succumbed to Khalid in 636 at the decisive battle of Yarmuk. Upon receiving the news of this disaster Heraclius left Syria and Palestine to the Muslims; north Syria fell from 637 to 647, and Jerusalem also surrendered (perhaps as early as 635 or as late as 638). In the next two years Muslim Arab tribes entered the Jazirah between the Euphrates and the Tigris in the north and ruled that vast and fertile area.

Conclusively, in only four years, the Muslims had occupied these provinces of the Byzantine Empire. Mountains to the north discouraged further advance into

The Spread of Islam

Byzantine Empire

Conquests of Islam to 632

Conquests of Islam to 656

HINDU KUSH

INDIA

Indus

ARABIAN SEA

TURKS

Jaxartes

ARAL SEA

Oxus

IRAN

Isfahan

CASPIAN SEA

CAUCASUS

Ctesiphon

IRAQ

ARABIA

Tigris

Kufah

Euphrates

Medina

Mecca

Persian Gulf

Damascus

SYRIA

PALESTINE

Jerusalem

RED SEA

Nile

EGYPT

Fustat

Alexandria

CYPRUS

BLACK SEA

MAGYARS

Constantinople

BYZANTINE EMPIRE

CRETE

MEDITERRANEAN SEA

BULGARS

AVARS

Danube

SLAVS

ITALY

SICILY

LOMBARDS

Venice

Ravenna

Rome

ALPS

CORSICA

SARDINIA

Rhône

BERBERS

FRANKISH KINGDOM

Rhine

Aachen

Loire

Tours

Poitiers

PYRENEES

SPAIN

Toledo

Córdoba

Seville

ATLANTIC OCEAN

400 mi

600 km

200

300

0

0

Inset map

Justinian's conquests 527–565

Byzantine Empire 527

FRANKS

OSTROGOTHS

ITALY

VANDALS

VISIGOTHS

400 mi

600 km

0

0

Byzantine lands or the vigorous pursuit of the emperor's armies. Arab generals and many tribes, however, looked for new opportunities. Amr ibn al-As decided upon an expedition toward Egypt. Although Alexandria, the second city of the Byzantines and an important naval base, was strongly tied to Constantinople by sea routes, the loss of Syria and Palestine cut off Egypt from the rest of the empire. Egypt, the chief granary of Constantinople and one of the richest and most populous areas of the Middle East, was very inviting to an ambitious general like Amr. Umar gave his assent to the campaign, but reluctantly. Amazed at the extent of the territory already occupied by his armies, he was fearful lest they be spread too thinly.

Leaving Palestine by the historic route along the coast, Amr and 4000 men entered Egypt late in 639 and then moved toward the apex of the Nile delta. Joined by a larger Arab contingent under one of the Companions of the Prophet ("those who knew Muhammad"), Amr moved on Alexandria and forced its surrender in 642. It was a great and rich metropolis whose public buildings, harbor facilities, and defense walls and towers were a cause of wonder to the desert and town Arabs. To protect his position Amr pushed on westward into Libya and received tribute from tribes around Tripoli. Egypt, from Alexandria south up the Nile to a point well beyond modern Cairo, was now a Muslim possession.

Umar also conducted extensive military campaigns in the east. At the moment of Umar's accession to the caliphate, the brilliant Bedouin general al-Muthanna, commander of the Muslim armies in Mesopotamia, was in Medina pleading for reinforcements. He begged that troops be raised among the Arab tribes guilty of opposing the Muslim state upon Muhammad's death, rightly judging that, however weak and chaotic Sasanian society and government might be, surrender to the Arabs would not occur without a struggle.

Although the lifting of the ban against apostates brought streams of warriors into Mesopotamia, superb Persian generalship, the use of elephants, the size of the armies, and the wealth available to the Sasanian kings more than matched the fervor of al-Muthanna's tribesmen. Ravaging far and wide, even to the gates of Ctesiphon, the Sasanian capital, the Arab forces acquired vast herds and immense stores of grain. Yet they had to retire from Mesopotamia into the western desert when finally faced by an organized Persian army under royal leadership.

Umar soon recognized that to hold Mesopotamia and secure its borders it would be necessary to destroy the main Persian army and reduce the capital at Ctesiphon. A major force was gathered, and in a decisive four-day battle at Qadisiyyah in 637 the Persian army was routed. Ctesiphon capitulated, and other battles—especially at Nihavend in 642—destroyed the Sasanian forces. There ensued the consolidation of Muslim control over the lands bordering on the Tigris and Euphrates rivers as far north as Mosul. These years saw the permanent conquest and occupation of Mesopotamia (now to be called Iraq).

The booty that fell to the Arabs suddenly showered upon them great wealth and unknown luxuries. After the battle of Qadisiyyah each soldier received 6000 pieces of silver; at the fall of Ctesiphon each received 12,000 pieces. Gold became as common as silver, and fabulous objects, such as a life-size silver camel with a rider of gold or a golden horse with trappings of gold, emeralds for teeth, and its neck set with rubies, became the prizes of the day. One Bedouin who sold a female slave for 1000 pieces of silver was chided by another for having sold her for so little. The excuse offered was that he had not known any sum larger than ten hundred. From the palace of Ctesiphon the army sent to Umar the royal banquet carpet, measuring 105 by 90 feet (32 by 27 m.) and portraying a landscape. The ground was represented by gold and the paths were silver; meadows were made of emeralds; streams were cascades of pearls; trees, flowers, and fruits were depicted by diamonds, rubies, and other precious stones. Some suggested that the carpet be kept as a trophy, but when many pointed out that earthly goods were but passing things, the carpet was cut into pieces.

Over the next several years Muslim parties raided Khuzistan and advanced toward Isfahan. Persian forces rallied at Hamadan, but with the removal of Umar's ban on advances into Persia (now to be called Iran), Muslims overran most of that land. In the ten years of Umar's caliphate Muslim armies had in an almost unbelievable sweep conquered Iraq and western Iran. They repeatedly crushed armies that only a few years previously had been able to conquer much of the Byzantine Empire. This success was even more remarkable when one considers that other Arab armies at the same time were engaged in conquering Syria and Egypt. During Umar's caliphate Iran, Iraq, Syria, Palestine, and Egypt became parts of the Muslim world. They, together with Arabia (and later Anatolia), constituted the heartland of the Islamic Middle East.

PROBLEMS OF ADMINISTRATION

These conquests alone would have assured Umar the position of second founder of Islam. But Umar's orders regarding the occupation and administration of the new territories were equally important in setting the Muslim pattern that has persisted to the present. Except in some parts of Syria and a few other places, the people of the conquered provinces continued to work and live as they had for centuries, generally with the advantage of paying less in tribute than they formerly paid in taxes. Armies were destroyed and administrators either departed or were employed in similar capacities by the Muslims, but most inhabitants were hardly touched. The strife, destruction, and plagues in the time when the Byzantines and the Sasanians fought each other incessantly were ended, and reconstruction and stability began to take effect.

Indeed, in some instances, Arab domination was not only tolerable but welcome. In Syria and Palestine urbanites had acquired a Hellenistic orientation and many of them, especially in Syria, left with the defeated Byzantine armies; but the local peoples had retained contact with desert and town Arabs, thus easing the transition to Arab rule. In Iraq, native tribes rejoiced in the Sasanian defeats. In Iran, however, the Arabs were never as fully accepted, and the rapidity of the Muslim conquest can be attributed in part to the collapse of the Sasanian dynasty and royal government.

In Syria, Palestine, and Egypt, heavy imperial taxes and the arrogant, high-handed attitude of officials from Constantinople embittered the provinces. More aggravating and more emotional were the persecutions inflicted upon local Christians and Jews. The orthodox Council of Chalcedon in the year 451 condemned the Monophysite doctrine according to which divinity and humanity make one compound nature in Christ. This Monophysite approach to Christianity was persecuted savagely by many emperors without success, until Heraclius, under whose rule these provinces were lost to Islam. In Syria and Egypt, the churches were ardently Monophysite. Thus, when it became apparent that Muslim rule meant religious freedom as well as lower taxes, the Arabs had little difficulty in obtaining cooperation from the local peoples. Since at this time Muslims paid no taxes, this toleration of taxpaying Christians and Jews is the origin of the often repeated but little understood Muslim formula of the three-way choice—Islam, taxes, or death—offered to conquered peoples.

Except in Iran the armies of occupation were held aloof from the established urban centers as much as possible. Umar ordered that camps be placed in the open near the desert. Later, camp cities were established in the newly won provinces— Basrah in lower Iraq, Kufah in central Iraq, Jabiyah in Syria, Ramlah in Palestine, and Fustat in Egypt.

In Syria, Muslim soldiers and local Arabs took over partially deserted towns and some lands whose owners, being Byzantine supporters, had departed. Some 20,000 of the Muslims moved into Hims and Damascus, but the Christians were more numerous. Jealousy and strife arose over available houses and lands, so much so that Umar visited Syria and made an evenhanded redistribution among everyone.

In all the conquered territories governors were appointed to collect taxes and maintain order. Only a handful of administrators accompanied the governors, and, in general, bureaus of government were staffed by previous officials. Non-Muslims could not bear arms and were subject to their own laws, a practice that established Islamic society as one of the most tolerant of all ages and developed into the famous millet (or semiautonomous religious community) system of the Ottoman Empire. Arabs from Arabia were eventually not permitted to own agricultural lands in conquered territory. Later, this injunction evolved into a complex system of landownership and rights of tenancy. Considering all aspects of life, the conquered peoples of the Middle East were disturbed very little by Muslim occupation.

Many other developments occurred during Umar's caliphate. The character of Mecca and Medina began to change as wealth from victories poured in. There was great building activity, particularly in Medina, where apartments were needed for retired soldiers, administrators, and others who flocked to the capital city as well as for the old inhabitants whose wealth had now greatly increased. Umar decreed that grazing grounds in Arabia would be restricted to horses and camels that would be used in the holy wars.

Umar again enunciated Muhammad's policy that although prisoners and movable property belonged to the soldiers who won them, land and taxes from conquest belonged to the whole Muslim community, and one-fifth of all income from conquered territory was to be forwarded to Medina. To facilitate distribution among the Muslims, Umar had a census taken in Arabia and a register (diwan) made of the sum each was to receive annually from the public treasury. The list included Muslims of all ranks, from Aishah and other members of the Prophet's family down to the least prestigious ranks of women and children of non-Arab warriors. Aishah received 12,000 dirhams (a silver coin); Companions of the Prophet, 5000; and a child of non-Arabs, 200.

Perhaps Umar's regulation of the calendar best showed the belief that a new state and community had been born. Numbering the new era with the Prophet's emigration to Medina, Umar decreed that Muslim dating should be counted as so many lunar years after the hijrah and that he had therefore become caliph in the year A.H. 13.

As the years went by and wealth and opportunity grew, Umar had more and more difficulty with his provincial governors and their administrations. Since he had no power to enforce his will, the governors were nearly independent. Consequently, the required income from conquered lands was not always forthcoming; Syria, in fact, never sent any. Among the leaders of Islam, Umar was only first among equals. This was especially true in the camp cities of Kufah and Basrah, inhabited by many nomad warriors who were proud, hardy, political Muslims, resentful of Quraish rule. Al-Mughirah, Umar's governor of Basrah, was a brilliant, tough, scheming native of al-Taif, just the sort of rough-and-ready genius that a new city would require. But when he was caught in adultery, the protests from Basrah were so vociferous that he was recalled to Medina for trial. Although al-Mughirah escaped punishment by slipping through a legal loophole, Umar relieved him of his post. Later al-Mughirah was able to wangle the appointment to Kufah, which he retained for many years, augmenting its power and scope until he became one of the most powerful men in the Muslim world.

In 644, at the very height of Umar's power and prestige, he was assassinated at worship in the mosque of Medina by an Iranian Christian slave who had a personal grudge to settle. On his deathbed Umar selected six leading notables of Medina, all ex-Meccans, to choose his successor. Shortly after he had been buried beside Muhammad and Abu Bakr, the notables, probably on the basis of seniority and a pledge to follow the policies and practices of Umar, selected Uthman ibn Affan, who ruled as caliph from 644 to 656. Another leading candidate, popular with the older Medina families, was Muhammad's cousin Ali, who was passed by because he would not promise to follow in Umar's footsteps.

UTHMAN

Uthman was a member of the prominent and powerful Umayyad family of the Quraish. Noted for his mild manner and piety, his only distinction as a Muslim leader was having been a respected Companion of the Prophet. His three predecessors as leaders of the community had belonged to lesser Quraish families, as had most of the emigrants to Medina. Perhaps it was because of this that they had ignored the traditional Arab policy of nepotism and regarded all Muslims as members of one community and one brotherhood. This new social philosophy was one of the revolutionary aspects of Islam.

Although Uthman was seventy and not particularly energetic when he became caliph, he nevertheless sought greater control over the provinces. He was fortunate to have at his command within his own clan a number of vigorous governors and generals to carry forward the banners of Islam. His foster brother Abd Allah was appointed governor of Egypt with financial and civil control, while the conquering Amr was left as commander of the Muslim army. Outraged, Amr immediately went to Medina and refused to serve, with the acid remark: "To be over the army and not over the revenue was like holding the cow's horns while another milked her." Abd Allah carried on campaigns for booty to the west and south. His armies held Benghazi and Tripoli, ravaged Tunisia, and raided the Sudan for slaves. But Abd Allah's great contribution was the development of a Muslim fleet, including at least some Coptic Christian sailors. In 652 the Muslim navy repulsed a Byzantine armada before it could attack Alexandria.

In Syria, Uthman had as governor his shrewd and aggressive cousin Muawiyah ibn Abu Sufyan, one of the greatest administrators in Muslim history. Umar had appointed him governor of Damascus, and as other governorships in Syria fell vacant they were added to Muawiyah's territory until under Uthman he became the powerful ruler of all of Syria. He rebuffed a large Byzantine army in 647 and in subsequent years sent raiding parties into Anatolia. He, too, built a fleet, gained influence over Cyprus in 649, attacked the island of Rhodes, and in 655, in conjunction with Abd Allah's ships, destroyed a large part of the Byzantine navy.

Other cousins of Uthman were appointed as governors of Kufah and Basrah; during these years they led Arab armies in Iran, continuing to fan out eastward. Fars was fully subdued by 650; parts of Khurasan were taken in 651; inroads were made into eastern Armenia in the 640s; and before the end of Uthman's caliphate, expeditions reached Balkh, Kabul, and Ghaznah in central Asia and Afghanistan.

Even though the caliph might not be personally aggressive, the ability of the Muslim army and navy were no longer questioned in the Middle East. The growing problem was the impact of the new empire upon the Muslim community, which had so recently emerged from Arab society. Most of the original emigrants who still lived were now notables and exceedingly wealthy. One reputedly had 1000 slaves and a palace in each of the great cities; another left a fortune of 400,000 dinars; many had villas in Mecca and Medina or in the hills nearby.

A second and new generation was coming to full manhood. The amusements and luxuries of Alexandria, Damascus, Ctesiphon, and the camp cities of Basrah, Kufah, and Fustat were tempting. Wine, women, and gambling were the undoing of many. Gone were the days when, as Aishah easily recalled, Muhammad considered wheat bread a rare treat and usually made a meal of dates or milk but never had the luxury of both at the same time. Sumptuous living, however, was not the only change. Personal politics and the desire for power and prestige began to eat at the vitals of Muslim society, and certainly Uthman was not strong enough to stem the process that was disrupting the consensus of the community.

MUSLIM POLITICAL FACTIONS

Three political factions were developing in the area ruled by Muslims. The first considered itself the party of Muhammad. Led by members of the less important families of Mecca, it was composed of those who had established the Muslim community. Abu Bakr and Umar had been members of this group, and in most circles Ali, as the husband of Muhammad's daughter Fatimah, was looked upon as the leader. The strength of the party, sometimes called legitimists, lay in Egypt and Iraq.

Leaders of the second faction were members of the Umayyad family and their associates among the Quraish. It had been one of the two most wealthy and influential Meccan families in the pre-Islamic period—a family that had bitterly attacked Muhammad and had led the campaigns against the Muslims in Medina. Uthman was an Umayyad, as were Muawiyah in Damascus, Abd Allah in Egypt, and Marwan, who served as Uthman's executive secretary in Medina. Though latecomers to Islam, they possessed great managerial talent and were rapidly surging to the fore in administering the empire. Umar had used them and controlled them, but the legitimists contended that the Umayyads controlled Uthman through their great power and wealth in Syria.

The third faction was composed of Arab soldiers who had joined the Muslims just before or after Muhammad's death. They outnumbered the other two groups, but they were unorganized and their leaders did not have the prestige of the Quraish. Yet it was their swords that had been responsible for the rapid expansion of the domain of Islam, and since Islam acknowledged no distinctions among peoples or individuals, this faction resented the inferior political position forced upon them. The third party had followers everywhere, but their forces were concentrated in Arabia and the two great military cities in Iraq.

Having lost the election that followed Umar's death, the legitimists carped at Uthman for his policies and his inaction. He was censured for enlarging the square around the Kaba in Mecca and for rebuilding and embellishing the mosque in Medina. Even his standardization of the Quran (still the canonical text today) was attacked, with many feeling that he had no superior religious insight or authority for such an undertaking. But the most severe criticism was leveled at him for appointing so many members of the Umayyad family to high office and for distributing unjustly the spoils of war. His political opponents claimed that he was reverting to the old order of Arab society where blood ties had ruled. Muhammad had preached earnestly to create a unitary Muslim community wherein all members would be like a family and where social, economic, and political equality would prevail, yet after a mere dozen years the traditional preference for the family reasserted its consuming role.

Malcontents across the empire fed on the stories and rumors regarding the sale of positions and the power and wealth of favorites. Supporters of Ali in Kufah first raised the banners of revolt. When opponents arrived in Medina from Egypt and Iraq and surrounded Uthman's residence, the caliph would not permit an army to be raised in his defense and commanded Muawiyah not to come to his rescue. After a siege of several months in 656 the rebels, including Abu Bakr's son, stormed the palace and murdered Uthman. Anarchy reigned in Medina until a group of notables, under pressure from the rebels, elected Ali to the caliphate and restored order.

ALI

Ali, Muhammad's cousin, adopted son, and son-in-law, was a pious and esteemed Muslim who as an individual soldier in his younger days had shone as one of the great heroes of Muslim battles. He had already been disappointed three times in not being selected caliph, and he may have known of the move to kill Uthman. Generally throughout the Muslim world he was recognized as the caliph, although with reluctance. The new governor appointed by him for Syria was rejected by Muawiyah, who refused to resign. There were many individuals who did not acknowledge Ali as caliph, largely because of jealousy or shock over the murder of Uthman.

Disgruntled elements among the legitimists, aided by Aishah, who bitterly opposed Ali, hatched a rebellion in Mecca on the grounds that Ali had implicated himself by not punishing the regicides. Ali led his army from Medina, which from that day onward ceased to be the residence of any caliph, and defeated the insurgents near Basrah in the renowned "battle of the camel," when the fighting swirled around Aishah on her camel. (Women had earlier participated in battlefield activities during the days of the Prophet, and others would later take part in the struggle between Ali and Muawiyah.) In this first battle of Muslim against Muslim neither booty nor reprisal against the vanquished was taken. Many illustrious Companions of the Prophet were killed. Aishah was captured but was permitted to retain an honored status in Medina, where she served as a source of religious information as she lived on for twenty-two years in her apartment—the place where, beneath the floor, Muhammad, Abu Bakr, and Umar had been buried.

Denouncing Ali as an associate of the murderers of his uncle, the caliph Uthman, Muawiyah withheld his allegiance and met Ali's forces at Siffin on the banks of the Euphrates in northern Syria in 657. In the midst of battle, fighting between Muslims was dramatically halted upon agreement that the contest would be decided by referring to the Quran. Arbitration was unsuccessful; Muawiyah refused to accept Ali as caliph until Ali punished the murderers of Uthman, and Ali could not kill his supporters, nor would he abdicate. Each force, however, retired from the field, and a stalemate ensued.

Following the "battle of the camel," Ali had made his capital at Kufah. His episode with Muawiyah was, in part, a revival of the persistent rivalry between Syria and Iraq for dominance in the Middle East. It was also a struggle between the Umayyad Quraish, now located in Syria, and the settled Arab tribesmen of Iraq and the Hijaz.

At the "battle of the camel" so many of the legitimist party perished that it disappeared from the annals of Islam, leaving Ali, in Kufah, at the mercy of the dominant local and religious groups. In fact, some members took the name Kharijites ("Seceders") and revolted against Ali in protest against his willingness to arbitrate. Ali destroyed their force in 659 but was assassinated in 661 by a Kharijite in Kufah on the way to prayer. Hasan, Ali's eldest son, was declared caliph in Kufah, but Muawiyah was recognized as caliph in Damascus. A few months later Hasan reached an agreement with Muawiyah and retired on a royal pension to his palace in Medina. Muawiyah, thenceforth, was accepted throughout the Muslim Empire as the sole caliph, and the center of the state shifted to Damascus.

Thus ended the consensual era of the caliphate in which the rulers were selected for reasons other than birth or military might. Throughout the bulk of this period Medina still served as the capital of the Muslim world, and the leaders of the community had known the prophet Muhammad personally. It was an Arab state;

the conquered provinces were ruled by a relatively small minority of Arabic-speaking Muslims. Most Muslims of later times looked back upon this era as a golden age, when Islam was extraordinarily successful and the community of believers was governed with great piety and wisdom. With the transfer of the seat of authority to Damascus and the caliphate to Muawiyah of the Umayyad family, a new era was born.

References

References cited at the end of Chapter 3 relate to this chapter as well.

ARNOLD, THOMAS W.: *The Caliphate.* Oxford, England: Clarendon Press, 1924. A classic discussion of the formation and history of the rule of the Muslim state.

DABASHI, HAMID: *Authority in Islam: From the Rise of Muhammad to the Establishment of the Umayyads.* New Brunswick, N.J.: Transaction, 1989. An examination of the period from a sociological point of view.

DONNER, FRED MCGRAW: *The Early Islamic Conquests.* Princeton, N.J.: Princeton University Press, 1981. The standard account of the Muslim conquests of Syria and Iraq, this work also contains a valuable analysis of the relations between nomadic tribesmen and the Medina government.

IBRAHIM, MAHMOOD: *Merchant Capital and Islam.* Austin: University of Texas Press, 1990. An intriguing essay on the early history of Islam up to the Umayyad dynasty, emphasizing the role played by merchants.

KAEGI, WALTER E.: *Byzantium and the Early Islamic Conquests.* Cambridge, England: Cambridge University Press, 1992. Carefully traces both military and other causes of Islamic expansion based on Byzantine and Arabic sources. An excellent study.

KEDDIE, NIKKI R., AND BETH BARON, EDS.: *Women in Middle Eastern History: Shifting Boundaries in Sex and Gender.* New Haven, Conn.: Yale University Press, 1991. A wide variety of essays dealing with the theoretical and practical aspects of the history of women in the Islamic Middle East, including a discussion of Aishah.

KENNEDY, HUGH: *The Prophet and the Age of the Caliphates: The Islamic Near East from the Sixth to the Eleventh Century.* London: Longman, 1986. This detailed political history incorporates recent scholarly research as well as the original sources; the author considers, but ultimately rejects, revisionist historians who have attacked the reliability of the primary sources.

LEWIS, BERNARD: *The Arabs in History.* Oxford, England: Oxford University Press, 1993. A concise account of the rise of the Arabs, emphasizing the broad economic movements through the ages and correlating these developments with historical processes among the Arabs.

SHOUFANI, ELIAS: *Al-Riddah and the Muslim Conquest of Arabia.* Toronto: University of Toronto Press, 1973. A study of the wars in Arabia upon the death of Muhammad, showing that Arabia was far from united at the time of the Prophet's death.

SPELLBERG, D. A.: *Politics, Gender, and the Islamic Past: The Legacy of 'A'isha bint Abi Bakr.* New York: Columbia University Press, 1994. Discusses later views of Aishah's life and importance.

VAGLIERI, L. VECCHIA: "Ali ibn Abi Talib." *Encyclopaedia of Islam.* New ed. Vol. 1, pp. 381–386. Leiden: Brill, 1960. This article, like the following one by W. Montgomery Watt, shows the high standards and thorough scholarship of the authors in the *Encyclopaedia of Islam,* a basic reference tool for all who are concerned with the Islamic Middle East.

WATT, W. MONTGOMERY: "Abu Bakr." *Encyclopaedia of Islam.* New ed. Vol. 1, pp. 109–111. Leiden: Brill, 1960.

CHAPTER 5

The Spread and Organization of the Muslim Empire Under the Umayyads

The death of Ali left no serious rival to Muawiyah and his leadership over all Muslims. He established the rule of the Umayyad dynasty over the Muslim community and state, replacing the consensual system of the first four caliphs. The Umayyad Empire lasted only ninety years, but Muawiyah and his heirs accomplished much in the political, military, and administrative areas while at the same time providing the prerequisites for both cultural accomplishments and religious and factional disputes.

Proclaimed caliph at Jerusalem in 661 while in his fifties, Muawiyah established Damascus as his chief residence and seat of government. Until his death nineteen years later, he managed the provinces through energetic, capable, and forceful governors, who tried to maintain a strong discipline over the proud and turbulent Arab soldiery. In Iraq, however, the crowded garrison cities and determined leaders declared their autonomy so vigorously that Muawiyah had a limited degree of control. Muslim soldiers held the province and the Sasanian governmental lands as theirs by right of conquest and rarely sent any part of the income to Damascus.

At home Muawiyah ruled confidently and with good judgment as the first among equals. He discussed policies of state with the notables about him, frequently explaining the course of government publicly from the pulpit of the mosque. In truth, his power rested upon the personal loyalty of the Syrian army, which was the strongest and best organized of any in the state. More and more he built an administration in the Romano-Byzantine tradition; less and less was he the tribal Arab shaikh governing purely on a personal basis. He was the first Muslim ruler to execute a fellow Muslim for political reasons.

Five years before his death, Muawiyah induced the leaders of the empire to recognize his son Yazid as his successor. Thereupon, Yazid was taken to Medina and Mecca to have those holy cities accept him as the next caliph. This procedure was definitely a dynastic custom, and the Muslim elite of Medina, declaring the step to be a sinful innovation, refused to render the requested homage. Essentially, this method of succession made the position of caliph a hereditary one, or at least a family prerogative, and overtly established the Umayyad Empire, which lasted until 750. Succession was among the males of the Umayyad family, but not necessarily from father to eldest son; instead, the incumbent ruler could designate his heir or power might be seized by the ablest member of the dynasty.

In general and by comparison with other ruling families, the Umayyads produced a dynasty of talented, competent caliphs. They were much maligned by later Muslim historians, especially the pious religious scholars who wrote under the patronage of the succeeding dynasty and depicted the Umayyads as hard-riding, wine-bibbing, luxury-loving, worldly minded usurpers of the caliphate. But the Umayyads organized the Muslim state into a centralized force that once again carried forward the banners of Islam into distant places. They were realists who, in order to meet existing and evolving situations, could not always follow the principles of government and law being formulated by theologians and jurists in the holy city of Medina. However, the military successes of the Umayyad dynasty were balanced by the development of new concepts and dogmas within Islam that gave birth to numerous Muslim sects. Under the Umayyads the unity of theology, as well as politics, was lost in the Muslim world.

CAMPAIGNS AGAINST BYZANTIUM

The nearest and greatest rival power of the Umayyad state was the Christian Byzantine Empire with its capital at Constantinople; the nearest and richest land for the Muslims to raid was Anatolia, the heart of the Byzantine lands. Muawiyah, as governor of Syria, had already driven Byzantine armies from north Syria and twice defeated Byzantine fleets. He repeatedly raided Armenia, which was forced by 662 to pay tribute to Damascus. Muawiyah's army exploited the weakness of the rule from Constantinople by annual summer excursions through the passes into Anatolia as far north as Caesarea (later known as Kayseri). After he became caliph, Muawiyah's forces roamed far and wide over Anatolia, and he attacked Constantinople, but the land and sea walls of the city proved too great a barrier for the Muslim Arabs.

Another assault upon Constantinople was launched by the Umayyad caliph Sulaiman. His brother Maslamah, supported by land and sea forces, occupied both shores of the Bosphorus and held a tight siege of Constantinople for fourteen months. In 717, however, he was foiled by Greek fire and the brilliant defenses of the new emperor, Leo the Isaurian (a Syrian from Marash), and by the ravages of disease, hunger, and an unusually severe winter. At the same time the new caliph, Umar II, strongly opposed to all expansionist policies, ordered the siege lifted and the Muslim forces withdrawn. Several generations elapsed before the Muslims appeared again before the walls of Constantinople, which proved too thick and too strong for the Arabs to penetrate without the aid of gunpowder. (Byzantine history will be discussed more thoroughly in Chapter 13.)

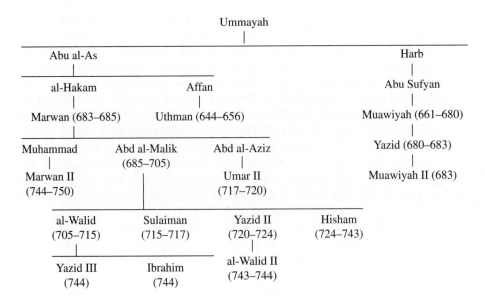

The Umayyad Caliphs

NORTH AFRICA AND SPAIN

The records do not disclose any planned pincers movement on Europe by the Umayyads, although simultaneously with their attacks upon Constantinople the greatest westward movement of Islam was being executed. Amr ibn al-As, governor of Egypt, sent a Muslim force into North Africa and resumed raids into Libya in the 660s. A camp city whose construction was begun in 670 at Qairawan in Tunisia served as headquarters to subdue Berber tribes and the coastal cities dependent upon Constantinople. Toward the end of the century Byzantine rule over the coast was ended by a joint army-fleet maneuver, which drove the Byzantines from Carthage as the new city of Tunis was founded. Appointed governor of northwest Africa sometime between 698 and 705, Musa ibn Nusair consolidated the region and added greatly to his military force by recruiting from among the Berber-speaking tribesmen. Most of Morocco, however, subsequently remained beyond the effective control of the Umayyad governors for decades.

One of Musa's Berber lieutenants led a small band across the Strait of Gibraltar in 710 and returned with such valuable booty that Tariq crossed on his celebrated raid in the early summer of 711 with several thousand men, mostly Berbers, and established a base on the strong height that still is called Tariq's mountain—Jabal Tariq, or Gibraltar. Crushing the Visigothic Christian forces of Spain, Tariq fanned out northward at will. Málaga, Córdoba, and Toledo fell; by winter Tariq found himself master of half of Spain, with an almost unlimited amount of booty at his disposal.

Scolding Tariq for acting independently, Musa joined his henchman in 712. Within two years nearly all of Spain had been overrun by Muslim forces. From Galicia, Musa looked down upon the waters of the Atlantic and the Bay of Biscay. At this time, a messenger ordered Musa to appear before the caliph in Damascus. Accompanied by Tariq, Musa made the long trek overland and presented to the court his trophies and many male and female Visigothic captives. Shortly thereafter a new caliph stripped Musa of his wealth and degraded him, perhaps because of fear or jealousy of Musa's great popularity. Musa died in poverty a few years later in the Hijaz, a strange fate for one who had opened Europe to the Muslims.

Within six or seven years the conquest of Spain was completed. The Arabs called the province al-Andalusia ("Land of the Vandals"), and it, or some part of it, remained a Muslim land for almost eight centuries. The Arab-Berber-Muslim (Moorish) culture left its indelible mark on Spain, which in turn had a profound influence on Islamic society. The speed and ease with which Spain was conquered indicated that it was in a state of near anarchy, following a struggle over succession to the Visigothic throne. The Visigoths ruled in an oppressive fashion and attempted to convert all Jews to Christianity by force.

In 720 Arab-Berber invaders seized Narbonne on the Mediterranean and established an arsenal and base for operations north of the Pyrenees. Raiding columns rode out of Narbonne every year, terrorizing the countryside and carrying off rich booty, especially from churches and convents. The greatest of these expeditions was the renowned foray of 732 led by the governor of Spain, Abd al-Rahman. The raiders turned back from their northward course only after the loss of their leader in the determined, bloody resistance put up by Charles Martel in the celebrated but indecisive battle of Tours. Never again did an organized expedition of Muslims approach so near to Paris.

Although Narbonne was not abandoned until 759, the Arabs and Berbers of Spain never fashioned a real hold upon southern France because of their lack of manpower, the distance from Damascus, and a running feud between Berber and Arab that led to violent insurrection in North Africa and Spain. Conversions to Islam among the Berbers were so extensive as to compromise the relationship between conquerors and vanquished in North Africa. Many Muslim Arabs looked down on the Berbers, who upon becoming Muslims anticipated equality with the proud Arabs. When the expected treatment was not forthcoming, rebellion burst out everywhere. From 739 to 742 North Africa was in flames from one end to the other. Berbers claimed that they were given semiarid plateau lands in Spain while the Arabs acquired all of the fertile areas.

In addition, factional strife among the Arabs existed at every turn. Political, religious, and family quarrels were at this moment rocking the Islamic world from the Pyrenees to the Indus, making incursions beyond well-established frontiers wholly ineffective. Furthermore, rivalry developed between Arabs from Arabia and the more recently arrived Syrian army sent to subdue Berber uprisings; their bickerings with the Arab governors and lords of Toledo and Córdoba were interminable. From the time of the battle of Tours to the landing of the Umayyad prince in Spain in 755, the term of the governorship of Spain averaged twelve months.

With such turmoil, uncertainty, and anarchy, permanent conquests in France were impossible.

EXPANSION IN ASIA

While the Umayyads were extending Islam westward into North Africa and Spain, a similar expansion carried Muslim rule to the Indus River and the frontiers of China in central Asia. Often territory was peacefully surrendered by treaty rather than conquered. Becoming viceroy of the eastern lands of the caliphate in 695, al-Hajjaj, a schoolmaster of al-Taif, gave his governor of Khurasan Arab troops to establish a strong base at Merv (Mary). These were added to the thousands of Arabs from Kufah and Basrah that Muawiyah had sent to settle in the oases around Merv; moreover, local Persian landowners, volunteers, and clients swelled the ranks of the Muslim forces. The army crossed the Amu Darya River (known then as the Oxus) and in a series of brilliant campaigns brought large parts of central Asia under Muslim domination. Bukhara and Samarkand in Uzbekistan and adjacent areas were subdued between 705 and 712 and soon became Islamic strongholds; Buddhist temples and monasteries were destroyed. Herat and Kabul in Afghanistan were also conquered. Native Turkish and Persian rulers were left in charge of civil affairs, although Muslim tax collectors and military inspectors represented the imperial authority. A generation later another caliph sent an Arab general beyond the Amu Darya River as far as Kashgar, on the borders of China, to reconquer the area and bring the Turkish rulers, some of whom had accepted Islam, again under caliphal authority.

Farther south, al-Hajjaj's son-in-law was authorized to lead a column toward India. Taking Makran, he occupied Baluchistan and subdued Sind. The Arab Muslims controlled the territory of modern Pakistan after 711 (and continued to rule there until 1026). Steady conversion to Islam, especially among Buddhists, eventually made this northwestern corner of India an important part of the Muslim world and laid the foundations for the Islamic state known today as Pakistan. Expansion beyond Sind to the east, or beyond central Asia to the east and north, did not take place for many of the same reasons as mentioned in connection with the situation of the Arab Muslims in southern France. In addition, the Muslims faced strong opposition from the military and political forces of Hindu Indian states as well as the power of China.

FISCAL DEVELOPMENTS

This wave of Muslim expansion under the Umayyads brought to a head certain economic and fiscal problems that had been developing at an accelerated pace. From the time of the hijrah in 622, Muslims were subject to a small tax to support their poor and unfortunate brethren, but there was no general taxation. Toward the end of the seventh century, with Arab Muslims scattered over the face of the earth and conversions among conquered non-Arab peoples growing by leaps and bounds,

The Umayyad and Early Abbasid Empires

TURKS

INDIA

Indus

Samarkand
Bukhara

Oxus

Balkh

ARABIAN SEA

Merv
Herat

Nishapur

ARAL SEA

Joxartes

CASPIAN SEA

Isfahan
IRAN
Shiraz

Volga

Hamadan

Tabriz

Persian Gulf

CAUCASUS

Baghdad
Ctesiphon

ARABIA

Basra

Tigris

IRAQ
Euphrates

Kufah

Aleppo

Medina

BLACK SEA

Damascus

Mecca

Dniester

Constantinople

S Y R I A

Jerusalem

Dnieper

EMPIRE

PALESTINE

RED SEA

BULGARS

Aswan

Danube

BYZANTINE

CYPRUS

EGYPT

Alexandria

Nile

Fustat

Dniester

CRETE

MEDITERRANEAN SEA

Rhine

ALPS

Venice

SICILY

ITALY

Rome

LOMBARDS

Loire

CORSICA   SARDINIA

Rhone

Qairawan

AGHLABID EMIRATE

PYRENEES

BERBERS

SPAIN
Toledo

Córdoba

Seville

ATLANTIC OCEAN

		400 mi
0	200	
0	300	600 km

Byzantine Empire

The Caliphate at 656

Conquests of Umayyads 661–750

Abbasid Empire, early 9th century

Abbasid Empire, late 9th century

questions of state annuities to worthy Muslims, landownership, and taxation arose to vex one caliph after another and ignited serious disturbances in Muslim society.

Besides the state's share of booty, which in the Umayyad era was very sizable, the principal source of revenue came in taxes from subject peoples and land. Each free non-Muslim was required to pay for his protection a poll tax (jizyah) of four, two, or one gold dinar or the equivalent in goods, according to wealth and position.

Land taxes were far more complex. In the days of the earliest conquests Muslim Arabs were forbidden to possess land outside of Arabia proper. Domain lands of ousted Byzantine and Sasanian governments and vacant lands fell to the caliph as agent for the Muslim community, and the income went into provincial coffers, with all surplus supposedly being forwarded to Damascus. As the Umayyad rulers established irrigation and agricultural development projects, the ensuing revenues from the provinces proved a valuable supplement to taxation. Ownership of other land was not changed, so peasants or local landlords who had owned the land under the Byzantines and the Sasanians continued in possession. In most cases the taxes (kharaj) remained the same and were collected by the same agents. As Arab Muslims acquired properties in Syria, Iraq, and other areas outside Arabia, freedom from land taxes usually prevailed. The state leased domain land to Muslim Arabs, who bought and sold the rights so that the land had the appearance of private property. Consequently, Arab laws governing landownership and tenure adhered generally to Byzantine, Persian, and more ancient practices and customs, thereby assuring to tillers of the soil throughout the Middle East a continuity that changed only slowly.

As the number of non-Arab Muslims increased through conversion, most deserted the land for the city in the expectation of living on state annuities as Arabs did. They paid no taxes on the land left behind in the village and ceased to pay the poll tax. This disastrously affected the treasuries, especially in North Africa, Iraq, and Khurasan—a large and rich province in northeastern Iran and central Asia.

Furthermore, in order to eliminate increasing resentment of non-Arab Muslims and to prevent incipient revolutions in several of the provinces, the Umayyad caliph Umar II decided to free Muslims, irrespective of origin or state, from paying poll and land taxes. The result was a lowering of revenues that upset the fiscal system of the government beyond the point of toleration. Caliph Hisham withdrew the order and instituted the policy, generally permanent in Muslim lands ever since, that although poll taxes "fell off" upon conversion to Islam, land taxes did not. Hisham also used land surveys and population censuses as part of the taxation system. At that time in the provinces the old tax measures were considered by non-Arab Muslims, the principal landowners, to be very inequitable. Great disaffection led to civil war in North Africa and proved to be a major factor in the overthrow of the Umayyad regime by the troops from Iraq and Khurasan.

SOCIAL ORGANIZATION

As the Arabs and the native inhabitants of the conquered territories began to coalesce, there arose four social classes: Muslim Arabs; clients, mostly Muslim non-Arabs; non-Muslim free persons (Christians, Jews, Zoroastrians); and slaves. The most numerous were the non-Muslim free persons—even at the end of the Umayyad Empire about 90 percent of the population was still non-Muslim.

The Muslim Arabs were the leaders of the Islamic order, and the Quraish of Mecca claimed to be the noblest of the Arabs. Wherever Islam spread, Muslim Arabs regarded themselves as the rightful leaders of society, and at first only they could live in the new garrison cities such as Qairawan and Kufah. Most Muslim Arabs outside Arabia lived in cities. Although Islam taught the equality of all believers and disavowed family connections in favor of religious ties, Muslim Arabs everywhere retained pride in their lineage: clan and tribe feelings ran high, and marriage between an Arab woman and a non-Arab man was considered a serious mistake. In the Umayyad period most Muslim Arabs were enrolled in the imperial registry, each receiving regular payments from the state treasury on the theory that the receipts of the Muslim community should be divided among all its members. In practice the Muslim Arabs acted as if it were decreed that the Arab minority would rule the non-Arab majority, Muslims as well as non-Muslims.

By the beginning of the eighth century, clients (mawali, singular mawla) outnumbered the Arab Muslims in most parts of the Umayyad Empire except Arabia. Most of the clients were non-Arab Muslims who became affiliated with an Arab Muslim tribe; in addition, even some poor Arab Muslims were not considered to be in the ruling Arab elite. Many clients were freed slaves. The masses in lower Iraq, Syria, and the cities of Khurasan were converted so rapidly that revenues in those provinces had dropped conspicuously. Rarely were these converts accepted as equals by the Muslim Arabs, and usually they attached themselves to a member of an Arab tribe or family (thus the term "clients"). Yet the converts were in many instances trained and educated individuals with skills not possessed by many Arabs. As several generations passed, because of the adoption of the Arabic language and considerable intermarriage, the Arabs from Arabia who had migrated to conquered territory had become intermingled among a variety of peoples, who jointly participated in a new common culture and customs in particular sections of the Middle East. In areas such as Syria and Iraq, where many Arab Muslims settled, non-Arab Muslims were absorbed relatively quickly, and Arabic became the dominant language of the masses. In more distant lands such as central Asia, India, and Spain, the few ruling Muslim Arabs dominated society and Islam spread, but indigenous languages prevailed in the long run. Non-Arab Muslims had a large role in cultural formation in the core areas of the Middle East; in the outer periphery of the Muslim lands they played an even more significant part.

Non-Muslims—Christians, Zoroastrians, Jews, pagan Berbers, and a few scattered others—were called dhimmis and were protected and recognized legally as second-class subjects on condition that they acknowledged the political supremacy of the Muslims. They were judged almost entirely in their own courts in accordance with their own laws and were permitted to worship in their own way and to live their personal lives as they wished. They were, nevertheless, greatly circumscribed in matters of civil rights and community affairs. Non-Muslims could not bear weapons; instead, they paid taxes. They were subject to many distinctive regulations concerning dress, types of saddles, and manner of riding. While dhimmis could not hold the highest public offices, many served in bureaucratic positions or as advisers to high Muslim Arab officials. In the Middle East many non-Muslims learned to speak Arabic in addition to the language they had earlier used, but the change to Arabic was slow and gradual and by no means universal. For a time Christians and Jews continued to produce theological thinkers of high quality, although as more and more of the population converted to Islam minority groups tended to become less innovative. Often the brightest and most ambitious members of the minorities were among the first to convert to Islam, and the lower social status of the dhimmis discouraged new thinking.

At the bottom of the social ladder were the slaves. Slavery in the Middle East had existed for many centuries before the birth of Islam in Mecca. Although Muhammad openly condemned it, saying that freeing slaves was pleasing in the sight of God, he declared slavery legal. In Islamic society, no Muslim could be enslaved legally; acceptance of Islam, however, did not give a slave freedom. Children of a slave woman remained slaves unless the male owner of the slave acknowledged them as his children. Marriage between master and slave was not permissible, although concubinage was. A concubine who presented her master with children could not be sold, was accorded special recognition as the mother of his children, and gained her freedom upon his death.

Slave trading was an active and profitable business in the Middle East under the Umayyads. Most slaves were acquired as booty in victorious campaigns and successful raiding expeditions, but many were purchased through regular slave channels. Greeks, Armenians, Turks, Kurds, Spaniards, Goths, Iranians, black Africans, and Berbers predominated, but there were slaves of every race and description. Prices rose and fell with the supply. Wealthy Arab Muslims frequently counted their slaves in the thousands.

POLITICAL ADMINISTRATION

When Muawiyah became caliph, his first task was to effect a systematic administration for the empire. Obviously following the practices of the Byzantine Empire formerly current in Syria, Muawiyah organized his government along three main functional lines: political and military affairs; tax collection; and religious administration, including courts and endowments. He also established rapid government messengers, the office of chamberlain, and a corps of guards.

The caliphs governed Syria including Palestine, and upper Iraq directly. The rest of the empire was divided by the Umayyads into several provinces, each with a governor appointed by the caliph; the provinces were often subdivided, merged, and reorganized. The religious officials, tribal army leaders, military police, and civil administrators in each province acted upon the authority of the governor. Administration was located in buildings usually located next to the chief mosque; government employees engaged in holding prisoners, supervising the treasury, and collecting taxes were housed together. Local expenses were defrayed by taxes collected in the provinces, with only the tax balances being forwarded to Damascus. Toward the end of the Umayyad regime when the administration began to weaken, provincial governors built up great personal fortunes by neglecting to forward the full balance to the caliph. Viceroys even remained in Damascus, hiring agents to go to the provinces to perform their functions. Frequently, special officers were sent directly by the caliph to collect taxes and to be responsible solely to him rather than to the viceroy, who resented the implied lack of confidence.

As the empire expanded, problems of trained and loyal personnel, of communications, and of money came to the fore. The number of qualified Arabs was too small to fill the positions required to keep the government functioning. In Syria, Iraq, and Egypt, Muawiyah retained the services of most of the government employees he found there upon the conquest. These employees used Greek, Persian, and Coptic to keep their records. Not until the time of Abd al-Malik was the conversion to Arabic as the language of government systematically begun. By the end of the Umayyad era, however, government affairs were recorded in Arabic, and clerks were Arabic-speaking and usually Muslim in faith. Mawali filled many prominent administrative posts, and there were even special contingents of these Muslim clients in the army.

At the time of their conquest, the Byzantine and Sasanian empires largely relied on a money economy with gold, silver, and copper coins in wide circulation. The Muslims took these over as mediums of exchange, sometimes with a phrase from the Quran stamped on the coins. True Muslim-Arabic coins, first minted at Damascus in the reign of Abd al-Malik, were similar in value to coins already in circulation. The gold ones were called dinars after the Roman denarius; the silver, dirhams, from the Greek drachma.

Muslim judges (qadis) for the various cities of the empire were usually chosen by the provincial governors and were responsible to them. Since these qadis were concerned only with the Muslims, there was little occasion for judges in the villages at this time. Caliphs and provincial governors also held court and handed out justice personally.

OPPOSITION AND OVERTHROW

As long as Muawiyah lived, his firm hand checked the development of opposition to the Umayyad dynastic rule of the Muslim community. After the death of his son Yazid I in 683 a civil war broke out; it was only resolved by the efforts of Marwan I and the reestablishment of Umayyad rule during the long reign of his son, Abd al-Malik, from 685 to 705.

Arab Muslim society tended to separate into two great groups, which were allegedly related to tribal groupings present in the Arabian Peninsula before Islam. Under the Umayyads with the rule of Abd al-Malik and his ruthless viceroy, al-Hajjaj, party strife reached a high point and influenced many aspects of political life in all parts of the empire. Reminiscent of the famous popular factions of the Byzantine Empire, the rivalry of the Arab parties became keen and often bitter. Although each group went by a variety of names, the two main divisions were often called the South Arabians and the North Arabians. Between the two parties any real differences of language, culture, and appearance had long since disappeared; only legend and rivalry remained to perpetuate the factions. Nevertheless, the feuding between the two groups was very real, as is attested by the oft-repeated incident of the two-year war in Damascus that was touched off because a member of one party stole a watermelon from a garden belonging to a member of the other party.

Beginning with Abd al-Malik until the downfall of the Umayyads, differences between the two parties became fixed upon two central issues, one political and one social. The first was the question of military campaigns of expansion. The South Arabians were opposed to these campaigns, and when Sulaiman, a sympathizer, became caliph in 715, he generally tolerated only expeditions that would consolidate frontiers. Umar II, a staunch supporter of this nonexpansionist view, stopped every campaign in 717 when he became caliph. His successors, however, were all expansionist North Arabians, and al-Hajjaj lieutenants were reappointed to high positions. They believed that the social and economic ills of the empire, such as pressures for equality in taxation, fiscal policies of stipends for all Arabs, and civil disturbances caused by some Arabs' refusing to go on campaigns, could be met by expansion on the frontiers, which would occupy the soldiers and avert civil wars, at the same time bringing in booty for soldier and imperial treasury alike.

The social difference was over assimilation—the granting of full status to non-Arab Muslims. The South Arabians believed that Islam recognized equality between Arab, Iranian, Berber, Egyptian, and all Muslims. The North Arabian view, on the other hand, held that Arabs formed a special elite. In general, South Arabians, as exemplified by Sulaiman and Umar II, felt that successful rule could be effected only by the consent and cooperation of those ruled. The North Arabian faction tended to rely more on authority, force, and favoritism to maintain order and peace. (In spite of their views concerning equal rights, the South Arabians excluded non-Arabs from their leadership, as did, of course, the North Arabians. For example, the caliph Abd al-Malik raised thirteen sons, but only the six born of Arab mothers could be considered as possible successors; even the capable Maslamah was ineligible because his mother was a non-Arab. This prejudice against Umayyad princes whose mothers were not Arabs lasted almost to the end of the dynasty in Damascus.)

Another source of opposition to the Umayyads emerged from two grandsons of the Prophet, the children of Ali and Fatimah—Hasan and Husain. Upon the death of Hasan, who had relinquished his caliphate in Kufah to make way for Muawiyah, his brother Husain became the head of the house of Ali. He remained at peace with the Umayyads until Muawiyah's death; then, refusing to recognize Yazid as successor and caliph, he and others from the families of Muhammad's early Companions rebelled openly. Husain set out for Kufah with a meager force and at Karbala in Iraq was surrounded and cut down by Umayyad supporters on the tenth of Muharram, A.H. 61 (October 10, 680). Although at the time it caused hardly a ripple across the Muslim body politic, his death was later observed by the Shiite sect of Muslims, who came to regard Husain and his brother Hasan as martyrs for the faith and as the rightful heirs to the leadership of the Muslims. Karbala has become a most holy spot, and frequently a kind of passion play is enacted by Shiites on the tenth of Muharram.

Husain's martyrdom left the opposition to the Umayyads in a very weakened position. When Medina, the center of remaining opposition, surrendered to Yazid's army, the rebels sought the protection of the supposed inviolability of Mecca but were pursued by the Syrian forces. In the midst of siege operations, which shattered the Kaba, news of Yazid's death led the Syrian army to withdraw. The North Arabian party in Mecca thereupon openly supported Abd Allah ibn al-Zubair, who was recognized as caliph throughout Arabia, Iraq, Egypt, Iran, and even in parts of Syria. Had he been willing to transfer his residence to Damascus, it is possible that all Muslims would have accepted his rule. Instead, Ibn al-Zubair's followers were defeated by the South Arabians in Syria, and the elderly Marwan, Muawiyah's cousin and formerly executive secretary to the earlier Umayyad caliph Uthman, took power. Nine months later Marwan was dead, and the task of reuniting the state fell to his son Abd al-Malik. In 692, eight years later, a Syrian army led by al-Hajjaj defeated Ibn al-Zubair after another destructive siege of Mecca and thus ended the second Muslim civil war.

This violent struggle of the Umayyads with Husain and Ibn al-Zubair was more than personal or dynastic; it was even more than a bitter outbreak of political party rivalry. In the first instance, the lesser families and clans of the Quraish of Mecca still resented and begrudged the power and dominance that the Umayyad clan had possessed in the decades just prior to the hijrah. Added to this jealousy was indignation over the fact that most of the Umayyads had opposed Muhammad almost to the very end; in fact, Muawiyah's father had driven Muhammad and the Muslims from Mecca. That this family should inherit Muhammad's mantle was more than the Prophet's Companions could stomach.

More serious in the long run was the moving of the center of the state to Syria. It was inevitable that the wealth and worldliness of that province would affect the ruling elite living there. Visitors from Arabia and religious scholars from Kufah were shocked at the elegance and pomp of the Damascus court and were scandalized by the flow of wine, the singing girls, and the devotion to hunting they saw. The Umayyads built luxurious hunting palaces in the desert, and many princes became patrons of poets, singers, musicians, and horse trainers. All these practices seemed far removed from the teachings of Muhammad. As the wealth and power of the ruling society increased, idleness, pleasure seeking, and disregard for Muslim virtues multiplied. Al-Walid II was the most shocking of the rulers among the pious; famous for his bathing in a tub of wine, he was extravagant, eccentric, sensual, and irreverent.

Such antics and increasing centralization alienated the provinces. The regime in Damascus, starting with the reign of Abd al-Malik, introduced greater centralization in government, an army reorganization, and more Arabization in the operations of the bureaucracy. These policies and the neglect of strict Muslim precepts fanned opposition among the pious. Shiite and Kharijite parties flourished especially in Iraq, Iran, and Khurasan. Iraqis disliked Syrian rule. In a sense it revived the old enmity between east and west exemplified in the wars of the Sasanian and Byzantine empires. Shiites, who held the view that the mantle of the Prophet rightfully belonged to the family of Muhammad and Ali and objected to the idea that might makes right, formed the nucleus of the opposition. At this time they were joined by the Kharijites, centered near Basrah, Fars, and the Arabian peninsula. They were religious democrats who proposed that piety be the criterion for selecting the leader of the Muslim community; they objected to prior designation or inheritance, as claimed by the Umayyads and the Shiites. Instead, the consensus of the faithful should determine the leader. Both groups were poorly organized and included people with a wide range of opinions on religious and political matters.

The third subversive party was that of the Abbasids, led first by Muhammad, a great-grandson of al-Abbas, who in turn was an uncle of the Prophet. This Muhammad circulated the story that one of Ali's grandsons on his deathbed had transferred the rights of the Alids (followers of Ali) to the Abbasid family. Beginning about the year 740, Abbasids posed as the leaders of the house of Hashim—Alid as well as Abbasid—and from their headquarters south of the Dead Sea gathered under their standard all anti-Umayyads of Islam. The Umayyads should have seen the handwriting on the wall when many Arabs in Syria, finding life too comfortable, refused to answer the call to arms.

The most valuable support to Alids and Abbasids came from Arab and non-Arab Muslims of Iran and Khurasan, who objected to an inferior position, demanded the equality preached in Islam, and rebelled against Marwanid policies of expansion and authoritarian rule. The organizational structure of the Umayyad Empire was decaying rapidly, as the Syrian troops that were the bedrock of military support for the Umayyads lost battles against external non-Muslim armies and were spread thinly throughout the extensive lands of the empire. An atmosphere of petty, vicious, and sometimes murderous rivalry surrounded the court; and in every corner of the empire there was strife between the two Arab parties. Such violent partisanship, coupled with what was viewed as the immoral life of many Umayyads, invited rebellion everywhere and played into the hands of non-Arab Muslims. The Abbasids utilized these factors to the full in their propaganda in the east and gathered Iranians, Khurasanians, Shiites, Alids, and others around their banner, for which they chose the color black. The Umayyads' and Alids' banners were white; that of the Kharijites was red.

In 747 the Abbasids raised the standard of revolt. Despite the execution of the initial leader, Abu al-Abbas, a great-great-grandson of al-Abbas, and his Iranian agent succeeded in directing a band of Iranians, Khurasanians, and South Arabians who took the city of Merv. Iraq fell in 749, and Abu al-Abbas was recognized in Kufah as caliph. Marwan II met the rival force early in 750 on the bank of the Zab, a tributary of the Tigris. The great Abbasid victory there opened all Syria, which had few soldiers in it, and Damascus surrendered in April. Abu al-Abbas moved the capital of Islam from Damascus to Kufah, establishing Iraq as the center of the Abbasid empire and placing a new family on the throne as leaders of the Islamic community.

At an infamous banquet near Jaffa some eighty Umayyads were murdered; others were hunted from one end of the empire to the other in an Abbasid attempt to wipe out the entire Umayyad family. Among the few who escaped was Prince Abd al-Rahman, who made his way to Spain and established an Umayyad state there. The political unity of the Islamic community was shattered from that time onward.

References

References cited at the end of Chapters 3 and 4 are pertinent to this chapter as well.

BLANKINSHIP, KHALID YAHYA: *The End of the Jihad State: the Reign of Hisham ibn Abd al-Malik and the Collapse of the Umayyads.* Albany: State University of New York Press, 1994. Emphasizes military defeats as the chief cause of the overthrow of the Umayyads.

CRONE, PATRICIA: "Mawla." *Encyclopaedia of Islam.* New ed. Vol. 6, pp. 874–882. Leiden: Brill, 1991. Treats the history of the clients in law, and for the Umayyad and Abbasid periods.

CRONE, PATRICIA, AND MARTIN HINDS: *God's Caliph: Religious Authority in the First Centuries of Islam.* Cambridge, England: Cambridge University Press, 1986. A detailed examination of the use of the title "caliph," and a revisionist interpretation of the role of the Umayyads as religious leaders.

GLUBB, JOHN B.: *The Great Arab Conquests.* Englewood Cliffs, N.J.: Prentice-Hall, 1964. A military history by an English general with long experience in the Middle East.

HAMILTON, ROBERT: *Walid and His Friends: An Umayyad Tragedy.* Oxford, England: Oxford University Press, 1988. A vivid account of the life of Walid II, with an emphasis on poetry.

HAWTING, G. R.: *The First Dynasty of Islam: The Umayyad Caliphate, AD 661–750.* Carbondale: Southern Illinois University Press, 1987. This is a careful and balanced political and military history with especially important information on tribal relations with the Umayyads.

LEWIS, BERNARD: *Race and Slavery in the Middle East: An Historical Enquiry.* New York: Oxford University Press, 1990.

MORONY, MICHAEL G.: *Iraq After the Muslim Conquest.* Princeton, N.J.: Princeton University Press, 1984. The continuity of Sasanid with Islamic Iraq is examined in the areas of administration, taxes, and ethnic and religious groups.

SHABAN, M. A.: *The Abbasid Revolution.* Cambridge, England: Cambridge University Press, 1970. A detailed history of the Arab conquest of Iran and Khurasan; highlights the importance of assimilation between Arabs and Iranians up to the Abbasid victory.

SHARON, MOSHE: *Black Banners from the East: The Establishment of the Abbasid State—Incubation of a Revolt.* Jerusalem: Magnes Press, 1983. The tangled early history of the Abbasids and their use of propaganda to gain victory over the Umayyads are thoroughly traced.

AL-TABARI, MUHAMMAD IBN JARIR: *The History of al-Tabari.* Vol. 18: *Between Civil Wars: The Caliphate of Muawiyah.* Translated by Michael G. Morony. Albany: State University of New York Press, 1987. This monumental and vitally important chronicle is being published in thirty-eight volumes, translated and annotated by various authors. They are essential original sources on which most subsequent historians have based their own work.

TAHA, ABDULWAHID DHANUN: *The Muslim Conquest and Settlement of North Africa and Spain.* London: Routledge, 1988. Detailed military and political history.

CHAPTER 6

The Flowering of the Muslim World Under the Early Abbasids

The destruction of the Umayyads marked the opening of a new age in the history of the Muslim community in the Middle East—the rule of the Abbasid dynasty in its early phase, which lasted until the middle of the tenth century. The Abbasids were Arabs whose relationship to the prophet Muhammad provided their chief claim to legitimacy. The political center of Islam shifted eastward to the Tigris-Euphrates valley since Arabia proper had become less significant in power and wealth and Damascus, with its interior lines of communication and transport, no longer held an advantage as the capital of such an empire. Iraq was more productive than Syria or Egypt and profited from extensive trade with India, China, Indonesia, and central Asia, whereas commerce languished in the Mediterranean and Europe. The markets of India and China were fabulous and their production was varied; the decaying economy of the west, except for Spain and Constantinople, was yielding rapidly to the demands of a self-subsistent agricultural life.

As has been pointed out, the Abbasids had shrewdly capitalized on the many grievances that various factions held against the Umayyads and, in an adroit propaganda campaign among the Muslim ummah, posed as the champions of each disgruntled group. However, hardly was Abu al-Abbas, the first of the line, seated on the throne than he openly showed the insincerity of Abbasid promises. Though he surrounded himself with theologians and pretended to take their advice, positions of authority and power were filled by Abbasids or by trusted family agents. The chief executioner, who was a new governmental official, always stood near the caliph's throne. The Alids who were the leaders of the Shiites were sometimes honored but powerless; Kharijites, who had generally opposed the Umayyads, received little consideration; viceroys, generals, and ministers who became too wealthy or too popular were executed. Indeed, many leaders who had engineered the Abbasid revolution were liquidated in the first years of the new regime by Abu al-Abbas, who was known as al-Saffah ("the bloodletter"). Abbasid rulers governed more imperiously than their predecessors; Harun al-Rashid was the first caliph to delegate to others the duty of the imam in leading prayer.

It was at the end of Abu al-Abbas's reign that the true installation of the new empire occurred with the ascension to the caliphate in 754 of Abu al-Abbas's brother, Abu Jafar. This ancestor of the next thirty-five caliphs took the name al-Mansur (meaning "rendered victorious").

Al-Mansur discovered that his personal safety was in question since his residence lay so close to hostile Kufah. The danger led him to build, in 762–766, a new capital on the Tigris, only 30 kilometers north of Ctesiphon, where a personal bodyguard of several thousand was on hand at all times. This new circular fortress-palace of al-Mansur grew within a few decades into the fabled luxury-filled city of Baghdad, which has thrilled the imagination of people from that time onward.

Like many of the Abbasids who followed, al-Mansur faced a struggle that eventually sapped the strength and effectiveness of the Abbasid government: the question of succession to the throne and the criteria for legitimate rule inside the royal family. Often the heir apparent was sent to Khurasan or Syria as governor, to learn how to be an able administrator. Succession did not necessarily go from father to eldest son; instead, rule might be transferred to any among the able male relatives. This was an issue that increasingly served as a vehicle by which social and governmental groups could strive for power. To obtain the recognition for his son al-Mahdi, al-Mansur gave prodigious bribes to his cousin, who had been named to the line of succession by al-Saffah. Nonetheless, al-Mahdi's elder son and designated heir, Musa al-Hadi, was almost passed over by the generals and court ministers in favor of his more popular younger brother, Harun al-Rashid. The court intrigues involving the accession of later caliphs grew even more heated as time passed. By the close of the ninth century, the question of succession overshadowed every act of the caliph and dominated the thoughts of the court. By the tenth century caliphs were removed, blinded, and turned out into the streets to beg.

Succession to the caliphate was not, of course, the only internal issue for the Abbasid government. Simultaneously, issues concerning theology and jurisprudence added fuel to the political fires, while differences in governmental philosophy complicated the political jockeying at the Abbasid court almost from the beginning until the rule of al-Mamun and his immediate successors. The religious scholars preached that the life of state and society should be based on the Quran and the practice of the prophet Muhammad, whereas the other main contestants for the caliph's ear, the civil secretaries and governing officials, looked for a political structure tending toward absolutism so that their decisions would be enforced. The latter group desired the guidance of an absolute ruler; the pious sought security in the collective wisdom of the community. Caliph al-Mamun looked in vain for a compromise between these two factions.

THE GLORY OF BAGHDAD

During the first century of the Abbasid caliphs Baghdad was the hub of the Middle East, with a population numbering in the hundreds of thousands. Officially named Madinat al-Salam (the "City of Peace"), Baghdad was a circular garrison fortress, situated on the west bank of the Tigris near a canal connecting with the Euphrates. The central area had a mosque and a green-domed palace with an audience hall

130 feet (40 m.) in height and was surrounded by a wall, a deep moat, and two thick outer brick walls. Numerous other luxurious palaces for princes and ministers of state were erected, and beyond these rose the busy metropolis of the Muslim world.

The setting of the Abbasids in the lavish fortress capital of Baghdad ensured that their rule would follow the pattern of the Persian and Oriental monarchies of earlier days. In comparison to the unabashed prodigality of royal life in Baghdad and to the difficulty an ordinary Arab had in approaching the caliph, the rule of the Umayyads seemed the essence of frugality and simplicity.

The wealth and magnificence of the court of al-Rashid (786–809) were renowned in his own day, and through the tales of the *Arabian Nights* the splendors of his court and life in Baghdad have captured popular fancy in later ages, although, in fact, he often resided elsewhere. The center of display was, of course, the palace of the caliph, where Zubaidah, al-Rashid's favorite wife, held sway. She insisted that all dishes be made of gold and the tapestries be studded with precious

The Early Abbasid Caliphs

gems. She outfitted several hundred of her most attractive maidservants as page-boys (a fashion that was soon all the rage in Baghdad), largely to amuse her son and to divert his affections from a favorite eunuch. At a festival celebrating the marriage of a prince, a thousand matched pearls were showered upon the couple as they sat upon a jewel-encrusted mat of gold.

In Baghdad, the wheel of fortune turned easily. This aspect of Abbasid rule was exemplified in the life of Khaizuran, a slave from Yemen and the mother of al-Rashid. Given to al-Mahdi, she became his favorite and ultimately his wife, and her sons were recognized at an early age as the heirs to the throne. The intelligent and able Khaizuran exerted considerable influence in the capital: she had her family brought to court; her brother became governor of Yemen; and her sister married a prince whose daughter was the famous Zubaidah. Before Khaizuran died she held vast properties bringing in an annual income of more than 160 million dirhams. The preference of the generals and courtiers for al-Rashid over al-Hadi was stimulated considerably by Khaizuran's acknowledged favor for the former. (Although Khaizuran's fortunes seemed to have steadily improved, wealth, position, and favor in Baghdad were always precarious, as the sudden fall of many favorites and advisers attested.) While Khaizuran's life demonstrated the influence women could exercise, the system of segregating upper-class urban women from men in public places was already being developed, as shown by al-Mansur's construction of a separate bridge across the Euphrates designated for women only.

At the court any word or act of flattery, a song or poem that pleased, or a deed well done was rewarded handsomely: 60,000 dinars tossed to the singer of a pleasant tune with complimentary lines; 100,000 dirhams to a poet who beguiled at the right moment; a landed estate to an entertainer or a dancer! For a sonnet extolling Harun al-Rashid on a trivial occasion a poet was given 5000 gold pieces, a robe of honor, ten Greek slave girls, and a horse from the imperial stables.

From the four corners of the known world came royal embassies bearing gifts and seeking the caliph's favor. Most publicized of these, at least in the west, was the mission sent by Charlemagne in 797 to secure greater safety for Frankish pilgrims to Palestine. The trophies brought back from the journey, the most fantastic being an elephant, so magnified the incident for the west that Baghdad became a romantic, incredible, and fabulous place and Harun al-Rashid a person in some far-off never-never land.

Intellectual interests of the Abbasids, hand in hand with imperial munificence, produced a great cultural flowering. The learning of the Greco-Romans, the Iranians, and the Hindus was translated into Arabic and assimilated into Muslim culture. Arabic became the common language not only for theology and jurisprudence but for philosophy, science, and the humanities. History, political treatises, literature, poetry, and etiquette came largely from Iran; astronomy and mathematics, from India; philosophy, medicine, and science, from Greece. By the middle of the ninth century the main works of Aristotle, Plato, Euclid, Ptolemy, Hippocrates, and Galen had been translated into Arabic and were known the length and breadth of the Islamic world. Royal patronage set the stage for translations and the expansion and dissemination of knowledge. Many princes, governors, and high officials followed the same course and became, on a lesser scale, patrons of scholars.

ADMINISTRATIVE ORGANIZATION

The Khurasanian soldiery was the power that had raised the Abbasids to the caliphate, and for several generations a Khurasan bodyguard maintained imperial authority in Baghdad and elsewhere. Even in this time, however, some army units still consisted of Arabs from Syria and Iraq. In the first decade of Abbasid rule the army conquered the area south of the Caspian Sea. Harun al-Rashid later launched his army against the Byzantine capital of Constantinople, but two sieges failed to take the walled city on its fortified peninsula. By the 830s mawali clients formed some units in the Abbasid army, along with slave groups recruited originally from non-Muslim peoples, as the army became diverse in its origins.

Iranian influences grew apace at the court. After the building of Baghdad, Iranian dress, manners, and techniques spread quickly throughout the empire, especially in fashionable society, although Arabic remained the language of administration and court culture, while the earliest bureaucrats to work for the Abbasid dynasty were often drawn from the same Arab families that had served the Umayyads. Converts to Islam no longer needed to become the clients of Arab Muslims, though freed slaves often continued to affiliate themselves in this way.

The Umayyads had advisers and ministers heading various departments of the government. Under the Abbasids, however, there arose the office of chief minister, the vizir, who became the alter ego of the caliph. The vizir's power was almost unlimited, and the office was frequently handed down from father to son. The first family of vizirs was the famous Barmakids of the second half of the eighth century. Khalid ibn Barmak, son of a Buddhist chief priest of Balkh, held the confidence of al-Saffah and al-Mansur. Khalid served as minister of finance and then as governor, became a general, and acted as guardian of al-Rashid. Khalid amassed a great fortune; on one occasion he was forced to pay 3 million dirhams of taxes which as governor he had not forwarded to Baghdad. His son, Yahya, served al-Mahdi as vizir but fell into disfavor and was imprisoned by al-Hadi.

The apogee of Barmakid fortunes was reached under al-Rashid. Yahya became the first true grand vizir, issuing orders and managing the empire with great skill and profit. He favored a policy of strict centralization, in both provincial government and taxation. He became alienated from the military, who generally preferred decentralization, which advanced their interests in the provincial garrisons. Yahya's sons al-Fadl and Jafar also exercised great power. Al-Fadl followed in his father's footsteps as governor and vizir, while Jafar became al-Rashid's boon companion and confidant. The Barmakids lived in a sumptuous manner, and their generosity to their own favorites and clients became proverbial throughout the Islamic world. Yahya, however, was distressed by Jafar's personal and intimate relationship with al-Rashid, fearing that it would bring disaster. The family could not hope for social, political, or religious equality with the Abbasids. In 803, without warning, Jafar was beheaded because of policy differences in regard to Khurasan and because he had used al-Rashid's friendship to impinge too far upon royal prerogatives; Yahya, al-Fadl, and two others were imprisoned; and the Barmakid fortune—palaces, lands, and some 30 million dinars in cash—was confiscated.

Other families of vizirs rose and fell, and with them rival generals and armies.

Under the Abbasids, generals were a significant force in obtaining the throne. Following al-Rashid's reign, intense rivalry arose between two of his offspring, the sensual al-Amin, son of the famed Zubaidah, and the more serious and steady al-Mamun, son of an Iranian slave girl. Al-Mamun had the better generals, and with the full support of the Khurasanian army he attacked Baghdad and beheaded his caliph brother. Al-Mamun's rule of twenty years was marred by insurrections that were overcome only very slowly. Egypt was brought to obedience by 827; the Aghlabids in Tunis paid tribute, but most of North Africa was lost to the empire. On the other hand, mountainous Azerbaijan and the Caspian shores were conquered.

By 861, the succession to the throne was to be decided for a time by the leaders of the army. The rulers al-Mamun and al-Mutasim had brought Turks and Persians, some slave and some free, to Baghdad and Samarra in northern Iraq (Samarra was the capital from 836 to 892) in such numbers that they dominated the imperial bodyguard, which in turn controlled the caliph.

After the beginning of the tenth century, the Abbasid caliphs receded into the background as puppet rulers. Diverse groups from the geographic margins of the empire began to influence its center. The old elites, including the Arab tribal leaders, the descendants of the Khurasanians long settled in Iraq, and the Abbasid family, declined in importance. Arab ancestry was still a source of pride, but more and more often non-Arab Muslims became leaders of society. Powerful captains in the eastern and western provinces, some Arabs and some non-Arabs, seized authority and established autonomous Muslim states. The political unity of Islam, which had already been cracked in the 750s by the establishment of the Umayyad state in Spain, was gradually shattered, starting with the advent of the military groups who controlled the Abbasid caliphate.

ECONOMIC AND SOCIAL LIFE

The bases of Abbasid wealth rested on agriculture and a century of relatively capable, honest, and stable administration of the provinces. Caliph al-Mansur established such a vigilant and judicious system of government throughout the empire and enforced such thrift that it took more than a century of spending to dislocate the state budget. In central Iraq the ancient canal system initially was operated so efficiently and extended to such a degree that productivity rose. In that same century imperial revenues from Egypt, Syria, and Iran showered great wealth upon the ruling circles and the inhabitants of the capital cities.

As a natural corollary to this organized agriculture and governmental stability, there arose a flourishing commerce and, for that age, an advanced technical production. The great preponderance of commerce was in the nature of domestic trade. Caravans plied the trade routes from the Indus to the Pyrenees, distributing the wares of each province throughout the empire and exchanging manufactures of Iran for those of Egypt, carpets of Tabaristan for paper of Baghdad. Handsome profits were realized, but great fortunes were as easily lost.

The bulk of foreign trade was with the Far East. From Baghdad and Basrah, Muslim merchants carried their goods by sea via the Persian/Arabian Gulf to China and India, while the main overland route to China went through Samarkand and central Asia. A flourishing trade across the Sahara subsequently developed between the North African Muslims and the populations of the Senegal River region. Although trade with western and eastern Europe was undoubtedly profitable, it seemed so trivial that Muslim traders left it for the most part to Christian and Jewish itinerants. Goods from the Middle East were expensive, and Europe beyond the lands of the Byzantines had little other than furs to offer in exchange. A type of banking with letters of credit and double-entry bookkeeping arose to facilitate the extensive commerce that stretched across much of the eastern hemisphere.

Concurrent with the rich agriculture and brisk commerce of the Abbasid empire there developed an active artisanal production in every province. Artisanal traditions of the ancient Middle East had not perished, and under a relatively secure political system these crafts revived and expanded. Textiles of linen, cotton, silk, and wool were the most important. Although each area produced high-quality fabrics of many types, every city or province excelled in some particular pattern or technique; carpets from Bukhara, silk kerchiefs from Kufah, linens from Egypt, damask from Damascus, and brocades from Shiraz gained fame. Special skills were often localized, and families guarded trade secrets, which were passed on as prized possessions from father to son through the centuries.

The science of papermaking was acquired from China, and by the tenth century paper mills existed in Iran, Iraq, Arabia, and Egypt; in the twelfth century one was built in Spain. Paper made from flax facilitated the production of books on an enormous scale. Private and public libraries spread widely; paper was even made that was light enough to be transported by carrier pigeon. Fine glass was produced in Egypt, and the glass industry flourished in Syria. The ceramic industry in the Middle East reached back into the most distant past, and the Abbasid era created some of the finest potteries and glazed tile; tin glazing and luster painting were used to create painted ornamentation. Samarkand, Rayy, Baghdad, and Damascus won fame for their decorated porcelains and their fine shades of blue, green, and turquoise. Middle Eastern artisans were equally skilled in metalwork using iron, steel, copper, brass, silver, and gold; the ewers made at this time were especially famous. Other crafts included making dyes, perfume, jewelry, leather, inlaid and decorated wood, and enamelwork on wood and metal. Soap manufacture in Syria produced hand soaps and colored, perfumed toilet soaps.

The Middle East in the eighth and ninth centuries utilized many of the arts and techniques of China, India, Iran, and the Byzantine Empire, and those of the early civilizations of Greece, Egypt, and Mesopotamia. The synthesis of these influences gave great life to Muslim civilization and production, which was regarded in Europe as the marvel of the ages. The slow movement of Middle Eastern know-how across the Mediterranean and over the Pyrenees gave rise to the development of similar handicrafts in Europe.

The Abbasid championing of non-Arab people within the Muslim Empire ironically took place at the same time as a rapid Arabization of the empire. Iranians, Berbers, Syrian Christians, Egyptian Copts, Jews, and others began to speak Arabic in their daily lives. Science, philosophy, literature, and books of knowledge from other cultures and tongues were rendered into Arabic. And an Islamic civilization evolved in which poets, scholars, musicians, merchants, soldiers, viziers, and concubines were considered cultural Arabs; little heed was given to parentage or birthplace for Muslims, and non-Muslims also contributed substantially to society and culture.

Local rulers followed the common patterns of Abbasid government and administration, and Muslim civilization continued to prevail. Political loyalties might differ as more often than not religious doctrines did; but artists, men of letters, scientists, merchants, and travelers were as much at home in Córdoba as in Cairo, Baghdad, or Samarkand. Provincial governors imitated as sumptuously as they could the Baghdad court. From India to Spain palaces and mosques were built where petty princes lived in the grand manner among poets, scholars, soldiers, dancing slaves, and fawning courtiers.

DECENTRALIZATION UNTIL 945

Although Islamic civilization prevailed in the Abbasid era from the borders of China to the Pyrenees, there was never more than a fleeting political unity. The followers of Ali and his descendants were never completely mollified, and more and more religious sects arose to battle against authority. As more of the subject population became Muslim the cohesion of the Muslim ruling elite and its mutual loyalty declined; instead, local attachments and loyalties grew, while allegiance to the central government and the caliphate relatively decreased. Social and economic ills periodically disturbed the empire. The caliphs starting with al-Mutawakkil frequently allocated the right to collect taxes from a given region to army generals. Ambitious and not-too-loyal soldiers sought to carve out their own principalities whose armed forces increasingly were based on professional cavalry, often recruited from Turks or Berbers. Centered upon a land area, communications and transportation over most of the Abbasid empire were costly, slow, and tedious. Distant provinces were difficult to control, and, as caliphs grew less and less concerned with the grueling task of governing, even nearer provinces flaunted the wishes of the Abbasid rulers. Revenues declined by about one-half from 788 to 915. The increasing salinity of the soil in central Iraq sharply reduced agriculture and the taxes derived from it— resources located at the center of the empire and formerly very important. The canals in Iraq were not properly maintained; taxes were raised and collected in a harsh manner, often through a system of tax farming; and the insurgencies of the late ninth century created widespread havoc. When Abbasid caliphs became mere puppets in the hands of bureaucrats in Baghdad and then were dominated by generals, governors and soldiers in the provinces opted for local autonomy.

Shiite claimants to the leadership of the community emerged in several places. With the death of the eleventh imam or leader of the chief Shiite lineage in 874 and the apparent disappearance of his son shortly thereafter, one source of opposition to Abbasid claims was temporarily removed, but other groups, both Sunnites and Shiites, posed many challenges to the Abbasid caliphs.

In the west—Spain and North Africa—Abd al-Rahman, grandson of the Umayyad caliph Hisham, escaped from Abbasid vengeance, and, making his way in disguise through Syria, Egypt, and North Africa, reestablished the Umayyad dynasty in Spain in 756. First as amirs and then in the tenth century as caliphs, the rulers maintained at Córdoba a court that enjoyed an eminence that rivaled the Abbasids in Baghdad. Many distinguished scholars, scientists, and literary figures in the Muslim world flourished under their patronage. At its zenith in the tenth century, Córdoba had 500,000 inhabitants, 700 mosques, 300 public baths, and a royal palace comprising 400 rooms that ranked second in size and splendor only to those at Baghdad and Constantinople. Umayyad power, however, began to deteriorate toward the middle of the tenth century. The palace chamberlains seized control, and Muslim Spain disintegrated into smaller states (Seville, Málaga, Toledo, Saragossa, and Granada) under the leadership of various families.

In 788 in Morocco Idris, a descendant of Ali, established an independent Sunnite regime. From their capital at Fez the Idrisids ruled most of Morocco for two centuries, firmly implanting Islam in that corner of Africa and establishing a flourishing trade with sub-Saharan Africa. Arabic became the dominant language in the towns, while Berber was used widely in the countryside. The Idrisids ultimately succumbed to the Umayyads of Córdoba.

Harun al-Rashid appointed Ibrahim ibn al-Aghlab governor of Algeria and Tunisia in 800. For a century the Aghlabids ruled as free amirs from Qairawan in Tunisia. Their fleets ravaged the coasts of Italy and France, seizing Malta, Sicily, and Sardinia; by 835 the Aghlabids had learned how to use the "Greek fire" liquid incendiary, which had first been employed by the Byzantines in 674, in naval warfare. The great mosque of Qairawan was built by the Aghlabids and soon became for western Muslims a venerated shrine, next in importance and holiness to Mecca, Medina, and Jerusalem. But in 909 the Aghlabids were engulfed by a Shiite uprising that placed on the throne the Fatimid dynasty, which claimed descent from Fatimah, the Prophet's daughter.

Meanwhile, beginning with the middle of the ninth century, a succession of clever governors and two short-lived Turkish dynasties, the Tulunids and Ikhshidids, ruled Egypt in the name of the Abbasids, who received some revenues from that province but exercised no real power there. Conversion to Islam had been slow, and the Muslims remained largely an urban-based minority group. Foreign slave and mercenary armies were recruited by the new dynasties. In the second half of the tenth century Egypt was conquered by the Shiite Fatimids of North Africa, whose claim of descent from Ali and Fatimah persuaded many to accept them as the valid leaders of the Muslim community.

South and east of Baghdad the Abbasid empire was likewise succumbing to the laxity of the caliphs' rule and was falling into the hands of aggressive soldiers and leaders who founded local dynasties, even though some of these groups acknowledged the nominal overlordship of the Abbasids. The greatest dangers were south of Baghdad and closest to hand: the rebellions of the Zanj and the Qarmatians.

Since early Islamic times the marshlands of southern Iraq, a perfect area for guerrilla warfare, had been the scene of a kind of slavery, based on large-scale agricultural estates, which was not seen elsewhere in the empire; the slaves, who were harshly treated, were mostly of east African origins. Under the leadership of Ali ibn Muhammad, an Arab from Iran, and with the help of Arab tribal allies, they rose against their owners in 869, took Basrah, and were a major threat to the Abbasid political and social order as they espoused Kharijism. In 883, the Abbasid caliph finally conquered the Zanj in southern Iraq, but the prosperity of that region was ruined. The Qarmatians were Ismaili Shiites (like the Fatimids in Egypt) who, starting in the ninth century, steadily attempted to overthrow Abbasid power, basing their forces in Kufah, among the nomadic tribes of Syria, and in Bahrain and eastern Arabia generally. In 923, they conquered Basrah, and in 930 the Qarmatians raided Mecca and carried off the sacred Black Stone from the Kaba. Internal disputes stopped their expansion, the Black Stone was returned to Mecca, and the Qarmatians became a local force enjoying peace and prosperity until the late tenth century. Although their enemies accused them of practices contrary to Islamic morality, they were most noteworthy for the existence of an advisory council whose opinions the ruler was obliged to consider, as well as approaches to gender relations based on equal treatment for men and women.

To the east, the Abbasids succeeded in crushing a peasant revolt based in Azerbaijan, but they lost effective power in their easternmost provinces of Sind and Makran, on the borders of India and Pakistan, after the middle of the ninth century. Three local dynasties dominated the central regions of the eastern part of the empire in the ninth century. The Tahirids, starting in 820, extended their sway from Merv to the frontiers of India. They were a family of local governors who sent extensive taxes to the Abbasid caliphs, and they played a major role in the internal political life of Baghdad. From 867 the Saffarid dynasty spread outward from Sistan, destroyed the Tahirids, invaded and conquered most of eastern and southern Afghanistan for Islam, and ruled with the investiture of the caliphs until 900, when they were reduced to only a local influence in southeastern Iran. Also in the late ninth century the truly independent Persian Sunnite Samanid dynasty was acknowledged by the caliphs as local governors; by the tenth century, they seized all of Khurasan but settled in central Asia, establishing Bukhara as their capital and Samarkand as the leading city of the state. Culture continued to flourish under Samanid rule, and the new forces were quickly assimilated, as illustrated by the Samanid ruler who invited the young Ibn Sina (Avicenna) to Bukhara and gave him free run of the state library. Under the Samanids, Firdawsi wrote his first poetry, marking the rebirth of Persian literature. From the Muslim conquest to the Samanid period, Arabic had been the language used everywhere by scholars and men of letters; this new era signaled the advent of the brilliant works of Muslim Iran, written in Persian, not Arabic.

In Baghdad itself, the authority of the Abbasid caliph vanished almost completely. Only the title and some of the prestige remained. Turkish captains of the bodyguard deposed caliphs almost at will; at one time three blind ex-caliphs were beggars on the streets of Baghdad. Taking the title *amir al-umara* (literally, "commander of commanders," but better, "prince of princes"), the de facto ruler imprinted his name on coins and insisted that his name be coupled with that of the caliph in the Friday prayers.

In 945 a Shiite Iranian, Ahmad ibn Buwayh, entered Baghdad with a strong army and was recognized by the caliph as the commander of commanders. Making and unmaking caliphs openly, the Buwayhid control of the Abbasid caliphate publicly and clearly changed the nature of political power and ushered in another new era in the political history of the Islamic Middle East. Before these new political changes took place, the development of Islamic theology, law, and philosophy, along with the creation of a complex and flourishing Islamic civilization, had already provided elements of continuity and creativity for the peoples of the Middle East, whose lives had been considerably changed as a result.

References

References cited at the end of Chapters 4 and 5 contain material pertinent to this chapter.

ABBOTT, NABIA: *Two Queens of Baghdad: Mother and Wife of Harun al-Rashid.* Chicago: University of Chicago Press, 1946. Not only does this volume discuss the lives of Khaizuran and Zubaidah, but it is full of the color and life of Baghdad in the eighth and ninth centuries.

ABUN-NASR, JAMIL M.: *A History of the Maghrib in the Islamic Period.* Cambridge, England: Cambridge University Press, 1987. An excellent survey.

BLIGH-ABRAMSKI, IRIT: "Evolution Versus Revolution: Umayyad Elements in the 'Abbasid Regime 133/750–320/932." *Der Islam* 65 (1988): 226–243. As the author makes clear, there were some links between Umayyad practices and the new Abbasid state.

DANIEL, ELTON L.: *The Political and Social History of Khurasan under Abbasid Rule, 747–820.* Minneapolis, Minn.: Bibliotheca Islamica, 1979. This detailed book follows the victory of small landowners in a key province and their subsequent fate, with attention to tax policy and regional particularism, as well as rural unrest.

FRYE, R. N., ED.: *The Cambridge History of Iran.* Vol. 4: *The Period from the Arab Invasion to the Saljuqs.* London: Cambridge University Press, 1975. Seven chapters on Iran's political history, followed by other excellent chapters on social, cultural, religious, and intellectual history.

GERVERS, MICHAEL, AND RAMZI JIBRAN BIKHAZI, EDS.: *Conversion and Continuity: Indigenous Christian Communities in Islamic Lands, 8th to 18th Centuries.* Toronto: Pontifical Institute of Mediaeval Studies, 1990. Twenty-six diverse essays on religion in the Middle East, especially useful for the contributions of Christians to Islamic society.

LASSNER, JACOB: *The Shaping of Abbasid Rule.* Princeton, N.J.: Princeton University Press, 1980. Separate essays cover the topics of crises over the succession to the throne, the clients of the Abbasids, the army, the city of Baghdad, and the royal palace.

SALIBI, KAMAL S.: *Syria under Islam.* Vol. 1.: *Empire on Trial, 634–1097.* Delmar, N.Y.: Caravan Books, 1977. The complicated history of the tribes of Syria is carefully presented and analyzed, along with a general discussion of Syrian history during this period.

SHABAN, M. A.: *Islamic History: A New Interpretation.* Vol. 2: A.D. *750–1055 (A.H. 132–448).* Cambridge, England: Cambridge University Press, 1976. This valuable and occasionally polemical book centers on the themes of trade, taxes, and regions as bases for interpreting the history of the Abbasids and their successors.

WAINES, DAVID: "The Third Century Internal Crisis of the Abbasids." *Journal of the Economic and Social History of the Orient* 20 (1977): 282–306. In the ninth century an internal economic and political crisis gripped the Abbasids; the crisis is ably analyzed and shown to be as important as the external threats to the empire's central authority.

WATT, W. MONTGOMERY: *A History of Islamic Spain.* Edinburgh, Scotland: Edinburgh University Press, 1965. Concise coverage of all aspects of the Muslims in Spain.

CHAPTER 7

Islam

THE RISE AND SPREAD OF ISLAM

Throughout the centuries that followed the life of the prophet Muhammad the central beliefs of Islam remained consistent, easy to understand, and inspiring to the growing numbers of Muslims in the ummah. Despite increasing theological sophistication, splits in the community, and ensuing differences of interpretation, there nevertheless remained a considerable common core. The central belief of all the approaches to Islam retained the simple monotheistic religion preached by Muhammad. Even though the rapidity of expansion and conversions admitted to Muslim society many whose knowledge of Islam was limited, the core of the faith remained, as the interpretation of the basic elements of Islam became richer and more varied.

During the rule of the four early caliphs in Medina and in the era of the Umayyad Empire the Muslims gained access to the Hellenistic philosophy and theology of Egypt and Syria, which rapidly affected Islamic theology. Ultimately the new concepts and dogmas within Islam gave birth to different Muslim sects; under the later Umayyads and early Abbasids the complete unity of theology, as well as politics, was lost in the Muslim world.

Acceptance of monotheism was the most important facet of religion to Muhammad. To be a Muslim was to profess the unity of God, to surrender to the will of God, and to admit Muhammad as God's messenger. God had ninety-nine names, each with a related attribute. The mere recitation of some of these would remind humanity of God: omniscient, omnipotent, the judge, the mighty, the creator, merciful, compassionate, self-subsistent, forgiving, magnificent, everlasting, most generous, and most high.

Of the infinite qualities of God, Islam constantly stressed everlastingness. God was the creator of creation and existed through all eternity. All people were God's creatures, and God "misleads whom He will and guides whom He will." Fear of God and the day of judgment was particularly emphasized in the early revelations in Mecca to impress the materialistic society there; but God was also visualized as a loving, bountiful, and forgiving protector, "closer to a man than his own jugular vein." The Quran repeatedly refers to God as merciful and compassionate. A third important attribute of God was mystical in nature: God was termed the light of the heavens and of the earth. In later centuries theologians developed this quality into various organized mysticisms that served as powerful forces in the spread and influence of Islam.

THE QURAN

The basis for Muslims' views of God and religion and for the central beliefs of Muslims of every sect rested upon the Quran ("lecture" or "recitation"), the collection of revelations sent to the prophet Muhammad. Consisting of 114 chapters, called *surahs*, made up of 6236 verses (77,934 words), the earliest versions were assembled soon after Muhammad's death. Most of the revelations had been written down in his later years by his secretaries; these and other revelations were memorized and recounted word for word by his companions. Tradition has it that after a battle in which many reciters of the Quran perished, the caliph Abu Bakr ordered the full Quran to be committed to parchment so that it would not be lost. Later, Uthman established the copy held in Medina as the true Quran. In the tenth century the methods of reciting the text were regularized from different readings that had arisen because of the lack of vowels and diacritical marks in the early Arabic script.

Except for the first, which is a short prayer, the chapters were arranged according to length, so that the later but longer Medinan chapters are located at the beginning. The Quran is about two-thirds the length of an Arabic version of the Christian New Testament.

Muslims regard the Quran as the word of God, transmitted to Muhammad by the angel Gabriel. It furnished the basis for law in the Islamic world; like a modern constitution, it was the skeleton of the legal and judicial systems. It also prescribed a pattern of daily individual and community living that distinguished Islamic civilization from all others. Since translations were frowned upon, Quranic Arabic served as a common religious language and a bond for all Muslims from one end of the world to the other. The Quran was also a schoolbook, and committing it to memory was standard practice for children everywhere. The very sound of the Arabic words stirs the emotions of Muslims; read silently, the Quran loses much of its power.

The major part of the Quran is concerned with God, whose attributes are cited and powers proclaimed; the individual's relations to God are defined. Associated with a vivid explanation of the day of judgment are portrayals of the resurrection, paradise and hell, and angels and devils. Religious and ethical paths to follow in life are sometimes presented directly, but for the most part they are contained in parables and stories, many of which are similar to those in Jewish and Christian holy books and their associated literature. Adam, Noah, Abraham, Joseph, Moses, David, Solomon, Elijah, Job, Zachariah, John the Baptist, Mary, and Jesus are all set forth so as to show that God rewards the righteous and punishes the wicked.

A perusal of the Torah, the Bible, and the Quran discloses a number of very similar passages. Surah 21, verse 105, is identical to Psalm 37, verse 9: "For evil doers shall be cut off; but those that wait upon the Lord, they shall inherit the earth." Despite this and other similarities, the Christians of Constantinople and western Europe branded Islam as a Christian heresy—a castigation that led to the abhorrence of Muslims and an exaggeration of the differences between Christianity and Islam. In reality, Judaism, Christianity, and Islam have a great deal in common. The dissimilarities are more in language, style, and form than in substance. Through each of these three religions runs a strong message of personal salvation for righteous individuals. This message of hope gives to the individual a sense of significance and equality that is not ordinarily available in cultures where other religions prevail.

HADITH

Following the Prophet's death it became obvious that God's revelations did not provide an answer to every problem that arose in daily life. Muhammad always distinguished carefully between his own individual thoughts and divine revelation. God's word was law; Muhammad's words were only guides to a wise and holy life.

As the years slipped by, leaving fewer and fewer Muslims who knew from their own memories what Muhammad had said and done, collections of his comments and deeds were considered vital for following his precedents. Traditions by the hundreds of thousands appeared; these have been used to establish the bases for the sunnah, the custom, usual procedure, or behavior of the Prophet. The sunnah of the Prophet in turn became a most important guide to life and belief for Muslims. Each of the different sects and parties that developed in Islam accepted certain hadith and rejected others as forgeries to prove the correctness of the party's views, no matter whether the contention affected militarism or pacifism, predestination or free will, mysticism or realism, asceticism or worldliness.

By the second or third century after the hijrah, hadith had become very intricate in response to the philosophical and theological demands of the scholars of the time. In the early days of Islam, hadith had comprised the simple, unvarnished ideas and stories that Muhammad had voiced or that his friends had repeated word for word. They are of varied topics, for Muhammad had definite opinions on all types of subjects. On one occasion he said: "God curse the woman who wears false hair and the woman who ties it on." When his wife Aishah acquired a pictured cushion, Muhammad exploded: "Verily, the makers of these pictures will be severely punished on the Day of Resurrection." On slavery he remonstrated: "A slave must not be given a task which he is unable to perform." Muhammad sometimes perceived the difference between legality and righteousness, as when he observed: "Of the things which are lawful the most hateful to God is divorce." In a similar vein he declared: "There is no man who receives a bodily injury and forgives the offender but God will exalt his rank and diminish his sin." Having been an orphan, Muhammad was always concerned with such unfortunates and proclaimed: "The best house amidst the Muslim community is that which contains an orphan who is well treated, and the worst is that wherein an orphan is wronged." Perhaps best known is the attitude Muhammad held toward moneylenders. In commenting on persons paying or charging very high rates of interest, he proclaimed, "They are equally culpable." Among Muslims one of his often quoted commands indicated Muhammad's view that sexual activity and piety could coexist: "No monkery in Islam!"

DOGMAS

Muhammad was not a systematic theologian, but after his death Muslim theologians and philosophers classified the faith into three fundamentals: religious beliefs (iman), religious duties (ibadat), and good works (ihsan). First and foremost, of course, is the belief that God is one and has all of the attributes ascribed to God. It has never been clear, however, how the attribute of omnipotence ought to be interpreted, and this problem has engendered controversy among Muslims from the days of the first caliphs to the present. In the early unaffected period, God's omnipotence simply meant that the individual is completely subordinate to God and can do nothing unless God permits it. Yet all persons are responsible for what they do and will be rewarded or punished accordingly. Muhammad preached incessantly on this point and declared that people would fall into evil ways if they did not believe in God. Submission to the will of God is the key to Islam.

Muhammad and the first Muslims referred so frequently to the day of judgment and the resurrection that belief in these two has become one of the significant aspects of Islam. When the cataclysmic day comes, the faith and deeds of each man and woman will be weighed, one's body will rise, and one will either enter paradise or be cast into hell. Martyrs for the faith do not wait for the day of judgment but immediately enter paradise. The latter is clearly described as a beautiful garden by a flowing river where the blessed rest on silken couches, partake of heavenly food and drink, enjoy spiritual joys, associate with their families, and are entertained by dark-eyed maidens and wives of perfect purity. The terrors of hell are almost beyond description. Waters boil; sinners' bellies are filled with molten brass. Into this fiery hell go the unbelieving, the covetous, and those who worship other gods.

Another basic point in the religious belief of Muslims is the role played by angels and jinn. Heaven and earth are populated by these invisible spirits who serve as God's messengers and record one's deeds. Gabriel is recognized as the leading angel and the spirit who brought the Quran to Muhammad. Rebellious jinn are devils and, like humans, will be cast into hell on the day of judgment. The leading devil did not bow down to Adam and continues to seduce people into evil ways until the resurrection.

Muslims believe that God has sent many human messengers to teach the world and that the last and greatest was Muhammad. The Quran specifically mentions twenty-eight prophets besides Muhammad, including four Arabs and one Greek (Alexander the Great); three (Zachariah, John the Baptist, and Jesus) are also in the Christian New Testament; the remainder are mentioned in the Torah or the Christian Old Testament. The most important of all the prophets are Adam, Noah, Abraham, Moses, and Jesus. Of all these, the last is Muhammad, whom God sent as the "Seal" of all. Prophets did not perform miracles except on special occasions when God gave them these powers. Divine revelation was granted to Moses in the Jewish

Torah, to David in the Psalms, to Jesus in the Gospels, and to Muhammad in the Quran, which was his only miracle. All of them preached salvation through the recognition that God is one.

Muslims are to accept and believe all of these scriptures, for they are the word of God and they corroborate each other. The final word of God, the Quran, attests the revelations in the other scriptures, clarifies all previous uncertainties, and brings perfect truth. After some controversy, it came to be felt that the Quran is eternal and uncreated; its earthly reproduction is identical in language and spelling to the heavenly original, every word and letter of which is sacred and divine.

DUTIES

The second essential in Islam as taught by Muhammad comprised religious duties. These actions are less obligatory than those of faith, but their performance constituted the individual's recognition of the omnipotence of God. These duties have usually been termed the "five pillars" or acts of worship of Islam; they are the easiest to observe and, unfortunately for many uninformed non-Muslims and even for some Muslims, have been mistaken for the true religious substance of Islam.

The first and foremost pillar is the open profession of faith. Often reduced to the Quranic formula "There is no god but God, Muhammad is the messenger of God," this declaration is used throughout a Muslim's life and suffices to ensure one's acceptance as at least a nominal Muslim.

Muhammad emphasized worship as the second obligation for Muslims. The Quran mentions directly no set ritual for worship but bids the faithful to worship frequently. Before Muhammad's death it had become customary for Muslims to pray formally five times daily: just before daybreak, at noon, in the midafternoon, at sunset, and in the evening. A Muslim should pray wherever he or she may be, but it is preferable to pray in unison with others and in a mosque if possible, with one acting as leader (imam) and the others standing in rows behind, all facing Mecca. Each prayer is composed of a certain number of bows: two at daybreak, three at sunset, and four at the other times. Each bow consists of seven distinct acts: (1) placing the open hands at each side of the head and repeating, "God is most great"; (2) standing upright and repeating the opening prayer of the Quran and at least one other Quranic passage; (3) bending from the hips and touching the knees with the hands; (4) straightening up, saying, "God listens to the one who praises Him"; (5) falling to the knees and prostrating oneself with the forehead touching the ground; (6) sitting on the haunches; and (7) a second prostration. Most Muslims include individual prayers to God, and devout Muslims pray frequently at other times during the day and night. Certain events such as burials, eclipses, serious decisions, and religious celebrations demand special prayers. The Friday noon prayer is the great congregational prayer at which a sermon (khutbah) is usually delivered. At first the sermon was delivered by Muhammad, then by the caliph or his representative, and now by a learned Muslim, who also offers a prayer on behalf of the ruling head of the state.

At the time of prayer one must be in a state of spiritual and physical purity, which is determined in various ways. Usually before prayers, simple purity, as defined in the Quran, is achieved by washing the hands and arms to the elbows, the face, and the feet up to the ankles. In the absence of water, sand may be used.

Of all the features of Islam, prayer in its public form has been the most constant democratizing force. Side by side at prayer are common soldier and general, prince and pauper, merchant and holy man. No distinction is made, and the proudest individual bows in humble prostration to the omnipotent and omniscient God.

The third pillar of Islam is almsgiving. Muhammad at first regarded giving to the poor and needy as a personal atonement and a means of salvation. Sometime in the Medinan period of his prophecy almsgiving was regularized to become a 2.5 percent voluntary tax on all produce and revenue of each Muslim above a certain minimum of goods. Termed *zakat*, the proceeds were used to support the poor, to erect religious buildings, and to help defray government expenses. In later years when states were much weaker, it was not possible to collect alms on any such basis and it became solely a freewill offering. Alms are also to be given generously for various religious and human charities such as mosques, hospitals, poorhouses, and schools. Likewise, beggars and the destitute are not to be turned away empty-handed. An ethical and egalitarian society is envisioned where excess wealth will be used for the benefit of the whole community.

Fasting, the fourth pillar of Islam, was enjoined upon all Muslims during Ramadan (the ninth lunar month), a month of fasting. From the very first flush of dawn to nightfall, food, drink, and smoke are not to pass the lips; sexual intercourse is also forbidden. When Ramadan fell during the summer months, compliance with fasting was particularly difficult in the Middle East. Voluntary sacrifice reinforced the spiritual commitment of the faithful. Fasting is also considered the best means of expiating one's sins of the year.

The fifth pillar of Islam, that of the yearly pilgrimage to Mecca (hajj), stands as the symbol of Muslim unity. It was assumed that each Muslim, man and woman, should participate in the pilgrimage each year if possible. Later, as the Muslim world grew, it became too arduous for many to go from Iraq, Syria, and Egypt; when Islam had spread to India and Spain, the pilgrimage became obligatory only once in a lifetime and only for those who could afford it. Occurring in the twelfth lunar month, the pilgrimage ritual is celebrated on certain days by elaborate rites at the Kaba in Mecca and at other sacred spots nearby. Since Muhammad's farewell pilgrimage in 632, non-Muslims have not been permitted to be present in Mecca during the pilgrimage; in general they are forbidden entry into both Mecca and Medina.

Throughout the entire course of Muslim history the pilgrimage has been a most valuable unifying factor within Islamic civilization. Pilgrims have come to Mecca from the four corners of the Muslim world. The interchange of thoughts, the acquisition of knowledge, the exchange of products, and the interplay of political forces in Mecca have been factors in maintaining a common Muslim link among the diverse peoples embracing Islam.

To some Muslims a sixth pillar of Islam has been added: that of jihad, which can be striving on an individual basis for one's own correct behavior or striving for the faith in holy war. Many consider that every Muslim bears the duty to expand the frontiers of Islam, by force if necessary, until the entire world has been won.

VIRTUES AND SINS

It might well be thought that after professing the religious beliefs of Islam and performing the various duties of a Muslim, the circle of religion had been completed. In addition, however, the Quran imposes upon all a course of righteous living and doing good works. There is a religious character for both private and public acts; only in a just society can one easily be a good Muslim, while it is the duty of a Muslim to strive for justice in society.

From the virtues extolled, Islam can be seen as moralistic and sometimes puritanical. In the area of gender, the Quran limits the number of wives to four and then adds: "But if you fear that you will act unjustly among them, then marry only one." Many other commandments raised the status of women in Arabian society. Settlements are required to be made upon a woman if she is divorced; a widow can marry whomever she wishes; and the burying alive of daughters is prohibited. Personal modesty in clothing is urged upon men and especially upon women; the caliph Umar decreed that men and women should pray separately from each other, so as to preserve modesty during the ritual. Some women mentioned in the Quran are meant to serve as examples of virtue or sin for the believers.

Spiritual and earthly penalties are promised for murder, adultery, homicide, theft, armed robbery, fraud, perjury, libel, and in general corruption. Injunctions are delivered against gambling, usury, and monopolistic practices. The use of wine and the eating of pork are forbidden. Idolatry is most sinful, and the making of images is only one step removed from worshiping other gods. Most of these declarations of right living are injunctions against practices that were common in the pagan and hedonistic society of Mecca at the time of Muhammad. Instead of this behavior the Quran and the hadith encouraged alternatives, leading to just behavior according to the shariah, the holy law of Islam.

In view of the comprehensive scope of the faith with respect to religious beliefs, religious duties, and virtues, the early Islam of Muhammad must be regarded as very successful. Since Islam required individual belief and morality, the tribal morality of pre-Islamic Arabia was replaced by the personal responsibility of the individual Muslim as a member of the universal Muslim community. By the end of the first Abbasid period in 945 the core of Islamic belief was clear. The approach to understanding God, the belief about God's will for this earth, and the way of salvation were soundly established. Ultimately they changed the life and philosophy of hundreds of millions of people in the Middle East and the wider Muslim world.

References

Also see materials cited at the end of Chapter 3.

ALI, ABDULLAH YUSUF: *The Holy Qur'an: Text, Translation and Commentary.* Washington, D.C.: The Islamic Center, 1978. One of the best translations, with comments and analysis, and the English and Arabic texts facing each other.

ARBERRY, ARTHUR J.: *The Koran Interpreted.* New York: Macmillan, 1955. The translation catches much of the majesty and beauty of the original; it should be used in conjunction with Watt's *Companion to the Qur'an,* cited on the next page.

AYOUB, MAHMOUD: *The Qur'an and Its Interpreters.* Vol. 1. Albany: State University of New York Press, 1984. This presentation and analysis of the first two chapters of the Quran shows the ways Muslims have analyzed the text.

BURTON, JOHN: *The Collection of the Qur'an.* Cambridge, England: Cambridge University Press, 1977. A radical interpretation of the history of the text of the Quran that maintains that Muhammad himself was involved in its compilation and editing.

DENNY, FREDERICK MATHEWSON: *An Introduction to Islam.* 2d ed. New York: Macmillan, 1994. This general survey of Islam, now the best available for the beginning student of the religion, deals with all aspects of the subject, with an emphasis on mysticism and personal faith as well as historical development from pre-Islamic days to the present.

MARTIN, RICHARD C.: *Islam: A Cultural Approach.* Englewood Cliffs, N.J.: Prentice-Hall, 1982. A broad and easily understood survey of most aspects of Islam.

PETERS, F. E.: *A Reader on Classical Islam.* Princeton, N.J.: Princeton University Press, 1994. This work provides basic sources on early Islamic thought.

RAHMAN, FAZLUR: *Major Themes of the Qur'an.* 2d ed. Minneapolis, Minn.: Bibliotheca Islamica, 1989. Spiritual insights into Quranic discussions of God, humanity, society, nature, revelation, the day of judgment, evil, and the ummah written by a profound Muslim thinker.

SAID, LABIB AL-: *The Recited Koran.* Translated by Bernard Weiss et al. Princeton, N.J.: Darwin Press, 1975. The history of the Quran is discussed in the first part of this book, while the making of the first complete recording of the Quran is examined in the second part.

SCHIMMEL, ANNEMARIE: *Islam: An Introduction.* Albany: State University of New York Press, 1992. A general survey of Islam, with an emphasis on India and Sufism.

STOWASSER, BARBARA FREYER: *Women in the Qur'an, Traditions, and Interpretation.* New York: Oxford University Press, 1994. This sophisticated book includes views of early, medieval, and modern Muslims about women mentioned in the Quran.

WATT, W. MONTGOMERY: *Companion to the Qur'an: Based on the Arberry Translation.* London: George Allen and Unwin, 1967. Certain sections of the Quran are explained or put in context.

———: *What Is Islam?* New York: Praeger, 1968. A survey of the background of Islam, the historical perspective, the work of religious intellectuals, and the Islamic worldview.

WELCH, A. T.: "Al-Kur'an." *Encyclopaedia of Islam.* New ed. Vol. 5, pp. 400–429. Leiden: Brill, 1981. A complete account of the various controversies, the arrangement of the text, the meaning of different sections, the final compilation, and the importance of the Quran for Muslims.

WILLIAMS, JOHN ALDEN, ED.: *The Word of Islam.* Austin: University of Texas Press, 1994. A very useful reader; includes excerpts from the Quran, hadith, shariah, mysticism, theology, and various sects.

Muslim Theology and Law

The uncomplicated, direct, and ethical religion and law preached and practiced by Muhammad appealed to the townspeople of Mecca and Medina and to the nomads of the desert. In general, they were easily adjusted to the needs of the theocratic state under Muhammad and the first four caliphs who immediately followed him.

When Islam, Muslim rule, and the need for law based on the faith spread beyond Arabia, Muslims faced unforeseen conditions. Succeeding generations of Muslims were exposed to the intellectualized philosophies and law codes current in the acquired provinces and developed a finely drawn Islamic theology and varied views on how to interpret law. A mystical approach to Islam and the separation between Sunnite and Shiite Muslims also became prominent during the Umayyad and early Abbasid periods.

THEOLOGY

Though the political capital of Islam was transferred to Damascus and then to Baghdad, Medina maintained its ascendancy as a center of Muslim theology for several centuries. Opinions not subscribed to by the thinkers of Medina were declared to be in error. Divergent views led to the formation of a number of groups with a wide variety of interpretations of Islamic theology and philosophy, which in many cases were branded as heretical by the Medinan theologians. Three schools of thought—the Kharijites, Murjites, and Mutazilites—were especially influential in the classical Islamic period.

At the time of the dispute between Ali and Muawiyah, the Kharijites broke away, rejecting the concept of compromise that Ali proposed. They believed that might does not make right and that only God can judge among people. A Muslim who committed great sins was no longer a Muslim. They nevertheless professed their way of life to be the right way, and when they quoted the Quran ("be patient until God judges between us") they meant that the fight should be continued until God granted them victory. The Kharijites were against both Ali and Muawiyah and opposed the growing organized structure of society in which they were being enveloped. Coming from a nomadic background, they found settled life in large groups alien to their spirits. The Kharijites eventually evolved into a sect that held that good works are the measure of faith and the only path to salvation. They also insisted on openly and literally pursuing egalitarianism and the commandment to preach to all persons a righteous life and to restrain them, by the sword if necessary, from doing evil. Their emphasis upon the centrality of the Quran influenced all other Muslim groups.

Laxity of life in Damascus induced others to uphold belief in the adequacy of inherent faith in attaining personal salvation. In essence, these Murjites, as they were termed, were opposites of Kharijites, for they readily accepted rulers whose conduct was sinful. They held that as long as persons profess God's unity, they should not be judged because of their sins but should be accepted as believers. In the first two centuries of Islam, the Murjites' concern was to preserve the unity of the Muslim community. Rebuked by Medina, they eased their ethics to political accommodation under the Umayyads. When the Abbasid revolution approached, Murjites supported the Umayyad claim to the caliphate, but once the Abbasids had won, they found no reason to oppose them.

In the formative period of Muslim theology Mutazilites held a view between these two extremes. By the time of the Abbasid caliph Harun al-Rashid, Mutazilites, accepting the doctrine of free will, were entangled in Aristotelian and Hellenistic Christian philosophies and engaged in adjusting Islam to Greek logic. Adhering to rationalism, free will, and philosophical theology in the ninth century, they lost much of their following when Muslim theology was pronounced in the tenth century by al-Ashari of Baghdad and fixed in the early twelfth century by al-Ghazali of Khurasan.

A myriad of theological questions appeared for these three groups as for others, several arising over and over again. Foremost was the question of God's omnipotence in relation to human responsibility or, as it devolved to the religious plane, the problem of predestination and free will. The second great problem related to the nature of the Quran: Was it uncreated and eternal or was it created? The third troublesome subject centered upon the nature of God and his attributes. If God could hear, see, and speak, was not his unity in doubt?

Mutazilites held that if God rendered punishment for deeds that had been predetermined, he would be an unjust God, and that therefore the human being does have free will. They professed that the Quran had been created in time by God and that between God and his creation, the human being, there is no resemblance. On other points Mutazilites believed that God does not forgive the grave sinner except after repentance and that, being just, he punishes all persons equally. They stood between Kharijites and Murjites with regard to the Umayyads and their sins, saying that judgment should not be rendered. On the question of one's duty to judge others, they asserted that one should command one's fellows to follow the right path. Wrongful actions should be forbidden—which meant that armed revolt against an unjust ruler was justified when there was a chance of success.

According to the theologian al-Ashari (d. 935), the apparent contradiction embodied in the concepts of predestination and free will was explained by the doctrine that human beings are responsible for their actions but only because God has so willed it. For al-Ashari and others, the Quran was preexistent and eternal; the words or expressions were created and revealed by the angels to the prophet Muhammad only as guides to the eternal word. The apparent contradiction between the unity of God and his other, more human attributes referred to in the Quran was explained by the belief that God is one and eternal but that his existence is not the same as existence in the world; therefore, one should not seek to specify how the Quran's descriptions of God in human terms can be reconciled with God's infinite character.

Many other theological points were established by al-Ashari, including the dogma that right and wrong are what they are because God declared them to be so, and that God could inflict pain in this world or in the next without being unjust. Even al-Ashari, however, was criticized by the religious men of Medina because they considered his theology too rationalistic and too far removed from the Islam of Muhammad. Asharite thinkers remained unpopular in Baghdad until the advent of al-Ghazali, whose writing and teaching united the modified Greek logic and philosophy of al-Ashari with Muhammad's religion to create a faith that has remained the basis of the mainstream of Islam to the present day.

SUNNITES AND THE SCIENCE OF TRADITION

When the word of the Quran did not appear to give the answer to some specific problem, the men of religion (ulama; singular, alim) of Medina and the pious throughout Islam looked for guidance in the words and actions of Muhammad or in those he had allowed. Arab tribes were devoted to traditions and normal practice, and custom (sunnah) was a powerful force in their lives. In the new community established by Muhammad and severed from many tribal customs, the life of Muhammad served as the touchstone for proper Muslim thought and conduct.

Early in Muslim history great collections of the statements and deeds of Muhammad were made. Aishah was the source of hundreds, and the city of Medina, where a great many Companions resided, became a center of the compilations. Each saying was called a *hadith,* or a tradition, and the whole body of these traditions was known as the *hadith.* Each hadith eventually had an introduction giving its full pedigree of transmission. Scholars developed a science to establish which of these traditions were authentic and which spurious. Many traditions were fabricated, particularly in Iraq, starting in the eighth century, and the task of selecting which ones were sound and which were forged became a difficult one. Each sect of Islam and each theologian chose the most suitable traditions on which to base some contentions or to press a point.

The first written collections were begun for judicial ends. By the ninth century the literature on the subject had grown so voluminous that it brought about the science of hadith. The scholar al-Bukhari (d. 870), published a collection of over 7000 hadith that was generally pronounced the most authoritative source of tradition. One of the largest collections was that of Ahmad ibn Hanbal, who assembled nearly 30,000 hadith to form a corpus that served as the basis of his legal and theological ideas. Each major Muslim city or province eventually adopted as standard practice the collected traditions of one of the noted theologians.

Acceptance of a body of traditions in time led to the establishment of the sunnah—a new customary, or common, law. Attachment to these traditions and a willingness to abide by the consensus of the community and its religious ulama identified Muslims as following the Islamic sunnah and thus gave them the name of Sunnites. This meaning of the term became clearly articulated only by the tenth century.

MUSLIM LAW

Early Muslims, pious and devout, perceived hardly any difference between law and religion. Only God knew the perfect law, and coexisting with him was natural law, comprising right and justice. Islam, then, was the ideal system, and its law pointed the "right path" (shariah) to an individual's salvation; divine law recognized good and evil. Law and justice were the chief duties of the state. If the state failed to enforce the law, the state's validity ceased. The caliph as head of the state was charged principally with the enforcement of law. Shariah was theoretically unchanging, allowing no consideration for time or place. Law upheld the common good of the community and served individual interests only when these conformed to those of the Muslim community as a whole. Islamic law had to be observed in good faith and sincerity.

Muslim systems of law, both Sunnite and Shiite, grew largely from two roots: the Quran and the traditions. However, caliphs and their judges, even in Medina, discovered early on that the Quran and the traditions did not address many situations with which they had to deal. In the absence of a definite statement, judges resorted to the use of analogy to some instance in the Quran or the traditions in deciding cases brought before them. Although the strictest judges did not practice analogy, on the grounds that it left too much to human judgment, it was nevertheless adopted widely in the eighth century as a legal aid and became an integral part of the shariah. In the same century Malik ibn Anas, a jurist-theologian of Medina, compiled a book of traditions that incorporated many of the local juridical customs and practices. This procedure introduced the institution of consensus (ijma), which at first was reserved to Medina.

In the next generation the jurist al-Shafii drew together these several elements and expanded consensus to include the Muslim community at large. In thus helping to establish Sunnite Islam, al-Shafii was instrumental in advancing the idea of following the practice as recognized by the ulama. Questions of law were to be resolved ultimately through the four fundamental principles: the Quran; the traditions, as communicating the sunnah; analogy; and consensus. Al-Shafii's general doctrine became widely accepted, with the modification of restricting consensus to that of ulama rather than to the whole ummah. The inclusion of consensus in the principles of the shariah established the classical Sunnite theory of the roots of jurisprudence and enabled Islam through the centuries to adapt its institutions to a changing world.

An additional source of Muslim law has been private opinion (ray), which was never quite accepted as a fifth principle of the shariah but was widely practiced. Early caliphs employed it extensively until bitter complaints that human legislation corrupted divine law forced its abandonment. Nevertheless, most caliphs and later rulers were compelled by administrative necessity to issue laws and decrees that were sanctioned almost wholly by opinion; such laws and regulations were later termed kanuns. In addition to the theoretical and theological bases of the law, and the decrees of the rulers, Islamic law in the Middle East was also influenced in practice by the preexisting Roman, Sasanid, and Greek laws of the provinces conquered by the Muslim armies.

FOUR SUNNITE SCHOOLS

The Sunnite jurists all accepted the shariah but differed as to which traditions were genuine and the weight that ought to be allowed to analogy, consensus, and opinion in establishing a viable Muslim code of law. At the time of the Abbasid caliph al-Mansur, it was suggested that he codify and enforce the diverse laws in the empire. Local particularism, however, won the day, and numerous systems prevailed among the Muslims. Since the eleventh century four principal schools of legal practice have been recognized as permissible by the Sunnites.

In point of development the earliest school was the Hanafite. Abu Hanifah (d. 767), a Murjite legal scholar of Kufah and Baghdad, held a tolerant view on the use of analogy and consensus and particularly emphasized the value and necessity of private opinion and judgment by those administering the law. By the eleventh century, however, a strong conservative movement closed the door on further innovations in the matter of juridical opinions. Henceforth, judges could allow only previously rendered opinions and were required to adhere closely to the Hanafite teachings. The Hanafite rite was the established procedure followed in the Ottoman Empire, parts of India, and central Asia.

Historically, the second orthodox school was the Malikite. Malik ibn Anas of Medina, who died in 795, codified the traditions of Islam and acknowledged the authority of the consensus of the Medina community. Malikite jurists, however, never equivocated in their stand against general consensus, private opinion, and the broad use of analogy. The Malikite school was accepted in Spain and still prevails in North Africa, Upper Egypt, and eastern Arabia.

Next to the Hanafite school in general acceptance has been that of the Shafiite. The jurist al-Shafii studied under Malik in Medina and taught in Baghdad and Fustat (Cairo), where he died in 820. The Shafiite rites permitted wider use of consensus than those of the Malikites, and al-Shafii asserted that consensus was the safest and highest legislative authority in Islam. The Shafiite school dominates legal practice in Palestine, Lower Egypt, eastern Africa, western and southern Arabia, parts of India, and Indonesia.

The Hanbalite school was the fourth and smallest among the orthodox schools. It was named after Ahmad ibn Hanbal, a student of al-Shafii who rebelled against the teachings of his master. The Hanbalites accepted neither private opinion nor analogy and scorned the use of consensus. They maintained that the only valid basis of Muslim law, besides the Quran, was the traditions. For his refusal to disavow his views Ibn Hanbal was beaten and persecuted by al-Mamun and al-Mutasim. Despite Ibn Hanbal's apparent personal appeal, as suggested by the hundreds of thousands of mourners who attended his funeral in Baghdad in 855, Han-balism outside Baghdad was too rigid to be popular or practical over the centuries and had only scattered followers. After the Ottoman conquest the doctrine was re-vived in the eighteenth century by the Wahhabis in central Arabia, where the Han-balite rites are still observed.

In addition to the four principal codes of law, another body of law evolved from a court practice of submitting the summary of involved and important cases to a learned jurist (a mufti), as a consultant, for an opinion known as a fatwa. Fatwas, which presented the legal issues and indicated the proper decision, were later col-lected and used as guides to the courts in rendering judgments. Until the advent of the Ottoman Empire, muftis more or less remained free from control or restraint by the government.

RATIONALISM

In essence, all of these ulama were attempting to fashion a system of law by a syn-thesis of Islamic truths and the highly refined and developed rationalism of the Greek philosophers. In the Umayyad period, those favoring the introduction of Hellenistic logic into Muslim theology were called Mutazilites. The arguments re-garding the nature of God and the Quran rocked the empire. The debates lasted for several centuries, and the particular views of the reigning caliph determined which opinion flourished at any given time. Caliph al-Mamun persecuted all but Mu-tazilites and ruthlessly suppressed those who did not support free thought. Caliph al-Mutawakkil then ousted the Mutazilites. Eventually, theologians under al-Ashari and the learned founders of the schools of religious law brought the controversy to rest and established theology, tradition, and law as separate from, and occasionally antagonistic toward, the caliphate and the state apparatus it controlled.

The great philosophical efforts, however, had the effect of taking Islam away from the people and ran the danger of destroying it as a practical religion. People desired a living experience of God, not a metaphysical or conceptual discussion of religion. To the simple Muslim, God was a personage always near at hand. One could talk to God, as a Bedouin's prayer in a time of drought attested: "O God of the devotees, what is the matter with us and You? You used to give us water—What has possessed You? Do send rain down on us. Exert Yourself!"

ASCETICISM AND MYSTICISM

In the first years after Muhammad, piety in Islam sometimes took the form of as-ceticism. Pious Muslims seeking knowledge of God and salvation for themselves adopted and preached asceticism. Study of the traditions of the Prophet, prayer, fasting, solitary meditations, and prolonged vigils would lead the soul to God. Poverty, humility, patience, repentance, and silence in this world would save be-lievers seeking godliness from eternal chastisement and permit them to come into the presence of God by means of the annihilation of the self, to taste the joys of paradise, and to abide therein to eternity.

In spite of a waning of ascetic tendencies in the Abbasid period, the mysticism remained strong among both male and female Muslims across the centuries. Sultans, generals, rich merchants, judges, and scholars might not adopt ascetic practices themselves, but they usually paid open deference to those who did.

Toward the end of the eighth century, mysticism entered into Islam with a great force. Theology and philosophy had not greatly affected the masses, and after the first half of the ninth century the majority of the literate community found little of interest in the hairsplitting of the ulama. For religious experience the masses turned to mysticism. Knowledge of God was to be achieved by the inner light of the individual soul, not by the intellectual methods of the philosopher.

Muhammad the Prophet came to be seen as the perfect or ideal human being, without sin, and popular piety viewed him as a model for what human life should be. The major roots of Islamic mysticism were the Quran and the traditions of Muhammad; to them were added the quietism and occult practices and beliefs of Buddhist stories, Hindu monism, Zoroastrian dualism, Gnostic ideas from Iraq, and miracles from the Gospels. The second coming of Christ became the doctrine of the coming of the Mahdi, the rightly guided one, who would bring complete victory to Islam.

The essence of mysticism was love, an ecstatic communion with the divine, and final absorption into the godhead. Nothing existed but God. To know and love God and to be united with him, without any thought of reward or salvation, was an emotional means of purifying the soul. God was eternal beauty, and the path leading to him was love. The mystic sought to lose the self in life with God, and he felt a sense of union with the godhead that offended nonmystical Muslims. The process of commingling self with God could best be achieved by love and thought of God.

Until the twelfth century, popular preachers who based much of their message on mysticism and won their wide appeal through mysticism and miracles were despised by philosophers and theologians and were frequently judged guilty of heresy. Then, as al-Ashari had made rationalism and Islamic theology compatible, so al-Ghazali led the learned and pious doctors and jurists to accept mysticism.

Born in Iran in 1058 and appointed professor at the Nizamiyah at Baghdad in 1091, the legal scholar Abu Hamid al-Ghazali had the court and the scholars at his feet, and for four or five years his fame spread far and wide. Apparently secure for life, he experienced some sort of personal admonition and abandoned everything to become a mystic. After about a decade of wandering, contemplation, and writing, he returned to society and taught at the Nizamiyah at Nishapur, and eventually died in his hometown of Tus in 1111. His great contribution, largely through his writings, was initially viewed by early medieval Muslims as his works on law, but in the longer run he vitalized Islam by making personal experience and emotion a part of religion. Islam began to live again for the ordinary man, through both law and mysticism.

FRATERNAL ORDERS

At the time of the appearance of mysticism a holy man was called a sufi, meaning "one garbed in wool." Sufis preached to the masses, and they lived a life of example for their admirers. Without question the conversion to Islam of many on the frontiers of the Muslim state was the accomplishment of the Sufis.

For several centuries Sufism was an unorganized movement throughout Islam. Certain Sufis obtained a devoted following on a personal basis. Before the end of the tenth century, however, groups of Sufis formed compact brotherhoods. The master Sufi, or shaikh, was the teacher and initiated disciples into the order. The members, by study, ritual, and piety, proceeded up the ladder of the order until they were ready to leave to establish a branch center.

By the thirteenth century, thousands of lodges dotted the Muslim landscape from Morocco to India. Each order had its own peculiar ritual and liturgy (dhikr). Some were elaborate and others simple, but all were mystical efforts to reach God. Most fraternities had hundreds, sometimes thousands, of lay members who went about their normal occupations in city or town. At stated times they met at the lodge to observe their ceremonies. A few of the orders increased the mystical stimulus by an accompaniment of music or by dancing or whirling.

It was not possible to know how many different orders existed at any one time; new splinter fraternities sprang into being and others disappeared at regular intervals. One of the strongest and best known was the Qadiriyah, founded by the Hanbalite Abd al-Qadir al-Jilani in the twelfth century, which had its center in Baghdad and spread throughout Islam. More conservative than most, its members have been noted for their philanthropy and humility. Another order, the Rifaiyah, was famed for glass eating, fire walking, and self-mortification. In Anatolia, the two best-known orders were the Bektashi, to which most of the Ottoman janissaries belonged, and the Mevlevis, whose members were popularly called "whirling dervishes" because of certain aspects of their ritual. In the central and eastern parts of the Middle East, there was the Naqshbandiyah order.

As a great social and religious development, the significance of the fraternal orders lay in the members' extensive participation in the spread and popularization of Islam, resulting in the majority of the people in North Africa, Sudan, Anatolia, central Asia, certain parts of India, and Indonesia becoming converted to Islam. In this process, much to the horror and disapproval of Muslim theologians, local beliefs and religious customs were grafted upon the original doctrines to form a popular Islam. In most instances, therefore, popular Islam in different parts of the world became exceedingly diverse in form and practice. Sufis could also be either Sunnites or Shiites, although most mystics apparently were Sunnites.

SHIISM

Differences of opinion and belief have usually been accepted in Islam. Variations in practice and doctrine among the four main Sunnite legal systems, the many conflicting interpretations of tradition in vogue throughout the Muslim world, and the confusing welter of exotic ideas rampant in popular Islam have made a definitive imputation of heresy difficult to verify on purely theological grounds.

Until comparatively recently, rulers throughout the world usually persecuted subjects whose religion was at marked variance with theirs. Nonetheless, Islam was relatively tolerant, as the treatment of Christians and Jews testifies, and the caliphs

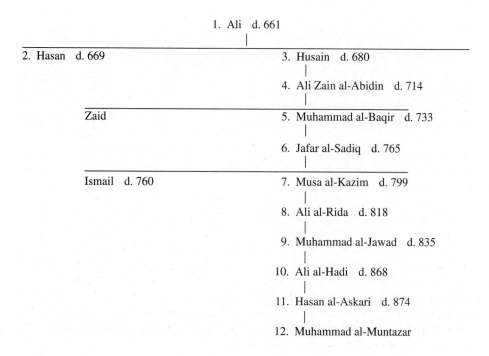

The Twelve Imams

permitted many types of religious deviation. In general, deviation became a serious matter only when religious doctrines denied to the caliph the right of his position and his power. Therein lay the true seeds of accusations of heresy.

Following the death of Ali and the ascension of the Umayyad caliphs, Alids contended that the rulers were usurpers and that the imamate, as they called the leadership position for the Muslim community, should be lodged in the house of the prophet Muhammad, through Ali and Fatimah. Within that family, succession to the imamate could be decided according to one or more criteria: strictly hereditary succession from Ali's son Husain; designation by the previous imam, which would be given to a member of the family but not necessarily the eldest son; self-designation through action against the enemies of the family, as Alid pretenders rose against the Umayyad and Abbasid caliphs. For more than two centuries, intermittent political and military attempts were made by the Shiites (the partisans, or sect, of Ali) to unseat the caliph. Constant opposition to established authority made the Shiites into a general umbrella movement that attracted numerous social and economic groups antagonistic to caliphal policies and the existing order. Although successful in reaching political power in some places at certain times, the Shiites usually were ruled by Sunnites, and the Shiites developed an intricate theology, heavily influenced as of the eleventh century by Mutazilite thought, which engendered some dogmas opposed by Sunnites.

The Shiites held that Ali had been the legitimate imam ("leader") and that the imamate was rightfully transmitted to his descendants. Ali had been given an esoteric power to interpret the Quran, a knowledge that was handed on, in turn, to his sons and grandsons. (Later, some extremists even professed that God's revelations had been intended for Ali but that the angel Gabriel had mistakenly given them to Muhammad.) Ali's descendants, therefore, ruled by a divine right that was handed down to them from Adam; they were infallible, impeccable, and certainly beyond human censure, and therefore not subject to the consensus of the Muslim community.

To substantiate their theological and political claims, the Shiites offered their own interpretation of the early history of Islam. They rejected the legitimacy of the first three caliphs—Abu Bakr, Umar, and Uthman—and claimed that Muhammad had announced in 632 that Ali (who they said had been the first or second convert to Islam) was his rightful successor. Muawiyah and the Umayyads in general were particularly criticized by the Shiites because they had overthrown Ali, and they were responsible for the murder of Ali's son, Husain, in 680, as he led an unsuccessful rebellion against the caliph Yazid. The tragic martyrdom of Husain became the most fervently celebrated event in the Shiite religious calendar and the chief emotional impetus for the spread of the faith.

The Shiites have been divided into numerous sects since the eighth century. The majority, the Twelvers, adhered to the belief that there was a succession by prior designation of twelve imams to Muhammad al-Muntazar ("The Expected"), who in the 870s disappeared in a cave and who will return as the savior (Mahdi) of humanity. In his absence the law and the creed were interpreted originally by four agents who acted for him, but upon the death of the last of these in 940 the "great occultation" or concealment began, and no definitive interpretation of the will of the imam was possible. This meant that historical precedent and the faith could not be interpreted in an absolutely binding way after 940, and intellectual speculation and judicial ingenuity could be exercised by Shiite scholars and jurists. Thus, in law, the Twelver Shiites accepted only the Quran, the sunnah of the prophet Muhammad, those traditions of Muhammad narrated by a recognized imam and the imams' own views on law and theology as compiled in the tenth and eleventh centuries, and a scholar's or judge's personal opinion when it could be upheld by tradition or precedent established by an imam. Justice was strongly emphasized, and oppression and tyranny were considered to be great evils. Analogy and consensus among the learned scholars were restricted in application, and their use was not widely accepted until a much later time.

Aside from petty ritualistic differences, the chief characteristics of these Shiites were the allowance of temporary marriage and the practice of dissimulation. The latter permitted Shiites to deny their faith to avoid persecution when Sunnites attacked them for disavowing caliphal authority.

The Twelver Shiites held political power only occasionally before the sixteenth century, as in the Buwayhid dynasty that controlled the Sunnite Abbasid caliphate in Baghdad at the close of the classical Islamic period, and several Syrian and Iraqi tribal dynasties. However, other types of Shiites established themselves in various parts of the Middle East in the ninth and tenth centuries, while in the late twentieth century the majority of Muslims in Iran and Iraq are Shiites of the Twelver persuasion.

The most conservative of the Shiites are found in Yemen. In parts of northern Yemen the Zaidi sect, which arrived there in the ninth century, at about the same time the sect was also flourishing in northern Iran, recognized a series of imams who were descended from Zaid, a son of the fourth imam. The Zaidis allow for little supernaturalism in their theology; succession to the imamate was by ability, among the descendants of Ali and Fatimah, and not by designation by the incumbent imam.

More extreme Shiite groups included a score or more of divergent sects. Of these the Ismailis, or Seveners, has had the greatest following. They regarded Ismail as the rightful seventh imam. At first, Jafar al-Sadiq named Ismail, his eldest son, as successor, but Jafar designated another son, Musa, as successor. The Seveners rejected this substitution, arguing that the imam was incapable of erring and his original choice must have been correct. Seven became a sacred and mystical number. The essence of the universe came in seven steps: God, universal mind, universal soul, matter, space, time, and earth and the human being. Since Muslims needed guidance, there must be an imam present to lead the Sevener community at any given time.

The Ismailis were masters of organization and tactics. Sent out by the true founder, Abd Allah ibn Maimun, from Salamiyah in Syria, missionaries traveled through the Muslim world, preaching that the language of the Quran was an occult veil covering an inner and true meaning that could be revealed only to the adept. Initiation of the novice proceeded in seven graded degrees, wherein was divulged secret knowledge such as transmigration of souls, the divinity of Ismail, and the coming of the Mahdi. One part of the Ismaili sect established its rule in North Africa early in the tenth century. The Fatimids, who claimed universal dominion as their goal, ruled much of the western portion of the Muslim world, while the Qarmatians, who were also Ismailis, ruled much of eastern Arabia, although the majority of the Muslims of the Middle East remained Sunnites.

Another Ismaili sect was the notorious Assassins, founded in Iran by Hasan ibn al-Sabbah, who studied Ismaili rites and doctrine in Fatimid Egypt and then returned to his home as a missionary. In 1090, near Qazvin in the Elburz Mountains, he seized the fort of Alamut, which became the residence of the grand master of the order. Below him were priors and propagandists; at the lowest rank stood the fidais, who risked death for the faith. Their familiar name, Assassins, was derived from the Arabic word for hashish, which they were said to use in their fearless raids from mountain fortresses. Exact knowledge about these Ismaili groups is lacking, however, because many of their records and books were destroyed in 1256 when the Mongols razed Alamut. Spreading westward earlier, the Assassins in the twelfth century held numerous castles in north Syria. The assassination of the famous vizir Nizam al-Mulk in 1092 was the first in a series of assassinations of prominent individuals. The western branch of the order was eliminated by the Mamluks in 1272.

Other Ismaili sects were the Nusairis or Alawites of northern Syria and the Druzes of Lebanon, Syria, and Jordan. The Nusairis were devotees of the eleventh imam but nevertheless adhered to the main tenets of the Seveners. They looked upon Ali as the incarnation of God and possessed a liturgy with many Christian borrowings. The Druze sect was an eleventh-century splinter group from Fatimid Egypt. Its members settled in Syria and the Lebanon mountain region, where they developed an elaborate ritual and a pattern of life distinctive even in minor detail. Both the Druzes and the Nusairis maintained strict secrecy with respect to their faith and practices.

Probably the best-known Ismaili in the twentieth century was the incomparable Agha Khan III of Bombay, London, Paris, and the Riviera, who traced his descent through the last grand master of the Assassins at Alamut to the seventh imam. Regarded as infallible and impeccable by his followers in Syria, India, Pakistan, and Zanzibar, he received a tenth of their revenues.

In addition to the sects and divisions of these branches of Islam already described, there have been many more. Thus, the Quran and the sayings of the prophet Muhammad passed through the fires of Greek logic, Hellenistic Christianity, and Persian dualism to evolve a finely drawn legal system and intellectual theology, a highly charged supernatural religion, and a flourishing mystical tradition. The apocryphal words of Muhammad have apparently been fulfilled: when told that there were seventy-two varieties of Christianity, the Prophet was supposed to have said that Islam would have seventy-three!

References

References for Chapters 3, 5, and 7 relate to the subject matter of this chapter.

ARBERRY, A. J.: *Sufism: An Account of the Mystics of Islam.* New York: Harper and Row, 1970. This succinct book by an expert in the field looks at the Quran, Muhammad, ascetics, mystics, the Sufi orders, and Persian mystical poets.

AZAMI, MUHAMMAD MUSTAFA: *Studies in Hadith Methodology and Literature.* Indianapolis, Ind.: American Trust Publishers, 1977. Hadith criticism and the chief compilers of hadith are examined in a traditional manner.

DAFTARY, FARHAD: *The Isma'ilis: Their History and Doctrines.* New York: Cambridge University Press, 1990. A very detailed and definitive work on all aspects of the subject; for advanced readers.

JAFRI, HUSAIN M.: *Origins and Early Development of Shi'a Islam.* London: Longman, 1979. The author follows events from the days of Muhammad to Jafar al-Sadiq from the point of view of Shiite Islam.

JUYNBOLL, G. H. A.: *Muslim Tradition: Studies in Chronology, Provenance and Authorship of Early Hadith.* Cambridge, England: Cambridge University Press, 1983.

KHALIDI, TARIF: *Classical Arab Islam: The Culture and Heritage of the Golden Age.* Princeton, N.J.: Darwin Press, 1985. Thoughtful essays on a broad range of subjects, including mysticism, reason, nature, and the prophet Muhammad.

KNYSH, ALEXANDER: " 'Orthodoxy' and 'Heresy' in Medieval Islam: An Essay in Reassessment." *The Muslim World* 83 (1993): 48–67. Shows the diverse approaches to Islam and to what is considered orthodox, especially prior to the fourteenth century.

LIEBESNY, HERBERT J.: *The Law of the Near and Middle East: Readings, Cases and Materials.* Albany: State University of New York Press, 1974. A systematic treatment of the subject from early to modern times.

MASSIGNON, LOUIS: *The Passion of al-Hallaj: Mystical Martyr of Islam.* Vol. 1: *Life.* Translated by H. Mason. Princeton, N.J.: Princeton University Press, 1982. The moving account of the life of one of the most extreme and famous of the mystics.

MOMEN, MOOJAN: *An Introduction to Shi'i Islam: The History and Doctrines of Twelver Shi'ism.*

New Haven, Conn.: Yale University Press, 1985. Shiism as a political, religious, and intellectual movement is thoroughly examined in a detailed manner.

PETRUSHEVSKY, I. P.: *Islam in Iran.* Albany: State University of New York Press, 1985. Despite its title, the book covers the whole geographic range of Islam, and its political and religious history, from the point of view of a Soviet scholar.

RIPPIN, ANDREW: *Muslims: Their Religious Beliefs and Practices.* Vol. 1: *The Formative Period.* London: Routledge, 1990. A revisionist introduction that casts doubt on many accepted interpretations.

SCHACHT, JOSEPH: *An Introduction to Islamic Law.* New York: Oxford University Press, 1964. The best book in the field and more than an introduction, as the author sheds light on the importance of al-Shafii.

SCHIMMEL, ANNEMARIE: *Mystical Dimensions of Islam.* Chapel Hill: University of North Carolina Press, 1975. This is a synthesis of Sufi theory and practice, its history, psychological and social significance, and literary output.

WATT, W. MONTGOMERY: *Muslim Intellectual: A Study of al-Ghazali.* Edinburgh, Scotland: Edinburgh University Press, 1963. A full study of this great theological philosopher.

————: *The Formative Period of Islamic Thought.* Edinburgh, Scotland: Edinburgh University Press, 1973. A detailed study of Islamic ideas from 632 to 945. This important work closely relates the effect of the development of ideas and beliefs upon political events.

————: *Islamic Philosophy and Theology: An Extended Survey.* 2d ed. Edinburgh, Scotland: Edinburgh University Press, 1985. An excellent short introduction and summary.

WILLIAMS, JOHN ALDEN: *Themes of Islamic Civilization.* Berkeley: University of California Press, 1971. Readings in chronological order drawn from original sources, with informative introductions, on the topics of the community, the perfect ruler, the will of God, the Mahdi, holy war, and mysticism.

Muslim Civilization in the Middle East

The Muslims burst from the cities of the Hijaz and the deserts of Arabia into the existing complex civilizations of the Middle East. Everywhere they demonstrated a remarkable genius for assimilating various attributes of existing cultures and blending them with their own to form a new and varied Muslim civilization. For the classical Islamic period during the first few centuries following the death of Muhammad in 632, Arabic remained the universal language; non-Arab Muslims and non-Muslims alike, if they learned the Arabic language, could and did participate in most aspects of Muslim culture. Jews, Christians, and others made substantial contributions to the development of the new civilization that often transcended religious as well as political and geographic differences.

Despite the political and military changes that altered the nature of Muslim governments in the early medieval period from 950 to about 1250, the development and refinement of Muslim civilization in the Middle East continued and even accelerated. There was little specialization in knowledge; most thinkers were accomplished in several fields of research. The cultural and intellectual accomplishments of the Muslims in the Middle East included major advancements in human knowledge in diverse fields, spanning various arts and sciences.

PHILOSOPHY

The emergence of the Mutazilites indicated that Greek logic was studied during the Umayyad era. Not until the reign of the Abbasid al-Mamun, however, was the bulk of Hellenistic thought and science translated into Arabic. Beginning with a majority of the works of Aristotle and Plato, translators soon rendered most earlier philosophers of the Mediterranean area into Arabic. It was upon this base and religious disputation that Muslim philosophy was erected.

The earliest of the prominent Arab philosophers was the Basran al-Kindi (d. ca. 865), a tutor to the son of the caliph al-Mutasim. He excelled in the study of optics, chemistry, medicine, and music, but above all he was a philosopher. Al-Kindi studied the ideas of Aristotle and Plato. He intermingled philosophy and theology, holding that the world of intelligence is supreme. Immortality results from having the correct knowledge of God and the universe. A century later, al-Farabi (d. 950), a Turk from central Asia who lived much of his life in Aleppo, blended Aristotelian, Platonic, and Sufi mystical thought. He presented his philosophy in a political treatise by describing a model city where the ruler was a moral and intellectual being and the happiness of all was the governing force. Al-Farabi's classification of the sciences influenced Muslim scholars for centuries to come. However, he shocked Muslims by claiming that the world was not created and had no beginning.

Muslim philosophers better known to the Western world were Ibn Sina (d. 1037; known as Avicenna) and Ibn Rushd (d. 1198; known as Averroës). The former, called by the Muslims "the shaikh and the prince of the learned," was born in 980 in a village near Bukhara. An Iranian, Ibn Sina lived as a young man in Bukhara, where he acquired an encyclopedic knowledge of medicine, mathematics, astronomy, and philosophy. Since he was able to write concisely, yet in a popular style, Ibn Sina's numerous works on these diverse subjects had a wide vogue among Muslims and greatly influenced the advancement of philosophical thought in medieval Europe. Pursuing Aristotelian philosophy, Ibn Sina developed and passed on to the West the notion that there are two intelligibles—the concept of an object such as a chair, and the pursuant or logical concept of a chair in relation to its abstract universal concept. He taught that the idea of a chair existed before the chair was created, that in each chair existed the idea of chair and that from many chairs came the idea of chair.

Ibn Rushd, the Malikite Muslim judge and philosopher, lived in Córdoba, Seville, and Marrakesh. He wrote in the fields of philosophy, medicine, mathematics, law, and theology. As the last of the classical Muslim philosophers of Spain, he built on the systems of al-Farabi, Ibn Sina, and his fellow countrymen. He declared that active human reason and possible reason or knowledge are one and present in everyone. Ibn Rushd's commentaries on Aristotle were more popular and influential in Christian Europe than they were in the Muslim world.

From Aristotle, Plato, and other Greek philosophers the Muslim scholars, writing in Arabic, created a school of philosophy that had a profound and recognized influence on Christian philosophers of medieval Europe. More significant to the Middle East, however, was their permanent impact upon Muslim intellectuals. Summaries, treatises, and commentaries on these philosophers and scores of others less well known were read and discussed. Scientific method itself became a field of controversy where philosophers, theologians, and the practitioners of the individual sciences fiercely debated theories of knowledge and investigation.

MEDICINE

Muhammad supposedly declared that there exist two sciences: theology and medicine. Consequently, throughout classical and medieval Islamic history most Muslim philosophers and scientists were students of medicine; frequently they were also practicing physicians. Muslims first became aware of medical knowledge at the Damascus court of the Umayyads, through their Greek, Syrian, and Iranian physicians, whose skills were based almost exclusively on works of Greek scientists. A few Greek or Syriac treatises were translated into Arabic, and the Alexandria medical school was transferred from Egypt, first to Antioch and later to Iraq.

Great strides in medicine were made under Abbasid rule in Baghdad. The medical works of Galen and Hippocrates were especially important when translated into Arabic. Galen was highly influential in forming medical theory. Several schools of medicine developed, and a physician took state examinations to obtain a license to practice his profession. In the year 931, there were 869 physicians registered in Baghdad; they swore to work for the benefit of humanity and for the relief and cure of the sick and not to give deadly medicines. Some traveling clinics for the poor were supported by the state, and hospitals were introduced into the Muslim world by the Abbasid caliph Harun al-Rashid. Most physicians were general practitioners, but there was specialization in ophthalmology and surgery. On most of his campaigns the Seljuk Turkish sultan Malikshah had with him a mobile hospital, carried on forty camels. Pharmacists were also examined and licensed, and schools of pharmacy and drugstores were established.

In 765 the Nestorian Christian Jurjis ibn Bukhtishu, dean of the academy of medicine of Jundishapur in southwestern Iran, came to the court of al-Mansur to cure the Abbasid caliph's stomach ailment. Fortunes were made by court physicians, who passed on their professional skills and practices as valued possessions from father to son for generations. Ibn Bukhtishu's grandson understood psychiatry; through a form of hypnosis, he cured one of al-Rashid's slave girls of hysterical paralysis by pretending to disrobe her publicly. Descendants of Ibn Bukhtishu served the Abbasid court for nearly three centuries.

The arrival of physicians from Jundishapur opened the way for medical investigations beyond the works of the ancient Greeks, and the ninth century in Baghdad was a period of many advances in medical knowledge. The compendium by Thabit ibn Qurra of Harran (d. 901) discussed general hygiene. It stated causes, symptoms, and treatment for diseases of the skin and every part of the body from head to foot. Infectious diseases were classified; fractures and dislocations were described; and the importance of climate, food, diet, and sex was explained.

The most ingenious Muslim physician was the Persian al-Razi (d. 925), chief of the Baghdad hospital from about 902 to 907, then a practicing physician and philosopher in Rayy. Considered the best original mind and clinician of the medieval period, he treated bladder and kidney stones, and presented the first clinical report on measles and smallpox. He had some fifty-six monographs on medicine and surgery to his credit. His comprehensive medical encyclopedia was based on clinical observations and experimentation.

The most famous Muslim medical work was al-Qanun, written in the eleventh century by Ibn Sina, whose philosophical accomplishments have been mentioned earlier. Encyclopedic in character, it showed the advances of Muslim knowledge and the originality of Ibn Sina in this field. Among other things, it explained the contagious nature of tuberculosis, showed that disease could be spread through water, recognized pleurisy, and described 760 different drugs. Al-Qanun, along with the works of Galen and Hippocrates, was among the chief medical books of the Middle East and western Europe from the twelfth to the seventeenth century.

Muslim Spain possessed superior physicians and surgeons. The ablest surgeon was Abu al-Qasim of Córdoba, who practiced the art of crushing bladder stones, cauterized wounds, and advocated dissection of bodies, even though Muslims generally did not engage in dissection. His surgical writings were translated and became the surgical manual at the medical schools of European centers. At the time of the Black Death in the middle of the fourteenth century, two Muslim physicians of Granada, Ibn al-Khatib and Ibn Khatima, recognized the disease's contagious character; in their treatises they noted that a patient's symptoms were identical to those of the person from whom he had been infected. Although religious law denied contagion, Ibn al-Khatib held that "experience, investigation, the evidence of the senses and trustworthy reports" established without a doubt the reality of infection from the afflicted.

Building on earlier sources, Muslim physicians expanded the frontiers of medicine. Their practice, monographs, and compendiums demonstrated originality and ingenuity up to the thirteenth century. The diversity and number of their works, translated into Latin and eventually printed, further established the place of Muslim physicians in the history of world medical science. Since the chief hobby of countless leading Muslims was the study of medicine, every medical practitioner was encouraged to reach the pinnacle of his ability and capacity.

MATHEMATICS AND ASTRONOMY

Muslim scholars also found mathematics an attractive and useful science, especially in company with astronomy and astrology. By far the greatest achievement of the Arab mathematicians was the adoption and wide use of "Arabic numerals." It is not known whether they were brought from India or developed locally. In any case, these numerals, including the use of zero and the placing of the digit in a series to denote units, tens, hundreds, and so on, made "everyday arithmetic" possible and simplified calculations, enabling Muslims to take the square and cube roots of numbers with ease. The word *cipher,* meaning zero, was taken directly from the Arabic sifr, meaning "empty."

Building on Indian and Greek works, Middle Eastern scholars advanced mathematical knowledge considerably. Muhammad al-Khwarazmi of Khurasan (d. 850) did a study on Indian numerals that later circulated in the west. Through his name came the word "algorism." He wrote on the solution of quadratic equations, and from part of the title of one of his books was derived the word *algebra* (al-jabr: "integration"). In the same century, the mathematician, astronomer, and physician Thabit ibn Qurra developed new propositions and studied irrationals. The Iranian al-Battani (d. 929) was the first to present ideas on trigonometric ratios.

One of the most distinguished mathematicians was the Iranian poet Umar Khayyam (d. 1130). He advanced far beyond al-Khwarazmi, establishing procedures for the solution of cubic and quadrinomial equations and developing analytic geometry in numerous ways. The last great medieval mathematician of the Middle

East was the Iranian Nasir al-Din al-Tusi (d. 1274), who assembled his laboratory in northwestern Iran under the patronage of the Mongols. Here he wrote his famous *Treatise on the Quadrilateral* and conducted his brilliant studies in the field of spherical trigonometry.

Mathematics and astronomy were closely related, especially since in the construction of any mosque it was necessary to fix the direction of Mecca, and accurate timekeeping was important to determine the occasions for prayers. Furthermore, since astrology was popular and the latitude and longitude of one's birthplace entered into one's horoscope, the movement of the stars was significant. Folk astronomy was used for fixing the lunar months and calculating times of prayers, while mathematical astronomy was more specialized. Muslim astronomy started from Iranian, Greek, and Indian contributions.

When the Abbasid caliph al-Mansur decided to build his new palace in Baghdad, the Iranian astronomer Naubakht was employed to draw the plans. Many palaces in Baghdad had private astronomical observatories. The main professional observatories were at Jundishapur and Baghdad. Scientists at the time of al-Mamun measured a degree on the meridian precisely, with only a 2 percent error. Although the Muslim religious calendar was based on lunar months, rather exact astronomical tables and solar calendars were also prepared.

Thabit ibn Qurra determined the altitude of the sun and computed the length of the solar year; Muhammad al-Battani recorded his observations on the appearance of the new moon, the inclination of the ecliptic, and eclipses of the sun. The astronomer and geographer al-Biruni (d. 1048), while at Ghaznah in Afghanistan, proposed the idea that the earth rotates on its axis and reckoned quite accurately latitudes and longitudes for every important city in the Middle East, as well as writing excellent cultural geographies.

Near Córdoba lived the great astronomer al-Bitruji, who computed the length of the Mediterranean and found it to be 42° of longitude, a nearly correct measurement. He advanced the idea of diurnal movements of the earth and explained the movement of the stars by the turning of the earth on its axis as well as by its circling about the sun.

One of the finest observatories was established by the Mongols at Maraghah, where the scientist Nasir al-Din al-Tusi developed the most precise instruments of medieval times. Because of his excellent equipment his Ilkhanian tables were long regarded as the most exact of astronomical tables.

The Arabic names of many stars and constellations and the Arabic origin of such words as *azimuth, nadir,* and *zenith* vouch for the brilliance of the Middle Eastern astronomers and the acceptance of their contributions by the west. Besides assimilating and transmitting to posterity the mathematics and astronomy of the ancients, Middle Eastern scholars up to the fifteenth century made many original contributions in the practical and theoretical branches of the subjects. The widespread use of numerals gave arithmetic an everyday value. Algebra became an exact science, and solid foundations were laid in the fields of analytic geometry and plane and spherical trigonometry. Through Spain and Sicily most of these ideas passed at an early date to the Western world, where they influenced the science of Europe, while the same knowledge was also passing to the great civilizations of India and China.

SCIENCES

In addition to medicine, mathematics, and astronomy, Middle Easterners investigated and frequently brought about fundamental redefinitions in the basic and natural sciences. It is not possible here to detail the various advances made in each science. Some examples would include works on botany, chiefly in connection with drugs for the pharmacist and physician. Zoological studies were made, some for use by veterinarians. Al-Masudi, who died about 957 in Cairo, discussed earthquakes, described windmills, and advanced a theory of evolution. In his book on geology, Ibn Sina suggested several ideas about earthquakes, winds, climate, and geologic sedimentation.

However, the greatest strides in the sciences were taken in chemistry and physics. The word *chemistry* is derived from Arabic. Chemistry was studied mostly in connection with alchemy, although some famous scientists, such as Ibn Sina and al-Kindi, did not believe in the transmutation of metals. Alchemy was founded on the belief that all metals contain the same essences and that it is possible to transmute one to another. Further, it was believed that gold is the purest form of metal and that some substance exists that can transform baser metals into gold. Throughout the Muslim world countless individuals engaged in the search for this substance and the technique of its use. Celebrated philosophers and physicians gave their time and genius to the quest. One of these men, al-Razi, distinguished volatile and nonvolatile bodies and classified all matter as vegetable, animal, or mineral. Others in their research determined the specific weights of stones and metals.

The greatest chemist, or alchemist, was Jabir ibn Hayyan, who lived in Kufah toward the end of the eighth century and died in 815. Jabir advocated experimentation and recognized the importance of confirming by careful observation theories that are based only on previous writings and hypotheses. He was able to prepare arsenious oxide, lead acetate, sulfide of mercury, and sal ammoniac. Jabir presented new and improved methods of evaporation, filtration, sublimation, melting, crystallization, and distillation. His works, translated into Latin in the twelfth century, proved to be the foundation of western alchemy and chemistry. The Arabic origin of such words as *alkali* and *alcohol* attests to western dependence upon Middle Eastern discoveries in this branch of science.

In physics the widest interest lay in theoretical and applied mechanics as related to problems of irrigation, the construction of mills, and the flow of water. Waterwheels and water clocks were built in many cities of the Middle East, some of the clocks being exceedingly ingenious in design. (Clock design was one of the very few areas of science and technology where European innovations were brought into the Islamic world; generally, the flow of knowledge went the other way.) In the twelfth century, al-Khazini observed the greater density of water when it was nearer the center of the earth, and he displayed a strong preference for experimentation rather than theorizing.

The most significant developments in physics, however, were in the field of optics. Many prominent scientists of the age investigated the subject. The most outstanding was Abu Ali ibn al-Haitham (d. 1039), who flourished in Cairo at the time of the Fatimids and who also extensively studied momentum and gravity. He refused to accept Euclid's and Ptolemy's theory that the eye emits visual rays; instead he advanced the theory that vision is due to the impact of light rays. Experimenting with reflection and optical illusions, he studied refraction through spherical segments filled with water. He also proposed that light is fire reflected at the spherical limit of the atmosphere; from observing phenomena at twilight he reckoned the atmosphere to be about 10 miles (16 km.) high. Ibn al-Haitham's studies greatly influenced, through translation, the works of such Europeans as Leonardo da Vinci.

GEOGRAPHY

The religious obligation of a pilgrimage to Mecca once in a lifetime undoubtedly reinforced a persistent urge among many in Islamic lands to travel and see the world. Because geographic data were needed by these travelers as well as by traders and administrators, travelers wrote detailed books on where they had been and what they had seen. Geography became one of the most popular pursuits of the medieval periods of Islamic civilization in the Middle East.

Muslim geographers had difficulty in freeing themselves from earlier Greek, Persian, and Indian concepts of the world. The scientist al-Khwarazmi, at the caliph al-Mamun's command, prepared a great map of the earth and a companion text that was used by geographers until the fourteenth century. Largely following the ancient Ptolemy, al-Khwarazmi pictured the world encircled by a continuous ocean from which the Mediterranean and the Indian Ocean branched to separate the land of the earth, which was divided into seven climate zones. The western prime meridian ran through the Canary Islands, and the easternmost area discussed was China. Iraq was considered to be in the center and the most fortunate of places.

Fortunately, the conservative and classical geographers were ignored by travelers and sailors who recognized irregular coasts strewn with gulfs and peninsulas and stated that the Indian Ocean, in certain directions, has no limit. The tales of these voyagers came down through the ages as the stories of Sindbad the Sailor. They described China in the ninth century and Russia in the tenth. Their road books were a mine of historical topography and economic and political geography. The tenth-century scholar was frequently on the move. The greatest globe-trotter was al-Masudi (d. 956), who visited most of the countries of Asia, Zanzibar, and much of North Africa. His thirty-volume work became one of the two recognized geographic encyclopedias of the medieval period. One of the last discerning voyagers was Ibn Battutah of Morocco. Living in the fourteenth century, he was on the move for nearly three decades. He made four pilgrimages to Mecca and visited India, China, Byzantine Constantinople, and parts of Africa.

The most noted geographer of the Muslim world was al-Idrisi, born in Ceuta in

1100 and for many years the chief geographer for the Christian King Roger II of Sicily. In his writings and discourses in Arabic, he summed up the ideas and contributions of Ptolemy, al-Khwarazmi, and al-Masudi. Using silver, al-Idrisi constructed for his patron a celestial sphere and a disklike map of the earth; the latter distinctly showed the source of the Nile to be a lake in central Africa.

The last eminent medieval Muslim geographer was Yakut ibn Abd Allah al-Hamawi, a Greek slave from Anatolia who was educated and given his freedom. Before his death in 1229 Yakut compiled a famous and vast encyclopedia of geographic information. Arranged alphabetically, it summed up the whole fund of knowledge available to him in this field and thus became an invaluable source book for all scholars.

POETRY AND LITERATURE

Poetry was the single most important expression of literature in the Islamic world, although other genres also flourished. In pre-Islamic Arabia poetry was a favorite vehicle of expression. A talented poet was highly esteemed, and the cultured person was one who appreciated fine poetry and could recite an endless quantity of verse. Muhammad found much of this poetry distasteful, since the way of life extolled was not the way of Islam, although he had the support of several poets of the day.

The advent of the Umayyad regime set the stage for the return of poetry to its pre-Islamic popularity. The poet Umar (d. 712) wrote with charming grace of free and erotic love, and his directness and simplicity influenced generations of Arab poets. Singers and entertainers found his style well suited to their ballads. Lyric poetry reached its height in the Majnun-Laila romance. The author-hero became mad (majnun) because of his burning passion for a woman whose father compelled her to marry another. The deranged lover roamed the world seeking his beloved. Ever after, Majnun was the typical hero of unrequited-love poems throughout the Middle East. In addition, there reappeared in the Umayyad period many writers of eulogistic and epic poetry of the pre-Islamic style. Noted for their erotic language and political invective, these poets pleased their patrons and their poetry revealed the life and morals of the age. Many Umayyad caliphs were themselves poets.

With the coming of the Abbasids, the court moved to Baghdad and the poets followed. Persian influence and rich caliphal patronage introduced an elegance and an openness in sexual matters. One of the first poets in this period was the blind Bashshar ibn Burd (d. 783), whose paeans of love were so popular and so apt for singing that the caliph al-Mahdi had him executed in 783 for endangering public morals. The boon companion of Harun al-Rashid was the sparkling and lusty Abu Nuwas (d. 811). Not all poetry, however, dealt with wine, women, and song; much political poetry was also written.

At the court and in wealthy society poetry was on the lips of all, and every elegant household had its poet. The immediate material rewards were great, as was, consequently, the quantity of verse, much of it praising a patron or meant only for the moment. Since the golden days of Baghdad the poetry of that classical age has retained its favored position among educated Arabic-speaking Middle Eastern peoples.

The zajal and the muwashshah (the ballad and folk song), developed in Muslim Spain, were popularized and spread by wandering minstrels. The epoch of the troubadour in northern Spain, Italy, and France was largely dependent upon this Spanish development; the idealization of the lady and love found in the troubadour songs was a Christian characterization of themes prevalent in Arabic lyrics of the Muslim world.

At the other end of the Muslim world in the province of Fars and especially in Shiraz, there arose the school of Persian-language poets. Firdawsi, who died in 1020, presented his epic Shahnamah, or book of kings, written in Persian, to the ruler Mahmud of Ghaznah. No poetry has ever stirred the soul of the Iranian people as has Firdawsi's Shahnamah; even today illiterates recite legends and history from Firdawsi's poetry with great emotion.

The famous Iranian scholar and poet Umar Khayyam wrote a set of quatrains; this Rubaiyat as translated into English, even though often far from the original texts, has come in the west to be popularly regarded as the very best of Middle Eastern poetry. Khayyam's poems beautifully expressed the hope for love accompanied by disillusionment of twelfth-century Nishapur and were merely a side thought of Khayyam, an illustrious mathematician.

Besides Firdawsi, the other poets regarded as truly gifted by Iranians were Nizami (d. 1209), whose romantic stories were exceptionally popular and whose rendition of the Majnun-Laila theme was depicted in countless miniature paintings; Jalal al-Din Rumi, the mystic poet who founded the Mawlawi (Mevlevi) dervish order and died at Konya in Anatolia in 1273; Sadi of Shiraz, another mystic whose writings were among the favorite poems of Iran; and the fourteenth-century Hafiz, the master of Persian-language lyricists, a materialist yet a mystic, whose love for the shady gardens, wine and women, and the laughter-loving people of Shiraz was shown in his collection of odes.

The Umayyad period featured letters addressed to the caliphs and others, often written by the newly Arabized bureaucrats and secretaries in Damascus. The Arabic language was thoroughly studied, and its grammar and style were analyzed as many dictionaries were compiled. Under the Abbasids government officials and others composed administrative manuals, collections of biographies, and "mirrors for princes" that were written to inform the young about how to govern. Another literary form was represented by the ninth-century essayist, humorist, and litterateur al-Jahiz of Basrah (d. 869)—a notable and witty example of the cultivated writer of polite and amusing stories who set high standards for subsequent authors.

For the most part, the literature of the medieval Middle East consisted of the writings of men who were famous philosophers, theologians, bureaucrats, geographers, historians, and travelers. They wrote under the patronage of rulers and officials. Prose fiction and advice-to-kings literature were not so highly regarded among the Muslim Arabs; not until the tenth century did Persian contacts influence the general taste to produce Arabic literature of this type. Rhymed prose emphasized elegant form over substance; it was often embellished with unusual words. In Muslim Spain a type of anecdote, frequently introducing a moral lesson through the adventure of some dashing hero, became the prototype of the Spanish picaresque novel. In his rhetorical tales al-Hariri of Basrah (d. 1122), whose works became enormously popular and were often illustrated by miniature painters, subtly criticized the existing social order.

A number of delightful anthologies, treasuries of poetry, literature, and history, serve as invaluable sources for the study of Muslim civilization. An example is the twenty-volume *Book of Songs* gathered by Abu al-Faraj al-Isfahani (d. 967).

Of all the literature of the Middle East the most colorful, fanciful, and noteworthy through many centuries has been the *Arabian Nights*. Taking the core of the stories and names of leading characters from old Indian and Persian tales, al-Jahshiyari in the first half of the tenth century in Iraq blended local color and current episodes and romances of the courts of al-Rashid, al-Mamun, and other caliphs to produce the great *Alf Lailah wa Lailah* (*One Thousand and One Nights*, known as the *Arabian Nights*). Its present form was achieved in the fourteenth century in Mamluk Egypt. Subsequently translated into other languages than Arabic, it has delighted many children and adults throughout the world, while it also can provide much information on social history.

HISTORY

The Muslims of the Middle East produced a number of notable historians. Political controversies in the early days of the Muslim ummah led to an emphasis on history writing. Shiites were especially active in writing history, as reference to the early history of Islam was crucial to their political and theological positions.

Umayyad historians were largely suppressed by the succeeding Abbasid dynasty. By the middle of the eighth century, historical works, especially biography and genealogy associated with religion, attracted the attention of Muslim scholars. The first known biography of the prophet Muhammad was composed by Ibn Ishaq, who died in 767. In the ninth century, accounts of the early battles of Islam, tales of the astonishing Arab Muslim expansion, and biographical dictionaries of historical figures appeared. The two best were those of Ibn Abd al-Hakam (an Egyptian), the story of the conquest of Egypt, North Africa, and Spain, and of al-Baladhuri (an Iranian), a carefully compiled and balanced narrative of Muslim expansion.

The histories produced in the Abbasid era were numerous and varied. Every century and court had professional chroniclers. One of the more noted was al-Tabari (838–923), who traveled widely and studied at many important Muslim centers. A most prolific writer for more than forty years, al-Tabari left a commentary on the Quran but is most noted for his monumental historical chronicle, often used by subsequent generations of historians. His contemporary from Baghdad, the Twelver Shiite al-Masudi, dealt with the same material but treated the unfolding of civilizations topically instead of chronologically as al-Tabari had done. Written after years of travel, al-Masudi's work ran to thirty volumes.

Probably the best known of Muslim historians is the Tunisian Ibn Khaldun (1332–1406). A citizen of the Muslim world, he studied and held important political positions in Fez, Granada, Algeria, and Cairo. His history of the Muslim states and peoples, especially the sections about North Africa, was a significant contribution to knowledge. But Ibn Khaldun's fame rested on his history's first volume, entitled *Muqaddimah* (*Prolegomena*), in which he presented his philosophy of the cyclic development of civilization, social solidarity, and the relationship of nomadic and settled groups, and explained how the historian should record and study the interrelated forces of society. Since he considered climate, geography, economics, and culture as the basic causes of major events, so as to provide lessons and rules about the patterns of history, Ibn Khaldun can be called the first modern historian.

THE MINOR ARTS

In the whole field of the so-called minor arts Muslims in the classical Islamic and early medieval periods carried on the skills and techniques of antiquity in a notable fashion. Far ahead of western Europe in each of the minor arts, at least until the European Renaissance of the fifteenth century, the Middle East produced outstanding rugs, silk and cotton textiles, leatherwork, fine glass, highly glazed ceramics of many types, and exquisite metal pieces in gold, silver, copper, brass, and bronze, many of the pieces heavily inlaid with other metals or encrusted with precious gems. The illumination of manuscripts and the painting of miniature pictures developed into a fine and precise art. Skilled penmanship produced a calligraphy so graceful and so pleasing that it became the predominant decorative art form, with many different decorative and cursive regional styles. Images of living beings were not present in religious buildings, but in secular life they were sometimes depicted. Elaborate designs based on intricate geometric and vegetal patterns were used in many different media.

Between the seventh and thirteenth centuries, proof of the real unity of the Muslim world was the ease and extent of exchange of knowledge and movement of individuals. Such a circulation dictated a considerable universality of Muslim civilization, and the minor arts are an excellent example. From Spain and North Africa on the west to central Asia in the east, each of the great cities boasted reputable craftsmen and artists in all of the arts.

From the foregoing survey of the many aspects of Muslim civilization and its development in the classical Islamic and early medieval periods, it can be seen that Muslim civilization was formed in its most important aspects during the times of the Umayyad and Abbasid empires. In the early medieval period Islamic civilization reached new heights. The Muslims appropriated and adapted from other civilizations and societies valuable ideas, experiences, and skills to create Muslim civilization, while innovative and original contributions were also made by Muslim and non-Muslim artists, writers, and scientists.

Few civilizations have been able to endure for long or to pursue any dynamic course when isolated either geographically or intellectually. Cultural growth is accelerated by the exchange of knowledge among peoples; the greater the exchange, the faster the acceleration. During the Umayyad and Abbasid empires many diverse groups were brought into close contact. Although by the end of the classical Islamic period the power of the central government had greatly lessened, the history of culture and intellectual activity in the early medieval Muslim Middle East reveals a continuing refinement and growth. In the later medieval period of the thirteenth to fifteenth centuries scientific and cultural productivity continued but slowed substantially; cultural development would reach another peak of creativity in the great empires of the early modern period.

References

Among the volumes already cited, those of particular value for this chapter are in Chapter 6.

AHMAD, S. MAQBUL: "Djughrafiya." *Encyclopaedia of Islam.* New ed. Vol. 2, pp. 575–587. Leiden: Brill, 1965. A useful survey of geography.

ASHTIANY, JULIA, ET AL., EDS.: *The Cambridge History of Arabic Literature: 'Abbasid Belles-Lettres.* Cambridge, England: Cambridge University Press, 1990. Twenty-four chapters on all aspects of literary history.

BEESTON, A. F. L., ET AL.: *The Cambridge History of Arabic Literature: Arabic Literature to the End of the Umayyad Period.* Cambridge, England: Cambridge University Press, 1983. A thorough study of the subject written by several authors.

BREND, BARBARA: *Islamic Art.* Cambridge, Mass.: Harvard University Press, 1991. Sophisticated analysis of art in each period and region, with many illustrations.

DODGE, BAYARD, ED. AND TRANS.: *The Fihrist of al-Nadim: A Tenth-Century Survey of Muslim Culture.* 2 vols. New York: Columbia University Press, 1970. Translation of a compendium of all knowledge written in the tenth century.

DUNLOP, D. M.: *Arab Civilization to A.D. 1500.* New York: Praeger, 1971. Covers literature, history, geography, philosophy, science, and famous women.

DURI, ABD AL-AZIZ: *The Rise of Historical Writing Among the Arabs.* Edited and translated by Lawrence I. Conrad. Princeton, N.J.: Princeton University Press, 1983. Especially valuable for developments in Medina and Iraq during the seventh, eighth, and ninth centuries.

FAKHRY, MAJID: *A History of Islamic Philosophy.* 2d ed. New York: Columbia University Press, 1983. A substantial and comprehensive history of Islamic theoretical philosophy, theology, and mysticism.

GIBB, H. A. R.: *Arabic Literature: An Introduction.* 2d ed. Oxford, England: Clarendon Press, 1963. Still a valuable beginning point.

GRABAR, OLEG: *The Formation of Islamic Art.* Rev. ed. New Haven, Conn.: Yale University Press, 1987. The author's treatment is very sensitive, his insights are thought-provoking, and his expression superb. He defines the originality and uniqueness of Islamic art.

HASSAN, AHMAD Y. AL-, AND DONALD R. HILL: *Islamic Technology: An Illustrated History.* Cambridge, England: Cambridge University Press, 1986. One of the very few works on this subject; although written by specialists it is accessible to beginners in the field.

HUMPHREYS, R. STEPHEN: *Islamic History: A Framework for Inquiry.* Rev. ed. Princeton, N.J.: Princeton University Press, 1991. An outstanding introduction to the sources and problems of Middle Eastern history from 600 to 1500, and an excellent guide to further reading.

IRWIN, ROBERT: *The Arabian Nights: A Companion.* London: Allen Lane, 1994. The best introduction to the stories and their context.

KHALIDI, TARIF: *Arabic Historical Thought in the Classical Period.* Cambridge, England: Cambridge University Press, 1994. Perceptive essays on historiography from the eighth to the fourteenth century.

KRAEMER, JOEL L.: *Humanism in the Renaissance of Islam: The Cultural Revival During the Buyid Age.* Leiden: Brill, 1986. Buwayhid political history is related to religious and cultural life.

KRITZECK, JAMES: *Anthology of Islamic Literature from the Rise of Islam to Modern Times.* New York: Holt, Rinehart and Winston, 1964. Discusses all forms of literature from the Quran and early commentaries to political theory, history, stories, and Ottoman puppet plays.

LEAMAN, OLIVER: *An Introduction to Medieval Islamic Philosophy.* Cambridge, England: Cambridge University Press, 1985. Al-Farabi, Ibn Sina, al-Ghazali, Ibn Rushd, and Maimonides on the creation of the world, immortality, God's knowledge of particulars, ethics, and happiness.

MCNEILL, WILLIAM H., AND MARILYN WALDMAN, EDS.: *The Islamic World.* New York: Oxford University Press, 1973. Original sources in translation, dealing with poetry, history, literature, and so on.

MORRISON, GEORGE, JULIAN BALDICK, AND SHAFII KADKANI: *History of Persian Literature from the Beginning of the Islamic Period to the Present Day.* Leiden: Brill, 1981.

NASR, SEYYED HOSSEIN: *Science and Civilization in Islam.* Cambridge, Mass.: Harvard University Press, 1968. A discussion of the development of science, technology, and scientific methodology in medieval Islam.

———: *Islamic Science: An Illustrated Study.* London: World of Islam Festival Publishing Company, 1976. Beautiful illustrations of various scientific inventions and charts; also links science to broader questions of the meaning of the universe and creation.

PETERS, F. E.: *Aristotle and the Arabs: The Aristotelian Tradition in Islam.* New York: New York University Press, 1968. A study of the synthesis of Hellenism and Islam.

RAHMAN, FAZLUR: *Health and Medicine in the Islamic Tradition: Change and Identity.* New York: Crossroad, 1987. Very readable general account of religion and medicine; emphasizes earlier time periods.

ULLMANN, MANFRED: *Islamic Medicine.* Edinburgh, Scotland: Edinburgh University Press, 1978. Brief review of translations of medical works, and of physiology, anatomy, pathology, disease transmission, dietetics, and the occult.

YOUNG, M. J. L., ET AL. EDS.: *The Cambridge History of Arabic Literature: Religion, Learning and Science in the 'Abbasid Period.* Cambridge, England: Cambridge University Press, 1990. Superb essays on a wide variety of cultural fields.

Social Patterns

By the end of the early Abbasid period in the middle of the tenth century, Islamic civilization in the Middle East gradually had evolved certain social patterns that became associated with political, religious, economic, and cultural institutions to form a long-lasting synthesis. These patterns involved a number of groups and issues, such as the role of women in society and gender relationships. The places and buildings in which people lived and the ways they earned their livelihood also profoundly influenced the social history of the era. Keys to understanding social patterns were the education and recreation available for the population.

While some information is available about these subjects, relatively little is known about the life of the bulk of the population who lived in the countryside in villages or about the smaller number of people who earned their living by herding animals as nomads. Most historical accounts dealt with city people and chiefly the prominent individuals among them. Social patterns also differed from region to region as well as from era to era. Tracing significant changes and then relating the patterns of social history to political, religious, economic, and cultural events is extremely difficult to do.

THE ROLES OF WOMEN AND MEN

Unfortunately, very little is known about the history of most women in the classical Islamic period, but it does seem clear that by the tenth century the role of wealthy and middle-class urban women in the family and in society had undergone a marked change from earlier times. Veiling, seclusion of upper-class urban women in a harem, and the general segregation of women from men were practiced by Muslims and by many non-Muslims in the Middle East. The origins of these practices and the reasons for their introduction are not certain, but the best indications point to Byzantine civilization as the main influence. Initially only the wives of the prophet Muhammad were secluded, but gradually this pattern of living became more widespread. Most people placed a high value on privacy.

Some urban women still shopped for goods, and Muslim women who were escorted by male relatives continued to make the pilgrimage. With the general and wide acceptance of concubinage, the rank of the actual wife was greatly elevated. Slave girls might sing, dance, and entertain quite openly and freely for the guests of their masters, but not wives. Thus, the veil and seclusion grew as a protection and a mark of distinction. However, the freedom and the public role of women such as enjoyed by Aishah, the wife of Muhammad, and in Abbasid times by Khaizuran and Zubaidah, lessened.

The social segregation of the sexes encouraged the widespread expression of homosexuality, which was often celebrated in verse, even though condemned by theologians. Al-Wathiq, an Abbasid caliph, devoted much of his poetry to a male lover. Muslims also condemned prostitution, adultery, and suicide; people engaged in prostitution and adultery were subject to rigorous punishments, sometimes including death.

Despite gender segregation, women appeared in courts, where their testimony was accepted, though it carried less weight than that of men. The legal status of Muslim women varied in part according to which one of the Sunnite schools of law they and their families followed; Hanafites were particularly open to interpretations that favored the status of women. In accordance with religious law, a woman's share in an estate was usually only about one-half that of a man. It seems likely that in some cases male-dominated families denied women their due rights so as to reduce the splintering effect of the division of estates or simply because of greed.

Women's roles in society were affected by the practice of birth control, through both contraception and abortion. Scientific, legal, and popular literature was written on the subject, and the authors assumed a free wife could choose to avoid contraception so as to have children, if she wished, while the rights of a slave wife were somewhat limited, and those of a concubine in this area were nil. The ulama, or men of religion, differed on the issue of abortion, with some holding that abortion during the first three months of pregnancy was permitted, while the majority held that it should not take place at all unless the life of the mother was threatened. Women and men regarded childbearing, and particularly having sons, as a way of improving the social status of individual women and benefiting the family's future economic situation.

Most men and women entered into marriages during their teenage years; chastity before marriage was socially expected. Families would usually consult with matchmakers to arrange marriages. If one marriage partner died, remarriage usually took place in a short time, since widows and especially widowed mothers of young children would often be poor. Marriage was a legal contract and was governed by religious laws. Society expected that women would obey their husbands, but actual practice in this and many areas of gender relations must have varied widely depending on personal tastes, abilities, and preferences. While Muslim men could theoretically marry as many as four wives at one time if they treated each wife equally, in practice very few men were polygamous. Only rich men could afford the expenses involved in marrying and maintaining several wives.

Although men were legally dominant in marriage, women retained the marriage settlement as their own property in the event of a divorce, which could be instituted by the husband or, rarely, by the wife. Divorce was viewed as abhorrent and a last resort for couples. Marriages were arranged and contracted between individuals or families of roughly equal status; the marriage of a Muslim woman to a non-Muslim man was uniformly opposed by the legal scholars. Prestige in marriage seemingly came chiefly from the man's family, but the status of the woman's family also influenced the esteem enjoyed by the couple. Families were the central unit of society, and for most people loyalty to the family was far more important than the loyalty owed to any other social group.

Women could and did own property; however, the management of real estate and commercial investments was sometimes difficult because of social restrictions on women. Many occupations were limited entirely to men, including such important posts as judges, clerks, and soldiers. Some wealthy women supervised endowed family charitable foundations (awqaf; singular, waqf). Usually women worked inside the home; peasant women probably also worked in some capacities in the fields, and nomadic women helped with the herds. Urban women frequently worked on textile production in their own homes, and some were employed as servants, entertainers, midwives, and perhaps as assistants to males engaged in craft production. Men often passed on their skills to related females, so, for instance, in a family of calligraphers one would occasionally find women who became expert writers.

Some women, including female religious scholars and teachers, became prominent despite the difficulties placed in their way. Examples include the eighth-century celibate mystic Rabiah al-Adawiyyah of Basrah (d. 801), who was one of the most influential of the early mystics and ascetics. In later times other famous Sufis were women. Several female poets gained some renown, especially the eleventh-century Spanish Umayyad princess Walladah. Many women were included in biographical lists: at least 400 of 1000 women mentioned in an Egyptian biographical treatise had studied Islam by memorizing the Quran, working with a scholar, learning hadith, and receiving a certificate of completing a course of study. Asma al-Dajai (d. 1498), a female alim in Yemen, was a Quran reciter, a recounter of the hadith of the prophet Muhammad, and an expounder of the meaning of religion. She mostly taught other women, but even a local male ruler consulted her. More frequent, though still rare compared with the total number of women in society, were the female students who sought instruction from male and female teachers of religion, although outside the higher institutions of learning, whose formal students were exclusively males.

A few women who influenced the politics of various Muslim Middle Eastern states will be discussed in later chapters. Exceptionally, two queens who were members of the Shiite Sulayhid dynasty in Yemen ruled in the eleventh and twelfth centuries; a few other instances of women rulers also were known. On a number of occasions women managed the political order on behalf of their sons who were minors.

CITIES AND MOSQUES

The peasants who lived in villages constituted the majority of the population in most parts of the Middle East. It was the villagers along with the animal-raising nomads who jointly provided the agricultural surplus of production above consumption that fed the cities. Villagers and nomads themselves needed some goods and services from the cities and the skilled craftsmen who lived in them, so there were mutual interchanges among all three locales. And some people worked and lived in intermediate ways, including those who resided in settled villages and then in other parts of the year moved with herds of animals from one grazing place to another, city-based traders who visited both villagers and the nomads who came to marketplaces, and nomads who might occasionally live for periods of time in the outskirts of cities. Trading and marketing provided an economic base supplemented by artisanal handicraft production in the cities. Urban-based government, religion, and culture also provided services, including education and law, while extracting resources from the countryside.

In the larger cities of the Islamic Middle East general patterns for organizing work and living existed across the area, although to refer to these frequently found characteristics as constituting "the Islamic city" implies more uniformity than actually existed. Almost all cities were walled, for instance, and most cities were organized into quarters or districts, often named after the chief market in the vicinity or after a local mosque or Sufi saint's tomb. Yet despite these and many other similarities, differences also existed, as, for instance, between relatively new cities such as Cairo (founded in 969) and much older cities such as Damascus.

Residential areas with a few hundred or a few thousand people were the norm, and they had a strong sense of local identity that was reinforced by a mutual responsibility for maintaining law and order. While the poor lived in huts, middle-income people lived either in apartment buildings of three or more stories or in separate homes usually built around courtyards. Homes were designed so as to provide maximum privacy; they generally contained little furniture. Religious and ethnic minorities and new immigrants to the city tended to live in separate areas, but a wide variation in housing patterns could exist, where people of varying backgrounds would live side by side. Craftsmen and shopkeepers who dealt in similar goods usually worked in the same neighborhood. Differences in status were reflected in style of housing but also in clothing, by which a person's religion, gender, and standing in life could be judged visually.

Skills were passed from one generation to the next and the units of production were small, with only a few larger factories employing animal power or sometimes water power. Crafts differed in prestige, with some occupations such as tanning leather regarded as obnoxious because of the smells associated with the work, while others such as working in precious metals carried greater social approval. Since streets were narrow, so as to provide shade from the sun and to keep the size of the city within its walls small, porters (as well as donkeys) carried goods from one place to another. Many poor people had no permanent employment, while the rich and powerful enjoyed extraordinary luxuries.

Government, soldiers, and rulers usually resided outside the city center in fortified and somewhat isolated palaces and compounds. A web of interests linked the governing elite to the city people; each needed the other. Some examples of this interdependence included the ruler's need for urban tax revenues and the merchants' need for market inspectors to regulate business. Intermediary officials between the rulers and people facilitated communication and the maintenance of order. Leaders of city quarters, the heads of guilds, representatives of the Christian or Jewish minorities, spokesmen for the merchants, and prominent ulama all put forward the respective needs and desires of the rulers to the people, and the requests and complaints of the people to the rulers.

Muslims of all backgrounds and occupations often went to worship in mosques. The first mosque was none other than the house of Muhammad in Medina, which resembled the typical house of the town Arab in Muhammad's time—a simple enclosure, usually square, with a few huts along the edge. Before he died it assumed a public character, for here the followers congregated to pray with Muhammad and to hear his revelations and sermons. Along one side palm trunks were set up and covered with palm leaves as a protection from the sun. Muhammad stood on a piece of a palm trunk so as to be heard. A pointer indicated the direction of Mecca so that prayers could be made facing the Holy City. Bilal, an early follower of Muhammad, stood on a rooftop to call the Muslims to prayer. Thus were established the essentials of a mosque.

As the Arab Muslims expanded into other lands, they employed local craftsmen in the building of mosques. Consequently, techniques and materials differed from place to place. But the fundamentals of a congregational mosque remained unchanged. A large part of the mosque area was an open courtyard, usually with a fountain where ablutions could be performed and sometimes with a narrow covered arcade on three sides. On the fourth side was the mosque proper. In most mosques in Iraq, Syria, Egypt, North Africa, and Spain, the mosque proper consisted of a system of arches supported by piers or columns arranged in series of parallel aisles and upholding domes, vaults, and a roof. Where the dome covered a square chamber or area, a transition from the arch was necessary. Stilted and horseshoe arches appeared early in the development of Islamic architecture, largely because the available cut columns taken from older structures were not long enough to hold the roof at the desired height. At Córdoba this problem was met by using a series of columns and arches superimposed upon another series.

At one or more of the corners of the enclosure there stood a minaret. First appearing at the mosque in Damascus, it was a square towerlike structure from which the call to prayer was given. Round or pencil-shaped minarets did not develop until late in the medieval period, although circular ziggurat-type minarets are known to have existed in ninth-century Iraq and Iran.

In the wall of the mosque on the side toward Mecca a mihrab, or niche, was constructed to indicate the exact direction of the Holy City. This was particularly helpful in converted churches, since they were often not correctly oriented. A pulpit (minbar) was a necessary piece of furniture of a congregational mosque, enabling the person who delivered the Friday sermon to be seen and heard by all. The façade encasing the main entrance of the mosque enclosure, as well as the inner façade around the doorway to the mosque itself, in time was elaborately decorated, taking on the appearance of an external mihrab. Semidomes, vaults, marble paneling, and molding surrounded these entrances and made peerless approaches for the mosques. In Iran and the east some mosques had unusually lofty and imposing portals. The prevalence of the distinctive stalactite or honeycomb vault occurred in the late eleventh century.

The exterior and interior decoration of the mosques was based upon matched and quartered panels of marble, porphyry, and other types of stone, different-colored stones being used in alternate courses in the walls. Spaces were often covered with finely carved geometric and floral patterns; in many instances the walls were given color, warmth, and depth by the use of plain or figured tiles. One of the most frequent and pleasing patterns employed in stone, wood, or ceramics was that composed of highly stylized Arabic letters, almost invariably a verse from the Quran. Human and animal figures almost never appeared in a mosque, although human figures were depicted in palaces and in book manuscripts.

Some of the imposing mosques of the Middle East that date from the classical Islamic period are the Umayyad mosque of Damascus, begun in 706; the Mosque of Ibn Tulun in Cairo, finished in 879; the Great Mosque of Qairawan, built about 836; the Great Mosque of Córdoba, begun in 785 (now the cathedral); and the Friday Mosque of Isfahan, built about 760 but much changed at later times. Although it is not a mosque, probably the most widely known sacred building in the Muslim Middle East is the revered Dome of the Rock in Jerusalem. A ringlike structure, it was begun about 685 by the Umayyad caliph Abd al-Malik to cover and enshrine the spot from where Muhammad made his nocturnal journey to heaven; it is also close to the spot where, according to Muslim belief, Abraham (Ibrahim) had prepared to sacrifice his son Ismail, and very close to the site where the Jewish temple had stood in antiquity. The Dome of the Rock comprises an octagon surmounted by a dome that rests upon an interior circle of piers and columns. The space between the inner circle and the octagonal wall was too wide to be spanned by beams, necessitating an intermediate octagon of arches borne by piers and columns. Thus were formed two rings that were used for ceremonial circumambulation. Originally the upper part of the exterior was covered with mosaics, but these were replaced with decorated tiles. The style of the building was a composite of Syrian, Roman, and Byzantine traditions and contained a number of novel adaptations. The style, however, was followed in later Muslim architecture only in technical and decorative details and not as a general model for other structures.

In the east the Ghaznavid and the Seljuk dynasties in the early medieval period used mud brick or baked brick to rapidly build monumental structures, usually decorated with stucco or stone, including mosques with a courtyard surrounded by four vaulted niches framing a portal. The dramatic height of the portals and niches contrasted with the smaller proportions of the courtyard at ground level. Mausoleums were usually square chambers covered by domes; they also came in the form of tomb towers, cylindrical or polygonal towers with conical roofs.

Although mosques and great mausoleums have been the most permanent of Middle Eastern buildings of the classical and early medieval period, various books contain descriptions of numerous libraries, hospitals, bazaars, palaces, forts, shrines, and public baths in Baghdad and other cities. One of the most famous, enduring, and beautiful of the palaces was the Alhambra of Granada, Spain. Begun in the thirteenth century, the fortified residential palace became world-renowned for its luxurious gardens, spectacular views, and sumptuous decorations. Some of these structures were open for all to visit, but many were intended solely for the wealthy patrons who constructed and maintained them. In any case, few peasants or nomads visited such urban sites.

EDUCATION

Formal education was similarly linked primarily to the cities, although much training and exchange of information took place informally in the family, while working on the job as apprentices, and in social institutions and organizations. In the early days of the Muslim ummah, the ruling Arabs held that a man was educated if he learned the basics of religion, to read and write, to use the bow and arrow, and to swim. A man should be taught courage, endurance, justice, hospitality, honesty, and generosity, while women were expected to attain skills relating to the household as well as the basics of the faith. By the opening of the eighth century most leading Muslims employed tutors or owned slaves to teach their children. The only education available for the masses was that obtained from Quran readers in the mosques.

In the Abbasid period, the number of elementary private schools increased, so that many children, especially in the cities, were taught to read and write. The curriculum centered on the Quran, allied religious texts, and Arabic grammar, and memory achievement was the goal. Children of wealthy and prominent families continued to get rigorous and comprehensive individual instruction. It was still not easy to acquire an advanced education, although to make one's way about the Muslim world in quest of great teachers was less arduous than in earlier days. Various study groups, academies, and mosques where one could study existed, some with waqf charitable endowments, but they were unorganized and did not furnish any systematic education. Children began systematic study inside the family or as apprentices at an early age, perhaps around eight years old; when urban children ultimately mastered a given craft, skill, or book of knowledge the supervising instructor or master craftsman issued the student or apprentice a certificate.

One of the most famous of the Islamic institutions for advanced study was al-Azhar in Cairo, founded by the Fatimids in the latter part of the tenth century. Through the centuries al-Azhar maintained a reputation for scholarship and a high quality of education, especially in the fields of theology and law, which it still has to this day. College-mosques often provided residential facilities for students and teachers. Sufi groups had separate educational locations, where mystics studied traditions, their own approach to law, and the mystical path to knowledge. A bureau for translation, a library, and an observatory in the Abbasid caliph al-Mamun's House of Wisdom in Baghdad served as a kind of collegiate institution, while libraries were widespread throughout the cities of Islam.

The honor of creating one of the first centers of learning in the east fell to Nizam al-Mulk, the ingenious eleventh-century vizir for the Seljuk dynasty. His Nizamiyah in Baghdad, intended as a private institution to teach Shafiites religion, was part of a trend that led throughout the Muslim world to construction of many madrasahs—schools for higher education chiefly in religion and law. In the leading cities of the Middle East, near each of the larger mosques, eventually there were privately organized and funded madrasahs, where religious and legal subjects predominated. Waqf pious foundations provided the money to support teachers and students. Professorial chairs were endowed, and fellowships were granted to advanced students. Philosophy, mathematics, medicine, and the natural sciences were taught in the homes of scholars, bookstores, hospitals, and sometimes in the madrasahs as auxiliary to religious subjects. Despite the popularity of the madrasahs, education continued to be available in many other settings, including homes, mosques, study groups, and religious festivals.

Rote learning and an emphasis upon the transmission of knowledge without much questioning until one mastered approved approaches to issues predominated—as in most educational establishments elsewhere throughout the ages. But the need to acquire dialectical skills and to defend viewpoints while deriving legal opinions encouraged analysis and synthesis for some thinkers. The obligation to show the relation between the ideas they imparted and the ethical and social requirements of society was recognized by noted Muslim teachers.

RECREATION

The great mass of people in the medieval Middle East, as in all other regions and in other periods except for the present, had little time or energy for higher education or for recreation and entertainment. However, people of moderate means, including villagers, nomads, and city people alike, could enjoy certain kinds of recreation, while other types were in practice reserved for the urban wealthy and the elite. Among the more widely accessible were poetry and some kinds of music.

Although many religiously oriented people criticized music, which was often associated with moral laxity, song and music from various instruments were exceedingly popular. Chanting the Quran was a valued skill. Religious poetry was often sung, and sometimes it was accompanied by musical instruments, especially among the Sufi mystics. In secular arenas, and in particular at the courts of rulers, accomplished musicians were praised, highly rewarded, and accepted as companions in high society. Slaves with musical talent and training commanded high prices. The elite themselves sometimes performed, and the Abbasid caliph al-Rashid's brother Ibrahim was regarded as a truly accomplished musician. Musical theorists included many prominent thinkers such as al-Farabi, al-Jahiz, al-Masudi, and al-Ghazali, who have already been discussed in Chapter 9 in other connections. The principles of performance and composition were based on improvising; dividing into clear internal units; repetitively reformulating earlier motifs, phrases, and sections; following a single melodic line; using few long notes; and constructing short but seemingly infinite patterns of musical expression. Performers used a wide variety of instruments such as the short-necked lute, flute, drums, and fiddles.

Upper-class urban men (and, separately, women) relaxed at home or at a public bath that served as their club, open for the sexes on alternating days. Baghdad in its heyday boasted several thousand such establishments. After soaking and steaming and a vigorous massage the patron might sip cool sherbet, listen to music, and engage in a game of dice, backgammon, or chess. Inside the home chess and playing cards were used for recreation. Chess was an ancient Indian game that came to Christian Europe by way of Iran and the Muslims. Playing cards also came from India to the Middle East, probably around 1300.

Outdoor sports were many; favorites were archery, javelin throwing, fencing, polo, and a ball game that may have been the ancestor of tennis. Hunting, with its allied sports of hawking and falconry, was much in vogue in the Umayyad and Abbasid eras, and later as well. The art of falconry was greatly refined, and there were numerous books on the subject. Caliphs and generals organized great hunts in which thousands participated in driving the game into confined quarters where the hunters could shoot the quarry without much effort. However, certain wild game at close range frequently provided a dangerous and exciting sport, as depicted in painting and ceramic decoration.

The most royal of all sports in the Middle East was horse racing. In ancient Iran, in Greece, and in Roman and Byzantine times, racing was the sport of kings and the favorite of the masses. The Arabs loved and prized horses, and the Muslim rulers quickly took to racing their horses in Syria, Iraq, and Egypt. Caliphs had their own stables, and al-Rashid apparently took great pleasure in seeing his horses win their races. Betting accompanied horse racing, as it did other sports, and made the races and games more exciting. Pedigrees and an interest in the breeding of horses advanced to the point where Arabian horses were recognized and valued throughout the Muslim world.

While only the rich could engage directly in such activities, everyone had to eat, and dining provided a form of recreation when family members and friends visited each other. Picnics were a particularly frequent pastime. Rural and provincial town cuisines were imported into the governing centers, and new delicacies soon became known throughout the whole region. The earliest still extant Islamic-era cookbook dates from about 800. Professional chefs working for the rich prepared lamb, chicken, game, and fish, especially by stewing; many vegetables and fruits were served; and a variety of spices were employed. The key foods for the poor were wheat bread, olive oil, and vegetables.

AGRICULTURE

Most of the first Muslims in the Hijaz were not farmers; however, intensive and irrigated agriculture was widespread in parts of Yemen and Oman, areas that contributed many soldiers to the Muslim armies and settlers in the newly conquered empire. In the rich agricultural lands of Iraq, Syria, and Egypt, the Muslims quickly came to appreciate the methods needed to efficiently cultivate the soil. As the native populations of these provinces and other fertile areas (such as Spain and Khurasan) were converted to Islam, Muslims were engaged directly in agriculture. Accordingly, the governing classes, the landowners, and the actual farmers or peasants all were concerned with agricultural progress. Most peasants had little margin for experimentation, however, because of their poverty; sharecroppers were especially poor because much of the profit of their operation went to landowners, who often provided seeds as well as the right to farm the land.

In the Middle East in Islamic times, the prime factor in agriculture has been water; the need for irrigation increased as new crops were introduced that required water in the summer when little rain fell. Problems of irrigation and canal building were not private affairs, and everywhere rulers paid strict attention to digging, reopening, and repairing water channels. Under Muslim governments gardens flourished, with many different plants, vegetables, and fruit trees being propagated. Rulers often sought to acquire new plants, and Arab manuals on farming and botany were written. The Arabs had known numerous varieties of dates, and families treasured their own species with favored qualities of flavor, sweetness, and moisture. The same interest and care were given to other produce of the land as Islam spread into new areas and new crops were grown, mainly fruit trees, grains, and vegetables, as well as flowers and ornamentals.

Agricultural productivity rose with higher-yielding crops and more specialized land use, including greater development in rotation of crops, labor-intensive methods, and a summer growing season. The agricultural surplus became so great it could support much larger rural and urban populations.

Cultivators were interested in improving the quality, cash value, and variety of their crops, and they took specimens wherever they went. Many crops were introduced from India through sailors and merchants from Oman and Yemen who carried knowledge of irrigation technology as well as seeds and cuttings from South Asia to the Middle East. On pilgrimages to Mecca, and on other travels, people exchanged information on agriculture. Thus, the best varieties of plants were distributed far and wide. The cultivation of cotton, sugarcane, apricots, peaches, and rice was introduced even as far as Spain on the distant edge of the Islamic world. Spanish authors produced many treatises on agriculture; one of the best-known and most beautiful gardens of the world was near the Alhambra. The technique of controlled pollenization was known and frequently practiced with special and prized varieties of the date palm and fruit trees. European Crusaders learned to value Middle Eastern agriculture and acquired a taste for many of its products. Yet it was largely through Sicily, Spain, and Cyprus that agricultural knowledge and skills slowly passed to Christian Europe.

The patterns of social activity that had appeared by the end of the classical Islamic period around 950 were further elaborated and developed during the early medieval era, when new political and military structures reshaped the public life of the Muslim community.

References

Also see works cited in Chapters 4 and 7.

ABU-LUGHOD, JANET: "The Islamic City—Historic Myth, Islamic Essence, and Contemporary Relevance." *International Journal of Middle East Studies* 19 (1987): 155–176. After a considered evaluation of methodological debates, the basic nature of cities is discussed.

AHMED, LEILA: *Women and Gender in Islam: Historical Roots of a Modern Debate.* New Haven, Conn.: Yale University Press, 1992. An excellent, balanced view of the topic, valuable especially for its discussion of Egypt.

AHSAN, MUHAMMAD MANAZIR: *Social Life Under the Abbasids, 170–289 AH 786–902 AD.* London: Longman, 1979. The author examines costume, food, housing, hunting, games, and festivals, and gives many specific examples.

CRESWELL, K. A. C., AND JAMES W. ALLAN: *A Short Account of Early Muslim Architecture.* Rev. ed. Aldershot, England: Scolar, 1989. A detailed survey of Creswell's earlier works, covering Umayyad and Abbasid days.

DURING, JEAN, ET AL.: *The Art of Persian Music.* Washington, D.C.: Mage, 1991. Sensitive treatment of early as well as more recent music.

ETTINGHAUSEN, RICHARD, AND OLEG GRABAR: *The Art and Architecture of Islam: 650–1250.* New York: Penguin, 1987. Specialized analysis with many valuable illustrations.

FARUQI, ISMAIL AL, AND LOIS LAMYA AL FARUQI: *The Cultural Atlas of Islam.* New York: Macmillan, 1986. Broad coverage of nearly all aspects of culture and history makes this work a useful introduction to many topics.

GOITEIN, S. D.: *A Mediterranean Society: The Jewish Communities of the Arab World in the Documents of the Cairo Geniza.* 5 vols. Berkeley: University of California Press, 1967–1988. Monumental works of scholarship that study the life of Jews in the Arab world but also illustrate general social and economic history.

LEVY, REUBEN: *The Social Structure of Islam.* Cambridge, England: Cambridge University Press, 1957. Although somewhat dated, this work still provides a valuable survey and introduction.

MAKDISI, GEORGE: *The Rise of Colleges: Institutions of Learning in Islam and the West.* Edinburgh, Scotland: Edinburgh University Press, 1981. This, the best advanced study now available on the subject, includes the role of religion, curricula, students, the position of professors, and a variety of other aspects of the topic.

MUSALLAM, B. F.: *Sex and Society in Islam: Birth Control Before the Nineteenth Century.* Cambridge, England: Cambridge University Press, 1983. A valuable and unusual study of an often neglected subject.

NASHAT, GUITY, AND JUDITH TUCKER: *Restoring Women to History: Middle East.* Bloomington, Ind.: Organization of American Historians, 1988. An excellent survey from antiquity to the present; issued as part of a series on various parts of the world.

RODED, RUTH: *Women in Islamic Biographical Collections.* Boulder, Colo.: Lynne Rienner, 1994. An essential discussion of Muslim women from the days of the prophet Muhammad to about 1500.

STANTON, CHARLES MICHAEL: *Higher Learning in Islam: The Classical Period, A.D. 700–1300.* Savage, Md.: Rowman and Littlefield, 1990. A very clear introduction to the content and methods of education.

TUCKER, JUDITH: *Gender and Islamic History.* Washington, D.C.: American Historical Association, 1993. This pamphlet surveys the topic concisely and is the best short introduction now available.

WAINES, DAVID: *In a Caliph's Kitchen.* London: Riad El-Rayyes, 1989. Entertaining analysis enlivens a short book of medieval recipes.

WALTHER, WIEBKE: *Women in Islam.* Updated edition. Princeton, N.J.: Markus Wiener, 1993. Emphasizes art, poetry, and social history.

WATSON, ANDREW M.: *Agricultural Innovation in the Early Islamic World: The Diffusion of Crops and Farming Techniques, 700–1100.* Cambridge, England: Cambridge University Press, 1983. A significant breakthrough in research on Islamic agriculture, this work is crucial reading.

CHAPTER 11

The Early Medieval
Middle East

The early medieval Middle East from 945 to 1250 was marked by political fragmentation. Even before 945, local dynasties of Muslim rulers had emerged in many parts of the Abbasid Empire. After 945 the Abbasid caliphs still ruled in Baghdad but only in name; real power there was in the hands of the Buwayhid dynasty. However, the unity of newly emerging Islamic civilization and social patterns preserved a sense of common identity for the ummah despite political fragmentation and military divisions. The Abbasids lost their power while keeping a kind of prestige basically because the territories they controlled were too large and diverse to be ruled centrally, given the technology of the age, and because they could not find a means of keeping the support of the Muslim community. An enormous gap developed between the Islamic ideals of political life and the reality of government, a gap that neither Sunnite nor Shiite rulers could easily close.

A bewildering series of successor states to the Abbasids was sometimes more successful in providing a government suitable to local conditions than had been the all-encompassing empires of the Umayyads and the Abbasids. Power fell into the hands of regional dynasties that were often drawn from or based upon foreign military groups, converts to Islam, and aliens to the vast majority of the people whose lives they controlled. As the general population withdrew from public life, the new Islamic civilization flourished despite political diversity bordering on chaos. Not until the appearance of the Ottoman Turks and the Safavids in the sixteenth century did the Middle East again experience large and centralized Muslim empires that reunited political, military, and cultural accomplishments on the scale of the Umayyads and Abbasids.

Muslim successor states in the early medieval period should be seen not only in comparison to the enormous empires that preceded and followed them but also in their own terms. The accomplishments of many regional dynasties particularly set off the early medieval period from the somewhat lesser achievements of the late medieval era after about 1250. Comparisons of the early medieval period in the Middle East with the medieval period in western and central Europe are also useful, but it is important to note that the characteristics that define early and late me-

PERIODIZATION IN THE HISTORY OF THE ISLAMIC MIDDLE EAST

Antiquity: from the rise of civilization to the coming of Islam

Classical Islamic period: from the life of the prophet Muhammad to the middle of the tenth century A.D.

The early medieval era in the Middle East: from about 950 to about 1250

The late medieval era in the Middle East: from about 1250 to about 1500

The early modern Middle East: from about 1500 to about 1800

The modern Middle East: from about 1800 to the present

dieval times for the Islamic Middle East differed somewhat from the structures of medieval European history.

SPAIN AND NORTH AFRICA

In the eleventh century, resurgent Christian Spain began a long and difficult series of campaigns that finally ended in 1492 with the capitulation of the ruler of Granada, the last Muslim prince in Spain. (Though Muslim law and government were terminated, the deportation of the Spanish Muslims was not enforced until a special edict was issued in 1609.) Sardinia, Sicily, and Malta also fell to Christian rule in the eleventh century.

Two Muslim dynasties in Spain and North Africa resisted the Christian advance. Also in the middle of the eleventh century a reformist and fundamentalist religious-military-tribal group, the Murabit dynasty (Almoravids) conquered western Algeria, Morocco, and southern Spain and established Marrakesh and Seville as their capitals. The Murabits governed with the support of the Malikite ulama and the military backing of the tribes. When Christians began to take districts in Spain from the Murabits, their legitimacy declined while their dogmatism offended many Muslims. Murabits in the twelfth century were replaced by the Muwahhids, a band of Muslim Berber reformers originating in Morocco. The founder of the Muwahhids claimed to be the Mahdi (the expected deliverer), and he reinforced this religious claim with tribal military alliances. His successor, Abd al-Mumin (r. 1130–1163), destroyed the Murabits and conquered part of Spain. Responding to the Norman expansion from Sicily into North Africa, he gained control of Algeria and Tunisia, and took Tripoli in Libya. He then established the principle of succession to power through dynastic inheritance within his family, and thereby transformed the nature of the state. The Muwahhids became patrons of philosophers. They united most of northwestern Africa economically, providing prosperity and

The Early Medieval Middle East, ca. 1100

the basis for considerable accomplishment in architecture and the decorative arts. Rebellions in Tunisia, the inevitable gap between religious ideals and political reality, tribal disaffections, deportation from Spain, and the rise of new and vigorous alternative leaderships led to the disintegration of the Muwahhids in the middle of the thirteenth century. Only a small province in the southeast of Spain remained in the hands of Muslim rulers, who nevertheless constructed there the beautiful palace of the Alhambra.

The Shiite Ismaili Fatimid dynasty had also begun its rule in North Africa in the early tenth century. With the help of North African Berber troops, the Fatimid dynasty overcame the Aghlabids and various Sunnite and Kharijite forces, built a navy, and recruited slaves for an expanded army. Upon their conquest of Egypt in 969, the Fatimids took the title of caliph and transferred their capital from Tunisia to the new city of Cairo, which they planned and built.

Under the Fatimids, the Egyptian court and its society experienced prosperity and a great burst of accomplishment in commerce, art, culture, and learning. One outstanding example of their cultural policy could be seen in the Azhar mosque-university complex in Cairo. Elaborate processions and public rituals organized by the Fatimids also provided legitimacy to the regime. Fatimid prosperity came from the peace and security given to the peasants of Egypt, and from imports of gold from Nubia, a sound coinage, textile manufacturing, and a flourishing international trade, especially by sea. The majority of the population became Muslims at this time, but they were mostly Sunnites, unlike their rulers. The Fatimids helped create institutions of urban governance based on a codification of Shiite law, a hierarchy of judges, market inspectors, a police force, prisons, and a separate appeals process for complaints against the government. Fatimid Egypt participated greatly in the artistic and intellectual endeavors of the Muslim world; many outstanding works of early medieval Muslim art and architecture still extant in Egypt date from the Fatimid period.

The Fatimids gained control of territory beyond Egypt: Syria, Palestine, the Hijaz, and Yemen. With difficulty, they ultimately defeated the Qarmatians in Syria and various nomadic and Turkish groups. Thus, at their height, about the year 1000, the Fatimids ruled most of the western Muslim world except Spain, while northern Syria was under Byzantine control; the Fatimid caliph's name was mentioned in the Friday prayers from Tunisia to the Euphrates. Their influence acting through Shiite agents even reached as far as India. However, because of eccentric and idle rulers, quarrels among the various ethnic units in the armies, and the inability to convince the masses of the central Middle East that Fatimid Shiism was the true version of Islam, the Fatimid empire began to break up early in the eleventh century. Viziers dominated the caliphs by the 1070s, and these ministers became heads of both the military and civil branches of government. The assassination of the caliph al-Amir in 1130 opened a period of internal strife over power, when no single military faction could gain a lasting degree of success. Salah al-Din al-Ayyubi (Saladin) eventually ended the Fatimid rule in Egypt in 1171. To a considerable degree it was the disintegration of the Fatimids that permitted first the continuation of Byzantine power in northern Syria and, second, the late eleventh-century incursion of the western knights called Crusaders, who penetrated, captured, and held the Christian Holy Land of Palestine and the Syrian coast in the twelfth and thirteenth centuries.

THE EASTERN AND CENTRAL REGIONS

In the first years of the early medieval period the eastern lands of the Muslim Middle East were controlled by the Ghaznavid, Buwayhid, and Seljuk ruling dynasties. This era witnessed the eventual triumph of Sunnite Islam over various Shiite challengers in the east and the incursions of Turkish-speaking nomadic groups who decisively influenced the subsequent history of the central and eastern regions.

A Turkish leader among the slave soldiers of the Samanid dynasty, Alptigin, rose through the ranks to struggle for power. Forced to flee from the Samanid domain, he captured Ghaznah and in 961 established the famed Persianate Sunnite Ghaznavid empire of Afghanistan and the Punjab in India. The most eminent of the Ghaznavid family was Mahmud (998–1030), who led nearly a score of expeditions into India and laid the foundations of the permanent Islamization of north and northwest India. Loot from Hindu temples gave him the material strength to destroy the Samanids and extend his state to include most of the eastern provinces of the Muslim world. The army was so important an element in providing the basis for government that in effect it became the state. Although a vestige of the Ghaznavid empire remained at Lahore until 1186, decline followed rapidly on the death of Mahmud in 1030. Muslim independent states in India broke away, central Asia remained under separate rule, and the Seljuk Turks appeared in western areas of the Ghaznavid empire where the Ghaznavids confronted the Buwayhids.

The Shiite Persian Buwayhid federation of rulers was usually led by the member of the dynasty residing in Shiraz, who took various titles such as "king" or "king of kings," thereby harking back to the pre-Islamic Sasanian dynasty. The Buwayhids beautified Shiraz and brought to it many learned men, while the dynasty portrayed itself as an heir of the pre-Islamic Persian kings. For a century Shiraz rivaled Baghdad, Ghaznah, Bukhara, Cairo, and Córdoba in culture and splendor, while massive irrigation projects improved agriculture in the countryside. In Iraq, however, Buwayhid administration was less successful as nomadic groups gained control of most of the countryside. The Buwayhids assigned revocable government revenues as grants to specific employees of the state, usually for a short time, so as to pay for services. This system—sometimes mistakenly called feudalism—was subsequently adopted with modifications by other dynasties such as the Seljuks and became a hallmark of decentralized administration. In the middle of the eleventh century Buwayhid fought against Buwayhid for the position of king; this, along with the internal disagreements of their troops and the diversion of international trade to the north and south of the Buwayhid lands, made them easy prey for the Turks riding in from the east.

Turkish nomads from the Kirghiz steppes in central Asia wandered into the Khurasan region around 970 and became partially settled there. Unlike earlier Turks who had served individually as professional soldiers, the new arrivals came as tribal groups, preserving their identity and seeking permanent control of grazing lands for their animals. Their military prowess gave impetus to a general trend throughout the Middle East, whereby cavalry replaced infantry as the more crucial element in armies, except for sieges. One of their chieftains, or khans, under the Samanids was Seljuk. For three centuries his Sunnite and strongly pro-Hanafite dynasty played an outstanding role in the Muslim world from Syria eastward and dominated the Turkish elements of society.

The true founder of the dynasty, Seljuk's grandson Tughril (r. 1038–1063), ascended to power rapidly in Khurasan. Defeating the Ghaznavids and ejecting the Buwayhids from Iran, Tughril entered Baghdad with an army in 1055; the Abbasid caliph of the day recognized him as king of the east and the west and sultan (the holder of power). Henceforth, these Seljuk Sunnite Turkish-speaking rulers adopted *sultan* as their chief official title. They dominated but did not totally control the Abbasid caliphs in Baghdad, who preserved an occasional local autonomy.

Tughril's nephew Alparslan followed as sultan and succeeded in gathering within his domain the vast lands of the Muslim world from the frontiers of China to the Mediterranean. Having expanded into Armenia and taken the Byzantine emperor prisoner in the decisive battle of Manzikert in 1071, Alparslan opened Syria and Anatolia to his Turkish and Kurdish nomads. His horsemen camped on the shores of the Sea of Marmara and lay astride the commercial and pilgrim routes of Anatolia. His son, Malikshah, pushed southward, taking Damascus, Jerusalem, and parts of Arabia, and threatening Fatimid Egypt, while making Isfahan his capital.

As the Seljuks became strong, they encountered numerous rivals, including Kurds, Ismaili Shiites, and pagan nomadic Chinese rulers in central Asia (the Qara-Khitai). The Kurdish tribal states were established in the Zagros Mountains, the mountains of northern Syria and southeastern Anatolia, and in Azerbaijan, subsequent to the decline of the Abbasids between 950 and 1050. The Kurds, who had their own language and culture, established their rule based on nomadic groups and

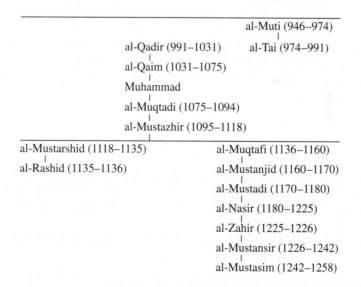

The Later Abbasid Caliphs

brought a good deal of economic prosperity to the diverse regions they controlled. They were in deadly competition with the nomadic Turkish tribes for pasturage—a competition won by the Seljuks, in part because of their superior political organization. As nomads expanded their grazing areas, peasants suffered and the amount of land under cultivation shrank. Ismaili Shiites called Assassins also opposed Seljuk rule and killed several prominent Seljuk officials. In the case of some opponents the Seljuks would use marriage as a means of forming an alliance or deflecting potential enmity.

The political genius through the reigns of Alparslan and Malikshah was Nizam al-Mulk, their principal vizir. A cultured and versatile Iranian, Nizam al-Mulk founded the renowned Nizamiyah, an academy in Baghdad, and wrote the Siyasat-namah, a scholarly work on the science of government. Nizam also revised the calendar and is perhaps best known as a patron of the Persian astronomer-poet Umar Khayyam and the famous thinker al-Ghazali. While Nizam al-Mulk was the most famous of the bureaucrats who served the Seljuks, the rulers cleverly utilized the administrative skills of other civil servants, while also allying themselves with the urban notables, the Sunnite ulama, and an army divided between Turkish nomads, freedmen, and Turkish slave soldiers. The Seljuks were famous patrons of the arts and architecture. Book illustration, metalwork, and silk textiles reached new heights under their influence.

Unity among the Seljuks vanished in 1092 on the death of Malikshah and the assassination of Nizam al-Mulk. In prior years, there had been numerous civil wars among members of the family; upon the demise of these two leaders what little central control that had existed over the various petty western Seljuk states was gradually lost. The chief reason for the collapse of the central Seljuk state was the difficulty the dynasty had in balancing so many contradictory groups and forces (nomads, soldiers, bureaucrats, and ulama) while also maintaining a delicate balance of power among the members of the royal family. One son succeeded to the sultanate in Baghdad. A brother held Damascus and Aleppo, although these cities were soon seized by different sons. A cousin ruled Anatolia from Konya; others possessed Jerusalem, Mosul, Diyarbakir, Amasya, and Edessa (Urfa). Soon afterward, the appearance of the Crusaders from the West disrupted Seljuk rule in Syria even further, though the main branch of the dynasty maintained its hold upon Baghdad until about 1152, and Sanjar (1118–1157) kept the eastern provinces relatively united and prosperous for a time. Ultimately the Chinese Qara-Khitai dynasty gained control of much of central Asia and even defeated the Seljuks in 1141; northern Iran also gained independence under another dynasty.

Economic productivity in Iraq under the Seljuks fell as agricultural conditions for the peasants worsened. The revenue grants system the Seljuks borrowed from the Buwayhids evolved into a form whereby the soldiers or administrators who received grants sometimes became powerful local magnates who governed autonomously.

The death of Malikshah and the collapse of the central Seljuk state heralded for early medieval times the end of a Muslim political entity strong enough and sufficiently organized to dominate the eastern and central Middle East. Under the rule of Malikshah, a merchant could travel alone unmolested with his goods from Samarkand to Aleppo. But within a few years of his death intraregional political anarchy and disastrous military chaos helped lure the Crusaders eastward and, much later, the Mongols westward.

CRUSADERS AND AYYUBIDS

In preaching the Crusade, or holy war, in 1095, Pope Urban II was unquestionably governed by religious spirit. Christian pilgrims returning from Jerusalem brought tales of the woe that recent Seljuk conquests had inflicted upon them in Anatolia and Syria. They also reported that disunity and internecine warfare among the petty Muslim states of Syria would make possible a victory. Furthermore, Emperor Alexius Comnenus sent a desperate appeal for help and promised the cooperation of the Byzantine army and fleet.

The western European feudal Catholic states had developed economically, socially, and politically to a degree that they could outfit and send expeditionary forces overseas. Gathering at Constantinople as an advance base, the Crusaders, almost always called Franks by Middle Easterners, departed for Palestine in 1097. Taking by force Iznik (Nicaea) and Eskishehir, the Crusaders were next welcomed with enthusiasm by the Armenian Christians in Edessa. The main Frankish army conquered Antakya (Antioch). Then the Crusaders successfully stormed the walls of Jerusalem on July 15, 1099. After the conquest, Muslims and Jews were barred from living in the city. In the ensuing decade one after another of the coastal cities of Palestine and Lebanon fell to the merchant fleets of Pisa, Venice, and Genoa, the allies of the Crusaders.

Shortly after the conquest of the Holy City, Godfrey of Bouillon became the "defender of the Holy Sepulchre," where Jesus had been buried, and the titular head of the kingdom of Jerusalem. Other prominent Crusaders scattered along the coast to become the count of Edessa, prince of Antioch, and count of Tripoli in Lebanon, these newly created principalities being held as fiefs of Jerusalem. Most of the Crusaders returned home as soon as the first victories were won, and those who stayed on were continuously hard-pressed to retain their possessions. In fact, they were a minority of the total population (where there was a Muslim majority), and the Crusaders would have been lost at an early date had not an uninterrupted stream of knights appeared from the west and had not the merchant cities of the western Mediterranean helped them.

Eventually the kingdom of Jerusalem was extended eastward across the Dead Sea and southward in a narrow tongue of land to touch the Gulf of Aqaba. In the north the county of Edessa reached eastward to the headwaters of the Tigris. Elsewhere, the Franks clung close to the coast, in some places holding a strip barely ten to fifteen miles wide. They never gained possession of such interior cities as Aleppo or Damascus.

The great majority of western successes sprang from the complete disunity of the Muslim rulers. The amirs of Syria were delighted by the Crusaders' defeat of the Seljuks in Anatolia, and during the siege of Antioch emissaries from Egypt proposed an alliance of the Crusaders and the Fatimids. Alliances by Muslim princes with Crusaders against fellow Muslims, or by Franks with Muslim amirs against fellow Crusaders, were commonplace.

The Crusades, 1140

The Crusades, 1190

The Crusades, 1204

Before a decade had passed only newly arrived Crusaders carried the religious spirit and fervor that had launched the First Crusade. In the Middle East the European knights reverted to the search for fiefs and the constant fighting they had known in the west. Nevertheless, the more advanced civilization of the Middle East began to influence the barbarous westerners. Crusader nobles emulated the ways and adopted the higher standard of living of the Middle Eastern ruling classes, thus opening the way for some of the knowledge of the east to find its way to western Europe and hasten the coming of the Renaissance.

Baghdad and the eastern Seljuk sultans were hardly bothered by the inroads of the Crusaders, especially since within a few years the latter followed the general preexisting political pattern of the Middle East. Resistance to the West awaited the appearance of a vigorous leader capable of creating an extensive Muslim state that might serve as a base for an attack upon the Franks. Such a man was the blue-eyed Imad al-Din Zangi, Turkish lord of Mosul. Consolidating the northern arc of the Fertile Crescent from Mosul to Aleppo into one Muslim state, Zangi stormed and took Edessa in 1144, an act that touched off the Second Crusade, whose chief effect was to bring fresh recruits to ward off other blows and hold the line. The Zangid principality subsequently augmented its power as both Seljuk rule in Baghdad and Fatimid power in Cairo waned. Zangi's son, Nur al-Din (r. 1146–1174), added Damascus to his state, conquered all of the county of Edessa, and wrested territory from Antioch and Tripoli. Bypassing the Franks in Jerusalem, his armies forced the Fatimid caliph of Egypt to surrender control of that still Muslim region to a Zangid lieutenant, Salah al-Din al-Ayyubi (Saladin).

Of Kurdish family origins, Salah al-Din sought to unify Islam and destroy the Crusaders. In 1171, he refused to recognize the Fatimid Shiite caliph and restored Egypt to the Sunnite creed, and the Abbasid caliph's name was once again mentioned in public prayers. Upon the death of the Zangid Nur al-Din, Salah al-Din used his Kurdish, Turkish, and Arab Bedouin army to seize Syria and eventually was accepted as the sultan in the Hijaz and Yemen as well. Long-distance trade flourished, and the spices of the East were a major source of wealth. Salah al-Din and the Zangids before him encouraged education and the construction of schools and other buildings in the cities of Syria, while Salah al-Din's citadel above Cairo dominated that city. The historian Ibn al-Athir (d. 1234) documented the record of the Zangids and Salah al-Din, while drawing on a wide variety of sources.

Turning upon the Franks, Salah al-Din wiped out the cream of the knights' armies at the battle of Hattin on July 4, 1187. This victory enabled him to retake Jerusalem and most of the principal cities. Salah al-Din's new fleet unsuccessfully contested control of the eastern Mediterranean with the Europeans. Jerusalem's fall to the Muslims initiated the Third Crusade, which gave rise to more romantic episodes in the history and literature of Islam and western Christendom alike than any of the other Crusades. Philip Augustus, Frederick Barbarossa, and Richard the Lionhearted could not recapture Jerusalem, but after a siege of two years Acre (Akka), which became the new Crusader capital city, fell to Richard in 1191. When the demanded ransom was not forthcoming, Richard decreed the execution of the garrison of 2700. This was in sharp contrast to Salah al-Din's clemency following the fall of Jerusalem, when all who were not ransomed were set free. An armistice was concluded, leaving a narrow coastal area and the island of Cyprus in possession of the Crusaders.

Upon the death of Salah al-Din in 1193 the usual political dismemberment developed, and his Ayyubid dynasty lasted only about fifty more years. One son held Damascus; others governed at Cairo and Aleppo. A brother ruled Jordan and conquered Syria and Egypt. Upon his death division and anarchy again ruled the Ayyubids' principalities until their own slaves destroyed them in 1250.

The recurring Muslim turmoil seemed to play into the Westerners' hands, leading to the Fourth Crusade, whose most significant triumph was the conquest of Orthodox Christian Constantinople in 1203, and eventually the Fifth Crusade's vain attempt to conquer Egypt. Salah al-Din's nephew, al-Malik al-Kamil, forced the Crusaders to abandon Damietta, where they had landed hoping to seize Egypt and the Red Sea, and their commerce with India and the east. Nevertheless, he made friendly treaties with the Italian city-states, entertained and discussed theology with Saint Francis of Assisi, and gave Jerusalem to Frederick II, the Holy Roman Emperor, as part of the Sixth Crusade in 1229. In Palestine disputes over succession to the throne of Jerusalem, quarrels of Venetians against Genoese and of baron against baron prevented lasting Crusader achievements.

Louis IX's Seventh Crusade to Egypt fell victim to the plague in 1249; at that same time the Ayyubid family of Salah al-Din in Egypt was supplanted by Turkish generals from its slave army. A new era in Muslim history was emerging—the Mamluk (slave) period. Baibars, the fourth Mamluk sultan, captured much of Palestine and Antioch. In 1291 another Mamluk took Acre. This was the signal for the few remaining Crusader towns to surrender. An episode in the history of the Middle East had ended.

The significance of the Crusades for western Europe was mixed. Most of the Crusaders remained in the Middle East a short time and profited little from the experience. Trade between east and west in the Mediterranean did, however, increase markedly, especially via a network of Jewish merchants in Cairo. Exports of sugar extracted from sugarcane were especially valuable Eastern goods in western markets. Furthermore, returning crusaders created an expanded western market for Eastern goods, since even those who remained in the Middle East only a brief time often acquired a taste for Oriental foods and a preference for its superior manufactured goods such as textiles, cutlery, metalwares, and leather goods. However, the main channels of Muslim influence upon western Europe were through Sicily and Spain. The concept of crusading continued even after the Europeans were expelled from Palestine; subsequent Crusades were launched in Spain, the Balkans, and elsewhere.

The effects upon the Muslims of the Middle East were much less significant. They became convinced that the Westerner was a ruthless soldier, semibarbarous in nature, ignorant, and uncivilized. For centuries, Crusaders' castles dotted the landscape, but these did not alter in any measurable degree local military architecture. Incessant fighting, particularly in Palestine, severely weakened the local economy. Indigenous Christians were the object of suspicion by their Muslim rulers, and their position in society declined after the departure of the Crusaders. The Middle East was politically disunited when the Crusaders arrived; it was still in fragments when they departed. In the interim, to be sure, the Ayyubids and then the Mamluks united the Muslims from the Nile to the Tigris, but this had no relationship to the Crusades; it was only an example of the recurring pattern of centralizing and decentralizing political forces continually at work in the area. In general, it can be said that the Crusaders were more destructive than constructive, and that the Middle East was poorer because of the experience.

The power of Muslim rule in the Middle East was threatened by Christian Europeans in Spain and the eastern Mediterranean area, but this challenge was successfully met by the Ayyubids and their successors. Many other issues and challenges were also at least tentatively resolved during the early medieval period. Sunnite Muslims repressed the attempt of various Shiite groups to gain control, although Shiism by no means disappeared from the Middle East. Militarily, the early medieval period usually saw the victory of nomadic groups—the Seljuks and Berbers, to name two—over settled societies. The economic prosperity of the central Middle East continued, especially in the twelfth century, although the turmoil that accompanied the incessant fighting among the Seljuks challenged the well-being of merchants, peasants, and townspeople alike.

Throughout the early medieval Middle East the political and military fragmentation that followed the loss of effective power by the Abbasid caliphs was accompanied by cultural, economic, and religious accomplishments. Even with the introduction of the Turkish peoples and the revival of the Persian language, Arabic remained a common tool for high culture, religion, and government. Certain common institutions, such as pious endowments and concepts of justice, also served to link the Islamic Middle East. In the later medieval Middle East the Mongols from central Asia, disease, and the rule of slave soldiers posed new challenges to the established order.

References

Many volumes already cited bear upon this chapter, including several in Chapters 4, 6, 8, 9, and 10.

ASHTOR, E.: *A Social and Economic History of the Near East in the Middle Ages*. Berkeley: University of California Press, 1976. An extremely important synthesis of earlier work, with discussions of agriculture, feudalism, city life, Iraq and the Mediterranean areas, and the Mamluks.

BACHARACH, JERE L.: "African Military Slaves in the Medieval Middle East." *International Journal of Middle East Studies* 13 (1981): 471–495. A careful look at a controversial subject that involves questions of race as well as slavery and the military.

BOYLE, J. A., ED.: *The Cambridge History of Iran*. Vol. 5: *The Saljuq and Mongol Periods*. Cambridge, England: Cambridge University Press, 1968. Beginning with the political and dynastic history of Iran from 1000 to 1217, the volume describes the internal structure of the Seljuk empire and its religion. It continues with a discussion of the Il-Khans, the Ismaili state, and the Mongols. Chapters on poetry and prose, the arts, and sciences are most useful.

EHRENKREUTZ, ANDREW S.: *Saladin*. Albany: State University of New York Press, 1972. Still an extremely interesting study of Salah al-Din, this work examines his liquidation of the Fatimid dynasty in Egypt, the establishment of his house as a princely family, and the unification of Egypt and Syria.

HODGSON, MARSHALL G. S.: *The Venture of Islam: Conscience and History in a World Civiliza-*

tion. Vol. 2: *The Expansion of Islam in the Middle Periods.* Chicago: University of Chicago Press, 1974. The author discusses the establishment of the international Islamic civilization.

HOLT, PETER M.: *The Age of the Crusaders: The Near East from the Eleventh Century to 1517.* London: Longman, 1985. Holt is the leading historian of the period for political history, and this broad and detailed work examines all aspects of the subject.

HUMPHREYS, R. STEPHEN: *From Saladin to the Mongols: The Ayyubids of Damascus, 1193–1260.* Albany: State University of New York Press, 1977. This author explains the Ayyubid confederation of principalities.

LAMBTON, ANN K. S.: *State and Government in Medieval Islam.* Oxford, England: Oxford University Press, 1981. An authoritative look at religion, politics, law, community, the individual, and the state.

————: *Continuity and Change in Medieval Persia: Aspects of Administrative, Economic and Social History, 11th–14th Century.* New York: Bibliotheca Persica, 1988. Very useful for the Seljuks and Mongols.

LE STRANGE, GUY: *Baghdad During the Abbasid Caliphate.* London: Oxford University Press, 1924. A still interesting description of the great city at its height.

LEV, YAACOV: *State and Society in Fatimid Egypt.* Leiden: Brill, 1991. Detailed discussion of Fatimid government, military, and society.

LEWIS, ARCHIBALD R.: *Nomads and Crusaders, A.D. 1000–1368.* Bloomington: Indiana University Press, 1988. This book adroitly presents a broad picture of the eastern hemisphere; useful for putting the Middle East into the general historical scene.

MORGAN, DAVID: *Medieval Persia: 1040–1797.* London: Longman, 1988. In this short book the author gives a useful overview and a starting point for subsequent reading.

MOTTAHEDEH, ROY P.: *Loyalty and Leadership in an Early Islamic Society.* Princeton, N.J.: Princeton University Press, 1980. This fascinating exploration of the values prevalent in Buwayhid society examines oaths of allegiance, patron-client relationships, membership in social categories, and the role of the king as arbiter of society.

PIPES, DANIEL: *Slave Soldiers and Islam: The Genesis of a Military System.* New Haven, Conn.: Yale University Press, 1981. In a broad essay, the author examines the evolution of Muslim military history.

RILEY-SMITH, JONATHAN: *The Crusades: A Short History.* New Haven, Conn.: Yale University Press, 1987. The best short introduction now available.

SOURDEL, DOMINIQUE: *Medieval Islam.* Translated by J. Montgomery Watt. London: Routledge and Kegan Paul, 1983. The author provides a sophisticated discussion of a number of disputed interpretations.

WINK, ANDRE: *Al-Hind: The Making of the Indo-Islamic World.* Vol. 1: *Early Medieval India and the Expansion of Islam, 7th–11th Centuries.* Leiden: Brill, 1991. A wide-ranging discussion of the eastern Islamic world.

ZACOUR, NORMAN, AND HARRY W. HAZARD, EDS.: *A History of the Crusades.* Vol. 5: *The Impact of the Crusades on the Near East.* Madison: University of Wisconsin Press, 1985. Part of a six-volume history of the Crusades, this work is an outstanding source of detailed information on every aspect of the Crusades.

The Late Medieval Middle East

From about 1250 to 1500 the late medieval Middle East witnessed a considerable variety of political and military regimes. In the thirteenth century pagan Mongols from central Asia conquered most of the eastern regions and destroyed the Abbasid caliphate in Baghdad. At about the same time Mamluk slave soldiers established in Egypt and adjacent lands an unusual but long-lasting regime that for a time provided security and prosperity. While the Mongol devastation was in many ways repeated under the conqueror Timur, his descendants ruled only a relatively small area. And in Anatolia the growing power of the Ottoman state projected a regional force that subsequently dominated most of the central Middle East in the early modern period.

Disease, destruction, internal strife, and other factors weakened the chief political units, especially after the middle of the fourteenth century. By the fifteenth century much of the Middle East was poorer than it had been since the rise of Islam, although cultural contributions were still being made in some centers of art and religion such as Cairo and Herat. Few areas other than Granada in Spain were permanently lost to non-Muslim control; the contrary was true—Islam was expanding dramatically on the margins of the Middle East and in areas beyond it.

THE MONGOL INVASIONS

In the early thirteenth century, as the Crusades were waning, devastation rode in upon the Muslim Middle East from central Asia. Born about 1165 in the neighborhood of Lake Baikal, Genghiz Khan came to rule over shamanistic Mongol nomad horsemen; by adding to his army the cavalry he had defeated, this self-styled "scourge of God" consolidated military power in his hands. Genghiz and his hordes of bowmen moved westward to Iran in 1219, conquering all lands in their path. Merv, Nishapur, Herat, and many other centers of civilization were stormed and sacked. Inhabitants were slain by the hundreds of thousands, perhaps millions.

PERIODIZATION IN THE HISTORY OF THE ISLAMIC MIDDLE EAST

Antiquity: from the rise of civilization to the coming of Islam

Classical Islamic period: from the life of the prophet Muhammad to the middle of the tenth century A.D.

The early medieval era in the Middle East: from about 950 to about 1250

The late medieval era in the Middle East: from about 1250 to about 1500

The early modern Middle East: from about 1500 to about 1800

The modern Middle East: from about 1800 to the present

Iraq, Syria, and areas to the west were spared by Genghiz's death in 1227 and by the subsequent division of the empire among his sons. But heirs maintained the great empire and pressure continued upon the Middle East. The Seljuk Turks in Anatolia were defeated in a ruinous battle in 1243, and the Mongols levied tribute upon them. Under Mongke, the third successor to the position of Mongol supreme khan, a great expedition moved westward under the direction of Mongke's younger brother Hulegu. Starting in 1252 to rid the world of the Assassins and to destroy the Abbasid caliphate, Hulegu Khan razed Alamut, the Assassin headquarters.

The Abbasid caliph al-Nasir, who reigned from 1180 to 1225, had managed to restore some real political power to the caliphate in Iraq. But now in 1258 Baghdad and the Abbasids were to come into the hands of the non-Muslim Mongols. Following a siege of several months, the city fell and was given over completely to the troops. Destruction continued for a month, and the Abbasid caliph was killed, thus ending the Abbasid line's long rule in Baghdad. Some of the Mongol armies, including local auxiliaries from the Middle East, then proceeded westward as far as Damascus. They were halted by Baibars, a Mamluk leader of Egypt, in a historic battle in 1260 at Ain Jalut, near Nazareth, as the Crusaders stayed neutral. Egypt was spared Mongol violence; Baibars, who became sultan, pressed his victory, freeing Syria from Mongol control.

In their conquests the Mongols helped themselves to whatever they wanted and destroyed the rest, not knowing what to do with it. They could not garrison the cities adequately; they were pagans; and the first generations neither understood nor appreciated the cultures and civilizations of the peoples they conquered. The effects of the devastation wrought by the Mongols lasted for centuries. Millions of people perished; cities vanished; canals silted and irrigation decreased; lands became barren and deserted; governments disintegrated; civilization foundered; and life returned to the bare essentials. Taxes were sharply increased and collected in an unusually brutal fashion. Since the initial Muslim conquests, conquering armies and peoples had come and gone as customs, religions, knowledge, and culture had been modified, developed, and altered. But through all this time the Middle East had never suffered such a cataclysmic shock as it received from the Mongol invasions.

MAMLUK RULE BEGINS IN EGYPT

Untouched by the Mongol devastation, Egypt suddenly became the great stronghold of Muslim civilization, even though it had just entered into a new and different era of its own domestic history. Upon the death of the Ayyubid sultan in 1249, his widow Shajar al-Durr seized power. After she had a second husband—a Turkish slave general—murdered seven years later, she was beaten to death by his slave soldiers. The rule of Egypt then passed briefly to his son and then to other slave generals, one after another until 1517, when Egypt was conquered by the Ottomans. This long period of two and a half centuries of Egyptian history was termed the Mamluk ("slave") era. Until 1382 the Mamluks were mostly Turkish and Mongol in origin, and they were called Bahri ("river") Mamluks. Between 1382 and 1517, they were generally Circassians and were known as the Burji ("citadel") Mamluks. The Mamluks were not a dynasty.

Begun by the later Ayyubids as a slave army and bodyguard of foreign origin, the Mamluks evolved into a Turkish-speaking, self-perpetuating urban slave military oligarchy. The recruit was purchased, usually in a Black Sea slave market, by the agent of a slave general or officer and transported to Egypt by Christian Italian merchants. In Egypt, he became a Muslim and was rigorously trained in the arts of war, especially cavalry, within a household where he would form a sense of common identity with his fellow Mamluks. As he developed and progressed toward the top, he would be freed, though in turn he would make new purchases of slaves, who would become the next generation of Mamluks. (The sons of the Mamluks might become part of the army, but they usually lacked the prestige and special position of their fathers; they were not Mamluks themselves.) Some Mamluks served in the civil administration, though most were in the military. A score of generals or amirs at the summit intrigued and battled for supremacy, held the chief posts of government, and chose the successor to the late Mamluk sultan. Sometimes during Bahri times the sultan would name one of his relatives as his successor, an example being the descendants of Qalawun (r. 1279–1290), many of whom subsequently became sultans. Under the Burjis a ruler picked on this basis would not rule long before he was ousted by an ambitious general. Many of the wives of the Mamluks were brought to Egypt from the Black Sea region, although in the Burji era intermarriage with Egyptians was more widespread. Some Mamluks never bothered to learn Arabic and were Sunnite Hanafite Muslims in name only. Aloof from the native Egyptians, whom they despised, the Mamluks usually showed toleration for religious minorities although conversion to Islam was widespread. The Mamluks supervised the pilgrimage to Mecca, and many went to the Holy City themselves.

Although frequently illiterate, the Mamluk sultans were usually crafty, and some were capable organizers and redoubtable generals. Nevertheless, their lives were fearfully uncertain, the average reign of the forty-seven Mamluk sultans being less than six years. The most resourceful, and one of the most enduring, Sultan Baibars (r. 1260–1277), the real founder of the Mamluk system, not only turned back the Mongols in Palestine but also cracked the strength of the Crusaders in Syria. Understanding diplomacy and statecraft, he established friendly relations with Sicily and Seville, sent envoys to the Byzantine emperor, and made an alliance with the Kipchak Turks of the Volga River basin (his own birthplace) against the Mongols of Iran and Iraq. He reestablished the Abbasid postal system for quickly taking news to Cairo. Bringing from Damascus a refugee Abbasid prince, Baibars originated the practice of having an Abbasid in Cairo as caliph but without actual power. Abbasid caliphs resided there up to the time of the Ottoman conquest, and their presence gave Mamluk rulers a degree of legitimacy.

Under the Mamluks (as earlier the Buwayhid and other dynasties), a system of revocable government grants to individuals in return for services spread in Egypt and elsewhere in their domains. In the tenth and eleventh centuries, as the power of the Abbasid government had declined, military officers and various civilians were assigned provinces and estates from which they collected taxes for their own support. For these privileges and benefits they were expected to serve the caliph or sultan, often in a military capacity. Land grants of this type were frequently changed from one individual to another under the Mamluks, especially after a cadastral survey. The fate of peasants in Mamluk Egypt was perhaps particularly harsh, as the state constantly increased exactions from them. Gradually most of the revenue from the lands of Egypt was granted to Mamluk officers who had to support, equip, and ensure the service of a number of soldiers, the number depending upon their rank and the size of the grant. However, after 1315, about one-half of the revenues from these grants was assigned to the sultan himself, for the same purposes.

THE IL-KHANS AND TIMUR

The major portion of the central Middle East under the Mongol Empire was split into a variety of provinces; all of these regions were part of the Mongol domain in the Middle East, but other branches of the royal family also ruled in China, Mongolia, and southern Russia. Contests with other Mongols as well as the Mamluks of Egypt dominated foreign policy, while government and wealth tended to move eastward. From time to time in the century following the conquests of Hulegu, peace among Genghiz Khan's descendants allowed for passage of traders and travelers such as Marco Polo (d. ca. 1324) and Ibn Battutah (d. ca. 1378). But the persistent military violence, direct or threatened, harmed middle-class merchants and tradesmen. In Herat a local Persian dynasty ruled and flourished from 1245 to 1383 while accepting Il-Khan sovereignty, while at the other side of the Mongol Middle East, the Armenian state in southeastern Anatolia also acknowledged Mongol supremacy.

Domestic policy was based initially on the fact that the Il-Khans, or Mongol rulers of Iran and Iraq, with their chief capital at Tabriz, remained non-Muslims and were tolerant protectors of the Christian and other minorities of the region. The Mongols themselves were subject to their own separate law, but Muslims and other

The Late Medieval Middle East, ca. 1300–1400

KHANATE OF THE GOLDEN HORDE

KHANATE OF CHAGATAI

EMPIRE OF THE GREAT KHAN

INDIA

Delhi

Otrar

Bukhara

Samarkand

Balkh

Qandahar

Jaxartes

Oxus

ARAL SEA

Merv

Herat

Nishapur

KHURASAN

DOMINION OF THE ILKHAN

PERSIA

KERMAN

Isfahan

Shiraz

FARS

Persian Gulf

ARABIAN SEA

MAZANDARAN

Hamadan

Baku

CASPIAN SEA

AZERBAIJAN

Tabriz

Baghdad

IRAQ

Basra

ARMENIA

Tiflis

GEORGIA

Kur

Erzerum

Tigris

Mosul

Euphrates

Trebizond

EMPIRE OF TREBIZOND

Sinope

BLACK SEA

Aleppo

Antioch

LITTLE ARMENIA

Damascus

SYRIA

Jerusalem

Tripoli

Beirut

Gaza

CYPRUS

SELJUK TURKS

Konya

Ankara

Izmir

Bursa

Constantinople

Edirne

BYZANTINE EMPIRE

OTTOMAN EMPIRE

Danube

CRETE

MEDITERRANEAN SEA

Alexandria

Cairo

MAMLUK SULTANATE

EGYPT

BARCA

RED SEA

Nile

Indus

Legend:
- Byzantine Empire, 1405
- Timur's Empire, 1405
- Byzantine Empire, 1400
- Ottoman Empire, 1400
- Timur's campaigns

Scale:
- 0 200 400 mi
- 0 300 600 km

137

groups continued to be tried according to their preexisting religious systems. After a period of strife over the succession after 1282 was ended with the accession to the throne of Ghazan in 1295, the dynasty became Muslim and sympathetic to Sufism. The shariah once again was the law backed by the state, although Mongol customs undoubtedly continued. Revenue-yielding land grants to soldiers probably became more widespread, as Ghazan reformed and regularized taxation, administration, and succession to the throne. Turkish began to replace Mongol as the language of the elite. Persian speakers dominated the civil administration, whose chief function was to extract taxes for the benefit of the Mongols. New Turkish nomadic groups also entered the Middle East during the Mongol period, and nomads gained ground from peasant agriculturalists, while much land was simply abandoned.

Abu Said (r. 1318–1335) was the last of the Mongols to rule over a united Iran and Iraq. He even succeeded in making peace with the Mamluks, but he left no heir to the throne, so civil war and puppet rulers followed each other after his death, and small and ephemeral dynasties came to rule a disease-racked area where the Mongols had once dominated. Moreover, in 1368, the founder of the Ming dynasty in China conquered the Mongols there and closed the overland Silk Road trade routes from central Asia into China, diverting commerce with the Mediterranean to the sea route through the Indian Ocean, the Red Sea, and Egypt.

Some cultural accomplishments took place under Il-Khanid Mongol rule: the Persian historian and statesman Rashid al-Din (1247–1318) wrote a famous world history; the study of astronomy was widespread; and great writers such as Sadi (d. 1291) and Hafiz (d. 1390) produced beautiful literature. Chinese medical texts were translated and used in Iran, while in the visual and plastic arts blue-and-white pottery and exquisite tiles became famous. Architecture was marked by the use of glazed bricks, more colorful decorations, and carved plaster. Female members of the royal family were patrons of the arts, sciences, and religion.

The final blows to the highly developed Muslim culture and civilization of the late medieval period in Iraq, central and eastern Anatolia, and parts of Iran were administered by the Mongolian Turks. For a quarter of a century, 1380–1405, the east was in turmoil because of the eruption of the Mongolian Turks led by the Sunnite Muslim Timur Leng ("Timur the Lame," or Tamerlane). Son of a Turkish-speaking chieftain of Mongolian extraction, Timur first won control of much of central Asia, which served as a base for expansion, both eastward and westward. He called himself by the title *amir,* while retaining the fiction of Mongol overlordship by descendants of Genghiz Khan. In 1380, his hordes of steppe cavalry archers began the conquest of Afghanistan, Iran, and Kurdistan. In rapid succession he captured Baghdad, Isfahan, Delhi, Aleppo, Damascus (where he interviewed at length the historian Ibn Khaldun), Ankara, and Izmir—but not Egypt. Timur's death in 1405 and the subsequent anarchy among his heirs brought relief to the Middle East, but the desolation wrought at his hands was difficult to repair. His most notorious custom was the construction of pyramids of human heads after the sacking of cities; at Isfahan 40,000 heads were built into such markers. Schools, libraries, and mosques were destroyed, and only the walls of the famed Umayyad mosque in Damascus were left. Skilled artisans and their families were deported to Samarkand, Timur's capital, where they erected magnificent buildings; however, many ancient skills that had survived through the ages were now lost forever in the central Middle East.

DECLINE IN IRAN AND EGYPT

Simultaneously with the development of the Middle Eastern revenue grants system came the spread of a more self-subsistent economy. As the uncertainties of government mounted and the difficulties of transportation and communication increased, industry and commerce were depressed and the money economy was greatly weakened. Political anarchy and civil wars destroyed the controls over the nomads within the Middle East, and the perpetual battle between the "desert and the sown" was resumed as agricultural production in most parts of the Middle East decreased. A number of factors contributed to this: the overuse of resources; an inability or unwillingness to overcome technical barriers so as to deal with past farming problems, such as increased salinity of the ground; a rigid social conservatism that opposed most forms of innovation; and reduced social mobility as many judicial and educational posts were held for long periods by the same family. Widespread disease, as in the case of the Black Death in the middle of the fourteenth century, and subsequent plagues killed millions of people, disrupted urban life, and at least temporarily decreased long-distance commerce. The Middle Eastern lands entered into this new era piecemeal over a long period of time.

After the death of Timur, three major regions still dominated in the Middle East: a fragmented Iran; a broken and reduced Ottoman state; and the wealthy if tumultuous Mamluk state of Egypt. Fifteenth-century affairs in the Middle East revolved around the economic, political, and international problems and relationships of these three powers.

In about 1409 eastern Iran came under the rule of Timur's son Shah Rukh (d. 1447), who made his capital in Herat and established a peaceful and prosperous regime. Until 1506 the succeeding Timurids were able to rule most of eastern Iran and Afghanistan, where they were great patrons of the sciences and arts. Miniature painting reached a brilliant stage of accomplishment in Herat, and a new calligraphic script and mosaic tilework flourished. Trigonometry, astronomy, and history were extensively studied. Sufi themes in poetry were frequent, as in the works of the biographer and poet Jami (d. 1492). The later Timurids, however, battled among themselves to such an extent that they were unable to control the Turkish nomadic tribes of the area. Despite some attempts by Timurid rulers to undo the damage done by the Mongols and by Timur himself, the general economic situation was bleak. New groups and families arose to divide Iran and to render it impotent in the struggle for power in the Middle East. Raids by Uzbeg tribes and the absence of trade to the east led the center of population and importance to shift westward, although one of the Timurid princes went south, where ultimately he and his descendants founded a new empire—the Mughal dynasty of India.

In the westward regions of the Caucasus and the highlands of eastern Anatolia, Turkish tribes under the leadership of the Qara Quyunlu (Black Sheep Turkomans) seized control of Armenia and Azerbaijan. For a time in the fifteenth century after the death of Timur, the Qara Quyunlu ruled Baghdad and western Iran, establishing Tabriz as their capital and building the famous "Blue Mosque" there. Other Turkish tribes in a Sunnite Aq Quyunlu (White Sheep Turkomans) federation were established in Armenia and northern Iraq with Diyarbakir as their capital. The pinnacle of Aq Quyunlu power came under Uzun Hasan, who ruled Iraq, much of eastern Anatolia, and nearly all of Iran from about 1467 until his death in 1478. Married to a daughter of the Greek emperor of Trebizond (Trabzon), Uzun Hasan through his in-laws was approached by Venice to fight battles against the Ottomans. However, he found the Ottoman sultan Mehmed II a formidable foe, especially since Venice made no move to engage the Ottomans in another quarter. After the death of Uzun Hasan the Aq Quyunlu state disintegrated, preparing the ground for the rise of the Safavid dynasty under Shah Ismail.

The fortunes of the Ottoman state are considered in more detail elsewhere in this volume. Here it is sufficient to point out that the Ottoman state was reunited by Sultan Mehmed I within fifteen years after the debacle of his father at the battle of Ankara in 1402, when Timur captured the Ottoman sultan. The process of building an empire by adding provinces in the Balkans and Anatolia was resumed, with Constantinople finally falling to Sultan Mehmed II in 1453. Following that renowned event, the Ottomans in their expansion southward and eastward came into conflict with both Iranians and Mamluks. Mehmed II in 1473 turned back Uzun Hasan of Iran, and Selim I soundly trounced Shah Ismail, clearing Anatolia of most of the Iranian sympathizers and fellow Shiites. Under Mehmed II border disputes flared in southeastern Anatolia between the satellites of the Mamluks and the Ottomans. In the 1490s Bayezid II was engaged in several indecisive campaigns against the Mamluks. Twenty years later (1517) the Ottoman Sultan Selim I and his army marched victoriously into Cairo.

Before the Ottoman conquest the Mamluk Empire remained as a vibrant society, although it had declined in some ways from the earlier days of its foundation and strength in the late thirteenth and fourteenth centuries. The Mamluks controlled most of the east-west commerce, especially in spices, after the collapse of the central Mongol Empire. The trade of south and southeast Asia passed to Europe through the Red Sea and to the Mediterranean either by way of Egypt or by the historic caravan routes in the Hijaz to Jordan and Syria. As this trade grew steadily in the fourteenth century, it, together with the natural productivity of the Nile valley and the skilled artisanal manufactures of Egypt, gave to the Mamluk-Arab society a brilliance unrivaled in any other Arab land.

What cultural life and quest for knowledge remained in the Arab world found refuge and patronage in Cairo, probably the largest city in the Middle East and one that drew scholars and students from many parts of the Muslim world. Mamluk Egypt and Syria in the fourteenth century excelled in the production of beautiful enameled and gilded glass, especially mosque lamps, and calligraphy, heraldry, and bookbinding flourished. Inlaid metalwork, as in brass candlesticks, was also noteworthy, while decorated textiles and carpets later became valued exports to Europe. Although originality had largely passed, religion, science, and literature were cultivated by students and supported by the court and the wealthy. In Damascus the theologian Ibn Taimiyya (1263–1328) contributed substantially to Hanbalite interpretations of Islam, criticized Sufism, and emphasized the basic elements in the faith. The general urban public enjoyed processions, festivals, Sufi activities, carnivals, tournaments, archery displays, and shadow puppets, as well as such earlier genres as the recitation of poetry and tales.

The greatest activity was in the construction and endowment of madrasahs, Sufi residences, and mausoleum-mosques in the great cities of the Mamluks, in particular Cairo and Jerusalem. Of these the most outstanding in Cairo was that of Sultan Qaitbay, who died in 1495. Noted for its alternate red and white stone courses, the mosque-tomb-school has a stately high dome over the tomb chamber. The exterior of the dome is covered by an elaborate geometric pattern interspaced with intricate floral designs. The minaret, several stories high, is one of the most handsome in Cairo.

Yet, despite all the trade and wealth and the escape from invasion and devastation, society and civilization in Egypt were changing in ways that adversely affected most people. Government was uncertain. Mamluk sultans succeeded each other with frequency and violence. In the fifteenth century, there were twenty-two changes of sultan; on one occasion there were three sultans in a single year. The system of training Mamluk officers and soldiers broke down, and the quality of new slaves deteriorated as it became more difficult to purchase slaves in the Volga and the Black Sea areas. Law became the whim of the ruler, and the ruling class was beyond the law. Graft, corruption, and inefficiency within the Mamluk order mushroomed. As land revenues declined, government officials grew more corrupt.

Sultan al-Nasir's death in 1340 signaled the end of a period of clear economic growth and of the tight control of government by the sultan, and began a time of internal strife. The Black Death of 1347–1350 killed tens of thousands of people in Cairo alone, and many more died in the rest of the Mamluk domains. After 1382 the Circassian Mamluks' regime brought even more factionalism. Bedouin unrest, increased taxation, state monopolies that reduced business flexibility, outbreaks of disease and subsequent depopulation (especially among the Mamluks themselves), the devastation of Syria in the period of warfare initiated by Timur, inflated prices, neglect of irrigation by the government, and famine all contributed to a decline of the Mamluk state.

The chasm between native Arab-Egyptian and Mamluk widened; the community of interests decreased. Personal insult was added to exploitation and civil degradation until the Mamluks, although Muslims, were loathed by most Egyptians. Nevertheless, rich merchants flourished in Cairo, and the presence of such wealth gave the city an aura of prosperous strength that misled most European visitors.

The Mamluk Empire included the Hijaz and Syria as well as Egypt, and in the 1370s the Armenian state in southeastern Anatolia was added. The outlying provinces were held through semiautonomous amirs. Syria was loosely tied to Cairo when the sultan was weak, and frequently at such moments the amirs played the dangerous game of flirting with the reviving Ottoman state or with whatever prince ruled in Iran. Border disputes were inevitable, and when a war broke out between rivals for the throne of Dhu al-Qadr (Dulgadir) in 1485, the Ottoman sultan

Bayezid II backed one contender while the Mamluk sultan Qaitbay supported the other. During the subsequent wars at one time the Ottomans occupied Aleppo; at other times Mamluk generals penetrated Anatolia. The Mamluks won the battles but could not achieve victory, and in 1491 peace was arranged.

Within a decade after this successful defense of the distant frontiers of the state, Mamluk good fortune was irretrievably lost. The Mamluk households' loyalty to their leaders declined and was replaced by insubordination and mutiny. Training for the Mamluk cavalry was of poor quality, and the Mamluks were reluctant to use cannons and handguns on the battlefield. Repeated attacks of disease also devastated Egypt and Syria. Then the Portuguese rounded Africa and strongly established themselves in the Indian trade, where they could afford to pay higher prices for goods than the Mamluks. Portuguese ships threatened the port of Jidda on the Red Sea, and in 1506 the Portuguese occupied and fortified the island of Socotra near the entrance to the Gulf of Aden. The small Mamluk fleet was damaged in 1509 by the Portuguese, but with Ottoman help the Red Sea was defended against further incursions.

When the Ottoman sultan, Selim I, arrived in Syria, conditions in the Mamluk Empire were in disarray. The Mamluk sultan brought his army to Aleppo to threaten the rear and flank of Selim, who was engaged with the Safavid Shah Ismail of Iran. Selim turned quickly, crossed the Taurus Mountains, and routed the Mamluks at Marj Dabiq in August 1516. Previously, the Mamluk army had been well paid and well equipped, but the force before the Ottomans here was a sullen, dispirited, and unpaid mob using obsolete armament, whereas the Ottoman armies had powerful and mobile cannons. Selim proceeded southward, taking all of Syria with ease. Cairo was taken by assault in January 1517, and the last Mamluk sultan was seized and hanged. Egypt became an Ottoman province, and the Abbasid puppet caliph, al-Mutawakkil, was taken to Istanbul.

With Selim I's destruction of the Mamluks and his temporary defeat of the Safavids, the political, economic, and cultural center of the Middle East shifted to Istanbul and the Ottoman Empire. An age had wearily come to an end. Turkish or Mongol sultans, generals, and slaves had ruled in Arab countries and Iran for several centuries, and the newly dominant power in the Middle East was still another Turkish empire, that of the Ottomans. The Ottomans and other successful dynasties employed gunpowder weapons and destroyed states that did not adopt them.

Other general characteristics of the late medieval period included the relative decline in importance of Arab Iraq and the growth of celebrated literatures in Turkish and Persian. Cultural creativity continued in Arabic, which remained the chief language for the study of religion, but Arabic's near monopoly of high culture was expanded to include other languages. Sufi mystical brotherhoods, some now structured and organized, others engaging in radical forms of behavior, became even more prominent than earlier. The Sufis spread Islam widely. While a majority of the population had converted in the early medieval period, now a much larger majority of the people were Muslims. Christians and Jews persisted as small minorities.

Economic decline affected many areas but was not universal. Peasants were particularly hard hit by the violence and exactions of oppressive governments, yet pastoral tribes often benefited from the same events that injured the villagers. City people probably suffered even more than peasants or nomads from the frequent bouts of epidemic disease that devastated so many parts of the Middle East during the late medieval age.

References

Volumes already cited bear upon this chapter, including several in Chapters 9, 10, and 11.

ABU-LUGHOD, JANET L.: *Before European Hegemony: The World System A.D. 1250–1350.* New York: Oxford University Press, 1989. A brilliant essay on the interconnections of eastern hemisphere societies and merchants, including the Middle East.

ATIL, ESIN: *Renaissance of Islam: Art of the Mamluks.* Washington, D.C.: Smithsonian Institution Press, 1981. Beautifully illustrated, with chapters on manuscripts, metalwork, glass, ceramics, and textiles.

BERKEY, JONATHAN: *The Transmission of Knowledge in Medieval Cairo: A Social History of Islamic Education.* Princeton, N.J.: Princeton University Press, 1992. Instruction, careers, the role of women, relations with Mamluks, and the general public are all touched upon in a careful analysis.

BLAIR, SHEILA S., AND JONATHAN M. BLOOM: *The Art and Architecture of Islam, 1250–1800.* New Haven, Conn.: Yale University Press, 1994. An excellent general survey.

DANIEL, NORMAN: *Islam and the West: The Making of an Image.* Oxford, England: Oneworld, 1993. This revised version of a 1960 classic work recounts and analyzes Christian Europe's views of Islam and Muslims, chiefly during the medieval period.

DOLS, MICHAEL W.: *The Black Death in the Middle East.* Princeton, N.J.: Princeton University Press, 1977.

DUNN, ROSS E.: *The Adventures of Ibn Battuta: A Muslim Traveler of the 14th Century.* Berkeley: University of California Press, 1986. Ibn Battutah (1304–1368) journeyed through most of the Muslim world; his lively and entertaining observations form the basis of this work.

GLUBB, JOHN BAGOT: *Soldiers of Fortune: The Story of the Mamluks.* London: Hodder and Stoughton, 1973. A thorough account of the rivalry for power among the cliques and various military contingents and the utter ruthlessness of the process.

IRWIN, ROBERT: *The Middle East in the Middle Ages: The Early Mamluk Sultanate, 1250–1382.* Carbondale: Southern Illinois University Press, 1986.

JACKSON, PETER, AND LAURENCE LOCKHART, EDS.: *The Cambridge History of Iran.* Vol. 6: *The Timurid and Safavid Periods.* Cambridge, England: Cambridge University Press, 1986. A detailed examination of the political history of the age in various chapters is followed by discussions of administration, European contacts, trade, social affairs, sciences, religion, art and architecture, and literature. Invaluable for all serious readers.

KARAMUSTAFA, AHMET T.: *God's Unruly Friends: Dervish Groups in the Islamic Later Middle Period, 1200–1550.* Salt Lake City: University of Utah Press, 1994. Discusses the radical Sufi groups; particularly useful for the early Ottoman Empire.

LAPIDUS, IRA MARVIN: *Muslim Cities in the Later Middle Ages.* Cambridge, Mass.: Harvard University Press, 1967. Centered on Cairo and Damascus, this book is extremely important for Mamluk social history.

LENTZ, THOMAS W., AND GLENN D. LOWRY: *Timur and the Princely Vision: Persian Art and Culture in the Fifteenth Century.* Washington, D.C.: Smithsonian Institution, 1989. Sumptuous and informative.

MANZ, BEATRICE FORBES: *The Rise and Rule of Tamerlane.* Cambridge, England: Cambridge University Press, 1989. A biography with an emphasis on tribal and military factors.

PETRY, CARL F.: *The Civilian Elite of Cairo in the Later Middle Ages.* Princeton, N.J.: Princeton University Press, 1981. The quantitative methodology employed here for fifteenth-century

Cairo represents one of the relatively few attempts to use these analytic tools in the study of the medieval Middle East.

————: *Protectors or Praetorians? The Last Mamluk Sultans and Egypt's Waning as a Great Power.* Albany: State University of New York Press, 1994. A thorough account of the last years of the Mamluk system.

SPULER, BERTOLD: *The Mongol Period: History of the Muslim World.* Princeton, N.J.: Markus Wiener, 1994. This reprint of the 1969 edition discusses the Mongols and their influence on the Mamluks, Timur, India, and Russia.

THORAU, PETER: *The Lion of Egypt: Sultan Baybars I and the Near East in the Thirteenth Century.* Translated by P. M. Holt. London: Longman, 1992. Examines critically all aspects of his life.

WOODS, JOHN E.: *The Aqquyunlu Clan, Confederation, Empire: A Study in 15th/9th Century Turko-Iranian Politics.* Minneapolis, Minn.: Bibliotheca Islamica, 1976.

The Ottoman and Safavid Empires

The Byzantine Empire

Throughout the centuries when the faith of Islam spread in the Middle East the Christian Byzantine Empire persevered as rival, enemy, and sometime trading partner. For over 1100 years the Byzantines ruled in parts of the eastern Mediterranean, Anatolia, the Balkans, and the Black Sea region. As discussed in earlier chapters, from the seventh century on the Byzantines profoundly influenced the Middle East during the early days of the Islamic ummah, the Umayyad and Abbasid dynasties, and the early and late medieval periods. In architecture, institutions, culture, imperial customs, economic structures, and many other aspects of life the Byzantine historical experience affected not only the empire's earlier contemporaries but also its chief successor—the Muslim Ottoman Empire, which at last destroyed the Byzantine state in the fifteenth century.

ESTABLISHMENT OF THE STATE

In a sense the Byzantine Empire was the continuation and heir of the Roman Empire after the last western emperor in 476, but with three significant differences from the old Roman Republic and Empire: the Byzantine state was Christian, not pagan; its dominant language was Greek, not Latin; and its center was in the eastern Mediterranean, not in Italy. Byzantine history begins with the era of the emperor Constantine and his dedication of the new city of Constantinople on the site of ancient Byzantium in 330.

Except for a period in the thirteenth century when western European knights of the Fourth Crusade occupied it, Constantinople was the hub of the Byzantine or Eastern Roman Empire until its fall to the Ottomans in 1453 (after which the city was known as either Istanbul or Constantinople). In choosing a site for a new imperial capital Constantine placed his chief residence close to the populous part of the empire and in a situation for the defense of the Balkan (southeastern European) provinces.

The eleven centuries of Byzantine rule witnessed, especially in Constantinople, the preservation and propagation of the Christian faith and its theology; the knowledge of the Roman and Hellenistic ages; the art and architecture of the ancient world; and many techniques of government discovered through centuries of Roman rule. In Constantinople, the emperor was the accepted absolute monarch with power strictly centralized in his hands. Except in a very few provinces, civil and military powers were separated, and a regular civil service system for the various bureaus of government was expanded on the basis of merit and seniority. Starting with Constantine the emperors and the Christian churches of the east closely cooperated. They participated in Christian affairs by calling general councils of the church, and they used their imperial power to try to achieve uniformity in Christian doctrine. The resulting union of state and church and the interdependence of emperor and patriarch were known as the Caesaro-papism of the Byzantine Empire.

From its first days, therefore, the Byzantine state embodied Roman imperial tradition, Christian orthodoxy, and Hellenistic culture—forces that gave direction to government, religion, and society in Constantinople for a thousand years.

POLITICAL HISTORY

Following Constantine, more than seventy emperors or empresses belonging to several dynasties held the imperial throne of Constantinople before its fall in 1204 to Fourth Crusaders. A relatively large number of these rulers were capable leaders; many were outstanding. Theodosius I (r. 379–395) made Christianity the official and sole religion of the empire. Theodosius II (r. 408–450) published the code of Roman law bearing his name and constructed the storied land walls of Constantinople, which stretched from the Sea of Marmara five miles to the Golden Horn. Without a doubt this formidable barrier on countless occasions saved the imperial city, and therefore the empire, from northern barbarians and the Muslims.

Justinian I (r. 527–565) was particularly noteworthy. Many of his structures still stand in Istanbul (the former Constantinople), the noblest of which are the incomparable Church of Hagia Sophia and the majestic aqueducts north of the city. Equally celebrated were the Justinian codes of laws. These codes remained the foundation of law through the years in the Byzantine Empire; they appeared in Italy in the twelfth century and served as the basis for the reintroduction of Roman law in western Europe. Probably the main reason for publication of the laws was Justinian's need for rigorous control of the empire and efficient collection of taxes to provide funds for his military campaigns in North Africa, Italy, and Spain.

The next gifted emperor, Heraclius (r. 610–641), an Armenian soldier, was the reviver of the empire. It was under him that Greek became the official language of the empire. Upon his accession he found disturbed conditions, with Slavs and Sasanians threatening the empire's existence. By reuniting church and state, by revitalizing the army and navy, and by reinstituting strict economy, Heraclius defeated the Sasanians in a series of brilliant campaigns and freed Syria and Egypt from their control. However, the financial strain of these wars and the cost in manpower left him unable to meet the Muslim Arabs in a favorable posture, and the recovered provinces were lost to Islam in Heraclius's last days.

During the remainder of the seventh century the frontiers contracted under the rule of the Heraclian dynasty, North Africa was lost, to be followed by the Byzantine portions of Italy in the next century, and the economy of the state materially weakened as population drastically decreased. Muslim armies ravaged Anatolia, camped near Constantinople, and took to the sea in the eastern Mediterranean. But the empire was preserved following the accession of Leo III (r. 717–740). Besides shielding the empire from eastern onslaughts, he favored legal and religious reforms, and advanced Heraclius's administrative system of themes, which were provinces where the military general was also governor. At first only a few areas were organized in this manner, but by the time of the Fourth Crusade thirty-eight provinces had been transformed into themes, the most important of which were in Anatolia facing the Muslims.

A contemporary of the Abbasid caliph Harun al-Rashid, the empress Irene (r. 797–802) was the Greek wife of Leo's grandson and the power behind the throne for twenty years. Irene blinded her son and ruled alone as emperor until overthrown by a revolution. She paid tribute to the Abbasid caliph Harun al-Rashid, an indication of the decline of Byzantine power. Domestically, she gave her support to factions in the capital that opposed iconoclastic policy, disclosing the deep-seated religious division that persisted in the empire. Many with Monophysite Christian tendencies, especially those from eastern reaches of the empire, were iconoclastic; that is, they objected to icons, images, and pictures in church services and decorations. Leo III, over the protests of many bishops and monastics in Constantinople, forbade the use of icons, an act pleasing to the soldiery of his eastern themes. Irene made a political alliance with orthodox churchmen, and for their favor in her struggle for imperial position and power she pursued orthodox doctrines of anti-iconoclasm. The debate over iconoclasm racked the empire not only in Irene's reign but for a period of about 125 years, from 717 to 843.

The empire suffered a loss of power until the ascent of Basil the Macedonian (r. 867–886). Maintaining its supremacy until 1056, his Macedonian dynasty led the empire during one of the more brilliant periods of its long life. Basil, of humble origin, rose from the imperial stables, where his superb physique and feats of prowess attracted the attention of the emperor. Soon coruler, Basil I took the next step and had his patron murdered. Nevertheless, he and his successors, particularly Basil II (r. 976–1025), were capable emperors, republishing old codes of laws, restoring harmony in the church, sponsoring a classical cultural revival, and pursuing a vigorous expansion of the state against Muslims, Armenians, and Bulgarians. Byzantines controlled northern Syria for over a century after 969.

From the death of Basil II until the fall of Constantinople to the Fourth Crusaders in 1204, a series of calamities befell the Byzantine state, reducing its effective power to an alarming degree. Beginning in the tenth century, transformation of the rural society and economy proceeded relentlessly. The free peasant and the free landholding soldier, especially in Anatolia, were disappearing as a result of the expansion of great estates held by the landed military aristocracy and the church. Even though there was a clear increase in economic activity between 1000 and 1200, and the population grew, especially in the European provinces, heavy taxes, famine, and insecurity caused the peasants to lose their lands to powerful lords. The stronger the magnates became, the more certain they were to obtain privileges, reduced taxes, and many other concessions from the central authorities. In turn, these events weakened the Byzantine fiscal position, lowered the available supply of loyal soldiers, harmed the theme military system, and created a powerful class in the provinces that was able and eager to threaten or overthrow an unwary or unco-operative emperor. By the middle of the tenth century, emperors began to issue de-crees to halt this process of aggrandizement, but to no avail.

When the strong hand of Basil II was removed in 1025, intense rivalry between the landed military aristocrats of the provinces and the powerful bureaucrats of the capital flared openly in the competition for the throne. The bureaucrats controlled the central administration, the imperial navy, the troops around the emperor, and the finances of the empire. In their party were included a number of aristocratic families, many senators, most of the cultured segments of society, and almost all the important administrators. From 1025 until 1057, the civilian government thwarted some thirty rebellions and exiled, executed, or blinded a long list of gen-erals who had mounted these insurrections. But the bureaucracy, looking for com-pliant emperors, found for the most part incompetents.

Since the main strength of the great Anatolian families lay in their control of the armies stationed in their midst, the bureaucrats set out to dismantle these local troops by withholding financial support from them, dismissing competent generals, and terminating obligations of various groups that owed military service. This was done at a time when Seljuk Turks were pressing on the frontiers in the east, the Normans of southern Italy were expanding, and others were invading the Balkans. The result was an increasing use of foreign mercenary troops, who lacked loyalty to the Byzantine state. In addition to the ease with which they changed sides, these mercenaries frequently ravaged the Anatolian countryside, held towns for ransom, and invariably reduced the flow of taxes to the imperial treasury. The economy of the empire sagged and the power of the state ebbed as the rival parties for political power, in spite of all consequences and at all costs, vied for supremacy.

With the accession of Alexius I Comnenus to the throne in 1081 the generals began a reign that lasted until the fall of Constantinople in 1204. During most of that time the Comneni dynasty ruled the empire, spanning the years of the early Crusades. Despite the successes of Alexius, under his heirs civil wars continued un-abated, with generals and leading families feuding among themselves and seeking to establish semi-independent principalities. Not least among these rivals were for-mer mercenary leaders, many of them Normans and Turks. Alexius I found himself between Turk on the east and Catholic Frank on the west, hardly knowing which to fear more. His daughter, Anna Comnena, left a most interesting account of the ar-rival of the First Crusade at Constantinople; the contrast in culture and civilization of the two Christian societies of her day was sharply drawn. In 1054, the western Christian church, led by the bishop of Rome, had officially declared the eastern church, headed by the patriarch of Constantinople, to be schismatic. The division between the two parts of Europe—the Catholic west and the Orthodox east—was even more emphatic in light of the flourishing of Byzantine culture, especially in the areas of rhetoric, history writing, theology, and the making of icons and other forms of art.

During most of the twelfth century the Comneni contained the dangers from the west, using a strong fleet against the Normans, tactful diplomacy against the papacy and Crusaders, and a balance-of-power strategy with Venice. In the east, the Byzantines allied with Orthodox Georgia and traded peacefully with the Seljuks of

Anatolia, but they faced strong opposition from Armenians and the Crusader states. In the 1180s internal quarrels and foreign reverses began a downward spiral. A large influx of western Catholics into Constantinople coincided with many influential government positions being given to them, much to the displeasure of the local bureaucracy. A strong popular antiwest reaction ensued. In 1204 Constantinople fell to Venetians and Fourth Crusaders, an act that ended the true Byzantine Empire. What later passed for that empire proved to be only a shell of its former power, grandeur, and significance.

THE ORTHODOX CHURCH

Before discussing this later phase of the empire, it may be well to study a few institutions of society as they were at the height of Byzantine glory, for their forms persevered into the weak last days and even beyond into the Ottoman period. The strongest and most vital arm of the emperor was the Christian church. After the demise of paganism in the fourth century, Constantinople, the Balkans, and Anatolia were devoted in their support and loyalty to the church. The church's tight organization, with the patriarch at its apex, gave powerful support or presented determined opposition to the emperor and government. Consequently, the emperor always tried to control the selection of the patriarch, while the patriarch had a strong influence with the emperor; there was a close and intricate relationship between the two posts.

Church monastic orders were socially, economically, and religiously important, and the monks were often popular heroes. Frequently, the government found it necessary to follow doctrines espoused by the populace, even though other dogmas were preferable for reasons of imperial policies. Whenever an emperor compromised with what was deemed heresy to mollify a distant province or the army in some Asian theme or entered into an understanding with the Roman papacy regarding the universal Christian church, orthodox voices in Constantinople were heard in opposition. And the Orthodox church strongly opposed Islam, condemning it on theological as well as political grounds.

In a way, the church resembled an administrative department of the government, and the patriarch acted as a minister of state in charge of religion. A dynamic emperor chose, appointed, and dismissed patriarchs; an energetic patriarch bent weak emperors to his will—yet at most times, the emperor was supreme and the church was subordinate to the state. It was this interrelationship that has been called Caesaro-papism.

AGRICULTURE, ARTISANS, AND TRADE

After the loss of Egypt to the Muslim Arabs, Constantinople and other cities of the empire were supplied with necessary food by Anatolia, Thrace, and the Balkans. The lot of the peasants was hard, and few envied them. Yet they seldom lacked food, clothing, or shelter, and famines were rare; charity to the poor was largely supplied by the churches and monasteries. Land was fundamental to the economy, and livestock such as oxen increased productivity. Monasteries in the capital and elsewhere possessed numerous estates that provided monks with their living. One bought and held land for the money income that it produced.

Although agriculture was the mainstay of the empire, artisanal production and commerce gave it wealth and luxury. In the great cities of the empire compact populations were engaged to a considerable degree in making articles of everyday use. Many, too, produced luxury goods of great value, which were used in rituals and services of thousands of churches and monasteries and were vital to the pageantry of the imperial court. Sumptuous living was much enjoyed, and the wealth of silk fabrics, gold brocades, jewelry, enameled wares, fine glassware, and all the precious and refined luxury of the age dazzled visitors. Crafts and skills of Hellenistic artisans prevailed for a thousand years in the Byzantine world.

The most active commercial city of the Byzantine Empire, Constantinople, was filled with warehouses, depots, banks, money changers, and other aids to foreign and domestic commerce. Trade from the Black Sea area and most of Russia centered upon Constantinople. Goods from the Far East and western Asia passed down the Bosphorus to quays on the Golden Horn. Domestic imperial production also gravitated to the capital for exchange and transshipment. Ships plied regularly between Constantinople and Trebizond, Salonica, Venice, and Genoa. A standard tax of 10 percent, levied on all imports and exports, brought to the imperial government a large part of its revenue. Italian cities, however, found it possible to obtain tariff concessions from the emperors, which allowed them to dominate long-distance trade.

Commerce and artisanal production were strictly regulated by the government. Controls were exercised over prices, quality, and quantity of goods produced or imported, profits, locations of business, labor conditions, and movement of workers. Implementation of these controls was effected by individual guilds, which were highly organized and fully developed before A.D. 900. Governments granted most guilds special privileges and monopolies. To some extent guilds were restrictive and conservative in character. Yet they prevented speculation and collusion, protected rights of individuals in local and distant markets, and performed many social and legal functions for members. The state appointed the heads of the guilds, and by regulating their activities, it controlled much of the urban economy.

THE CRUSADES

In 1071, when Emperor Romanus IV Diogenes was defeated by the Seljuk sultan Alparslan at the battle of Manzikert near Lake Van, the rout was so complete that soon eastern and central Anatolia were overrun with Turkish bands. Food supplies and raw materials, revenues, commerce, trade routes, and manpower supplies were lost; this further contraction of the empire ultimately spelled its doom.

However shocking this major defeat in 1071 may have been, it had been in the making for the half century since the death of Basil II. For more than a decade prior to the battle of Manzikert the domestic conflicts to control Constantinople had denuded the Anatolian provinces of their military might, opening the way for Turkish invaders. When Romanus IV Diogenes marched out to meet Alparslan, not only was his military equipment woefully inferior but half of his soldiers were merely untrained city youths and the other half were unreliable mercenaries. On his way to battle he had to subdue his own unruly Germans; his predecessors also had alienated many Armenians. In the heat of the battle Andronicus Ducas, leader of the contingent of bureaucrats in the emperor's army, spread the word that Romanus was being defeated and withdrew his men. Turkish forces, witnessing the anarchy, attacked the Byzantine army in flight and captured the emperor. It had been more than 250 years since an emperor had been taken prisoner in battle!

The humiliation of the battle of Manzikert accelerated the fragmentation of society. When the Turks set Romanus IV free, civil war over the throne erupted, further destroying military power in Anatolia and creating a power vacuum. Petty independent states sprang up everywhere: Normans in Bithynia; Seljuk Turks at Nicaea; Armenians in the southeast; and Turkish (Turkoman) tribes everywhere. As a result, Byzantine cultural borrowing and military dependence increased. Before the able general Alexius I Comnenus seized the imperial throne in 1081, several contenders had even relied on Turkish armies in their battles against each other. These actions and the encouragement of Alparslan to Turkoman tribes to invade Anatolia brought Turkish sieges of many walled towns and the general ravaging of the countryside in every corner of Anatolia.

At last Alexius I Comnenus sent out a desperate call to western Christendom for aid. The Crusades were the response, but in the long run they did more harm than good for the Byzantine Empire. The west expended little sentiment over the Byzantine Empire, as the Fourth Crusade demonstrated. The fall of Constantinople to Venetian merchants and soldiers in 1204 abruptly terminated the Byzantine Empire, and its society and civilization collapsed. The Orthodox church was Latinized; monasteries disappeared; the wealth of the churches was carried off; learning and literature vanished; books and libraries were lost; and works of art were destroyed.

The flight of the Byzantine court and ruling classes from Constantinople in 1204 had the immediate effect of producing several independent Greek principalities in the Byzantine provinces. At Nicaea, Theodore Lascaris gathered many of the old aristocracy and had the patriarch crown him emperor, thereby gaining a prestige never enjoyed by his rivals. Meanwhile, the Latin empire of Constantinople hardly had a chance. Fraught with internal feuding and largely deserted by the west, the Crusaders were hemmed in by the expanding second Bulgarian kingdom (founded around 1186) and by Byzantine states. Finally, in 1261, Michael Palaeologus, a general who usurped the Lascaris throne, overthrew the Latins and reestablished the Byzantine state in Constantinople under Palaeologi rule. Greece and the Aegean, however, continued as several Latin-ruled states.

THE END OF BYZANTINE RULE

From 1261 to 1453 Byzantine rule held in Constantinople, but it cannot justly be regarded as a restoration of the Byzantine Empire. It was never more than a small

Greek kingdom, and for the final half century nothing more than the capital city itself. The old empire was broken beyond repair. Furthermore, the Mongol invasions weakened the Seljuks of Anatolia, who controlled much of Anatolia. The resulting power vacuum opened the way to the new Ottoman state, which was built upon the Seljuk and Byzantine legacies.

The Palaeologi tried to maintain a style of imperial government unjustified by the extent of their actual domain. Only a small part of northwestern Anatolia remained in their hands, and most of the Balkans were held by Bulgarian and Serbian rulers. The Byzantines now had no imperial navy. Land revenue was extremely low, as fiscal, judicial, and administrative affairs increasingly fell into the hands of the church, towns, and local landlords. Revocable government grants of revenue became hereditary, and the services owed by the grant holders were frequently ignored. The peasants in the fourteenth century were becoming even poorer as the central government lost power and authority. Indeed, with so much trade passing to western Europe through Mamluk Egypt the imperial crown jewels had to be pawned in Venice.

One mediocre ruler succeeded another; palace poverty and intrigue spawned civil wars and revolutions. Toward the middle of the fourteenth century the poor rose in Constantinople and massacred the aristocracy and the rich, while in 1347 bubonic plague devastated Byzantine cities. Interminable strife also marked the history of the church. The Palaeologi, in their desperation for aid, repeatedly made and accepted bids to subordinate the Orthodox church to the pope of Rome and his authority. Monks, churchmen, and the people objected, and religious unity with the west was continually being postponed or abandoned.

Foreigners gained more power in the empire. From their docks and counting houses of Galata, a suburb across the Golden Horn from Constantinople, the Venetians and Genoese yearly grew more powerful and more insolent in their dealings with the Palaeologi. The most spectacular group of foreigners that came to the Byzantine state was the mercenary Catalan Grand Company of soldiers, who were hired in 1302 to combat the mounting aggression of the Turks. The emperor, however, was soon more terrified of the Catalans than he was of the Turks. No longer could the state afford a regular standing army; the mercenaries, smallholders, and heavy cavalry grant holders could be paid and supported only when a crisis arose or a threat appeared.

In the century and a half preceding the fall of Constantinople international politics in the Byzantine area consisted almost entirely of constantly shifting alliances and realignments among the Byzantine successor states, of which the Greek state was only one. However, when Venetians and Serbs banded together to seize Constantinople, Orhan, the Ottoman ruler, was given the hand of Theodora, the daughter of John VI Cantacuzenus, as partial inducement to bring his forces across the Dardanelles into Europe to defend Thrace from that combination. A rival emperor in alliance with the Genoese drove the Ottomans back to Asia and sent his predecessor to a monastery, where he spent the rest of his days writing his brilliant memoirs. Deposed by his own son and the Genoese, the new emperor called for Ottoman support, which returned him victoriously to Constantinople in 1379.

From that time on Ottoman sultans were deeply involved in Byzantine affairs.

Emperors frequently recognized sultans as their suzerains, sent their sons as hostages to the Ottoman court, and sometimes led the Ottoman fleet on adventures into the Black Sea. Sultans plotted palace revolutions in Constantinople, and emperors sponsored rivals to the sultan's throne and intrigued with other Turkish principalities against the Ottomans. Manuel II (r. 1391–1425) and Mehmed I personally discussed affairs from their respective galleys on the European shores of the Bosphorus and then crossed to the Asiatic side for a picnic, although the emperor did not descend from his galley. When an emperor died childless in 1448, Murad II approved the selection of Constantine XI, whose niece married Mehmed II. The various groups in the area had much in common, despite religious differences; their leaders and societies were coming to resemble each other in many ways. Still, the Ottoman Muslim dynasty was a rival to the Byzantines.

At first the Ottomans were invited and hired by Byzantine emperors to fight in battles against Serbs, Bulgars, and Italians or for one faction of Palaeologi against another. Later they settled in Europe, and before the close of the fourteenth century they had become masters of Thrace, Macedonia, Bulgaria, and parts of Serbia. Constantinople was isolated but obtained a fifty-year reprieve from Timur's crushing defeat of the Ottomans at the battle of Ankara in 1402. Constantinople was all that remained of the Byzantine Empire. That it did not fall to the Ottomans after their state was re-created under Mehmed I can be credited almost wholly to its superb defensive position. Protected by water on three sides and the marvelous Theodosian Wall between the Golden Horn and the Sea of Marmara on the fourth side, the inhabitants of Constantinople felt secure. Any attacker had seemingly insurmountable obstacles to overcome.

By building castles on the European shore of the Bosphorus in 1452 the Ottoman ruler Mehmed II was able to blockade Constantinople by sea. Control of the Balkans gave him complete freedom to mass an army equipped with heavy artillery before the land walls in the spring of 1453. The plight of the city was obvious to all. When the walls were breached and his navy transported from the Bosphorus over the hills of Pera to the Golden Horn, the fate of Constantinople was sealed. Constantine XI died on the walls, Muslim prayers were recited in Hagia Sophia, and bells tolled in Europe. The once great and vigorous Byzantine Empire finally succumbed of old age after a long and painful illness. The young Ottoman Empire ushered in a new day for the great imperial site on the Bosphorus.

Through the ages and up to the present, writers have maligned the Byzantine Empire, its civilization, and particularly its rulers. Intrigue, court politics and palace revolutions, the sharp business acumen of the merchants, and the mercenary character of some aspects of its life all led historians to use the word *byzantine* in a derogatory manner. Nevertheless, a close study of Byzantine records reveals a complex society that possessed an efficient government and excellent public services, managed and directed by an educated and sophisticated bureaucracy, and protected by an army of high tactical ability. At a time when western Europe was semibarbaric, some inhabitants of the Byzantine Empire were enjoying literature, philosophy, urban social culture, and a much higher standard of living. Certainly the Byzantine Empire had a great impact on the peoples and governments of the Middle East and especially on the Ottoman Empire.

References

Volumes cited at the end of Chapters 4, 5, and 11 are also important for this chapter.

BARTUSIS, MARK C.: *The Late Byzantine Army: Arms and Society, 1204–1453.* Philadelphia: University of Pennsylvania Press, 1992. Excellent though detailed examination of military matters and their political and social impacts.

BROWNING, ROBERT: *The Byzantine Empire.* New York: Scribner's, 1980. A profusely illustrated general introduction.

DIEHL, CHARLES: *Byzantium: Greatness and Decline.* Translated by Naomi Walford. New Brunswick, N.J.: Rutgers University Press, 1957. An English translation of the French classic.

HARVEY, ALAN: *Economic Expansion in the Byzantine Empire, 900–1200.* Cambridge, England: Cambridge University Press, 1989. This complex revisionist analysis finds general economic and demographic growth, in opposition to the prior view of decline and contraction.

HUSSEY, J. M.: *The Orthodox Church in the Byzantine Empire.* Oxford, England: Clarendon Press, 1986. The story of patriarchs and emperors, theology, and the spiritual life of the church.

MAINSTONE, ROWLAND J.: *Hagia Sophia: Architecture, Structure and Liturgy of Justinian's Great Church.* New York: Thames and Hudson, 1988. A beautifully illustrated historical introduction.

MANGO, CYRIL: *Byzantium: The Empire of New Rome.* London: Weidenfeld and Nicolson, 1980. Social history is related with care, as the author discusses cities, heresies, the economy, monasticism, education, and intellectual life and self-image.

NICOL, DONALD M.: *Church and Society in the Last Centuries of Byzantium.* Cambridge, England: Cambridge University Press, 1979.

———: *The Last Centuries of Byzantium, 1261–1453.* 2d ed. Cambridge, England: Cambridge University Press, 1993. A perceptive account of late Byzantine political history.

OBOLENSKY, DIMITRI: *The Byzantine Commonwealth: Eastern Europe, 500–1453.* New York: Praeger, 1971. An excellent study of Balkan and eastern European relations to Constantinople under the Byzantine emperors.

OSTROGORSKY, GEORGE: *History of the Byzantine State.* New Brunswick, N.J.: Rutgers University Press, 1969. The standard political history of the Byzantine Empire.

VASILIEV, A. A.: *History of the Byzantine Empire, 324–1453.* Madison: University of Wisconsin Press, 1952. A valuable history of the Byzantine Empire, especially regarding political and military matters.

VRYONIS, SPEROS, JR.: *Byzantium and Europe.* London: Thames and Hudson, 1967. A concise survey of Byzantine history by a leading scholar, with great insight into the complete life of the empire.

———: *The Decline of Medieval Hellenism in Asia Minor and the Process of Islamization from the Eleventh Through the Fifteenth Century.* Berkeley: University of California Press, 1971; paperback reprint, 1986. A landmark in scholarship for its concepts of developments in later Byzantine times.

CHAPTER 14

Ottoman Origins and Early History

The Ottoman Empire destroyed the Byzantine state, but the major role the Ottomans played in the history of the Muslim Middle East should be viewed in the context of a broad range of accomplishments. This empire lasted for more than 600 years, it ultimately ruled over large parts of three continents, and its ruling family became the best-known and most important example of a Muslim dynasty in the Middle East during the early modern and modern periods.

Throughout its long history the Ottoman Empire was marked by three characteristics: allegiance to the imperial dynasty founded by Osman, adherence to Sunnite Islam, and dominance by a Turkish-speaking elite. Although the capital of the empire changed, the center of the state and the economy was constant, located where Asia and Europe met, and where the Black Sea and the Mediterranean-Aegean seas adjoined.

The origins of the Ottomans have been the subject of much scrutiny, not only because of the historical importance of the Ottoman Empire but also because so few sources are available about its early history that many different hypotheses could be entertained. The chief elements that enabled the Ottomans to establish themselves as a leading dynasty were the legacy of the Seljuk Anatolian experience, Byzantine weaknesses, the process of Turkification, competition with other Turkish dynasties, and the contribution of ghazi and tribal values. Once established, the Ottoman principality flourished not only because of these factors but also because of the personal abilities and policies of its rulers and their various deeds.

THE TURKISH SELJUKS IN ANATOLIA

The battle of Manzikert in 1071, in which the Seljuk Alparslan routed the Byzantine army, ranks as a decisive historical event: it opened Anatolia to Turkish settlement and created the first element in what was to become the Ottoman Empire—the Seljuk experience as a model. A second factor in explaining the rise of the Ottomans existed at about the same time as the Seljuk Anatolian state flourished—

a power vacuum around Constantinople resulting from the weakness of the Byzantine Empire.

Within ten years Turkish forces fanned out over Anatolia. The ease with which Turks conquered much of Anatolia resulted not only from their war skills but also from popular resentment against Byzantine policy. March warriors (akritoi) and Armenian areas were disaffected, and gave the Byzantines little aid. Turkish Muslim frontier warriors (ghazis), independent Turkoman nomads, and other Turkish princely dynasties overran Anatolia.

The First Crusade helped Byzantine forces to stem the Turkish tide. Nicaea was retaken, and western sections of Anatolia were restored to Byzantine control, while central and eastern Anatolia remained Turkish. It was only during the reign of the Seljuk Kilij Arslan II (1156–1192) that a truly local Seljuk administration in Anatolia was created, with its capital at Konya, as the administration of the central Seljuk empire to the east collapsed. Kilij Arslan II subdued other ghazis and obtained from Emperor Manuel Comnenus recognition as the commanding lord of Anatolia. However, the central power of the Anatolian Seljuks declined once Kilij Arslan II assigned governorships to his twelve sons, who declared their independence in their father's declining years.

Because of the great prestige of the Seljuk name, Konya attracted ulama to teach in its schools; mystics, Sufis, and poets frequented its court. The Seljuks established Muslim financial administration throughout their state and built mosques, mausoleums, schools, palaces, and caravansarais. Christian churches and monasteries remained in many urban centers, even though they owed their allegiance to the Orthodox patriarch in Constantinople. A mixed culture prevailed in rural areas, in former ghazi districts, and definitely at the frontiers toward the Byzantine Empire.

As the Seljuks expanded their rule, some Greeks fled westward; others were killed or enslaved; many became Muslims and gradually learned to speak Turkish. A decisive victory by the Seljuk sultan over the Byzantines in 1176 meant the Byzantine emperors gave up any idea of reconquering Anatolia, and the Seljuk sultans felt secure from any serious attack from Constantinople. Now the Seljuks, other Turkish rulers, ghazi bands, and Turkomans controlled Anatolia except for a small district around Trebizond on the Black Sea coast and the area near Constantinople.

Thus, through most of the century from 1150 to 1250, the Seljuk sultanate of Konya shone brightly. Muslim and Christian traders frequented its markets, and a considerable share of Far Eastern trade passed through the area to enrich various treasuries. Schools were crowded and the arts flourished. Armenian stonecutters, Persian poets, and Arab calligraphers practiced their crafts. Ghazis settled down, Turks became villagers, communities were established, stone caravansarais were built, and life in central and eastern Anatolia prospered.

Early in the thirteenth century, refugees fleeing the Mongols settled in Seljuk Anatolia, which was soon invaded. At the fateful battle of Kosedagh in 1243 the Seljuk armies were crushed and the Seljuk rulers, thenceforth, were only puppets or vassals of the Mongols to whom they had to pay a high yearly tribute. All respect for Seljuk rulers by other Turks of Anatolia vanished, and the dynasty itself disappeared in the early fourteenth century. Since Mongol rulers did not themselves establish a firm authority in Anatolia and the Mongol Il-Khan state collapsed after

1335, their invasion politically fragmented the peninsula but did not lead to any permanent new order. Mongol traditions and governmental practices did, however, ultimately influence the small Turkish states that succeeded the Seljuks, including the Ottomans. Almost simultaneously with the Mongol conquests the Byzantine emperors regained Constantinople from the Crusaders and became involved immediately in Balkan affairs so that their Asian provinces were neglected. Turkish ghazis and Turkoman tribes discovered not only that the restraining hand of the Seljuk sultan could be ignored but also that Byzantine frontiers could be easily penetrated.

TURKIFICATION OF ANATOLIA

The third element in creating the prerequisites for the emergence of the Ottoman state was the transformation of Anatolia from a Greek and Armenian Christian society to a Turkish Muslim land. Throughout the twelfth and thirteenth centuries and on into the fourteenth, pressure was exerted on every aspect of Christian life and society. Decisive victories for Muslim armies, continual battles and marches across the land by hungry soldiers and rapacious mercenaries, sacking of cities, and scorched-earth policies generated massacres, flight, enslavement, plague, and famine. Those Christians who remained were filled with insecurity and a sense of helplessness.

As various areas fell into Turkish Muslim hands, certain factors made it fairly easy to assume the customs and manners of the victors. In the first place, non-Muslims were tolerated but nevertheless discriminated against in many ways with regard to dress and life; unquestionably they were second-class subjects. Converts, on the other hand, escaped discrimination—as well as many taxes. Furthermore, Christian communities became leaderless at a time of great psychological and economic crisis. Consequently, whole villages turned Muslim overnight, at first in the interior and later along the coasts of Anatolia. By about 1300 a majority of the population of Anatolia was Muslim.

The Seljuk state also actively supported Islamic institutions. Within a few decades Anatolia was blanketed with mosques, madrasahs (advanced schools), hospitals, caravansarais, and even halfway houses for converts to Islam. Most of these were endowed as waqfs by leading Turks or by the state from confiscated Christian property and the income from Christian villages. Moreover, Anatolia was saturated by Sufis who preached a mystical popular Islam that reached the people. They presented a kind of religious syncretism that equated Islamic practices and holy men with those of the Christians. The twelve apostles became the twelve imams and the Trinity came to consist of God, Muhammad, and Ali. This phenomenon of cultural change continued in Anatolia until the mid-fifteenth century when the Ottoman Turks captured Constantinople, recognizing the patriarch as subject to the sultan and in essence institutionalizing and protecting the Orthodox church as a part of the state. As a consequence, Christian communities could look to the patriarch and bishops without fear of reprisal, and the church hierarchy felt responsible for its flock throughout the Ottoman domain.

OTHER TURKISH STATES

A fourth element in the rise of the Ottomans was the long competition between that family and other small Turkish Muslim dynastic states whose political and social patterns dominated Anatolia for several centuries. Originally the amirate founded by Osman near Eskishehir was quite insignificant, even though eventually it conquered or annexed all the others. Probably the most important of these was the Karaman principality with its capital at Konya. The founder of the dynasty, Karaman, was the son of a Sufi mystic. Other Turkish principalities along the Aegean coast established navies that raided commerce.

The Turkish amirates of Anatolia were quite similar to each other, and that established by Osman had few attributes different from usual ghazi traditions upheld in these principalities. Ibn Battutah, the fourteenth-century Moroccan globe-trotter, visited Anatolia and left a record of his impressions of these amirates. Entertained at the courts of many, he reserved no special tribute for Orhan, Osman's son. It was the competitive struggle among the principalities that helped the Ottomans evolve patterns of behavior and institutions that subsequently held them together through times of adversity.

GHAZI SOCIETY

A fifth factor in bringing about the later success of the Ottomans was their leadership of ghazi warriors. The Ottoman dynasty, in addition to its desire for expansion and glory, also sought to foster Islam by armed force. (The ghazi traditions and attributes were not limited to the Ottomans; indeed, most Muslim dynasties on frontiers with non-Muslim peoples had something resembling the Anatolian ghazi experience.)

Ghazi war bands brought back rich plunder, including slaves. Ghazis were equal socially and politically; aristocracy was derived from actions and leadership rather than from blood. It was a typical rough frontier society. Another feature of ghazi life was acceptance of the futuwwa, a set of rules by which the virtuous should live. Mutual fidelity among the membership was particularly emphasized. Likewise, almost every ghazi brotherhood recognized a spiritual leader; in most cases this leader was a Sufi.

Ghazi society lacked administrative, institutional, and governmental apparatus and stability that could maintain control once conquest ceased. This problem confronted the Ottomans constantly in their meteoric path across Anatolia and the Balkans. The success with which they solved this continuing problem determined, in considerable measure, the permanent or ephemeral character of Ottoman conquests.

OTTOMAN ORIGINS: OSMAN AND ORHAN

In addition to the external factors that helped open the way to the rise of the Ottoman dynasty, the personal abilities of the rulers and their individual accomplishments played a very important role in the establishment and growth of the state. Osman, founder of the Ottoman state, was the son of Ertogrul, a Turkish frontier warrior whose holdings on the western edge of the Seljuk domains were given him by one of the later Seljuk sultans. Although little is known about Ertogrul's ancestry or background, probably he was one of the countless seminomadic Turkomans looking for a place to settle in Anatolia.

Like any other frontier warrior, Ertogrul led raiding excursions into Byzantine territory; the conquest and absorption of neighboring villages and fortified places began only in the 1280s or 1290s. This was presumably after Osman had married the daughter of a Sufi leader. Osman established ties with ghazi groups and their futuwwa moral and ethical ideas. (The word *Ottoman* was an Italian corruption of *Uthman,* the originally Arabic name Turks pronounced as Osman; in Turkish the dynasty was often called the sons of Osman.)

Osman, as a leader of tribesmen, began to acquire by capture or alliance a number of small towns. Between 1300 and 1320 Osman seized the countryside west of the Sakarya River, and west and north to the Sea of Marmara. Yet he was not strong enough or sufficiently well equipped to take the walled towns. Not until after Osman died in 1323 or 1324 did his followers under the leadership of his son Orhan take Brusa (Bursa), which surrendered without a struggle after several years of siege. Bursa became the Ottoman capital and center of government. The fall of Bursa was the signal for Byzantine collapse in that corner of Anatolia. Orhan occupied Nicaea (Iznik) in 1330. Later, he dispossessed the quarreling sons of a neighboring Turkish amir and placed Ottoman rulers over still another amirate. Thus, by

Osman (1281–1324)

Orhan (1324–1360)

Murad I (1362–1389)

Bayezid I (1389–1402)

Mehmed I (1403–1421)

Murad II (1421–1444; 1446–1451)

Mehmed II (1444–1446; 1451–1481)

Bayezid II (1481–1512)

Selim I (1512–1520)

Suleiman I (1520–1566)

Ottoman Rulers, 1281–1566

1345, the Ottoman state included the entire northwestern corner of Anatolia from the Aegean to the Black Sea.

Several factors prepared the way for this accelerating growth of the Ottoman state. The personality and spirit of Osman counted heavily since his followers were loyal and devoted to him. Byzantine force weakened rapidly, and such towns as Bursa and Iznik were summarily abandoned to their fate. Unlike other nearby Muslim dynasties, the Ottomans kept their lands intact under one ruler, rather than dividing them among various family heirs.

A most important element in the growth of Ottoman forces was the policy of welcoming any and all fighting men as part of the fluid, open religious and social atmosphere of the Anatolia of that time. Mikhal, a Greek who became a Muslim, was one of Osman's favorite comrades. His descendants (the Mikhaloglu) held prominent positions through centuries of Ottoman history. Osman and Orhan used slave soldiers who were part of their household entourage. In 1305, some of the Catalan Grand Company joined the Ottoman camp; defeated Mongol raiders, given clemency, joined Orhan. Fighting men from various tribal, ghazi, and Byzantine Christian backgrounds flocked to the Ottoman infantry and cavalry as their successes multiplied. Some Christians worked as bureaucrats for the Ottomans in the early fourteenth century. Orhan also accepted the Muslim practice of allowing Christians and Jews to live in a Muslim land by paying taxes and special tribute.

In the first half century under Osman and Orhan, Ottoman expansion was gradual enough to permit the organization of some governmental administration. Moreover, the Muslim world was in such disorder that Muslim artisans, merchants, bureaucrats, theologians, jurists, teachers, and scribes were attracted by opportunities in this new frontier Muslim state. Schools of theology were built in Bursa and Iznik soon after their capture, and Bursa remained the center of learning and philosophical discussion for the Ottomans.

Furthermore, the immigrant artisans and merchants who were known as akhis formed corporations somewhat like European guilds. These akhi guilds were closely knit bodies subscribing to specific futuwwa codes of conduct very similar to the ghazi code of honor. A close alliance and understanding between ghazi and akhi gave to Ottoman society an economic strength that was lacking in other ghazi states. Silver coins were minted, and a lively trade developed in the prosperous towns, while charitable foundations (waqfs) were endowed. The early arrival of Muslim judges, theologians, and ulama expanded the social structure beyond the ruling ghazi and Turkoman family circles. Thus, at an early date social and economic disturbances in towns passing into Ottoman hands were largely minimized. Life went on in much the same way, with considerable intermingling of people. Orhan himself married Nilufer, a daughter of the Greek lord of a captured town. By the middle of the fourteenth century Orhan had become amir or prince of a sizable state facing the historic Straits and Europe beyond.

OTTOMAN EXPANSION: ORHAN AND MURAD I

Turkish ghazis were long accustomed to raiding parties in Thrace and Macedonia. An example of this raiding took place when Orhan and his men became allies of the Byzantine emperor John VI Cantacuzenus in 1345 to fight against a rival emperor. Part of Orhan's bargain was the privilege of plundering; another part was the hand in marriage of Theodora, Cantacuzenus's daughter. Six thousand Ottomans ravaged the hinterland of Constantinople and the Black Sea coast and were instrumental in taking Adrianople (Edirne). In most years thereafter Ottoman soldiers amassed fortunes in booty through raids in Thrace and the southern Balkans. Byzantine resistance to Ottoman expansion was also weakened by the Black Death, which reached Constantinople first in 1347, and by a severe earthquake in 1354, which demolished the walls of Gallipoli on the European shore of the Dardanelles. Ottoman forces in Europe rushed into Gallipoli, asserting that God had given it to them, and Ottomans colonized the city, much of whose population had been carried off by the Black Death.

From this bridgehead in Europe, Ottomans stormed over eastern Thrace, seizing all areas between the Aegean and the Black seas except, of course, the imperial city of Constantinople. The Serbian empire collapsed in 1355 and Bulgaria became weak in the 1360s, also opening the way to Ottoman expansion. Adrianople surrendered in 1369 to Murad, third in the Ottoman line of rulers, and for nearly a century that city (which the Turks called Edirne) stood as the chief Ottoman city in Europe.

Murad I, the younger son of Orhan and Nilufer, followed in his father's footsteps, vigorously pushing one campaign after another northward and westward into the Balkans. Rival emperors of Constantinople, Serbian and Bulgarian tsars, independent princes of Greece, the city-states of Venice and Genoa, popes, and Crusaders kept the Balkans in such constant turmoil and confusion that Murad in his expeditions did not have to worry about facing a consolidated offensive and usually had several Christian allies in his camp. Under Murad's leadership (r. 1362–1389), Ottoman armies and raiders succeeded in conquering most of Bulgaria, Macedonia, and parts of Serbia.

Likewise, Murad made extensive advances in Asia. He took Ankara and, through a combination of prestige, power, money, and diplomacy, nearly doubled his Anatolian possessions. Marriage of his son Bayezid to the daughter of an amir brought the town of Kutahya as a dowry. Murad forced another Turkish amir to "sell" most of his domain and will the balance to the Ottomans. Campaigns were launched against the Karaman princes but with little success, perhaps because ghazis fought with less enthusiasm against fellow Muslims. In these Anatolian campaigns Murad's most loyal supporters were contingents of his Slavic allies and mercenaries. Western Crusaders also were involved in conquests in Anatolia: from 1344 to 1402 Izmir, an important port, was held by them, not the Ottomans.

During the battle of Kossovo in 1389 against the Serbs, Murad lost his life. When Bayezid I succeeded as ruler or sultan of the Ottomans, he inherited a state that in the brief span of a century had grown from a petty principality to a dominant power stretching from the Danube River in Europe to the Taurus Mountains in Asia.

BAYEZID I

Bayezid I seized the reins of government on the field of Kossovo in 1389. His only brother, Yakub, was assassinated by the supporters of Bayezid, leaving him the only male alive in the Ottoman royal family. Having the example of bitter and destructive rivalries of the Byzantine dynasties before him, Bayezid judged that executing his brother was for the best. Practices of this kind became standard procedure for a new sultan upon accession to the throne and prevailed in the Ottoman family for more than 200 years.

With the rise of modern nationalism, Kossovo was viewed by Serbs as a catastrophic defeat despite an equality in losses, but in 1389 no great ill feeling seemed to be generated. A Serbian royal princess was married to the victorious Bayezid, who became devoted to her; and Serb contingents remained loyal to Bayezid throughout his reign. In succeeding years Ottoman forces raided Bosnia and Hungary, even crossing the Danube, and Bayezid brought greater numbers of Turks into Europe, especially into Thrace.

Indeed, beginning in 1391, all of Thrace was occupied up to the very walls of Constantinople: the city was virtually blockaded from the land side. Bayezid attempted to close the Bosphorus and the Dardanelles to ships destined for the imperial city. But attacks, first in Europe and later in Asia, saved Constantinople for half a century.

Sigismund, then king of Hungary, but later Holy Roman Emperor, was concerned over successful Ottoman aggressions. The building of an Ottoman navy, which began depredations in the Adriatic Sea, helped lead Europe to heed Sigismund's loud cries for a crusade. The romantic crusade of Nicopolis of 1396 was the result. Nobles from England, France, and the German states, and armies from Hungary and Wallachia, all laden with wine and women, joined as if on a picnic. They foolishly charged the center of the Ottoman forces, commanded personally by Bayezid, who had left the siege of Constantinople to meet the knights of Europe. Utterly outmaneuvered, the flower of western nobility fell on the battlefield of Nicopolis, and thousands were captured. Those under twenty years of age were taken for the janissary corps or the sultan's court. Many were held for ransom, and others were impressed to row in the galleys as ordinary slaves. This encounter brought disaster to the new Crusaders and for several decades squelched any thought of another crusade on their part.

After raiding Hungary, Bayezid turned his attention to Greece, where Ottoman armies overran Thessaly, entered the Peloponnesus, and captured towns and smaller cities. Ottomans were settled in the northeastern corner of the Peloponnesus, then called Morea, and land grants were handed out in northern Greece. But fortified cities that could still be supplied from the sea were, like Constantinople, still beyond Ottoman reach.

Bayezid's involvements in Europe and the attempts at choking Constantinople did not deter him from campaigns in Anatolia. His burning ambition was to unite under his rule all Muslim lands of Anatolia and perhaps of the entire Middle East. Although this sort of goal was common in the expansion and unification attendant upon the rise and growth of a new state, Bayezid's haughty manner and ruthless tactics plus the rise of a brilliant enemy spelled his ruin.

In rapid succession between 1390 and 1397 Ottoman forces, frequently led by Bayezid in person, captured and annexed old ghazi and Turkoman amirates such as Karaman. The dispossessed princes, instead of being given responsibilities to weld them into the Ottoman system, fled with revenge in their hearts to the court of

Expansion of the Ottoman Empire, 1300–1574

RUSSIA

Syr Darya

Amu Darya

ARAL
SEA

INDIA

Indus

ARABIAN
SEA

CASPIAN SEA

Volga

CAUCASUS

IRAN

• Isfahan

Persian Gulf

Dnieper

BLACK SEA

CRIMEA

Tabriz •

• Trebizond

Aleppo • Mosul •

IRAQ

Tigris

Baghdad •

Euphrates

• Basrah

ARABIA

Medina •

• Mecca

RED SEA

Istanbul •

Dniester

HUNGARY

Danube

BALKANS

Damascus •

SYRIA

Jerusalem •

PALESTINE

CYPRUS

• Cairo

EGYPT

Nile

AUSTRIA

Vienna •

ITALIAN
STATES

Rome •

CRETE

MEDITERRANEAN SEA

Rhine

Loire

Rhone

FRANCE

ALGERIA

SPAIN

ATLANTIC
OCEAN

	200	400 mi
0		
	300	600 km
0		

Ottoman Turks, 1300

Acquisitions, 1300–1451

Acquisitions, 1451–1574

165

Timur Leng (Tamerlane). With Bayezid engaged in subduing Bulgaria and in besieging Constantinople, the Karaman leaders judged that a revolt might be successful. However, Bayezid transferred his troops to Asia with amazing speed and destroyed the Karamans in front of Bursa. He did this so completely and so quickly that his soldiers dubbed him Yildirim (meaning "thunderbolt" or "lightning").

Except for a few walled towns like Constantinople and Athens, Bayezid was now master of the land from the Adriatic and the plains of Hungary to the Euphrates. In barely a decade he had doubled his Asian possessions and gained recognition as lord of the Balkans. In 1395 Serbian princes and Byzantine emperors rendered homage. The uncomplicated Ottoman state of Osman and Orhan had vanished.

ECONOMIC, SOCIAL, AND POLITICAL CHANGES

Two great trade routes met in Anatolia, and as the Ottomans conquered the peninsula they gained control of this rewarding commerce. The extension of the Mongol Empire into Anatolia in the thirteenth century had established profitable east-west trade routes, especially for Chinese and Persian silks. At the same time, merchants following north-south routes brought spices and fabrics to Konya and then to the principal markets of Anatolia and to Constantinople. In the fourteenth century, with the disintegration of the Mongol state and the rise of the Ottomans, more and more of this trade found its way to Bursa, which by the year 1400 had become the most important trading city in Anatolia. As Bayezid extended his rule, merchants could travel safely from Tabriz and Aleppo to Bursa, where merchants from the Italian cities bought their goods.

The Ottomans were interested in commerce and industry, and the akhi groups were influential members of their society. Ibn Battutah noted in 1333 that Orhan, because he held Bursa, was the richest Turkish ruler in Anatolia. And as early as 1340 Orhan had built a bazaar and an enclosed market in Bursa where valuable goods could be safely stored and sold. Such interests had greatly aided the Ottoman successes.

In the time of Murad I the government began to grow; under Bayezid I expansion was rapid and very noticeable. The first cadastral registers, designed to record land revenue assignments, were compiled. Government organization by religious leaders and graduates of the schools of Bursa and Iznik introduced more efficiency yet also more rigidity in administration. At the same time evolution of the post of grand vizir or chief minister in the hands of Kara Khalil Chandarli aroused considerable opposition among most Ottoman soldiers, accustomed for generations to great freedom.

Dismay also stemmed from Bayezid's dreams of empire. In 1394 he sent an embassy to the Mamluk-controlled Abbasid caliph in Egypt, requesting to be invested with the title sultan of Rum (Anatolia). Even Bayezid's grandfather had used that title, and evidently it was commonly applied to Bayezid. Yet he wished recognition from the older Muslim world, perhaps because numerous Turkoman amirates that he engulfed looked upon him as a tyrant. Some ghazis may have objected to his Asian campaigns; Bayezid learned that in operations against fellow

Muslims he could be sure only of his janissaries and contingents sent by his European Christian vassals. Many Muslims in Asia could hardly escape questioning Bayezid's own faith when he led Christian soldiers against Muslims.

There were other ways in which Bayezid's actions alienated his subjects. The cultural background of Ottoman leaders left them open for many innovations, and with a medley of individuals appearing among them, eclecticism developed. Discussions among religious leaders of various sects within the Ottoman state even led to proposals for a common religion from a composite of Islam, Judaism, and Christianity. Undoubtedly this trend can be seen in the names of Bayezid's younger sons—Musa (Moses), Isa (Jesus), and Mehmed (Muhammad). Other sons were called Ertogrul (Turkish name), Mustafa (Muslim mysticism), Kasimir (Balkan Christian), and Suleiman (Solomon).

Even more objectionable to many Ottoman subjects were Bayezid's personal habits. Increasingly, he took on the ways of Balkan and Byzantine rulers and nobles. Manners and dress changed; court ceremony became more elaborate. Many still remembered the ease with which they could approach Orhan and contrasted the simplicity of Orhan's establishment to the complexity of Bayezid's. Bayezid, though brilliant and energetic, fell under the spell of grandeur and sumptuous living. He drank wine and engaged in homosexual behavior, both of which scandalized many Muslims. His harem was large, and he began to follow in the footsteps of the caliphs of old. Earlier Ottoman rulers had apparently married both Christian and Muslim women, including princesses; by the days of Bayezid males in the royal family more frequently had concubines than wives, and it was these non-Turkish concubines who were the mothers of the next generations of rulers.

DEFEAT AT ANKARA

Timur invaded Anatolia in part because of the unrest among Bayezid's subjects and the request to do so by exiled Anatolian amirs who were in his entourage. In addition, Bayezid had invaded territory beyond the Euphrates to the Tigris and given indications of ambitions in Syria, thereby threatening Timur's vassals.

Surprisingly overconfident, Bayezid moved leisurely to meet the threat. In the face of so great a danger he organized a huge hunting party, wasting valuable time and tiring his men. The contest came in 1402 at Ankara, where only the janissaries and the Christian vassals of the Balkans stood fast. Bayezid, a prisoner, was brought before Timur, who honored him until his haughtiness became insufferable. Within a few weeks he died, and his body was returned to Bursa, the chief Ottoman burial site.

Following his great victory, Timur marched across Anatolia to Izmir on the Aegean. He showed little desire to hold Anatolia directly, however. Ottoman conquests in Europe and the early holdings of Osman and Orhan in Asia were divided among Bayezid's remaining sons: Suleiman, Musa, Isa, and Mehmed. Anatolian amirates taken by Murad and Bayezid were restored to their previous hereditary families. Bayezid had a dream of empire, but it was shattered at Ankara. The Ottoman family was left only in possession of those holdings that were considered legitimately theirs. Bayezid's sons and all other amirs of Anatolia swore allegiance to

Timur. When Timur died three years later, the amirs of western Anatolia and the four heirs of Bayezid renounced all dependence upon the Timurids.

The duration of the united Ottoman state from about 1280 to 1402 had been equivalent to that of many other Muslim dynasties in the late medieval Middle East. Thus the destruction of the Ottoman army and the ensuing disunity were typical of what had happened often in the past to other groups, and the disappearance of the Ottoman state could be expected. What was surprising was that the empire was soon reunited and in fact became far more successful in the fifteenth century than it had been earlier. Causes for this revival can be found in many of the circumstances that had enabled the Ottomans to expand their principality between 1300 and the battle of Ankara, and in particular their dynastic, military, diplomatic, institutional, religious, and cultural accomplishments.

References

Volumes cited at the end of Chapters 12 and 13 are important for this chapter.

ALDERSON, A. D.: *The Structure of the Ottoman Dynasty.* Oxford, England: Clarendon Press, 1956. An important volume on the Ottoman family and the lives of the individual sultans.

CAHEN, CLAUDE: *Pre-Ottoman Turkey: A General Survey of the Material and Spiritual Culture and History, c. 1071–1330.* Translated from the French by J. Jones-Williams. London: Sidgwick and Jackson, 1968. The most important work on the subject.

COOK, M. A., ED.: *A History of the Ottoman Empire to 1730.* Cambridge, England: Cambridge University Press, 1976. Seven chapters by different authors; the essays are drawn from the *Cambridge History of Islam* and the *New Cambridge Modern History.*

IMBER, COLIN: *The Ottoman Empire 1300–1481.* Istanbul: Isis Press, 1990. Detailed political and military history is based on scrupulous analysis of primary sources; this is now the best beginning point for the time period and subjects covered.

INALCIK, HALIL: *The Ottoman Empire: The Classical Age, 1300–1600.* 2d ed. New Rochelle, N.Y.: Caratzas, 1989. A new chapter on rural society has been added to this thorough history by an outstanding scholar. In addition to political matters, the author discusses in a most enlightened way law, economic and social life, and culture.

ITZKOWITZ, NORMAN: *Ottoman Empire and Islamic Tradition.* New York: Knopf, 1973. This excellent introduction to the Ottoman Empire deals with the early history leading to the formation of the empire.

KAFADAR, CEMAL: *Between Two Worlds: The Construction of the Ottoman State.* Berkeley: University of California Press, 1995. This book, which emphasizes the importance of ghazis in early Ottoman affairs, should be read in connection with the work by Rudi Lindner cited here.

KINROSS, LORD (PATRICK BALFOUR): *The Ottoman Centuries: The Rise and Fall of the Turkish Empire.* New York: Morrow, 1977. A well-written, popular account of the history of the Ottomans.

KRAMERS, J. H.: "Murad I." *Encyclopaedia of Islam.* New ed. Vol. 7, pp. 592–594. Leiden: Brill, 1993. A brief but useful account.

LINDNER, RUDI PAUL: *Nomads and Ottomans in Medieval Anatolia.* Bloomington, Ind.: Research Institute for Inner Asian Studies, 1983. The author discounts the ghazi and emphasizes the tribal identity of the early Ottomans. There is also an excellent account of the treatment of Anatolian nomads by the Ottomans in the middle period of the empire's long history.

PITCHER, DONALD EDGAR: *An Historical Geography of the Ottoman Empire: From the Earliest*

Times to the End of the Sixteenth Century, with Detailed Maps to Illustrate the Expansion of the Sultanate. Leiden: Brill, 1972. Emphasis is on political geography.

SHAW, STANFORD: *History of the Ottoman Empire and Modern Turkey.* Vol. 1: *Empire of the Gazis: The Rise and Decline of the Ottoman Empire, 1280–1808.* Cambridge, England: Cambridge University Press, 1976. This is an outstanding contribution by a leading scholar in the field. He analyzes the many forces that produced the Ottoman Empire and relates the factors that led to its decline.

SHINDER, JOEL: "Early Ottoman Administration in the Wilderness." *International Journal of Middle East Studies* 9 (1978): 497–517. A review of earlier theories of Ottoman administration which acknowledges the influence of the Il-Khans but also points to Ottoman innovations.

SUGAR, PETER F.: *Southeastern Europe Under Ottoman Rule, 1354–1804.* Seattle: University of Washington Press, 1977.

VRYONIS, SPEROS: "Seljuk Gulams and Ottoman Devshirmes." *Der Islam* 41 (October 1965): 224–252. A very important article showing how the slave system developed and operated.

The Winning of the Ottoman Empire

Even though the Ottoman Empire was dissolved by Timur in 1402, by 1413 Mehmed I reunited it, in the process overcoming both internal and external enemies. As the strengthened and renewed state then expanded, the Ottomans encountered challenges on all fronts. One of the chief means by which they overcame these difficulties was their army, while diplomacy and the personal abilities of the ruling sultans also played a large role in their successes. Finally, the Ottomans aimed at capturing Constantinople, the great imperial city whose conquest had been the goal of several earlier Muslim dynasties.

MEHMED I REUNITES THE STATE

Timur's capture of Sultan Bayezid I at the battle of Ankara in 1402 destroyed the unity of the Ottoman Empire as it caused the remaining Ottoman provinces to be apportioned among his sons. Timur recognized Mehmed, probably the youngest son, as governor of Amasya. Isa was designated as lord of Bursa, the former capital of the Ottomans, and a town burned by Timur's troops. Suleiman, the eldest and formerly governor at Manisa, went to Edirne and ruled the Ottoman possessions in Europe. Musa, taken prisoner by Timur, was placed on parole at Kutahya. Shortly afterward, he was authorized to take his father's body to Bursa for burial and was then sent to the court of his brother Mehmed.

The transitory character of Timur's conquest permitted the four sons to quarrel among themselves over their patrimony. At first Mehmed and Musa teamed up against Suleiman and Isa, striking their first blows in Asia. Mehmed drove Isa from Bursa. Fleeing to Constantinople, Isa was encouraged by Suleiman, himself under pressure from Musa, to make a bid to regain his city. He was, however, beaten by Mehmed and vanished.

Meanwhile, having escaped from the Ankara disaster with Ali Pasha Chandarli and the leader of the janissaries, Suleiman arrived at Edirne, European headquarters for the Ottoman family. With the richest part of the state in his hands and supported by his father's chief ministers, Suleiman in 1403 claimed to be ruler of the Ottomans, and he extended his reign to include most of Ottoman Anatolia. But Mehmed and Musa refused to acknowledge his supremacy.

Rivalry among the three brothers endured for a decade. Its genesis was the example set by Bayezid I in killing his own brother. But competition among Suleiman, Musa, and Mehmed also arose from the factionalism in Ottoman politics that emerged in reaction against their father's attempts to consolidate and centralize the state.

The imperial clique found its candidate in Suleiman. Supported by the Chandarli and Evrenos families, by the governmental machinery in Edirne, and by the janissaries who survived the rout at Ankara, Suleiman reigned until 1411. Treaties with Venice and the Byzantine emperor recognized him as Ottoman ruler and facilitated trade and commerce in Europe, affairs in which the Chandarli family was personally interested. Suleiman failed, however, in his campaigns to dislodge Musa and Mehmed from the region east of Ankara.

With the aid of discontented Serbs and Wallachians, Musa carried the struggle against Suleiman to Europe in 1410. Unsuccessful in the first attempt, Musa caught Suleiman the next year in a surprise raid upon Edirne and had him strangled as he was fleeing to Constantinople. Ibrahim Chandarli, the Evrenos family, and the court immediately transferred their loyalty to Musa, who was now recognized as lord of Europe. Mehmed remained supreme in Anatolia.

Besides Balkan vassals and Ottoman European officialdom, Musa was supported by freethinking religious groups pursuing a theological eclecticism popular at that time. As chief judge in Ottoman European territories, he appointed one of the leaders of these groups, Shaikh Badr al-Din Simavni, who held views leading toward an egalitarian society and a union of Judaism, Christianity, and Islam. Some years later Shaikh Badr al-Din led an unsuccessful rebellion against the state, and in the mid-sixteenth century his views were still being preached by one of his descendants.

Musa was an energetic individual who sent out raiding parties into Europe and resumed the siege of Constantinople, but Mehmed aided the Byzantine emperor against his brother. Musa's revolutionary tendencies and his confiscations and executions drove many of his supporters, such as Ibrahim Chandarli, over to Mehmed, who carried on an active campaign for allies among high-placed Ottoman lords in Europe. Most of these went over to Mehmed; and in 1413, after Mehmed gained fresh troops from the Serbs and Dhu al-Qadr, Mehmed caught up with Musa near Sofia. Musa perished, and his body was returned with honor to Bursa to be buried beside Sultan Murad I.

In looking for factors in the success of Mehmed, his having first governed in Amasya, heartland of the old ghazi district, helped make him the champion of the ghazis. With the favor of this powerful faction, essentially the military foundation of the state, propaganda for him among frontier raiders and Ottoman colonists in Europe took root easily, while the slave troops and officials were lowered in position and rank. Mehmed represented the "good old days" of Osman and Orhan.

Another factor in the personal success of Mehmed was the role of his tutor and his early education. As was customary, Mehmed was sent as a boy to govern a province and learn the art of ruling. A high state dignitary accompanied the prince to advise in all matters. In this instance, the tutor was Bayezid Pasha, an Albanian by birth and a war captive retained by Murad and raised at court. Bayezid Pasha proved to be an outstanding general and a devoted slave to Mehmed, winning battles, organizing campaigns, and above all leading Mehmed to the task of reuniting the Ottoman state. Bayezid Pasha was one of the very first of a new type of high Ottoman official who in his attachment to his masters, the Ottoman family, showed his proclivity for a centralized state.

In strongly identifying himself with Anatolia and the old ghazi way of life, Mehmed avoided the mistakes of his father and his brother Suleiman in their European manners. He chose for his wife a daughter of the amir of Dhu al-Qadr, a Turkoman amirate of the Syrian frontier. Mehmed grew to be revered by the Ottomans for his gentleness, integrity, and modesty.

THE OTTOMAN ARMY

The institution of the Ottoman army also proved to be an important factor in helping to preserve the Ottoman dynasty to overcome the factionalism and divisions following 1402. Military traditions, processes, and history provided pressures for unity. The army had become more sophisticated and differentiated since the early days when under Osman criers simply went through the villages announcing that anyone who wished to participate in a raid should meet at a given place at a specific time. Orhan had organized the army. Moreover, in the wars of Orhan and Murad closer contacts with the Byzantine military provided examples from which the Ottoman army obtained useful suggestions.

The army was organized on a basis of units of 10, 100, and 1000 men, with a responsible officer over each group. This was as true of irregular infantry and volunteer horsemen and cavalry scouts as it was of regular cavalry (sipahi) and the janissaries (yeni cheri). Officers of the immediate family and entourage of the Ottoman ruler were placed in overall charge of the armies. The word *pasha* was a title used at this time by Ottoman officers.

The institution of the janissaries held a special place in Ottoman annals. The origin of this corps has been much debated since they were so important in innumerable Ottoman victories through several centuries. Janissaries as part of an Ottoman institution probably began in connection with the custom of Muslim states, beginning in the time of the prophet Muhammad, that the ruler as the embodiment of the state usually received one-fifth of the booty of war. Since human beings had long been valuable prizes of successful campaigns and since their lot was often one of slavery, the Ottomans under Orhan and Murad found more slaves on their hands than they knew how to employ in customary tasks. The answer was to turn them into soldiers to fight for their captors.

In the past caliphs and sultans had slave bodyguards, and in late medieval Egypt the ruling Mamluks had been slaves. Seljuk rulers used slaves by the thousands who were trained as soldiers, led their armies, and rose to become high officials. Most of them were Greek youths of Anatolia taken as prisoners or levied as a tribute from the Greek subjects. Youths captured in battle were kept as slaves by the Ottoman sultans as well. Nominally converted to Islam, they were banded together and trained as special corps in the army about the sultan. Their name, yeni cheri ("new soldier"), was corrupted to "janissary" by Europeans, who learned to fear their discipline, their esprit de corps, and their prowess with arms. Many younger captives were "farmed out" as apprentices to Ottoman officers for a number of years. During these years they learned some Turkish and how to fight.

In the days of Murad I the janissaries probably numbered around 1000; by the time of Bayezid I they had increased to about 5000. They were paid a small daily wage and did not marry while serving as active soldiers. Living together in barracks, drilling, training, and dressing alike gave the janissaries the status of a standing army. Some were cavalry; most were infantrymen; others were members of a specially honored left-handed guard. Many rose through the ranks and became high officers and trusted civil officials; a few were beheaded for dishonesty or disobedience. Before a century passed, only those who became regular infantry were known as janissaries. Other ranks and other corps had their own special designations.

Another important group were the sipahis, who answered the need for regular cavalry, for colonization of newly won lands, and for local provincial administration. Adapting Seljuk and Byzantine practices, Ottoman rulers rewarded fighting men with the revocable grants of the right to collect tax revenues from land farmed by peasants; the sipahis derived their living from these revenues. By the sixteenth century these grants tended to become hereditary. Each year when a campaign was announced, sipahis left their estates and appeared equipped to fight under a local officer whom they elected. This cavalry not only was the main force of the Ottoman armies but also was engaged almost continually in raids beyond the frontier. Sons went along on campaigns with their fathers and learned the profession of arms. They were eligible to become cavalrymen, and often they were awarded at least a part of the family holdings. By settling and rearing families on the land, the sipahi cavalry served as the first Ottoman colonizers and administrators of new territories.

Running strongly through the ranks of the Ottoman cavalry until the end of the sixteenth century was the ghazi spirit. In certain areas where the frontier had long been a battleground, as in Bosnia and Albania, a ghazi society emerged similar to those of earlier frontier areas in Anatolia. A thorough admixture of Ottoman warriors with local populations occurred, giving rise in the Balkans to Greek-, Serb-, and Albanian-speaking Muslims.

All these groups—janissaries, sipahis, frontier raiders, urban volunteers, and others—felt that the religious ideal of frontier warfare for Islam, their own particular and organizational interests, and the success of Ottoman Muslim society were intertwined with the glory and unity of the Ottoman Empire, which needed strong leadership. With the victory of Mehmed I the Ottoman state was reunited in 1413.

EXPANSION IN ASIA

There were in Anatolia many Turks, however, who were not considered Ottomans and who did not accept the idea of one united state. Although forces from Karaman and Dhu al-Qadr fought with Mehmed when he ousted his brother Isa from Bursa, the Karaman prince, the prime Ottoman rival in Anatolia, besieged Bursa when Mehmed was destroying Musa in Rumeli. (The European part of the Ottoman state was referred to as Rumeli—the land of the Romans, i.e., Byzantines.) The Karamans were defeated in 1415, but their state was not conquered.

Most of the other Anatolian states now recognized the dominant position of the Ottomans in central and western Anatolia. However, the disruption of society resulting from Timur's invasion and continued by the civil wars of Bayezid's sons generated many mystical sects in Anatolia. A number of Sufi orders founded by holy men from Iran date their origin from this period. Social unrest, too, was common. In 1416, Bayezid Pasha had to raise levies from most of Anatolia to quell a socioreligious revolutionary movement in Anatolia and in Europe—a movement led by the mystic Badr al-Din Simavni, onetime European army judge under Musa.

Mehmed could not ignore Europe, especially since Rumeli produced far greater revenue for the Ottoman government than did Anatolia. Mehmed intervened in Wallachia, built fortresses north of the Danube, and conquered parts of southern Albania, reaching the Adriatic Sea, although the sultan refused to resume the attack that his father and brothers had begun upon Constantinople.

Unquestionably, Mehmed reestablished Ottoman unity approximately to the extent that it had existed in his father's time. But a truly complete Ottoman Empire was not yet created, and it could not be created without Constantinople, geographic and economic center of the area. Mehmed's death from a stroke in 1421 may have saved the city from attack.

MURAD II

The idea of the continuity of the state and the sultan's relationship to governmental power had so grown that Mehmed's closest advisers, of whom Bayezid Pasha was one, concealed his death for forty days until his son and successor Murad II arrived in Bursa from Amasya to take charge. Nearly eighteen years old, Murad had resided with his advisers and tutors at Amasya. At the time of his father's death, Murad had three surviving brothers—two were blinded and therefore made ineligible for the succession; the third, Mustafa, afraid that Murad would kill him as Bayezid had strangled Yakub, fled from his Anatolian governorship with his tutors to the protection of the Karaman family in Konya.

Murad surrounded himself with representatives of old Ottoman families such as the Chandarli and Evrenos families, and with leaders of the new courtiers like Bayezid Pasha, although this latter group was less numerous. At the very outset of Murad's reign the Byzantine emperor freed the old pretender Mustafa, son of Bayezid I, who defeated and killed Bayezid Pasha, seized Gallipoli with the emperor's aid, and invaded Anatolia. Murad rallied and drove them back to Europe. In 1422 Genoese cooperation in transporting his troops across the Straits permitted him to catch and kill the pretender Mustafa and the rebels in Edirne.

Murad raged at the emperor for his duplicity and ordered resumption of the siege of Constantinople. With prodigious effort, much enthusiasm, and the use of breaching cannon for the first time in Ottoman history, Murad and his soldiers stormed the walls. After two months of failure Murad lifted the siege to meet a new threat in Anatolia: Byzantine diplomacy with the Karamans had brought Murad's brother Mustafa from his refuge in Konya to an unsuccessful attack upon Bursa.

Though Mustafa was caught and hanged, and the threat of a new lengthy civil war averted, Murad never resumed the attack upon Constantinople. The emperor agreed to pay the Ottomans a yearly tribute and surrender most Byzantine territory outside the walls. In Anatolia, Murad judiciously alternated between diplomacy and force. Murad married the daughter of one amir, and by 1430 he had brought all of western Anatolia fully under Ottoman control. Although the Karaman amir sued for peace, there was an uneasy relationship with Karaman; whenever Murad became deeply engrossed in Europe, war with the princes of Konya became imminent and sometimes necessary.

Murad's greatest efforts were expended in Europe, and there lay his greater gains. The sultan encouraged privateers whose ships in the Aegean Sea raided commerce, while he also organized an Ottoman fleet into which the privateers were ultimately incorporated. Using this naval strength based at Gallipoli as well as the army, in 1430 Salonica was retaken from Venice after a long struggle. Upon the accession to the throne of Hungary of Ladislaus, king of Lithuania and Poland, he invaded Ottoman territory, in 1443 winning numerous strongholds and bringing Murad to the edge of ruin. Nevertheless, Murad and King Ladislaus concluded an honorable peace in 1444, each promising not to invade the other's territory for ten years. Murad had also temporarily defeated the Karamans and John Hunyadi, Ottoman vassal governor of Transylvania.

OTTOMAN SOCIETY AND CULTURE

Evidently Murad felt that since he had made peace with his enemies the time was right for retirement from an active rule. He was forty years old and had been sultan for twenty-three years. His two older sons having died, Murad abdicated in favor of his young third son, Mehmed, who went to Edirne with Khalil Pasha Chandarli as grand vizir. Murad himself withdrew to his favorite residence in Manisa, where he intended to live in ease and peace with poets, mystics, theologians, and men of letters. He wished to pursue the futuwwa, the ideal life, modestly studying and writing in quiet contemplation.

It was the time of an incipient Turkish renaissance. The Turkish language, as spoken at the Ottoman court and in western Anatolia, became a medium of cultured expression. Konya and Bursa in Anatolia and Edirne in Europe were its centers; its patrons were the Karaman and Ottoman families and their courts. Heretofore, Persian and Arabic were the languages of poetry, records, and education. But Turkish was growing more popular. Many Persian and Arabic works were translated into Ottoman Turkish, and poets were held in high esteem. Sufis were numerous and earnestly venerated.

Ottoman history was first cultivated under Murad, when a "romantic" movement arose. Until this time, Ottoman chronicles were legendary sagas of ghazis and their great deeds. Under Murad, there developed a new and more formal Ottoman history, which included stories of illustrious ancestors going back to the most noble of Turkish tribes—the Oghuz tribe. Beautiful tales were written of Osman's ancestors riding with 400 horsemen into Anatolia. Naturally bringing victory to the side they aided, they were richly rewarded. In this manner the Ottomans are supposed to have received their start! It must be remembered that at the time of Murad's retirement 150 years had passed since Osman's first conquests, and that in a new and rapidly evolving society not many people could correctly relate the exploits of their great-great-great-grandfathers.

Murad's intellectual and cultural concerns were reflected in the education of his children. He employed distinguished scholars, many of whom also held important army or administrative positions, as teachers for the princes. Included with the princes in the palace school were other boys, some of whom were captives of war or sons of distinguished vassals of the sultan. Murad desired not only to educate his own sons but also to train other youths in discipline, integrity, and moral values that might serve state and sultan intelligently and faithfully. Proof of the value and thoroughness of this school was first demonstrated in the education and ability of Murad's son, Mehmed.

MILITARY DEVELOPMENTS

For a few months all went well in the Ottoman state. Murad had retired to Manisa, and the boy Mehmed II was surrounded by advisers and teachers at Edirne. But the Hungarians broke the peace in the autumn of 1444, perhaps thinking that the treaty with Murad was invalidated by his retirement and that victory would be possible against a boy ruler. Murad was recalled from his retirement and crushed the crusader invaders near Varna on the Black Sea. King Ladislaus, who had insisted upon breaking the treaty against Hunyadi's admonitions, lost his life, and his army was defeated and dispersed.

The Ottomans now easily overran Serbia and Bosnia. Since Ottomans were tolerant of Christianity whereas Hungarians in their brief sway had begun to impose Latin Catholic rites upon Serbian and Bosnian Orthodox churches, many fortresses freely opened their gates to Murad.

With this affair apparently settled, Murad abdicated a second time in 1445 and returned to Manisa. It was not long, however, before an open rebellion against Mehmed II by janissaries seeking back pay brought Murad back to active rule in Edirne. The ringleaders were executed, imprisoned, or exiled from the capital, and the sultan's authority was fully restored.

This episode was a harbinger of future grave difficulties that Ottoman sultans would experience with janissary and other imperial troops, who were hardened professional soldiers. Simply educated, reared and trained exclusively for warfare, and not too well paid because of the expectation that they would be richly rewarded from plunder won on campaigns, the janissaries felt their power and importance and were easily induced to demand favors of many kinds. Between them and other groups of Ottoman supporters—the sipahi cavalry and old families who provided administrators like those closest to Murad—rivalry was often bitter.

For this reason, in about 1430 Murad had reinstituted a draft (devshirmeh) procedure for the janissary corps. Every few years army officers toured the rural districts, conscripting Christian boys between the ages of ten and fifteen. These youths were brought to Edirne. As slaves of the sultan they were parceled out among court officers, the sipahis, and the sultan himself. The draftees from the Balkans were sent to Anatolia and vice versa. After a few years of growth, toughening, Islamization, and Turkification in language and customs they were returned to Edirne, where they received military training and were assigned to a janissary barracks. The more favored were attached to the palace; the very best attended the princes' school, whereupon any position in the state was open to them. At first employed to augment the ranks of the janissaries when wars and raids failed to yield sufficient captives, the draft was justified as another form of taxation for the subject communities, analogous to poll taxes except they paid taxes in boys! More significant was the fact that the most vigorous and capable youths were being removed from their villages and raised as Ottomans. Some observers remarked that this policy helped to keep the Christian population in subjection by drawing away future leaders. Some families turned to Islam rather than lose their sons.

It was also the custom for vassal Christian princes who were permitted to retain their lands to send sons as hostages to the sultan's court. One such hostage was George Kastriota, who was sent to Murad II. He was educated in the princes' school, served in various responsible posts under Murad, but deserted in 1443. Skanderbeg, as he was now called, returned to his native Albania, where for twenty-five years he led resistance movements and guerrilla warfare against Murad and Mehmed II.

After the janissary revolt of 1445 was put down, Murad did not again retire but engaged in campaigns in Europe. Twice he entered Albania in pursuit of Skanderbeg. Bulgaria was fully absorbed into the Ottoman system of direct rule, and much of it was settled by Turkish-speaking nomads. In 1448, Murad drove John Hunyadi (now in control of Hungary) out of Serbia, defeating him on the plains of Kossovo. Early in 1451, the aged warrior (about fifty years old) died in Edirne. The young Mehmed, now grown to manhood, when apprised in Manisa of his father's death, supposedly leaped on his horse and raced to the capital, Edirne, to take charge.

MEHMED II

In some ways Mehmed II's character was an extension of his father's. Since he had the benefits of the princes' school, his mind was well trained. He knew literary Turkish, Arabic, Persian, and Greek, and was able to converse in ordinary Serbian and Italian. He enjoyed philosophy and poetry, and was familiar with the classical poetry of Iran, Greece, and Rome. Mehmed was an accomplished poet himself and gathered about him poets from the four corners of the Muslim world. He loved history, particularly biographies of Alexander the Great and the Caesars. The study of war and of everything associated with war aroused his interest greatly. Every Ottoman, even of the royal family, had a trade—perhaps because of the akhi heritage—and Mehmed was an accomplished gardener. Later, between campaigns and for relaxation, he worked in the gardens of the royal palace.

With regard to administration, however, Mehmed was quite unlike his father. Thoroughness and efficiency combined with great energy and promptness became the order of the day whenever Mehmed was present. Delay and procrastination were foreign to his nature, and he was known for his furious temper. He showed remarkable toleration in religious matters.

In many respects Murad had not been very businesslike in his administration, and Mehmed spent the first year of his reign reorganizing the government, particularly the treasury. Tax rates were raised, monopolies established, and pious foundations (Arabic, waqf/awqaf; Turkish, vakif/evkaf) were confiscated to the benefit of the imperial treasury. The entire administration of the royal palace was surveyed, registers of the troops scrutinized, and soldiers' pay increased. Some provincial governors were removed; others were promoted on the basis of merit. One unhappy episode was Mehmed's order that his only brother, an infant, be drowned in his bath, thus perpetuating the custom begun by Bayezid I of eliminating rival heirs. Years later, Mehmed decreed that whoever of his sons seized the throne should execute his brothers.

CAPTURE OF CONSTANTINOPLE

With the coming of 1452 Mehmed began his plans for taking Constantinople. Peace with Serbia, Hungary, and the Karamans had been arranged, so as to deter their aiding the Byzantines. Munitions were gathered: armor, bows, arrows, mortars, cannon, balls, gunpowder, timbers, and war articles of every sort. Although Ottoman siege cannons were rather clumsy, they were quite effective and technologically equivalent to those first used by French forces in the 1430s. At Gallipoli a fleet was assembled and new ships built. To control the Bosphorus Mehmed ordered the construction of a fortress on its European shore opposite the fortifications built on the Asian side half a century earlier by his great-grandfather. Erected just above the narrowest point of the Bosphorus, this fortress harbored cannons whose range controlled the passage of ships.

While the siege began in 1452, the true attack upon Constantinople started in April 1453. More than 50,000 of the best soldiers that Mehmed could muster were assembled for the assault. The Ottoman fleet numbered about 200 ships. For fifty-four days cannonballs pounded the land walls of the city. The sea walls were bombarded by the fleet, but the walls along the Golden Horn could not be reached. Mortars from the shores of the Bosphorus did sink some Greek ships on the Golden Horn, but a heavy chain from Galata to Constantinople effectively closed the Horn to Mehmed's ships. Not to be thwarted, Mehmed constructed a greased wooden runway from the shore of the Bosphorus up the hill of Beyoglu (Pera) and down the slope to the Golden Horn. About seventy ships of the Ottoman fleet were hauled up over the incline and slid down to the Golden Horn, from where they threw their stone cannonballs on the city walls.

Cut off completely and bombarded from every side, the defenders of Constantinople still resisted the attacks. The Genoese and other Italians in Galata and Pera gave little assistance, and most of the 50,000 inhabitants of the once great city acted supremely indifferent to their fate, perhaps because Emperor Constantine in desperation had called for aid from the west and announced submission to the pope in exchange for promises of soldiers. A few came, but help was entirely inadequate.

A stupendous assault was launched on May 29, 1453; cannon fire breached the walls, and the city was taken. Following the custom of that age, the conquering troops had complete license to pillage the city and enslave its inhabitants, except that no public buildings could be touched. Mehmed entered the city, and the plundering ceased. He went to Hagia Sophia, where Muslim prayers were said. He then quickly turned to the problem of the city that the Ottomans usually called Istanbul. A governor was appointed; inhabitants were encouraged to remain by exempting them from taxes and by giving them back their houses; the sultan ransomed many on the condition that they would stay; the army was disbanded; and Mehmed temporarily returned to Edirne.

The economic, military, and cultural effects of the capture of Constantinople have usually been exaggerated. Later centuries developed a myth that the fall of Constantinople blocked the trade routes to the Far East, thereby forcing the age of discovery and the voyages of Columbus. According to another legend, the fall of Constantinople resulted in the migration of Greek monks and manuscripts to Italy, thus initiating the Renaissance. Another story has related that the fall of Constantinople removed the Balkan bastion, at once enabling the Ottoman Turks to conquer the whole peninsula of southeast Europe. All three of these myths have been exploded.

Nevertheless, the emotional impact of the fall of Constantinople on the people of the fifteenth century should not be minimized. To Christian Europe, both Orthodox and Catholic, the great imperial city had fallen. In a sense the Roman Empire had finally come to an end. Now Ottoman expansion seemed a more threatening and immediate danger. To Muslims, the fall of Constantinople was a great and glorious achievement that Islamic rulers and armies had attempted many times in the past. To them, Constantinople was the majestic city of imperial tradition whose conquest had been a goal of the great caliphs. Now a Muslim state had accomplished the impossible, and consequently Mehmed II received great acclaim and respect. To the Ottomans, it was the conquest of the natural capital and center of their state.

Since the time of Bayezid I the incorporation of Constantinople in the Ottoman state had been a logical and necessary step, but it had been long in coming. Its acquisition served as the keystone in the Ottoman Empire, which would now enter into a long period of dynamic expansion and development.

References

References in Chapters 13 and 14 are important for this chapter.

BABINGER, FRANZ: *Mehmed the Conqueror and His Time.* Edited by William C. Hickman. Translated by Ralph Manheim. Princeton, N.J.: Princeton University Press, 1978. This excellently annotated classic biography emphasizes diplomacy, military, and political history.

COOK, M. A., ED.: *Studies in the Economic History of the Middle East from the Rise of Islam to the Present Day.* London: Oxford University Press, 1970. All the articles are by major authors, and many explore new ideas.

INALCIK, HALIL: *The Ottoman Empire: Conquest, Organization and Economy.* London: Variorum, 1978. A collection of sixteen articles dealing with Ottoman conquests and organization, the economy, and decline and reform.

KRITOVOULOS: *History of Mehmed the Conqueror.* Translated by Charles T. Riggs. Princeton, N.J.: Princeton University Press, 1954. A contemporary account by a Greek in the service of the Ottomans.

RUNCIMAN, STEVEN: *The Fall of Constantinople, 1453.* Cambridge, England: Cambridge University Press, 1969. The author has scoured the sources and presented in great detail and with much understanding a very readable account of the taking of the city.

TURSUN BEG: *The History of Mehmed the Conqueror.* Translated by Halil Inalcik and Rhoads Murphy. Minneapolis, Minn.: Bibliotheca Islamica, 1978. In addition to a facsimile text of a manuscript of the work by Tursun Beg in the original Turkish, the translators have provided a summary translation and a discussion of the author.

Expansion of the Ottoman Empire

The reestablishment of the Ottoman Empire after Timur's destruction and then the conquest of Istanbul opened the way for rapid expansion of the imperial borders. Three rulers—Mehmed II, Bayezid II, and Selim I—directed the wars and diplomacy that resulted in a doubling of the size of the state. Despite struggles over succession to the sultanate, advances were made in rebuilding Istanbul as the imperial capital and making institutional arrangements for the governance of the many non-Muslim subjects added to the realm.

MEHMED II'S CONQUESTS

Beyond taking Istanbul (Constantinople) in 1453, Mehmed II, called Fatih ("the Conqueror") by his subjects, extended the periphery of his empire substantially. Campaigns were scheduled almost every year. Operations were conducted in the Balkans and Anatolia, and from Venice and southern Italy to Iran and the Crimea. Affairs of any one area involved those of others, and Mehmed was unable to isolate his many international and domestic problems to deal with one at a time. Moreover, Venetian envoys were plotting at every court to swell the number of his enemies and bring his downfall.

Ottoman campaigns, colonization, and government had been proceeding in the Balkans for a century. Nonetheless, Ottoman rule was still not effective in several regions, and many provinces that were tied to the Ottomans by a kind of vassalage or alliance were not integrated units of the state. Byzantine practices persisted in local administration, especially on church and monastery lands. Conversion to Islam was very slow; the languages of the conquered peoples persisted even when Ottoman judicial, fiscal, and landholding structures were introduced. The Ottomans ruled about 4 million non-Muslims in the Balkans, whose territory provided much of the revenue of the state. The sultan enacted a number of reforms; probably the most important was a land reform in the entire empire, whereby the state regained direct control of the taxes of thousands of villages that had fallen into private hands (this reform was reversed under Mehmed's successor). In addition, semiautonomous local lords were ousted in parts of the Balkans in favor of more direct rule, and Christians were retained as holders of some revocable land grants, although most of these grants were given to Muslims.

Pressure on the Balkans, however, was maintained continuously. Greece, except for a few Venetian ports, was conquered, with Athens falling to the Ottomans in 1456. In the 1460s Serbia and Bosnia were subjected to Ottoman rule and organized as regular imperial provinces. Wallachia and Moldavia were forced to become allies. Skanderbeg was checked in Albania, and after his death in 1468 much of Albania and Herzegovina became provinces of the empire.

Mehmed also pursued a vigorous policy in Anatolia and the east. The most resistant foe to the Ottomans had been the Karaman dynasty of the Bursa region; in 1468 Karaman opposition was broken. Later Cilicia in southeastern Anatolia was acquired, and as his reign closed Mehmed became involved in family quarrels of the Dhu al-Qadr of Diyarbakir. The entire Mediterranean coast of Anatolia was now in Ottoman hands. Since Istanbul and the Straits were now Ottoman, Mehmed moved northward and eastward, hoping to control the Black Sea shores. In 1461, with the cooperation of the navy from Gallipoli, Mehmed forced the surrender of the Greek emperor of Trebizond, thus obliterating the last remnant of the Byzantine Empire.

These activities led the Ottomans into conflict with the Aq Quyunlu, who dominated parts of Iran, Armenia, and eastern Anatolia. Venetian ambassadors traveled to the court of the Aq Quyunlu leader Uzun Hasan at Tabriz and encouraged war against Mehmed, so as to lessen Ottoman pressure upon Venice and its European territory. The danger to the Ottoman state was great, since the alliance of Venice, Hungary, Uzun Hasan, and the Karaman ruler threatened the empire on all fronts in the 1460s and early 1470s. However, Mehmed II collected a mighty army of more than 200,000 soldiers, including his two sons, Mustafa and Bayezid, his grand vizir, and Gedik Ahmed Pasha, a burly general who had risen from the ranks of the ordinary janissaries. Using cannons and handguns to which the Aq Quyunlu were unaccustomed, the sultan defeated Uzun Hasan in 1473 in eastern Anatolia; after this defeat the Karaman pretenders finally disappeared. Next the Crimea, which was ruled by Turkish Tatar khans, came under Ottoman aegis in 1475. Except for the coast between the Crimea and the Danube River, the Black Sea was now an Ottoman lake.

To the south of Istanbul in the Aegean Sea, conflict between Venice and the Ottoman Empire grew. To ensure control of the Aegean coast of Anatolia and permit Ottoman conquests in southern Greece, it was necessary to incorporate the Aegean Islands into the empire. This was particularly important because Venetians and pirates used these islands and their numerous harbors as bases to harry the Ottoman coast and hold up trade. Mehmed's fleet, therefore, captured these islands, and for fifteen years (1463–1478) he was at war sporadically with Venice. The Ottomans were unable to defeat Venetian fleets at sea, but they captured strategic bases that would later enable them to extend their naval power substantially.

Pressure on Venetian outposts along the Dalmatian coast in the Adriatic Sea area was also constant, and Ottoman raiders from Albania and Bosnia kept alarms sounding on St. Mark's Square in Venice. In 1477 Ottoman raiders descended to the Italian plain north of Venice. At night Venetian senators from the roof of St.

Mark's could see Ottoman campfires and burning villages. When autumn came the Ottomans returned home laden with booty. Venice concluded peace with Mehmed and recognized his island acquisitions.

In 1480 an Ottoman army under Gedik Ahmed Pasha crossed the Adriatic and took Otranto in the heel of the Italian peninsula, thus establishing a bridgehead for the conquest of Italy. Gedik Ahmed wintered there, but upon Mehmed's sudden death in May 1481 the expedition to Otranto was withdrawn, never to be launched again. The conqueror was dead. Secrecy was maintained in the Ottoman Empire until a successor could ascend the throne. Bells pealed in Europe when the news arrived.

ISTANBUL AND THE ORTHODOX PATRIARCHATE

Istanbul in 1453 was only a half-populated city, which had been dying slowly for more than two centuries. Mehmed II viewed the task of repopulating the city as even a mightier one than the actual conquest. He freed many prisoners, encouraged others to remain, exempted many from taxation, and conducted a census in 1455. In later conquests inhabitants of other towns were ordered to move to Istanbul, so by the end of the century Istanbul became the most populous city in Europe and the Middle East. Mehmed also supported the bazaar, including a covered market. Many pious endowments (awqaf) were established to promote the welfare of Muslims. The Christian population, as in most Ottoman cities, was not subjected to the devshirmeh.

When Mehmed "Fatih" entered Istanbul, he learned that the Orthodox Christian patriarch was dead. Appreciating the need for the election of a new patriarch, Mehmed indicated confidence in the teacher and philosopher George Scholarius, who had long been popular with the Greeks of the city and in disfavor with the last Byzantine emperor because he headed the anti-Catholic faction. Duly elected, Scholarius took the name Gennadios. Mehmed recognized him as leader of the Christians in Istanbul. Gennadios was charged with responsibility for the obedience, conduct, and life of the Greek Orthodox people and their relationship to the Ottoman government. Thus, in many ways Orthodox Christians were encouraged to reside in Istanbul and allowed to live according to their own ways and laws as long as they did not come into conflict with the administration of the government and the lives of Muslim subjects. In like manner, Mehmed II recognized a head of the Armenian Christian community in Istanbul, as well as other Armenian religious leaders for other regions. The chief Jewish rabbi of Istanbul was treated as preeminent among the rabbis of the empire, while the heads of local Jewish communities in other cities were acknowledged as locally autonomous leaders.

Islam and Muslims nevertheless received priority in government policy. Public buildings were reserved for the state, and many churches were converted into mosques; nearly 200 new mosques were built by the imperial authorities. The outstanding example was Justinian's great church Hagia Sophia, which became the Muslim Aya Sofya. Mehmed II and his successors gave much church-owned land to Sufi establishments. During the siege the Ottomans discovered what they claimed to be the burial site of the hero Abu Ayyub al-Ansari (Eyup), the standard-bearer of the prophet Muhammad, who had died in 668 during an earlier siege near the walls of Constantinople in the days of the caliph Muawiyah. Ayyub's remains were entombed in a mosque-mausoleum–Sufi residence near the Golden Horn, where subsequent Ottoman sultans were ceremoniously girded with the sword of their authority.

As his first residence Fatih built a large palace in the most populous part of the city; he occupied it for about twelve years whenever he was in Istanbul. Here, about the year 1465, a new palace was completed, which remained the chief domicile of sultans until the nineteenth century. The new palace was erected on the site of the acropolis of ancient Byzantium on the point of land between the Golden Horn and the Sea of Marmara. Facing the entrance to the Bosphorus, it was the most beautiful and spectacular spot in the city for an imperial residence. It was soon popularly called Topkapi Saray ("Cannon Gate Palace") because of the heavily fortified gate at the tip of the point of land. Yet Fatih passed many seasons at the palace in Edirne or in Bursa. Edirne remained the favorite summer headquarters of sultans until the eighteenth century.

BAYEZID AND JEM

When Mehmed II died in 1481, he left two sons. Bayezid, aged thirty-three, was governor of Amasya, the old ghazi center. Jem, aged twenty-one, was governor of Konya, the former Seljuk capital. Since Amasya was eight days' ride from Istanbul whereas Konya was only four, the younger son had an advantage in obtaining control of the central administration. The janissaries, the pages of the palace, and the government officials who were slaves of the sultan and recipients of the palace school training preferred Bayezid. Mehmed's last grand vizir, however, belonged by birth to the old Muslim families of Anatolia and was partial to Jem. He tried to conceal Mehmed's death and secretly dispatched couriers to Jem. However, Mehmed's death became known, whereupon the slave officials and the janissaries seized control, murdered the grand vizir, impaled his messengers to Jem, and awaited Bayezid's appearance. They chose the latter because they considered his residence of twenty-five years or more at Amasya as wedding him to the ghazi tradition, of which they were fast becoming the heirs. Moreover, recognizing the so-called law of fratricide, Bayezid had cleverly attached through marriages and political friendship several figures of the government hierarchy to his candidacy. Jem's chief difficulty was his comparative youth; Bayezid for years had been gathering his party for the eventual day. To break through a cordon of officers blocking the gate to the imperial palace of Topkapi, Bayezid pledged a handsome gift of money to every janissary, declared an amnesty for all crimes committed in the interregnum, and, most significantly, agreed to appoint to the vizirship only men who were soldiers or palace slaves.

Jem, with forces from Karaman and Konya, occupied Bursa and challenged Bayezid for the throne. Gedik Ahmed was recalled from Otranto and with the army that Mehmed II had gathered defeated Jem, who fled to Mamluk Egypt whence he made the holy pilgrimage to Mecca. Bayezid offered him a princely income if he would live peacefully in Jerusalem, but Jem returned in 1482 and made a second vain attempt at the throne. Escaping to the protection of the Knights of St. John on the island of Rhodes, he was held in custody by them and used to obtain a favorable treaty of peace with the Ottomans. The knights subsequently moved him to their castles in France, where he fell into the hands of Charles VIII. Later, Jem was presented to the pope, then was borrowed by Charles in 1494, from Pope Alexander VI, ostensibly to participate in a crusade against the Ottomans. Jem, however, died of a fever in Naples the next year.

WARS OF BAYEZID II

Between 1482 and 1495, Bayezid's fear of his brother's return somewhat restricted his foreign activities. Yet the organization of the Ottoman state was conditioned to aggressive expansion. When campaigns were not in progress, sipahis, janissaries, and the court became uneasy. During these years, therefore, a number of expeditions along the Dalmatian coast and into Hungary were undertaken and a large navy was built. Although these raids were usually indecisive, they were rewarding in plunder. Akkerman, on the Black Sea at the mouth of the Dniester River, was taken, and Wallachia and Moldavia were subdued.

In this early period of Bayezid's reign, war broke out with the Mamluk sultans of Egypt. Persistent dynastic difficulties among the Dhu al-Qadr involved the Mamluks and Ottomans in disputes. In 1484, after aid and asylum had been given to Jem, open war broke out. The peace concluded in 1491 left Egypt in possession of the disputed border areas, but no difficulties appeared for two decades.

Following Jem's death, Bayezid pursued a more aggressive policy in the west. The tempo of Ottoman raids along the Dalmatian coast increased; ports rang with the noise of carpenters, coopers, and caulkers constructing war galleys. When war broke out with Venice in 1499, the Ottoman navy of about 250 vessels defeated the Venetian fleet in a great sea engagement at Navarino. Peace was not concluded until 1503. The war further eclipsed Venetian power in Greece and the eastern Mediterranean, and Ottoman sea power became strongly established. Thereafter in Bayezid's reign, contingents of the Ottoman navy raided throughout the Mediterranean, and Ottoman merchants prospered throughout the great inland sea.

Back in the east, about the time the war with Venice ended, a new figure emerged on the Ottoman frontier—the Shiite Shah Ismail of Iran, who kindled a religious and military enthusiasm in the peoples of Iran and eastern and southern Anatolia. Shah Ismail's doctrines proved popular, and open revolt among the Turkoman tribes developed in 1511. Ismail's followers were called qizilbash ("red head") because of the red hats they wore. The rebels besieged and took Konya, seized Kutahya (Ottoman Anatolian army headquarters), and impaled the Ottoman commander in chief. Despite the eclectic nature of Ottoman Sunnite Islam and the fact that Bayezid II was enough of a mystic that one of his nicknames was Sufi, the Ottomans could not permit the religious ideas of a foreign monarch free rein within their state. The Safavid rebels were defeated in a battle against an army that included 4000 janissaries under the grand vizir and three Ottoman princes.

SELIM'S SUCCESSION

After the end of the Venetian war Bayezid suffered poor health and was often carried on a stretcher so that the troops might see him and know he still lived. With each illness his sons became exceedingly nervous about the future. Of his eight sons, only three remained in 1511: Korkud at Manisa; Ahmed at Amasya; and Selim, the youngest, at Trabzon. Each was jockeying for advantages and seeking favors and strategic appointments for friends and sons as the protracted struggle for power weakened the central government. The janissaries and the soldiers preferred Selim, since he was the most devoted to warfare. Bayezid and the high officials advanced Ahmed as a solid administrator. The poets, philosophers, and theologians supported Korkud, for he was one of them.

Selim moved his forces to Edirne, and when Bayezid and his close advisers began granting authority to Ahmed, Selim seized that city. To gain friends in Anatolia, Ahmed had donned the red hat of the qizilbash. Upon this development the staunchly Sunnite Bayezid called Selim to Istanbul in 1512 and abdicated in his favor. A month later Bayezid died while en route to retirement.

For thirty-one years Bayezid II, a peace-loving, scholarly, and contemplative person, had governed the Ottoman Empire. He spent years in organizing the administration of the government and took great interest in the palace school, often quizzing the students himself. Trade flourished, with merchants from Venice and Genoa thronging to Istanbul, and merchants from the east and the Arab lands coming to Bursa. The Ottomans exported copper and timber and imported silk, wheat, and spices. Bayezid and many janissaries and court officers belonged to Sufi orders, yet he was strict with Muslims because his father's unorthodox ways had disturbed him. One of Bayezid's first acts as sultan was to clear from the palace the pictures of his father painted by Gentile Bellini. Despite this religious rigor, during his reign about 200,000 or more Jews came to Istanbul, Izmir, Edirne, Salonica, and Palestine when they were driven from Spain even before but especially during 1492.

Selim I (nicknamed Yavuz, meaning "stern" or "inflexible") gave a bonus to each soldier upon his accession, as had become the custom in securing the throne. But he entered the palace by a side gate in order not to bow openly to their demands. The facts were that he held only Rumeli with Istanbul, Ahmed controlling most of Anatolia from Amasya. Upon Selim's enthronement, Ahmed tried to take Bursa. Selim crossed to Asia and carried the attack against Ahmed, who resisted until the following spring, when he was defeated and strangled. Meanwhile, five of Selim's nephews and his brother Korkud were similarly disposed of. Because Ahmed had obtained considerable support from the qizilbash of Anatolia, Selim decided to curb the growth of the sect, particularly since it was popular in the difficult mountainous and frontier areas of Karaman and Diyarbakir. Late in 1513, Selim stationed troops in all parts of the empire, and at a given notice about 40,000 were cut down. By transporting others to Europe, Selim hoped that he had eradicated religious dissent in Anatolia.

WAR AGAINST SAFAVID IRAN

In this ferocious way Selim acted against Shah Ismail in Anatolia, where he was supported by qizilbash and regarded by many as a holy saint. Following Ismail's interference in the affairs of Dhu al-Qadr and the Ottoman succession, and Iranian invasions, Selim sent the fleet with his commissariat to Trabzon. With several thousand janissaries, the grand vizir, and troops of Rumeli and Anatolia, supported by batteries of light artillery, he marched eastward. Shah Ismail scorched the earth as he retreated; Selim's soldiers complained as they were driven on, but Selim would not turn back. In August 1514 at Chaldiran, northeast of Lake Van and not far from Mount Ararat, Selim's cannon and his army's superior numbers turned the tide against the Iranian cavalry. Ismail fled, leaving even his harem to be captured.

Although the victory at Chaldiran momentarily settled Selim's problems on his eastern frontier, in no way did it destroy the new state arising in Iran or eliminate the Safavid dynasty and its spreading of Shiite Islam. (Safavid Iran will be discussed at greater length in Chapter 19.)

THE CONQUEST OF EGYPT

With Shah Ismail's defeat, Sultan Selim began to use the title shah and sometimes shahinshah ("king of kings"), or padishah ("father of kings"). More important, the balance of power among the three largest Middle Eastern Muslim states—Safavid Iran, Mamluk Egypt, and the Ottoman Empire—was fully upset in favor of the last. Ismail had written to the Mamluk sultan for aid against Selim, and in 1516 the Mamluks at last marched into Syria in full force. Selim as usual took the offensive, crushing the Mamluk army at Marj Dabiq, north of Aleppo. Again it was a victory of artillery and muskets in the hands of a well-disciplined, well-paid, and well-supplied army over an undisciplined, unpaid, and disloyal motley force. Aleppo, Damascus, and Jerusalem opened their gates to the Ottomans. New governors were appointed everywhere, but little else was changed. Taxes continued to be farmed; the amirs of the Lebanon Mountains became only nominal vassals; and Jews and Christians were treated well.

By January 1517, Selim I and his army were on the outskirts of Cairo, which they stormed and took after several days of fighting. A quarter of a century earlier, the Mamluk power had defeated the Ottomans in several campaigns over successive years. Now Selim took their measure with little difficulty and captured the Mamluk Empire in one campaign. The Mamluk government had become impoverished and could no longer meet its commitments or protect the state.

Selim was sultan from the Danube to the cataracts of the Nile. By extension, he became sovereign of Mecca and Medina, along with Jerusalem the principal holy cities of Islam. Shah Ismail hastened to congratulate him on his new territories, and in most parts of the Middle East the Ottoman Empire was now the dominant power after the conquest of the central Arabic-speaking lands.

By midsummer 1518, back in Istanbul after an absence of two years, Selim faced the question of the meaning of the extensive conquests. At Aleppo the puppet Abbasid caliph al-Mutawakkil, whom the Mamluks brought along on the expedition, fell into Selim's possession. Selim took the caliph to Istanbul, where he was confined to the state prison. Much later, in 1543, he was permitted to return to Cairo, where he died, thereby finally ending the last shadow of the Abbasid dynasty. The Ottoman ruler had used the title of "caliph" since Murad I, a title that was now nearly meaningless. With the new dominions, they added to their titles "servant of the two holy sanctuaries" of Mecca and Medina, and saw themselves as protectors of Islam and the pilgrimage to the Hijaz, and as the most powerful of the Muslim rulers, in accordance with the will of God.

In Selim's long absence his only son, Suleiman, wielded power in Edirne; Piri Pasha, the great admiral, managed Istanbul; Bursa was governed by Hersekoglu Ahmed Pasha, several times grand vizir and cavalry officer under Mehmed II and Bayezid II. Even under such able guidance the affairs of state suffered and the treasury was depleted. Selim remained in Edirne and Istanbul, straightening out accounts, collecting back taxes, and preparing a navy adequate for an attack upon Rhodes. However, cancer struck him in the spring of 1520 and he died that autumn.

SELIM I

Yavuz Selim was a controversial figure. Yavuz means "good," "just," "stern," "inflexible," "ferocious"; he was all of those. He massacred many thousands of qizilbash in his land. Vizirs and generals lost their heads at seemingly the slightest failure. A standard curse came to be, "May you become Selim's vizir!" He was an excellent general, a brilliant poet, and a skillful administrator. His court supported philosophers, historians, theologians, and literary figures of many kinds. His tastes were simple; he read widely, slept little, and was uninterested in his harem. Some attributed his moods to an addiction to opium, but there is no evidence that he used the drug before cancer troubled him.

In Selim's brief reign of eight years Ottoman territory increased greatly—almost exclusively in Asia at the expense of other Muslim states. Dominating the Middle East, the Ottoman Empire became the outstanding Muslim empire of the area, heir of the Umayyad and Abbasid empires, and ruler of the Muslim holy lands. Selim's sole male heir, Suleiman, would reign over the Ottomans for forty-six years. Longer than any among his forefathers, Suleiman's rule brought the Ottoman Empire and the life of its people to the pinnacle of power and luster. The fabric of society and the sources of power and wealth, however, were well fixed by the time of Selim's death. The eminence of Suleiman's period rested on the firm building of his ancestors. A new stage in the history of the Middle East would begin as the Ottoman Empire and its great Muslim rival, the Safavid Empire of Iran, entered into the early modern era.

References

Works mentioned at the end of Chapters 12, 13, 14, and 15 relate to this chapter.

BRUMMETT, PALMIRA: *Ottoman Seapower and Levantine Diplomacy in the Age of Discovery*. Albany: State University of New York Press, 1994. An excellent account of commerce, diplomacy, and warfare during the reigns of Bayezid and Selim.

BRYER, ANTHONY, AND HEATH LOWRY, EDS.: *Continuity and Change in Late Byzantine and Early Ottoman Society*. Birmingham, England, and Washington, D.C.: University of Birmingham Centre for Byzantine Studies/Dumbarton Oaks Research Library and Collection, 1986. Detailed discussions by eight authors on local changes in various regions from late Byzantine to early Ottoman times.

FISHER, SYDNEY NETTLETON: *The Foreign Relations of Turkey, 1481–1512*. Urbana: University of Illinois Press, 1948. Deals with the period of the reign of Bayezid II.

HODGSON, MARSHALL G. S.: *The Venture of Islam: Conscience and History in a World Civilization*. Vol. 3: *The Gunpowder Empires and Modern Times*. Chicago: University of Chicago Press, 1974. This concluding volume in a magisterial survey of the Muslim world's history emphasizes the period from about 1500 to 1900.

INALCIK, HALIL: "Istanbul: An Islamic City." *Journal of Islamic Studies* 1 (1990): 1–23. Istanbul is described during its first years as an Ottoman city, including discussions of Mehmed II's policies and urban institutions.

INALCIK, HALIL, AND DONALD QUATAERT, EDS.: *An Economic and Social History of the Ottoman Empire, 1300–1914*. Cambridge, England: Cambridge University Press, 1994. With outstanding contributions by the editors, Suraiya Faroqhi, Bruce McGowan, and Shevket Pamuk, this lengthy work is a crucial source of information for the history of the Ottoman Empire and its peoples.

LEWIS, BERNARD: *Istanbul and the Civilization of the Ottoman Empire*. Norman: University of Oklahoma Press, 1963. A brilliant survey of the city at its heyday.

MIHAILOVIĆ, KONSTANTIN: *Memoirs of a Janissary*. Translated by Benjamin Stolz, with historical commentary and notes by Svat Soucek. Ann Arbor: University of Michigan Press, 1975. This volume contains the Czech original along with the translation. Very interesting and illuminating.

RUNCIMAN, STEVEN: *The Great Church in Captivity: A Study of the Patriarchate of Constantinople from the Eve of the Turkish Conquest to the Greek War of Independence*. Cambridge, England: Cambridge University Press, 1968. The author contends that under the sultans the patriarch became a lay ruler of a state within a state and that the church endured as a great spiritual force.

CHAPTER 17

Institutions of the Ottoman Empire

At the same time the Ottomans dramatically increased the size and power of their empire through military and diplomatic successes, they also maintained and developed institutions that preserved and strengthened the state. The sultan was at the apex of society through his military leadership, assertion of legitimacy, and supervision of the administration of justice. By using the elaborate imperial palace services, including training facilities in the palace school, the sultan gave direction to a differentiated and flexible system of government. Military, administrative, scribal, financial, and religious officials functioned efficiently, while non-Muslim subjects and foreign residents were carefully regulated. During the fifteenth and sixteenth centuries the Ottoman Empire was a formidable power in the eastern hemisphere in large part because of its institutions.

THE SULTAN

At the head of the Ottoman Empire and at the pinnacle of the various social strata stood the sultan. In the west his government was called the Sublime Porte, presumably because edicts emanated from the principal gate of the palace, called the Gate of Felicity or the Exalted Gate. The sultan's authority was derived from the military power that he controlled, from the allegiance and obedience his subjects gave him, and from his religious legitimacy for Sunnite Muslims.

All military power was under his command. Whether slaves, sipahi cavalry, irregular infantry, vassal troops, or sailors of the fleet, all were supposed to obey his orders. Not that they always did, of course. Groups frequently went on unauthorized raids into Christian lands, often to the embarrassment of the sultan. On numerous occasions the army insisted on abandoning arduous campaigns that took them from the pleasures of Edirne and Istanbul during winter months or from their homes in the provinces. And the janissaries came to demand bonuses from the sultan upon his accession to the throne.

Nevertheless, the armed services were generally loyal, and certainly they were more obedient than similar forces in western Europe were to their kings and emperors. Upholding the sultan was the long tradition of leadership by his family; no other family possessed the prestige of the Ottoman dynasty. Moreover, the slave status of most of the commanding officers and the nature of their rearing gave the sultan such a hold over their lives that deviation from his wishes was risky.

The sultan was head of the Islamic state, defender of the faith, protector of the pilgrimage to Arabia, executor of sacred law, and preserver of the holy relics associated with the prophet Muhammad captured in Cairo by Selim I. Sultans used court ceremonies, special clothing, banners, thrones, and other symbols that emphasized their glory, power, and wealth, and thereby helped create a sense of awe and allegiance among those who saw them. Sunnite Muslims in the empire rendered obedience to the sultan as the most important leader of the faith. Indirectly, Christians and Jews did likewise, since the sultan appointed some of the leaders of their communities.

In general, Ottomans followed the law of Sunnite Islam as developed formerly by earlier Muslims. Four distinct bodies or sources of law existed. Foremost and supreme over the other three stood sacred law (shariah), in accordance with the interpretation of the Hanafite school. Sultan and judges were bound by sacred law, and to ignore it invited disaster. Second stood kanuns, or decrees of sultans, which either were administrative in character or were said to be supplementary to the shariah. Kanuns, for example, dealt with intricate ceremonial law of the Ottoman government and with military, financial, taxation, and police law. Last in the strata of law were adet and urf. Adet was customary law as observed by Turks from time immemorial, by Ottomans, and by peoples conquered by them. Thus, adet in Bosnia might be different from adet in Greece, and both might be different from adet in Ankara. Urf, the sovereignty or will of the ruling sultan, might contravene adet. Kanuns could change adet and urf and could annul or amend other kanuns. Shariah, however, was thought of as inviolable.

The great institutions of the state, established by either sacred law or kanuns, were accepted as emanating from God or from the sultan's supreme will; in no sense were they considered to flow from the will of the people. In examining governmental institutions of the Ottoman Empire it becomes apparent that over the 600 years of the empire's existence the structure and procedures of government were not identical from one century to the next. Ceremonial forms may have often remained the same, but the power, realities, relationships, and types of personnel varied from period to period. All the personnel and their families can be said to have belonged to the ruling class.

At the time of the accession of Suleiman I in 1520 there were four principal divisions of government: the palace services; the military-governing administration; the scribal-financial bureaucracy; and the religious-judicial establishment. In theory and in practice the sultan supervised all of these, and the officials in each were directly or indirectly answerable to him. In common speech all the officials belonged to the military category, and in fact many went on campaigns with the sultan, even if they were not trained to fight. This terminology was used to differentiate them from the reaya category—those Muslims and non-Muslims who did not belong to the Ottoman service and system. The leaders and upper echelons in these four branches of government were, certainly, the elite of state and society, even though many members of these branches, except those of the religious establishment, were technically the slaves of the sultan.

THE PALACE SERVICES

Since the sultan was the supreme head of the government with absolute power, the center of the government was wherever he happened to be. Thus his household gained a special significance and power through the influence that could be exercised upon him. Technically, individuals of the ruling category, with the exception of the land-grant holders, enjoyed membership in the sultan's court and were expected to be a part of his retinue on ceremonial occasions and sometimes in camp. More specifically, the court consisted of the harem of the women, the Inside Service, and the Outside Service.

Until about 1540 there were relatively few in the harem, which was quartered in the Old Palace in Istanbul or in the palaces in Edirne and Demotika. It formed a palace within a palace and included consorts of the sultan (whether wives or concubines), other female relatives, female servants of the court, eunuchs, and girls in training, who ultimately were married to court officers unless they had moved up the well-defined hierarchy in the harem. The greatest woman of the harem was the sultan's mother (valide sultan); after her came the mother of the sultan's firstborn son, and then mothers of other sons.

Male functionaries who took care of the sultan's personal affairs constituted the Inside Service, which was also a kind of harem, in the sense that it preserved the same sense of privacy as the harem of the women. Chief of the entire Inside Service was the general of the gate, a white eunuch. He was invariably a high state dignitary, who served also as grand master of ceremonies for the palace, director in chief of the palace school, and confidential agent of the sultan.

Aside from the white eunuchs, members of the halls were called pages and were young men usually chosen from the elite of the captives and tribute children. Those who did not obtain advancement joined the sultan's cavalry at various levels or received other appointments. The pages remained as court officials or were appointed as provincial governors, high officers in the janissary corps or cavalry, or as officials in the Outside Service or another principal branch of government.

Whereas the Inside Service controlled the relations of the sultan's life within the palace, the Outside Service coordinated his relations with the world outside. In the Outside Service the most important officials for the military-governing administration were the grand vizir and the remaining vizirs. Other high functionaries included the commanders of the janissaries and the sultan's cavalry divisions; officers responsible for palace security, discipline, and protocol; the kitchen service; gardeners; tent pitchers; masters of the hunt and equerries; officers of supply; the treasurer and record keepers; the personal bodyguard; and learned associates of the sultan. These learned associates were members of the religious-judicial establishment, constituted by the sultan's religious teacher and adviser, preachers, muezzins, chanters, readers, astrologers, physicians, and surgeons. The bodyguard was drawn from sons of high officials, choice graduates from the Inside Service, and veteran janissaries—in all about 400 men. Many palace guards were responsible officials, including ambassadors and executioners. The treasurer and record keepers were members of the scribal-financial bureaucracy, which was just beginning to form at this time. Others tended the palace gardens or rowed the sultan's boats on Bosphorus excursions.

At the time of Suleiman I the sultan's court with its three services numbered in the neighborhood of 10,000 persons. Earlier Ottoman sultans lived more simply; several accounts of public ceremonies in mosques and other places report that it was difficult to distinguish the sultan from his attendants. In the court of Mehmed II, magnificence in ceremony appeared. After the conquest of Istanbul, Mehmed II introduced into his bodyguard a company of 100 halberdiers, copied in arms, costumes, and manners from the Byzantine emperor's bodyguard. Rituals of each section of the services became so elaborate and rigid that a law of ceremonies was drawn, and observance of procedure equaled in importance the fulfilling of duties.

Until the reign of Suleiman I the court and its personnel seldom directly affected government and administration. The court served the personal needs of sultan and palace. However, insofar as court officers had direct access to the sultan, they could be influential persons whose favor was eagerly sought. To have a friend highly placed at court was a precious asset.

THE PALACE SCHOOL

In the years of Mehmed II's reign the expanding state, with its growing diversity of population, needed more trained personnel to operate the government. Murad II had faced a similar problem and had resolved it by placing the most promising of his young slaves in a school beside his own sons. Mehmed met the crisis by creating the palace school of Istanbul, which maintained continuous operation until the twentieth century. Students, called pages, were selected after a very careful screening from the boys between ten and fourteen years old among war captives and those drafted from Christian provinces. At the palace school, they received a thorough education in languages, literature, music, law and theology, military science, mathematics, philosophy, administration, taxation, finance, physical training, personal conduct, and sports. It was thought fitting that each should learn a trade in case he should some day have to earn a living as a craftsman. Only the very best lasted through the ten to twelve rigorous years of the course; those unable to continue drew governmental positions equal to their abilities.

Graduates were appointed to administrative posts in various sections of the government. The instructors were drawn from the finest teachers in mosque schools of Bursa, Edirne, and Istanbul and from high administrative offices of the government. All in all, a tremendous spirit was induced in the students; graduates of the palace school formed a firmly knit group that stood apart in conduct and loyalty to the sultanship. Trained by one sultan, they often served his son or held the government together until a successor was determined. At the time of the great success, efficiency, and strength of the Ottoman central government, the entire system was based chiefly on merit. Training and merit would bring appointment to government office and subsequent promotions.

THE MILITARY-GOVERNING ADMINISTRATION

The administrators in the sixteenth century who ran the government and the army were usually products of the Inside Service of the palace. From the end of Mehmed II's reign through most of the following century, the great majority were recruited chiefly, though not entirely, from the tribute and captive children. At the top was the vizir, or chief minister; later, when four ministers had the title of vizir, one was designated first vizir or, under Suleiman I, grand vizir. The sultan delegated his political and executive authority only to his vizirs. When they were in the provinces or on campaign, they could even impose the death penalty. The grand vizir by the law of Mehmed II had power and ceremonial precedence greater than all others and was in all matters the sultan's absolute deputy. He was also entrusted with the sultan's personal seal (the taking away of which signaled dismissal from office). The grand vizir was responsible for a wide array of duties, including personally inspecting the bread supply of Istanbul, so as to make sure that the people of the capital city would have enough to eat.

Murad I had appointed the first grand vizir from one of the prominent Ottoman families. Murad II chose vizirs from the religious-judicial establishment and from the army. Mehmed II picked them from the graduates of the palace school and from Ottoman families of Anatolia, but from the accession of Bayezid II until late in the sixteenth century all were from some part of the palace service.

The vizirs, under the chairmanship of the grand vizir, made up a council, or divan, with whom the sultan conferred on matters of state. Other members of the divan, also often called vizirs, were the head of the janissaries; two chief judges—one for Anatolia and one for Rumeli; two defterdars, or treasurers, again one each for Anatolia and Rumeli; the chief secretary of state; and the chief admiral of the navy. The divan met with the sultan for several hours every Saturday, Sunday, Monday, and Tuesday to decide all matters of government. Analogous to a modern cabinet meeting but also bearing some resemblance to a supreme court, the divan meeting served as a kind of union and capstone to the several branches of the Ottoman government. However, by the time of Mehmed II the sultan, rather than attending divan meetings himself, after each session would receive the divan members to consider their decisions.

It was a rule that no one, not even the other vizirs, could be privy to the grand vizir's dealings with the sultan and to their secret decisions. Yet there were many checks on the authority of the grand vizir, for he was obliged before making any important decision to consult with the other members of the divan. Failure to abide by this procedure was an important factor in the dismissal and execution of the grand vizir Ibrahim in 1536. In addition, the heads of the janissaries, the treasury, and the judiciary also dealt directly with the sultan. (As stated by Mehmed II, not a single penny would enter or leave the treasury unless the head of the treasury ordered it.) The various vizirs and other officials maintained households similar to that of the sultan, with the number of slaves, pages, and aides usually dictated by the position. Rustem Pasha, one of Suleiman's grand vizirs, had 1700 slaves at the time of his death.

Among the various functional divisions of government supervised by the vizirs, the military was the most important. (The earlier conditions of the army were discussed previously in Chapter 15.) By the middle of the sixteenth century the armed forces numbered about 100,000. The heart of the Ottoman army was the janissary corps of over 10,000, many of whom used handguns in battle. The janissaries were commanded by an aga (general) who was directly responsible to the sultan. Usually this aga was an officer trained in the palace, although sometimes he rose from the ranks like other janissary officers. In addition to the ordinary janissaries there were a number of specialized units.

The regular cavalry, generally called sipahi of the Porte to distinguish it from the sipahi land-grant holders, was drawn principally from the ordinary janissaries and the pages of the palace. One special battalion was a kind of foreign legion, consisting of non-Ottoman Turks, Kurds, Arabs, Christian renegades, and horsemen from sources outside the sultan's court.

The Ottomans gave special attention to the technical services, and European observers at that time marveled at the equipment, food, transport, and routes provided for Ottoman armies. Most important were the artillery corps and ordnance services, which cast cannon and manufactured gunpowder. These branches more than any other brought victory after victory to Ottoman armies.

Beginning with Murad II, the navy became an effective but expensive division of the armed services. Development of sea power advanced reign by reign until under Selim I and Suleiman I the navy applied its force widely. Ships were built at many different ports from the Black Sea to the Adriatic, even in the Red Sea. Master shipbuilders working with Greek and Turkish builders, frequently by flares at night, kept the navy in fighting trim. The navy was manned by experienced seafaring men from North African coasts and the eastern Mediterranean area who maintained fleets of 300 to 400 ships. Some Ottoman corsairs raided civilian shipping in much the same fashion as cavalry on land raided Carinthia and Styria, but most of the navy was used for protecting commercial ships and for regular warfare against the enemies of the empire.

One of the most important parts of the Ottoman army came from the provincial sipahis. Whenever a campaign was announced, the governors of most provinces assembled the cavalry who held land grants from the sultan, although some areas of the empire such as Egypt were not part of the sipahi system. Each sipahi came with a predetermined number of warriors in his entourage. They elected their own immediate leaders, although their provincial commander was an appointee of the sultan (after the time of Murad II, frequently a graduate of the palace school). Prior to the period of Suleiman I supreme command of these cavalry rested on the shoulders of two generals—the beylerbey of Anatolia and the beylerbey of Rumeli. (At a later time additional beylerbeys were designated for areas such as Syria, Hungary, and Baghdad.) These two generals acted as vizirs, attended meetings of the divan when convenient, and commanded the wings of the army in battle.

Other branches of the armed forces included irregular, unpaid, volunteer caval-rymen or foot soldiers who answered the call to arms in hopes of booty or the gift of a land grant for valor. In any battle these soldiers usually were used as front-line troops to absorb the first shocks of contact with the enemy.

THE SCRIBAL-FINANCIAL BUREAUCRACY

The scribal-financial bureaucracy consisted of private secretaries, a corps of scribes, and personnel attached to high posts. On a broader base, however, three main branches of the bureaucracy evolved into the executive office of the divan, the chancery, and the treasury. In the early days, individuals holding these offices had usually come from the palace, but by the middle of the sixteenth century most were recruited from the families of Ottoman officials and their clients and from sons and relatives of members of the bureaucracy. Clerks entered the bureaus as apprentices and learned on the job, often simultaneously taking courses to enhance their knowl-edge of law and religious sciences. Promotions in the bureaus came at regular inter-vals, and diligent and intelligent clerks could work their way to the top. Changing from one bureau to another was possible but unlikely except when one had reached a fairly high position.

The divan had a secretarial staff, and as time passed a regular bureau was for-malized to draw up orders. The head of this bureau, in turn, became the first secre-tary of the grand vizir, and in later centuries became a minister of state and foreign minister. The chancellor, who was a member of the divan, checked on all appoint-ments to office (including the assignment of grants of land revenue); had responsi-bility for the land surveys and censuses; kept records of salaries; and recorded all ordinances and commands of the sultan, the divan, the vizirs, and other officials, affixing the seal of authority and the sultan's signature to official documents. The treasurer collected state income and was charged with accounting for all receipts and expenditures of the central government. Until the time of Mehmed II, collec-tion of taxes was generally administered directly by the treasury, chiefly through the land-grant holders, but difficulties in collections later led to a system of tax farming. The Ottoman Empire was greatly decentralized financially; provincial governments collected and spent their own funds; and the religious establishment was supported by revenues from waqf properties granted as endowments and not always funneled through the treasury. Total revenue for the central government in the 1520s has been estimated at about 9.7 million ducats, a greater sum than that spent by contemporary governments in France, Spain, and Iran. The treasurer, like the chancellor, was a member of the divan and responsible only to the sultan.

In addition to these main departments of government, there were a number of others, including the mint, the customs bureaus, commissionerships, governors in the provinces, courts, and endowments that developed bureaucracies of their own. Consequently, there were thousands of secretaries and scribes in the Ottoman Em-pire in the sixteenth century—as evidenced by the tons of records still in the archives in Istanbul.

THE RELIGIOUS-JUDICIAL ESTABLISHMENT

Parallel with the three main branches of government already described stood the religious-judicial establishment. In many ways it was quite separate from the others but not fully independent of them. Since Islam was the religion of the government (with the sultan responsible for the enforcement of Islamic law) and all officials by this time were Muslims, every aspect of government was touched by the religious-judicial establishment. Government personnel at the top levels often moved to other branches of government, particularly from the religious-judicial group into the others. Functionally, this establishment had three main divisions: religion, education, and law.

The learned ulama included such religious functionaries as preachers, mosque caretakers, muezzins, professional leaders of prayers in mosques, heads of Sufi brotherhoods, and sharifs and sayyids. Waqf mosque endowments provided for regular attendants and leaders in mosque activities on a full-time basis. Sufis preached holy wars, spread the faith, and inspired emotional public demonstrations. Sharifs and sayyids traced their descent from Hasan and Husain, grandsons of the prophet Muhammad, wore green turbans, and had numerous personal prerogatives. One was the sultan's standard-bearer and ranked above all officers of the army.

Every mosque, large and small, had a primary, or reading, school, where pupils studied reading, writing, Arabic, and the Quran. Schools of higher learning, called madrasahs (medreses in Turkish), taught grammar, logic, metaphysics, geometry; advanced madrasahs gave courses in law and theology. Students were partially supported by waqf religious endowments; those in law were completely subsidized. Madrasahs were numerous throughout the empire, and in Istanbul every sizable mosque had one or more attached to it. Each stage of education was rigidly graded; those who completed the courses belonged to the learned class. A graduate received a degree and became qualified to teach in a primary school. Further study raised the holder to higher ratings, which permitted him to be a professor, jurist, or judge.

A learned individual who completed a law course, especially those given in Istanbul, usually received an appointment as a teacher, then as a judge (qadi in Arabic, kadi in Turkish) or as a legal consultant (mufti), or as an assistant in the office of one of these. In cities and large towns the sultan appointed a judge who exercised juridical control over the surrounding territory. Slaves of the sultan, sharifs, and sayyids had their own judges and courts. Except in cases that involved Muslims, foreigners and non-Muslims were subject to their own laws. Local officials, beylerbeys, and vizirs also administered justice in their courts except in cases involving the shariah.

The hierarchy of judges was based on carefully classified grades, and advancement usually proceeded from one grade to another. At the top of the system of judges were two judges—one for Europe and one for Asia—who nominated all the other judges of the empire. Appeals progressed from court to court, and sentences were executed by the civil authorities.

Associated with the judge of many cities was a mufti, who was assigned to interpret sacred law for the judge and government officials. Appointed for life, the muftis remained private citizens; in legal matters they had no initiative of action. When a judge, or even a private citizen, was faced with a legal problem, he or she submitted the question in point to the mufti for legal opinion. The mufti examined the law and gave his answer. In Istanbul the mufti, who was usually selected from the ranks of the judges and teachers rather than other muftis, ranked above the judge; and since the sultan and vizirs might pose important questions vital to the life of the whole empire, he became a significant official. Mehmed II added to the mufti's dignity by conferring upon him the title shaikh al-Islam (Şeyhülislam in Turkish), "Leader of Islam," and in ceremonies he took precedence over the grand vizir.

The Muslim religious-judicial establishment within the Ottoman Empire, from the shaikh al-Islam to the lowliest teacher in a mosque primary school, welded the empire together under one type of education and one body of law. Any male Muslim child, if he studied hard and passed the various examinations, might rise in the ranks, just as fighting men and the sultan's slaves advanced on merit in their branches of government. Poverty was no barrier to advancement, but important friends or relatives did help.

Perhaps one-third of the land of the empire was set aside as waqf endowment for various religious activities. In Anatolia and Europe cash endowments were also established, despite the opposition of some men of religion. The money that constituted the basis of the foundation was lent to peasants and townspeople, leading to their increasing indebtedness. Both sorts of endowments, in land and in cash, could be given by sultans and private individuals, and were, at least theoretically, intended for the support of some specific mosque, library, school, almshouse, hospital, bridge, inn, or fountain. The imperial treasury actually handled the funds established by the sultan, and an official was designated as trustee. Private donors often stipulated in the deed of transfer that their own descendants should be administrators of the endowment; thus, much of the revenue from the endowment could be diverted for private and personal gain. Slaves of the sultan found this method a convenience in providing perpetual and inalienable income for their descendants. However, in many cases the property and wealth of men of the state were confiscated by the sultan upon their deaths.

NON-MUSLIM SUBJECTS AND FOREIGNERS

Ottomans were tolerant of non-Muslims in the fashion of the older Muslim world. Christian and Jewish groups were given their religious and cultural freedom; many Balkan communities preferred such autonomy under the Ottomans to the religious and cultural restrictions and persecutions suffered under Hungarian and Hapsburg Catholic rule. In the first centuries of the empire's existence, some non-Muslims served as holders of revocable land grants and warriors; by the late sixteenth century this practice seems to have stopped. By the 1530s probably less than one-tenth of the population of Anatolia was Christian or Jewish, but in the European provinces the proportion was reversed and only one-fifth of the population was Muslim, while the vast majority of the subjects in the countryside were Christians.

The various religious groups were termed *communities* (and, much later, *millets*), which meant a group of people with a particular religion within the Ottoman Empire. Each community—while considered inferior to the Sunnite Muslims—still had the legal right to use its own language, develop its own institutions, collect taxes and render them to the imperial treasury, and maintain courts for trying members in all cases except those involving public security and crime. Each millet had a leader or leaders who were responsible to the sultan for the payments of taxes and for the good behavior and loyalty of members of the community. Christian and Jewish subjects of the state, resident non-Ottoman Muslims, and non-Muslims who were subjects of other Muslim states were all subjected to a special extra poll tax. Shiite Iranians began to be treated as a somewhat separate category in at least some of the Ottoman provinces in a later time.

Paralleling these religious communities were groups of foreigners, chiefly merchants residing in Istanbul, such as the Genoese residents in Galata across the Golden Horn. Each group lived under provisions of a formal treaty drawn up between the sultan and the foreign authority; the agreements were periodically renewed. The trading privileges or capitulations that the French had enjoyed under the Mamluk sultans in Egypt since 1251 were reconfirmed by Suleiman in 1528; and a regular treaty with France was concluded, though not formally ratified, in 1536—a treaty similar to those made with Venice, Florence, and Hungary by Mehmed II and Bayezid II.

The general tenor of these treaties was exemplified in the Treaty of 1503 between Bayezid II and Venice. Among other things, the sultan agreed that a Venetian consul might come to Istanbul with his family and reside there for three years. Although Venetians could live in certain designated cities of the empire for a limited time, they could travel about only with the consul's permission. The consul should settle all cases and disputes among Venetians; and Venetian testimony was recognized as valid in courts of Christian and Jewish Ottoman subjects. In criminal cases Venetians were guaranteed justice in regular Ottoman courts.

These treaties recognizing certain rights and obligations for European residents in the Ottoman Empire were based on the assumption that since foreign Christians could not fare well under the shariah, they would have to live by their own laws. However, in later years, when the balance of power between western Europe and the Ottoman Empire shifted, such arrangements evolved into the famous capitulatory treaties, which gave nationals of other governments a privileged position in the Ottoman Empire. Those years were still far away, however, in the fifteenth and sixteenth centuries, when Ottoman governmental institutions provided the empire with great resilience, legitimacy, efficiency, and power.

References

In addition to general studies on Muslim institutions, references in Chapters 14 and 16 are of particular importance.

BIRGE, JOHN KINGSLEY: *The Bektashi Order of Dervishes.* Hartford, Conn.: Hartford Seminary Press, 1937. A significant work on this Sufi order and its relationship to Ottoman society.

BRAUDE, BENJAMIN, AND BERNARD LEWIS, EDS.: *Christians and Jews in the Ottoman Empire: The Functioning of a Plural Society.* 2 vols. New York: Holmes and Meier, 1982. This excellent collection of twenty-nine articles emphasizes the late Ottoman period and deals extensively with the Arab lands as well as the central government.

DE BUSBECQ, OGIER G.: *Turkish Letters.* Translated by Edward S. Forster. Oxford, England: Clarendon Press, 1927. De Busbecq was an ambassador to the Ottoman Empire for many years; his observations were singularly objective and discerning.

GIBB, H. A. R., AND HAROLD BOWEN: *Islamic Society and the West: A Study of the Impact of Western Civilization on Moslem Culture in the Near East.* Vol. 1 (in two parts): *Islamic Society in the Eighteenth Century.* London: Oxford University Press, 1950, 1957. While subject to much valid criticism, this work remains a penetrating study of Ottoman institutions as they existed in the eighteenth century and as they had evolved from earlier forms since the fourteenth century.

GOODWIN, GODFREY: *The Janissaries.* London: Saqi, 1994. A popularly written account of janissary life and how the janissaries affected Ottoman events.

KNOLLES, RICHARD: *The Generall Historie of the Turkes, from the First Beginning of That Nation to the Rising of the Othoman Familie: With All the Notable Expeditions of the Christian Princes Against Them. Together with the Lives and Conquests of the Othoman Kings and Emperours.* . . . London, 1603. This is still the most extensive and longest Ottoman history in the English language, written by an Englishman, long a resident in Turkey. There are many later editions.

LEWIS, BERNARD: *The Jews of Islam.* Princeton, N.J.: Princeton University Press, 1984. A thorough and well-written treatment of the subject.

MANDAVILLE, JON E.: "Usurious Piety: The Cash Waqf Controversy in the Ottoman Empire." *International Journal of Middle East Studies* 10 (1979): 289–308. An interesting examination of the flexibility of Ottoman legal thinking.

MASTERS, BRUCE: "Trading Diasporas and 'Nations': The Genesis of National Identities in Ottoman Aleppo." *International History Review* 9 (1987): 345–367.

MITLER, LOUIS: "The Genoese in Galata: 1453–1682." *International Journal of Middle East Studies* 10 (1979): 71–91.

NECIPOGLU, GULRU: *Architecture, Ceremonial, and Power: The Topkapi Palace in the Fifteenth and Sixteenth Centuries.* Cambridge, Mass.: MIT Press, 1991. This beautifully illustrated volume provides a detailed examination of every part of the imperial palace and of the rituals and symbols that inspired awe and allegiance.

REPP, RICHARD C.: *The Müfti of Istanbul: A Study in the Development of the Ottoman Learned Hierarchy.* London: Ithaca Press, 1986. Traces in an extremely careful and detailed way career patterns and lives of individuals who held the post of Mufti.

SIMSAR, MUHAMMED AHMED: *The Waqfiyah of Ahmed Paşa.* Philadelphia: University of Pennsylvania Press, 1940. A fine translation with notes on a perpetual trust established in 1511 by Ahmed Hersekoglu Pasha, who was the son of the last duke of Herzegovina and who became an Ottoman vizir.

The Ottoman Empire as a World Power

During the early modern period of Middle Eastern history, from about 1500 to about 1800, the Ottoman Empire dominated the region and much of the eastern hemisphere in terms of institutional, political, military, religious, and cultural accomplishments. Other states existed in Morocco and elsewhere in the Middle East, but only the Safavids in Iran and the Hapsburg dynasty in western and central Europe provided a real challenge to Ottoman supremacy.

The sixteenth-century reigns of Suleiman I and Selim II were particularly noteworthy for their success in military expansion to both the east and the west, by both land and sea. Changes in the organization of the court and in administration also marked the era from 1520 to 1574, while imperial sponsorship of architecture, art, and literature helped create remarkably beautiful symbols of Ottoman glory.

SULEIMAN I

The institutions and personnel of the Ottoman Empire were so well organized, capable, and effective under Mehmed II, Bayezid II, and Selim I that the government could function well even without much direction from a sultan. When combined with an extraordinary leader, the Ottoman state could accomplish even more, as took place during the long reign of Suleiman I. Since Selim I left only one son, for the first time since the accession of Mehmed Fatih the transfer of authority in 1520 generated no civil war or execution of royal relatives. Suleiman, moreover, was born in the year A.H. 900, the opening year of the tenth century of Islam, and was the tenth of his dynasty. Because of these portentous beginnings his subjects believed he was destined to rule over a great part of the world.

The youthful Suleiman, only twenty-five years old when he became sultan, was called "the Magnificent" by Europeans and Kanuni ("the Lawgiver") by his own people. He appeared as a magnificent sovereign, certainly the match of his contemporaries Ismail I of Safavid Iran, the Mughal Babur of India, Charles V of the Hapsburg family of Holy Roman Emperors, Francis I of France, and Henry

---

PERIODIZATION IN THE HISTORY OF THE ISLAMIC MIDDLE EAST

Antiquity: from the rise of civilization to the coming of Islam

Classical Islamic period: from the life of the prophet Muhammad to the middle of the tenth century A.D.

The early medieval era in the Middle East: from about 950 to about 1250

The late medieval era in the Middle East: from about 1250 to about 1500

The early modern Middle East: from about 1500 to about 1800

The modern Middle East: from about 1800 to the present

VIII of England. Suleiman reigned for forty-six years. During those years the Ottoman Empire, built on solid foundations by his predecessors, reached its height as a conquest state in terms of power, wealth, and brilliance.

During the latter years of Bayezid II's reign Suleiman was assigned as governor of Bolu and then was transferred to Kaffa in the Crimea, where his mother, daughter of a khan, had been reared. After his father seized the throne, Suleiman was called to govern Istanbul, while Selim fought against brothers and nephews. Suleiman then governed Edirne during his father's long wars in Iran and Egypt. Only upon Selim's return to Istanbul in 1517 was Suleiman sent to rule the province around Manisa in western Anatolia. Thus Suleiman attended the pages' school in Istanbul and resided for more than five years at the palaces of Istanbul and Edirne. In addition, he had nearly six years of experience as provincial governor, surrounded by teachers, advisers, and graduates of the palace school. No prince of his time had better training or more practical preparation for the responsibility of ruling a great empire.

SULEIMAN'S COURT

After initial military campaigns against Belgrade and Rhodes, for the following three summers Suleiman remained in Edirne and Istanbul enjoying peace. He loved the gardens of the palace, and one of his greatest pleasures was boating on the Bosphorus and the Sea of Marmara. Frequently he would be rowed across to the Asian shore to walk in his gardens there.

It was also during these years that a Ukrainian-Polish slave girl named Hurrem caught his fancy. She soon completely captivated Suleiman, became his legal wife, and dominated him until her death in 1558. Suleiman's mother ruled his harem until her death in 1534; after that date Hurrem became Suleiman's confidant and counselor. Her chief rival, the concubine Mahidevran, mother of Suleiman's oldest living son, Mustafa (b. 1515), left for Manisa in 1533 in the company of her son when he was established there as governor. As a concubine Hurrem departed from Ottoman tradition not only by marrying the sultan but also by bearing him more than one child. She ultimately gave birth to six children, including Mehmed; Selim (b. 1524); Bayezid; Jihangir, a hunchback; and a daughter, Mihrimah. Hurrem did not leave Istanbul, as had Mahidevran. Competition in the harem for Suleiman's affections and intense rivalry among the mothers for the advancement and protection of their sons brought affliction upon Suleiman in later days, but the royal family also provided a source of strength as the sultan's female relatives were married to prominent vizirs.

In 1523 Suleiman advanced to the grand vizirate his favorite and boon companion, Ibrahim. The son of a Greek sailor, Ibrahim had been captured by pirates and sold to a lady of Manisa, who gave her slave an excellent education. As a prince in Manisa, Suleiman recognized Ibrahim's talents, enjoyed his violin playing, and brought him to Istanbul as chief falconer and head of the pages of the inner chamber. For the following thirteen years Ibrahim governed the empire, year by year relieving his brother-in-law Suleiman of more of the tiresome duties of ruling. He even took the title of seriasker-sultan ("commander in chief of the armies," with the power of sultan). He dined with Suleiman, was with him at all hours, and even slept in the sultan's apartments. Between 1523 and 1536 no policy of state was reached without Ibrahim's consideration and approval.

Unfortunately, Ibrahim's rapid advancement to grand vizir ran counter to the system of promotions based on merit and service. There could be no question that Ibrahim was a brilliant and successful administrator and adviser. Still, others who had proved their abilities through service were passed over by the sultan's personal favorite.

The first demonstration of Ibrahim's genius came in Egypt. The second vizir in 1523 had asked for and received as a consolation the governorship of Egypt. Within months after his arrival in Cairo he was deeply involved in treason and was murdered in his bath by loyal Ottomans. Other revolts by Arab tribes and Mamluks led Suleiman to commission Ibrahim to go to Egypt to inaugurate a more stable regime. Finances, administration, law, and trade procedures were thoroughly overhauled, and future Ottoman governors were given more responsibility. Ibrahim went on to show his abilities in many subsequent activities.

Eventually, however, Suleiman came to feel that Ibrahim was amassing too much power. One evening in 1536 Ibrahim dined as usual with Suleiman and retired for the night to his customary place in Suleiman's apartments. The next morning his strangled body was found outside the palace. No explanation was ever given. His immense wealth reverted to the sultan, since he was Suleiman's slave. In later years Suleiman tried to avoid promoting officers too rapidly or elevating them too obviously over the heads of their seniors.

BELGRADE, RHODES, AND VIENNA

Suleiman expanded the size of the empire significantly, both in the Balkans and against eastern foes. His numerous European campaigns began with the goal of taking Belgrade in 1521. At Sofia, he gathered his army and supplies, including 3000 camels carrying ammunition and 30,000 laden with grain. At least 10,000 wagonloads of grain were requisitioned locally, and 300 cannon were brought up the Danube from Istanbul.

As expected, there was little opposition from Europe. The Hapsburg Charles V was busily engaged preparing for war against Francis I of France and also deeply involved with Martin Luther and imperial problems. Belgrade held out for three weeks as Ottoman cannon, implanted on an island in the Danube, ended all resistance; many Serbs were transplanted to the outskirts of Istanbul. The capture of Belgrade opened the Hungarian plains and the upper Danube basin to the Ottomans.

The following year, Suleiman assembled his forces in Asia for the heralded attack on the island of Rhodes. Rhodes lay only 6 miles off the coast of Anatolia, astride the sea route from Istanbul to Alexandria, where the Knights of St. John had continually harassed Ottoman trade. Rhodes was a highly fortified port, and large contingents of knights arrived to defend the citadel. (Venice sent her fleet, but to protect Cyprus!) Massing 300 ships and 100,000 men, Suleiman personally led the attack, which lasted from July until December. Thousands of stone cannonballs bombarded the walls, and a few rudimentary explosive shells were hurled into the town. Effective attacks were launched in conjunction with sapping and mining operations against the walls, with heavy casualties. The knights surrendered on Christmas Day 1522. They were allowed to depart with all who desired to leave.

The janissaries and palace troops grew restless with several years of inactivity and little booty. In April 1526, Suleiman, Ibrahim, and other vizirs set out from Istanbul with 100,000 men and several hundred cannon. Early in August the Ottomans crossed the Drava River and moved toward Mohacs, where a crushing victory opened all of Hungary. Early in September, Buda surrendered to Suleiman; two weeks later Pest, across the river on the east bank of the Danube, was burned. The following day Suleiman and his army began the long trek homeward, reaching Istanbul in the middle of November. But the expedition into Hungary ended only as a magnified raid. Suleiman did not possess adequate manpower to garrison such distant cities as Budapest and Mohacs. No land grants were handed out to Ottoman officers, and Hungary remained a political vacuum.

Subsequently, John Zapolya, duke of Transylvania, occupied Budapest and was crowned king of Hungary. Then Ferdinand of Hapsburg, archduke of Austria, defeated Zapolya in 1527 and claimed to be the Hungarian king. In desperation, Zapolya turned to the Ottomans. Suleiman moved in 1529 to oust the Austrians from Hungary. Not until the middle of May did the army leave Istanbul, and continuous drenching rains impeded its march. The larger cannon had to be abandoned along the way. Mohacs was reached only in mid-August; Budapest was reached a month later. Soon afterward Ottoman raiders penetrated into Austria like swarms of locusts, and the attack upon Vienna opened on September 29. Although Ferdinand had all summer to meet the threat, forces to defend Vienna assembled less than a week before the siege began.

Ottoman mining operations and assaults raged day after day. On October 12, 1529, mines seriously damaged the walls, and infantry attacks almost succeeded. Both sides grew weary, however, and on October 15 the Ottomans retired. To the defenders of Vienna it seemed miraculous, for they were on the point of surrender.

In truth, the retreat was forced by the janissaries, who wanted to reach Edirne and Istanbul before winter. Ferdinand recognized Suleiman's hold upon Hungary in a peace treaty in 1533.

Vienna had not been taken by Suleiman because his communications were so extended that his forces could not be effective. Incessant rains in the Balkans and in Austria made the long marches arduous and the hauling of the heavy cannon that took Belgrade almost impossible. The army left Istanbul only after the mud dried late in April, and it insisted upon returning before the winter rains began in December. Neither the janissaries nor the sipahis wanted to campaign in the winter. Vienna was thus beyond Ottoman reach, although Christian Europe failed to appreciate the full facts of the sultan's limitations.

NAVAL ACTIVITIES

While Suleiman was engaged in Hungary combating the Hapsburgs, the French looked to him as a useful ally in their struggle against the Hapsburg Holy Roman Emperor, Charles V. Relations with the French led the Ottomans to extend their interests to the entire Mediterranean. Since the conquest of Istanbul Ottoman navies had grown in competence. In 1480 Mehmed II was able to support an expedition across the Adriatic to the heel of Italy. Under Bayezid II, Ottoman sea power came of age, controlled the eastern Mediterranean, and repeatedly plundered the shores of Spain. Under Suleiman the navy occupied and added much of North Africa to the empire.

The key figures in this conquest were the Barbarossa brothers. While Selim I was conquering Egypt, Aruj Barbarossa and his more famous brother, Khair al-Din, appeared in Tunis to lead fleets against Christian Europe. Their father was an Ottoman grant holder from Rumeli who had settled on the island of Mytilene following its conquest by Mehmed II, and they followed the sea-ghazi tradition. After retaking Algiers, Aruj lost his life in an assault upon Tlemcen. Khair al-Din, who inherited his brother's name of Barbarossa, sent word that he would consent to Selim's overlordship in exchange for aid and official position. Appointed beylerbey of Algiers and North Africa with absolute authority to rule those provinces and to raise and organize a janissary army, Barbarossa went to Istanbul in 1533; he would exercise Ottoman power in the Mediterranean until his death in 1546. His ships raked the coasts of Spain and maintained unceasing pressure upon Charles V. Barbarossa's men were of all backgrounds, and thus truly Ottoman, but his personal bodyguard was composed exclusively of Spanish renegades.

Barbarossa's conquest of Tunis in 1534 was soon challenged by Charles V, who employed a large fleet and a powerful army to dislodge the Ottomans from Tunis. But Barbarossa escaped with a score of his ships to Algiers to pillage Minorca. Then he proceeded with his loot to Istanbul—where Suleiman appointed him admiral and made him responsible for all naval activities. After the treaty with France in 1536, French ships frequently cooperated with Ottoman fleets in the western Mediterranean. In the winter of 1543, the harbor of Toulon was given over entirely to Barbarossa's ships and men as the inhabitants moved out.

After Khair al-Din died in 1546, his role was filled by Turgut (Dragut), Piyale

Pasha, and Khair al-Din's son Hasan. Tripoli of Libya was stormed and became the headquarters of Turgut, who was named its beylerbey. The strategic island of Jerba off the coast of Tunisia fell to Piyale Pasha. The Ottomans now ruled nearly all of North Africa, except for Morocco, which under the Saadian dynasty used gunpowder weapons to successfully defy both Ottoman and Iberian invaders. Morocco never did become part of the Ottoman Empire.

In 1565, Suleiman sent Piyale with 200 ships and a landing force of nearly 30,000 men, including sipahis and janissaries, to take the strategic island of Malta from the Knights of St. John, whom he had driven from Rhodes more than forty years earlier. After several months of costly assaults upon the island fortresses, the Ottomans had to withdraw. Despite this failure, Ottoman supremacy upon the Mediterranean continued for many years after Suleiman's death.

EASTERN CAMPAIGNS

On several occasions in the early years of Suleiman's reign, there were difficulties with the Safavid shah of Iran. The Ottoman court, being Sunnite, looked with contempt upon the Shiites of the east. They also feared any successes of the Shiite Safavid followers who lived in various parts of the Ottoman Empire. Although Selim I had defeated Shah Ismail and killed thousands of his followers, border chieftains in eastern Anatolia vacillated in their loyalty from the Safavid capital of Tabriz to Istanbul, and then back to Tabriz again as advantages shifted from one to the other. Such changing allegiances helped cause large conflicts between the two great empires and also perpetuated minor engagements, all of which tended to cause the depopulation of the border districts of the Caucasus.

The first eastern campaign conducted personally by Suleiman was in 1533. The Ottomans took Tabriz, but since they were not able to come to grips with Shah Tahmasp, they moved southward and captured Baghdad. There Suleiman passed the winter, arranging the administration of this new addition to his empire. In 1547 Shah Tahmasp's brother appeared in Istanbul, seeking help in a bid for the Iranian throne. Suleiman left Istanbul in 1548, recaptured Tabriz, wintered in Aleppo, and spent all of 1549 pillaging cities and pursuing the elusive Tahmasp, who never dared risk a battle.

Again in 1553, perhaps believing that the Ottomans were fully engaged in Europe, Tahmasp adopted an aggressive policy and seized Erzurum from the Ottomans. Rustem Pasha, the grand vizir for most of the years from 1544 to 1561, headed a large army against the Safavids. Despite numerous victories the Ottomans recognized the futility of trying to hold all their eastern conquests, so they arranged a peace that allowed them to retain Iraq, including Baghdad, and a port on the Persian Gulf, as well as most of Kurdistan and western Armenia.

Suleiman also took an interest in developments in the Red Sea area and along the shores of the Arabian Sea. In 1538, an Ottoman admiral sailed from Suez, installed governors in Aden and Yemen, and then passed on to the Malabar coast of India, where he landed and unsuccessfully besieged Diu. Suleiman also found that the Portuguese blocked the exit from the Persian Gulf, in part nullifying his capture of Baghdad and Basrah. When the famous geographer–sea captain Piri Pasha failed to oust the Portuguese from the Strait of Hormuz, he was beheaded for cowardice. (The Portuguese kept Hormuz from 1515 to 1622.) Nonetheless, the Ottomans retained control over the Persian Gulf, Aden, Yemen, and the Red Sea, including the coastal areas of the Sudan and portions of Ethiopia, while the spice trade to Egypt through the Red Sea then revived.

HUNGARY AGAIN

Suleiman had too many irons in the fire to press his eastern campaigns vigorously. In the latter half of his reign he became involved again in Hungary, occupying Budapest in 1541 and for the first time merging central Hungary directly into his empire. Some twenty-five provinces were formed, each with a governor under the beylerbey of Budapest. Ferdinand of Austria tried to retaliate, but his siege of Budapest failed. Peace treaties were signed in 1547; each party retained the lands in his possession, and Austria paid a tribute of 30,000 ducats a year to the Ottomans. The Hapsburgs, however, violated the peace, and in 1552 Suleiman's forces incorporated the Banat of Temesvar (Timishoara), northeast of Belgrade, into the empire.

Maximilian II succeeded his father, Ferdinand, in 1564. He, too, refused to pay the tribute and attacked Ottoman territory. When governors clamored for support in 1566, Suleiman set forth on his seventh campaign into Hungary. Over seventy years of age and no longer able to ride a horse, he traveled in a carriage. On the night of the fall of the fortress at Sziget—the eve of the consolidation of Hungary, the fulfillment of the conquest that had begun with the fall of Belgrade in his first year of campaigning—Suleiman died. Mehmed Sokollu, the grand vizir, kept Suleiman's death a secret for over three weeks while he sent a messenger to Kutahya to summon his father-in-law, Selim, to the succession.

THE SUCCESSION OF SELIM II

Suleiman had had eight sons, but only one outlived him. Mehmed, who was Suleiman's favorite, died in 1543 at the age of twenty-one. In 1553 elements of the army apparently began to suggest that the sultan's eldest son, Prince Mustafa, should take the throne, so as to respond to attacks launched by the Safavids. Egged on by Hurrem, who was plotting for the succession for one of her sons, Suleiman took the field, then summoned Mustafa to Eregli, where he was strangled. Thus, for the first time since Murad I, a sultan executed an adult son.

The remaining two rivals, Selim and Bayezid, were Hurrem's sons. Selim, the elder of the two, formerly governor of Konya and Manisa, drank to excess. The soldiers preferred Bayezid, who resembled Suleiman. Each brother had a following at court, and rivalry between the two had been intense. Selim and his friends employed every means to advance his power. Especially after Hurrem's death in 1558, Selim's fortunes were watched over by the grand vizir Rustem Pasha. The latter was the husband of Hurrem's and Suleiman's daughter Mihrimah, who had as much power over her father as her mother did. Civil war between the brothers broke out in 1559. Suleiman ordered the provincial governors in Anatolia to give active support to Selim, who was then victorious. Bayezid fled to the court of the Safavid Shah Tahmasp. Eventually, on the payment of 400,000 ducats, he and his sons were turned over to Suleiman's agent, who executed all of them. Thus, when Suleiman died, there remained of his sons only Selim, known as "the Drunkard"— a fat and fun-loving person.

IMPERIAL ADMINISTRATION

The succession of Selim II was symptomatic of the rapidly changing dynamics of imperial government. Expansion into eastern Anatolia, Syria, and Egypt by Selim I was followed without much breathing space by Suleiman's conquests in Serbia, Hungary, North Africa, and Iraq. The result was that in two decades the empire experienced an astonishing increment not only of power and wealth but also of responsibilities.

More and more provinces were created, with a proportionate increase in the number of governors, judges, tax collectors, and clerks. The janissary corps doubled in size. The imperial household became larger and more complex, and power became centralized within it. As wealth poured into Istanbul, high officers of the court adopted a life of pomp and splendor. (To celebrate the circumcision of Mustafa, Mehmed, and Selim in the summer of 1530, high dignitaries gathered in Istanbul for festivities that lasted three weeks.) Each vizir had a magnificent court of his own, modeled after that of his master. Mehmed Sokollu, the grand vizir at the time of Suleiman's death, had become Suleiman's slave when the chief treasurer was executed and his property confiscated in 1534. Ayas Pasha, Ibrahim's successor as grand vizir and a slave of Albanian origin, lived in the grand manner. At his death from the plague, it was noted that he left 120 children!

As governmental administration became vaster and more complex, institutions, standards, and values began to change. The situation was abetted by the haphazard growth of Ottoman law and legal procedures. Suleiman, therefore, reissued and modified numerous kanuns, or decrees, dating from his predecessors' reigns, and codified old kanuns, particularly those affecting the provinces, in an attempt to regularize his administration. (It is on the basis of this legal activity that he has been known in Ottoman history as Suleiman Kanuni—"the Lawgiver.") Many laws related to matters of inheritance, salary, rank, and ceremony for officers of the court. Market and guild regulations were modified, and one of the greatest collections of laws was that fashioned for the land-grant holders in 1530. It was designed to make sure that all grants were made directly by the central administration and not by the beylerbeys.

A social problem also emerged in connection with the relatively new drink, coffee, which had come into general use in the fifteenth century. Opposition to coffee first emerged among some governmental and religious circles in Mecca and Cairo, despite the economic advantages created by the trade in coffee during the sixteenth century. Popular coffeehouses were viewed with suspicion by the central Ottoman government officials as likely to lead to sloth and sedition, but despite condemnations the coffeehouses spread ever more widely and increased the male public's opportunities for social interaction.

Suleiman's revenues were greater than those of any contemporary monarchs in Europe. Income was derived from many sources. Since the Ottomans usually followed the customs that were practiced in a province before its conquest, the sources varied from one province to another. Tithes on land, poll taxes, special taxes on lands of non-Muslims, trade, animals, produce, markets, mines, confiscations, and booty annually brought Suleiman about 12 million ducats. Even so, Suleiman was often hard-pressed for funds, and in his later years he forced gifts from his officers upon their appointment to a higher position.

SELIM II

Throughout his reign of eight years Selim II retained his father's last grand vizir, Mehmed Sokollu, who administered the government and might well be called the actual ruler. Virtually afraid of his grand vizir, Selim generally deferred to him and to other high officials of proven abilities. Selim was highly emotional, sensitive, and a truly gifted poet, but he was also self-centered. He was unaware of how the court and the soldiers felt toward him, and he lived in the company of, and was easily influenced by, fawning courtiers and unscrupulous adventurers.

Since Sokollu continued as grand vizir throughout Selim's reign and on into that of his successor, there was no break in governmental procedure or policy, although there was some difficulty at the onset. Selim erred in not comprehending the power and fearlessness of the janissaries, and at first he declined to give the customary accession donations to the soldiers. Complaints and a show of force followed until Selim promised the money.

Otherwise, the course of events proceeded as it had under Suleiman as military expansion took place. Piyale Pasha took the island of Chios from the Genoese, peace was made with Austria and Poland, and more of Yemen was subjugated. An ambitious project was undertaken in 1569: forces were sent to conquer Astrakhan at the mouth of the Volga River at the Caspian Sea; meanwhile, engineers started digging a canal to connect the Don River and the Volga at a point where they are only about 30 miles apart. The purpose was to enable ships and military supplies to be sent from the Black Sea to the Caspian Sea so as to support attacks upon Iran. The garrison at Astrakhan withstood the storm, however, and an army drove away the Ottoman workmen on the canal. The enterprise was abandoned, and peace between Muscovy and the Ottomans was reestablished.

Sokollu had a similar dream of cutting a waterway across Suez to link the Mediterranean and Red seas, but affairs in Yemen and Arabia and then Selim's insistence upon war against Venice for the conquest of Cyprus stopped the work. The whole island of Cyprus was subdued at heavy cost by 1571. Cyprus became a unified part of the empire (and Selim could now command the entire output of Cypriote wine of which he was so fond).

The attack on Cyprus and the extraordinary naval preparations of the Ottomans not only alarmed Venice but instigated the formation of a powerful naval league that included Spain, Venice, Savoy, the pope, and the Knights of Malta. Commanded by Don Juan of Austria, the Christian fleet met the Ottomans at the Gulf of Lepanto in October 1571. A furious battle ensued, with the Ottomans losing over

150 ships and many men. The allied fleets suffered less, and victory was theirs. To the Ottomans the battle of Lepanto was a severe loss in a long series of naval engagements. However, a new fleet was built that winter in the naval yards of Gallipoli and Istanbul; by the spring of 1572 the Ottoman naval position, other than the loss of trained personnel, was largely repaired. To the Christians, however, it had seemed a notable victory; it gave them courage and proved that the Ottomans were not invincible upon the sea. Nevertheless, they failed to follow up the victory. In 1574 Tunis joined Algiers and Tripoli as Ottoman strongholds on the north shore of Africa and remained an Ottoman possession until the nineteenth century; in the eastern Mediterranean only the island of Crete remained outside Ottoman control. Ottoman maritime commerce became prosperous and flourished.

Late in 1574 Selim was inspecting a new bath at the palace, and to protect himself from any dampness of the fresh plaster, he drained an entire bottle of Cypriote wine. Being slightly unsteady, he fell on the floor and suffered a brain concussion from which he died a few days later. His death, followed a year later by the assassination of Mehmed Sokollu, terminated an era in Ottoman history. The expansionistic and dynamic Ottoman Empire soon turned into a more stable and satisfied but still powerful state, with new policies and procedures in the long seventeenth century.

OTTOMAN ARCHITECTURE AND ART

In the illustrious period of Ottoman history during the reigns of Suleiman and Selim (and including some of their successors), the most viable and lasting examples of the empire's greatness and magnificence were the majestic mosques that still silhouette much of the skyline of Istanbul. Sultans, grand viziers, admirals, princes and princesses, and women of the harem—all built impressive pavilions, tombs, mosques, and mosque complexes (the latter centered around the mosque but including madrasahs, hospitals, etc.) to memorialize themselves. Most of the prominent mosques of the empire, and of Istanbul in particular, date from the sixteenth century, beginning with the mosque of Sultan Bayezid II (completed about 1500) and ending with the Blue Mosque of Sultan Ahmed I (1617). They surpassed the already high standard of imperial architecture established at Bursa and Edirne.

The simplest style and form, exemplified by the mosque of Sultan Selim I in Istanbul, consisted of a plain square building carrying one large dome. The transition between square and circle was accomplished by flat and spherical triangular pendentives. The second type of imperial mosque evolved in the mosques of Bayezid II and Suleiman I. These mosques showed that Ottoman architects studied Hagia Sophia and appreciated its solution to the problem of building a domed open square or rectangular structure suitable for congregational worship. In these two mosques, the great rectangle was roofed by a large dome on spherical pendentives that effected the transition from the dome to the four broad pointed arches resting upon four piers. The dome was abutted longitudinally by semidomes fitted to their rectangles by pendentives or small semidomes, which in the Suleimaniye mosque were anchored to their corners by stalactite pendentives. The pendentives confused the eye and thereby hid the awkwardness, thus serving much the same function as the colored mosaics of the Byzantines. The strong buttresses in the lateral walls were admirably concealed by external porches.

Sinan (d. 1588), a janissary and a military architect, became the master designer of all sorts of buildings. Sinan contended that his early Shehzade mosque in memory of Suleiman's son Mehmed was the work of an apprentice; his later mosque for Suleiman was the work of a journeyman; and Sultan Selim II's mosque in Edirne, completed in 1574, was the work of a master. In Shehzade, Sinan presented a new style aimed at opening the entire edifice into one spacious congregational hall so that every worshiper could see the mihrab. The post-Sinan great mosque of Sultan Ahmed I (built 1609–1616) followed the same principle and achieved its goal by replacing the small domes of the lateral aisle with one large semidome. The central dome at Ahmed was supported by large circular piers. Upon entering Ahmed, one noticed immediately that the whole area was unified and that the central space was vaster than in Hagia Sophia.

At the mosque of Sultan Selim II in Edirne, Sinan developed another type of imperial mosque. The dome, 31 meters across, was supported by an octagon of arches, pendentives of stalactite corbels, and eight sturdy paneled piers, which Sinan called "elephant feet." In all these mosques the flood of light that entered the central halls played a large role in the fascination and admiration felt by so many worshipers and other visitors.

The internal centers of the domes were usually decorated with flowered and calligraphic frescoes, and the walls were embellished by panels of colored and veined marble or colored ceramic tiles. The Ottomans were more conscious of aesthetic external lines and composition than were Byzantine builders, and this accounts for the architectural evolution that gave to the Istanbul horizon its splendor of domes and slender minarets. Ottoman architecture, with its distinctive domes and minarets, spread from Istanbul throughout the empire, serving as a source of visual unity.

Mosques and palaces were furnished with the richly colored and geometrically patterned carpets and rugs for which the Ottoman Empire became so famous, and also with pottery, whose style was initially influenced by Chinese porcelain models. By the middle of the sixteenth century, Ottoman pottery and tiles, especially those produced at Iznik and Damascus, developed a variety of beautiful colors and motifs that dazzled as they pleased. Calligraphy was an art form that was favored by the sultans and had close connections to the Sufi mystics. The imperial court also sponsored bookbinding and miniature painting. Styles of painting were influenced by Safavid artists in the early and middle sixteenth century; later Ottoman artists developed a more independent style. The "minor" arts also flourished; Sultan Suleiman was himself a goldsmith and a calligrapher, as well as a patron of art on an enormous scale. Ottoman silk weavings were much sought after in Europe. All the various forms of art were largely produced in workshops organized by the imperial government, which consumed most of their production. Officials of the state, grandees living in the provinces, and the wealthier members of the protected religious minorities also patronized similar artists and artisans.

OTTOMAN LITERATURE

The sixteenth century led in architectural achievement, but it was also a period of brilliant literary activity. Suleiman had a strong historical feeling; he emphasized the parallelism of Ottomans and Byzantines, so that Mehmed II and the emperor Constantine were viewed as similar, and Suleiman equated himself with Justinian. Like the Byzantine emperor Justinian, Suleiman was lawgiver and law codifier, builder of remarkable religious edifices and aqueducts, leader of armies, and generous patron of scholars and men of letters.

A quarter of all the eminent Ottoman poets and writers belonged to the period of Suleiman and Selim II. Poetry and history were the outstanding forms of literary effort. Lyric poetry often had a Sufi content and was expressed in forms heavily influenced by Sufi mysticism. Many themes were persistent for centuries—the garden; the lover/beloved; an urban orientation, especially toward Istanbul; and images of roses, nightingales, and wine. From an earlier time the female writer Mihri Hatun (d. 1506) produced exquisite love poetry, while Jem, son of Mehmed II, wrote poetry reflective of his life and its melancholy circumstances. The Turkish-Iraqi poet Mehmet Fuzuli (d. 1556) produced a panegyric on Suleiman's conquest of Baghdad and became famous for his romantic poems. Sufi poets and wandering minstrels recited poetry for the masses in the countryside, poetry that strikingly differed from that of the palace and the capital city. Both Suleiman and Selim were accomplished poets themselves, Suleiman writing in Persian and Turkish under the pen name Muhibbi (one who loves). The shining lyric poet of that age and perhaps of the Turkish language of all ages was Abd al-Baki, whose elegy for Sultan Suleiman was his greatest public work.

Historians flourished. Their works were sometimes general in scope and sometimes specific, describing only one phase or incident of the period, and were often sumptuously illustrated with miniature paintings. Early histories had been straightforward and written in a popular style, but Sultan Bayezid II commissioned a more ornate comprehensive history of the Ottomans. The ornate style first involved works written in Persian and Arabic, and later an infusion of words and grammatical units from those languages into Turkish. Cultural intermingling, amalgamation, and synthesis were reflected in language, but the gains in literary elegance were counterbalanced by the increasing gap between the style of the imperial court and the learned elite on the one hand, and the great mass of Turkish speakers on the other. The latter often could not understand the new high-flown rhetoric of the imperial style.

Among the historians, Ramazan wrote of the capture of Rhodes; Kemalpasha-zade, whose career included service as a sipahi and, much later, as shaikh al-Islam, narrated the victorious campaign of Mohacs, and wrote a general history of the dynasty. One of the most revered of Ottoman historians appeared late in the sixteenth century in the person of Saad al-Din. Tutor of Suleiman's grandson Murad III, he wrote and compiled *The Crown of Histories,* which, in numerous volumes and an analytic manner, covered the gamut of Ottoman history. Continued by Saad al-Din's son, for several centuries it dominated concepts of Ottoman development from the earliest times to his own day. The prolific bureaucrat, poet, and historian

Mustafa Ali of Gallipoli (d. 1600) wrote an important book of counsel for sultans and a history of the world and the Ottoman Empire, begun in the year 1100 after the hijrah (A.D. 1591–1592). For such writers, historical chronicles were literary accomplishments, reflecting the increasingly complex and rich nature of Ottoman Turkish, as well as following the format of chronologically arranged annals.

The conquests chronicled by the historians were due in large part to Ottoman success in using gunpowder weapons and to the flexibility the empire demonstrated in adapting its military to new needs. Ottoman history in the sixteenth century and the nature of its rulers were typical of the range of experience found in other Middle Eastern and European countries of the time. Selim I had been harsh, brilliant, demanding, and energetic; he set the government in motion toward momentous conquest. Suleiman I was a dignified, orderly, just, conscientious, and artistic soldier and gentleman who gave the Ottoman Empire a sense of distinction and cultural urbanity. Selim II was a talented, irresponsible, emotional, dissolute drunkard who helped hasten the transformation of the state in new directions. Through all three reigns the Ottomans accomplished much in cultural areas as well as in the military and administration. During the sixteenth and seventeenth centuries they successfully matched the threat posed by the Shiite Savafids of Iran.

References

Most titles already cited for the chapters discussing the Ottoman Empire are relevant to this chapter. Especially noteworthy are those in Chapters 14 and 16.

ANDREWS, WALTER G.: *Poetry's Voice, Society's Song: Ottoman Lyric Poetry.* Seattle: University of Washington Press, 1985. This excellent study places Ottoman lyrical poetry in the context of modern literary analysis and examines the meaning of poetry.

ATIL, ESIN: *Süleymanname: The Illustrated History of Süleyman the Magnificent.* New York: Harry N. Abrams, 1986. Lavish display of miniatures from a history of the sultan.

————: *The Age of Sultan Süleyman the Magnificent.* New York: Harry N. Abrams, 1987. The text and pictures illustrate all aspects of the art of the age.

COOK, WESTON F., JR.: *The Hundred Years War for Morocco: Gunpowder and the Military Revolution in the Early Modern Muslim World.* Boulder, Colo.: Westview, 1994. A thoughtful analysis of Moroccan events in the sixteenth century that also provides comparative insights for Ottoman and Safavid history.

FLEISCHER, CORNELL H.: *Bureaucrat and Intellectual in the Ottoman Empire: The Historian Mustafa Ali (1541–1600).* Princeton, N.J.: Princeton University Press, 1986. A sophisticated analysis not only of the life of this particular historian but of historiography for the entire period.

GOODWIN, GODFREY: *A History of Ottoman Architecture.* Baltimore: Johns Hopkins University Press, 1971. Reissued, London: Thames and Hudson, 1992. An outstanding work, covering Bursa, Edirne, Istanbul; includes Sinan's works and an excellent chapter on the Ottoman house.

————: *Sinan: Ottoman Architecture and Its Values Today.* London: Saqi, 1993. A short but valuable introduction to the superb Ottoman architect and his work.

GUILMARTIN, JOHN FRANCIS, JR.: *Gunpowder and Galleys: Changing Technology and Mediterranean Warfare at Sea in the Sixteenth Century.* London: Cambridge University Press, 1974. A masterful study on ships, sea battles, and their influence on politics and economy.

HATTOX, RALPH S.: *Coffee and Coffeehouses: The Origins of a Social Beverage in the Medieval*

Near East. Seattle: University of Washington Press, 1985. This charming and convincing book is an excellent example of research on Ottoman social history.

KORTEPETER, CARL MAX: *Ottoman Imperialism During the Reformation: Europe and the Caucasus.* New York: New York University Press, 1972. A study of relationships of political units in the great span between Europe and the Caucasus.

KURAN, APTULLAH: *The Mosque in Early Ottoman Architecture.* Chicago: University of Chicago Press, 1968. Develops the idea that the basic unit in early Ottoman architecture was the domed square. Scholarly and authoritative.

MENEMENCIOGLU, NERMIN, AND FAHIR IZ, EDS.: *The Penguin Book of Turkish Verse.* Harmondsworth, England: Penguin Books, 1978. Translations and commentaries on a wide range of Ottoman poets and modern Turkish poets as well.

MERRIMAN, R. B.: *Suleiman the Magnificent, 1520–1566.* Cambridge, Mass.: Harvard University Press, 1944. An adequate summary of the life of the great sultan.

PEIRCE, LESLIE P.: *The Imperial Harem: Women and Sovereignty in the Ottoman Empire.* New York: Oxford University Press, 1993. This outstanding analytic work concentrates on the period from 1520 to the middle of the seventeenth century; an indispensable work of historical revisionism.

PETSOPOULIS, YANNI, ED.: *Tulips, Arabesques and Turbans: Decorative Art from the Ottoman Empire.* New York: Abbeville Press, 1982. Informative chapters by a number of authors on many aspects of Ottoman art.

PRYOR, JOHN H.: *Geography, Technology and War: Studies in the Maritime History of the Mediterranean, 649–1571.* Cambridge, England: Cambridge University Press, 1988. While covering a wide array of groups, this book is especially interesting for the fifteenth- and sixteenth-century Ottomans.

ROGERS, J. M.: *Islamic Art and Design, 1500–1700.* London: British Museum, 1983. Treats Ottomans, Safavids, and Mughals of India comparatively.

CHAPTER 19

The Flowering and Decay of Safavid Iran

In the early modern period of Middle Eastern history the Shiite Safavid dynasty dominated Iran, establishing a large empire beginning in 1501 that lasted for about 220 years. During this time Iran gained a religious and political identity separate from that of its Sunnite neighbors—the Ottomans, the Mughals of India, and the Uzbegs of central Asia. Military competition with the larger Ottoman Empire strongly affected the Safavids, whose vigorous rulers such as Ismail and Abbas the Great often fought the sultans of Istanbul, even while interacting with them culturally. In the two centuries up to its abrupt demise in 1722, the Safavid state usually witnessed a capable administration, religious conversion on a large scale, economic prosperity, and cultural flowering.

ESTABLISHMENT OF THE SAFAVIDS IN IRAN

As the Mongol Il-Khan state declined in the late thirteenth and fourteenth centuries, many Turkoman tribes became autonomous. At about the same time numerous independent Sufi orders appeared. Some of the Turkoman tribes and the Sufi orders converted to Shiism, as Sufi leadership became hereditary and combined religious and military roles.

After the Mongols destroyed the city of Ardabil in northwestern Iran in 1220, it subsequently revived but only as a small provincial town. A Sufi order in Ardabil was called Safavid after its first leader, Safi al-Din, a Sunnite, who died in 1334. The tomb of the Safavid leader became a shrine, and the complex of buildings around it served as a place of pilgrimage. Political chaos, which disturbed the town and northwestern Iran, enabled the Safavid family to maintain their local freedom and gain great wealth. They became Shiites at some time after 1392 and by the 1450s were seeking political power as allies of the Aq Quyunlu Turkomans. Raids against Christian Georgia earned the Safavids the title of ghazi. Following the death in battle of the Safavid Haydar in 1488, his son took the title padishah (king or emperor), and in the late fifteenth century the charismatic Safavids claimed to be the Hidden Imam of the Twelver Shiites, who came to that position as a result of inheritance and not by designation of a predecessor. In time, powerful Turkoman tribes and Sufi groups in western Iran and eastern Anatolia accepted and supported the Safavid order. (As mentioned earlier, the Sufis were called qizilbash, or "red head," a term derived from their distinctive hat—a scarlet cone-shaped affair with twelve scallops, or gores, one for each of the twelve Shiite imams.)

Ismail, a younger son of Haydar, became the leader of the Safavid dynasty. With the indispensable aid of Turkish-speaking qizilbash tribes and a small group of advisers, Ismail defeated the Aq Quyunlu, took Armenia and Azerbaijan in 1501, and, at the age of fourteen, was proclaimed shah in Tabriz.

As leader of the Safavid religious order, Ismail regarded himself in his poetry—and was accepted—as a divine reincarnation. He was worshiped during his lifetime as a saint who possessed supernatural attributes and who, consequently, was invincible; his subjects prostrated themselves before him as before God. His state was based on the principles of Twelver Shiism, and his task in Iran was to spread that sect. Wherever his edict reached, the choice was fixed: conversion to Shiism or death. Though most Iranians had been Sunnite Muslims, Ismail's cruelty, coupled with his policy of confiscating properties of Sunnites, expropriating endowments of Sunnite Sufi orders, executing or exiling Sunnite religious leaders, bringing into Iran Shiite scholars from the Arab world (especially from southern Lebanon), and the already existing Shiite sentiment in Qumm and Khurasan and among guilds, all changed Iran into a Shiite state by the time of his death in 1524. His power was based on the support of the Turkish tribal leaders, held by a mystical

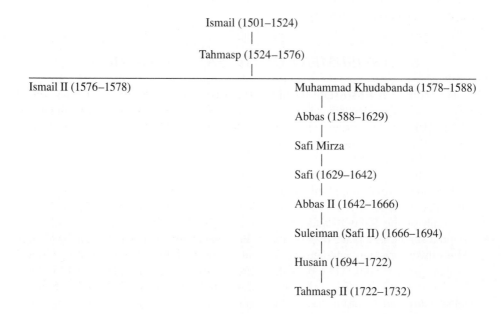

Ismail (1501–1524)
|
Tahmasp (1524–1576)
|

Ismail II (1576–1578)

Muhammad Khudabanda (1578–1588)
|
Abbas (1588–1629)
|
Safi Mirza
|
Safi (1629–1642)
|
Abbas II (1642–1666)
|
Suleiman (Safi II) (1666–1694)
|
Husain (1694–1722)
|
Tahmasp II (1722–1732)

The Safavids

allegiance and tied to urban populations who were devotees of the Safavids. The tribal and Sufi leaders together could be called a kind of religious fraternity. With economic interests shifting into the hands of the Shiites, a permanent attachment to the Safavid dynasty occurred, and peace and prosperity were sought. In return for soldiers and revenue, each qizilbash chief was given a province, with the power of life and death over its people and the obligation to convert all to Shiism.

Claiming descent from the prophet Muhammad, Ali, and the seventh Shiite imam and also from Aq Quyunlu Turks and Byzantine emperors, Ismail united Iranians, Turks, and Shiites in devotion to his mystical being. Ismail established a theocratic state in western Iran with his principal strength in the north. Ismail gained control of central and southern Iran in 1503, and of Baghdad and southwest Iran in 1508. To the west, he seized most of the Tigris-Euphrates basin including Diyarbakir in 1504, and later he reached Dhu al-Qadr and the frontiers of the Ottomans. Expanding eastward, he successfully waged war against the Sunnite Uzbegs of central Asia, killing Muhammad Shaibani, their chieftain, in 1510. Herat now became the second most important city in the state and the residence of the heir to the throne, despite the temporary resurgence of the Uzbegs in 1512.

Ismail sent religious-political agents to Anatolia, where they took advantage of the economic distress of the Turkoman tribes to urge revolt against the Ottomans. To overawe the Ottoman sultan Bayezid II, Ismail had the Uzbeg chieftain's skin stuffed with straw and sent to him as a warning. (In an even more typically macabre gesture Ismail had that same victim's skull rimmed with gold and set with jewels, using it for a while as his drinking cup.)

A governing apparatus of three main divisions was formed: military, religious, and bureaucratic. At first, no sharp distinction in the ruling establishment existed between military and civilian officers: all were members of the monarch's household. (The only real distinction was that most of the military spoke Turkish and most of the civilians spoke Persian.) As political centralization gained momentum, the reins of government were gathered into the hands of Ismail's associates and officials.

At the top of the hierarchy stood the viceroy, who exercised both temporal and spiritual authority. He took a leading role in political affairs, acted as a military commander, and influenced the selection of officials. The viceroys spoke Persian, a fact deeply resented by the qizilbash Turkish leaders. In the midst of a battle against the Uzbegs in 1512, the qizilbash forces deserted, guaranteeing the defeat and death of the viceroy. After another viceroy was killed in the battle of Chaldiran in 1514, the position was limited to supervision of the bureaucracy and the civil administration. Next in line stood the commander in chief, a post that was originally held by the viceroy and that, in addition to controlling the military, had considerable influence in administrative and political matters. In 1509, Ismail chose an obscure officer for this post in an obvious move to weaken the power of the Turkoman leaders. Persian-speaking individuals also held the posts of supervisor of the ulama and vizir. Naturally there developed among these officials a great deal of rivalry for power and for Ismail's favor.

When Selim I seized the Ottoman throne in Istanbul in 1512, he became involved in the raging quarrel in Anatolia over the qizilbash tribes. Selim set out to destroy Ismail. At the battle of Chaldiran in 1514 the Ottomans outnumbered the Safavids; in addition, the Ottoman forces enjoyed the superiority of janissary muskets and Ottoman artillery over the Safavid swords, spears, and bows. (The Safavids had used cannons in sieges, but they were reluctant to use cannons and handguns, and did not successfully integrate handguns and artillery into their military; the Ottomans, on the other hand, adapted their warfare to the new technology.) Most Turkoman qizilbash leaders and many high Iranian officials were killed. The Ottomans temporarily occupied the Safavid capital of Tabriz, but the long lines of transportation back to Anatolia, the opposition of the soldiers to such a distant campaign, and the bitter cold induced Selim to retreat. The Ottomans did, however, gain and keep Diyarbakir and most of eastern Anatolia.

Ismail's spirit was crushed. It is said that he never smiled again, and he began to drink excessively. Henceforth the Turkoman leaders tended to doubt Ismail's claim of supernatural powers. But with Selim seizing Kurdistan and Diyarbakir, and wiping out qizilbash rebellion in Anatolia, the Turkoman qizilbash seemed to have had no choice but loyalty to Ismail. The shah never again led troops into battle. He tried to put civilians into positions of trust and power in order to break the might of the qizilbash leaders, although he could not control all the provinces, especially Khurasan. With his death in 1524 at the age of thirty-six, the full extent of the decline of the ruling institution became apparent.

SHAH TAHMASP I

Because when Ismail died his eldest son, Tahmasp, was only ten years old, Turkoman leaders were able to regain their power. Civil war among the Turkoman tribes kept the state in turmoil until Tahmasp subdued the rebellions and ended the strife by seizing power for himself and appointing an Iranian viceroy in 1533. Tahmasp then established his personal authority, civilian rule as set by Ismail became dominant, and the Safavid state survived. The Sufi organization was unsuccessful in penetrating or subverting the administrative system of the Safavid government. During this period in Iran the main lines of monarchy were worked out, the capital was fixed first at Qazvin and later in Isfahan, and Shiism became the established official religion.

Despite this political turmoil, textiles, ceramics, calligraphy, and miniature painting flourished during Tahmasp's reign. The shah himself was a noted poet, calligrapher, and painter. Illustrations for Firdawsi's *Shahnamah* commissioned by Ismail and Tahmasp were especially splendid. In religious matters, Tahmasp did not regard himself as being semidivine; instead, he designated a leading cleric as the deputy of the Hidden Imam (a concept later called the mujtahid of the age).

External enemies threatened the Safavid lands. The Uzbegs took Khurasan but were defeated by Tahmasp in 1528, in large part thanks to cannons provided by the Portuguese. To the west, when the Ottoman sultan Suleiman I threatened Iran over its support of various Turkoman chiefs, Tahmasp in vain sent envoys to Charles V

for aid. In 1534 the Ottomans invaded, sacking Tabriz and Gilan, and capturing Baghdad. (Central Iraq remained in Ottoman hands for ninety years.) Another campaign occurred in 1548 when Tahmasp's brother induced the Ottomans to send an invading army that seized Azerbaijan. Peace was arranged in 1555, but the shah lost Iraq to the Ottomans. Although a shortage of artillery and muskets was a disadvantage to Tahmasp, his scorched-earth strategy, distances from Istanbul, difficult terrain, problems in the Danube basin and the Mediterranean, and the psychology of Ottoman fighting men stopped the Ottoman forces from permanent conquest. Thus, Tahmasp was able to enforce his rule from the Tigris to central Asia and from the Persian Gulf to both sides of the Caspian Sea. Border provinces lost their autonomy and were directly incorporated into the state.

Within the Safavid lands there was competition between the qizilbash Turkomans and Persian-speaking groups. Shah Tahmasp attempted, as his father had before him, to find an alternative to the power of unreliable Sufis and qizilbash. Nearly every province was held by one of their leaders, and their incomes and retainers gave them an independence difficult to offset. Between 1540 and 1544 Tahmasp sent four expeditions to Georgia, bringing back 30,000 prisoners, most of whom were boys who would be trained as ghulams—slaves to serve in his army or in administration. The girls served as concubines whose sons also entered the shah's service. This policy of creating a Georgian, Circassian, and Armenian counterweight to the qizilbash in the end proved disastrous, as civil war broke out between them in 1572 when Tahmasp grew old and feeble. Also, his many sons and their mothers began to intrigue for the succession. Two leading candidates were Prince Ismail, whose mother was a Circassian, and Prince Haydar, whose mother was a Georgian. In the end the qizilbash declared they would support sons of Turkish mothers only.

In 1576, Tahmasp was poisoned and the qizilbash had the power to put Ismail, his fourth son, on the throne. Having been incarcerated for twenty years by his father, he was brutal toward his royal relatives. He killed all the royal princes except Prince Muhammad Khudabanda, who was nearly blind and not considered a threat. The shah attempted to return Iran to Sunnism, and he executed many qizilbash and Sufi leaders who had supported his brothers. Ismail II finally gave orders to have his sole remaining brother executed. Before the deed could be committed, however, the shah died mysteriously; it is possible he was poisoned.

Shah Muhammad Khudabanda ruled as a puppet in Turkoman hands for ten years until 1588. During this time of Safavid weakness the Ottomans began a war that lasted from 1578 to 1590 and resulted in their reconquest of Tabriz. Shah Muhammad was overthrown and killed by Turkoman leaders who seized Qazvin, the capital, and who put his sixteen-year-old son, Abbas, on the throne. Ruling for forty-one years, Abbas ushered in a new age in Iranian history. By 1587, religious zeal for Safavid rule had lessened, and over the century the shah's position as the head of a secular state dominated. There had been a gradual change and evolution under Tahmasp, with acceptance of the idea of a central government. He strengthened the state by moving the capital from Tabriz to Qazvin, which was safer from Ottoman assault. Moreover, Shiite doctrinal unity had been achieved to a great extent, making religion much less of an emotional issue. One could now recognize the consolidation of Safavid Iran into a state of considerable permanence.

SHAH ABBAS THE GREAT OF ISFAHAN

Only about one-half of the Safavid Empire was still intact when Abbas came to the throne. After the qizilbash chieftains left Herat for Qazvin to install Abbas on the Safavid throne in 1588, the Sunnite Uzbeg tribes had invaded and captured Herat. Shah Abbas met them at Meshhed, but crucial rebellions of local princes in his western provinces demanded his immediate return. With combined forces of local qizilbash tribes and an army improvised from Georgian prisoners and held together by his personal leadership, Abbas was able to put down a serious uprising in Shiraz and soon had central Iran pacified. The Ottoman attack in the west could not be thwarted, however, and by the peace of 1590 with Murad III, Tabriz, some Caspian ports, and surrounding areas were ceded.

During the following seven years Abbas consolidated his position and power, his initial step being the weakening of qizilbash forces. Their leaders were killed and their provinces and lands confiscated. With the income from these holdings plus the funds of the royal household, Abbas formed a standing army of 10,000 horsemen and 12,000 foot soldiers from prisoners and slaves from Armenia and Georgia. In addition to this strengthening of manpower, Abbas significantly improved his firepower.

In 1598, Robert Sherley, along with other Englishmen, arrived in Isfahan, the new capital, to discuss trade and an alliance against the Ottomans and the Dutch. The Englishmen helped Abbas train musketeers and taught his men how to cast cannon. Within a few years, Abbas had a force of 12,000 artillery men equipped with 500 brass and bronze cannons with which he effectively challenged the Ottoman armies as well as internal dissidents. A new corps of 12,000 mounted musketeers was raised from the peasantry, and another 10,000 Georgian prisoners were added to the army. Throughout his reign Abbas continued the policy of turning prisoners of war into soldiers and administrators: on one occasion 20,000 Armenians were taken from the region of Erzurum and pressed into service; on another, an expedition into Georgia, tens of thousands of prisoners were taken and moved into his state in various areas and capacities.

By 1602, Abbas cleared the eastern frontiers of challengers. He drove the Uzbegs from Meshhed, Herat, and Khurasan and moved eastward to Balkh. Abbas attempted to stamp out Sunnism in eastern Iran. To defend Khurasan he transported thousands of Kurdish horsemen and their families to the frontier, establishing them so securely that many of their descendants still reside in that area. War against the Ottomans erupted in 1603, and Tabriz was recaptured. With the decline of Ottoman military force in eastern Anatolia, Abbas took Kurdistan and Shirvan from Ahmed I and in 1623 recaptured Baghdad, Mosul, and Diyarbakir, restoring to Iran the territories held at the time of Shah Ismail. On other fronts, Abbas defeated the Mughals of India, taking Qandahar (Kandahar) in Afghanistan; seized the Bahrain Islands in the Persian Gulf; and with British aid drove the Portuguese from Hormuz in 1622, founding the important Persian Gulf trading post of Bandar Abbas. When Shah Abbas died in 1629, his lands enjoyed peace and prosperity. In contrast, the Ottoman Empire had been defeated, Russia was recovering from its Time of Troubles, and the Mughals in India were beginning to lose hold of south Asia.

ADMINISTRATION AND TRADE UNDER ABBAS

By the year 1606, Shah Abbas had established his direct rule over most of the provinces of Iran. Warfare was relegated to the frontiers and was fought by professional soldiers as well as qizilbash. The administration of most of the provinces was overseen by governors subservient to the royal will. Like Allahverdi Khan, governor of Fars and one of Abbas's first appointees, many of these officials were slaves. In due course, more than a fifth of the central government came from the ghulam slave ranks. Still, a majority of the civil administration was drawn from Persian-speaking free people.

Over one-half of the population consisted of peasant farmers living in villages; the next largest economic group was made up of nomads and seminomads, organized usually into tribes; and the smallest category consisted of town and city dwellers. Revocable grants of revenue from each of these groups constituted the chief form of payment for government officials and soldiers. Each city had its mayor, responsible for taxes and civil order. The numerous craft guilds were strictly regulated, their chief masters meeting with the mayor to debate taxes and matters of general concern; on occasion they protested government restrictions and officials' oppressions. Most imperial revenues came from the tax on land.

The shah created numerous religious endowments as symbols of his commitment to Twelver Shiism. Abbas enhanced the post of sadr, an administrative official and head of the religious and judicial hierarchy, who gained in power by becoming charged with the administration of many religious endowments or waqfs. Madrasahs, courts, and mosques were flourishing, but they were not as efficiently organized and as subservient to imperial authority as in the Ottoman Empire. The shah ordered the compilation of a legal treatise that became the basis of law for the century. Shiite ulama were brought to Iran from the Arab theological centers of southern Lebanon and Bahrain, and the shah persecuted the Shiite Sufi orders. The great philosopher and metaphysician Mullah Sadra Shirazi (d. 1640), writing in Arabic, espoused Gnostic views. As a result, he was strongly attacked by the Shiite ulama.

Abbas had a special concern for commerce, both domestic and foreign. To connect all major cities, Abbas provided a network of roads that every 20 miles (32 km.) or so had a secure caravansarai where several caravans could spend the night safe from marauders. The shah showed similar initiative with regard to the important and highly profitable silk trade. Since Armenian communities were basic in the silk trade, with one of their centers at Julfa on the Aras River in Azerbaijan, Abbas imported 3000 Armenian families and created New Julfa for them on the outskirts of Isfahan, exempting them from various taxes and permitting them to elect their own mayor. A monopoly over the silk trade was established, with the Armenians running it for the shah. They prospered so greatly that some Armenian merchants lived in the style of the Safavid imperial court. Armenian religious manuscript illumination reached new heights, and the printing of Armenian secular works took place in 1608.

To exploit European enthusiasm for fine porcelain from China, Abbas brought 300 Chinese potters to Isfahan to create pottery in the Chinese style. Not only was an additional export developed but an important tradition was established, for the most skillful and resourceful potters since the seventeenth century have been in Isfahan.

It was not long before Iranian artisanal goods were highly esteemed and their quality and artistry became legendary. Among the more important were silk and wool carpets and textiles of all types, porcelains, miniature paintings and albums, enamelwork, glassware, dyes, jewelry, lacquered woods, bookbindings, leather goods, gold and silver plates, vases, and fine steel swords. Since many of these items were the product of court workshops, they were of a design and workmanship that were nearly always superb. As commercial relations with Europe and particularly the Netherlands increased in the seventeenth century, export goods declined somewhat in quality and were more influenced by foreign motifs.

Undoubtedly the best-known articles have been the Persian carpets. The finest of these carpets were made in court workshops for the court and the wealthiest patrons, few if any being exported. Only materials of the highest quality were employed in their manufacture. Sheep were specially bred for their delicate wool and were tended like children so that the wool would never be soiled or roughened. Even the water for washing the wool was important. Court painters designed the carpets, often using medallion patterns and also employing refined stylized motifs that incorporated gardens, animals, and pools. At the time of Abbas, great carpet factories were located at Kerman, Herat, Hamadan, Tabriz, and Karabagh, but other cities and provinces also produced fine carpets that were much in demand, especially in Europe. Rugs manufactured for export, though of a lesser quality, were nevertheless rich in color, design, and fabrication, most coming from workshops closely allied to the court. Outside the imperial capital the carpet weaving of nomads and villagers followed the old traditions and was often of high quality, particularly in the making of plain-weave, lightweight kilims used for travel.

Skills in other arts were also highly developed. Velvets, brocades, and embroideries were produced with the greatest care. Painting and the decorative arts were of a highly intricate style that displayed a keen sense of blending floral and geometric patterns to create a pleasing whole. The work of goldsmiths and silversmiths has hardly been surpassed. Potters learned how to decorate their wares in many colors, often firing seven or more colors at once on large tiles. Shah Abbas was so fond of fine calligraphy that he is said to have personally held a candlestick so that his favorite artist could see better as he wrote.

THE SPLENDOR OF ISFAHAN

The internal stability established by Shah Abbas the Great encouraged a vast increase in trade, raised levels of production, opened wider avenues of opportunity for many, and ensured a great prosperity for much of the population. At the court in Isfahan the resulting wealth transformed the style of life to a degree of lavishness seldom seen. European visitors gave nearly incredible descriptions of the dazzling opulence: Abbas on his throne surrounded by several hundred courtiers clothed in gold and silver with an array of gray, scarlet, yellow, green, plum, blue, and maroon silks embroidered with the rarest of jewels. What Abbas lacked in terms of the size of his palaces he made up for in number—over 100 in Isfahan alone. Each of these palaces was a masterpiece of design and decoration, as can be seen from Ali Kapu and Chihil Sutun, which still stand.

In the center of the new, planned district of Isfahan, Abbas surrounded a great open square, 560 yards (512 m.) by 174 yards (159 m.), with magnificent buildings. The square was used for polo—the popular sport of the courtiers at that time—horse races, fireworks displays, and executions. On one side of the square was the Ali Kapu, an entrance to a palace, featuring a lovely pavilion in which Abbas liked to lounge with his courtiers and watch the festivities of the square. On another side was the imperial mosque, Masjid-i Shah, masterpiece of Safavid architecture. An impressive pointed archway more than 80 feet (24 m.) high led to an inner courtyard surrounded by a graceful two-storied arcade. Opposite the entrance was another portal leading to the mosque proper, whose walls carried a large dome, the exterior of which was covered by exquisite polychrome tiles with arabesque patterns in dark blue and green on a sky-blue background. On another side of the area was a great covered bazaar with a monumental arched entrance. The dome of the imperial mosque served as a landmark of the center of the heavily walled city, which had 600,000 inhabitants and boasted 1802 caravansarais, 162 mosques, 273 public baths, 48 colleges and academies, and numerous coffeehouses. Isfahan, with its rich verdure, pools, bridges, and watercourses, was a flower lover's paradise, its gardens displaying roses, jasmine, lilies, irises, poppies, and many other flowers. Abbas himself laid out the gardens, planned the buildings, and even gave detailed instructions to the workmen.

UZBEG CENTRAL ASIA

At the time when the Safavids were accomplishing much in the cultural and military arenas, in the arid steppelands of central Asia the heirs of Timur were driven into India, where they subsequently created the Mughal Empire. In their place, the Shaibanid and Tuqay Timurid descendants of the Mongol conquerer Genghiz Khan established Sunnite states based on Uzbeg Turkish-Mongol tribes. Succession in the royal families to the position of khan or leader usually went to the senior male in the family, and military and fiscal power often was decentralized among various royal princes. The Turkish Uzbeg and Persian Tajik nomadic, village, and urban populations also provided military and Sufi leaders. Administration was less formal and thorough than in the Safavid Empire; for instance, the rulers did not have a formal standing army. Holders of revocable grants played a large role in tax collection and provincial administration. The Hanafite rite of Islam dominated the shariah courts as supported by the political leadership.

Muhammad Shaibani Khan, the grandson of an earlier Uzbeg leader, rose from a cavalry soldier to governor of Tashkent by 1494. He based his claim to power on descent from the Mongol conqueror Genghiz Khan. After Muhammad Shaibani's capture of Samarkand in 1501 he expanded the new Uzbeg state to Herat in 1507, but following his defeat and execution by Shah Ismail the khanate was more limited geographically, including chiefly Bukhara, Samarkand, Tashkent, and Balkh. Although the Shaibanids defended themselves against Mughal and Safavid attacks, internal divisions limited their military power. Civil wars between 1550 and 1582 ultimately resulted in the victory of one Shaibanid clan, which united all of the region. Abd Allah Khan (1583–1598) overcame the Safavids and seized Herat and most of Khurasan, but upon his death and the assassination of his heir, anarchy ensued. The Safavid Abbas the Great regained eastern Iran, while in central Asia the Shaibanid dynasty disappeared.

Rule over Uzbeg central Asia fell into the hands of another group of descendants of Genghiz Khan, the Tuqay Timurid clan. They consolidated their power during the decade of the 1600s, gaining their capital Bukhara, as well as Samarkand and Balkh, but ultimately ceding Tashkent to the expanding power of the Kazakhs. The long and relatively peaceful reign of Imam Quli Khan (1612–1642) was followed by civil war and Mughal invasion, and finally the reestablishment of the Tuqay Timurids, who ruled from both Bukhara and Balkh. In the last half of the seventeenth century the Tuqay Timurids maintained their state against numerous foes, supported the ulama and Sufis, and fostered the pilgrimage to Mecca.

Both branches of the Genghiz Khan family, the Shaibanids and the Tuqay Timurids, built mosques, madrasahs, Sufi centers, and royal palaces in central Asia. The Tuqay Timurid khans endowed shrines with waqf properties to provide money for expenses. Literature written in eastern Turkish dialects provided a basis for a common culture heavily influenced by Safavid Iran, and miniature painting modeled on the style of Herat flourished in Bukhara, which was the intellectual capital of Muslim central Asia.

In the first half of the eighteenth century central Asia experienced a general crisis, including political disintegration, economic decay, urban collapse, the enhancement of tribal power, and the decline of settled agriculture. Government revenues lessened as commerce decreased, while local groups successfully challenged the power of the various royal families. Samarkand was completely abandoned and devastated. The Tuqay Timurid khans in Bukhara lost all real power, although they remained symbols of legitimate rule. Kazakh tribes expanded their influence, while Turkmen groups moved into Khurasan and parts of central Asia. As a result, an ethnic and linguistic patchwork of settlements emerged, where widely varying groups of people lived side by side.

SHAHS SAFI AND ABBAS II

South of Uzbeg central Asia in Iran, the last century of Safavid rule began with the relatively uneventful reigns of Shahs Safi and Abbas II, who preserved the basic institutions and boundaries of the empire between 1629 and 1666. Personally the shahs were capricious and cruel, and, as was perhaps to be expected, they could not maintain the level of rule of Abbas the Great. During this time a transition took place from an expansionist military and foreign policy to a more internally oriented leadership; for most Safavid subjects the change was probably at first beneficial.

The empire was preserved intact by a multitude of factors: the widespread acceptance of Shiism as a common bond among the people, the strength of the administration, the quality of many officials, the vitality of commerce, the general peace, the internal tranquillity, and the weakness of opponents beyond the frontiers. Without these, the dynasty and the state might well have become weak earlier than was actually the case.

A decline in the experience and ability of the rulers was caused by Abbas I. Because he feared the popularity of his own sons, he had his eldest executed and two others blinded, making them ineligible to rule. In addition, he instituted the practice of keeping the royal princes as prisoners within the palace, in the company of women and servants who satisfied their every sensual whim. Catapulted to the throne after years of polite imprisonment, their incompetence was compounded by the influence of court officials, women of the harem, and slave officials. Effective control of administration frequently fell into the hands of the grand vizir. Often naive and upright when ascending the throne, a young shah would be intentionally corrupted by court attendants to enable them to rule without his interference.

Consequently, upon his death in 1629, Abbas was succeeded by his young grandson, Shah Safi, whose debauchery was thoroughgoing. He murdered his mother, a sister, his favorite wife, army generals, provincial governors, and many of the court officials. Nevertheless, the government under Safi did have the strength and will to repel Uzbeg incursions into Khurasan and suppress rebellions in Gilan, although the Mughals repossessed Qandahar and the Ottomans retook Baghdad in 1638. There ensued a peace treaty that ended the incessant Safavid-Ottoman wars—at the cost of Iraq becoming Ottoman. The shah was a noted patron of miniature painting, thus continuing Isfahan's reputation as the center for great successes in this art form.

Safi died from drinking too much and was followed in 1642 by his ten-year-old son, Abbas II, who started with real promise and at the age of sixteen showed vigor and flashes of his great-grandfather's character by leading an army in the recapture of Qandahar. Despite this success, Abbas II usually chose peace with his neighbors. During his reign an intellectual form of Sufism and Gnosticism reached a high level. He appointed slave ghulams who were converts to Islam to high posts in the provincial governments, while the shah personally took a direct interest in the administration of justice. Still more lands were taken from the governance of notables and directly administered by the central authorities. Abbas II's rule was marred, however, when he turned to drink and personal indulgences, murdering many around him and forcing the conversion of Isfahan Jews to Islam.

Some cultural and artistic successes were achieved. In ceramics, armor, textiles, miniature paintings, and drawings, works of considerable beauty were still being created. However, European styles began to influence painting by the late seventeenth century, and literature and poetry were in decay, despite new opportunities for poets and folktale reciters in coffeehouses. The ruling dynasties of India and the Ottoman Empire offered many inducements to Persian writers, prominent thinkers, and artists to entice them to leave Iran. The sciences in Iran were stagnant, except for limited advances in medicine and in the production of astrolabes.

THE DECLINE AND END OF SAFAVID RULE

In addition to a steady decline in the quality of the shahs, the power of the central government over distant regions weakened. The economy contracted as the value of exports fell, foreign competition increased, gold was in short supply, and insecurity on the trade routes worsened. Silk production may have decreased after 1670, although wool exports increased. Transportation of bulky goods continued to be so expensive that while grain surpluses existed in some areas, famines took place elsewhere. The government debased the coinage and reallocated spending away from the military so that close to one-half of expenditures went to the harem and the royal family. Customs collections were farmed out to tax collectors, a practice that in the long run contributed to budgetary woes. Most important of all, the number and effectiveness of tribal cavalry soldiers fell even as spending on the ghulam standing army was also cut.

Moreover, at the same time as this economic and military decline, Shiism became ever more widespread among the peoples of Iran. The Shiite ulama gained more influence at court and among the faithful. At the instigation of the ulama many of the Sufi orders were repressed by the state and eventually Sunnites were harassed. As the shahs lost legitimacy and backing, the Shiite ulama gained support.

Upon the death of Abbas II in 1666, his seventeen-year-old son first took the title Safi II but because of disasters chose to take a new regnal name and was re-crowned the following year as Shah Suleiman. He reigned (it could not be said that he ruled) for twenty-eight long years, dying in 1694. Shah Suleiman was a drunkard who loved peace and thought little about the state: once, when told that an attack was expected, he replied that it made no difference to him, as long as he could keep Isfahan. Perhaps inadvertently this policy of peace worked well, and Iran enjoyed long years of respite from foreign wars.

In 1669 Shah Suleiman built the famous palace called "Eight Paradises," known for its pavilions and tile work. The shah had many government officials executed, leaving more of the administration to his ghulam palace cronies, although he had sense enough to employ an able grand vizir. When he died in 1694, he had already executed his eldest son and left the choice between his other sons to the eunuchs and courtiers of the palace. They chose Husain. Having been shut up in the harem of the palace for twenty-six years, Husain was ignorant, superstitious, and easily influenced—just the kind of shah the courtiers desired.

Subject to excessive piety, Husain inaugurated his reign by prohibiting the use of wine: he had all the wine jars in the palace broken and would not permit the Armenians who controlled the wine trade to sell in Isfahan. As a youth he had become a partisan of religious teachers and leaders, or mullahs, so much so that many jokingly called him Mullah Husain. Religious minorities—Christians, Jews, and Sunnites—were persecuted. In 1706, the shah organized a pilgrimage to the holy shrine at Qumm, the site of the family tombs, accompanied by over 60,000 people. This venture proved so enjoyable that he went with an equal number of retainers on the 600-mile (965-km.) pilgrimage to Meshhed, remaining there a whole year. The extravagance of this expedition not only emptied the treasury but ruined all the provinces through which it passed.

Thanks to an aunt who prevailed upon him to permit her to drink in the palace, Husain did not remain abstemious for long. Soon wine flowed freely everywhere. Husain became licentious, and his agents were constantly on the lookout for attractive faces to kidnap for his harem. Unable to curb his lavish habits and faced with the mounting cost of maintaining a standing army with cannon and muskets, the shah's ministers had to find additional income. Government officials created artificial bread shortages in the capital of Isfahan and then made fortunes selling grain at inflated prices. Another lucrative device was to squeeze more revenue from the provinces. Even before this, provincial administration had already suffered under Safi I and Abbas II, when many provinces had been transferred to the royal household and their governorships sold to court favorites, who reimbursed themselves by gouging the inhabitants. The right to collect revenue was sold more and more often, thereby also increasing the tax burden on the peasants.

Upon the raiding of Qandahar by Baluchis, Shah Husain sent a Georgian general as the new governor in 1704, who adopted such severe measures against the Sunnite Ghilzai Afghan inhabitants that they rose in revolt under Mir Vays in 1709. Shah Husain sent an army from Isfahan in 1711 to destroy Mir Vays, but being poorly-paid and divided by jealousies among three different components, it was routed in front of the walls of Qandahar. Mir Vays thus became an independent ruler, calling himself regent of Qandahar.

In 1715 Mir Vays was succeeded by his sixteen-year-old son, Mahmud, an ambitious youth who began to attack the shah's kingdom, advancing to a point close to Isfahan. The battle for the Safavid capital was joined in 1722, with Mahmud occupying the Armenian suburb of New Julfa and investing the city. After a six-month siege that saw 60,000 inhabitants killed by starvation or epidemics and 20,000 killed in fighting, Husain surrendered. In a humiliating ceremony Husain went out to Mahmud's headquarters and there, with his own hands, took from his turban the imperial plume of heron's feathers set with jewels—the sign of sovereignty—placed it on Mahmud's head, and bade him rule. Safavid power had collapsed.

During the siege Tahmasp, one of Husain's older sons, escaped from Isfahan and made his way to Qazvin, where he was recognized as Shah Tahmasp II. Affairs were not, however, favorable to his candidacy for rule. The Ottomans seized Tiflis, Tabriz, and Hamadan. Peter the Great of Russia, outfitting a fleet on the Caspian Sea, took Shirvan and Gilan, and compelled Tahmasp II to sign a treaty in 1722, ceding to Russia Darband, Baku, Gilan, Astarabad, and Mazandaran in exchange for Peter's commitment to drive the Afghans from Isfahan. When Mahmud learned of the proposed Russian incursion to place Tahmasp II back on the throne in Isfahan, he had all the members of the Safavid family assembled in the palace court-yard; he and two of his friends then hacked them to death, except for Husain and two small children whom Husain shielded with his own body. Mahmud, who had rapidly grown insane, died in 1725, being succeeded by his cousin Ashraf. The Ottoman armies pressed forward into Iran, asserting that they planned to restore the Safavids to their rightful possessions. Ashraf thereupon had Husain executed and sent his head to the Ottoman commander to forestall his attack on Isfahan.

Meanwhile, Tahmasp II gathered an army in Mazandaran in 1727, being supported by two qizilbash tribal leaders: Fath Ali Khan, the chief of the Qajars, and Nadir Khan of the Afshars, each bringing several thousand experienced soldiers. They marched into Khurasan and recaptured Meshhed and Herat from the Afghans in 1729; along the way Nadir Khan murdered his rival, Fath Ali, and thus became the sole commander of the royal army. Nadir routed the Afghans under Ashraf, expelling them from Isfahan and Shiraz. Tahmasp II returned as shah to Isfahan but gave most power to Nadir. In 1732 Nadir dethroned him and sent him as a prisoner to Khurasan, where he was later killed. Nadir put Tahmasp's infant son on the throne as Abbas III, but the child died in 1736 and Nadir assumed the title shah, the powers of which he had been holding for several years. Safavid rule had ended.

The Safavids left a profound legacy for Iran, as they determined its Shiite religious identity, established many of its borders, encouraged a cultural flowering, and provided stable government. Notable Safavid shahs—Ismail, Tahmasp I, and Abbas the Great—arranged a balance of power among their backers so that qizilbash, ghulams, ulama, and bureaucrats functioned effectively. Isfahan during the reign of Abbas I was especially splendid. The decline and collapse of the Safavids, however, ushered in a long era of chaos and catastrophes for the people of Iran. During the seventeenth century the Ottoman Empire faced many of the same challenges and opportunities encountered by the Safavids and the Uzbegs of central Asia, but the Ottomans were more successful in responding to changes. While the Safavid and Uzbeg dynasties collapsed, the Ottomans endured for several more centuries.

References

Works relevant to this chapter are listed in Chapters 11, 12, and 18.

ARJOMAND, SAID AMIR: *The Shadow of God and the Hidden Imam: Religion, Political Order, and Societal Change in Shi'ite Iran from the Beginning to 1890.* Chicago: University of Chicago Press, 1984. A review of religion and politics from a social scientist's viewpoint.

FORAN, JOHN: "The Long Fall of the Safavid Dynasty: Moving Beyond the Standard Views." *International Journal of Middle East Studies* 24 (1992): 281–304. Adds new dimensions to the analysis presented in the book by Laurence Lockhart cited below.

———: *Fragile Resistance: Social Transformation in Iran from 1500 to the Revolution.* Boulder, Colo.: Westview, 1993. This important sociological and historical study puts Iran's experiences into a comparative framework.

KEYVANI, MEHDI: *Artisans and Guild Life in the Later Safavid Period: Contributions to the Social-Economic History of Persia.* Berlin: Klaus Schwarz, 1982.

LOCKHART, LAURENCE: *The Fall of the Safavi Dynasty and the Afghan Occupation of Persia.* New York: Cambridge University Press, 1958. Deals largely with the eighteenth century; excellent for political history.

MATTHEE, RUDI: "Administrative Stability and Change in Late-17th-Century Iran: The Case of Shaykh 'Ali Khan Zanganah (1669–89)." *International Journal of Middle East Studies* 26 (1994): 77–98. An interesting account of the life and policies of a Safavid grand vizir.

McCHESNEY, ROBERT D.: "Waqf and Public Policy: The Waqfs of Shah Abbas, 1011–1023/1602–1614." *Asian and African Studies* 15 (1981): 165–190.

———: *Waqf in Central Asia: Four Hundred Years in the History of a Muslim Shrine, 1480–1889.* Princeton, N.J.: Princeton University Press, 1991. The economic, social, and political history of Balkh is splendidly illuminated by this thorough study.

———: "Central Asia vi. In the 10th–12th/16th–18th Centuries." *Encyclopaedia Iranica.* Vol. 5, pp. 176–193. Costa Mesa, Calif.: Mazda, 1992. Valuable detailed discussion of political and military history.

MONSHI, ESKANDAR BEG: *History of Shah 'Abbas the Great.* 2 vols. Translated by Roger M. Savory. Boulder, Colo.: Westview, 1978. A monumental "insider's" look at Safavid court history.

SAVORY, ROGER: *Iran Under the Safavids.* Cambridge, England: Cambridge University Press, 1980. In addition to political events, there is full discussion of foreign policy, the arts, the city of Isfahan, social and economic history, and intellectual life. A brilliant and impressive work, crucial for the era.

TITLEY, NORAH M.: *Persian Miniature Painting and Its Influence on the Art of Turkey and India.* Austin: University of Texas Press, 1984. Includes Mongol, Timurid, Safavid, and Qajar art, with an emphasis on individual painters and their styles.

WELCH, STUART CARY: *A King's Book of Kings: The Shah-Nameh of Shah Tahmasp.* New York: Metropolitan Museum of Art, 1976. Sumptuous and beautiful.

The Transformation of the Ottoman Empire

Unlike the Safavids, the Ottomans were able to adapt to changing situations while retaining both internal legitimacy and military prowess. During the long seventeenth century between 1574 and 1699 the government of the Ottoman Empire went through a gradual transformation. Many in the ruling Ottoman elite viewed the changes in leadership, the military, the economy, and society as a decline from earlier times, but it is possible to see them as a readjustment with some positive as well as negative characteristics. In the fifteenth and sixteenth centuries the Ottoman state had been expansionist, with sultans who were activist warriors. Now the empire expanded only slightly even though it fought many long wars, and its sultans were for the most part less competent and usually sedentary in Istanbul. Power was shared in a different way in the capital, while in the provinces the transformation favorably affected the interests of some groups while harming others.

THE TRANSFORMATION OF THE SULTANATE

The Ottoman political system with an absolute sultan as the keystone of the arch of power changed as the military, administrative, and religious establishments lost power to the palace. A dozen sultans ruled during the period, and many of them were personally incompetent and in some cases even disastrous rulers. The causes of this obvious change in the quality of the sultans were in part the need for a regency for the four who were under sixteen years of age when they succeeded to the throne and also the fact that most of the rest of these sultans were undisciplined young men with little training to be rulers. Transformation of the sultanate was an evolving process discernible for a number of years rather than an abrupt change associated with the personalities or characteristics of a single ruler.

As the sultanate changed, the women of the royal family, especially the mothers of the sultan and the sultans' favorite concubines, gained great influence and even on occasion formulated policy. One example was Sultan Murad III (1574–1595), who was controlled by his mother and by his harem favorite, Sultana

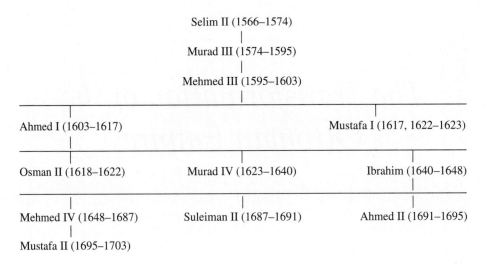

Ottoman Rulers, 1566–1703

Safiye. It was Safiye who actually ruled the empire later while her son Mehmed III (1595–1603) occupied the throne. For a time Murad was so faithful to Safiye that his mother and sister, the wife of Sokollu, fretted over her undue power and made presents of pretty slaves to distract Murad's attention. In at least one respect they were obviously successful: Murad fathered over 100 children, of whom 20 sons and 27 daughters survived him.

The women of the harem also used the marriage of princesses to state officials as a means of cultivating loyalty and influence. Women in the royal family became prominent philanthropists, sponsors of elaborate buildings, and creators of waqf foundations. A sultan's mother served many roles: regent during the minority of a young sultan, protector of her son against intrigues, adviser to him, and a channel whereby outsiders could pass on information.

Another transformation took place in the succession to the throne. In most earlier cases, Ottoman royal princes battled for their father's sultanate, with the victors executing the losers. Ahmed I (1603–1617), upon his accession to rule, decided upon a new procedure where succession was based on seniority. Unlike his father, who had had his own nineteen brothers strangled, Ahmed allowed his nearly insane brother, Mustafa (1617, 1622–1623), to be his heir and to live closeted in the palace. Royal princes were kept in the palace after the reign of Murad III, so the sultans came to the throne without experience of outside life, but the new system did stop the violent struggles for succession among the princes. The sultans were now sedentary in Istanbul and not often leaders in battle, which allowed them to stay in the center of power rather than risk their lives in battles on the distant frontiers of the empire. While in the prior fourteen generations of Ottoman sultans succession went from a father to a son, for the next three centuries the eldest male of the dynasty, usually a brother or nephew of the incumbent, succeeded upon the death, deposition, or abdication of the sultan.

The sultans were surrounded by fawning officials and courtiers. In such an atmosphere intrigue flourished. Personal spies, forgeries, intercepted letters, and gossip became acknowledged techniques of government. Sultans usually found it impossible to differentiate the important from the petty and frequently were of a mentality that bordered upon derangement. Mustafa I was, in fact, quite mad.

The saddest chapter in seventeenth-century Ottoman history was the period embracing the reign of Ibrahim (1640–1648) and the minority of Mehmed IV (r. 1648–1687). Ibrahim, the only male of the royal family alive in 1640, initiated a reign of eight years that was one long series of wild caprices. Among many other things, Ibrahim disrupted divan meetings. Ibrahim had a great passion for furs and commanded that the floors and walls of his apartments be carpeted and covered with sable. The sultan commissioned a trusted woman of the harem to make the rounds of Istanbul baths to seek out special beauties who were then installed in his harem. No person and no property were secure against Ibrahim; he even seduced the daughter of the shaikh al-Islam. In 1648 the janissaries and ulama, led by the shaikh al-Islam, deposed Ibrahim as unfit to rule and placed his seven-year-old son on the throne. Ten days later when the sipahis rioted in favor of Ibrahim, the executioners were sent to his cell. For eight years the Ottoman central government had been the scene of intrigue, military insubordination, judicial venality, local oppression, and provincial revolt. Sultana Turhan, Mehmed IV's mother, saved the day for her son by appointing in 1656 an old, experienced, and honest official (Mehmed Köprülü) as grand vizir with absolute power and authority.

Even before the advent of Köprülü there were flashes of the earlier style of sultanic leadership as seen in the reign of Murad IV (1623–1640). At Murad's accession the treasury was empty, the coinage debased, and the soldiery of Istanbul unruly and lawless. His mother had talent and preserved the sultan's authority for several years until he came of age. In 1632 the sipahis rose in revolt and called for the heads of high officials, including the shaikh al-Islam and the grand vizir. For two months terror reigned at the palace. Murad IV perceived that his own turn might easily come unless he acted swiftly. Obtaining the support of the janissaries and the judges, he executed the leaders of the rebellious sipahis and through vigorous measures restored order to Istanbul and the provinces.

Twice Murad personally led expeditions eastward. In 1638, he reconquered Baghdad from the Safavids, personally performing prodigious feats with his sword, but in the same year Yemen was lost to the Zaidi Shiite imams. As time passed, however, he grew hardened to the presence of the executioner. Frequently through mere caprice he removed someone's head, perhaps just for crossing the road in front of him. Furthermore, he took to drinking bouts that carried him to the grave at the age of twenty-eight.

FISCAL, ADMINISTRATIVE, AND MILITARY TRANSFORMATION

Among the most important causes of the transformation of the central government were economic and financial issues. From its earliest days, the Ottoman state supported itself in considerable part from raids and conquest, but as frontiers in Europe and Asia were extended, campaign costs became staggering. The booty obtained hardly met expenses, and little was left for palace extravagances, which nevertheless continued. Fireworks, public festivities, processions, and sumptuous luxury were on display to the public in Istanbul and Edirne, especially for the circumcision ceremonies of the royal princes. The widow of Sultan Ibrahim ordered the construction of a large mosque complex beside the Golden Horn, and Murad IV added impressive new buildings to the Topkapi Palace. Such expensive buildings and ceremonies were designed to show the legitimacy, power, and glory of the ruler.

A gradual shift in world trade from the Mediterranean to the Atlantic brought a marked decline in Ottoman revenues from international trade. Simultaneously, Europe and the Mediterranean world were experiencing a continuing monetary inflation. Government income never quite met expenditures.

To make up for the loss of revenue, officials were obliged to give liberal sums to the sultan upon promotions. During the reign of Murad III the sultan obtained bribes for appointments, and by the time of Sultan Ibrahim there was open trafficking in offices. An example was the Orthodox Christian patriarchate, which saw sixty-one changes in office in the seventeenth century, with bribes and appointment fees accompanying each new patriarch. Such a personnel system quickly filtered down to the lowest officials, so ability became less important than access to cash.

With the doubling of the size of the empire in the early sixteenth century, administrative problems became more and more difficult. As the work of governing increased to overwhelming proportions, the sultan left more affairs of state to the grand vizir, whose role in decision making naturally increased. In 1654 Mehmed IV finally gave the grand vizirs a residence and set of offices outside the imperial palace.

Later sultans frequently were unwilling to perform any onerous duties as head of the state and gave themselves up to a life of voluptuousness and frivolity. Since the sultans nevertheless could dismiss and even execute any official, there resulted an unfortunate separation between power and responsibility. Meanwhile, leading officers drew unprecedented power into their hands. Beginning with Murad III, the sultans gave high office to their favorites, who were usually ill fitted for the jobs to be done.

As the slave recruiting system fell out of use, personal loyalty to the sultans also declined somewhat and greed played a larger role in motivation. The corruption and venality should not, however, be overly emphasized, for despite a transformation in values and the other changes appearing in the Ottoman central government, there persisted a remarkable devotion to the dynasty and the state among a substantial body of capable, trained, and loyal officials. Such leaders helped in a new collection and revision of the imperial decrees, or kanuns, in 1673 so as to take into account the transformation of the state. And the administration of justice according to the shariah in the major towns remained swift, flexible, equitable, and fair even to the poorer groups in society.

For about three centuries the Ottomans had expanded continuously. But now campaigns in Austria, Russia, Iran, and North Africa were proving too costly to be pressed fully. Further expansion would not pay. When the conquests ended, ambi-

The Transformation of the Ottoman Empire, 1574–1798

INDIA

Indus

ARABIAN SEA

ARAL SEA

Syr Darya

Amu Darya

CASPIAN SEA

• Tehran

IRAN

Volga

RUSSIA

CAUCASUS

1783 to Russia

Persian Gulf

Baghdad •

Basrah

Tigris

Euphrates

Mosul •

IRAQ

Aleppo •

Trebizond •

TAURIDA 1783 to Russia

1792 to Russia

BLACK SEA

Damascus •

SYRIA

Jerusalem •

PALESTINE

Medina •

Mecca •

ARABIA

RED SEA

CRIMEA 1783 to Russia

Kuchuk Kainarji

Istanbul •

CYPRUS

CRETE

EGYPT conquered temporarily by France 1798

Nile

PODOLIA 1699 to Poland 1793 to Russia

BUKOVINA 1775 to Austria

Dniester

TRANSYLVANIA 1699 to Austria

BANAT 1718 to Austria

HUNGARY 1699 to Austria

AUSTRIA

Vienna •

Karlowitz

Passarowitz

Danube

IONIAN IS. to Venice till 1797 1797–99 to France

MOREA 1699 to Venice 1718 to Ottomans

MEDITERRANEAN SEA

ITALY

Rome •

Rhine

Rhone

Loire

FRANCE

SPAIN

ATLANTIC OCEAN

TUNISIA

ALGERIA

400 mi

200

600 km

300

0

0

Ottoman Empire, 1574

Acquisitions, 1574–1683

Losses, 1638–1683

Losses, 1683–1699

Losses, 1700–1718

Losses, 1719–1798

Ottoman Empire, 1798

tious members of the military and civil elites had to readjust their expectations as opportunities decreased.

Compounding this problem was the increased military sophistication of European enemies, which created a growing need for improved Ottoman manpower and weaponry. Between Suleiman's accession to the throne in 1520 and the end of the century, the janissaries increased from 8,000 to 37,000 and the sipahis of the palace from 5,000 to 21,000. By 1600, the total of the sultan's household troops had grown to around 85,000. Unlike the provincial sipahis who held land-revenue grants, the sultan's standing army had to be paid in cash. The provincial sipahis continued to provide large numbers of cavalry, but the heavy casualty rates they endured as a result of frequent wars decimated their ranks. During the seventeenth century they more often stayed in their local grant area rather than be transferred from one province to another.

The central and provincial governments formed new troops in Anatolia called sekbans, who were trained in the use of firearms. Money had to be found to pay the salaries of larger armies, at the same time when government income was declining. As payless days arrived the sekbans ravaged the countryside. Joined by landless villagers and penniless students, they, under the name of jelalis, menaced Anatolia for many years, beginning in 1595. Their rampages left many dead and large areas deserted. Government troops finally gained control, integrated many of the jelali leaders into the governing elite, and tried to resettle abandoned villages; the government also inaugurated the policy of stationing salaried janissary contingents in the provinces. Almost immediately the janissary leaders joined the merchants, the guild masters, and the ulama as provincial notables. They amassed great fortunes by tax farming, acquiring vast tracts of land and forcing villagers to become sharecroppers. From this janissary infusion came many of the local dynastic families that dominated the provinces in the eighteenth century, weakening the central government still more.

These changes among the sultans, the high officers of the state, and the military invited insubordination and rebellion from the rank and file of the armed forces. By the time of Mehmed II the janissaries and sipahis of the palace were already headstrong groups that had to be placated by gifts at festivals and, especially, at accessions of new sultans. Even in the days of Bayezid II and Suleiman I the janissaries had frequently dictated policies. Beginning with the reign of Murad III, soldiers often stormed the palace to demand the head of a particular official, usually one who was corrupt and whose rapacity or incompetence inflicted hardship and injury upon them. Once this type of action proved successful, ambitious officials through clever appeals instigated movements among the troops to remove rivals.

Equally debilitating were civil wars between different branches of the services and open revolts of garrisons or local forces in the provinces. Bad blood developed between the janissaries and the sipahis of the court. In the reign of Murad III warfare broke out in the streets of Istanbul. Under Mehmed III the janissaries, at the bidding of his mother, Safiye, broke the insubordination of the sipahis. Wishing to weaken the power of the janissaries, Osman II (1618–1622) entered into war against Poland with the purpose of thinning the janissaries' ranks; he then intended to gather an army of Kurds and Turkomans to fight the janissaries, a project that led to his dethronement and murder.

THE FUNDAMENTAL CAUSES OF TRANSFORMATION

Basic social, cultural, and economic developments helped bring about the transformation of the sultanate and the central government. Population growth was one of the most important of these factors.

Until about the 1580s, life and society in the Ottoman Empire, especially in Istanbul and the central provinces, seemed to be stable and secure. Incomes were ensured, prices were relatively constant, and food and goods were abundant. With this well-being, the population had increased in some parts of the empire over the sixteenth century—by 40 percent in villages, 80 percent or more in some towns. Population pressure on the available land began to be felt, and deforestation ensued in much of Anatolia and the eastern Mediterranean area. The influx of people into cities was altering their character.

Likewise, a smugness and an opposition to innovation arose among so many of the ulama that they developed a dislike for inquiring creatively into theology and intellectual sciences. Those supporting innovation in thought or belief were condemned by popular preachers from Istanbul pulpits. Society was much affected by the use of tobacco, a new product brought to the Middle East by the English; it soon spread, and smoking was associated with the flourishing coffeehouses, despite the objections by the men of religion, many of whom despised it. Coffee from Yemen, song, tobacco, and intellectual sciences were attacked by the ulama in the same breath with luxury, lax morals, and injustice, all as factors supposedly undermining religious faith. An uprising led by these preachers was quelled by Mehmed Köprülü, who exiled them. Despite this intellectual conservatism, the Ottomans maintained sophisticated technical skills in such fields as mining.

One example of cultural stagnation could be seen in the reaction against Murad III's building an astronomical observatory in 1579. Shortly thereafter an outbreak of the plague was attributed to God's vengeance against those who had penetrated divine secrets. The shaikh al-Islam petitioned the sultan to have the observatory dismantled, and the janissaries leveled it to the ground. Fanaticism and stagnation triumphed along with anti-intellectualism.

The cultural and artistic life of the imperial court continued at the high standards of the mid-sixteenth century for some decades. It was only in the late seventeenth century that decline became noticeable in a number of areas. Originality of design and fineness of execution in Iznik pottery and tiles deteriorated, although miniature painting took the new form of studies of single figures, which were often beautifully drawn. Several sultans were noted both for their own calligraphy and for their patronage of calligraphers. Creative genius still remained, as could be seen in the work of the great calligrapher Hafiz Osman (d. 1698), who created a style that served as a basis of imitation for later generations; he influenced the imperial court directly as a teacher of Mustafa II (1695–1703) and Ahmed III (1703–1730).

History writing for the sultans became institutionalized as the post of court chronicler was officially established. In some of the provinces governors and notables imitated the sultans as patrons of the arts.

If not the root causes of all these changes of fortune, as some economic historians contend, the following at least were major complicating factors: the massive influx of gold and silver into Europe and the Middle East from the Americas; the ensuing monetary and price inflation; debasement of the imperial coinage; and the failure of the Ottomans to adopt a mercantile economy. The biggest impact of these changes came in the 1580s, producing tremors felt throughout the next century. Silver began to flood the market. In 1580, one gold coin equaled 60 silver ones; but by 1590 it took 120 silver coins to buy a gold coin; by 1640, it took 250. During the sixteenth century the price of wheat increased by nearly twenty times. People on fixed incomes—central government officials, judges, janissaries, sipahis, waqf endowment holders—were ruined unless they turned to bribery and corruption. For the central government it was fully as disastrous. In 1534 the treasury had an income of 5 million gold ducats, but by 1591 it was only half that, for taxes were levied in silver.

To counteract the fall in revenue, new taxes were added, more tax farming was tried, and local communities were asked to make lump sum tax payments. During the seventeenth century tax farmers usually held the right to collect taxes for only three years, but in 1695 the central government in some provinces also authorized the sale of the right to collect taxes from the peasants for the lifetime of the tax farmer. Many of these measures had the effect of increasing the decentralization of the empire, and thereby exacerbating the fiscal crisis.

Domestically, the government tried to hold down prices in the face of tremendous increases. The resulting price differentials stimulated the smuggling of significant quantities of wheat, copper, wool, and other raw materials from the empire, producing local shortages and even greater inflation. Because of the enormous profits to be had, peasants and landowners conveniently located for this trade began to be oriented to a commercial agrarian regime. This export orientation in some regions did not change the basic organization of agriculture: small peasant farmers, not large landlords, continued to predominate in most regions during the seventeenth century, while much land was turned into waqf property. Local craft production continued, with credit available at interest rates of 10 to 20 percent; a higher rate of annual interest was labeled by the courts as usury and was condemned. International commerce was centered around Istanbul, Izmir, Aleppo, and Cairo. The balance of trade was probably negative; precious metals flowed to India and Persia. As people lost faith in the value of the money, Ottoman mints nearly stopped producing new coins in the middle of the seventeenth century; instead, foreign coinage was widespread.

Against new western mercantilist policies the Ottomans clung to old ideas, concerned primarily with providing the home market with necessities such as food. The empire encouraged imports and discouraged exports, prohibiting the export of certain commodities for fear of domestic shortages. It saw no danger in extending capitulations to foreigners, since in the seventeenth century foreigners and their local aides were still under the control of the empire. Ottoman subjects dominated most aspects of trade by land, and guilds were widespread. Artisanal production was not yet substantially disrupted by European competition.

Social patterns and gender relationships apparently remained intact, without major change. In seventeenth-century Egypt, Syria, Anatolia, and Cyprus, as presumably throughout the empire, urban women took part in court cases, frequently were owners and administrators of real property (mostly in the cities but occasionally including village farmland), inherited estates, and lent money. Women engaged in cottage industry but seldom belonged to guilds, and males maintained their legal and political superiority.

The Ottomans saw little reason to change their society. In cultural, religious, social, and economic matters they were still convinced of their own superiority.

CHANGES IN THE PROVINCES

The political situation in the provinces varied tremendously from one region to another. As the central Ottoman government in Istanbul lost much of its power, local elites in many of the provinces gained more autonomy. They welcomed the transformation of the sultanate and the administration because it often resulted in an effective transfer of authority to themselves, as leaders of the great cities or tribes, and as provincial tax farmers or officeholders.

If the imperial court retained the ability to name governors on its own, rather than bowing to the wishes of local elites, the governorships were often given to court favorites and estates were left vacant so that their income would devolve upon the governor. Governorships were for shorter terms than formerly; they were sold to new courtiers every year or two, and a succession of governors seeking the money payments needed by Istanbul often led to overtaxation. The elaborate households of the provincial governors were an added expense. Many peasants fled the high taxes; some peasants became nomads.

Local leaders usually remained within the Ottoman system: they acknowledged the overlordship of the sultans, used their names in the Friday noon prayers, remitted some revenues to Istanbul, provided troops for the imperial armies when asked, and made no attempt to establish an independent foreign policy or to mint coins in their own names. The provinces closest to Istanbul, which were crucial to the provisioning of the capital and to providing money to the treasury, were especially closely supervised. At least some of these areas, such as Bursa, were as prosperous in the seventeenth century as they had been in the sixteenth. They were more fully integrated into the Ottoman political and military structures than were the more distant lands.

Some leaders did not follow this pattern. A prominent example was Ali Janbulad (Jumblat), who led a rebellion in northern Syria aiming at real independence, suppressed only with the greatest difficulty in 1607. The Manid amir of southern Lebanon, Fakhr al-Din, similarly sought so much freedom of action in running his local administration as to provoke an Ottoman invasion and his ouster in 1633. Southern Iraq was autonomous for the first half of the seventeenth century, as tribes and local notables directed affairs, but it was brought more closely under Ottoman control after 1668.

Egypt was reorganized in the 1520s after revolts, and the Ottomans controlled the country during the rest of the sixteenth century. The viceroy of Egypt was appointed by the sultan, while the revenues of local districts, especially those along the upper Nile, were farmed out to tax collectors. The sipahi and revocable land-tax system was not established in Egypt, and Ottoman military contingents in Egypt were eventually infiltrated by a revived Mamluk military system. During the seventeenth century competition for power among these groups and factions turned the Ottoman governors into figureheads; real authority resided with military leaders, most of whom were Mamluks. Occasionally, when the local forces grew too anarchic or were perceived in Istanbul to be too strong, the central government would directly intervene. Following an insurrection in 1711, Ottoman power decreased, and Mamluks dominated the country. However, justice was enforced in Ottoman Egypt in the seventeenth century with remarkable fairness; both holy law and secular decrees provided the bases for social legitimacy. The population of the larger Arab-Ottoman cities such as Cairo increased from the sixteenth through the eighteenth centuries, despite political uncertainties and rivalries. Other signs of the relative social peace and prosperity of Egypt included the integration of the tribes of upper Egypt into the local governing system, the flourishing of Sufism, and the development of guilds.

The northern Balkan vassal states in Moldavia and Wallachia represented a different pattern of provincial control—they were tributary to the Ottoman Empire. They acknowledged Ottoman overlordship, and in return the Ottomans granted them the right to select their own rulers as long as they paid tribute, supplied food to Istanbul, and permitted some Ottoman garrisons on their territories. The local princes and nobles otherwise controlled their own affairs. Ottoman power in Transylvania was still lighter, as the amount of tribute demanded was small.

EXTERNAL AFFAIRS: EUROPE, THE MEDITERRANEAN, AND THE EAST

Despite the numerous difficulties posed to the Ottomans by their military transformations, the empire remained intact and, on balance, even expanded slightly. The Ottomans fought numerous long, exhausting wars and suffered heavy casualties, but until the end of the seventeenth century they won most of the time or the wars ended in a draw.

The war with Austria from 1593 to 1606 was marked by a great victory of Ottoman arms in 1596 at Mezö Keresztes, which kept the Hapsburgs at bay. Since each side was worn out, peace was signed in 1606 on the basis of the status quo. This was the first time an Ottoman peace treaty had been negotiated outside the empire, as well as the first time the Hapsburg ruler was recognized as a fellow emperor who did not have to pay tribute. Fortunately for the Ottomans, whose depleted treasury would have made further military engagements precarious, the Thirty Years' War engulfed the Hapsburgs and other European powers between 1618 and 1648.

The question of the security of the eastern Mediterranean was perennial. Wheat, barley, and other vital supplies came from Egypt, as did an annual surplus revenue, sometimes amounting to half a million ducats. With Venice threatening the routes from Egypt because of her use of the new broadsided tall ships, in 1645 the Ottomans began a war aimed at capturing Crete from Venice; the ensuing conflict lasted until 1670. In June 1656, one in a series of inept admirals, whose only qualification was his position as son-in-law of the sultan's mother, led the fleet out of the Dardanelles to total destruction. Venice blockaded the Straits, and Istanbul was in a panic as prices of foodstuffs soared. Ahmed Köprülü turned his attention to the island of Crete, where Candia, the ancient Knossos, had resisted sporadic Ottoman assaults for twenty years; to the Ottomans it had become like a running sore. Köprülü conducted a three-year siege of Candia until it fell in 1669; Crete, in Venetian hands since the Fourth Crusade, finally was incorporated into the Ottoman Empire.

On the outer peripheries the empire was under attack from all quarters. Ottoman naval power could no longer be projected into the Indian Ocean. The empire was able to maintain some control in the Red Sea, although English and Dutch pirates began to operate there in 1613 and Ottoman forces in the Persian Gulf became ineffective. Cossacks raided at will north of the Black Sea. Meanwhile, the sultans increasingly lost their hold on North Africa, which came to grant only a nominal acknowledgment of Ottoman legitimacy.

From 1578 to 1639 the Ottomans often had successful military adventures in the east. Aid from the Crimean khan kept them at Darband on the Caspian Sea, and Kars was converted into a fortress in 1579. Baghdad, Mosul, and all of Iraq were formally annexed in 1586, and a favorable treaty in 1590 with Iran left Tabriz in Ottoman hands. But then Shah Abbas I began the war of 1603–1618, in which the shah captured Tabriz, much of the Caucasus, and Kars. In 1623 another Ottoman army was crushed, and Abbas took Baghdad and the rest of Iraq. By the middle of the next decade, however, Murad IV seized Erivan and recaptured Baghdad in 1638. The peace that was arranged in 1639 settled eastern affairs for many years, leaving Iraq and Kars to the sultan and Azerbaijan to the shah.

MILITARY RESURGENCE UNDER THE KÖPRÜLÜS

When Mehmed Köprülü assumed office as grand vizir in 1656, he inaugurated a period of centralization and military expansion. He was filled with a ruthless determination to purge the government. In 1658, he repressed the rebel Anatolian governors who had defied the power of Istanbul since the 1620s. In five years of his grand vizirate some 30,000 officers, officials, judges, and theologians were executed for acts contrary to the interests of the sultan. His son Ahmed Köprülü succeeded to the post and remained grand vizir until his death in 1676. Restoration of central control under these two vizirs revealed that the coercive strength of the state had not been sapped beyond repair.

Although Mehmed IV gave himself up completely to hunting and to the harem, he remained steadfast in his support of the Köprülüs. In 1663 Mehmed placed the battle standard in the hands of Ahmed Köprülü, who then led the largest force assembled since the campaigns of Suleiman I to Belgrade and beyond. However, Ahmed Köprülü was repulsed at the renowned battle of St. Gotthard in Austria. Ahmed succeeded, however, in capturing Crete and thereby successfully ending the long war with Venice.

Next, the scene shifted to Galicia and the Ukraine. Cossacks of the Dneiper River region threw off Polish rule and sought Crimean and Ottoman protection. When the cossack leader came to Istanbul in 1672, he received a two-horsetail standard and was named leader of the Ukraine. Poland protested, and the grand vizir led an army that forced Poland to surrender its Ukrainian territories and to pay an annual tribute. Several more campaigns followed, and a treaty in 1676 incorporated the western Ukraine into the empire.

Three days after the signing of this treaty Ahmed Köprülü died. Unfortunately, Mehmed IV filled his place as grand vizir with his court favorite, Kara Mustafa, who was also related by marriage to the Köprülü family. In 1683 he organized the last attack upon Vienna. Early in the spring the ambitious Kara Mustafa gathered about 150,000 men and reached Vienna in the middle of July. For two months the army mined and bombarded the walls of Vienna, which were defended by a force of only 15,000 men. As September approached, the weakness of Vienna and the depletion of its garrison were obvious. The janissaries felt confident that Vienna would fall, but Kara Mustafa held back, hoping that the city would surrender: if it did, its wealth would be his, whereas if the soldiers took the city by storm, it would be theirs to loot. Meanwhile he ignored the approach of King John Sobieski of Poland with an army of 76,000 to relieve the city. When Sobieski encamped on the heights outside Vienna, Kara Mustafa virtually dismissed his presence. The Ottomans were thoroughly defeated on September 12, 1683, with only about one-half of the army escaping. Kara Mustafa was subsequently executed by the sultan for incompetence.

MILITARY DEFEATS

In the next four years one military calamity after another descended upon the empire. Venetians captured southern Greece and Athens. In the siege of Athens the Ottoman defenders made their last stand on the acropolis, which the Venetians shelled, exploding the beautiful Parthenon, which was serving as a powder magazine. The Austrian forces followed up their victory at Vienna by a lengthy war in which they took Budapest and seized Hungary. In 1687 the loss of Mohacs so infuriated the Ottoman soldiers that they forced Mehmed's deposition and placed his younger brother on the throne as Suleiman II (1687–1691). The new sultan, who had been incarcerated in the palace for forty-five years, did not know how to cope with the situation. Janissaries and sipahis rioted in Istanbul and partially sacked the city; a sort of civil war broke out between sekbans and janissaries. Belgrade fell in 1688, as did Vidin and Nish in 1689.

Previously when Ottomans had suffered reverses, they recouped their losses quickly and returned to fight in strength. This was notably true before Vienna in 1529 and at Lepanto in 1571. But the transformations of the seventeenth century had weakened the military. By the late seventeenth century when the call for a campaign was sounded, the sipahis hid on their estates or bribed a commanding officer to excuse them. At one time a census was ordered, compelling all sipahis in Europe to register in order to expose unfit and fraudulent grant holders, but the inspectors were incompetent and no one was caught. However, the sipahis were no longer as important as they had been, since few were equipped with up-to-date firearms and they lacked the new skills needed in warfare. Instead, many land grants were sold or rented by the imperial government so as to gain the money to pay the sekban musketeers. By the eighteenth century there were only about 25,000 sipahis, and they were relegated to digging trenches and hauling cannons.

The changes among the janissaries, the sipahis of the court, and palace soldiers were no less substantial. Captive boys and renegades diminished in numbers as the seventeenth century progressed since there were so few new territories added to the empire. The drafting of Christian boys ceased entirely during the reign of Murad IV. In his attempt to restore the vigor of the state, Ahmed Köprülü reinstituted the program and collected 3000 boys in 1675, but the policy was dropped after his death. Free local Muslims, the sons of janissaries, and even unsuited persons joined the ranks. Worst of all was the practice of ignoring merit in questions of promotion, for it meant that officers were not skilled in military affairs. Many janissaries had other occupations and were members of the corps only on payday, although it should be noted that janissary engagement in commerce and leasing shops was traceable as far back as the early sixteenth century. European commanders in the late seventeenth century observed the mediocre leadership of Ottoman armies and outmaneuvered them time and time again. By the beginning of the eighteenth century the janissaries had become an ill-disciplined, turbulent gang, frequently more dangerous to their own government than to foreign aggressors.

After the loss of Nish in 1689 Suleiman II recognized the desperate plight of his empire and appointed as grand vizir Mustafa Köprülü, brother of the late Ahmed Köprülü. The genius of the Köprülü family ran strong in the new grand vizir. He instituted financial measures that made it possible to assemble an army and regain Nish and Belgrade. Köprülü attempted again the following summer to drive the Austrians farther back but lost his life in battle.

The energy of Mustafa II, an opponent of the Köprülü faction, brought a series of minor Balkan victories; but when faced by Prince Eugene of Savoy in 1697 at Zenta, the Ottoman units were crushed, and Hungary and the lands north of Belgrade were lost forever.

TREATY OF KARLOWITZ, 1699

In the face of these reverses Mustafa called to the grand vizirate Husain Köprülü. Negotiators met at Karlowitz, north of Belgrade, where the hostile participants agreed on the general principle that each power should retain what it possessed and concluded in 1699 the Treaty of Karlowitz. In addition, the sultan pledged to give his Christian subjects consideration and protection, as he customarily had. Venice gave up Athens but retained part of southern Greece and Dalmatia. Austria obtained most of Transylvania and Hungary. Poland received back parts of the Ukraine the Ottomans had earlier taken. Russia opted for a truce but in 1700 accepted the Karlowitz arrangement as a basis for peace. Karlowitz underlined the military weakness of the state and thereby encouraged rebels in 1703 to depose Mustafa II.

Karlowitz marks a definite change in the relations of the Ottoman Empire and Europe. Since it was largely arranged by England, the treaty seemed to acknowledge that many European states were rightfully concerned with Ottoman issues. It recognized the special interest and importance of the Russian state with respect to the Ottoman Empire. The treaty showed how the sultan's Christian subjects would become a major concern of European foreign offices.

At the peace conference of Karlowitz, European emissaries worked largely through the Ottoman-Greek interpreter, Alexander Mavrocordatos, and carried away the erroneous impression that he was chief of the Ottoman delegation. But his important role signified a transformation in the Ottoman civil service. For a century the great majority of Ottoman officials had been Turkish-speaking Muslims, many of whom did not know much about Christian Europe. Many were not educated in the palace, and their schooling was less secular than in previous generations, so they became dependent upon Christian subjects, chiefly Greeks residing in Istanbul, for interpreters and counselors.

As for Europe, Karlowitz ended the fear of an Ottoman invasion of central Europe and opened an avenue for European expansion toward Istanbul. When Europe was engaged in its own internal struggles, Ottoman forces were still able to win victories, but from the beginning of the eighteenth century, Ottoman armies and navies would be no match for first-rate European soldiers. No longer was the Ottoman Empire a grave military question. As one writer aptly put it, its importance became diplomatic.

Despite the military and diplomatic weakness the treaty of Karlowitz signaled, the transformations the Ottoman Empire had undergone between 1574 and 1699 also had some favorable consequences. Most subjects were still loyal to the sultanate, Ottoman institutions functioned reasonably well, religion provided a strong basis of identity, local groups using gunpowder weapons were integrated into provincial elites, and some areas even flourished. The Ottoman Empire responded flexibly to new circumstances. On the other hand, the incompetence of many sultans, the recurring fiscal crises, the insubordination in the military, the social and intellectual resistance to technological change, and the rapid growth of European power presented grave threats for the future.

References

Works relevant to this chapter are listed in Chapters 10, 14, 16, 17, and 18.

ABOU-EL-HAJ, RIFA'AT 'ALI: *Formation of the Modern State: The Ottoman Empire, Sixteenth to Eighteenth Centuries.* Albany: State University of New York Press, 1991. This extended essay raises many theoretical questions about Ottoman history.

ABU-HUSAYN, ABDUL-RAHIM: *Provincial Leaderships in Syria, 1575–1650.* Beirut: American University of Beirut Press, 1985. Traces the tangled web and diversity of Ottoman Syria, with attention to political history.

BARKEY, KAREN: *Bandits and Bureaucrats: The Ottoman Route to State Centralization.* Ithaca,

N.Y.: Cornell University Press, 1994. The author shows how jelalis were incorporated into the Ottoman structure.

CHELEBI, EVLIYA: *The Intimate Life of an Ottoman Statesman, Melek Ahmed Pasha (1588–1662) as Portrayed in Evliya Chelebi's Book of Travels (Seyahat-Name).* Translated and with a commentary by Robert Dankoff. Albany: State University of New York Press, 1991. A grand vizir's biography that also vividly illustrates life in Istanbul and the provinces.

COOK, M. A.: *Population Pressure in Rural Anatolia, 1450–1600.* London: Oxford University Press, 1972. Examination of population trends of the period and their effects.

FAROQHI, SURAIYA: "Political Activity Among Ottoman Taxpayers and the Problem of Sultanic Legitimation (1570–1650)." *Journal of the Economic and Social History of the Orient* 35 (1992): 1–39. Useful especially for the jelali revolts.

GERBER, HAIM: "Social and Economic Position of Women in an Ottoman City, Bursa, 1600–1700." *International Journal of Middle East Studies* 12 (1980): 231–244. A trailblazing study based on legal documents.

————— : *The Social Origins of the Modern Middle East.* Boulder, Colo.: Lynne Rienner, 1987. Traces the impact of landholding patterns in the Ottoman Empire from early days up through the twentieth-century Middle East.

————— : *State, Society, and Law in Islam: Ottoman Law in Comparative Perspective.* Albany: State University of New York Press, 1994. Examines the way courts operated in Bursa and Istanbul during the seventeenth and eighteenth centuries.

GOFFMAN, DANIEL: *Izmir and the Levantine World, 1550–1650.* Seattle: University of Washington Press, 1990. Interesting account of changes brought about by European traders in western Anatolia.

GRISWOLD, WILLIAM J.: *The Great Anatolian Rebellion 1000–1020/1591–1611.* Berlin: Klaus Schwarz, 1983. A wide-ranging study of this question, including discussions of Syria and Ottoman policy toward the Safavids.

HOLT, PETER: *Egypt and the Fertile Crescent, 1516–1922.* Ithaca, N.Y.: Cornell University Press, 1966. Authoritative on Ottoman-Arab relations.

KEYDER, CAGLAR, AND FARUK TABAK, EDS.: *Landholding and Commercial Agriculture in the Middle East.* Albany: State University of New York Press, 1991. A collection of useful essays covering the sixteenth through the nineteenth centuries.

KUNT, I. METIN: *The Sultan's Servants: The Transformation of Ottoman Provincial Government, 1550–1650.* New York: Columbia University Press, 1983. An outstanding study of Ottoman administration.

MASTERS, BRUCE: *The Origins of Western Economic Dominance in the Middle East: Mercantilism and the Islamic Economy in Aleppo, 1600–1750.* New York: New York University Press, 1988. A superb example of the trend toward detailed social and economic histories of seventeenth-century Ottoman provinces, as also seen in excellent studies by Daniel Crecilius, Haim Gerber, Halil Inalcik, and Ronald C. Jennings.

MATUZ, JOSEF: "The Nature and Stages of Ottoman Feudalism." *Asian and African Studies* 16 (1982): 281–292. An analytic approach to the subject, especially for the Balkans and Anatolia.

RAYMOND, ANDRÉ: *The Great Arab Cities in the 16th–18th Centuries: An Introduction.* New York: New York University Press, 1984. A refreshingly written and informative survey.

RYCAUT, PAUL: *History of the Turkish Empire, 1623–1677.* 2 vols. in one. London: Clabell and Roper, 1680. A detailed account by an eyewitness.

————— : *The Present State of the Ottoman Empire.* London: Clabell and Roper, 1686. Really a third volume to the reference cited above.

TIETZE, ANDREAS, TRANS. AND ED.: *Mustafa 'Ali's Counsel for Sultans of 1581.* Pt. 1. Vienna: Austrian Academy of Sciences, 1979. Ottoman self-view of the causes of decline and corruption.

WINTER, MICHAEL: *Egyptian Society Under Ottoman Rule, 1517–1798.* London: Routledge, 1992. Excellent account of social and political matters, including discussions of Sufism, guilds, tribes, ulama, minorities, and life in Cairo.

ZILFI, MADELINE C.: *The Politics of Piety: The Ottoman Ulema in the Postclassical Age (1600–1800).* Minneapolis, Minn.: Bibliotheca Islamica, 1988. Discusses Sufism and puritanical movements as well as the careers of the ulama.

The Retreat of the Ottoman Empire Begins

The changes that transformed the government of the Ottoman Empire in the seventeenth century continued into the next century, but the challenges the empire faced increased as the power of its European adversaries grew, leading to the beginning of a retreat of the Ottoman state. By the end of the period 1703 to 1789 the Ottoman Empire was weak in comparison with its two chief military challengers, Russia and Austria. Changes in international commerce also started to affect the Ottomans adversely. Internally, local elites in the provinces gained more and more autonomy, thereby decreasing the effectiveness of the central government. Despite these factors, the Ottomans still attained some successes in military, cultural, and economic fields, especially in comparison with the chaotic situation of Iran in the eighteenth century.

THE SULTANATE

Power in the central government was allocated in the same way as in the seventeenth century: the palace dominated administration, and the sultans were greatly influenced by those closest to them.

The five sultans who ruled in the eighteenth century lacked the education and training to enable them to be leaders. They were unable to cope with the growing corruption, inefficiency, and incompetence that marked the period. Each of the sultans came to the throne after decades of confinement; none had an opportunity to learn the art of statecraft. Usually, his mother or the harem favorite dominated the sultan. The rulers could not bring about substantial changes so that the central government could adapt itself to new times. The sultans were still the ceremonial leaders of the army, but they did not participate in battles.

Increasingly, the grand vizir and sultan called special councils, composed of prominent officials, to debate the severe problems facing the empire. By this means, responsibility for difficult decisions could be spread among a wider number of people. Sultans also changed their grand vizirs so frequently (their terms averaged around seventeen months) that few were able to carry out any long-range projects. Ability within the Muslim religious establishment declined, and posts of high authority went to unqualified favorites of the ruler. Training of about one-half of government officials took place in the households of major officeholders rather than inside the palace. Household factions dominated key posts.

Many of the rulers were artists. Ahmed III (1703–1730) was interested in his tulip gardens, and also was a calligrapher and a patron of poets. He spent fortunes on festivals and illuminations for the women of the court. Ahmed also had a more serious side—by playing his enemies against each other he regained a good deal of power for himself. He then embarked upon a naval reorganization, and he expanded the rural sipahis and the standing armed forces.

Sultan Mahmud I (1730–1754) loved literature and surrounded himself with poets and men of letters. The rest of his energy was devoted to building mosques, palaces, and kiosks. Osman III (1754–1757), Mustafa III (1757–1774), and Abdulhamid I (1774–1789) were well along in years when they ascended the throne; they proved to be mild, ineffectual rulers. Abdulhamid may at least be commended for the freer life he permitted his nephew Selim, the heir apparent, for with Selim's accession in 1789 began the more vigorous attempts at reform that marked the nineteenth century.

WARS WITH RUSSIA AND AUSTRIA

Austria and Russia contested the power of the Ottomans throughout the eighteenth century. During the period 1711–1739 the Ottomans lost little territory, even though they were often defeated.

Tsar Peter of Russia (r. 1682–1725) was not content with the 1699 Treaty of Karlowitz: the Black Sea, the Straits, and, most important, Istanbul all beckoned the Russians on against the Ottomans. However, when Peter led his army across the Pruth River in 1711, he fell into an Ottoman trap. To escape, he restored to the sultan the territories and privileges gained at Karlowitz. Ahmed III dismissed the grand vizir for agreeing to such easy terms when the Ottoman army might have destroyed Peter and crushed the Russians.

Peace with Russia and Austria freed the Ottomans to regain their possessions lost to Venice at Karlowitz. The grand vizir swept Venice from southern Greece in 1715. These victories enticed Austria to break with the Ottomans, and Prince Eugene won several smashing engagements, capturing Belgrade. Then Britain arranged the Treaty of Passarowitz of 1718, which ceded to Austria all the conquered territory in Serbia but permitted the Ottomans to retain the lands taken from Venice.

In response to Russian provocation, the Ottomans declared war in 1736. Russia overran the Crimea, and Austria entered the fray. As an Ottoman resurgence in 1739 pushed the fighting back to the walls of Belgrade, the French ambassador skillfully engineered the amazing Treaty of Belgrade, which returned that city to the Ottoman Empire. Even though Russia won great victories, it gained little.

After this, for thirty-five years from 1739 to 1774 there was peace in Europe for the sultans, although they fought wars against Iran during that time. As a result,

Ottoman Rulers, 1703–1839

the growing weakness of the Ottomans compared with European states remained unrevealed. In fact, by "depriving" the Ottomans of military experience for a full generation, the Treaty of Belgrade accelerated Ottoman weakness. Even though the Ottoman forces adopted some European-style technical reforms, the military gap between the skills and abilities of western and central Europeans and the Ottomans increased throughout the century. Another factor causing Ottoman military decline was internal: Ottoman soldiers rejected the use of new weapons, such as the bayonet, because they would hurt the vested interests of the officers.

COMMERCE AND THE CAPITULATIONS

While internal commerce inside the empire was most important, trade with Europe increased substantially in the eighteenth century. European merchants were governed by a series of agreements known as capitulations. France and England, and to a lesser extent the Netherlands, had valuable commercial interests in the Middle East. Ottoman wars with Austria and Russia disturbed their trade, a factor that animated English, French, and Dutch mediation in Ottoman wars.

Ottoman commerce with India was probably equal to European trade. The Ottomans exported precious metals to India and various commodities, such as cotton and tobacco, to Europe. In the Red Sea and Black Sea most merchants were Ottoman subjects, but in the Mediterranean Europeans gained control of trade. Much Ottoman commerce remained in the hands of Armenians, Jews, and Greeks. Traders on land were mostly Ottomans, not Europeans, while textile production remained steady despite European competition.

Earlier capitulations granted by the sultans to various Europeans and especially to the French were reaffirmed. As of 1740, capitulations changed from temporary trading arrangements granted by the sultan in expectation of reciprocal rights for Ottoman merchants to relatively permanent arrangements given European countries in return for their diplomatic support of the empire. The significant points of a treaty of 1740 with France, to which almost all similar treaties of later dates refer, granted the French the right to travel and trade in any part of the empire. French diplomats had jurisdiction over French subjects. The French were allowed to possess and erect churches of their own and to worship freely, special considerations being made for French Christians in Palestine.

Most important was the article that gave France the privilege of enrolling under its flag and protection foreigners who had no ambassador or consul at Istanbul. All Roman Catholics were considered and treated as French, giving them a very special consideration among Christians in the Ottoman Empire. Furthermore, France and other nations that had such an article in their treaties (England, Austria, the Netherlands, and later Russia) could bestow special trading privileges to Ottoman subjects, usually Christians and Jews. As a result of these circumstances, a large portion of the exterior trade of the Ottoman Empire was beyond imperial control.

TREATY OF KUCHUK KAINARJI

Upon the termination of the Seven Years' War in 1763 the powers of Europe were free to turn their attentions to Poland and the Ottoman Empire, with unfortunate consequences for both. Upon the advice of the French ambassador, Mustafa III unwisely rushed into war against Russia in 1768 when his demands with respect to Poland were not met. Since the Ottoman armies were unprepared, the Russians occupied Bucharest and within two years held all of Moldavia and Wallachia. Meanwhile, a Russian fleet sailed from the Baltic Sea around western Europe to the Aegean Sea, where it proceeded to destroy the Ottoman fleet. Nonetheless, the Ottomans, with French advice, had repaired the fortifications along the Straits leading to Istanbul sufficiently to thwart the Russians, who sailed off to Egypt to threaten the Ottomans from that direction.

Russian successes in the Danubian Principalities caused the Austrians to sign a secret treaty with Istanbul in 1771, pledging military support if the Russians crossed the Danube. Informed of this maneuver, Prussia prevented war between Austria and Russia by speeding the partition of Poland among its three neighbors and simultaneously inducing Catherine II of Russia (1762–1796) to relinquish her conquests from the Ottomans. Partition of the Ottoman Empire was saved by the sacrifice of Poland! Desultory fighting came to a halt in 1774 upon the signing of the Treaty of Kuchuk Kainarji. This famous treaty was a landmark in Russo-Ottoman relations for more than a century. The sultan regained possession of Moldavia, Wallachia, and the Aegean islands, but Russia's political (though not religious) control of the Crimea was confirmed. Navigation on the Danube was freed, and the Black Sea was opened to Russian shipping. A permanent Russian ambassador was accepted at Istanbul.

Of particular significance for the future were two articles that stated in vague terms that the sultan promised to protect the Christian religion in his empire. More important, Russia as a "neighboring and sincerely friendly Power" could offer the sultan representations in behalf of his Christian subjects in Moldavia and Wallachia. These two articles served Russia in the nineteenth century as useful devices to advance its ambitions in the Balkans.

Since Austria had diplomatically supported the Ottomans against Russia, the Austrians demanded from the sultan the province of Bukovina as a reward for non-belligerency during the Russian war. When Vienna ordered the occupation, the sultan recognized his helplessness and ceded Bukovina to the Hapsburgs.

The Ottomans reacted to the new military situation with a naval construction campaign, the building of a more modern artillery corps, changes in military education, and a purge of the janissaries so as to eliminate those who were soldiers in name only. French advisers provided new approaches to warfare, and traditional reforms were also undertaken.

PEACE OF JASSY

For a decade and a half the sultan was left in peace, while Russia and Austria discussed the possibility of further Ottoman disintegration. The "Greek project" of Catherine II and Emperor Joseph of Austria in 1782 marked the first specific design for partitioning the Ottoman Empire. The fate of the Crimea was established when Russia annexed it in 1783, thereby discarding the limited rights of the Ottoman sultan.

Still another war broke in 1787. Austria and Russia won initial victories, but international complications in Europe and serious internal disorders in the Hapsburg realm enabled the Ottomans to obtain the peace of Sistova with Austria (1791) and the peace of Jassy (Iashi) with Russia (1792). The former returned the frontier to the status quo ante, but the latter allowed Russia to advance its frontier to the Dniester River. The outbreak of the French Revolution in 1789, the second (1793) and third (1795) partitions of Poland, and the death of Catherine II of Russia (1796) gave the new Ottoman ruler, Selim III (1789–1807), a short relief from European expansion.

DOMESTIC CHANGES

Internally, the Ottoman court supported cultural accomplishments, while bringing about changes in taxation and the status of non-Muslims. A new system of governing Moldavia and Wallachia had particularly important consequences.

Peace between Russia, Austria, and the Ottomans in 1718 allowed the fun-loving Ahmed III to begin a period known for its luxury, its love of flowers (especially tulips), its imitation of European styles, and its translations of works from Persian, Arabic, and European languages into Turkish. Cultural innovations of all types flourished. An Istanbul printing press began to issue a small number of nonreligious books in Ottoman Turkish in 1729, although few were printed after 1745; Jewish and Christian groups had printed books in other languages long before the eighteenth century. Rococo and, later, baroque decoration modeled on that of Europe abounded in the capital, just as Ottoman styles influenced western European art.

The new imperial mosques, fountains, and kiosks that were built reflected the elegance, grace, and lightheartedness of the rococo style as modified by Ottoman traditions. Wall paintings showed western conceptions of perspective. Later, the famous poetess Fitnat (d. 1780), a member of a distinguished ulama family, wrote sonnets that celebrated such classic themes as tulips, roses, and the season of spring.

Some cadastral surveys for fiscal demarcation were reinstituted after a lapse of a century. This and other measures raised money needed for the imperial court, but they also caused mounting opposition to the sultan's policies. Ahmed III was overthrown in 1730 after suffering a defeat by Iran, and his changes temporarily were suspended.

In the seventeenth and eighteenth centuries some provincial administrators, sipahis, and managers of pious endowments hired tax farmers to manage the collection of revenues. As the power of the central government's bureaucracy decreased after 1695, some tax farms auctioned in Istanbul were converted to positions whose incumbents held them for life; these tax farms became quasi-hereditary. It was hoped that the increased security of tenure would encourage the tax farmers to foster economic growth, but the hereditary tax farm tended to weaken the Istanbul administration, since it reduced flexibility in making appointments.

Other changes took place among religious groups. Christian and Jewish religious minorities came increasingly into contact with their coreligionists outside the empire. Most Ottoman Christians remained members of Orthodox churches, but the Roman Catholic Church established small Uniate churches that, while linked with Rome, also preserved their own liturgies. Jews suffered from lawless attacks by janissaries and also from prejudiced treatment by Christian Ottomans and foreign European Christians. The Ottoman central government in the eighteenth century reissued rules about clothing non-Muslims could wear, but these regulations were usually circumvented by bribes to officials. Among Muslim ulama, especially those in Mecca and Medina, there was a broadening of interest in reform of the faith. This found expression in a renewed study of hadith and a strengthening of Sufi brotherhoods.

One of the more significant developments in Istanbul was the rise of the so-called Phanariotes. In the seventeenth century the Orthodox patriarch lived in a district bordering the Golden Horn, taking its name Phanar from the Greek word meaning "lighthouse." Earlier, most Greeks who served the sultan had become Muslims, but by the end of the seventeenth century it was no longer necessary for Greeks to adopt Islam to hold office. Out of this circumstance grew the term *Phanariot,* used to designate a Greek or Hellenized Christian in Ottoman service. (Most Orthodox Ottoman Christians were thoroughly under the control of the Greeks, even though such peoples as Bulgarians, Arabs, and Romanians were not Greek-speaking.)

The ascendancy of the Phanariotes took place gradually in the last half of the seventeenth century. From the Phanariotes and their associates came Orthodox patriarchs, merchants, bankers, government translators, ambassadors, and the governors of Moldavia and Wallachia from 1714 to 1821. Of these posts, the most lucrative and therefore the most expensive to purchase were the governorships. Consequently, Phanariot governors found it necessary to rule over their subjects in an extortionate fashion. The prosperity and cultural accomplishments of Moldavia and Wallachia in the seventeenth century were ended as local armies were abolished, intellectual contacts with central Europe decreased, and landlords controlled a majority of the peasants. By the end of Phanariot rule the peasants and nomads had fallen to an estate lower than any in the Balkans.

Yet the Danubian Principalities (and Bulgaria) remained the larder of Istanbul. The empire as a whole was self-sufficient in food, but the capital city needed to import grain and store it in case of emergency. Wheat, butter, cheese, honey, and cows were transported by the central authorities, and more than 500,000 head of sheep were moved every year. As the production of Anatolia became less available, the Danubian Principalities assumed greater importance as an imperial granary. Nevertheless, the frequent wars of the eighteenth century fought on Danubian soil and four Russian occupations increased the misery of the peasants.

The Danubian Principalities were freer from the political and financial control of the Ottoman central government than many provinces of the empire. However, by the middle of the eighteenth century the process of disintegration had reached a point where an energetic and ambitious governor in almost any province could build up his own independent military, political, and economic power and even try to defy the sultan. Throughout the empire, the local wealthy, urban, elite families gained power as the central government's writ was progressively weakened, and the nomads moved into cultivated areas, thereby decreasing the number of villages and the taxes paid by them.

REBELLIOUS PROVINCES

To describe each one of the petty provincial lords and to relate the incidents of his local government would be superfluous. In Europe the best known were Ali Pasha of Janina, who ruled Epirus from 1788 to 1822, and Osman Pasvanoglu of Vidin, who terrorized the lower Danube from Belgrade to the sea. Both recognized the sultan's theoretical sovereignty and occasionally sent Istanbul tribute; yet, unlike seventeenth-century local leaders, each also regularly defied the central government and entered into diplomatic relations with European powers. They established order in their own areas, and their rule, though harsh, was at least less destructive than the circumstances created by the near anarchy that prevailed where robber bands and ex-janissaries held sway.

The most famous of the quasi-independent lords in other parts of the empire were the rulers of the city-states of North Africa. Even in the sixteenth century, at the heyday of the sultan's power, the authority of the Ottoman central government in Algiers, Tunis, and Tripoli was never very substantial. In the eighteenth century, North African local dynasties and corsairs recognized the sultan's overlordship but retained local control in their own hands, as could be seen in Tripoli under the Qaramanli dynasty from 1711 to 1835.

More significant in the process of the weakening of Ottoman central government and in its loss of revenue were developments of the eighteenth century that occurred in Egypt, Iraq, Syria, and Anatolia. The Mamluk system in Egypt was never fully eradicated, and once the reins from Istanbul were loosened the Mamluks flourished again from 1711 to 1798. Ali Bey, the Mamluk leader of Egypt from 1760 to 1772, secured military and fiscal power, centralized the civil administration, expanded contacts with Europe, and directed Egypt on an independent course, even minting coins using his name rather than the sultan's. In 1786 the Ottoman central government conquered Egypt again but was unable to directly govern such a distant province, so it reverted to Mamluk control and ensuing economic decline.

From 1704 to 1831 Baghdad was in the hands of a Mamluk dynasty, and Mosul was held for more than a century by the Jalili family. The al-Azm family ruled strongly on behalf of the central government in Damascus and adjacent areas of Syria, where they created private homes of great splendor as well as some degree of public order. Other families held Jerusalem, and the province of Aleppo was so torn with strife and civil wars that between 1765 and 1785 hundreds of villages disappeared.

The most adventurous career was that of Ahmed Jezzar (Ahmed the "Butcher"). Of Bosnian origin, he obtained his nickname from his ruthless tactics while employed by Ali Bey of Egypt. Gaining the favor of Istanbul, he became pasha of Sidon and Acre along the Mediterranean coast (1785–1805), later augmenting his territory to include Damascus. Ahmed Jezzar Pasha maintained a private army, built a fleet, suppressed the nomads, drastically increased taxes on the peasants, established monopolies, made commercial agreements with western merchants, and created an efficient governmental organization. All this was done in the name of the sultan, and his policies gained Ahmed the approval of Istanbul.

Even in Anatolia, closer to Istanbul, a similar situation existed in the eighteenth century. Derebeys (valley lords), who were leaders of local families, seized power. The central government was compelled to appease them to obtain any compliance with respect to law, taxes, and military support.

SEARCH FOR REFORM

Beset by foreign powers and enfeebled by internal political decentralization, the empire nevertheless retained the support of many groups as its leaders considered reforms. In Istanbul and other cities the many trade and craft guilds served as a powerful bonding agent, giving individuals a sense of security and a definite place in society. (There were even guilds for prostitutes and pickpockets!) Guild members found their lives regulated by their guild, experienced their social life in the guild, and had their contacts with government chiefly through guild leaders. In the countryside, landowners avoided political association as much as possible, and peasants were concerned only with their landlords. Simple village life was the chief aim of the peasants.

Many Ottomans in top positions believed the state was stagnating and falling behind European states. They predicted that the empire was surely doomed unless reforms were undertaken. In sciences such as astronomy Ottomans kept informed about European discoveries in a timely fashion, but military defeats spurred ex-officials of the government to write treatises deploring corruption and inefficiency. Notable essays on these points appeared in 1616, 1630, 1657, 1725, and 1772; each condemned the selling of offices and recounted specific abuses by officials from the sultan down to the lowliest scribe. In a book written in 1725, a former imperial treasurer prescribed as a remedy a return to the higher values that had allegedly prevailed two centuries earlier in the reign of Suleiman I.

No reforms could be initiated with success unless they were supported by the sultan. Many sultans of the eighteenth century desired reforms but did not know how to inaugurate them. A reorientation of the government also demanded the labor of dedicated persons who understood Ottoman conditions in relation to developments in Europe. Unfortunately, money needed for military reforms was in short supply as the revenues available to Istanbul declined and at the same time the needs of the state grew.

NADIR SHAH AND CHAOS IN IRAN AND CENTRAL ASIA

While the Ottoman Empire witnessed a relative decline in its power compared with most of Europe, the fate of Iran in the eighteenth century was far worse. After the fall of Isfahan to the Sunnite Afghans in 1722, Safavid Shiite Iran disintegrated. Even though the military adventurer Nadir Shah temporarily established a large empire, neither he nor the capable Karim Khan Zand was able to stop the impoverishment and anarchy that affected most of Iran and central Asia.

In 1731 the weak Safavid shah Tahmasp II had to cede Iranian holdings in the Caucasus to the Ottomans. The real power in the land, Nadir Khan Afshar, removed Tahmasp from the throne, and then Nadir managed to revitalize his forces and effect the recovery of Azerbaijan and the southern Caucasus. The Russians evacuated Gilan, Baku, and Darband. Nadir, crowned shah in 1736, placed his capital at Meshhed, not far from where he had been a shepherd boy of the qizilbash Afshar tribe.

Nadir owed his position to the strength of his army and his ability to lead it, rather than to internal prosperity and popular support. Under his rule for several decades the state's economy worsened. Taxes on the peasants doubled, and internal trade was impaired by constant warfare. A standing army with artillery and muskets was so expensive that the only way Nadir could keep his regime in funds was through conquest and loot. First he successfully pressed the Bakhtiyari chieftains in the southwest to accept his rule, many of them enrolling their tribal followings under his banner. In 1738 he took Qandahar after having laid siege to it for over a year.

Nadir proceeded to Kabul, and through the Khyber Pass to India. Here he found rich stores of money with which to support his army. In 1739 he defeated the Muslim Mughal emperor at the battle of Karnal. Victory allowed him to proceed triumphantly into Delhi, where the emperor handed over his immense wealth. (The most famous trophy in this loot was the peacock throne, built of gold and covered with priceless pearls and jewels, which became the throne for the ruler of Iran.)

In 1745 Nadir defeated an Ottoman army and captured its artillery and military stores, but then concluded peace with Mahmud I. The shah began to build a navy in the Persian Gulf, but this attempt was ultimately without result since the state Nadir had fashioned was crumbling. A military adventurer, Nadir never appreciated the relationship between military means and political ends. He administered the state poorly, and the bureaucracy was neglected. His experiment in the reconciliation of Shiite with

Sunnite Islam was a failure, and the independence of the Shiite ulama actually increased. By the time of his assassination in 1747, he had become a bloody tyrant who marked his triumphs by having his victims' skulls stacked into high pyramids.

Immediately upon Nadir's murder, his army broke up into segments under tribal leaders. One chief, Ahmad Shah Durrani, subsequently became ruler of Afghanistan (1747–1773). For most of the following half century, Iran suffered under a frightful anarchy among contenders for the throne. The land was rife with massacres and wholesale blindings. When Kerman fell to Aga Muhammad, for instance, he ordered that 20,000 pairs of eyes be presented to him!

In central Asia, the disintegration of the Tuqay Timurid state in the first half of the eighteenth century matched the chaotic and dangerous conditions of Iran, but no local figure equal to the conqueror Nadir Shah emerged as descendants of Genghiz Khan finally lost their legitimacy after 500 years of rule. On Nadir's return from India he occupied Herat, and in 1740 he invaded the lands of the Uzbegs, taking Bukhara and Khiva, which he controlled loosely thereafter. Upon the death of Nadir two tribally based Uzbeg dynasties gained power, and, as trade with Russia increased, a certain degree of prosperity returned to parts of central Asia in the late eighteenth century.

There was a hiatus to the savagery following the death of Nadir for some parts of Iran with the rule of Karim Khan Zand, who maintained his capital at Shiraz. Karim upheld justice, was a patron of music, and gave much of Iran two decades of internal peace, low taxes, and general prosperity. He temporarily extended Iran's control over Basrah in southern Iraq and unsuccessfully tried to assert Iranian power in Oman, all the while continuing his modest fiction of simply being the deputy of a puppet Safavid prince. But upon Karim's death in 1779 confusion again engulfed Iran, with cities falling to one attacking force after another, in many cases suffering devastation that was felt up to the twentieth century. In 1794, Aga Muhammad, the leader of the Qajar qizilbash tribe, won over all rivals, and his chief residence of Tehran thus became the capital of Iran. This shah, who had been castrated at the age of six by Nadir's nephew, nevertheless established a Qajar rule that held sway in Iran until 1921.

The eighteenth-century wars and devastation that affected much of Iran and central Asia were not as prevalent for the subjects of the Ottoman state. In the early part of the century the Ottomans even enjoyed some diplomatic successes and witnessed cultural growth. By the end of the century, however, internal disagreements and rebellious provincial leaders bedeviled the Ottomans, and their chief challenge came from Russian and Hapsburg Austrian expansionism. As of 1789 the need for administrative change and military reform was great, although many groups still opposed it or were unsure how to bring it about.

References

Important for this chapter are books cited in Chapters 14, 16, 17, 19, and 20.

Abou-El-Haj, Rifaat Ali: *The 1703 Rebellion and the Structure of Ottoman Politics.* Istanbul: Netherlands Historical-Archaeological Institute, 1984. In addition to an account of the rebellion, this valuable work contains an analysis of the Ottoman Empire in the seventeenth century.

AKSAN, VIRGINIA H.: "Ottoman Political Writing, 1768–1808." *International Journal of Middle East Studies* 25 (1993): 53–69. Useful analysis of reformers' ideas on military change and westernization.

ANDERSON, M. S.: *The Eastern Question, 1774–1923: A Study in International Relations.* London: Macmillan, 1966. A detailed study of European diplomacy as it related to the Ottoman Empire.

AVERY, PETER, ET AL., EDS.: *The Cambridge History of Iran.* Vol. 7: *From Nadir Shah to the Islamic Republic.* Cambridge, England: Cambridge University Press, 1991. Twenty-four chapters cover all aspects of the subject; indispensable.

BARBIR, KARL: *Ottoman Rule in Damascus, 1708–1758.* Princeton, N.J.: Princeton University Press, 1980. An excellent book showing the subtlety of Ottoman-provincial relations.

COHEN, AMNON: *Palestine in the 18th Century: Patterns of Government and Administration.* Jerusalem: Magnes Press, 1973. Authoritative.

CRECILIUS, DANIEL: *The Roots of Modern Egypt: A Study of the Regimes of Ali Bey al-Kabir and Muhammad Bey Abu al-Dhahab, 1760–1775.* Minneapolis, Minn.: Bibliotheca Islamica, 1981.

FISHER, ALAN W.: *The Russian Annexation of the Crimea, 1772–1783.* Cambridge, England: Cambridge University Press, 1970. Based on Russian and Ottoman archival materials, this work shows that the idea of Russian liberation of the Crimea was a myth.

GEORGESCU, VLAD: *The Romanians: A History.* Translated by Alexandra Bley-Vroman. Columbus: Ohio State University Press, 1991. This study deals with the subject from earliest times to the 1980s.

INALCIK, HALIL: "Imtiyazat ii.—The Ottoman Empire." *Encyclopaedia of Islam.* New ed. Vol. 3, pp. 1179–1189. Leiden: Brill, 1971. An important discussion of the capitulations by a leading scholar.

ITZKOWITZ, NORMAN: "Eighteenth Century Ottoman Realities." *Studia Islamica* 41 (1962): 73–94. Still essential reading for an understanding of Ottoman government.

JELAVICH, BARBARA: *History of the Balkans.* Vol. 1: *Eighteenth and Nineteenth Centuries.* Cambridge, England: Cambridge University Press, 1983.

LEVY, AVIGDOR: "Military Reform and the Problem of Centralization in the Ottoman Empire in the Eighteenth Century." *Middle Eastern Studies* 18 (1982): 227–249.

MARCUS, ABRAHAM: *The Middle East on the Eve of Modernity: Aleppo in the Eighteenth Century.* New York: Columbia University Press, 1989. An exceptionally valuable and richly rewarding picture of social life in all its manifestations.

MURPHEY, RHOADES: "Provisioning Istanbul: The State and Subsistence in the Early Modern Middle East." *Food and Foodways* 2 (1988): 217–263.

NAFF, THOMAS, AND ROGER OWEN, EDS.: *Studies in Eighteenth Century Islamic History.* Carbondale: Southern Illinois University Press, 1977. Sixteen chapters by various experts on government, economy, and culture, mostly in the Ottoman Empire.

PANZAC, DANIEL: "International and Domestic Maritime Trade in the Ottoman Empire During the 18th Century." *International Journal of Middle East Studies* 24 (1992): 189–206. Especially valuable for discussion of Mediterranean trade.

PERRY, JOHN R.: *Karim Khan Zand: A History of Iran, 1747–1779.* Chicago: University of Chicago Press, 1979. Outstanding discussion of political, military, provincial, economic, and external events as they affected Iran in the second half of the eighteenth century.

SHAW, STANFORD J.: *The Jews of the Ottoman Empire and the Turkish Republic.* New York: New York University Press, 1991. A well-written and thoroughly researched account.

THOMAS, LEWIS V.: *A Study of Naima.* Edited by Norman Itzkowitz. New York: New York University Press, 1972. A perceptive study of the life, ideas, and contributions of the great Ottoman historian and chronicler of the late seventeenth and early eighteenth centuries.

ZILFI, MADELINE C.: "Elite Circulation in the Ottoman Empire: Great Mollas of the Eighteenth Century." *Journal of the Economic and Social History of the Orient* 26 (1983): 318–364. In this and later articles the author carefully examines Ottoman administration, legitimacy, and religion.

The Nineteenth-Century Middle East

The Era of the French Revolution and Napoleon

Three crucial events marked the end of the early modern era and the beginning of the modern period in Middle Eastern history: the accession of the reform-minded Selim III as sultan of the Ottoman Empire in 1789, the 1798 invasion of Egypt by Napoleon Bonaparte, and the establishment of the new Qajar dynasty in Iran around 1794. The reforms undertaken by Selim III, based in part on trends already seen in the eighteenth century, brought about many changes in the military. A rapid French conquest of Egypt opened the way for multifaceted struggles and changes along the Nile during the next decades and showed the Ottomans how weak they were compared with western Europe. Qajar rule in Iran ended the chaos and fragmentation that had devastated much of that land since the destruction of Safavid rule in 1722.

A common factor linking the central Ottoman lands, Egypt, and Iran was a perceived need for military reforms along western European lines. The far-reaching wars and diplomacy of the era of the French Revolution and Napoleon from 1789 to 1815 emphasized the military imbalance between Europe and the Middle East. Despite this, some groups, such as the Saudi dynasty in central Arabia or the Ottoman janissary corps, reacted against European encroachments by opposing any type of reform, even limited military modernization.

THE REFORMS OF SELIM III

Selim III became Ottoman sultan in 1789 just before the outbreak of the French Revolution. The new ruler desired to restore the power of the sultanate over other institutions and groups in Istanbul and to establish governmental authority in the provinces. That he thought of himself as a reformer in a modern sense is doubtful. But he did understand that techniques pursued in Russia and the west had placed great power in the hands of the ruler and his government. In 1789, Selim was about twenty-seven years old and had studied more widely than most of his immediate predecessors. At first, wars with Austria and Russia tied his hands. The French

---

PERIODIZATION IN THE HISTORY OF THE ISLAMIC MIDDLE EAST

Antiquity: from the rise of civilization to the coming of Islam

Classical Islamic period: from the life of the prophet Muhammad to the middle of the tenth century A.D.

The early medieval era in the Middle East: from about 950 to about 1250

The late medieval era in the Middle East: from about 1250 to about 1500

The early modern Middle East: from about 1500 to about 1800

The modern Middle East: from about 1800 to the present

Revolution, however, distracted the European powers, gave the Ottoman Empire a few years of respite from western imperialism, and offered Selim an unexpected opportunity to show his true character.

In the central government Selim sought to curb the powers of the grand viziers by reorganizing the imperial divan and by commanding that it be consulted on all important measures. Specialized commissions and advisory councils, each for a particular matter, were formed, and the divan ministers were ordered to consider their recommendations. One of the greatest difficulties in administering any reform was the lack of officials who thought of their position as anything but an opportunity for personal profit at the expense of the state.

In the provinces Selim found that his word received little heed and foresaw that reforms would be ineffective unless a thorough transformation could be carried out in the army. The janissaries and standing sipahi cavalry had for some time been of little value; the training and weapons of all were hopelessly obsolete. Following the peace of Jassy in 1792, Selim recruited a corps of 600 men, who were outfitted in European military garb and trained in European tactics. When Selim suggested to the divan that the janissaries adopt similar uniforms and be drilled in the same manner, he was able to appease mutineers only by withdrawing the request.

Selim instituted similar reforms in the old army units by reorganizing the financing of the army and giving the administrative duties of the commanders to other officers, thus allowing the janissary agas to concentrate on military effectiveness. Fortunately, French revolutionary governments sent several of the latest pieces of artillery, artillerymen, and army engineers to advise in the use and manufacture of the new weapons and drill sergeants from French regiments to organize and train a new Ottoman army.

A new force, called the Nizam-i Jedid (Army of the New Order), came into being about 1792 and grew slowly, first hardly more than a toy for Selim's amusement. By 1801 there were over 9000 men in the new army; in 1807 there were 25,000. But because of the rapidity of this expansion, training and discipline were superficial. Since a majority of the recruits came from villages, they were unaccustomed to a confining life; they became unruly and took to plundering Istanbul suburbs. The janissaries refused to adopt any "Christian" devices and objected to serving alongside the Nizam-i Jedid. Thus these troops played only a token role in the 1806 and 1807 campaigns against the Serbs and Russians, leaving the main fighting to the relatively ineffective janissaries and sipahis.

Selim encouraged the founding of schools, especially engineering academies, which he felt were necessary adjuncts to any military reform. The Imperial Naval Engineering School included courses in naval architecture, and the arsenal was improved. By 1798, forty-five naval vessels had been launched. In all, there were twenty ships of the line and twenty-five frigates with 40,000 sailors. The navy could compete with European fleets whereas the army could not. A cannon foundry was built and a new gunpowder plant set up. Other scattered technical improvements included the founding of the naval school of medicine and the reintroduction of printing establishments that made possible the printing of mathematical and technical books, some translated from western sources.

Military reform was a limited goal, with no evidence that Selim felt a need for innovative political, social, and economic reforms to support the military and technical changes. To improve foreign policy, permanent Ottoman embassies were sent to London, Paris, Vienna, and Berlin. The published reports of many of the Ottoman ambassadors contributed to the limited, but growing, Ottoman knowledge about conditions in Christian Europe. Ottoman artists also came to follow European conventions and methods in some fields, as seen in book illustrations, landscape painting, and architectural decoration but not in such cultural areas as music and literature.

Selim sought greater governmental efficiency and therefore issued orders to reduce the number of officials, doing away with the positions of many who did no work. He increased taxes, debased the coinage, seized private property, and melted down gold and silver utensils, sending the bullion to the mint. But these measures were merely palliative, leading to inflation, hunger, and, ultimately, economic disaster. In Istanbul earlier decrees to regulate costumes of persons according to creed, profession, trade, and position were openly flouted. To reduce violence and disorder on the streets, Selim demanded that laws be enforced, including those regarding rules for clothing according to personal status, and even went out in disguise to catch offenders himself. Another attempt to bring law and order to the capital and to reduce its burgeoning population was an edict to cut down on the number of taverns and coffeehouses, to forbid the building of any new hotels or lodging houses, and to send idlers back to their villages. When grain became scarce, Selim controlled the supply and the trade: bakers had to buy their grain and sell their bread at fixed prices. Many of the reforms failed because of the sultan's personal weakness and lack of determination; the reforms lapsed entirely when General Napoleon Bonaparte invaded Egypt.

NAPOLEON INVADES EGYPT

The sultan's authority in Egypt had been only nominal for nearly a century. As the power of Istanbul waned, Mamluks grew wealthy and independent. Ostensibly,

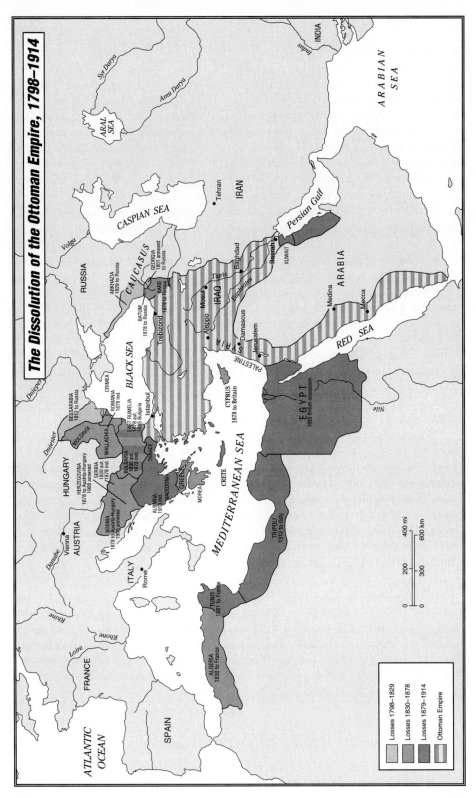

The Dissolution of the Ottoman Empire, 1798–1914

INDIA

Indus

ARABIAN SEA

Syr Darya

Amu Darya

ARAL SEA

CASPIAN SEA

Tehran

IRAN

Persian Gulf

Volga

RUSSIA

ARKHAZIA
1829 to Russia

CAUCASUS

GEORGIA
1801 annexed
to Russia

Baghdad

Basrah

KUWAIT

ARABIA

KARS
1878 to Russia

BATUM
1878 to Russia

Trebizond

Tigris

Mosul

IRAQ

Euphrates

Aleppo

SYRIA

Damascus

Medina

Mecca

Dnieper

BLACK SEA

Istanbul

Jerusalem

PALESTINE

RED SEA

BESSARABIA
1812 to Russia

CRIMEA

ROMANIA
1878 ind.

CYPRUS
1878 to Britain

EGYPT
1882 British occupation

Nile

MOLDAVIA

EAST RUMELIA
1878 aut.
1885 Bulgaria

THRACE

Dniester

HUNGARY

WALLACHIA

HERZEGOVINA
1878 to Austria-Hungary
1908 annexed

BULGARIA
1878 aut.
1878 ind.

SERBIA
1830 aut.
1878 ind.

MACEDONIA

GREECE

CRETE

MEDITERRANEAN SEA

BOSNIA
1878 to Austria-Hungary
1908 annexed

ALBANIA
1913 ind.

MOREA

Danube

Vienna

AUSTRIA

ITALY

Rome

TRIPOLI
1912 to Italy

Rhine

Rhone

Loire

FRANCE

SPAIN

ATLANTIC OCEAN

TUNIS
1881 to France

ALGERIA
1830 to France

400 mi

600 km

200

300

0

0

	Losses 1798–1829
	Losses 1830–1878
	Losses 1879–1914
	Ottoman Empire

Bonaparte invaded Egypt to destroy the Mamluks, who were proving so troublesome to his supposed ally Sultan Selim III. However, Bonaparte's real objective was probably to attack the route to British-controlled India, while the possession of Egypt would widen the French commercial sphere in the Mediterranean. In view of Napoleon's known regard for the importance of Istanbul, perhaps he also intended to take Egypt as a base for moving upon Istanbul, the Balkans, and Austria.

In any case, Bonaparte, accompanied by engineers, historians, archaeologists, architects, mathematicians, chemists, and Egyptologists, set sail in May 1798 to take Malta and Egypt. He landed on July 1, took Alexandria on July 2, and defeated the outnumbered Mamluks at the famous battle of the Pyramids outside Cairo on July 21. The rapidity of the French defeat of the Mamluks can be explained by the technical superiority of the revolutionary armies of the Republic, the military genius of their general, and the dreadful economic circumstances of Egypt in the 1790s. Napoleon's victory was partially overcome, however, when his fleet was destroyed by the British at Aboukir Bay; his line of supply was thus cut and his freedom of action impeded. Nevertheless, the French were able to suppress a revolt in Cairo by the Egyptians.

Since Egypt was a province of the Ottoman Empire, the attack brought a declaration of war from the sultan, who joined with England and Russia in a coalition against France. This alliance scandalized the ulama, who considered the treaty as too subservient to the infidels and contrary to the shariah. Selim gave Ahmed Jezzar, governor of Sidon and Acre, command of the army in Syria, and a fleet and army were collected at Rhodes for the relief of Egypt. Napoleon marched on Syria in 1799 in the hope that discontented Sunnites, Druzes, and Christians would rise against the Ottomans. He took Gaza and Jaffa, where in cold blood he murdered 2000 Ottoman prisoners. But Jezzar, with reinforcements landed by an English squadron, held off Napoleon's attack at Acre. Repulsed there, Napoleon hurried to Egypt to meet a landing of Ottoman infantry and cavalry at Aboukir Bay. These he drove into the sea, regaining his heavy-handed mastery of Egypt. He then deserted his troops and sailed for France, where he executed his famous coup d'état and seized power in the government.

The French forces remaining in Egypt were not conquered or evacuated until 1801. Several Ottoman expeditions, in collaboration with an English army and naval squadron, forced the surrender of the French and gave them a guarantee of safe-conduct home. British forces held Egypt and kept the several local competing factions from open warfare until a short peace in 1802 required the departure of the British. At that point Mehmet Ali (Muhammad Ali), leader of one of the Ottoman factions, took advantage of the prevailing political and military anarchy and set the course of his meteoric ascent. His rise was of great significance for the Middle East, but it separated to a degree the affairs of the Nile from those of Istanbul.

At the time of the 1802 peace, agreement was reached between Selim III and Napoleon. Selim was also at peace with England, Russia, and Austria. The Russians and British, however, used every device to offset French influence and to gain the Ottomans as allies for their European policies. Trade revived in Ottoman ports, and shipping was brisk on the Black Sea.

UPRISINGS IN SERBIA AND ARABIA

Upon the general establishment of peace in Europe, Selim expected to proceed with his reforms, but calamity befell him in Serbia and the holy cities of Arabia. The combined effect of these rebellions contributed mightily to his eventual overthrow and execution.

The 1791 peace of Sistova had provided for the return of Belgrade to the sultan, but it also stipulated that the janissaries, who previously ruled the area in a ferocious manner, would not be permitted to return. Selim's new governor gave Serbia the most peaceful, prosperous, and enlightened rule it had known for nearly a century. However, to appease Pasvanoglu Pasha of Vidin, Selim agreed to the return of the janissaries to Belgrade in 1799. Murdering the enlightened governor, four janissary leaders defied Selim's authority and divided Serbia among themselves. Outrage upon Christians and Muslims followed outrage, until there occurred the famous uprising of 1804 against janissary rule.

Aided by Austrian arms and led by the Serbian Kara George, insurgents were successful in destroying the janissaries. Selim sought to reestablish Ottoman rule in Belgrade, but the Serb leaders insisted that the terms of settlement be supervised by an Austrian commissioner. Selim declared he could not consent to foreign interference in domestic affairs, and Austria refused to break the peace of Sistova. When the Serbs then turned to Russia, the Ottomans sent troops against the rebels. Victorious, the Serbs organized a provisional autonomous regime and again defeated the Ottomans. In 1806 the outbreak of war between the Ottoman Empire and Russia enabled Serbia to clear Ottoman arms from the entire province. Thereupon Serbian affairs became a part of the European tangle of international diplomacy and power politics.

When Selim removed the two pro-Russian governors of Wallachia and Moldavia, replacing them with pro-French officials, Russia invaded the Danubian Principalities in 1806, and the Ottomans declared war and closed the Straits to Russian ships.

In central Arabia, well beyond the reach of Ottoman soldiers, Prince Muhammad ibn Saud, a local prince in the small oasis town of Diriyyah, in 1745 concluded an alliance with Muhammad ibn Abd al-Wahhab (d. 1792), a Hanbali Sunnite religious reformer. Muhammad ibn Abd al-Wahhab and his followers (usually called Wahhabis) emphasized the unity of God, sought to return Muslims to the principles and practices of the earliest days of the ummah in Medina, opposed so-called innovations in the faith such as Sufi orders, and energetically sought to expand their control. From the Saudi-Wahhabi point of view, the Ottomans were among the chief enemies of true Islam. By the time of the death in 1765 of Prince Muhammad ibn Saud the Saudi-Wahhabi group had conquered much of central and eastern Arabia. Saud I (r. 1803–1814) captured Mecca and Medina, thereby taking control of the pilgrimage from the Ottoman Empire and causing Selim III to order expeditions to be sent from Egypt against Saud.

OVERTHROW OF SELIM

A change of equipment for the garrisons on the Bosphorus incited the janissaries to demand the dismissal of the divan. And since payments due them were in arrears, the janissaries overturned their soup kettles, the traditional sign of revolt. The ensuing uprising by unruly janissary trainees precipitated Selim's deposition and the elevation of his cousin Mustafa IV in May 1807. Formal charges against Selim were that he incited revolution by military innovations and that he had fathered no children after more than seventeen years of rule.

As has been indicated, Selim did not possess the resolute ruthlessness necessary to cope with the turbulence of the age. Surrounded by self-seeking, dishonest, and insubordinate officials, he was thwarted at every turn. He realized that his only hope was to play one faction against another. Each suggested innovation jeopardized some vested interest, the most perceptibly threatened group being the janissaries whose distress brought his downfall. The masses were agitated over prices and by fears of uprisings in many of the provinces. French and Russian threats kept everyone on edge, and the presence of a growing number of Europeans in influential positions disturbed the political elite.

Mustafa IV was an ineffectual person, the puppet of those who had overthrown Selim. Although the French officers and technicians were dismissed, the new sultan and Napoleon concluded a truce which ironically was disastrous for Mustafa and the rebellious janissaries, since it freed the Ottoman armies on the Danube. An Ottoman army of Bosnians and Albanians, commanded by Bairaktar, governor of Ruschuk, marched on Istanbul and camped near the capital. Bairaktar called many leaders to his camp and in July 1808 moved upon the city and the palace. Before Bairaktar's men could force the gates, Mustafa executed Selim and gave orders for the strangling of his own brother Mahmud. The insurgents, however, quickly imprisoned Mustafa and placed on the throne Mahmud II, who had been hidden in an empty furnace of the palace.

MAHMUD II AND THE NAPOLEONIC WARS

Mahmud II gave the office of grand vizir to Bairaktar, and the movement for reform proceeded along the lines drawn by Selim. After the organization of a new Europeanized army, Bairaktar permitted his Bosnians and Albanians to return home. Thereupon the janissaries rose up and destroyed Bairaktar. Civil war raged in the streets of Istanbul for a week, with fires, explosions, and chaos, during which Mustafa was executed. Mahmud, now the sole surviving male of the Ottoman dynasty, was fairly safe, but friends of the janissaries controlled the government, and military reforms were out of the question.

The French and Russians were furious as Mahmud seemed to favor Britain; the tsar sent his troops to the Danube and into the Caucasus, taking several towns. Fortunately for Russia, the 1812 Peace of Bucharest with the Ottoman Empire was signed a month before the French attack on Russia was launched. As a result of the treaty, the Ottomans gained back most of the territory they had lost, except Bessarabia (Moldova), which came under the control of Russia. Mahmud II dismissed the grand vizir and executed the negotiators for giving Bessarabia to the tsar, but the Peace of Bucharest did permit the Ottomans to stay neutral in the enormous struggle between Russia and the French Empire.

The treaty also abandoned the Serbs to the sultan, who pledged that Serbs could manage their own internal affairs. The Russian regiment left Belgrade, and the Ottomans attempted to rule the province. Although Kara George departed, a new leader, Milosh Obrenovitch, continued the Serbian revolt. The Congress of Vienna in 1815 allowed the Serbs to retain their arms and gave them a voice in the management of their own government through an elected parliament. As a result, the sultan's sovereignty over Serbia was hardly more than a legal fiction, and most of the taxes that the Serbs collected remained in Serbia. The empire had lost effective control over several peripheral provinces, but its core remained intact, although in need of military strengthening.

THE QAJAR DYNASTY

The Shiite Qajar tribe of northern Iran was a major player in the chaotic struggle for power in eighteenth-century Iran. Aga Muhammad Shah of the Qajars, who won out in 1794 over other rivals for the throne of Iran following the demise of Karim Khan Zand in 1779, had as a child been captured and castrated. Subsequently freed, he had gained ascendancy in the leading Qajar clan as a young man and then passed many years as a political hostage at the court of Karim Khan. After Karim's death in 1779 Aga Muhammad made his way to the north, where he organized a force, drove the Russians from the southern Caspian coast in 1781, established his capital in Tehran by 1786, and had so strengthened his position that with the fall of Kerman in 1794 major resistance to Qajar rule was eliminated in the central Iranian lands. In 1796 Aga Muhammad crowned himself shah and girded himself with the sword of the Safavid Shah Ismail.

Aga Muhammad, attacking the Georgians and their Russian allies, took Tiflis and Erivan, before conquering Meshhed. When the Russians in 1796 occupied Baku and Darband, his position would have been hopeless had not the death of Catherine the Great that year brought about a Russian withdrawal. He managed to pacify Kurdistan and subdued parts of Khurasan and fortified it against Uzbeg forays.

Aga Muhammad was generally recognized to have had four passions: power, avarice, revenge, and hunting, the greatest being power. He was often ruthless and cruel, but was very effective in establishing justice in the countryside. He was murdered by his personal servants in 1797.

The shah had chosen as his successor his nephew Fath Ali. Governor at Shiraz at the time of his uncle's assassination, Fath Ali hastened to Tehran while a Qajar general held the throne for him. Scions of the Afshar and Zand tribes made bids for the throne, but Fath Ali's army gave him sufficient edge to overwhelm them. When the early Qajar shahs died, several contenders might battle for the imperial turban and plunge the state into disorder. Two centuries earlier the central government's acquisition of artillery and muskets gave the opposition little chance, but at the outset of the nineteenth century many groups in Iran possessed these weapons and could question the succession even of a designated heir. Eventually, however, the throne passed more peacefully, even though the government's army, consisting largely of cavalry, was weak. British and Russian contingents more or less guaranteed a regular succession, since they wanted to avoid a civil war.

Fath Ali Shah maintained a close and lasting association with many of the ulama and welcomed, at times, their participation in governmental matters. He knew that an appearance of piety was useful and sometimes necessary, and so he built mosques and commissioned theological works. To the great pleasure of the ulama, he also suppressed the Sufi orders.

The monarchy was the dominant feature of Iranian politics, and the shah's word was final within the central government. If he made prudent decisions, the state prospered; if he made unfortunate ones, all suffered. The shah appointed some of his numerous sons to be provincial governors, where they gained experience in administration and the central bureaucracy was increased in size. But Iran was not truly unified: there was little social cohesion, so the absolutism of the shah was a myth. Within the royal family and among the elite there was a mixture of self-interest and self-indulgence often combined with considerable efficiency and effectiveness in administration.

DIPLOMACY IN IRAN

For Fath Ali and his ministers Russian power and aggression engendered apprehension throughout his entire reign. During the French Revolution and the Napoleonic Wars in Europe, French, British, and Russian envoys and military missions journeyed to Tehran, vying for Iranian alliances. The French were looking for aid against the British in India, and the British were cajoling Iran to stand firm against France. The Russians sometimes were allies of the French and usually opposed the influence of the British. Britain also had an interest in Iranian policies since to a certain degree British India's northwest frontier was more peaceful when Iran blocked Russia and held the Afghans in check.

In addition to these issues of grand strategy, for Iran the fate of the Caucasus helped determine its alliances. Russia annexed Georgia in 1801, added portions of the western Caucasus in 1803–1806, and gained some of the eastern Caucasian khanates and Baku between 1804 and 1813. Since Iran considered the southern Caucasus to be an integral part of its own domain, this caused considerable friction with Russia.

Until 1805, British missions to Tehran and Fath Ali's to Bombay discussed relations with the Afghans. French approaches in 1805 proposed that Fath Ali sever his undertakings with the British and invade India with French support. At the same time an alliance against Russia was suggested with the idea of French aid in regaining Georgia from Russia. Sent to France to undertake negotiations, Prince Reza caught up with Napoleon at Tilsit and signed the Treaty of Finkenstein in May 1807. By its terms, Iran pledged to declare war on Great Britain, to incite the Afghans to attack India, and to grant French troops right of passage across Iran; the French meanwhile recognized Iran's right to Georgia, agreeing "to compel Russia to relinquish Georgia," and committed a military mission to Tehran. General Claude Gardane and seventy officers and technicians soon arrived to train the Iranian army in European warfare. This was a monumental task, compounded by the poor pay of the soldiers, the absence of any heavy artillery, and the tribal composition of the fighting units.

Sorely disappointed by the Treaty of Tilsit because it contained no mention of Iran, Fath Ali did not declare war against Great Britain. In 1809 the British envoy presented the shah with an exceptionally large diamond and signed a treaty that promised an annual subsidy to Iran as long as Great Britain was at war with Russia and pledged a mission of British officers to train the Iranian army. General Gardane was replaced by British officers. One in particular, Captain Henry Lindsay Bethune, an artillery officer who was 6 feet 8 inches tall, so captivated the Iranians that he remained there for many years and became commander in chief of the Iranian army. The shah sent one of the princes to London to learn how the substantial subsidy was to be paid, and from these negotiations the Treaty of Tehran of 1814 was signed. According to this treaty all alliances between Iran and European powers hostile to Great Britain were null and void; Iran agreed to induce the rulers of Bukhara to prohibit armies from marching against India; frontiers between Iran and Russia were to be determined by Iran, Russia, and Great Britain; and a large subsidy was to be given each year to Iran by the British. Frequently called the Definitive Treaty, this arrangement was the basis of relations between the two countries for many years.

The costly Russo-Persian War of 1804–1813, which was declared a jihad by the ulama, finally ended with the humiliating Treaty of Gulistan, by which Iran ceded to Russia, Georgia, Baku, Shirvan, and other areas in the Caucasus, with the stipulation that Iran would have no navy on the Caspian Sea. The Treaty of Gulistan also committed Russia to support Prince Abbas, son of Fath Ali Shah, for succession to the throne.

REFORM IN IRAN

Even before the Gardane mission arrived in Iran, Prince Abbas as governor of Azerbaijan had been reorganizing the Iranian army along European lines. Russian officers were employed to train the soldiers of this "new army," the Nizam-i Jedid, who were recruited on a permanent basis with fixed pay, disciplined and dressed as European troops, and equipped with modern weapons. They were similar to the new army of Selim III in Istanbul, and the ulama in Iran, who were gaining in power and self-confidence, objected to them just as those in the Ottoman Empire had. (Prince Abbas drilled with the new soldiers but had to do so in private so that his religious faith would not be questioned.) French officers replaced the Russians in 1808, only to be replaced in turn by the British, who continued in the role of military advisers for several decades. Prince Abbas began many other reforms in Tabriz and was energetic in improving the systems of taxation and justice. He also encouraged the production of local cloth. These changes represented the first elements of westernization and modernization in the social structure of Iran.

The Qajar dynasty began a new era of recovery from the devastation of most of the eighteenth century. Modern Iranian history commenced with the establishment of the Qajars, their diplomatic activities during the wars of the French Revolution and Napoleon, and their halting steps toward military reforms.

The Ottoman Empire by 1815 had also, on balance, successfully weathered the cataclysms of the 1789–1815 period. It was true that Bessarabia was lost, a semiautonomous regime was legalized in Serbia, Egypt was recovering from foreign occupation, and the Hijaz in Arabia was dominated by the Saudis; also two sultans had been slain by military revolts. Little change resulted in the internal organization of the empire, and Selim's military changes seemed dead along with him. Nonetheless, the seeds of reform were sown by wide movements of people and ideas, and a growth in commerce raised incentives to a new high. The Ottoman Empire, Iran, and Egypt were on the threshold of a new age.

References

Among volumes already cited, those of particular value for this chapter are in Chapters 14, 19, and 21.

ANDERSON, ROBERT, AND IBRAHIM FAWZY, EDS.: *Egypt Revealed: Scenes from Napoleon's Description de l'Egypte.* Cairo: American University in Cairo Press, 1987. A good introduction to the massive publication on Egypt compiled by the French scholars accompanying Napoleon in 1798.

ATKIN, MURIEL: *Russia and Iran, 1780–1828.* Minneapolis: University of Minnesota Press, 1980.

DALLAL, AHMAD: "The Origins and Objectives of Islamic Revivalist Thought, 1750–1850." *Journal of the American Oriental Society* 113 (1993): 341–359. Compares Wahhabis with other Muslim religious reformers.

FASA'I, HASAN-E: *History of Persia Under Qajar Rule.* A translation by Heribert Busse of Farsnama-ye Naseri. New York: Columbia University Press, 1972. This detailed account of the Qajar dynasty and rule to 1882 is factual, anecdotal, and illuminating.

FINDLEY, CARTER V.: *Bureaucratic Reform in the Ottoman Empire: The Sublime Porte, 1789–1922.* Princeton, N.J.: Princeton University Press, 1980. An able analysis of the transformation of the scribal service into a civil bureaucracy; also discusses with great insight the general political transformation of the Ottoman Empire.

HUREWITZ, J. C.: *The Middle East and North Africa in World Politics: A Documentary Record.* Vol. 1: *European Expansion, 1535–1914.* New Haven, Conn.: Yale University Press, 1975. The first of three volumes; indispensable for diplomatic events.

ISMAIL, F.: "The Making of the Treaty of Bucharest, 1811–1812." *Middle Eastern Studies* 15 (1979): 163–192.

JABARTI, ABD AL-RAHMAN AL-: *Napoleon in Egypt: Al-Jabarti's Chronicle of the French Occupation, 1798.* Translated by Shmuel Moreh. Princeton, N.J.: Markus Wiener, 1993. This account vividly conveys how an Egyptian scholar regarded the invasion and, along with other items printed in the book, is extremely informative.

KELLY, J. B.: *Britain and the Persian Gulf, 1795–1880.* Oxford, England: Clarendon Press, 1968. A monumental work dealing with British activities on all sides of the Persian Gulf.

LANDEN, ROBERT G.: *The Emergence of the Modern Middle East: Selected Readings.* New York: Van Nostrand Reinhold, 1970. Very useful readings of original documents in translation; concentrates on the Ottomans and Arabs.

LEWIS, BERNARD: *The Muslim Discovery of Europe.* New York: Norton, 1982. A fascinating discussion of Muslim views of Europe as seen in language, media, scholarship, religion, and culture, and on a personal level.

SHAW, STANFORD J.: *Between the Old and New: The Ottoman Empire Under Sultan Selim III, 1789–1807.* Cambridge, Mass.: Harvard University Press, 1971. A comprehensive description by a leading authority.

YAPP, M. E.: *The Making of the Modern Near East 1792–1923.* London: Longman, 1987. This history concentrates on political and economic events; it is especially useful for comparing one region with another.

Mahmud II: Greek Nationalism and Ottoman Reform

The Ottoman Empire, Egypt, and Qajar Iran sought military reforms along European lines, but they faced many obstacles. In particular, ethnic nationalism, another European innovation, caused difficulties for the multiethnic, religiously based, dynastic Ottoman Empire. Nationalist revolution in Greece brought about international complications for Sultan Mahmud II, whose drastic changes in the military were not sufficient to meet new dangers from Russia and Egypt.

THE GREEK REVOLUTION

The French Revolution of 1789 and the ensuing reorganization of much of Europe along nationalist lines contributed to the rise of Greek nationalism. Eighteenth-century liberal Europeans wished to emulate ancient Greek culture; they particularly admired Greek political ideas. Therefore, as Greeks increased their contacts with Europeans at the turn of the century, they were impressed with their own heritage and fostered an intellectual renaissance in Greek communities from Odessa to Marseilles. Before 1820, over 3000 books had been published in modern Greek.

Greek intellectual patriots roused their countrymen to arms and formed a society to cast off Ottoman rule. They glorified the heroic deeds of ancient Greeks and advanced the reconstruction of modern Greek by condemning colloquialisms that had crept into the ancient tongue. The labors of such patriots were aided by the Greek Orthodox Church, which had preserved the identity of the Greek community, and by Greek schools, which trained churchmen and taught many people to read and write Greek.

As the military power of the central Ottoman government in its provinces decreased in the eighteenth century, many outlaw bands emerged in the mountains of Greece. They created a nucleus of Greeks familiar with the handling of weapons. Also, as in antiquity, many Greeks were drawn to the sea and foreign commerce; their knowledge of the ways and languages of the Middle East proved extremely beneficial in trade between Ottoman and Mediterranean ports. From 1768 to 1815 they reaped enormous profits.

In 1814, a group of Greeks in Odessa founded a secret band named the Philike Hetaeria (Friendly Society) to organize a rising against the Ottomans. Similar to contemporary European secret societies, the Philike Hetaeria grew rapidly with the commercial depression after 1815. Its members could not be restrained, and in 1821 Alexander Ypsilanti, a distinguished Phanariot Greek and a general in the Russian army, unfurled the banner of revolt. He crossed the Pruth River from Russian Bessarabia into Moldavia, but this was not the most propitious spot from which to launch a Greek revolution, since the native Romanians hated Phanariot Greeks as much as Ottoman Turks, and local Romanian notables had gained a good deal of autonomy from the Ottomans. Ottoman Turks in Jassy were impaled, and the leader of a simultaneous Romanian revolt was killed by Ypsilanti. The other European Great Powers induced Russia to strike Ypsilanti's name from Russian army rolls and disown the adventure. When an Ottoman army drove him from Bucharest, he fled to Hungary.

Within a few weeks of the crossing of the Pruth, the revolution was in full swing in the Peloponnesus of Greece, where Greek speakers constituted a majority of the population. Ottoman Turks were massacred and the population of surrendered towns put to the sword. When the Ottoman provincial capital fell, over 8000 Ottoman Turks were butchered. Athens, except for the acropolis, was conquered by the insurgents. Immediately the Ottomans fought back; on Crete and some of the Aegean Islands reprisals and counterreprisals were common among Ottoman Muslims and Greek Christians.

The rebellions in the Danubian Principalities and the Peloponnesus led Sultan Mahmud II (r. 1808–1839) to take action against suspected Greek nationalists in Istanbul. A number of leading Phanariotes were executed, and on Easter Sunday the Greek patriarch was hanged from the gate of his residence by janissaries despite his denunciation of the rebels. Of all the Aegean Islands, Chios was the most wealthy, and its inhabitants showed no interest in the uprisings on the mainland. Early in 1822, however, Greek adventurers took over the island against the wishes of the Chiotes. Thereupon, an Ottoman admiral landed and the Ottomans leveled villages, put Chios to the torch, and massacred nearly 25,000 Greeks. Shortly thereafter, Ottoman soldiers surrendered the acropolis in Athens on the pledge that their lives would be spared. The promise was not kept.

One of the factors that had led to these uprisings was Sultan Mahmud's decision to settle some scores with Ali, the rebellious Albanian pasha of Janina in northern Greece. Indeed, because Ottoman forces were dispersed, Mahmud's withdrawal of the best of his soldiers to subdue Ali virtually ensured Greek success. A mixture of eighteenth-century European Enlightenment, pro-Sufi sentiments, and devotion to ancient Greek literature, Ali had ruled as a benevolent tyrant for thirty years, corresponding with Napoleon and the British. In 1820, Mahmud sent an army to Epirus to bring in Ali's head. During this campaign the Ottoman garrisons in Athens and other Greek towns were reduced to the minimum, leaving the towns defenseless against a popular uprising. When, however, Ali Pasha's head and those of his sons and grandsons were exhibited on a silver platter outside the sultan's palace in Istanbul in 1822, Mahmud's forces began the long but ultimately success-ful campaign to restore Ottoman authority in Albania. They also could intimidate the Greeks since, although the sultan's forces were exhausted, the Greeks were torn already with dissension.

INTERVENTION BY EGYPT AND THE GREAT POWERS

The European Great Powers (Great Britain, France, Prussia, Austria, and Russia) looked upon the Greek activities with considerable misgivings, but pro-Greek com-mittees in England and France compelled their governments to take an interest. Furthermore, in 1824 the Greek provisional government obtained the first of a se-ries of loans from British bankers, a move that guaranteed a continuing interest from London. Considerable romantic publicity accompanied the enlistment of Eu-ropean volunteers; the most famous of these was the English Lord Byron, whose death in 1824 in Greece created more sentiment for the Greek nationalists than any other single event in the long struggle.

In 1824, Mahmud commissioned his powerful vassal of Egypt, Mehmet Ali (Muhammad Ali), to aid in suppressing the insurrection. His son Ibrahim, ap-pointed governor of the Peloponnesus, proceeded to establish his authority by fire and sword. Meanwhile, an Ottoman army subdued western Greece and recaptured Athens. Greek independence seemed very doubtful.

The victories of Mahmud's lieutenants hastened the intervention of the Great Powers. The Treaty of London, signed in 1827 by Britain, Russia, and France, de-manded an armistice from the Ottomans and the Greeks and the mediation of any differences. Since Mahmud refused to declare an armistice, the British navy inter-cepted supplies and reinforcements destined for Ibrahim. The battle of Navarino on October 20, 1827, completely shattered Egyptian and Ottoman naval forces, and a French army then compelled Ibrahim to withdraw from Greece.

Russian interests in Greece were tied to the affairs of Serbia and the Danubian Principalities. Even before Russia agreed to the London treaty, an ultimatum had been delivered to Istanbul demanding cession of Kars and other eastern provinces; evacuation of Moldavia and Wallachia, whose governors would be elected by the Romanian aristocracy and could be removed only upon Russian consent; and im-mediate autonomy for Serbia. On the last possible day Mahmud accepted the terms, which were incorporated in the Convention of Akkerman of 1826.

After the destruction of the Ottoman navy at Navarino, Russia could not resist taking advantage of Ottoman weakness. A peculiar kind of war was declared in 1828: Russia became a belligerent in the Balkans and the Black Sea but remained a neutral in the Mediterranean. One Russian army advanced in the Caucasus with considerable success, taking Ardahan and Erzurum; another took Varna on the Black Sea, crossed the Balkans, and entered Edirne.

TREATY OF ADRIANOPLE

Upon the advice of Prussian and British envoys Mahmud sought peace. The Treaty of Adrianople (Edirne) of 1829 reestablished the frontiers much as they had been before the war and compelled the Ottomans to pay a heavy indemnity to Russia. The Straits were open again to Russian trade. The two Danubian Principalities no longer had to supply grains, wood, and sheep to the sultan's government; only the annual tribute to Istanbul was continued. Governors held their posts for life and ruled in consultation with native assemblies. The ties with the Ottomans were reduced to a minimum, and Russia moved into the vacuum.

Other provisions of the treaty stipulated that the articles of the Convention of Akkerman should be put into immediate effect. Another article declared that the Ottomans adhered to a second Treaty of London, which England, France, and Russia had concluded earlier in 1829 and which established an independent Greek kingdom. In consequence of its inclusiveness the Treaty of Adrianople was an important landmark in Balkan development as well as in the relationship of the Ottoman Empire to the great European states. Greece became an independent state in 1832, but it was small, with most Greek speakers still living outside its borders.

DESTRUCTION OF THE JANISSARIES

An event of vaster proportions and ramifications, however, preceded the Treaty of Adrianople and was in part responsible for it. In 1826, Mahmud destroyed the janissaries. For many years Ottoman sultans found the janissary corps unruly, and since the beginning of the seventeenth century these soldiers frequently vetoed policies of state, and grand viziers were beheaded at their behest. Through the eighteenth century several of the sultans contrived to modernize the army and equip the janissaries with more efficient weapons, but each attempt was rebuffed. Since the sultan's authority in the provinces was continually snubbed by recalcitrant governors, a reliable standing army had to be created before he could reassert his power. Although Ali Pasha of Janina and Mehmet Ali of Egypt possessed competent standing armies, the sultan depended upon janissaries, irregular levies, and the remnants of the sipahis. The modernization of the army became even more urgent as Ottoman units met with Austrian and Russian regiments, to which they compared adversely.

Selim III had earlier lost his life in the attempt to modernize the army, so Mahmud II plotted more warily. The sultan had to maneuver into key positions officials who would support him and his policies. Ottoman artillery was carefully improved, and more than 14,000 artillerymen were gathered in Istanbul. When the blow was readied, Mahmud had the loyalty of the artillerymen, the grand vizier, the shaikh al-Islam, the chief of the janissaries, and a sizable force of Anatolian levies stationed across the Bosphorus.

In 1826, Mahmud forced the divan to order some janissaries to drill in European fashion. An uprising broke out, as was expected. The artillery mowed down the janissaries as they charged the palace and then shelled their barracks into a mass of ruins, burying 4000 beneath the rubble. Victory was followed up in the provinces, where many janissaries were either killed or completely scattered. New troops were assembled, and Mahmud planned to organize and train an army of 40,000. Although the Russian attacks in 1828 and 1829 were launched before the new troops were trained and weakened them permanently as the Russians had hoped, Mahmud rid his state of an anachronism that had retarded the process of military modernization in the empire. It was a first step in destroying the power of the governors in outlying provinces and in rebuilding the centralized control that had proved so effective in the fifteenth and sixteenth centuries. Military spending represented about 70 percent of the government's expenditures, but now other reforms could also occur.

MEHMET ALI AND MAHMUD II

But there was hardly any time for sound reform. Peace was no more than established when Mahmud faced rebellion and serious attack by Mehmet Ali, his governor of Egypt. The actions of this dynamic newcomer affected the Ottoman Empire profoundly, particularly in its relationship to the Great Powers.

For lending aid to the sultan, Mehmet Ali had been given Crete and the governorship of the Peloponnesus for his son Ibrahim. The latter promise could not take effect, however, because the Great Powers established the kingdom of Greece; and Crete by itself was inadequate, so Mehmet Ali diverted his attention to Syria, which he requested for Ibrahim in place of the Peloponnesus. When Mahmud refused, Mehmet Ali invaded Syria.

Ibrahim, meanwhile, waged a combined land and sea attack upon Acre, which finally fell in 1832 after a prolonged siege. Mahmud hardly lifted a finger to aid Acre; Ibrahim easily routed an Ottoman army collected in central Syria; and in rapid succession Damascus and Aleppo in Syria, and Adana and Konya in Anatolia were occupied by the Egyptian army. Up to this point the Great Powers were unconcerned; France even looked with favor upon the expansion of Mehmet Ali's territory. Ibrahim defeated the main Ottoman army near Konya and pushed on to Kutahya in western Anatolia, on the route toward Istanbul. At this point Mahmud grew frantic and begged the Great Powers to rescue him. Only Russia responded. Early in 1833 a Russian fleet anchored in the Bosphorus, and 14,000 Russian marines landed to protect Mahmud from Mehmet Ali and to guarantee the treaties the Russians had obtained from the Ottomans since 1774.

Meanwhile, Russian and Ottoman envoys in Cairo were discussing peace terms with Mehmet Ali, while French diplomats were pressing Mahmud to accept some of the Egyptian demands. Compromises were effected. Syria was assigned to Mehmet Ali on the condition that he pay the central government an annual tribute; he was also to retain Adana, which would give him easy access to the Taurus passes and Anatolia. Ibrahim's troops were recalled from Anatolia. The Russian fleet, however, postponed its departure from the Bosphorus. Two days before the Russians reembarked from the Bosphorus village of Hunkiar Iskelesi, where they had encamped, a treaty was signed that achieved for Russia a long-sought goal. The Treaty of Hunkiar Iskelesi of 1833 was a straightforward alliance between Russia and the Ottoman Empire, providing for friendship, peace, and mutual assistance. The provocation lay in a secret article, which did not remain unknown very long, stating that upon Russian request the sultan would close the Straits to the extent of "not allowing any foreign vessel of war to enter therein, under any pretext whatsoever." Although diplomats questioned the significance of the secret article, the value of Hunkiar Iskelesi to Russia rested on its right to interfere in Ottoman affairs "to the exclusion of the alliance and intervention of the Powers."

MAHMUD'S REFORMS

Mahmud II used the peace he had so dearly purchased to carry forward the reform of the government. Reform was pushed beyond purely military and technical changes to include government administration and a broad array of policies. Destruction of the janissaries and the formation of new troops, known as Muslim Soldiers, were only the most publicized aspects of his military innovations.

The 1831 attempted abolition of the sipahi system ruined the cavalry and levies upon which sultans had depended and which had proved valuable for Mahmud. Income from land grants to support sipahis now went directly to the treasury, and officers of the sultan enlisted recruits from these areas. The best sipahis were enrolled in four new squadrons of cavalry and the rest were pensioned, while in 1834 a national militia was organized to give rudimentary military training in the provinces. A group of Prussians participated in training Ottoman officers; other Ottomans studied in England.

Military and medical colleges were opened in 1830. Connected with these colleges and previously established engineering schools were primary and secondary schools where a mostly secular education was given to prepare students for advanced training. In 1824 Mahmud declared a primary education compulsory for all, but means for carrying out this decree never materialized. The best primary-secondary school was the one attached to the medical college at Galatasaray. With instruction given in Turkish and French, it became a leading source of elite education in the latter part of the nineteenth century. Medicine, mathematics, and physics now began to be understood as in western Europe; old concepts in these fields gradually faded away.

Since the ulama had opposed previous attempts at reform, Mahmud attempted to weaken them and the Sufis, and symbolically to change traditional culture. In 1826 he gave an office building to the shaikh al-Islam and appointed him as head of a regular department of government; courts for Muslim subjects came under its authority. However, the appointment of teachers and the control of schools passed to the new Ministry of Education and the selection of judges and the administration of law went to the Ministry of Justice. Even more damaging to the ulama, and to the chief officers of the state who also had their own pious endowments or awqaf, was the creation of a Ministry of Pious Foundations to which was given the income of most religious and charitable endowments. This ministry paid out what was needed to the various foundations, placing the remainder in the treasury. The financial independence of Sufi orders was attacked. Bektashi Sufi leaders were exiled and the order's buildings confiscated, supposedly because of the order's heretical views but actually as part of the suppression of the janissaries, with whom many Bektashis had been associated. However, Bektashis secretly continued to operate in parts of the empire, even in Istanbul, until the twentieth century. The fez was adopted as the new headgear for government officials. The frock coat was also adopted, and within a few years the fez, the frock coat, trousers, and black leather boots became the standard dress in urban centers. When the shaikh al-Islam objected, Mahmud removed him, giving public notice of his earnestness in these matters. On the other hand, Mahmud was not completely opposed to earlier culture: he was himself a master calligrapher.

Changes in the military were used to centralize power in Istanbul. Independent local lords in Anatolia were checked, Iraq was subdued in 1831, and other governors began to feel and respect the sultan's authority. In 1835 the Ottoman army occupied Tripoli in Libya, thereby ending the local autonomous rule of a prominent family; however, it would take the Ottomans twenty more years of campaigning to bring the whole of Libya under direct imperial control. To a certain extent the war with Egypt resulted from Mahmud's desire to project his power into every corner of the realm. As a further curb on local rulers, governors were forbidden to execute anyone without referring the case to Istanbul. This removal of the death sentence from a governor's whim gave people throughout the empire a deeper sense of security.

In addition to ministries already cited, two bureaus within the office of the grand vizir were formed into ministries: foreign affairs and civil affairs. This development took away the power of the grand vizir as an all-powerful deputy of the sultan and made him a prime minister, for a number of years holding this title instead of that of grand vizir. Even when the latter title was restored, the grand vizir remained merely chair of the Council of Ministers. One of the more important innovations came after the Greek revolution when Greek Phanariotes were no longer trusted to serve as translators and interpreters. Within a few years a translation bureau was attached to the Ministry of Foreign Affairs, and officials in this bureau became significant members of the government, many later in the century rising to be grand vizirs. Departments of government were staffed by better-trained civil servants, whose higher salaries tended to lessen bribery, and more attention was given to promotion on merit.

To a significant degree the changes that were instituted came as a result of closer contact with western Europe. The first steamship arrived in Istanbul in 1828, and within a few years regular schedules were established between Istanbul and western Mediterranean ports. The length of a trip from France was cut from a month to twelve days. Thus, the 1830s saw an influx of western visitors, merchants, and missionaries joining Istanbul and other Ottoman coastal cities such as Izmir to the west as nothing previously had done. As a result, European techniques were studied and employed in many ways.

The end of the wars with Russia and Egypt left the empire almost bankrupt. Foreign observers commented on the wealth and produce of the country, but inefficiency in the collection of taxes reduced the sultan to penury. Under new procedures the central government tried to assume direct responsibility and sent out its own agents, thereby reducing the number of hands through which the taxes passed, although tax farming also continued. Non-Muslims had to pay higher poll taxes. New roads improved trade, and Muslims were encouraged to enter business by the abolition of the Court of Confiscations in which the government had seized the property of an exiled or condemned individual. Creditors henceforth felt less personal danger in pressing the government and its high officials for the payment of debts. In general, these measures were effective by the end of Mahmud's reign in 1839, despite numerous outbreaks of epidemic diseases and some recurrent famines.

Mahmud also recognized the stimulus to reform that a general circulation of books and newspapers would generate. Presses were established in Istanbul and Izmir, publishing with those of Mehmet Ali in Egypt several thousand books in Turkish and Arabic between 1830 and 1840. The military and medical colleges introduced many young Ottomans to French and German literature. Newspapers in French were founded in Izmir in the 1820s; and in 1832 the first Turkish-language newspaper appeared in Istanbul with official support from Mahmud.

Mahmud II's reforms broke the conservative grip of the janissaries and ulama upon government. The increase in the power of the central government was a mixed blessing since some groups were adversely affected—nomads lost much of their freedom, villagers' taxes were increased, provincial notables were no longer as influential—while other segments of society, especially merchants and townspeople, benefited from the increase in law and order.

Military and administrative reform did not accomplish its chief goal of acquiring equality with the chief European powers or Egypt, as shown in the Treaty of Adrianople and an 1839 defeat of Mahmud's forces by Mehmet Ali. Also, the success of Greek nationalism was only a beginning: nationalist movements in other parts of the empire later grew and flourished, posing increased dangers to the state. Nevertheless, after Mahmud's changes a return to the old order was impossible, and a commitment to reform would prevail.

References

Works containing material pertinent to this chapter are cited in Chapters 21 and 22.

BARNES, JOHN ROBERT: *An Introduction to Religious Foundations in the Ottoman Empire.* Leiden: Brill, 1986. An excellent discussion of the origins of pious foundations, the Ottoman land system, and the actual administration of the foundations.

CLOGG, RICHARD: *A Short History of Modern Greece.* 2d ed. Cambridge, England: Cambridge University Press, 1986.

CUNNINGHAM, ALLAN: "The Sick Man and the British Physician." *Middle Eastern Studies* 17 (1981): 147–173. Europeans who visited or commented upon the Ottoman Empire are thoroughly discussed.

FRANGAKIS-SYRETT, ELENA: "Greek Mercantile Activities in the Eastern Mediterranean, 1700–1820." *Balkan Studies* 28 (1987): 73–86. Shows impact of European wars on growth of Greek-Ottoman commerce.

KEDDIE, NIKKI, ED.: *Sufis, Scholars and Saints: Muslim Religious Institutions Since 1500.* Berkeley: University of California Press, 1972. A fine collection of articles dealing with the learned and popular aspects of Islam in various parts of the Muslim world.

LEWIS, BERNARD: *The Emergence of Modern Turkey.* London: Oxford University Press, 1961. A first-rate account of the development of the Ottoman Empire in the nineteenth century.

RALSTON, DAVID R.: *Importing the European Army: The Introduction of European Military Techniques and Institutions into the Extra-European World, 1600–1914.* Chicago: University of

Chicago Press, 1990. Comparative studies of military modernization in Europe, Russia, the Ottoman Empire, Egypt, China, and Japan.

SHAW, STANFORD J., AND EZEL KURAL SHAW: *History of the Ottoman Empire and Modern Turkey.* Vol. 2. *Reform, Revolution, and Republic: The Rise of Modern Turkey, 1808–1975.* Cambridge, England: Cambridge University Press, 1977. This substantial volume touches upon every aspect of change in the Ottoman Empire and Turkey. It is especially strong in explaining governmental structure.

Mehmet Ali, Ismail, and the Development of Egypt

Nineteenth-century Egypt was largely the creation of Mehmet Ali. Mamluk leaders of Ottoman Egypt in the 1770s and 1780s had increased contacts with Europe, and some social and economic changes commenced before 1805, but it was Mehmet Ali and his descendants, acting as Ottoman governors of Egypt, who created the basic administrative, military, and economic structures that marked a new period in Egyptian history. Egyptian military reform and expansion threatened the central Ottoman government and were ultimately curbed by the European Great Powers, but domestic reorganization and development continued until bankruptcy opened the way for a British occupation in 1882.

RISE OF MEHMET ALI

Mehmet Ali arrived in Egypt in 1801 as second in command of part of an Ottoman army sent by Sultan Selim III against Napoleon. Mehmet Ali was a Sunnite Muslim Ottoman, probably of Albanian descent and then about thirty-two years old. (His name as spelled here follows the Turkish form, by which he referred to himself; in Egypt and the Arab world he is called Muhammad Ali.)

His political talent was manifested in Egypt, where he was soon responsible for several thousand Albanian and Bosnian troops. At that time three major powers existed in Egypt: the Ottoman governor, who ruled in the name of the sultan; the Mamluks, who held landed estates and were split in jealous factions; and the Albanians. The people of Cairo constituted a weak fourth.

Mehmet Ali played his cards extremely well. When the British left Egypt in 1803, he sided with the Mamluks and drove the Ottoman governor from Cairo. Mehmet Ali then turned one Mamluk faction against another. Finally, with the aid of the Cairo populace, he chased the Mamluks into the desert and deposed the new governor, becoming himself recognized as governor by the citizens of Cairo. In 1805 Mehmet Ali asserted his submission to Sultan Selim, who appointed him governor of Egypt.

Dynasty of Mehmet Ali

Affairs in Europe in 1807 pushed the Ottomans and Mehmet Ali along with them into the French camp. In league with Mamluk remnants, the British occupied Alexandria but were defeated and withdrew. After the Treaty of Tilsit, which allied England and the Ottoman Empire, Britain renounced all designs upon Egypt. Mehmet Ali was now the actual as well as the titular holder of power in Egypt.

Finances cramped him severely. On several occasions even Mehmet Ali's own Albanians, their pay considerably in arrears, shot at him as he passed in the streets of Cairo. The economic catastrophes of the 1790s and repeated wars in connection with the French occupation of Egypt in 1798 had disrupted agriculture and trade, thereby lessening taxes collected. Under the Mamluks taxes had supported an Egyptian army, but Mehmet Ali found revenues to be quite insufficient. Consequently, he ordered a detailed cadastral survey of all landholdings and confiscated properties with irregular titles. Later he seized many land grants, modified the system of land tenure, collected taxes more harshly, and expropriated tax farms. Taxes on land usually produced over half of his revenues. Even awqaf belonging to religious institutions were appropriated. Despite all these measures, real revenues increased only gradually during the next twenty-five years, after accounting for inflation.

As land taxes increased, Mehmet Ali turned his attention to commerce and established a government monopoly on the export of grain. In several of these years the Nile valley possessed the only exportable surplus available to the British. Demand was brisk, and profits in the grain trade often reached 500 percent.

Mehmet Ali's power and the loyalty of his troops rose in direct proportion to his improved finances. One long-standing score remained to be settled, not only for himself but for the authority of his sovereign, the Ottoman sultan. The Mamluks, particularly those in Upper Egypt, had never been fully subjected. For several years Mehmet Ali threatened, cajoled, and attacked them. His entreaties induced many to settle near Cairo, and in 1811 they were tricked into entering the citadel of Cairo, where the Albanian soldiers slaughtered them. A year later another thousand were executed in Upper Egypt. The destruction of most of the Mamluks confirmed Mehmet Ali as the chief authority of the land.

ARABIA, THE SUDAN, AND GREECE

Organization of the finances of Egypt and destruction of the Mamluk power enabled Mehmet Ali to consider widening his rule to nearby areas. Since the Ottoman central government was challenged by the Saudi-Wahhabi uprising in Arabia (discussed in Chapter 22), Mehmet Ali willingly responded to an order from Istanbul to send his new armies there. The sultan was eager to suppress the Saudis so as to restore Ottoman control of the Meccan pilgrimages and to reestablish Ottoman prestige as protector of the holy cities of Mecca and Medina, while Egypt sought to restore its Red Sea trade.

In 1811 Mehmet Ali's son Tusun headed an expedition to subdue the Hijaz. Not until 1818, however, under the able leadership of Mehmet Ali's son Ibrahim, did the superior equipment and discipline of the troops from Egypt turn the scales against the Saudi-Wahhabi forces. The Saudi capital was taken and razed, and the Saudi ruler was conveyed to Istanbul, where he was executed. Ibrahim became governor of the Hijaz and Ethiopia, the latter consisting then of a few Red Sea ports that served as outlets for the Sudan.

Mehmet Ali looked upon the Sudan as a boundless area full of gold and slaves. He also believed that he could develop an army of black slaves from the Sudan, thereby securing independence from his unruly Albanians. An expedition went southward in 1820. The Sudan was politically divided and had become the refuge for some Mamluks who had fled Egypt. The sedentary tribes along the Nile capitulated after little resistance, and the Funj sultanate was conquered, but gold proved to be relatively scarce. Khartoum became the capital of Egyptian administration.

The experiment with an army of Sudanese slaves proved a failure. Disease and fatalities among the Sudanese constrained Mehmet Ali to build an army around Egyptian soldiers and Turkish, Circassian, and European officers. Over 30,000 Egyptian peasants were in a short time drilled into effective soldiers, and eventually a military of over 150,000 was conscripted (at great cost to the lives of the soldiers' families). Meanwhile, Mehmet Ali assembled a fleet. One ship mounting sixteen guns was built at Suez; others were bought in India, Europe, and the Greek islands.

While these developments were in progress, the Greek rebellion upset the eastern Mediterranean area (as discussed in Chapter 23). Sultan Mahmud II offered the governorship of Crete and part of Greece to Mehmet Ali and his son Ibrahim, whose army of 16,000 men and a navy of sixty-three ships left Alexandria in 1824. Various islands were attacked and plundered, Mehmet Ali replacing his losses with new ships from France and Italy; he even bought some from Greek shipbuilders! Ibrahim landed in Greece in 1825, but that adventure was extremely costly for Mehmet Ali: his fleet was ruined, and his trained and disciplined army returned to Egypt crippled.

CONQUEST OF SYRIA

But Mehmet Ali was not a ruler to be discouraged easily. From his ready income provided by the changed tax base he rapidly reconstituted an army. And by 1829

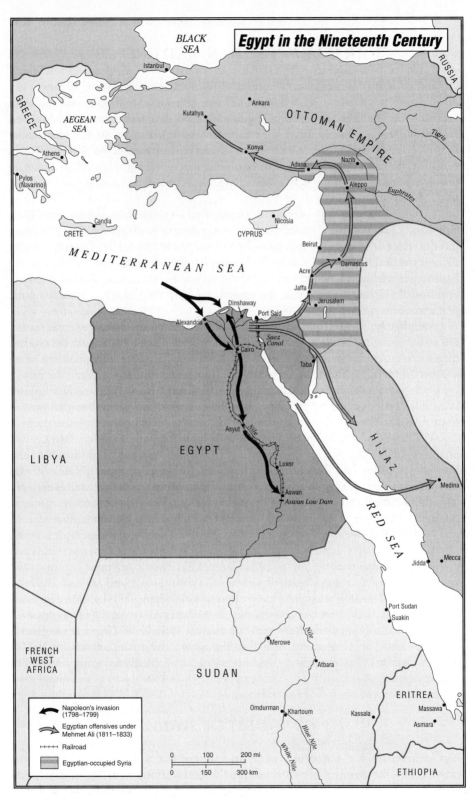

BLACK
SEA

Egypt in the Nineteenth Century

RUSSIA

Istanbul

GREECE

AEGEAN
SEA

Ankara

Kutahya

OTTOMAN EMPIRE

Tigris

Athens

Konya

Adana

Nazib

Pylos
(Navarino)

Aleppo

Euphrates

Candia

CRETE

Nicosia

CYPRUS

Beirut

Damascus

MEDITERRANEAN SEA

Acre

Jaffa

Jerusalem

Dinshaway

Port Said

Alexandria

Cairo

Suez
Canal

Taba

LIBYA

Asyut

Nile

EGYPT

HIJAZ

Luxor

Medina

Aswan
Aswan Low Dam

RED SEA

Jidda

Mecca

FRENCH
WEST
AFRICA

SUDAN

Merowe

Nile

Atbara

Port Sudan
Suakin

ERITREA

Massawa

Omdurman

Khartoum

Blue Nile

Kassala

Asmara

White Nile

ETHIOPIA

Napoleon's invasion
(1798–1799)

Egyptian offensives under
Mehmet Ali (1811–1833)

Railroad

Egyptian-occupied Syria

0	100	200 mi
0	150	300 km

the new self-sufficient naval arsenal at Alexandria had begun to turn out frigates, corvettes, and other men-of-war.

Syria was economically inviting, especially since its districts were pledged to Mehmet Ali as payment for his undertaking in Greece. Mehmet Ali sent Ibrahim against Acre, which fell in 1832. He then turned upon the Ottoman forces, reaching northward to the outskirts of Konya in Anatolia. Ibrahim's devastating victory at Konya carried him on to Kutahya, where peace between Mahmud and his rebellious viceroy was concluded in 1833. Egypt, Syria, Adana, Tarsus, and Crete were assigned to Mehmet Ali, for which he agreed to pay a tribute to Istanbul.

Ibrahim governed Syria for eight years. Taxes were regularized, justice was more secure for the religious minorities, commerce was encouraged, privileges for foreigners were less abused, education was stimulated, and law and order were more prevalent. The harsh rule that Mehmet Ali created in Egypt was also attempted in Syria. Had it been given a longer period of trial, it might have succeeded. Conscription, however, was resisted; the new taxes were hated; and rebellion faced Ibrahim on several occasions. Mahmud was rebuilding a modern army to threaten Mehmet Ali. Since the governorships of Egypt, Syria, and Crete were granted for only one year at a time, and since there were constant disputes over tribute, Mehmet Ali considered maintenance of an ever-ready army a prime requisite for his own safety. When, therefore, European governments urged abandonment of conscription in Syria, reduction of his armaments by half, and withdrawal of his troops from Syria, Mehmet Ali agreed only on the condition that Mahmud grant him hereditary title to his territories and that the Great Powers guarantee him against aggression.

Ottoman forces invaded Syria but were destroyed at Nazib by Ibrahim in June 1839. Five days later Mahmud II died, and before July was out the Ottoman fleet deserted to join the Egyptians at Alexandria. Mehmet Ali was now master of the situation, and the Ottomans prepared to surrender to his demands of hereditary control for all territories then in his possession.

DEFEAT OF MEHMET ALI

A joint note from the European Great Powers—Austria, Great Britain, France, Prussia, and Russia—recommended to the Ottomans that no action be taken on Mehmet Ali's claims without their approval. The British feared that Russia would call into operation provisions of the Treaty of Hunkiar Iskelesi or that France through Mehmet Ali would dominate Syria and Egypt and control all routes from the Mediterranean to India. The British, therefore, preferred a united action to Russian or French unilateral steps, and they prevailed upon Russia, Prussia, and Austria to sign the Treaty of London in 1840. This treaty was a diplomatic defeat for France, which nevertheless eventually agreed to its terms. The 1840 treaty allowed Mehmet Ali the hereditary governorship of Egypt if he agreed to the settlement. Otherwise, the four powers would blockade Egypt and support the central Ottoman authorities.

Since Mehmet Ali refused to budge, the only recourse was force. British agents in Lebanon and Syria helped raise a rebellion against Ibrahim, while a combined

British-Austrian fleet landed troops at Beirut and captured Acre. Mehmet Ali was forced to recall Ibrahim from Syria and accept British terms. He also withdrew from central and western Arabia, allowing the Wahhabis and Saudis to return to power in the central regions, and the Ottomans to regain Mecca. Egypt was left as a hereditary province to Mehmet Ali and his heirs, but the size of his army was limited to no more than 18,000 men.

ORGANIZATION OF EGYPT

The defeats of 1840 and the diplomatic negotiations of 1841 gave Mehmet Ali full political power in Egypt but left him an old and broken man. He lapsed into senility in 1847 and died one year later. For forty years Mehmet Ali had ruled Egypt, and every phase of life and society had interested him at one time or another. He had created a new government and developed a cabinet with ministers of war, navy, finance, commerce and foreign affairs, education, and security. Real power, however, had never slipped from the hands of the Pasha, as Mehmet Ali was known. Most of the top officials were related to him or were personally associated with his household. In the 1830s, when councils of notables were appointed to discuss governmental affairs, western travelers were greatly impressed. But the Pasha never intended that his rule be other than that of a benevolent despot.

In economic matters Mehmet Ali attempted to make many changes. Exports were partially oriented away from the rest of the Ottoman Empire and toward Europe. The trade monopoly for grain was extended to include cotton and tobacco, although the British terminated the monopoly system after the 1838 commercial treaty for the Ottoman Empire was eventually forced upon Egypt. He also extended the corvée, or forced labor of the peasants, which by 1840, along with various acquisitions of land, brought the state—that is, Mehmet Ali and his extended family—control of as much as half of the cultivable land in Egypt. This meant that many of the peasants were deprived of their land and some peasant rebellions took place; the government attempted to rigorously and directly monitor peasant life. The ruling family controlled the domestic market through state enterprises, and for more than a decade there was a monopoly over imports as well as exports. By the treaties of 1840 and 1841, however, Mehmet Ali was forced to abide by the sultan's laws, especially the capitulations and commercial privileges held by the Great Powers. Since taxes were paid in kind, the Pasha's government continued to be the principal participant in the export trade.

To promote agriculture, corn and rice were introduced. In many areas steam pumps and better canals allowed summer irrigation, enabling the peasants in the villages to double the yield by growing two crops a year. Great attention was given to the science of irrigation. Swamplands were drained, old canals opened, and new ones built. North of Cairo a great barrage on the Nile was constructed to raise canal levels, especially in years of scanty floods. However, since the engineering work was not sound, it proved ineffective until rebuilt in the 1880s.

The age of Mehmet Ali in Egypt coincided with rapid industrial growth in western Europe, and the Pasha became convinced of the value of industrialization. He built textile plants and sugar refineries. But technical knowledge, capital, suitable labor, power-driven machines, and supplies of coal and iron were lacking, while European pressure also restricted Egyptian opportunities. Even before Mehmet Ali died, the failure to industrialize Egypt was apparent.

Mehmet Ali's endeavors included sanitation and education. Great plagues raged every year, and annual deaths from smallpox, cholera, and bubonic plague sometimes rose to 10 percent or more of the population. Midwives were trained, a more effective quarantine was organized, and the foreign consuls in Alexandria were appointed to a board of sanitation, which was given ample funds and absolute authority. After 1840 health conditions in general improved somewhat, except for cholera outbreaks. A notable increase in the population was largely attributed to advances in public security, agriculture, and health.

The first new government schools were for the military—infantry, cavalry, engineers, navy, and artillery. Most of the instructors in these schools were French, and boys were sent to study in France, Italy, and England. In 1833, however, the Polytechnic School was founded with a staff composed almost entirely of Egyptian teachers. Soon preparatory schools for the Polytechnic were organized in Cairo and Alexandria, although the vast majority of school-age children either attended traditional elementary religious schools or had no formal education at all. In connection with the government schools an official press was set up near Cairo; most of its publications were translations of European technical works. Newspapers printed in both Arabic and French not only gave urban society access to western ideas but also made Egypt a leader in the new intellectual life of the Arab world.

A neoclassical cultural revival along indigenous intellectual lines also took place in the early years of Mehmet Ali's reign. The notable historian and religious scholar Abd al-Rahman al-Jabarti, who was antagonistic toward the ruler, compiled a massive and sophisticated history of the era. Turkish remained the language of the ruling elite and most government records throughout the Mehmet Ali era.

Mehmet Ali was impatient and tried to change society rapidly without a sufficient number of sympathetic officials. Many of his innovations were too hurried and too shallow to endure, and by the middle 1840s even he ended or slowed down many of them. Still, construction of canals brought Nile trade and traffic from Cairo to Alexandria and helped turn the latter into a cosmopolitan boomtown whose population increased from 15,000 in 1805 to 100,000 by 1850. During his reign, Mehmet Ali had ruthlessly established local autonomy for Egypt and even sown the seeds for the establishment of a separate state. Incredibly, this was done without incurring any substantial foreign debts.

ABBAS AND SAID PASHAS

Much of Mehmet Ali's work was undone by his successor, his grandson Abbas Pasha (r. 1848–1854). A conservative pro-Ottoman, Abbas Pasha disliked Europeans and resented their presence in Egypt, but he also realized that his interests paralleled those of the British. He shunned Frenchmen and permitted many of his grandfather's innovations to lapse. Uneconomic factories were abandoned, and schools were closed. Western influences and culture were weakened under Abbas, who banished some educators to Khartoum. Aggressive policies were curtailed, and Albanian mercenaries were brought into the army. Although a British firm constructed the first railway between Alexandria and Cairo, Abbas opposed French proposals to build a Suez Canal to join the Mediterranean and Red Seas. Egypt's economy was linked more closely to Europe, despite the policies of Abbas.

Upon Abbas Pasha's murder in 1854, authority passed to his uncle Said (1854–1863), Mehmet Ali's favorite son, who had headed the Egyptian navy for many years and who was pro-French. Said initially cut the size of the army from about 80,000 or more under Abbas to about 70,000, and even further by 1860 to about 25,000. Abbas and Said sent an army of 20,000 to help the central Ottoman government during the Crimean War, and Said borrowed large sums of money from European bankers, beginning thereby an ultimately disastrous process. Some reforms were initiated, including the opening stages of the Suez Canal, but the reigns of both Abbas and Said saw relatively few changes compared with the age of Mehmet Ali before them or Ismail after them. For most common Egyptians the period from 1849 to 1863 was uneventful and a welcome relief from the wars, exactions, and rapid Europeanization under Mehmet Ali.

In Said's youth he had formed a friendship with Ferdinand de Lesseps, son of the French political agent in Egypt, and shortly after his accession Said granted his friend a concession to construct a canal at Suez. The 1855 news touched off a long diplomatic struggle. The British government opposed the scheme, believing it would deliver control over the easiest means of trade and communications with their empire in India into the hands of the French and Egyptians, and that it would inevitably create an Egyptian question for European diplomacy. Because they were involved at the moment in the Crimean War, the Ottomans, still the ultimate source of sovereignty in Egypt, could not afford to antagonize England and thus did not ratify the project.

In 1856 an international commission of engineers surveyed the land and reported on the proposal, setting an estimate of £6 million as a maximum cost. Some stock in the Suez Canal Company went to Said for granting the concession and for furnishing the labor required to dig the canal. Other shares were held by the organizers or were given without cost to influential persons.

Until 1858 Napoleon III, emperor of the French, seemed unconcerned with the Suez Canal project, but it is believed that de Lesseps gave a substantial number of shares to members of Napoleon's court, if not to the emperor and empress themselves. Although Said warned that construction of the canal should not begin until approved in Istanbul, digging started in 1859. The British protested over the use of forced labor and were able to keep the sultan from ratifying the concession. Little work had been accomplished when Said died in 1863 and Ismail, Ibrahim's oldest living son, became Ottoman governor of Egypt.

THE SUEZ CANAL AND ISMAIL

At his accession Ismail accepted the commitments concerning the canal, and by 1866 the British no longer opposed it. Under pressure from Napoleon III the Ottomans gave their authorization. Ismail paid an indemnity for not supplying forced labor, and the construction proceeded rapidly. When the canal was finished in

1869, Ismail spent £1 million on the lavish opening ceremonies. Empress Eugénie was the guest of honor among 6000 guests. Verdi's famous opera *Aïda,* composed for this event, was later performed in Cairo at the opera house built for the occasion; the opera emphasized the glory of the ancient Egypt of the pharaohs.

For the first several years the Suez Canal operated at a loss, and the company was perilously close to bankruptcy. However, traffic increased, the canal showing profits continuously after 1875. The cost of the canal to Said and Ismail was estimated at £11.5 million, for which Egypt received little return. Egypt also spent large sums of money on other infrastructure projects. Ismail ordered the digging of thousands of miles of irrigation canals, the doubling of the railroad network, and the building of an extensive telegraph system. A government-run postal service used steamboats on the Nile.

ISMAIL'S RULE

Ismail was thirty-three years old when he gained power in 1863. He had been educated in Paris at the École d'État-Major and had gone for Said on missions to Istanbul, France, and the Vatican. From the moment of Ismail's accession until his deposition in 1879, life at the court in Egypt was sumptuous: money flowed like the waters of the Nile. Ismail showered lavish gifts upon all, and his trips to Europe and Istanbul were extravagant in every detail. Presents to the sultan on the order of £1 million and a diamond-encrusted solid-gold dinner service were not unusual. Ismail possessed a charismatic personality that dispelled opposition.

Shortly after Ismail's accession, Sultan Abdulaziz visited him in Egypt, being the first Ottoman sultan to come to Cairo since its capture in 1517. (It should be pointed out that these two rulers, who resembled each other in many ways, were cousins, their mothers being sisters.) In 1866–1867 Ismail visited Istanbul, where through gifts he won the title khedive (prince) and recognition of the succession to control of Egypt by the law of primogeniture, rather than the previous system whereby the eldest male descendant of Mehmet Ali had succeeded to the governorship. At the same time, for the doubling of his tribute he was allowed to strengthen his army, coin money, and bestow decorations and titles on his own. In 1869 he was received, entertained, and decorated by the crowned heads of Europe. However, Ismail was rapidly falling into the clutches of unscrupulous moneylenders and European bankers.

Before detailing Ismail's bankruptcy his reign should be examined to provide a balance against his financial profligacy by acknowledging his imagination and leadership. Egypt in 1879, the end of Ismail's rule, was a far cry indeed from the Egypt of 1863. Perhaps the most apparent change during Ismail's reign was the Europeanization in sections of some Egyptian cities. He forcibly changed parts of the cities by constructing some European-style residential quarters, squares, and parks along with water service, gas supplies, and street lighting. The social and cultural gap between the cities and the countryside widened greatly, as by 1880 as many as 100,000 Europeans were living in Egypt, mostly in Cairo and Alexandria. By 1882 the total population of Alexandria grew to more than 230,000, and urban populations in general were growing even more rapidly than the increases in the whole country. The bulk of the population, however, continued to live in villages and engage in agriculture.

Meanwhile, the leading citizens of Egypt sent most of their sons to Europe to be educated. Ismail's fondness for saying that Egypt was a part of Europe was not without foundation. In fact, it was the Europeanized elite, participating in government, education, and general culture, who maintained his programs and sustained most of his works.

In military and government matters, Ismail drastically increased the size of the military, which reached 35,000 in 1865 and ultimately more than 120,000. Egypt sent a contingent to participate in the Russian-Ottoman War of 1877–1878. New officers were recruited: while the upper ranks were reserved for Turks and Circassians, some Egyptians also became officers. While many in the ruling elite still spoke Turkish, most government records were now written in the Arabic language. In 1866 the khedive inaugurated the Assembly of Delegates, a quasi-parliamentary body, most of whose members came from the category of wealthy and influential village headmen. The assembly served Ismail as a kind of constitutional shield to offset the Turkish elite that was evolving from the privileged army officer and government official classes. Until 1875 the assembly meetings were superficial and under Ismail's thumb, but then the financial crisis emboldened the members to criticize foreign powers and to demand responsibility over government ministers. In a session in 1876 it suggested that the assembly supervise government expenditures, and in 1879 he dissolved the assembly.

The economy under Ismail was dominated by cotton, a labor-intensive crop. Long-staple cotton had been introduced in 1821 from the Ethiopian-Sudanese border, and Mehmet Ali had eagerly spread its cultivation. By 1850, a total of 35 million pounds (about 16 million kg.) was being grown annually, as Egypt became integrated into the world market dominated by Europe. During the American Civil War production soared to 250 million pounds (113 million kg.) per year, and the price increased by 400 percent to a total of over £25 million because Britain could no longer obtain cotton from the American south.

The rich especially profited from this bonanza, but with the end of the war prices tumbled and peasants were thrown into a miserable condition of mortgage foreclosures and indebtedness. By the 1870s about one-third of the peasants were landless laborers. Village headmen, foreigners, and prominent officials improved their own position by lending to their bankrupt neighbors. The dominance of the headmen in the assembly, formed at a time of peasant hardship and depression, was not a coincidence. Since cotton was a cash crop, it tended to destroy the old communal economy of the village; and in steps under Said and Ismail, family proprietorship with an individualistic economy began to prevail. The state monopoly over agricultural products was terminated, and in 1871 Ismail gave full right of ownership to villagers. Still, with heavy taxes a peasant flight from the land persisted. Big estates flourished and were subject to taxation only after 1854, though at a low rate. Village headmen remained important in the political, economic, and social life of the country, and their sons, subject to conscription under Said, began to improve the quality of the rank and file in the army and even to change its character as some higher ranks were opened to them. Large estates, swollen by abandoned lands, were owned by the khedivial family and the Turkish-speaking elite. Yet there was also a certain fluidity in ownership caused by personal mismanagement and indebtedness and the fractioning of landholdings under Muslim laws of inheritance. Ismail's economic policies and actions, including the building of roads, railroads, and canals, and the bringing of over a million acres (400,000 hectares) of new land under cultivation, were efforts to increase his own income; nevertheless, they did benefit the whole nation, as the population growth during his sixteen years of rule testified.

In the sphere of international affairs, Ismail had certain autonomous rights granted by the sultan but also many burdensome obligations. In addition to the ability to contract loans, Ismail could negotiate with foreign governments but only through consuls, never ambassadors. As a part of the Ottoman Empire, Egypt was subject to capitulatory treaties with fourteen countries, whose abuse ensured that law cases were settled by diplomatic pressure rather than on the basis of merit. The variety and number of foreign nationals residing in Egypt made cases of one foreigner against another difficult to adjudicate. Ismail's foreign minister, the Armenian Nubar Pasha, proposed a mixed court staffed by Egyptians and foreign judges, which would administer codes based on French law. It would deal with civil and criminal cases. Eventually a conference in Istanbul in 1873 authorized the Mixed Courts. The courts began in 1875 with a majority of foreign judges, and the French language used in all proceedings. Judges, Egyptian and foreign, were appointed by the khedive, although foreigners were nominated by participating governments. Establishment of the Mixed Courts, however, weakened the government and frequently frustrated its operation. They did not end the capitulations but modified them in an important way. Personal law for Muslim Egyptians remained the Islamic shariah.

Ismail's boldest foreign venture was the extension of Egyptian rule into the Sudan. Mehmet Ali had conquered parts of the region, and in 1842 the sultan had recognized him as governor-general of the Sudan. During the middle of the century under Abbas and Said, interest lapsed. Ismail set up a new southern province with Fashoda on the White Nile as its capital. Ismail was Europeanized to the extent of considering Egypt as a participant in the exploration and partitioning of Africa, and he devised ambitious schemes of expanding Egypt to the equator and including all of the basin of the White Nile. In 1869, he declared that steps were being taken to end the slave trade in the Sudan and set up a government in the equatorial region. Expeditions to the equatorial lakes district resulted in the attachment of Bahr al-Ghazal to the Sudan. Ismail sent the Briton General Charles George Gordon toward Ethiopia in 1875 and 1876. Gordon was so successful in curtailing the slave trade as to disturb the local economy and dislocate the principal occupation of local leaders. Gordon departed in 1877, and by 1879 the Sudan was left in a state of near anarchy. Taxes throughout the period of Egyptian rule were high, and the depopulation of many areas and the disruption of much of the economy ensued. Without financial resources from Cairo, Egyptian governors were no match for the uprising led by Muhammad Ahmad of Dongola, who declared himself Mahdi, the expected savior, in 1881.

Ismail admired the social and cultural life he saw in his European travels, and he tried to create a similar society in Egypt. Hardly any facet escaped his attention. Societies were organized for archaeology, music, and poetry, for the construction of libraries (the Khedivial Library in 1870) and museums (the Egyptian Museum in 1863) for the advancement of Egyptology, and in 1875 the Khedivial Geographical Society for African exploration. In 1868 Ismail opened a comedy theater in Cairo and brought in European companies to perform plays. The next year the Cairo Opera House was opened with a performance of Verdi's *Rigoletto* followed by the premiere of *Aïda*. Newspapers were encouraged, and the famous daily *Al-Ahram* (meaning "the pyramids") was born in 1876, while postage stamps had been used for the first time in 1866.

As neighborhoods, guilds, and religious groups began to be affected by change, the role of men in society remained predominant. However, many midwives were professionally trained, and some women participated in the new education or worked in factories. Women were active in the court system, and they took part in the general economy—buying, selling, inheriting, lending and borrowing, and pursuing debtors. As conscription and forced labor for the state increased in the country, family life was often disrupted. A frequent, though unintended, consequence of the reforms was to decrease the freedom of social action of many women.

Above all else, Ismail believed firmly that education would westernize his state. A Ministry of Education was established and headed at times by Ali Pasha Mubarak, a scholar and administrator. In 1873 the first school for girls was established. Specialized schools were started for military officers, lawyers, engineers, and administrators; Teachers College was founded in 1872; and the renowned School of Languages was reopened under the direction of Rifaa al-Tahtawi, a scholar and author who was to inspire many of the leaders of Egyptian public life for the following half century. During Ismail's reign literacy had climbed to perhaps 5 percent, and many more children were now taking part in formal education, whether in religious, government, or foreign schools.

BANKRUPTCY AND EUROPEAN INTERVENTION

At Ismail's accession Egypt had a combined foreign and domestic debt of £7 million. Thirteen years later it had a foreign debt of £68 million and a domestic debt of £30 million, which made Egypt on a per person basis one of the most indebted countries in the world at that time. Of the debt, nearly 35 percent was incurred in the form of discounts and commissions, none of which could be used for investment in Egypt. Interest charges mounted to £5 million per year, more than half the total annual revenue of the government. Ismail flogged the peasants to increase taxes and sought new sources of income. In 1874 he sold his shares of stock in the Suez Canal to the British government for nearly £4 million. But this only delayed the day of reckoning, which came in 1876 when Ismail ceased payment on his debts and Egypt became officially bankrupt.

There is no question that Ismail was exceedingly extravagant, although most of the proceeds from the loans was spent on useful and productive projects. The capitulations practically condemned Egypt to the role of an agriculturally based economy, which in the period following the Crimean War and the American Civil War reduced it to a level of relative inferiority compared with industrialized nations.

Hard times following the European financial panic of 1873 hurt Ismail; further loans were impossible to obtain, and state revenues were inadequate to cover interest payments.

To extricate himself, Ismail conducted a losing battle against European bondholders and their governments. In 1876 the debt was unified, and Ismail agreed to set up a public debt authority with members representing the British, French, Italian, and Austrian creditors. These directors (the British member was Evelyn Baring of the Baring banking family, who later became Lord Cromer) supervised revenues and expenditures in Egypt, channeling 60 percent of the revenues to pay off the debt and enabling the servicing of the debt to be met fully in 1877.

But Ismail had also been forced in 1876 to appoint dual controllers: Baring for the British and M. de Blignières for the French. The controllers could attend cabinet meetings, demand information, give advice, and report to their diplomatic representatives in the event advice was ignored. They became the real rulers of Egypt. A law was enacted squeezing the debt down to £85 million and reserving £4.5 million of the annual government income for the budget. All excess income, then estimated at £4 million, was to be employed to retire the debt. Unfortunately for the future development of Egypt, expanding revenues resulting from increased productivity and hard work would not benefit Egyptians or improve services of the government. Since the controllers were duty-bound to guard the revenue and pay off the debt, they could hardly fail to be unpopular with the Egyptians, to whom their regime appeared unduly restrictive.

An international commission demanded that Ismail accept a civil list for himself and the idea of ministerial responsibility. Moreover, a new cabinet was installed with Nubar Pasha as prime minister, Mr. Rivers Wilson as finance minister, and M. de Blignières as minister of public works, and with many Europeans serving in various offices at generous salaries. Times were hard; government expenditures were greatly curtailed; and the Nile flood of 1877–1878 was exceedingly low, drastically reducing crop yields. The crisis encouraged activity by many social groups, including the Assembly of Delegates, military officers, ulama, the press, artisan guilds, peasants, and nationalist clubs; all these played a role in the opposition to European control of Egypt.

In 1879 Ismail secretly instigated an attack on Nubar Pasha and Rivers Wilson by a group of army officers whose pay had just been cut. Ismail then dismissed Nubar Pasha and the cabinet, eventually appointing in its place an all-Egyptian cabinet. He summoned the consuls general to confront them with the discontent of the Assembly of Delegates, the disaffection of the army, and the disquiet of the public. A draft constitution was submitted to the assembly, giving it, among other things, full control of finances. There was great jubilation when the assembly accepted the constitution. The British and the French, however, were determined that Ismail be deposed. The European powers persuaded the sultan in Istanbul to send a telegram on June 26, 1879, addressed to the "former" Khedive Ismail informing him that rule had passed to his son Tawfiq (r. 1879–1892). Ismail left for Italy, where he died in 1895.

Soon after Ismail's deposition authority passed to the revived dual controllers, who naturally cut expenditures to the bone. The size of the army was reduced to

12,000; many officers were retired; civil budgets and personnel were pared. Yet a sizable number of foreign administrators came in at inordinate salaries. Opposition quickly formed in Egypt. The evolution of society under Ismail had brought four parties to the fore: a weak reactionary group; a vigorous Islamic modernist faction developed by Muhammad Abduh; a constitutional party of wealthy Europeanized Egyptian landowners organized by Sharif Pasha from membership in the assembly and from other groups; and an army group composed of Egyptians in the lower officer echelons and inspired by Colonel Ahmad Urabi. Only the first party acquiesced in the foreign dual control, preferring it to any of the Egyptian groups. The army was the most violent in its opposition because high-ranking officers were Turks or Circassians and the dual control did not remove these officers to the extent that it curbed the rise of native Egyptians.

When in January 1882 England and France presented a joint note to the khedive Tawfiq protesting the formation of a constitutional government, the army partly gained control of the cabinet. The army's leaders sought reforms within the context of Egypt's continued local autonomy inside the Ottoman Empire. England and France had to occupy the country or give up the dual control, and riots in Alexandria served as the pretext. A change in the French government, however, altered French policy; and England alone intervened. The British occupied Egypt in July 1882 to overthrow Colonel Urabi and reestablish European control through their influence on Tawfiq. Alexandria was shelled; the British navy occupied the Canal cities; and in September, British troops defeated the Egyptian army and took Cairo. At this point resistance to European control in Egypt collapsed.

European power and influence were increasing throughout the Middle East in the nineteenth century, even while Egypt, the central Ottoman Empire, and Qajar Iran engaged in military and economic modernization. As Egypt became incorporated into the European-dominated world economy, the Suez Canal made this Ottoman province led by the family of Mehmet Ali more and more important, both strategically and commercially. Britain would remain in control of Egypt for more than seventy years after 1882.

References

Readings for this chapter are also found in Chapters 20, 21, 22, and 23.

ABU-LUGHOD, IBRAHIM: *Arab Rediscovery of Europe: A Study in Cultural Encounters.* Princeton, N.J.: Princeton University Press, 1963. A study of Arab travelers and students in Europe in the century after Napoleon.

BLUNT, WILFRID S.: *Secret History of the English Occupation of Egypt.* London: Unwin, 1907. Written by a longtime resident of Egypt who was a friend of many of the leading Egyptian nationalists.

CANNON, BYRON: *Politics of Law and the Courts in Nineteenth-Century Egypt.* Salt Lake City: University of Utah Press, 1988. Especially useful for new views on the Mixed Courts.

COLE, JUAN R. I.: *Colonialism and Revolution in the Middle East: Social and Cultural Origins of Egypt's 'Urabi Movement.* Princeton, N.J.: Princeton University Press, 1993. A sophisticated and convincing discussion of Egyptian social, economic, and political history in the middle decades of the nineteenth century.

CRABBS, JACK A., JR.: *The Writing of History in Nineteenth-Century Egypt.* Detroit: Wayne State University Press, 1984. A very useful contribution to the historiography of the Middle East.

CUNO, KENNETH M.: *The Pasha's Peasants: Land, Society and Economy in Lower Egypt, 1740–1858.* Cambridge, England: Cambridge University Press, 1992.

DEEB, MARIUS: "The Socioeconomic Role of the Local Foreign Minorities in Modern Egypt, 1805–1961." *International Journal of Middle East Studies* 9 (1978): 11–22.

FARNIE, D. A.: *East and West of Suez: The Suez Canal in History, 1854–1956.* Oxford, England: Clarendon Press, 1969. A monumental work, derived from a vast range of western-language sources.

GOLDSCHMIDT, ARTHUR, JR.: *Modern Egypt: The Formation of a Nation-State.* Boulder, Colo.: Westview Press, 1988. The bibliography is especially valuable in this clear, concise, and thoughtful analysis of Egypt from Mehmet Ali to Mubarak.

GRAN, PETER: *Islamic Roots of Capitalism: Egypt, 1760–1840.* Austin: University of Texas Press, 1979. Stimulating discussion of Egyptian economic conditions and intellectual life.

HUNTER, F. ROBERT: *Egypt Under the Khedives, 1805–1879: From Household Government to Modern Bureaucracy.* Pittsburgh: University of Pittsburgh Press, 1984. A detailed study of the growth and changes in government and administration.

KUHNKE, LAVERNE: *Lives at Risk: Public Health in Nineteenth-Century Egypt.* Berkeley: University of California Press, 1990. An excellent study of medical theory and practice.

LANDES, DAVID S.: *Bankers and Pashas: International Finance and Economic Imperialism in Egypt.* Cambridge, Mass.: Harvard University Press, 1958. A significant case study of private banking in Egypt in the 1860s.

LANE, E. W.: *Manners and Customs of the Modern Egyptians.* New York: Dutton, 1923. Still the most valuable source for the social history of nineteenth-century urban Egypt, this book, originally printed in 1835, is full of interesting observations on life in Cairo.

LAWSON, FRED H.: *The Social Origins of Egyptian Expansionism During the Muhammad Ali Period.* New York: Columbia University Press, 1992. A controversial study that describes economic changes as the chief cause of Egypt's foreign expansion.

MCCARTHY, JUSTIN: "Nineteenth-Century Egyptian Population." *Middle Eastern Studies* 12 (1976): 1–40. A sophisticated analysis of a complicated issue, showing that substantial population growth was caused largely by civil order and political stability.

MARSOT, AFAF LUTFI AL-SAYYID: *Egypt in the Reign of Muhammad Ali.* Cambridge, England: Cambridge University Press, 1984. A valuable political biography that analyzes most aspects of Egyptian history of the period.

————: *A Short History of Modern Egypt.* Cambridge, England: Cambridge University Press, 1985. An excellent introduction to the subject.

MORSY, MAGALI: *North Africa 1800–1900: A Survey from the Nile Valley to the Atlantic.* London: Longman, 1984. Especially useful for discussions of the Sudan and the role of the Sahara in the history of North Africa.

OWEN, E. R. J.: *Cotton and the Egyptian Economy, 1820–1914: A Study in Trade and Development.* Oxford, England: Clarendon Press, 1969. A stimulating and scholarly analysis of the Egyptian economy.

REIMER, MICHAEL J.: "Colonial Bridgehead: Social and Spatial Change in Alexandria, 1850–1882." *International Journal of Middle East Studies* 20 (1988): 531–553.

RIVLIN, HELEN ANNE B.: *The Agricultural Policy of Muhammad Ali in Egypt.* Cambridge, Mass.: Harvard University Press, 1961. An outstanding work that considers the entire economy of Egypt.

SCHÖLCH, ALEXANDER: *Egypt for the Egyptians! The Socio-Political Crisis in Egypt, 1878–1882.* London: Ithaca Press, 1981. The best study of the political factors in the fall of Ismail and the rise of Urabi.

TOLEDANO, EHUD R.: *State and Society in Mid-Nineteenth-Century Egypt.* Cambridge, England: Cambridge University Press, 1990. A new and more favorable evaluation of Abbas Pasha and the social history of his time, emphasizing elite ties to Ottoman culture and fascinating insights into everyday urban life.

TUCKER, JUDITH E.: *Women in Nineteenth-Century Egypt.* Cambridge, England: Cambridge University Press, 1985. A pathbreaking work of great value for the urban history of Egypt and the role of women in Egyptian society.

VATIKIOTIS, P. J.: *The History of Modern Egypt: From Muhammad Ali to Mubarak.* 4th ed. Baltimore: Johns Hopkins University Press, 1991. A fine, detailed book on nineteenth- and twentieth-century Egypt. Strong on social and intellectual movements in the rise of Egyptian nationalism.

Ottoman Tanzimat and European Ambitions

Between 1839 and 1876 the Ottoman Empire undertook a series of reforms while struggling against the growing power of European imperialism. During the nearly forty years of this reform period, which was known as the Tanzimat, the military and civil sections of the central government witnessed many substantial changes. The reforms, nevertheless, did not yet directly affect regions such as northern Iraq, which were far removed from the effective reach of the reformers. Throughout the whole period the empire also faced a series of external challenges. Those in the Ottoman elite who favored internal reforms believed that the changes were inherently worthwhile since they would promote the modernization or Europeanization needed to save the state from being swallowed up by its enemies. At the same time reforms might gain favor with some European countries, particularly Great Britain, and thereby advance the diplomatic interests of the empire. The pattern of alternating and intersecting internal reforms and foreign crises sometimes made it difficult to focus successfully on one or the other.

HATT-I SHARIF

The reforms of the Ottoman sultan Mahmud II had strengthened the authority of the central government. After the destruction of the janissaries a more effective army was developed and many autonomous provincial governors were subdued. Mahmud's struggle with Mehmet Ali of Egypt, however, resulted in a disastrous defeat in 1839. With Mahmud's death in 1839, his sixteen-year-old son, Abdulmejid (r. 1839–1861), faced military catastrophe, only to be saved by the European Great Powers. The new sultan had only a scanty education. Since his view of the world hardly extended beyond the palace walls, his understanding of the problems of his empire was rudimentary. His personal whims led to constant shifts of grand viziers, frequently at the instigation of powerful ambassadors. He and the other sultans of the Tanzimat period—Abdulaziz (r. 1861–1876) and Murad V (r. 1876)—remained the source of political legitimacy and sovereignty, yet they played only a small role in governing, as power tended to gravitate toward the chief bureaucrats and grand viziers.

Shortly after his accession Abdulmejid declared the Hatt-i Sharif (Illustrious Rescript), theoretically changing many aspects of Ottoman political life. It abolished capital punishment without a trial; guaranteed justice to all with respect to life, honor, and property; and continued the Supreme Council of Judicial Ordinances, whose purpose was to frame laws, such as a new penal code against which no infringements would be tolerated because of personal rank or influence. Mixed tribunals, composed of Muslims and non-Muslims, were formed to handle commercial cases involving foreigners. Most significant, testimony by a non-Muslim against a Muslim was made admissible in the courts. The second reform measure of the Hatt-i Sharif was designed to end the system of tax farming and expand the direct collection of taxes by government officials. (In reality, some tax farms continued until World War I.) The decree's provisions pertained to all subjects, regardless of religious sect.

The Hatt-i Sharif was a demonstration to Europe that the Ottoman Empire was capable of self-preservation and reorganization to withstand pressures from Christian ethnic groups for independence. Its issuance made enactment of the London treaties of 1840 and 1841 concerning the integrity of the Ottoman Empire appear more reasonable and just, thus easing British adherence to the settlement. The Ottoman foreign minister, Mustafa Reshid, had served as ambassador in London and Paris, and recognized the appeal that the Hatt-i Sharif would generate in European capitals. Whether the Hatt-i Sharif was intended primarily for foreign consumption or as part of an internal reform process has been much debated. Though sometimes weak in holding to a course and often personally corruptible, Reshid became an advocate of both internal reform and a pro-British foreign policy.

The new spirit of reform was soon curbed. As soon as the Great Powers decided to drive Mehmet Ali back to Egypt, reaction set in. Reshid had introduced a new penal code, based somewhat on French models, but after he fell from office in 1841 over discussions of the new commercial code, which eventually was decreed in 1850, the course of reform took a different direction, emphasizing chiefly military matters. Under Riza Pasha, a conservative court favorite and commander in chief of the army, a more rigorous conscription among Muslims was effected and some foreign officers were hired. (Christians were excluded from conscription.) The regular army and the reserves were increased, although in practice Ottoman forces were often tied down in police operations. The currency situation was greatly improved by withdrawing most of the paper money in circulation and introducing a new silver coinage. Paid government officials who went out to collect taxes proved so incompetent that peasants—Muslims and Christians alike—clamored for a return to tax farmers as the lesser of two evils.

EUROPEAN INTERESTS IN THE OTTOMAN EMPIRE

Throughout the nineteenth century, Britain, France, Austria, and Russia maintained a continuing interest in the Ottoman Empire. Toward the end of the century

Germany became the fifth major European imperialist power involved in the Middle East.

Britain and France thought of the Ottoman Empire in terms of commerce, imperial geopolitical strategy, and military and naval alliances. France was interested in imperial expansion in North Africa and the Mediterranean; the French conquered Algiers in 1830. Since England rivaled France in the east and in southeast Asia, whichever power gained secure access to Middle Eastern routes could threaten and block the communications of the other. In 1839 Britain annexed the important trading center of Aden in Yemen. Britain tended to support the maintenance of the Ottoman Empire as a means of blocking Russian entrance into the Mediterranean. This policy impelled England to oppose partition of the Ottoman Empire and to seek to strengthen the sultan's government.

Dynastic expansion at the expense of the Ottomans motivated Austrian and Russian conquests. Austria and Russia were also apprehensive that each might gain Ottoman territory at the expense of the other.

Russia, the most consistent enemy of the Ottoman Empire, dreamed of gaining Istanbul and reestablishing a Christian empire in the city of Constantine. Russia also was expanding in central Asia and the Caucasus areas; felt a religious interest in Jerusalem; was concerned over the welfare of Ottoman Orthodox Christians; and sought the creation of friendly Slavic Christian satellite states in the Balkans. In 1840–1841 the European powers agreed that any Russian occupation within the Istanbul region to protect the sultan from Mehmet Ali had to be only temporary. With the expiration of the Treaty of Hunkiar Iskelesi no European state had any special privilege that others did not possess, even though Russia, on the basis of various agreements with the Ottomans, enjoyed specified rights in the Balkans and among certain Christian groups throughout the empire.

COMMERCE AND THE CAPITULATIONS

While most of the commerce of the Ottoman Empire consisted of local trade among Ottoman subjects, international commerce was steadily increasing throughout the nineteenth century, and this area of the economy was coming under the control of foreigners and Ottoman minority groups protected by foreigners. In 1838, the signing of the British-Ottoman commercial convention gave English merchants favorable terms for trading; other European merchants soon gained the same privileges. Furthermore, government monopolies were abolished on goods exported from the empire, a provision that specifically included Egypt. The effects of the convention for Ottoman traders were unfortunate, but the consequences were lessened when the agreement was ignored or circumvented in some provinces.

International commerce increased dramatically throughout the whole world during the nineteenth century. The 1838 commercial convention marked a definite upsurge in commerce between the Ottoman Empire and western Europe. As a result, port cities such as Beirut and Izmir grew rapidly in population and wealth. After 1846, the grain trade of the Ottoman Empire and especially of the Danubian provinces rose to unprecedented heights. Within a few years Britain was obtaining as much grain from the Ottomans as from Russia. In 1827 British exports to the Ottoman Empire were worth about £500,000; in 1849 they were more than £2,400,000. Britain became the chief trading partner of the Ottoman Empire. The trade of France and Austria also developed, though not as markedly as that of Britain.

Growing industry in western Europe found in the Middle East a source of foodstuffs and raw materials that could be obtained in exchange for the products of the new machines of the west. This trade affected cloth production in the Ottoman Empire, in some areas substituting machine-made textiles from western Europe for local homespun cloth and thereby helping to cause a decline in guild membership by the end of the century. Ottoman industry also suffered from a lack of capital, although in various fields of production Ottoman artisans and manufacturers proved to be adaptable to new circumstances, thereby retaining and even expanding their sales of goods.

Great Britain forced the Ottoman Empire, Egypt, and Iran to stop almost entirely their commerce in slaves. In the 1840s and 1850s the British secured measures to stop the importation of African slaves by sea and the public sale of slaves. By the 1880s the slave trade was officially banned and only small numbers of slaves were being smuggled into the Ottoman Empire. (Abolition of slavery, however, had to wait until the next century.)

Use of machines and new types of power made it possible for the west to forge far ahead of the Middle East in matters of material welfare and wealth. Industrial capitalism, the earlier agricultural revolution, vast strides in science and technology, new military techniques, and the political strength deriving from nationalism all contributed to the increasing power of western Europe. The imbalance of power and prestige of western countries over the mostly agricultural Middle East became more preponderant with each decade. The central government of the Ottoman Empire and the coastal regions of that state (and their immediate hinterlands) speedily developed into economic colonies of western Europe. The privileges known as capitulations hastened this process.

With great increases in trade and shifting power relationships in the nineteenth century, the capitulations allowed foreigners special privileges. Some Ottomans gained the status of foreign citizens, and outright sale of citizenship and passports was practiced by unscrupulous consuls. Since foreigners had the right to be tried in their own consular courts and Ottoman officials frequently relied upon the advice of powerful European ambassadors, consuls could usually have criminal cases against their nationals dropped. Foreigners were exempt from local taxes and were thus able to conduct business with less interference from the government and at a lower cost than Ottoman subjects. In the first half of the nineteenth century sultans granted special privileges to selected Ottoman merchants to help them compete with European traders.

Export tariffs were also established by the capitulations and could not be changed except by consent of each party in a specific treaty. Since each treaty also contained a "most favored nation" clause, it was necessary to change all treaties at once to make any successful change at all: to get all to agree was virtually impossible. Such a situation enhanced the commercial exploitation of the weak Ottoman Empire by the powerful European nations.

RELIGIOUS ISSUES

Into this picture of the capitulations was injected an additional feature: religion. France claimed to represent the interests of all Roman Catholics inside the Ottoman Empire, and Russia asserted a similar claim to protect all Orthodox Christians. European powers increasingly intervened in Ottoman domestic affairs on behalf of religious and ethnic minorities. This helped lead to an identification of religious creed with ethnic nationality, which seemed to make nationalism synonymous with religion.

Prior to the recognition of Greek independence, there were still only three millets (semiautonomous religious communal groups) in the Ottoman Empire. But by 1914 there were seventeen, and almost all enjoyed the sponsorship of a foreign government. Not entirely responsible for this movement but certainly encouraging it were foreign missionaries. Christian missionaries from Europe, especially Roman Catholics, had labored in the Middle East for centuries, but their number increased greatly in the nineteenth century. Different denominations established schools, churches, hospitals, printing presses, and a variety of service groups to carry the Christian message and western concepts of society to Middle Eastern peoples. Almost completely unsuccessful in converting Muslims, they concentrated their efforts upon indigenous Christian groups but sought to influence Muslims by westernizing them. Many Orthodox Christians in Anatolia became more prosperous and took part in a cultural flowering separate from the efforts of the missionaries and still within the framework of the Ottoman political system.

In 1860, with the founding of the Alliance Israélite Universelle, Jews in Europe began to better the welfare of Jews in the Middle East, especially through education. Most Jews in the Middle East did not have the diplomatic protection granted Christians by European governments; as a result, they suffered less from the rising antagonism directed by some elements of the Muslim population against minorities who depended on foreigners for advancement and security.

The Christian European governments often subsidized Christian Ottoman groups for ulterior, political aims. Russia and England, for instance, competed for the Armenians, and neither wished to see American missionaries enter the field. The greatest rivalry occurred in Palestine between the Russians and the French. Since medieval times Catholic clergy had attended the holy places in Bethlehem, Jerusalem, and Nazareth. Orthodox churchmen dated to the seventeenth century their right to protect the Holy Sepulchre, where Jesus had been buried. They protested against French claims, and crowds of Orthodox traveled thousands of miles to pray at the Holy Sepulchre. Beginning about 1840 there was rising interest in France over the position of the Catholic church in Palestine. In 1842, when the cupola of the Church of the Holy Sepulchre needed repair, a great commotion arose over which sect should enjoy the privilege, and actual fighting broke out in 1847 in

Bethlehem, where Catholic and Orthodox monks attacked each other with candlesticks and crosses at the Church of the Nativity. The Ottoman governor of Jerusalem posted soldiers inside the Church of the Holy Sepulchre to prevent bloodshed.

TANZIMAT

In the midst of these crises, Mustafa Reshid returned to office as foreign minister in 1845 and became grand vizir the following year. He reinvigorated the Hatt-i Sharif by initiating the Tanzimat (meaning "reforms"), a movement for reorganization, and he found an eager ally in the British ambassador.

Earlier military reforms continued and cost large sums of money. The regular Ottoman army grew from 24,000 in 1837 to 120,000 in 1850; during the Crimean War of 1853–1856 reserves were also mobilized, bringing the total force to about 250,000. A major difficulty arose from the insufficient number of trained officers and the inadequacy of support services.

The Tanzimat spirit was also manifested in the growing number of Ottomans who were educated in the west or in a western manner and who became more secular in their outlook. The best evidence of this growth was the newspapers and books that appeared in the 1840s. Politics, history, biography, and philosophy were popular subjects, and new ideas appealed to some in the younger generation. Everywhere in Europe revolts against conservatism were stirring, and Istanbul, on the edge of Europe, felt this movement. Nationalist sentiment among Greeks, Armenians, Bulgarians, and others could not fail to arouse Ottoman patriotism, too. A secular attitude was injecting new ideas of law and education into the Muslim as well as the non-Muslim communities: the individual was coming to be regarded as having rights outside of the group. Although many Muslims still opposed the idea, Ottomanism promised equality for all subjects, and Ottoman Christians and Jews were appointed to the reform councils.

Some of Reshid's reforms were extended beyond the capital and appeared in measures regarding equal justice, withdrawal of capital punishment from the hands of local governors, an increase in the size of the bureaucracy, and creation of elected local assemblies. These assemblies were usually composed of wealthy, influential notables and conservatives; ironically, they often prevented changes from being adopted. In addition to provincial assemblies, the grand vizir checked on actions of the governor by sending out commissioners to inspect a province and receive petitions from local groups.

No longer was the state to be viewed solely as an instrument for the sovereign to collect revenue, raise armies, and administer justice. Matters of education, public works, and economic development were of some concern to the rulers. This Tanzimat "reordering" spirit was also manifested in the modernization of law and diplomacy. Government administration was more efficient (except in finance), the number of bureaucrats increased substantially, and civil servants were recruited more broadly than in the past. No law or ordinance could become effective until it had been discussed by the Tanzimat Council and approved by the Council of Ministers.

The Judicial Council, including Christian as well as Muslim members, served as a court of appeals for cases arising from new, westernized civil laws but not from religious laws, as these were handled by millet courts. Many innovations were introduced, including the standardization of weights and measures under the metric system, postage stamps, a new nationality law, a lending bank for small businesses, and a reorganization of public instruction.

THE CRIMEAN WAR

Ottoman leaders could not concentrate exclusively on domestic reforms—they also had to deal with urgent foreign policy disputes. The Ottomans tried to satisfy both Russia and France in their argument over the Christian holy places in Palestine, but the Russians came to feel that they had been duped by the sultan. In 1853 they demanded full Orthodox privileges in Palestine, including the Russian right to repair the cupola of the Church of the Holy Sepulchre as well as a special treaty guaranteeing privileges for Ottoman Orthodox Christians and conclusion of a secret defensive alliance with Russia. Compromise was reached on some matters, while the sultan refused demands regarding Russian protection of Orthodox Christians, for to do so was tantamount to giving Russia the right to govern between 10 and 12 million inhabitants of the Ottoman Empire.

When the Russian tsar ordered the occupation of the Danubian Principalities, the British and French supported the Ottomans, who tried compromise again, but Muslim feelings now ran high, and this was regarded as the final appeasement. Bolstered by the recent arrival of a large Egyptian fleet at the Golden Horn, the Ottomans rejected new European proposals, declared war in 1853, and attacked the Russians on the Danube. Inconsequential Ottoman successes were obtained there and in the Caucasus, but real victory was won by the Russians when the Ottoman navy was destroyed in the Black Sea. Then the British and French governments sent their combined fleets into the Black Sea.

No European power was then prepared to allow the partition of the Ottoman Empire, so in the spring of 1854 Austria and Prussia joined in the concert against Russia by requesting assurances of the integrity of the Ottoman Empire. The Russian army retired from the Ottoman Danubian Principalities since the tsar was not prepared to face all Europe. Disturbances in Serbia were quelled, and British and French troops occupied Athens to force the Greeks to abandon an attack upon the Ottoman Empire. But sentiment in England and France, on the streets and in the governments, was for further war.

Acting with a treaty of alliance between Britain, France, and the Ottoman Empire, the three powers waged war against Russia. There is no need to dwell on the Crimean War here, since it was a European rather than a Middle Eastern war. Ottoman monetary debts to English and French bankers mounted as costs mushroomed. Cholera weakened the armies more than did battles, but the will to fight persisted. War continued until the fall of Sevastopol in the Crimea to the allies and the fall of Kars in Anatolia to the Russians in late 1855. Peace was speedily concluded at Paris in 1856.

The Treaty of Paris and additional agreements declared that the Ottoman Empire was a European power. In a separate treaty England, France, and Austria agreed to respect, defend, and guarantee the empire's independence and integrity. The Black Sea was demilitarized. Equally important was European acceptance of a new edict already promulgated by Sultan Abdulmejid, the Hatt-i Humayun, guaranteeing many reforms for Ottoman Christians. Domestic change was accelerated greatly by the Crimean War. The presence in Istanbul of large numbers of British, French, and Italians had substantial social repercussions upon the Ottomans, while the quantities of money expended by the Crimean War allies gave to many the opportunity of satisfying their desire for European travel.

Special vassalage status was conferred upon the Ottoman provinces of Wallachia and Moldavia, with the hope that a more independent rule for the Danubian Principalities would enable them to serve as a better buffer between the Ottoman Empire and Russia. In 1866 a member of the Prussian royal house, Carol (Charles) of Hohenzollern, became prince of a united Romania.

HATT-I HUMAYUN

Before the Treaty of Paris could be completed, a new reform document was issued. This was the Hatt-i Humayun (Imperial Rescript) of February 1856, which reendorsed the Hatt-i Sharif and the Tanzimat. But it was far more specific in its details and more extensive in scope than previous reform measures. The imperial decree was in the main concerned with the Christian and Jewish population; it granted non-Muslims the rights and privileges that the Muslim subjects possessed. Patriarchs and heads of communities (millets) were to be appointed for life, and through self-chosen assemblies each community was to control its own temporal administration. Freedom of worship was declared, and no one could be compelled to change religion. Religion or ethnicity could not be a hindrance to holding public office, employment by the state, entry into a school, or service in the army.

In matters of justice and court procedures, commercial and criminal cases between Muslims and non-Muslims and among non-Muslims of different sects were referred to mixed tribunals whose proceedings were open to the public. Equality of taxes among the various religious groups was pronounced, and foreigners were henceforth permitted to own real property in the sultan's realm.

Steps were supposed to be taken to reform the monetary and financial systems of the empire. Roads and canals were envisaged, and commerce and agriculture were to be encouraged, while every means was to be sought for the empire "to profit by the science, the art, and the funds of Europe."

On paper the Hatt-i Humayun contained the essentials necessary for a strong revival. The Ottomans sought to show this strength by extending their power over areas, such as Yemen, that had for long been independent of Istanbul. In 1849 they had landed there, and in 1872 they took Sana in the interior. But in many of the more distant provinces, such as Yemen or the Hijaz in Arabia, the Tanzimat reforms were unpopular and were for the most part not applied.

To make the reforms work both in the central government and in the provinces required the commitment of more people than were available. Moreover, the Hatt-i

Humayun ignored the rising tide of nationalism among non-Muslims and failed to appreciate the effect of foreign residents upon the millet system. Through their schools and literature the nationalists accepted the concept that people could only enjoy the greatest happiness when governing themselves. The capitulations in the Ottoman Empire, including Egypt, gave political, social, and economic privileges to foreign nationals. Thus the Hatt-i Humayun, in spite of the efforts of such men as Fuad and Ali Pashas, was doomed to failure almost from the beginning. Too many were opposed to it. On the other hand, the wars in Europe from 1859 to 1871 that accompanied the unification of Italy and Germany and the reforms that occupied Russia usually allowed the Ottoman Empire to follow her own political course.

LEBANON AND SYRIA

A series of bloody events in Lebanon and Syria furnished one pretext for European intervention in internal Ottoman problems. Since the time of Napoleon, Amir Bashir Shihab, the leader of a local dynasty that had been paramount in the area of Mount Lebanon after 1697, had ruled with ruthless calculation. His loyalty to Mehmet Ali allowed the Ottomans to replace him in 1840 with an incompetent nephew. Maronite Christians and Druzes soon fell to fighting. European pressure elicited a new arrangement from the sultan in 1843: the northern regions of Lebanon were governed by a Maronite, supported by the French; the southern portion was left to the Druzes, who were favored by the British.

An uneasy peace and prosperity reigned. However, a new and weak governor in the Maronite district, installed in 1854, permitted local notable families to abuse villagers, and population pressures were felt keenly. In 1858 a kind of social upheaval broke out, while in 1860 in the Druze-governed district, where many of the peasants were Maronites, and in the city of Damascus massacres of Christians took place. The Great Powers permitted Napoleon III of France to send a force of 6000 to restore order there. The Ottomans, however, firmly stopped the violence before the French arrived, and the Ottomans reestablished direct control over Syria as a European commission drew up a statute for autonomous rule in Mount Lebanon. Signed by Sultan Abdulmejid in 1861, it provided for an Ottoman Christian governor appointed with consent of the Great Powers. He was to have full executive power and was to be assisted by a central administrative council composed of members of all important sectarian communal groups. The first governor, Daud Pasha, an Armenian Catholic, proved exceptionally able as a diplomat and administrator; and rule under the statute, redrawn in 1864, remained in effect with a great degree of success until the Ottomans assumed direct control during World War I.

SOCIAL CHANGES AND POLITICAL REFORMERS

Western European influence was indirect as well as direct; it could be seen in books and secular ideas, which affected political affairs more and more noticeably after the Crimean War. By the early 1870s about 160 books were published each year, chiefly in Istanbul. Many elite Ottomans, including especially members of the religious minorities, imitated French poetry, art, philosophy, and social forms; nationalism was discussed; European-style plays were performed; and Persian elegance of phrasing became outmoded. French manners, urbanity, and sophistication were now the fashion. The effect, however, of this innovative group upon Ottoman society as a whole was still limited to the urban areas.

More immediately, European style was influential in the design of new imperial palaces. Ponderous, opulent, and westernized in their interior decoration, these palaces marked a transformation of Ottoman imperial artistic traditions. The sultans of the Tanzimat era moved from the beautiful Topkapi Palace in old Istanbul to the new Dolmabahche Palace along the Bosphorus in 1853. Many parts of Istanbul were changed as streets were widened and straightened, transportation was improved, and urban services were increased.

A conservative influence came from the millions of Muslim immigrants who arrived in the Ottoman Empire from the provinces that had been lost to Russian and Balkan state expansionism. Resettlement of the refugees from the Caucasus, the Crimea, and the various Balkan regions was a costly and laborious process, but one that the Ottoman government welcomed. The refugees were viewed as a source of additional agricultural labor to work on productive land that had been vacant. One consequence of the refugee settlements was that the proportion of the Ottoman Empire's population that was Muslim substantially increased. The total population probably remained roughly constant despite this immigration, since endemic diseases, occasional starvation, war casualties, and outward migration tended to counterbalance the numbers of immigrants.

The Ottoman Land Law of 1858 enabled the new immigrants and others already settled on the land to obtain deeds and more security of tenure. Land ownership in most parts of the Ottoman Empire probably remained in the hands of small holders, although some large estates were created by nomadic leaders who registered as their own property enormous amounts of land that had been collectively utilized by their tribes. The central government also sold land in public auctions, and large sections could be accumulated by absentee investors, especially in regions newly brought under the effective control of the state. The land law and protection from raids by nomads enabled peasants to extend their planting of crops into outlying regions, as in Syria, Jordan, and Iraq.

Some of the Tanzimat changes affected the role of peasant and urban women. Wealthy urban women were especially affected; for instance, their clothing became similar to that worn in western Europe. The central government began to train midwives, and thousands of girls attended new public and private schools by the end of the century. A women's teachers training school was established in 1870, and female education was supported by some male political leaders and reformers, although primary education remained in the hands of the relatively conservative ulama. Most families continued to be nuclear in structure, with a wife and husband and their children living together. New factories often hired women, especially in silk-reeling mills, and paid them very low wages, while many village and urban women worked in their homes producing such products as yarn, cloth, and carpets. Many western Europeans favored a change in the status of women, with the result that in the minds of conservative Ottomans feminism became associated with foreign claims of cultural superiority.

The Ottoman reformers were led by Reshid Pasha, who died in 1858. He had been for twenty years the most commanding figure in the Ottoman government, having held all the high offices at one time or another. As was the custom, he found young, talented men in the government service and advanced them to higher positions if their views agreed with his. Two, Mehmed Emin Ali Pasha and Kechejizade Mehmed Fuad Pasha, came to be regarded as Reshid's chief disciples. Both Ali and Fuad were liberals, reformers, and Freemasons; together they dominated the Ottoman government for fifteen years following the Hatt-i Humayun. Both were born in 1815, and for the decade from 1861 to 1871 one was always foreign minister while the other was usually grand vizir.

Ali Pasha, the son of an Istanbul shopkeeper, entered government service at the age of fifteen, moved into the famed translation bureau in 1833, became ambassador to London in 1841, foreign minister in 1846, and grand vizir in 1852 at the age of thirty-seven. During the Crimean War he served as foreign minister, and then in 1855 as grand vizir. In 1856 he attended the Paris Peace Conference as the Ottoman envoy. When Reshid Pasha died in 1858, Ali was named grand vizir again. He was to be, variously, and sometimes simultaneously, grand vizir, foreign minister, and minister of the interior for the next sixteen years.

A small, frail person who spoke hardly above a whisper, Ali Pasha knew when to be silent and possessed complete self-control. He was a hard worker and honest, although it was supposed that he received a sizable "gift" from Khedive Ismail of Egypt in 1866. Ali, as an Ottoman leader, endeavored to uphold order in the state, to ensure prosperity for all, and to initiate gradual changes in government and society. He believed in mixed schools where Muslims and Christians could study together, and hoped for the development of a full equality among Ottomans. He was, however, opposed to the introduction of an elected constitutional government, arguing that the people were not sufficiently educated for that.

The only rival permitted in Ali Pasha's circle was his fellow moderate liberal, Fuad Pasha, who teamed so well with Ali yet differed from him in so many ways. Fuad, who belonged to a well-known Istanbul family, graduated from the Galatasaray medical school, where instruction was in French, and then served in the army medical corps. His fluency in French was such that his witticisms in that language became famous throughout Europe. Entering the translation bureau in 1837, he soon became its highest officer. Fuad lived in London and conducted special negotiations in Spain, Russia, and Egypt. In 1852 he assumed the office of foreign minister, a post he was to hold on five separate occasions. He also served terms as grand vizir, the first in 1861.

Fuad was tall, handsome, talkative, and much more westernized in his habits than was Ali. Nevertheless, Fuad was also devoted to the service of the Ottoman state. He strongly believed that to survive the Ottoman Empire would have to change its political and civil institutions to keep pace with progress in Europe. Feeling that Islam was out of date in some respects, he argued that it should accept new truths no matter whence they came. He moved to dampen the growing nationalisms in the Balkans by calling for an Ottoman identity and equality, with liberties for all non-Muslims. Fuad accompanied Sultan Abdulaziz and his nephews Murad and Abdulhamid in 1867 when they visited Paris and London, a trip that helped persuade the sultan to support Tanzimat reforms.

Fuad and Ali were the guiding hands of the late Tanzimat period, but ultimate legitimacy and power remained in the hands of the sultans of the Ottoman dynasty. Though others might carp at the Tanzimat leaders for pushing too slowly for changes, Fuad and Ali recognized that politics is the art of the possible and that change must be gradual.

YOUNG OTTOMANS

The Tanzimat was opposed by conservative Muslims in society and in the palace. On the other hand, there were those who chafed at the slow progress: by the mid–1860s quite a number of young Ottomans, both Muslims and non-Muslims, who had studied in Europe felt this way. Young army officers, medical students, junior government officials, and others criticized the shortcomings of the government in the newspapers. Following the terminology of such groups in Italy, France, and elsewhere, Europeans labeled them the Young Ottomans. Foremost among them was Namik Kemal, whose father was court astronomer (astrologer). Namik Kemal was a clerk for a time in the translation bureau but left this job for journalism. A poet and an Ottomanist patriot, in 1873, his play *Vatan* (Fatherland) created such a stir that it was shut down by the government and Kemal was exiled.

Uprisings in Crete and appeasement of the Cretans by Istanbul infuriated the Young Ottomans. Abdulhamid Ziya joined Namik Kemal, turning his pen and influence against Ali, with whom he had a personal quarrel. An admirer of western science and Persian poetry, Ziya was an Ottoman patriot who in 1867 was exiled to Cyprus. Another Ottoman patriot was Ali Suavi, a man of humble origins who had attended traditional schools and had taught in secondary schools. Suavi assailed the government by delivering nationalist harangues in Istanbul's mosques. Early in 1867 he started a newspaper in which he praised Turkish qualities.

Many of the Young Ottomans went into exile in Europe, where they agitated for reforms in their homeland. Their lack of internal cohesiveness made it easy for the central government in the late 1860s and early 1870s to secure their services and separate them one from another.

MIDHAT PASHA AND THE CONSTITUTION

Those government officials who most strongly favored westernization and reform were led by Ahmed Midhat Pasha (1822–1884), an able provincial administrator. After he put many reform ideas into practice as governor of Nish, Midhat was recalled in 1864 to Istanbul, where he helped draw up new regulations for the provinces. The empire was divided into twenty-eight large provinces (vilayets), with mixed tribunals for cases involving Christians and Muslims and assemblies of notables to counsel the governor. Yet, since the power of appointing the governor rested in the hands of the sultan or his advisers, the quality of administration enjoyed by a province depended almost wholly upon the governor's personality and the sultan's backing.

The energetic Midhat returned to Bulgaria, where for a few years he served as governor of the new Province of the Danube. He established roads, bridges, orphanages, schools, hospitals, agricultural credit cooperatives, and an official newspaper. Even more important was his securing of law and order and his just treatment of the Christian population. On the other hand, Midhat Pasha ruthlessly suppressed outbursts of nationalism aimed at self-government and independence. In rapid succession following the Bulgarian assignment Midhat chaired the imperial council of state and was governor of Baghdad, where he also enacted many modernizing reforms. He became grand vizir for three months in 1872, held the governorship of Salonica, and then retired to private life in Istanbul.

The government of the Ottoman Empire had lacked strong leaders since the death, in 1869, of Fuad Pasha and, in 1871, of Ali Pasha. Bankruptcy and uprisings in the Balkans, with their corollary of European intervention, heartened Midhat Pasha to engineer the deposition of the incompetent Abdulaziz and install as sultan his nephew, Murad V, on May 30, 1876. In August Murad had a nervous breakdown and was replaced by his brother Abdulhamid II (r. 1876–1909), meaning that the Ottoman Empire had three sultans in one year. Midhat mistakenly assumed that Abdulhamid would support liberal political changes.

Under the direction of Midhat Pasha as grand vizir, on December 23, 1876, Abdulhamid proclaimed a written constitution that Midhat and others had been formulating since the deposition of Abdulaziz. Accepted with great rejoicing among the liberals of Istanbul, the constitution provided for a cabinet and an elected parliament. It reaffirmed that all subjects of the sultan were equal, regardless of race or creed. Freedom of religion, education, and the press were guaranteed.

The outbreak of war with Russia enabled Abdulhamid in 1878 to suspend parliament, exile Midhat, and quietly ignore the constitution. By the end of the war and the settlement at the Congress of Berlin, Abdulhamid and his entourage had control over the central government. In 1884 the sultan ordered Midhat to be strangled in his prison in al-Taif, near Mecca. Modernization through liberal political reform was killed along with Midhat.

OTTOMAN FINANCES

No matter which sultan reigned, the expenses of the state increased throughout the century. The central government in Istanbul needed increasingly large sums of money to pay for wars, military modernization, and other changes. Beginning with the Crimean War, the Ottoman government contracted loans to meet the extraordinary expenses of the army and navy.

Between 1854 and 1875 the Ottoman Empire borrowed $1 billion from western Europe; at the end of that period almost nothing remained to show for such a vast sum—except debts. The tax system was still antiquated, increasing income could not keep up with the costs of government, and there was a yearly excess of imports over exports. The great bulk of imports were consumer goods, and loans did not bring in the capital goods that in the end might have expanded Ottoman productivity and facilitated repayment of the loans.

Once the habit was fixed, loans were contracted almost every year, with the tribute from Egypt, Istanbul customs duties, tobacco and salt taxes, and various other revenues pledged as security. Interest rates were high, and as long as confidence could be maintained, European bankers had little difficulty in floating bonds, with enormous profits to be made. When one grand vizir balked at taking a loan, a British banker used his influence to replace him with a more willing borrower. The theory of the right of European governments to intervene in Ottoman affairs grew with the series of loans. Commissioners were appointed to investigate spending of funds and the financial feasibility of the loans and to supervise their collection.

By 1875 Ottoman foreign debts had risen to £200 million, bearing annual charges of £12 million, while the total revenue was only £22 million. This meant that the empire had one of the highest debts per person of any country in the world at that time. Severe famines in central Anatolia and a financial crisis in Europe contributed to the Ottoman dilemma; the government had to partially suspend payments of interest. The empire was bankrupt.

The growing financial crisis affected every part of the empire. The burden of the debt left the treasury a diminishing sum with which to meet expenses of government. Officials who went unpaid resorted to corrupt practices, while the government adopted harsher methods of taxation. Peasants everywhere were squeezed; the most serious rebellion burst in Bosnia.

BALKAN PROBLEMS

From their forested mountain retreats many local Muslim leaders had resisted the Tanzimat innovations. In 1831 they had fought Mahmud's reforms, and Bosnian Muslims rebelled again in 1849, only to be subdued in 1850. Financial difficulties called for rigid collection of taxes in Bosnia in 1875, even though there had been a scanty harvest the previous year. Serbian Christians in Herzegovina and other Balkan areas erupted over the stringent measures. Christian insurgents tasted considerable success—and Pan-Slavs in Russia and Serbia were jubilant.

The Balkan revolt spread to Bulgarian districts, where economic prosperity and a cultural revival had opened the way to ethnic nationalism. Long centuries of Ottoman rule had permitted Muslim notables and Greek Orthodox clergy to have local authority. By the 1830s Bulgarian schools, history, language, folklore, and national consciousness began to develop rapidly as the Bulgarian region became linked economically to western Europe. With the creation of a Bulgarian Orthodox Exarchate in 1870 nationalism grew ever faster and Macedonia became a battleground between Greek and Bulgarian. Further unrest arose when Muslim refugees from the Crimea and the Caucasus settled in Bulgarian regions; the refugees terrorized peasants and kept villages in a state of perpetual siege. Christian peasants also wished to gain control of agricultural land owned by Muslim notables. Irregular Ottoman militias perpetrated massacres, most notably upon the villagers of Batak, who were preparing to join in an uprising. Perhaps 5000 individuals out of 7000 in Batak were killed. Reports from correspondents, describing many shocking incidents, appeared in London newspapers.

Because of the high emotion aroused in Britain by the Bulgarian atrocities, Russia and Austria believed they could change the Balkan status quo. Montenegro and Serbia declared war against the Ottoman Empire in July 1876, but Ottoman armies defeated the Serbs, whereupon Russia gave the sultan an ultimatum, leading to a December 1876 conference of the Great Powers in Istanbul to discuss peace between Serbia and the Ottomans.

At the beginning of the conference, the sultan proclaimed a written constitution for his empire. Counting on the friendship of Britain, the Ottomans refused to go along with the Great Powers, and the conference broke up in January 1877. Peace was signed directly between Serbia and the sultan in February upon the basis of the status quo.

RUSSIAN-OTTOMAN WAR

Hoping to gain territory and influence, Russia declared war in April 1877. No one expected the war to last very long because neither contestant had much ready cash. The Ottoman navy dominated the Black Sea, but Romania declared full independence from the Ottoman Empire and aided the Russians, who passed the Danube and appeared to be on their way to Edirne and Istanbul. Then the Ottoman general Osman Pasha dug in near Plevna in Bulgaria, resisting the Russian siege from July until December. The Ottomans mobilized armies totaling about 250,000 men on the European and Caucasian fronts. Meanwhile, Ottoman forces were defeated at Kars by a Russian general, in Herzegovina by the Montenegrins, and at Nish by the Serbs. The Ottomans threw themselves upon the mercy of the European powers as Russia, Romania, Serbia, and Montenegro continued the war, occupying Edirne in January 1878. Muslims fled before the advancing armies, since Russian and Balkan armies were as brutal in their atrocities as Ottoman irregulars had been at Batak.

As the Russians approached Istanbul, they placed their headquarters at the village of Yeşilköy (San Stefano), only a few miles from the Ottoman capital. Under this threat, the Ottomans signed the disastrous Treaty of San Stefano in March 1878, recognizing the independence of Montenegro, Serbia, and Romania, each of which received considerable territory at Ottoman expense. Bosnia and Herzegovina obtained autonomous rule. Russia solidified its control of the whole Caucasus region, acquiring Batum and Kars, and eastern Anatolia up to Trabzon and Erzurum. Bulgaria was created within the Ottoman Empire as a large, self-governing Christian principality from the Aegean Sea to the Black Sea and westward to Albania, including Macedonia. As a final blow the Ottomans were to pay a large indemnity to Russia.

THE CONGRESS OF BERLIN

Almost before the ink dried, objections to San Stefano arose. The creation of "Big Bulgaria" produced a storm—Greece, Serbia, Romania, and Montenegro protested, and representatives of Albanian groups petitioned to be heard. Britain and Austria demanded a new settlement. First, the Anglo-Ottoman convention of June 1878, ceding the administration of Ottoman Cyprus to Britain, was announced, then at Berlin, on July 13, 1878, a galaxy of statesmen concluded new arrangements for the Balkans.

The Treaty of Berlin reduced the "Big Bulgaria" of the Treaty of San Stefano to a smaller autonomous principality, where the prince would be chosen by an assembly of Bulgarian notables and confirmed by the sultan. The province of Eastern Rumelia was constructed, where the governor-general was appointed by the sultan with consent of the Great Powers. Although the Ottoman Empire could maintain troops and erect fortresses there, the police were to be drawn from the native population. Romania, Montenegro, and Serbia became independent; and Austria-Hungary occupied and administered Bosnia and Herzegovina. Kars and Batum were given to Russia. Finally, the Ottomans pledged religious liberty and civil equality for the sultan's subjects in Europe and Asia alike. The dignitaries rejoiced when they signed the treaty because a troublesome question had been handled without a new war.

The loss of so much territory in Europe, bankruptcy, three sultans in one year, declaration of a constitution, and the cumulative effect of nearly forty years of reforms and foreign policy crises left the Ottoman state reeling by the time of the Congress of Berlin. European imperialism seemed stronger than ever. While Ottoman military reforms and expenditures had increased the power of the army, they had not been sufficient to defend the empire against Russia. Only foreign diplomatic intervention had stopped the humiliating San Stefano agreement from being put into effect; the Congress of Berlin arrangements, while an improvement, were still a major defeat for the Ottoman Empire.

Using the Hatt-i Sharif and the Hatt-i Humayun, the leaders of the Tanzimat had succeeded in reforming many bureaucratic practices, while Ottoman commerce increased dramatically and the Ottomans became part of the world economy. By the 1870s the reforms began to reach beyond the cities and towns to affect some of the peasants, although most of the villagers and the nomads were still unaffected. But European influence inside the empire was also growing, often by means of minority religious groups who identified their interests with those of external governments. The success of the Tanzimat was also limited by the size and complexity of the empire. Decreeing reforms in Istanbul was one thing, but executing the changes throughout the enormous empire was another. Since by the late 1870s the Ottoman Tanzimat seemed insufficient to save the empire from destruction, another approach to government, reform, and foreign policy seemed to be essential.

References

Many volumes mentioned in earlier chapters concerned with the Ottoman Middle East relate to subjects discussed in this chapter. Works cited in Chapters 16, 17, and 20 through 23 are especially pertinent.

ABU-MANNEH, BUTRUS: "The Sultan and the Bureaucracy: the Anti-Tanzimat Concepts of Grand Vizier Mahmud Nedim Pasha." *International Journal of Middle East Studies* 22 (1990): 257–274. Mahmud Nedim's favoring of the sultanate and conservative Islam rather than the bureaucracy and secularizing reforms is examined.

AUGUSTINOS, GERASIMOS: *The Greeks of Asia Minor: Confession, Community, and Ethnicity in the Nineteenth Century.* Kent, Ohio: Kent State University Press, 1992. A sensitive treatment of the subject for the period 1840–1880.

BLACK, CYRIL E., AND L. CARL BROWN, EDS.: *Modernization in the Middle East: The Ottoman*

Empire and Its Afro-Asian Successors. Princeton, N.J.: Darwin, 1992. Highly useful summaries of current knowledge; the first part deals chiefly with the late Ottoman period, while the second part covers the twentieth century.

BLAISDELL, DONALD C.: *European Financial Control in the Ottoman Empire: A Study of the Establishment, Activities and Significance of the Ottoman Public Debt.* New York: Columbia University Press, 1929. The most complete picture of this extraordinary episode of Ottoman history.

ÇELIK, ZEYNEP: *The Remaking of Istanbul: Portrait of an Ottoman City in the Nineteenth Century.* Seattle: University of Washington Press, 1986. An excellent study of urban change.

DAVIS, FANNY: *The Ottoman Lady: A Social History from 1718 to 1918.* New York: Greenwood, 1986. Along with charming anecdotes of upper-class Ottoman women, there are numerous bits of information on economic, cultural, and political activities of women in Ottoman cities, especially Istanbul.

DAVISON, RODERIC H.: *Reform in the Ottoman Empire, 1856–1876.* Princeton, N.J.: Princeton University Press, 1963. Still the best available study of this time period.

———: "Midhat Pasha." *Encyclopaedia of Islam.* New ed. Vol. 6, pp. 1031–1035. Leiden: Brill, 1991. An excellent introduction to this leading figure of the Tanzimat.

DEVEREUX, ROBERT: *The First Ottoman Constitutional Period: A Study of the Midhat Constitution and Parliament.* Baltimore: Johns Hopkins University Press, 1963. This work, with those by Davison and Mardin, makes a fine trilogy.

FAWAZ, LEILA TARAZI: *Merchants and Migrants in Nineteenth-Century Beirut.* Cambridge, Mass.: Harvard University Press, 1983. Traces the growth of the city and the changes in its social and economic composition.

FINDLEY, CARTER VAUGHN: *Ottoman Civil Officialdom: A Social History.* Princeton, N.J.: Princeton University Press, 1989. An impressive study of how the central bureaucracy changed from 1789 to World War I.

FINNIE, DAVID H.: *Pioneers East: The Early American Experience in the Middle East.* Cambridge, Mass.: Harvard University Press, 1967. Concerned with all American interests, from diplomats to navy men, shipbuilders, scholars, and missionaries.

ISSAWI, CHARLES: *The Economic History of Turkey, 1800–1914.* Chicago: University of Chicago Press, 1980. A wide variety of readings drawn from foreign and Ottoman sources that illustrate economic history.

———: *An Economic History of the Middle East and North Africa.* New York: Columbia University Press, 1982. An outstanding volume that concentrates on the nineteenth century.

JELAVICH, CHARLES, AND BARBARA JELAVICH: *The Establishment of the Balkan National States, 1804–1920.* Seattle: University of Washington Press, 1977. An excellent survey of the various Balkan countries.

KARPAT, KEMAL H.: *Ottoman Population, 1830–1914: Demographic and Social Characteristics.* Madison: University of Wisconsin Press, 1985. Very useful statistical information and fine analysis.

KUNERALP, SINAN, ED.: *Studies on Ottoman Diplomatic History.* Vol. 1. Istanbul: Isis Press, 1987. The first of a series, with each volume including essays based on Ottoman and European sources.

KUSHNER, DAVID: "The Place of the Ulema in the Ottoman Empire During the Age of Reform." *Turcica* 19 (1987): 51–74. Shows that despite secularizing reforms the ulama kept much of their influence in education, law, and administration.

LEWIS, NORMAN N.: *Nomads and Settlers in Syria and Jordan, 1800–1980.* Cambridge, England: Cambridge University Press, 1987. A stimulating study of nomadic tribes and their interactions with Ottomans and the national states of the twentieth century.

MA'OZ, MOSHE: *Ottoman Reform in Syria and Palestine, 1840–1861.* London: Oxford University Press, 1968. A well-balanced description of political, social, and religious conditions.

MARDIN, ŞERIF: *The Genesis of Young Ottoman Thought: A Study in the Modernization of Turkish Political Ideas.* Princeton, N.J.: Princeton University Press, 1962. The best study of early Turkish nationalism.

OCHSENWALD, WILLIAM: *Religion, Society and the State in Arabia: The Hijaz Under Ottoman Control, 1840–1908.* Columbus: Ohio State University Press, 1984. Points out that many Tanzimat changes were not put into effect in distant provinces.

OWEN, ROGER: *The Middle East in the World Economy, 1800–1914.* Rev. ed. London: Tauris, 1993. An excellent study.

PAMUK, ŞEVKET: *The Ottoman Empire and European Capitalism, 1820–1913: Trade, Investment and Production.* Cambridge, England: Cambridge University Press, 1987. A sophisticated analysis, based on the "dependency school" approach, which sees the Ottoman Empire as part of Europe's periphery.

PEARS, EDWIN: *Forty Years in Constantinople, 1873–1915.* New York: Appleton, 1916. Gives the flavor of events as seen by a British lawyer in Istanbul who corresponded with several London newspapers.

POLK, WILLIAM R., AND RICHARD L. CHAMBERS, EDS.: *Beginnings of Modernization in the Middle East: The Nineteenth Century.* Chicago: University of Chicago Press, 1968. Twenty papers by distinguished scholars on many facets of change in the nineteenth-century Middle East.

QUATAERT, DONALD: *Ottoman Manufacturing in the Age of the Industrial Revolution.* Cambridge, England: Cambridge University Press, 1993. A convincing essay showing that Ottoman household and workshop textile production adapted to new circumstances despite European competition.

RACCAGNI, MICHELLE: "The French Economic Interests in the Ottoman Empire." *International Journal of Middle East Studies* 11 (1980): 339–376.

ROSENTHAL, STEVEN T.: *The Politics of Dependency: Urban Reform in Istanbul.* Westport, Conn.: Greenwood Press, 1980. Traces the European-supported reform in municipal government in parts of Istanbul during the Tanzimat.

SHIELDS, SARAH D.: "Take-off into Self-Sustained Peripheralization: Foreign Trade, Regional Trade and Middle East Historians." *Turkish Studies Association Bulletin* 17 (1993): 1–23. Interesting for its theoretical approach as well as factual data, this study argues that Ottoman internal trade was more important than trade with Europe.

TOLEDANO, EHUD R.: *The Ottoman Slave Trade and Its Suppression, 1840–1890.* Princeton, N.J.: Princeton University Press, 1982. Based on Ottoman and European sources, this is a thorough treatment of a difficult topic.

Abdulhamid II
and Autocratic Reform

Sultan Abdulhamid II, who ruled the Ottoman Empire from 1876 to 1909, was the last of the Ottoman sovereigns to exercise real power. He was viewed by Ottoman and European liberals as a tyrant, and he did in fact suppress the constitution of 1876, oppose nationalism, and construct an elaborate system of spies. On the other hand, he also continued many elements of the Tanzimat, with an emphasis on technical, educational, and military modernization. Earlier reforms had begun slowly; now they finally began to take effect. The sultan sought to increase central control over the provinces despite growing nationalist opposition to Ottoman rule. In exercising political power Abdulhamid resembled his grandfather, Mahmud II, more than his Tanzimat-era father, Abdulmejid. Among Sultan Abdulhamid's chief policy concerns were European imperialism, the state's finances, and building railways.

ACCESSION OF ABDULHAMID II

The remarkable year 1876 witnessed three sultans ruling the Ottoman Empire: after Abdulaziz and then his nephew Murad V were deposed, Abdulhamid II became ruler. The latter came to the sultanate in a period of intense crisis. Internally, the tragic situation in Bulgaria and Bosnia had provoked rebellion and severe repression. A year earlier, in 1875, the empire had to suspend payment of interest on its bonds. International events set in motion by these events, which have been discussed earlier, included the Russian-Ottoman War, the Treaty of San Stefano, and the Congress of Berlin. By 1878 about one-third of the territory of the empire had been lost.

Faced with these problems, two political groups favoring different solutions emerged. One was distinctly liberal and pro-western European in its desire for constitutional government, fiscal reforms, and industrial and commercial expansion. The other was conservative and favored strong rule by the monarch. The liberals were led by Midhat Pasha and Husain Avni Pasha.

In May 1876 theological students demonstrated against Sultan Abdulaziz on the streets of Istanbul, obtaining, as had been done so frequently in preceding centuries, the dismissal of the grand vizir. On May 31 Midhat and Husain Avni deposed the extravagant Abdulaziz and brought Murad V to the sultanate. Two popular liberal journalists, Abdulhamid Ziya and Namik Kemal, became the sultan's private secretaries. Midhat proceeded to draft a constitution that limited the power of the sultan, created a parliament, and appealed to liberals in Europe. Unfortunately for the Ottoman liberals, the former sultan Abdulaziz committed suicide, a crazed officer broke into a cabinet meeting and assassinated four officials, including two ministers; the strain of rule proved too much for Murad, who became incapable of governing. Affairs of state stood still until in August Midhat deposed Murad in favor of Abdulhamid II.

The new sultan promised to support the liberal party and to retain Ziya and Namik Kemal as his private secretaries. Abdulhamid, however, had much more sympathy for the conservatives. Although Abdulhamid never appointed the liberals as his secretaries, he did make Midhat grand vizir and promulgated the constitution. However, Midhat was soon placed aboard the sultan's yacht and carried away to exile. Parliament met in March 1877, but Abdulhamid obtained its adjournment after a few weeks and, with the Russian army almost in Istanbul in February 1878, adjourned it and suspended the constitution. Until 1908 the constitution was printed each year in the official register but remained ignored. The war with Russia served as the excuse for its suppression and became the pretext for Abdulhamid to rule in the fashion of his pre-Tanzimat predecessors.

OTTOMAN PUBLIC DEBT ADMINISTRATION

Bankruptcy in 1875, followed so closely by defeat in the war with Russia, compelled Abdulhamid to accept measures limiting Ottoman sovereignty. In 1881, the Ottoman central government arranged with European bondholders' groups to reduce and consolidate the £210 million of the external debt of the empire to £106 million. The Council of Administration of the Ottoman Public Debt was authorized to collect and disburse revenues and taxes on behalf of the bondholders. The council consisted of seven members: five represented foreign bondholders; one was nominated by the Ottoman Bank, which was foreign-controlled; and one was appointed by the sultan. Largely the work of the British ambassador, the Ottoman Public Debt Administration regularized Ottoman finances and eventually reestablished the sultan's credit, although large sums of money had to be transferred abroad. By the late 1880s about one-fifth of all revenues were paid as interest on the debt. Once their good credit was established, the Ottomans resumed borrowing on a large scale.

Within a few years after its inception the Ottoman Public Debt Administration became more than merely a collecting and banking agency. Slowly, debts began to be liquidated and, even more important, Ottoman credit was rehabilitated so that money could be found to build railways and other western innovations. In almost every case in which Ottoman credit was involved, an agreement provided that the Ottoman Public Debt Administration should act for the government. Thus, by 1900 many railways in the Ottoman Empire were supervised by the Public Debt Administration, and railway bonds became the administration's obligations. It was so successful and in such good repute that the government itself used the organization to collect various unassigned taxes.

Sometimes the Ottoman Public Debt Administration served as an instrument of economic imperialism. By and large, however, it recognized that the interests of the bondholders would be best served by an improved economy. That its existence impinged upon Ottoman sovereignty there could be no doubt, but even the new regime after the revolt of 1908 was not strong enough to force its demise. Still later, after World War I, the Turkish Republic accepted the validity of the Ottoman debts but refused categorically to accept the kind of foreign intervention implied in the Public Debt Administration; the latter died quietly in 1923, when the Treaty of Lausanne omitted all reference to it.

CONTINUING REFORMS

Abdulhamid II eliminated the internal political opposition and stopped political liberalism. Some opponents were bought, while Midhat Pasha was strangled in Arabia and other illustrious Ottomans died in exile or in the inhospitable spots to which they were consigned. Abdulhamid, who eventually came to live in mortal terror of his own overthrow, had an elaborate system of spies. He took refuge at Yildiz Palace in Istanbul, which he enhanced and rebuilt and then protected with a double encircling wall.

Faced with so many problems, Sultan Abdulhamid embarked on a new policy that aimed at securing internal and external support for him as the caliph of the Muslims and the leader of the Pan-Islamic cause. Unlike most of his ancestors, who had viewed the title of caliph as only a minor one among many honorifics, Abdulhamid emphasized a claim to be the successor of the prophet Muhammad and leader of the ummah everywhere. Within the Ottoman lands this was an effective means of gaining legitimacy with many Sunnite Muslims, especially new refugees from areas seized by Christian states. Also, the empire's population consisted of a larger proportion of Muslims than had been the case earlier, because of the loss of many Christian-inhabited regions in the Balkans. Pan-Islamists argued that all Muslims should rally to defend the Ottoman Empire—the largest remaining independent Muslim state. Abdulhamid encouraged the growth of Pan-Islam by enlisting Sufi orders, using Ottoman diplomats abroad, subsidizing newspapers, and sending emissaries to all parts of the Muslim world. Some support for Pan-Islam emerged in areas such as India, Africa, and southeast Asia, thereby threatening the European imperial powers who controlled those regions and making them more willing to try to conciliate the Ottoman state.

Despite his firm determination to centralize all power in his own hands, in many ways Abdulhamid continued elements of the reforms that had characterized the Ottoman Empire since the days of Selim III. The sultan strongly favored military modernization and new weapons procurement. He employed Germans to train the army, while England was engaged to organize a police force. Fine new ships for the navy were ordered in England, France, and the United States.

Changes in government administration and society proceeded in those areas where Abdulhamid was not categorically opposed to reform. Government bureau-cracy increased dramatically in size, even though because of fiscal mismanagement the sultan was often not able to pay civil servants on time. As a result, employees often became corrupt and inefficient. In 1879, Abdulhamid appointed the minister of justice, Mehmed Said Pasha, as grand vizir, with the hope that Said would meet the pressing problems of the empire in a traditional fashion. Said had earlier reor-ganized the Ministry of Justice.

While minister of justice, Said Pasha had written a memorandum to Abdul-hamid proposing financial reforms to strengthen the state and improve the army, administrative reforms to end the drift toward local autonomy, and educational re-forms to achieve greater allegiance to Abdulhamid from his Muslim subjects. By this initiative Said Pasha became grand vizir, a post he held eight different times.

Said Pasha also understood the need to adjust the Ottoman system to the reali-ties of Europe, which were pressing upon the empire. In 1882 the Istanbul Cham-ber of Commerce was created to aid Ottoman merchants in meeting the impact of western business practices. After 1885, however, Said Pasha had difficulty in over-coming Abdulhamid's suspicion of innovation; Said's power waned, and his later terms as grand vizir were of short duration. However, Said's policy of increasing public education did continue to enjoy the support of the sultan.

THE PRESS, WOMEN, AND EDUCATION

The press had a difficult time during the reign of Abdulhamid, even though its cir-culation increased. In the 1860s several Turkish-language newspapers had been launched, most of which were liberal in their attitudes toward government. Ziya, Namik Kemal, and Ali Suavi were the most noteworthy and capable editors and writers. But Abdulhamid enforced a rigid censorship, and newspaper work meant "patriotic martyrdom," since editors and authors were almost invariably exiled. Ziya died a broken man in 1880 in Adana; Namik Kemal followed in 1887; and Ali Suavi was executed for his part in a plot against Abdulhamid in 1878. Many writers lived and published their works abroad and sent them into the Ottoman Empire through the protection of the various foreign post offices established under the ca-pitulations. Abdulhamid controlled the press and suspended opposition papers as they appeared. But he did not have enough spies to police the entire empire; conse-quently, attacks upon him could not be wholly suppressed.

Yet the effects of writers reached beyond the strictly political, educating the lit-erate population to developments and thoughts in the outside world. Over 300 books were published in 1890, many of them exciting French novels translated into Turkish that introduced Ottomans to a very different world. And phonographs reached the urban centers of the empire shortly after their invention, providing a new medium for cultural diffusion and entertainment.

Two authors, Tevfik Fikret and Ahmed Midhat, left their marks during these decades of Abdulhamid's rule. Fikret, whose writings flowered later, was editor from 1895 to 1901 of the *Servet-i Fünun* (Treasury of Science), which at first was an illustrated scientific and literary supplement to an Istanbul evening newspaper and then was an independent periodical. This pictorial news magazine was directed

to the educated elite and contained articles on biography, art, science, and literature. Because of censorship and the strict prohibition of even indirect political com-
ment, Fikret and other authors attacked social ills through fictional writing and introduced readers to European cultural and intellectual life.

The most prolific author of the period was Ahmed Midhat, the son of a humble
cloth merchant of Istanbul. Educated by his elder brother in a simple elementary
school, Ahmed Midhat entered government in the civil service, which he left in
1871 at the age of twenty-seven to be a printer and a writer. He fell in with liberals
and found himself deported to Rhodes for four years, returning with most of the exiles upon the deposition of Abdulaziz. In 1877 he published a book vindicating Abdulhamid's accession and title to the throne, an act that won for him the director-
ship of the state printing press and, subsequently, numerous official positions. For
the next thirty-one years this acquiescent mediocrity made a great contribution to
the development of Ottoman society.

Ahmed Midhat edited a daily newspaper, *Interpreter of Truth,* that had a
weekly supplement distributed to the students of the nation's elementary schools.
Most of the stories, serials, articles, and features were written or translated by
Ahmed Midhat, who at the same time was writing books, more than 150 in all, on
history, ethics, religion, philosophy, and science, as well as producing many works
of fiction modeled after contemporary European authors. He also wrote, in fourteen volumes, separate histories of European countries and a three-volume world
history. These were the first serious efforts to give the ordinary reader of Turkish a
view of history beyond the Islamic world. Because Ahmed Midhat did not possess
outstanding style or distinction and had little originality, men of literary talent were
contemptuous of his work. Yet his prodigious outpouring of books, periodicals, and
newspapers—particularly those for schoolchildren—probably did more to change
the outlook of the Ottomans, preparing them for a more secular and European
world, than the work of any other author.

A particularly incendiary cultural issue for the Ottomans was the status of
women. Political liberals like Namik Kemal tended to advocate female education,
while conservatives were opposed or skeptical. Upper-class, urban Ottoman
women still wore veils in public, but in the 1890s the veils became lighter and more
transparent. A few exceptional women wrote books of poetry or essays and managed to learn foreign languages; some Ottoman girls attended public or missionary
schools. In other cases women worked in new circumstances, such as newly established small factories. However, most village, nomadic, and urban women apparently continued to work in traditional occupations, especially in the home, assisting
in the fields or with the herds, and in handicraft production, as in the rapidly expanding area of carpet manufacture.

Public education for boys and girls was promoted in 1880, when, in a lengthy
memorandum, the grand vizir Said stressed the importance of an improved and
greatly extended educational system. Throughout the provinces the number of elementary and secondary schools was greatly increased and teacher training schools
were established, and in 1883 a special education tax was introduced to support
these schools. There were a million students in the public schools by 1895 plus tens
of thousands in foreign educational institutions, while the literacy rate increased
steadily throughout the nineteenth century—reaching perhaps 5 percent by 1876

and 10 percent by 1914. Said opened a school for training civil servants for the government; it had a modernized curriculum and boarding facilities for students from the provinces. Eighteen new professional schools or faculties were founded in Istanbul, teaching law, finance, fine arts, commerce, civil engineering, and veterinary medicine. Finally, the Imperial University in Istanbul opened in 1900.

The spread of western thought and the mixing together of pupils from many locales in Ottoman schools swelled the ranks of the discontented, some of whom fled as exiles to western Europe. Despite this, Abdulhamid continued to found many schools and even supplied the students with pocket money in hopes they would remain loyal to their patron. Perhaps because the teachers in the government medical and military schools had had the most European experience, their students were the most unsettled of all. In pursuing their studies many were exposed to French or German, which immediately opened to them the ideas of nineteenth-century Europe. As a result, army officers and medical men came to hold positions of political leadership all out of proportion to their numbers in society.

THE ARMENIAN QUESTION

Many Europeans disliked Abdulhamid most because of his treatment of the Armenian minority. As national aspirations had earlier stirred Serbs, Greeks, Romanians, and Bulgars, so some Armenians were moved in the latter half of the nineteenth century to seek a separate identity. Most of the Ottoman Empire's Armenians lived in its eastern Anatolian provinces; many Armenians were also subjects of the Russian Empire, living in the regions of the Caucasus close to the Ottoman border.

Muslim Turks and Kurds, Greeks, and Armenians in Anatolia were relatively prosperous between 1878 and 1911, as the peninsula's population increased by about one-half. Of the 17 million or so people living in Anatolia in 1911–1912, about 1.5 million were Armenians and about the same number were Greeks, while a large majority, about 14.5 million, were Muslims. Of the latter, most were Turkish speakers, but in the eastern provinces there were many Kurdish speakers as well.

Encouraged by the Russian government and stimulated by European and American missionaries, the three Armenian Christian religious communities—Gregorian, Catholic, and Protestant—and their respective educational institutions worked to develop national consciousness. Political societies flourished, and visions of an independent Armenia were encouraged by revolutionary committees in Russia.

Abdulhamid became frightened of the Armenian situation. He feared that six or more eastern provinces forming the Armenian highlands, where most of the Armenians were concentrated, and Little Armenia, or Cilicia, might become separated from the empire. To subdue the people, break their spirit, and forestall the possibility of an Armenian state, from 1894 to 1897 violent attacks upon the villages and massacres were perpetrated especially by Kurdish irregular Ottoman forces. Killings of Armenians occurred in many places, even in Istanbul. In all, perhaps 100,000 or more Armenians lost their lives.

These government atrocities had a very deep effect. The few revolutionary societies were wiped out; Armenians were entirely cowed; and many thoughtful Ottomans were genuinely depressed by their government's action. Charitable foreign aid societies provided some relief, but emigration appeared to be the only solution. Economic life in many areas was disrupted. The British, French, Italian, and American governments protested in vain against Ottoman treatment of Armenians. Newspapers, magazines, churches, and lecture halls echoed to stories of the "Terrible Turks." As a result, for several decades western governmental and diplomatic actions in the Ottoman Empire were guided to a considerable degree by unfriendly public opinion in the west.

CRETE

Anti-Ottoman feeling was already widespread on the island of Crete even before Abdulhamid became sultan. The quality of government on Crete varied greatly, since the distance of the island from Istanbul and the remoteness of certain parts of it left governors considerable autonomy. A small uprising occurred in 1841, and demands by local assemblies for reforms multiplied after the Hatt-i Humayun was issued. In the 1860s the better-educated subscribed to Greek nationalism, the first outburst for union with Greece taking place in 1866. Desultory fighting and Ottoman countermeasures persisted until 1870.

In 1885, a concentration of European naval units at Crete placed a damper on Greek preparations for war against the Ottomans and discouraged Cretan enthusiasts for union with Greece. Nonetheless, disorders of various origins continued to maintain tension. In 1896 and 1897, after bloody battles on the streets of Canea between Greeks and Turks brought matters to a head, Prince George of Greece cut off Ottoman reinforcements and the Great Powers occupied Canea. Boiling national sentiment in Athens compelled the king to initiate a war against the Ottoman Empire. The "Thirty Days' War," better known as the Greco-Ottoman War of 1897, was a series of Greek disasters. Only the intervention of the Great Powers saved Athens from an Ottoman occupation. The Peace of Istanbul, which restored the boundaries, placed a heavy indemnity upon Greece. Even though the Ottomans won the war, the European powers in Crete recognized Prince George as high commissioner under the suzerainty of the sultan. The Muslim minority gradually emigrated from Crete; by 1908, when union with Greece was finally achieved, less than 10 percent of the population was Muslim.

MACEDONIA

Problems with Armenians and in Crete were enough to keep the Ottoman state embroiled with the European powers and to stampede the sultan into some unwise and bloody decisions. It was the complex affairs of Macedonia, however, that sealed his fate and substantiated the charge that the Balkans were the powder keg of Europe. Populated by Turks, Bulgars, Greeks, Serbs, Albanians, Romanians, and other groups, Macedonia became the focus of the chauvinistic nationalisms rampant in the Balkans. A proviso of the Bulgarian Exarchate, permitting churches in Macedonia a choice between Greek and Bulgarian affiliation, touched off the explosion, as nationalism and religion interacted. Nationalistic schools, scholarships, newspapers, and books, as well as raids, village burning, kidnapping, and assassination, were among the tactics employed to achieve nationalist ends.

A committee purporting to advance a movement of "Macedonia for the Macedonians" was formed in Sofia, Bulgaria. It suggested the organization of an autonomous Macedonia with its own government at Salonica. The obvious intention was a repetition of the Eastern Rumelia episode and a union of Macedonia with Bulgaria. The proposition was rejected by all except the Bulgarians, and Macedonia sank into disorder and chaos. Ottoman police forces and the imposition of martial law were unable to cope with the situation. In 1903 the Mürzsteg Program, suggested by the Great Powers, went into effect. Accordingly, the British, French, Italians, Austrians, and Russians each policed an area of Macedonia. Although some regions were excluded from the agreement, European control was sufficiently successful to induce the Great Powers in 1908 to extend the Mürzsteg Program for another six years.

RAILWAYS AND ECONOMIC GROWTH

Despite international and internal turmoil, direct foreign investment in the Ottoman Empire tripled between 1890 and 1914, and France and Germany were the leaders in the development of the Ottoman infrastructure that ensued. It should be noted that Germany did not participate in the pacification of Macedonia. Until this era German imperial interests in the Ottoman Empire were negligible, since German leaders viewed the area as worthless to Germany, instead wanting only to keep Russia and Austria from fighting each other over the Balkans. But with the accession of Emperor Wilhelm II in 1888, Germany's role changed. In that year the Oriental Railway was completed from Vienna through to Istanbul, while a newly formed German syndicate, the Anatolian Railway Company, was granted a concession to construct a railroad from the Bosphorus to Ankara in central Anatolia; it was in operation by 1893.

German interest in the Ottoman Empire increased with the official visits of Emperor Wilhelm to Istanbul in 1889 and again in 1898; on the latter trip he went to Jerusalem and Damascus, where he uttered a famous speech promising Muslims that the German emperor would be their friend. But above all else, German interests focused upon railway concessions, which blossomed into the much-publicized Berlin-to-Baghdad venture.

Sultan Abdulhamid believed that railways would unify the empire and bring the central government more effective power over outlying regions. More of the resources of Anatolia and the Arab provinces would be developed, guaranteeing economic prosperity. The military capacity of the state would be improved and independence protected. Although railways and other such facilities like telegraph networks, ports, and roads were costly enterprises, it was thought that the advantageous results would amply repay the effort and money expended.

In the case of the Hijaz Railway, which linked Syria to Ottoman western Arabia, the Ottoman government itself financed and built a railroad between 1900 and 1908, reaching Medina by 1908. This project had a special religious character since it helped facilitate the Muslim pilgrimage to the holy cities. Other railways were foreign-built and foreign-owned. A favorite project of the sultan was building a railway from Istanbul's Asiatic suburbs to the Persian Gulf. British and French companies already had built and were operating several lines connecting Izmir with the Anatolian hinterland when the Anatolian Railway Company took over the British railroad from the Bosphorus to Izmit and extended it to Ankara. In 1896, other existing Asiatic railways included Jaffa-Jerusalem, and Beirut-Damascus-Aleppo lines. The government naturally desired to link all these together to form an integrated system, and also to push on to Iraq and the Persian Gulf.

The railway concessions usually called for a government subsidy to the construction firm, a guarantee of a minimum annual revenue, or both. For extending the line to Ankara, the sultan assured the Anatolian Railway Company at least 15,000 francs per kilometer annual revenue. This money was to come from the taxes of several provinces, the collection of these taxes being assigned to the Public Debt Administration.

Abdulhamid insisted that the railway should not approach the Mediterranean, where gunfire from enemy fleets could interrupt traffic. The Germans, therefore, proposed to proceed from Konya to Adana, then eastward to the valley of the Tigris near Mosul, and down the river past Baghdad, ending with a terminal on the Persian Gulf. Actually, British and French capitalists accepted the idea that the concession would be awarded to the Germans, and their governments were fully satisfied. In 1899 Britain safeguarded its military preponderance in the Gulf by an agreement to conduct all foreign relations for the shaikh of Kuwait; this permitted England to block the railroad's best terminus on the Persian Gulf and to gain an unofficial protectorate over Kuwait.

The Ottoman Empire paid tremendous sums not only for building the railway but also for guaranteeing annual operating receipts, as well as granting mineral rights on each side of the right-of-way. In October 1904, the first section was opened. Building cost less than was expected, and profits were high. In 1906 the European powers accepted a slight increase in tariffs to pay for further extensions. In 1909 a construction company was organized to undertake the second leg across difficult mountainous terrain. Certain bridges and tunnels in the Taurus Mountains were still not finished at the outbreak of war in 1914. Thus, a through route to northern Iraq or Syria from Anatolia was not opened completely to traffic until the post-World War I period.

The railways brought an agricultural revolution to Anatolia and Syria. New settlements were formed, greater amounts of produce were marketed, tax revenue from crops was increased, and more land was cultivated; grain and other heavy commodities were now much cheaper to ship. The companies initiated irrigation projects and agricultural training centers to stimulate traffic; in these details the Germans were the most efficient and thorough. By 1910 guarantees for annual receipts were no longer necessary and railways were even paying profits into the Ottoman treasury.

By opening up vast areas to inexpensive transportation, the railways changed local economic conditions and helped integrate many districts into the world economy. The railways also helped Ottoman growth in general, although an international economic depression between 1873 and 1896 lowered the world prices for Ottoman exports, especially grains. Ottomans enjoyed a long period of economic upturn from 1889 to 1911, except for temporary setbacks in 1894–1897 and 1907–1909. A sign of the times was the opening of modern bank offices in many distant provincial towns, although most credit to local enterprises was still offered by traditional lenders at high rates of interest. Immigrants continued to come into the domains of the sultan, including Muslims and Jews fleeing European Christian control and persecution in such areas as the Balkans, Algeria, Crimea, and the Caucasus. Emigration was also substantial, especially from Lebanon and Syria; hundreds of thousands of Christians (and some Muslims) from those regions went to the Americas, including the United States, seeking greater opportunities.

Despite the prosperity that was linked in large part to infrastructure development, the Ottoman government was constantly short of money to pay its troops, and the peasants who had to pay the agricultural tithe to tax farmers bore much of the burden of the empire's expenditures. By the 1900s, the Ottoman Empire had to pay about one-quarter of all spending for the interest and part of the principal of its debt, while expenditures on the military consumed 40 percent or more of the budget. Government civilian employment expanded to number about 500,000 people.

The railways helped bring not only economic growth but also German influence, which many Ottomans found to be a relief from British and French colonialism. Usually Germans were more tactful and considerate of Ottoman feelings. But German inroads into the Middle East frightened the British, who after 1904 and 1907 convinced the French and Russian governments to cooperate with them in trying to block German aspirations.

Sultan Abdulhamid II was able to block most of the European states who sought to gain direct control of the Ottoman Empire. After the disastrous losses at the beginning of his reign, little additional territory was taken from the Ottomans. Indeed, the only war the empire subsequently fought during his reign was marked by the victory over Greece. However, indirect European influence grew in the Ottoman Public Debt Administration, and in Macedonia and Crete, while most of the new railways were built by foreign capital. The sultan's Pan-Islamic policy became known to many foreign Muslims, but its chief effect was to reinforce the sense of loyalty of Ottoman Muslims.

Internally, the power of the central government was extended to many regions that had been part of the Ottoman Empire in name only; in Palestine, Iraq, and southern Syria, and in certain sections of Libya, the Hijaz, and Yemen Ottoman authority was established on a firmer basis. Even in autonomous Mount Lebanon the Ottomans managed to secure a long period of peace. But growing nationalism and political opposition threatened to overthrow the sultan. Autocratic reforms in such areas as railway construction were insufficient in the eyes of the young army officers who in 1908 sought a new path toward Ottoman reinvigoration.

References

Many readings touch upon this chapter. Those cited in Chapters 16, 21, 22, 23, and 25 are of particular value.

AKARLI, ENGIN D.: "Economic Policy and Budgets in Ottoman Turkey, 1876–1909." *Middle Eastern Studies* 28 (1992): 443–476.

————: *The Long Peace: Ottoman Lebanon, 1861–1920.* Berkeley: University of California Press, 1993. An excellent study of political history.

BERKES, NIYAZI: *The Development of Secularism in Turkey.* Montreal: McGill University Press, 1964. The most profound and stimulating book to appear on this subject.

DERINGIL, SELIM: "Legitimacy Structures in the Ottoman State: The Reign of Abdulhamid II (1876–1909)." *International Journal of Middle East Studies* 23 (1991): 345–359. Shows how the sultan tried to appeal to both Muslims and non-Muslims.

EARLE, EDWARD MEAD: *Turkey, the Great Powers and the Baghdad Railway: A Study in Imperialism.* New York: Macmillan, 1923. A classic.

EDIB, HALIDÉ: *Memoirs.* New York: Century, 1926. The life of a western-educated Ottoman Turkish woman.

GRAHAM-BROWN, SARAH: *Images of Women: The Portrayal of Women in Photography of the Middle East, 1860–1950.* New York: Columbia University Press, 1988. Numerous photographs combined with a superb analysis demonstrate many aspects of life and gender relations in the Ottoman Empire, Egypt, and Iran.

HADDAD, WILLIAM, AND WILLIAM OCHSENWALD, EDS.: *Nationalism in a Non-National State: The Dissolution of the Ottoman Empire.* Columbus: Ohio State University Press, 1977. Essays on the development of nationalism in the Ottoman Empire.

LANDAU, JACOB M.: *The Politics of Pan-Islam: Ideology and Organization.* Oxford, England: Clarendon Press, 1994. This authoritative study begins with Ottoman Pan-Islam but also discusses later developments.

MCCARTHY, JUSTIN: *Muslims and Minorities: The Population of Ottoman Anatolia and the End of the Empire.* New York: New York University Press, 1983. An excellent study of this very debatable issue; relies on census data from the Ottoman archives.

OCHSENWALD, WILLIAM: *The Hijaz Railroad.* Charlottesville: University Press of Virginia, 1980. Examines one aspect of Abdulhamid's Pan-Islamic policy and political centralization.

QUATAERT, DONALD: *Social Disintegration and Popular Resistance in the Ottoman Empire, 1881–1908: Reactions to European Economic Penetration.* New York: New York University Press, 1983. Excellent essays on various aspects of European economic investments in the Ottoman Empire. Especially valuable on the Anatolian railways.

SALT, JEREMY: *Imperialism, Evangelism and the Ottoman Armenians, 1878–1896.* London: Frank Cass, 1993. Using chiefly British and U.S. sources, this highly controversial work emphasizes the role of foreign promises and Armenian revolutionaries in provoking violent incidents.

The Young Turks
and Nationalism

In the years before 1908 a broad movement arose against the absolute power of Ottoman Sultan Abdulhamid II. This Young Turk opposition included a wide array of Ottomans, but its core consisted of Turkish-speaking Muslim army officers organized in the Committee of Union and Progress, who first limited the sultan's authority and then, in 1909, deposed him. During the short time from 1908 until the outbreak of World War I in 1914, the new government faced many foreign policy problems, including war with Italy and several wars in the Balkans. Domestically, there was a struggle for control of the central authority and a continuing process of defining the basic ideology of the state, with Ottoman, Islamic, and Turkish identities in dispute.

The ethnic nationalist separatism that had started with the independence of Greece and the autonomy of Serbia continued in the last years of the Ottoman Empire as Arabs and other Ottoman subjects of different linguistic, ethnic, and religious backgrounds agitated for new cultural and political roles. When the Committee of Union and Progress leaders learned of Arab nationalism, they sought to suppress the Arab secret societies, arguing that the desperate situation of the empire by 1914 necessitated unity.

SECRET SOCIETIES

The Young Turk revolution of 1908 was a reaction to the political absolutism and repression during the long reign of Sultan Abdulhamid II. Added to this was the growing westernization of certain Ottomans and the effect of contemporary European liberal ideas upon Ottoman youth. After the suspension of the constitution of 1876 dissident Ottomans living in exile in Europe dreamed of governmental reform at home.

In 1889, at the Istanbul Military Medical College, a group of students organized a secret society, the Ottoman Unity Society, which subscribed to nationalist ideas. Membership spread to other government schools. The sultan heard of the committee through his secret agents and took reprisals against the students. Nonetheless, the committee slowly grew. By 1896 more important elements of Ottoman society dominated the committee, and it attracted members who had belonged to such earlier groupings of rebellious spirits as the Young Ottomans and Young Turks.

Society members who escaped to Europe joined with other Ottoman malcontents. The best known of these was Ahmed Riza (1859–1930), whose newspaper became the society's official publication. At the same time, Murad Bey, a history teacher, fled to Paris and published a more popular newspaper. These two papers, which obtained easy entrance into the empire through foreign post offices, gathered a considerable following. The society's programs of action were as varied as its membership, but most of the members denounced any thought of overthrowing the reigning family; it preached reform and the value of science, promoted westernization, favored secularism, and advocated Ottoman nationalism and a strong government. Abdulhamid II should be removed, the constitution restored, and all would be well.

A series of arrests nipped in the bud the society's coup planned for 1896. The sultan only sent the leaders to remote parts of the empire, whence they slipped away to Paris and Geneva; by 1897 Abdulhamid enticed Murad Bey to Istanbul and shattered the now renamed Committee of Union and Progress.

Nevertheless, every class at the Military Academy was infected with the virus of revolution. At the General Staff Academy in 1905 a young leader named Mustafa Kemal (1881–1938; subsequently president of the Turkish Republic) was arrested as a revolutionary agitator on the very day he was commissioned. Later, when released and stationed in Damascus, he helped organize a secret revolutionary society among officers in Syria. Because Macedonia and its cosmopolitan center of Salonica were susceptible to revolutionary propaganda, Kemal sought a transfer there in 1907. In Salonica an influential secret society included in its earliest membership Mehmed Talat Bey, Fethi Bey, and Colonel Jemal Bey. This group spread rapidly throughout the European provinces. Pledged to overthrow Abdulhamid and establish a just government, the society drew to its ranks liberal and freethinking Turks, especially Bektashi and Melami Sufis, Freemasons, and military officers. When army officers fraternized with their European colleagues stationed in Macedonia, pursuant to the Mürzsteg Program of 1903, they compared their own unfavorable treatment with the pleasant life of European officers.

In 1907 fugitives from Salonica won over Ahmed Riza in Paris to the possibility of armed revolution. Abdulhamid's enemies joined them in a congress of Ottoman liberals, at which even an Armenian revolutionary society was represented. After this meeting the Paris and Salonica groups merged under the earlier-used name Committee of Union and Progress.

THE REVOLUTION

The real revolution began in the Middle East, not in Paris. Army mutinies became frequent in 1906, largely because of miserable conditions and arrears in pay. When rebellions were seen to bring immediate improvements, many more occurred in 1907, with civilians joining to protest against corrupt officials. In 1907 and 1908, there were crop failures in wide areas of the empire; the prices of grain and meat rose very sharply. Real income fell and inflation increased. Beginning in June 1908, mutinies broke out in Macedonia, as Russia and England planned additional reforms that might end Ottoman rule there. Both events hastened the action. Majors Enver and Niyazi and other officers took to the hills, and agents of the sultan were assassinated. Many officers demanded the restoration of the constitution. Messages from scores of cities and towns poured into Istanbul, and meetings of soldiers and civilians proclaimed the constitution. After a fateful telegram on July 23 announced that the units in Macedonia would march on Istanbul on behalf of the constitution, Abdulhamid reluctantly restored it and ordered elections for members of the Chamber of Deputies.

The summer of 1908 was spent in preparing for the elections and readjusting government ministries in accordance with the wishes of the Committee of Union and Progress. Even though the committee wanted to depose the sultan crowds in Istanbul cried out, "Long live the constitution!" and "Long live the sultan!" And Abdulhamid pretended that he was happy over the turn of events! The committee was not fooled but recognized that it did not have the force to depose him. In fact, no member of the committee even became a cabinet minister since it was believed then that a certain skill and rearing were required for conducting a minister's office, qualifications none of the committee members possessed. Abdulhamid, following the committee's wishes, appointed Kamil Pasha grand vizir, and thus the committee indirectly controlled state affairs; the palace was isolated.

On December 17, 1908, in the chambers where Midhat's parliament had met thirty-one years earlier, Abdulhamid opened parliament. Major religious and national groups of the empire were represented: attending were 147 Turks, 60 Arabs, 27 Albanians, 26 Greeks, 14 Armenians, 4 Jews, 5 Bulgars, 4 Serbs, and 1 Vlach. The best-organized group was the Macedonia branch of the Committee of Union and Progress, but it was far from having complete control of the situation. Ahmed Riza, who was chosen president of the Chamber of Deputies, served as a valuable figurehead for the anonymous members of the committee.

Members of parliament coalesced into three political groups. In addition to Union and Progress, there were the Liberal Unionists, who believed the solution to the ills of the empire could be found in creating a loosely federated state of locally autonomous provinces. The third group was the Muslim Association, which supported Pan-Islam and firm adherence to religious law. Union and Progress, however, showed its power in February 1909 by causing the downfall of the grand vizir on a motion of no confidence.

FAILURE OF THE COUNTERREVOLUTION

The Young Turks of the Revolution, as they were called, were inexperienced in government and few in number. Moreover, they harbored the illusion that the proclamation of the constitution would erase all evils. But it did not happen. Soldiers' pay was no better, and general conditions remained about the same. Social unrest ensued as Anatolian Railway Company workers and tens of thousands of other laborers went on strike, with both Muslims and non-Muslims often successful and acting together for economic goals. However, most of the people of the Ottoman Empire were not prepared to abandon the system of the millets and the political superiority of Muslims as compared with non-Muslims. "Under the same blue sky we are all equal; we glory in being Ottomans,"—these often-quoted words of Enver, one of the committee members who later rose to fame, stirred emotions but were not accepted as fact.

A counterrevolution struck on April 12, 1909, and leading members of Union and Progress went into hiding. Developing among lower-level ulama and soldiers in Istanbul, the counterrevolution was inspired by the cries of "Down with the constitution," "Down with the committee," and "Long live the shariah." Abdulhamid gave his blessing to the counterrevolution.

The Committee of Union and Progress, however, acted decisively. Mahmud Shevket Pasha, commander of the army in Macedonia, was invited to march on Istanbul to defend the constitution. On April 24, Istanbul was occupied, and a few days later parliament deposed Abdulhamid, having obtained approval from the shaikh al-Islam. The new sultan, Mehmed V, a mild gentleman born in 1844, declared he had not read a newspaper in the last twenty years. He had been completely surrounded by his brother's spies and had lost all initiative. He was the perfect constitutional monarch for the committee. And the constitution of 1876 was amended to give greater authority to the parliament, which was dominated by the committee.

WAR WITH ITALY OVER LIBYA

The task before the new government would have staggered the most experienced administrators. Internal problems commanded the highest priority as many bureaucrats and army officers sympathetic to the old order were purged, but foreign affairs and war rose to occupy the minds of the committee and consumed the meager funds available. In October 1908, Bulgaria cut all ties with the sultan, Austria-Hungary announced annexation of Bosnia and Herzegovina, and Crete revolted and declared union with Greece.

A far greater shock was delivered by the Italian ultimatum of September 1911, demanding that the Ottoman Empire in effect cede Libya to Italy. The Italian government had been seeking overseas territories in Eritrea and Ethiopia, and had secured some economic influence in Ottoman Libya even before 1911. After Italy declared war, Ottoman forces were driven from the coastal areas of Libya, although guerrilla warfare continued in the interior. Because of its naval superiority Italy was able to occupy Rhodes and the Dodecanese Islands and shelled the Dardanelles. Sentiment ran high in the empire. Enver Bey and Fethi Bey, both prominent members of Union and Progress and military attachés in Berlin and Paris, respectively, along with other officers of later distinction like Mustafa Kemal, made their way with difficulty to Libya, where they organized and for a time led a resistance movement in cooperation with various groups, including the Sanusi Sufi organization.

An Ottoman victory was hopeless, and when it appeared that the Balkan states were plotting a common war against the Ottoman Empire, the Ottomans hastily signed a treaty with Italy on October 18, 1912. Under the terms of the treaty the Ottoman Empire withdrew from Libya, while Italy withdrew from the Aegean Islands. Italy agreed to assume a share of the Ottoman debt, and the authority of the caliph was recognized in Libya. Italy, however, refused to evacuate its island conquests, while the Ottomans continued to incite guerrilla warfare in Libya. By 1914 Italy had control of most of Libya.

THE COMMITTEE OF UNION AND PROGRESS

Shortly after the deposition of Abdulhamid in 1909, the Committee of Union and Progress held a party congress and established a central executive committee that remained active until the party was dissolved at the end of World War I. The executive committee ruled the party and, when the party was in power, the government and the ministers. Provincial branches of the committee consisted of local notables, professionals, merchants, guild leaders, landowners, and soldiers, mostly Muslims and Turkish-speakers.

The many activities of the Union and Progress party began to tell on its popularity. Even before the defeat by the Italians, to stop a defeat in the Chamber of Deputies the committee had Mehmed V dissolve the chamber and call for a new election. The new chamber was also closed in August 1912, when radical young leaders of Union and Progress attacked a cabinet composed of men of more experience and prestige. Two ministries largely representing the Liberal Unionist party tried to curb the power of the Union and Progress group. The government, however, succumbed to a coup d'état by the Union and Progress party in January 1913, when extremists rebelled at surrendering Edirne to the Balkan states. From that moment until the end of World War I leaders of Union and Progress maintained firm control over the government.

The desires of Union and Progress flowed out in every direction. Their intention was to examine all the institutions of their society, changing any that had become outdated. The Finance Ministry was reorganized, tax farming was abolished, and strikes were outlawed. In education and social services reformers such as Ziya Gökalp (1876–1924) and Tevfik Fikret took the helm. General Liman von Sanders headed a German mission to transform the army under the direction of Enver. Secular law was gaining as the ulama were brought under the control of the state.

The Committee of Union and Progress changed the legal rights of women, and magazines and newspapers increasingly published essays dealing with the status of women. Women gained the right to work in the postal offices and telephone exchanges. During World War I reformers achieved basic changes in marriage laws, which now came under the Ministry of Justice. The writer and educator Halidé Edib (Adivar) and other women founded several women's organizations, while in 1916 the University in Istanbul admitted women students.

These Union and Progress leaders sought to improve the well-being of the great mass of Ottoman subjects. They deplored their poor quality of life and wished to give pride and dignity to the people. They recognized that the empire remained an exporter of foodstuffs and raw materials, and an importer of manufactured goods, with few heavy industries. They wanted to create a national consciousness; however, society lacked ethnic, linguistic, and national homogeneity, and there were religions by the score. Village, nomadic, and urban cultures and manners were so foreign to each other that little overlap seemed to exist.

OTTOMAN, ISLAMIC, AND TURKISH NATIONALISMS

The sociologist and essayist Ziya Gökalp and his friends debated these problems of early nationalism and at various times emphasized one factor over another. Because of the complexities, three overlapping yet distinct types of nationalism developed: Ottomanism, Pan-Islamism, and Pan-Turkism. Ottomanism possessed the greatest attraction in the earlier days of the revolution. It was based on acknowledging the mixed ethnic character of the Ottoman Empire, while the role of religion was downplayed. Language was less of a barrier as Turkish had long been the lingua franca of the Ottoman Empire. Ottomanist nationalists noted the common history and culture that upper-class Ottomans shared, whether Turks, Greeks, Arabs, Kurds, or Armenians, and also that peasants and artisans of various backgrounds were alike in many respects. Ottomanism was fashionable; thus, the rejoicing of many groups when the revolution came in 1908.

But ethnicity soon triumphed. Often non-Turks in the Chamber of Deputies voted as a bloc in opposition to the Turks. So-called programs for Ottomanization were branded as attempts to Turkify all others. By 1910 such moves provoked a revolt in Albania, where the tribes and nationalists resisted fiercely. Equality in the army, holding government posts, and paying taxes went against the customs and views of too many groups in the empire to be accepted voluntarily for very long. As soon as Ottomanism was advocated and practiced overtly, differences were highlighted and proved insurmountable.

The next move was toward religion and Pan-Islamism. Abdulhamid II had sought greater rapport among Muslim states and peoples and hoped to strengthen the position of the empire by building wider support for the Ottoman sultans as caliphs. Pan-Islamic missions were sent to Kabul, and Abdulhamid subsidized Jamal al-Din al-Afghani (1839–1897) in his work of preaching for reform in Islam. Many Turks in their nationalist enthusiasm found some satisfaction in Pan-Islamic dreams, even though most of the Committee of Union and Progress leaders were not very pious. Unfortunately, Islam as the basis of the state was seen as implicitly discriminatory against non-Muslim minorities inside the empire. Full responsibility for the atrocious massacres of Armenians in Cilicia in 1909 was never ascertained, but some blame should probably be shouldered by Ottomans who were Pan-Islamic. The measures of a Pan-Islamic nature adopted by the Union and Progress party from April 1909 to July 1912 led, at least in part, to its temporary downfall.

The third form of nationalism appeared in Pan-Turkism (Pan-Turanism), which espoused the cultural connections and political union of all Turkish peoples, including those in central Asia. The main efforts of the Pan-Turkists were devoted to the policy of Turkification of all non-Turks and to the task of instilling a national, historical, and linguistic common feeling among all classes of Turks within the Ottoman Empire. In literature, music, and cultural matters generally, Turkish nationalists espoused reforms that would emphasize what they saw as the Turkish core of Ottoman identity. To accomplish this the Committee of Union and Progress sponsored a program of adult education aimed at developing a national consciousness.

ARAB CULTURAL NATIONALISM

In the many Ottoman provinces where Arabic speakers formed a majority of the population at the opening of the twentieth century, the question of an Arab nationalism distinct from Ottoman or Egyptian patriotism was in the minds of only a very few. However, a cultural revival using Arabic had been under way for some decades. The cultural and the later political aspects of Arab nationalism at first affected mostly urban upper-class Ottoman subjects, especially those most in contact with Europeans and European thought. Initially, peasants, artisans, and nomads were largely untouched by both cultural and political nationalism.

In Syria and Lebanon, although Jesuits had arrived in the seventeenth century to teach in Maronite and Catholic communities, little rejuvenation of Arab thought occurred until after 1820, when American Presbyterian missionaries in Beirut organized schools that provided competition with Catholic institutions. Girls' schools were also opened. From its founding in 1866, the Syrian Protestant College (known later as the American University of Beirut) played an important role in training Muslim and Christian Arabs. Catholic missionaries, largely from France, settled in Syria in great numbers; in 1875 the University of St. Joseph in Beirut opened. Later, Ottoman and Egyptian state schools played an even more important role than the missionary institutions in spreading secular and patriotic concepts.

Numerous writers, thinkers, and teachers influenced the growth of Arab nationalism. Three of them were Christian Arabs from Lebanon. Nasif al-Yaziji taught Arabic near Beirut until his death in 1871. His masterly writings in Arabic pioneered a style, manner, and vocabulary suitable for expressing the life and ideas of the modern world and paved the way for an Arabic renaissance. Butrus al-Bustani (1819–1883) assisted American Protestant missionaries in translating the Bible into Arabic. His dictionary, encyclopedia, and periodicals helped to create a modern Arabic prose that could present the concepts of contemporary thought in language simple enough for use in newspapers; he is the father of so-called newspaper Arabic. He was at the same time both a Syrian Arab patriot and an Ottoman loyalist, and seemingly saw no contradiction between these two positions. The third Lebanese Christian was Jurji Zaydan (1861–1914), whose historical novels built a modern romantic Arab image of the Arab past.

In Egypt, still nominally part of the Ottoman Empire even after its occupation by Britain in 1882, an educational and literary renaissance was also under way. Cairo drew many intellectuals from every part of the Arab world. Books and newspapers published there spurred nationalism. British control ironically freed nationalists from the Ottoman sultan's surveillance. Egypt, along with France and Switzerland, became a haven for exiled Arab nationalists. One of these exiles was Abd al-Rahman Kawakibi of Aleppo (1854–1902), who wrote *Umm al-Qura,* a work on the future of Islamic society, and *The Attributes of Tyranny,* published in Cairo. Together these works analyzed the decrepit world of Arab society and called for a return to early Islam. Kawakibi attacked the ignorance of the masses and the obscurantism of the ulama who dominated the educational field. He was also one of the first to separate Arab national revival from Pan-Islamism.

An incomplete tally in 1913 showed 118 Arabic-language newspapers in the Ottoman Empire, excluding Egypt. In the last half of the nineteenth century, Arabic presses in several Ottoman cities were publishing original works and many translations of European books. From outside the empire ideas of patriotism, nationalism, Islamic reform, European science, and modernization were being developed, while the threat of expanding western Christian imperialism made new ideologies an urgent matter.

THE BIRTH OF ARAB NATIONALISM

For centuries Muslims in the Middle East had felt superior to westerners. After the Napoleonic Wars economic, cultural, military, and political contacts between the Middle East and western Europe expanded greatly, and the wealth and power of Europe became evident. Nineteenth-century thinkers such as Nasif al-Yaziji and Butrus al-Bustani put their faith in an educational revival as a means of catching up. Differences between Arabs and Turks were barely considered. Islam and Islamic civilization were regarded as the valid bases of the society that had produced the wondrous ages of the past. Accepting the fact that Arabic was the language of religion and Turkish the language of government and politics, the early thinkers supported the Ottoman Empire and argued that it would be necessary only to borrow certain things from the west, such as the natural and physical sciences (as in the case of the Darwinian theory of evolution), and the gap would close.

As the years passed and the obvious gap between the strength of the Middle East and the west widened, more penetrating questions began to be raised about Middle Eastern culture. Al-Afghani, his Egyptian pupil Muhammad Abduh (1849–1905), and the modernist Muhammad Rashid Rida (1865–1935) asserted that Islam was in a deplorable condition because over the centuries society had corrupted true original Islam. They believed in Pan-Islam and that Muslims should exercise reason and examine the bases of faith so as to be truly modern. None of these reformers was prepared at this time to overturn the Ottoman caliph-sultan.

Political changes led the way for conservative Ottomanism to become modernist Ottomanism, which in turn was transformed into Arabism. Rida, Kawakibi, and other Arab nationalists countered the Pan-Islamists by proclaiming that Islam was only one of the infinite glories of the Arab nation. They favored religious toleration among Arabs and called for ejecting alien influences from the Arab scene. After the revolution of 1908 many Arab thinkers became suspicious of Ottomanism and Pan-Islamism, though most Arab leaders remained loyal to the Ottoman Empire until the end of World War I.

THE YOUNG TURKS AND ARAB NATIONALISM

The program of the Young Turks before the counterrevolution in 1909 appealed to many Arab leaders, who saw in it the destruction of Abdulhamid's centralization policies. They subscribed to the program of the Committee of Union and Progress because they translated it to mean decentralization of the empire and equality of Arab with Turk.

An early test of the judgment of the Committee of Union and Progress in regard to policy in the Arab lands arose when they insisted that Abdulhamid designate Sharif Husain of the prophet Muhammad's Hashimite family as prince of Mecca. Although Husain had resided quietly for fifteen years in Istanbul, the sultan astutely judged the man to have ambitions to rule an autonomous Arab state and warned the Committee of Union and Progress of the folly of their recommendation. In September 1908, however, Abdulhamid appointed Husain to the post.

After the counterrevolution of 1909, centralization of government, Turkification, and secularism became veiled objectives of the committee. As political societies were suppressed, the Arabs, among others, went underground. Here, then, was the birth of passionate Arabism among the new professionals who were teachers, students, journalists, civil servants, military officers, lawyers, and local notables. Many such Arabs feared the loss of Arab Libya to Italy in 1911–1912 indicated that the Ottoman Empire could no longer protect other Arab provinces from European imperialism.

In Palestine, another source of Arab nationalism appeared in addition to the ethnic, cultural, intellectual, and political factors just outlined. Jewish nationalism, or Zionism, created a strong backlash as Arab Muslims and Christians who composed a majority of the total population in Ottoman Palestine felt increasingly threatened by Jewish settlers and their foreign supporters. Zionism had originated in Europe during the nineteenth century in response to new, more liberal circumstances for western European Jews, and also as a reaction against the harsh repressions directed against eastern European Jews. Some Russian, Polish, and other Jews argued that it was imperative to reestablish themselves in their ancient homeland and religious center of Palestine, where they could fully develop themselves culturally, politically, and spiritually. The possibility of massive numbers of Jewish settlers arriving in the area was disturbing to Ottoman officials and Arab residents alike, who feared that in the long run the Zionists might aim at gaining independence from the empire. As Zionists actually settled in parts of Ottoman Palestine, their aspirations became more real and substantial. Ottoman Jews were divided in their views of Zionism, with many favoring it and others opposed.

Palestinian and other Arab representatives in the Ottoman parliament after 1908 joined the Arabic press in harsh criticism of what they felt might be a Zionist goal for unilateral control of the land. Since the Ottoman authorities usually shared the views of the Arab nationalists on this question, many barriers were placed in the way of Zionism in Palestine before World War I—barriers that were often evaded with the help of European powers.

ARAB SECRET SOCIETIES

As usual in the development of ethnic nationalism, a welter of small societies sprang into being among Arabs in Istanbul, Damascus, Beirut, Cairo, Baghdad, Aleppo, and other Arab cities. An important one in Istanbul was the Literary Club, which disavowed political activities; it was a meeting place and library for Arabs living at the capital, but it also served as a forum for discussing political philosophy; guest speakers included Arab members of the Ottoman parliament and even the leaders of the Committee of Union and Progress.

Another important open group was the Ottoman Decentralization party, established in Cairo in 1912 by Syrian Arab Muslim and Christian public figures. Its objectives were to mobilize Arab and Turkish public opinion for the organization of an Ottoman Empire based on a federal system. The Decentralization party stressed party machinery and enjoyed partial success during the last half of 1912 when the Union and Progress party was out of power. Lebanese patriots who wanted to enhance the special status of Mount Lebanon within the empire worked together to agitate for new policies by the central authorities.

One interesting secret society was called al-Qahtaniya. (Qahtan was a legendary ancestor of the Arabs.) It advocated the creation of a dual Turko-Arab empire, much like the Austro-Hungarian Empire, in which "unity" of the two peoples could be attained by "separation." As the Turkish leaders of Union and Progress guided affairs definitely along paths of Turkification, aspirations for a Turko-Arab accommodation died.

Suppression by the Committee of Union and Progress drove many Arabs abroad. Like the Turks a decade earlier, they flocked to Paris, where in 1904 Najib Azuri (d. 1916) had already begun to write criticisms of the Ottoman Empire. In 1909 Arab refugees and students formed the society known as al-Fatat (Youth). A secret society, al-Fatat eventually rejected the idea of any integration within the empire and worked for full Arab freedom and independence. It became the most widespread and effective force among Arabs, moving its headquarters to Beirut and then Damascus.

In view of these activities and the Arab enthusiasm they evoked, the Union and Progress leaders adopted stringent measures to combat them. A committee of reform in Beirut in 1913 publicly announced a program for Arab home rule and won such wide acclaim that the government suppressed it. Under the leadership of al-Fatat a congress of Arabs held in Paris adopted the platforms of the Decentralization party and the committee of reform. The results of the congress were ostensibly accepted by an imperial decree in 1913 incorporating the declarations as stated policy in the Arab provinces. However, the reforms remained unenforced, and the Arabs believed they had been duped.

Partially in reply, an Arab, Major Aziz Ali al-Misri (1879–1965) of the Ottoman general staff, initiated a new society called al-Ahd (the Covenant). Aziz Ali had been a member of Union and Progress before 1908 and had won honors in the march on Istanbul in 1909, in a military mission to Yemen in 1910, and in the war against Italy in Libya. Al-Ahd was composed exclusively of army officers and became for the military what al-Fatat was for civilians. It had members in Beirut, Damascus, and Baghdad. In 1914, the Young Turks arrested Aziz Ali and condemned him to death. Public opinion became so indignant, especially in Egypt, that the British protested to Istanbul. Aziz Ali was pardoned and sailed for Egypt as a public hero, to lead al-Ahd from Cairo. Any hope that the Union and Progress leaders had for Arab nationalist cooperation and participation was now dispelled. Ottomanism and Pan-Islamism for Arab leaders disintegrated in the face of an obvious drift to Turkish nationalism shown in the actions of the radical Committee of Union and Progress.

THE ARAB PRINCES

Not only did the Ottoman Turks have difficulty with Arab nationalists and their many patriotic societies but they also discovered that Arab semiautonomous rulers employed every means to resist centralization. Unsuccessful expeditions were sent to bring the inner sections of Yemen, then under the rule of Imam Yahya, and Asir, ruled by Muhammad al-Idrisi, to heel. Tiring of the continual drain on resources, the central government reached an accord with the two, granting them many local powers. In central Arabia the Istanbul authorities found their support of the Rashid family unavailing against the young Saudi ruler Abd al-Aziz, who drove the Ottomans from the rich province of al-Hasa in eastern Arabia in 1913.

Had it not been for the Hijaz Railway, which connected Syria with Medina, Ottoman authority over Sharif Husain in Mecca would have been even weaker. However, the Hijaz was too dependent upon religion and the pilgrimage to welcome secular Arab nationalism. Husain did find substantial local help in his opposition to Turkification, centralization of power, the attempted introduction of conscription, the extension of the Hijaz Railway to Mecca, and the Europeanization espoused by the Committee of Union and Progress. An Ottoman garrison stationed at Mecca rendered overt revolt foolhardy without considerable strength and careful planning. Early in 1914, Prince Abd Allah, Husain's second son, an Arab member of the Ottoman parliament, hinted vaguely to the British as he passed through Cairo that his father would be open to rebellion against the Ottomans. These discreet overtures indicated that Husain was considering a treaty similar to that which the British had with Arab princes in the Persian Gulf area. Such treaties provided for British recognition of the Arab ruler's independence and protection, in exchange for British conduct of all foreign relations.

Suspicion that Husain was harboring these intentions drifted back to Istanbul, where the authorities planned to build the Hijaz Railway south of Medina toward Mecca and assigned a new governor to the Hijaz with instructions to destroy Husain. In the spring of 1914, the Ottomans came to understand that Husain had consolidated his position with the townspeople and tribes of the Hijaz; the new governor was ordered to make peace, and the railway extension was stopped.

Probably no substantial connection existed between the various Arab princes in the Arabian peninsula on the one hand and the revolutionary societies of the Ottoman Arab world on the other, although writers such as Rashid Rida tried to build up mutual cooperation. However, the princes and the nationalists were too different in beliefs and circumstances to make joint action possible. Some foreign governments were friendly to the secret societies; British and French officials in Beirut and Egypt gave encouragement to them.

When World War I began in 1914 the Union and Progress triumvirate realized that defection in Arab provinces was likely and that the loyalty of Arab officers was questionable. Yet Enver, Talat, and Jemal hoped that divisions of interest among the Arabs and a strong commitment to Islam would save the day. Their hope was justified. Many members of the secret societies in the urban centers were opposed to the autocratic rule of the Arab princes. Most Arabs remained loyal to the Ottoman Empire, either because they felt an emotional loyalty to it or because they feared its destruction would lead to the dissolution of the only remaining barrier against European imperialism. Equally apprehensive were the various princes, each of the other. But it was only a question of time before Arab nationalism would flare into the open. World War I hastened the day of Arab revolt.

THE BALKAN WARS

Other non-Turkish communities also bitterly resisted Turkification drives. In several districts in Anatolia trouble arose with Greeks and Armenians, whose boycotts and attacks caused serious dislocations of commerce. A violent storm broke in Albania, when in the process of Turkification the government took steps to enforce a decree forbidding the possession of arms. Albanians also objected to a census, taxes, and the drafting of young men to serve in Yemen (which was called the graveyard of Ottoman armies). The Albanian rebellion was quelled early in 1911 after diplomatic intervention by Montenegro and a grant of considerable local autonomy.

Concessions to the Albanians, however, aroused hopes among other nationalities; the Macedonians particularly hoped for the establishment of a regime similar to the one in Eastern Rumelia. These concessions also excited the ambitions and jealousies of officials in Greece, Bulgaria, Serbia, and Montenegro, who declared war on the Ottoman Empire in October 1912, after agreeing on the division of Macedonia. Within a month after the start of the war these allies, who possessed a decided numerical advantage over the Ottoman armies, overran most of Ottoman Europe. Many Muslims left the territories that came under the control of the European Christian states and fled to Ottoman land.

In December an armistice was signed and the five belligerents met in London to negotiate peace. The European powers demanded the cession of Edirne to Bulgaria, but when it became apparent that Kamil Pasha, the grand vizir, and the Liberal Unionists were willing to pay that price for peace, Enver Bey and about 200 members of Union and Progress staged a successful coup d'état. They assassinated the minister of war and returned to power. In February 1913 war was resumed. Edirne fell, and the Greek navy defeated the Ottoman forces outside the Dardanelles and occupied a number of the Aegean Islands.

In April a second armistice was arranged, and a peace treaty signed in London ceded to the victors almost all Ottoman European possessions and consigned to the Great Powers questions arising from the transfer of territory among the Balkan states. Then the establishment of Albania upon the insistence of the Great Powers goaded Greece and Serbia to demand a revision of their previous understandings with Bulgaria. Failure to reach agreement brought war between Bulgaria and Serbia on June 30, 1913. Greece, Montenegro, and then Romania entered the war against Bulgaria. In July 1913, the Ottomans invaded Thrace and Enver Bey reoccupied Edirne. The Treaty of Bucharest ended the Second Balkan War in August, although a separate settlement in Istanbul between Turkey and Bulgaria, which restored Edirne to the Ottoman Empire, was not drawn up until September.

When the Libyan and Balkan wars ended, the Ottomans had lost almost all their possessions in Europe and North Africa. The empire had ceded about a quarter of its population and 10 percent of its territory, including lands it had ruled for hundreds of years!

THE TRIUMVIRATE

The radical wing of the Committee of Union and Progress had seized power in January 1913, and Mahmud Shevket Pasha became grand vizir. But his assassination in June and the succeeding grand vizirate of Said Halim Pasha, a mild and weak Egyptian prince, permitted the reins of government to fall into the hands of a triumvirate of the committee: Talat, Enver, and Jemal.

Talat Bey (1874–1921), now minister of the interior, was born of a poor family near Edirne and began work as a telegraph operator in the government office at Salonica. Possessing a brilliant mind, he was one of the organizers of the revolutionary movement in Macedonia and served as minister of the interior in several cabinets. He was a dedicated man who stayed poor and remained modest throughout his career. Ruthless in his tactics, he made a distinction between personal and national morality, believing that many acts that would be entirely immoral and cruel if perpetrated by an individual were perfectly moral if performed in the interests of the state.

Enver Bey (1881–1922), minister of war, came from a lower-middle-class family and received a military education. Catapulted to public attention by his defiance of Abdulhamid and his flight to the Macedonian hills in the first stage of the revolution in 1908, Enver loved the heroics of Turkish nationalism and won fame in the war in Libya against Italy. He was a man of action and hasty decisions. As an attaché in Berlin, Enver fell under the spell of Prussian militarism and believed in the superiority of the German military machine. He, more than any other, brought the Ottomans into World War I as German allies. As he rose to power, he became vain—a development many of his former friends deplored. As one remarked: "Enver Pasha has destroyed Enver Bey." An advocate of Pan-Turkism, Enver died pursuing this policy in central Asia after the end of World War I.

Jemal Pasha (1872–1922), governor of Istanbul and later minister of the navy, was an early member of Union and Progress. He came from an old Ottoman family and had been a Pan-Islamist, but in the days of the triumvirate he became an ardent Turkish nationalist. The weakest of the three, Jemal served as a kind of policeman for the Young Turks, maintaining discipline and holding the faltering in line.

To the day of the entry of the Ottoman Empire into World War I, the young and rash triumvirate ruled with a strong hand. Disobedient party members were punished, opponents were eliminated, and uncertainty and terror returned to government circles. Thus, even before the carnage of World War I, the internal violence and external wars of the period from 1908 to 1914 created an atmosphere seemingly so threatening to the existence of the state as to justify extreme repression and radical reform.

The rejoicing that had greeted the Young Turks in 1908 faded away by 1914. While the Committee of Union and Progress did succeed in dominating the central government, its military leaders lost several wars and a great deal of territory during this short time. Continuing uncertainty about the allegiances linking the people to the state also weakened the regime. However, Arab nationalists and other ethnic groups seeking independence or autonomy had as yet little popular support among most of the subjects of the sultan. *Din ve devlet*—religion and the state, or Islam and the sultanate of the House of Osman—still commanded the loyalty of most of the population, except for some of the religious minorities who became increasingly alienated by the Young Turks. In Egypt, however, the fiction of Ottoman overlordship had been undermined since 1882 by the reality of British supervision. The already somewhat separate path of historical development Egypt had pursued since Mehmet Ali's days diverged even more from the central Ottoman experience in the three decades before the outbreak of World War I.

References

Many references mentioned in preceding chapters are important for this chapter; those of particular note are in Chapters 22, 23, 25, and 26.

AHMAD, FEROZ: *The Young Turks: The Committee of Union and Progress in Turkish Politics, 1908–1914.* Oxford, England: Clarendon Press, 1969. This important study points out that the committee did not hold absolute power during this period and was able to adapt to altering circumstances.

AHMIDA, ALI ABDULLATIF: *The Making of Modern Libya: State Formation, Colonization, and Resistance, 1830–1932.* Albany: State University of New York Press, 1994.

ANTONIUS, GEORGE: *The Arab Awakening: The Story of the Arab National Movement.* New York: Hamilton, 1938. Still a key work on this topic; its controversial conclusions have been revised by many scholars, as in the works of Dawn and Khalidi, cited below.

ARAI, MASAMI: *Turkish Nationalism in the Young Turk Era.* Leiden: Brill, 1992. Illustrates nationalist thinking through a study of periodicals.

CLEVELAND, WILLIAM L.: *The Making of an Arab Nationalist: Ottomanism and Arabism in the Life and Thought of Sati' al-Husri.* Princeton, N.J.: Princeton University Press, 1971. The life of an Ottoman Arab who chose to be an Arab nationalist after World War I.

DAWN, C. ERNEST: *From Ottomanism to Arabism: Essays on the Origins of Arab Nationalism.* Urbana: University of Illinois Press, 1973. Shows the subtle aspects of the Arab revolt and its relationship to Arab nationalism, bringing out many of the misconceptions about it.

DIVINE, DONNA ROBINSON: *Politics and Society in Ottoman Palestine: The Arab Struggle for Survival and Power.* Boulder, Colo.: Lynne Rienner, 1994. A useful summary for the period 1800 to 1918.

DURI, A. A.: *The Historical Formation of the Arab Nation: A Study in Identity and Consciousness.* Translated by Lawrence I. Conrad. London: Croom Helm, 1987. Traces the emergence of Arabic, Arab-Islamic culture, and Arab patriotism.

GAWRYCH, GEORGE: "Tolerant Dimensions of Cultural Pluralism in the Ottoman Empire: The Albanian Community, 1800–1912." *International Journal of Middle East Studies* 15 (1983): 519–536.

———: "The Culture and Politics of Violence in Turkish Society, 1903–14." *Middle Eastern Studies* 22 (1986): 307–330. An enlightening essay on the political and military problems of the time, including a discussion of the psychological atmosphere and literary developments.

HADDAD, MAHMOUD: "The Rise of Arab Nationalism Reconsidered." *International Journal of Middle East Studies* 26 (1994): 201–222. A careful evaluation of Young Turk policies and Arab reactions to them.

HANIOGLU, M. ŞÜKRÜ: *The Young Turks in Opposition.* New York: Oxford University Press, 1995. A detailed examination of the ideology, organization, and actions of the early Committee of Union and Progress from 1889 to 1902.

HOURANI, ALBERT H.: *Arabic Thought in the Liberal Age, 1798–1939.* New York: Oxford University Press, 1962. Brilliant, authoritative treatment of Arabic thought and Arab nationalism.

KARAKISHLA, YAVUZ SELIM: "The 1908 Strike Wave in the Ottoman Empire." *Turkish Studies Association Bulletin* 16 (1992): 153–177. Examination of the causes, events, and consequences of the strikes of 1908.

KHALIDI, RASHID: "Arab Nationalism: Historical Problems in the Literature." *American Historical Review* 96 (1991): 1363–1373. This excellent bibliographic essay is a good beginning point for reading about the topic.

KHALIDI, RASHID, ET AL., EDS.: *The Origins of Arab Nationalism.* New York: Columbia University Press, 1991. Essays on all aspects of the topic, concentrating on Syria, Iraq, and the Hijaz.

KHOURY, PHILIP S.: *Urban Notables and Arab Nationalism: The Politics of Damascus, 1860–1920.* Cambridge, England: Cambridge University Press, 1983. An analysis of the governing elite and who among them came to be Arab nationalists and why.

KUSHNER, DAVID: *The Rise of Turkish Nationalism, 1876–1908.* London: Frank Cass, 1977. This is a brief study of the intellectual origins of Turkish nationalism in the last decades of the nineteenth century.

MANDEL, NEVILLE J.: *The Arabs and Zionism Before World War I.* Berkeley: University of California Press, 1976. An excellent study of a very complex relationship that also involved the Ottoman government.

PARLA, TAHA: *The Social and Political Thought of Ziya Gökalp, 1876–1924.* Leiden: Brill, 1985. Also discusses his life, political career, and contemporary relevance.

QUATAERT, DONALD: *Manufacturing and Technology Transfer in the Ottoman Empire, 1800–1914.* Istanbul and Strasbourg: Isis and Strasbourg University, 1992. Excellent chapters on low-level technology, industrial factories, and silk manufacturing.

SHARABI, HISHAM: *Arab Intellectuals and the West: The Formative Years, 1875–1914.* Baltimore: Johns Hopkins University Press, 1970. Explains the intellectual and ideological background of modernization and transformation in the Arab world.

TAUBER, ELIEZER: *The Emergence of the Arab Movements.* London: Frank Cass, 1993. Thorough surveys of each group and analysis of their views and effectiveness.

ZEINE, ZEINE N.: *The Emergence of Arab Nationalism.* 2d ed. Delmar, N.Y.: Caravan Books, 1973.

ZÜRCHER, ERIK JAN: *The Unionist Factor: The Role of the Committee of Union and Progress in the Turkish National Movement, 1905–1926.* Leiden: Brill, 1984. A stimulating, revisionist interpretation that stresses the continuity between the Union and Progress period and that of the Turkish Republic.

British Occupation
of Egypt and the Sudan

From 1882 to 1914 Britain occupied Egypt, chiefly to control the Suez Canal and to stop Egypt from falling into the hands of any other country. Despite maintaining the fiction of Ottoman sovereignty and the governorship of Mehmet Ali's descendants, Britain gradually consolidated its military occupation, domination of civilian government, and influence on the economy. Opposition to the British presence increased, and Egyptian nationalism came to have a considerable impact on political and cultural affairs.

STABILIZATION OF BRITISH CONTROL

The British army occupied Cairo and took control of Egypt in September 1882. The British administration presumed that its occupation would be of short duration, hoping to put Khedive Tawfiq (r. 1879–1892) in a powerful position and then to withdraw. But the British cabinet argued that certain aspects of Egyptian government needed to be stabilized before evacuation was possible. For this purpose Lord Dufferin, British ambassador to Istanbul, was sent to Egypt to advise the khedive in establishing authority and in arranging for "the well-being of all classes of the population." Dufferin found Egypt in chaos. Colonel Ahmad Urabi, the national hero, who had surrendered to the British, had been turned over to the frightened and vindictive khedive for trial. Urabi was found guilty of treason and sentenced to be executed, but the British intervened and insisted instead that he be exiled to Sri Lanka.

Lord Dufferin spent months forcing changes in the Egyptian government. First the army and the police were reorganized in order to guarantee control of passage through the Suez Canal. A new Egyptian army, provisionally set at 6000, was created under an English general, with a number of British officers serving in various high posts. The British army of occupation was cut from 12,000 to 9500, the intention being to withdraw it entirely as soon as the new Egyptian forces could be trained. In the cities a police force was formed, commanded by Europeans.

The British believed that financial reforms were the second step to ensure stability and tranquillity. The dual control by France and England, terminated by the occupation, was replaced with a single British financial adviser, who in reality became fiscal master of Egypt. Also Dufferin placed in key ministries British advisers whose recommendations had the force of commands. In the provinces civil and criminal codes, based on Napoleonic codes, were adopted, and between 1883 and 1889 a system of lower courts and courts of appeal was decreed with Belgian and Dutch judges. However, then and for a long time thereafter, the courts and the justice dispensed by them were poorly understood by most Egyptians, who continued to regard them as unjust and foreign.

Lord Dufferin was also instructed to see to "the establishment of institutions favourable to the prudent development of liberty," a fond hope of many English liberals. In 1883 the khedive therefore decreed that there should be an advisory council elected in each province; a Legislative Council (some members appointed by the khedive, the remainder elected by the provincial councils) that could examine and debate proposed legislation but could only make suggestions to the government; and a General Assembly, consisting of cabinet ministers, the Legislative Council, and delegates from the provinces, whose chief function was to approve or disapprove new tax levies.

One of Lord Dufferin's more lasting reforms was the bringing in of engineers as irrigation advisers to the Ministry of Public Works. They set to work to rehabilitate the old Nile Barrage built by Mehmet Ali at the apex of the delta. In 1884, after the barrage was restored, the cotton yield was 30,000 tons greater than in the previous year. This increased Egypt's cotton income by over £1 million; the cost of the renovation had been only £26,000.

In the long run revenues from these and similar changes greatly increased; as a result, public and private profits made the British occupation of Egypt acceptable to the Great Powers and their bondholders and tolerable to Egyptian landlords. With the framework for a new regime in place, Lord Dufferin returned to his post in Istanbul.

LORD CROMER AND EGYPTIAN GOVERNMENT

In September 1883, Sir Evelyn Baring (1841–1917) became British agent and consul general in Egypt. Elevated to the peerage as Lord Cromer in 1892, he controlled Egypt autocratically until his retirement in 1907. His negative views of Egyptian national character served as a means of justifying English control of Egypt, while many Egyptians resented his condescending attitude toward them. He faced an interlocking and complex series of problems, including the indefinite status of Egypt and its desperate financial situation.

Egypt's status was not clearly defined: the dynasty founded by Mehmet Ali governed nominally as Ottoman appointees, and Egypt was supposedly part of the Ottoman Empire; locally, the khedive was formally in control of the autonomous area of Egypt; and several European countries claimed special privileges inside the country. In reality, though, England controlled Egypt, despite the fact that no formal machinery for control was established. The capitulations remained, as did the

Mixed Courts, and the public debt. Khedive Tawfiq continued as head of the administration, the cabinet and the ministries functioned, local officials governed the cities and provinces, and the courts and judiciary performed their duties. The ultimate power of decision, however, resided in the British agent. This indirect rule was facilitated by an unspoken alliance fashioned early between Lord Cromer and Tawfiq, in which Egyptian ministers either followed the advice of the British agent or lost their posts. Several prime ministers served under Cromer. Mustafa Pasha Fahmi served the longest continuous period and was so subservient to the British that he antagonized many Egyptians.

Lord Cromer and his British advisers and officials determined and administered trade policies, agriculture, communications, irrigation, health, and foreign affairs in addition to Egypt's army and finances. Education failed to fit into any program. The illiteracy of the masses was hardly touched, and the number receiving a secondary education was very limited. Sufi brotherhoods were brought more closely under the control of the Egyptian state; religion was one of the few areas that remained largely outside the sphere of the British.

In the short run the British occupiers faced a desperate financial situation. The French, embittered by Britain's unilateral occupation and the abolition of the dual control, used every device possible to embarrass the British. Revenues such as railway and telegraph receipts, customs duties, port fees at Alexandria, and proceeds from khedivial estates continued to be collected, but funds for the administration of government and payment of tribute to the Ottoman sultan were insufficient. By the end of 1883 government workers' salaries were in arrears and the floating debt had doubled. British proposals to reduce interest payments on the debt and transfer some funds to pay for administration were vetoed by the French.

Finally, at a London conference in 1885 agreement was reached to float an internationally guaranteed loan to pay off the current debt, to reduce interest payments, and to provide for Egyptian irrigation needs. Any surplus funds were to be divided equally between the administration and debt funding. By 1889 the Egyptian treasury began to show surpluses.

With Egypt's finances seemingly adjusted the British turned to the thorny problem of withdrawal from the country. Badgered from every side—and especially by France—to set a definite date and equally encouraged by Cromer to be vague on this issue, England tried to conclude in 1885 a withdrawal agreement in concert with Sultan Abdulhamid II and with the other European powers. The French and Russians protested so strenuously against British proposals that Abdulhamid failed to ratify the agreement. As a result, the British remained in Egypt, although with an anomalous status until 1914. British imperial military and diplomatic strategy shifted its focus to Cairo and Suez from Istanbul, where German influence was mounting, and British withdrawal from Egypt was now pushed to some nebulous future.

KHEDIVE ABBAS HILMI II vs. LORD CROMER

Mustafa Pasha Fahmi became prime minister in 1891. An elegant Turk, weak in resolve, gentlemanly, honest, hardworking, an ally of Ismail, a friend of Urabi, and devoted to Tawfiq, Fahmi continued as prime minister, with some interruptions, until Cromer's retirement in 1907. Affairs moved so smoothly during Fahmi's stewardship that Cromer allowed that he was almost bored. With imports and exports on the rise, treasury surpluses building up, and the cabinet and khedive docile, the British occupation appeared to be succeeding. Then, in January 1892, Tawfiq fell ill and died. His son and successor, Abbas Hilmi II, not quite eighteen years old, was studying in Vienna and was an untested and unknown figure. Cromer realized that the "alliance" had been broken; he would have to start afresh to educate the new khedive to reality.

Abbas had some acquaintance with French liberal ideas, and he tended to be suspicious of England. The new khedive wanted to show his independence of Cromer and evidently hoped that France would aid him in getting rid of the British. But the sultan's appointment of Abbas preoccupied him in the first few months of his rule, as Abdulhamid had excluded the Sinai peninsula from Abbas's territory. Cromer was intensely disturbed over his omission, jeopardizing the Suez Canal as it did, and fully supported Abbas in the final drafting in favor of Egypt.

Soon, however, Cromer was calling Abbas a foolish youth, for Abbas had decided to replace the seriously ill Fahmi with a prime minister of his own choosing. With London's backing, Cromer forced Abbas to dismiss the prime minister designate and declare that he "would always most willingly adopt British advice."

Suddenly Abbas became a hero to many of the budding Egyptian nationalists, who saw in him a young and vigorous voice for "Egypt for the Egyptians." Abbas now had the sympathies of many of the Egyptian people and especially of the Egyptian army, but timidity and caution kept him in subjugation. Moreover, in 1894 he discovered that the rather small army might hail him at one moment but abandon him in a contest of will with the British. Abbas and Horatio Kitchener (1850–1916), commander of the Egyptian army, were making a tour of inspection when Abbas remarked disparagingly to Kitchener on the performance of some troops. Kitchener took offense, accused Abbas of criticizing British officers, and demanded a public apology. Sensing this as a suitable opportunity to put Abbas in his place, Cromer supported Kitchener's stand. Abbas was forced to retract his remarks.

EGYPTIAN NATIONALISM

For support in his opposition to British occupation, Abbas then turned to the Egyptian nationalists, who had been increasing in number and influence. Cromer, never worried very much about Egypt's educated minority, had permitted a free press to exist. Now a number of teachers, lawyers, and writers, most of whom had studied or lived in Europe, were involved in the creation of a sense of Egyptian territorial patriotism or Pan-Islam, but not yet Arab nationalism. Few Egyptians identified themselves with the Arabic-speaking people to the east of Egypt, even though several Arab nationalists from the Syrian region were active in Cairo.

Egyptian nationalists began to appear early in the nineteenth century. One of the first advocates was Rifaa Rafi al-Tahtawi (1801–1873), who had studied at

Cairo's al-Azhar University and then in 1826 was sent by Mehmet Ali to Paris as the religious guardian of a group of Egyptian students. He remained there for five years, learning French and reading widely. After his return to Cairo, al-Tahtawi taught two generations of Egyptian students and wrote and translated many significant books, among them, *Guiding Truths for Girls and Youths* and *The Paths of Egyptian Hearts in the Joys of the Contemporary Arts.* These works championed the love of Egypt but pointed out that Egypt's destiny could not be attained until the ulama were modernized and the schools offered a more secular education.

Many other writers contributed to the intellectual and ideological ferment in Egypt in the time of Said and Ismail. One was Jamal al-Din al-Afghani, who lived, taught, and conspired in Cairo from 1871 to 1879. A Shiite from Iran, he posed as a Sunnite from Afghanistan (in Afghanistan he claimed to be a Turk). He had studied in Iraq and lived in Istanbul before coming to Cairo. Jamal al-Din's life can be summed up in a phrase used as the title of a book about him, *An Islamic Response to Imperialism.* In Egypt he found adherents who were swept up by his compelling personality, his lucid and persuasive presentation of ideas, and the innovation and dedication of his beliefs. He argued that when the Muslim ummah returned to the truth of Islam, society would cease to be weak; only then would there be a regeneration. Jamal al-Din believed that the essence of Islam was identical to that of modern rationalism. He believed that one should use one's mind freely to know and test all. Furthermore, every mind was capable of providing the individual with self-respect and a sense of equality. Lastly, Jamal al-Din was convinced that Islam was an active way of life; it was not a passive resignation to whatever might come but a responsible activity in doing the will of God.

These preachings, which were debated privately, were heady stuff. They were aimed against Christian imperialistic attacks upon Islam and against westernizing influences and materialism. Jamal al-Din al-Afghani was a Pan-Islamist who wanted to reform Islam by means of education and to adapt Islam to the conditions of modern life. He did not see how this could be done without revolution, the political unity of the Muslim world, and freedom from foreign domination. Wherever he went, whether in Cairo, Istanbul, or Tehran, he vigorously stirred the minds and imaginations of Muslims to react in defense of an embattled Islamic society and against its debasement by Christian Europe. He became so influential in Egypt that the government asked him to leave. The remainder of his life was spent in Iran, France, England, and Istanbul, where he died in 1897.

Jamal al-Din's most illustrious pupil was Muhammad Abduh, born into a peasant family, who had a distinguished career as a mystic, journalist, judge, and teacher. Differing from his mentor, Muhammad Abduh deplored the use of violence and believed that true reforms came only as a gradual process. He advocated a reform of Islam that would return it to its earliest, purest dogma, permitting a more flexible interpretation than was allowed in al-Azhar University. Abduh also worked for the development of Arabic into a more unified language, attempting to draw newspaper Arabic and the spoken vernacular together and bring both nearer to classical Quranic Arabic.

Abduh supported the Urabi movement, was an active member of the Nationalist party, and was exiled along with Urabi. He found his way to Paris to join al-

Afghani; together they edited a short-lived but influential Pan-Islamic journal. At Cromer's urging, Abduh was allowed by Tawfiq to return to Egypt in 1888. He was appointed a judge in a local court and in 1899 became grand mufti of Egypt, from which post he helped reform the religious courts and codify the shariah until his death in 1905. In France, Abduh had concluded that Egypt's poverty-stricken traditional society could neither mount a successful revolution nor drive out the British. Henceforth he taught that reason and the pragmatic accommodation of Islam to the modern world must supersede customary practice and belief; one should adopt what is reasonable and just for society.

Abduh and Cromer respected each other and met frequently. Abduh felt Egypt needed a benevolent despot and probably would have supported Cromer had he been an Egyptian. Cromer backed Abduh against the vindictiveness of Tawfiq and Abbas, which made them dislike and distrust Abduh. Abbas circulated such rumors about Abduh that only after Abduh's death was he fully accorded his rightful honors as a patriot, scholar, teacher, judge, and reformer.

Another prominent nationalist, a contemporary and sometimes rival of Muhammad Abduh, was Ali Yusuf. As a teacher at al-Azhar University he preached reform in much the same vein as did Abduh, but without the philosophical and intellectual substance. In 1889, Ali Yusuf founded *al-Muayyad* (The Supporter), a newspaper that within a few years became the leading pro-Egyptian journal. When Abbas II became khedive he befriended Ali Yusuf, subsidized the newspaper, and often took him on his travels. Naturally, *al-Muayyad* supported Abbas in his attempts to become independent of Cromer. In 1907 Ali Yusuf formed, under Abbas's patronage, the nationalist Party of Constitutional Reform, which died in 1911 with Ali Yusuf. Ali Yusuf was a conservative, orthodox nationalist who wanted Egypt governed by Egyptians. However, he doomed his movement by tying it to Abbas, for Abbas's surrender to Cromer had turned most Egyptian nationalists against him by 1905.

No nationalist was more fiery than Mustafa Kamil (1874–1908). Coming from the new educated class, he entered the School of Law in 1891 and went on to France, where he graduated in law in 1894. Returning to Egypt in 1896, he spent the remaining years of his life working for Egyptian national independence. A spellbinding orator who fired audiences with his ideals and ideas, Mustafa Kamil pleaded with all Egyptians of whatever origin or religion to unite into one nationalistic force to eliminate ignorance and to support the khedive as a rallying point against the occupation. His slogans, such as, "Had I not been born an Egyptian, I would have wished to become one," instilled in his followers a love of Egypt and a pride in its past glories. Kamil worked to erase the defeatism and the sense of inferiority generated by the capitulations and the occupation. In 1900 he founded the radical newspaper *al-Liwa* (The Standard) and created the Nationalist party shortly before his death. Something of a Pan-Islamist, whose goal was to achieve liberation of Egypt from British rule and autonomy within the Ottoman Empire under the sultan-caliph, he accused the British of impairing the authority of the khedive, destroying Arabic as the language of the educated, depriving Egypt of the Sudan, exploiting Egyptian agriculture, and excluding Egyptians from top government positions. Cromer called him a fanatic.

ECONOMIC AND CULTURAL CHALLENGES

Changes in agriculture and population, and debates over the status of women and cultural issues also played a role in the public life of Egypt during the first decades of the British occupation. The British apparatus in Egypt encouraged the government to invest large sums of money in irrigation projects, making perennial irrigation and two or three crops a year standard agricultural practice in many parts of Egypt. The British also paid the workers on these projects and sought to abolish forced labor under the lash. A dam at Aswan opened in 1902 made perennial cropping possible in large parts of Egypt, guaranteed water for summer irrigation, and ensured a high and increasing cotton yield. However, in the long run, perennial cropping posed an unintended but serious health and ecological hazard to the farmworkers and to the soil itself. The water-borne disease bilharzia came to affect as many as half of the peasants of northern Egypt. Despite this drawback, overall agricultural production substantially increased, even when calculated on a per capita basis.

Ownership of much of the agricultural land was concentrated in the hands of an elite: some 12,000 people owned about 40 percent of the cultivated area. On the other hand, a peasant-based middle group of small to medium landowners had about one-third of the cultivated area; they often rented land and also had to find work on land belonging to other people. And about one-third of the peasants owned very little or no land at all in 1896. The British occupiers organized a cadastral survey of the land, and agricultural taxes were equalized and reduced.

Egypt became a net importer of food as cotton was by far the greatest crop grown in the country. Food needs increased because of rapid population growth, especially in the cities, in which about one-fifth of the population resided by 1897. Despite several cholera outbreaks, the population of Egypt increased from about 8 million people in 1882 to more than 12 million in 1917.

The more than 100,000 foreigners resident in Egypt strongly welcomed British control, since the British in effect supported foreign domination of Egyptian finance, banking, and the export trade (including cotton). Technical and commercial modernization was part of, and a contributor to, the further integration of the Egyptian economy into the world economy. Some examples included the establishment of the first telephones in Egypt in 1884, construction of more railways, and the founding of the first European-style insurance company in 1890.

British liberals and most of the modern middle-class Egyptian nationalists agreed on the desirability of education for women. They favored more schooling for women, abolishing the veil (although rather few Egyptian women wore it in any case), and making polygamy more difficult. Qasim Amin's controversial book of 1899, *The Liberation of Women,* was especially influential, as it presented the argument that European political and scientific superiority was, in part, based on the relatively better-educated condition of women in Europe. Women's ignorance also created a harmful intellectual gap between wives and husbands and lessened the national strength of Egypt. Despite these and other arguments, very few women were enrolled in public elementary schools by World War I. A government primary school for girls in Alexandria, the second-largest city in Egypt, was opened only in 1917. On the other hand, traditional Muslim religious schools for girls had about 17,000 students by 1908; Christian and Jewish girls also were enrolled in religious community schools. Muslim benevolent societies provided increased educational opportunities in the 1890s, but mostly for males. Women's associations played a considerable role in literary and charitable enterprises, especially after 1908, as womens' magazines promoted education and discussed gender relations. Still, men continued to completely dominate public life, including elections.

Some aspects of popular culture remained as in earlier times; for instance, Quranic schools were the chief source of education for most students, while the majority of the population still lived, as in earlier periods, in villages near the Nile. However, European civilization did heavily influence new cultural genres and life in the major cities. Starting in the 1840s, plays were produced; often they were translations of European works, but by the end of the century original plays flourished. Newspapers by the 1870s gained a considerable audience among the minority of the population that could read. Foreign-run schools played a prominent role in education, while the nearly 1000-year-old al-Azhar theological institution nevertheless continued to be influential throughout the Sunnite Muslim world. The sons of elite families often went to Europe for higher education. A Museum of Arab (later Islamic) Art, which opened in 1884, supplemented the Egyptian Museum's specialization in the pharaonic period. European architects in Cairo designed buildings along European lines while incorporating some elements of Islamic design in surface decorations, and European scholars of Islam and the Middle East (Orientalists) substantially influenced the ways Egyptian intellectuals regarded the history and culture of Egypt and the Nile River valley.

THE ANGLO-EGYPTIAN SUDAN

Throughout the nineteenth century the governing forces in Egypt maintained a lively interest in the Sudan, just south of Egypt along the Nile River. Mehmet Ali sent an expedition into that area in 1820, and in 1842 the Ottoman sultan recognized him as governor-general of the Sudan. During the middle of the century the chief activities with regard to the Sudan consisted of conflicts with Ethiopia over Red Sea ports. A regular commerce in ivory and slaves developed, despite vigorous measures taken later by the khedive Ismail against the slave trade. Ismail extended Egyptian control up the Nile, to the east and west of the great river, and toward Ethiopia. Many of his appointees in the Sudan were European Christians who did not know Arabic and who were greeted with great hostility by the Sudanese. At the time of Ismail's ouster from office and the crisis over Urabi and the finances of Egypt, affairs in the Sudan were beginning to be difficult to manage.

In 1881 Muhammad Ahmad (ca. 1841–1885) of Dongola, an ascetic Sufi leader, proclaimed himself to be the Mahdi, the religious leader sent to complete the work of the prophet Muhammad and to signal the last days of the world. He gained support among the northern tribes and the western nomads, and he preached a message filled with appeals to revolutionary justice and Sunnite fundamentalism. He claimed to be recreating the circumstances of the early Islamic community in

Mecca and Medina. He said Egypt and the "corrupt" Islam practiced there were the enemy. The harsh rule of the Sudan by Mehmet Ali and his successors provided a powerful sense of resentment that fueled the Mahdist movement among the Sudanese. When revolt broke out south of Khartoum, affairs in Egypt were so chaotic and finances so desperate that the Sudan was left alone. However, in 1883 Khedive Tawfiq sent an Egyptian army to the Sudan. It was cut to pieces by the forces of the Mahdi, and the English insisted upon complete Egyptian withdrawal from the Sudan, largely for financial reasons. Charles George Gordon was then sent in 1884 to arrange for the evacuation of Khartoum, but he delayed the operation and a relief expedition from Cairo arrived too late. In 1885 Khartoum fell to the Mahdi, and Gordon and his men were slain.

For the following decade the Sudan was an independent theocratic state under the Mahdi and his successors. The Mahdi established a judicial system based on his own unique position as the recipient of communications from the prophet Muhammad. Sufi fraternities were outlawed, and the pilgrimage to Mecca was forbidden because Mecca was under the control of the Ottoman Empire. The Mahdi minted coins, collected the Quranic taxes, and permitted slavery and the slave trade once again to flourish. Following his death in 1885, the caliph Abd Allah of the western tribes overcame a series of revolts, bad harvests, and the outbreak of disease. He sought to conquer Ethiopia and Egypt but was disastrously defeated by the Anglo-Egyptians in 1889. Taxes were increased, and the major government positions were assigned to members of Abd Allah's tribe as the state authority came to resemble personal rule exercised through a bureaucracy rather than the charismatic appeal of the Mahdi.

In the 1890s, the Italian war in Eritrea and French pressure upon Ethiopia led the British to consider the reconquest of the Sudan. Kitchener took Dongola in 1896. Two years later, with the support of Indian and English troops, the Egyptian army moved up the Nile under the leadership of Kitchener, taking Omdurman and Khartoum and completely routing Caliph Abd Allah's forces.

In 1899, the Sudan Convention established what soon came to be known as the Anglo-Egyptian Sudan. Theoretically, it was a condominium, or joint rule, but the Egyptian voice in ruling the Sudan remained only nominal. Military and civil power was vested in a governor-general chosen by the British. Egyptian law was not valid in the Sudan, nor were the mixed judicial tribunals extended there. Import duties were not levied on goods coming from Egypt, and the slave trade was prohibited.

By World War I, the borders of the Sudan with its neighbors were determined. But within the country, British control was limited by vast spaces, the heterogeneous population, and inadequate funding. Egypt paid for the armed forces and provided a subsidy until the Sudanese budget was finally balanced in 1913. British officers in the Egyptian army and Egyptian civilians were the main sources of government employees. Personal law came from the Islamic holy law; tribal law dominated the nomadic tribal countryside; and secular law began to prevail in criminal matters. The southern Sudan was treated differently than the rest of the country: the English language was encouraged, missionaries were supported, and Islam, the Arabic language, and Arab customs were opposed. The condominium built railroads linking Khartoum to Egypt and to a new port on the Red Sea, and by the beginning of World War I the British were planning for massive irrigation projects that would enable a dramatic increase in the growing of cotton. Although the British and Egyptian flags were flown side by side over all public buildings, no one ever doubted which power ruled the Sudan.

TABA AND DINSHAWAY

Though the diversion of some resources to the conquest of the Sudan and nationalist attacks in the press made life more difficult for Cromer, he expected that improved economic conditions would blunt the campaigns of the educated few who mounted the opposition and would allay the antagonisms of the Egyptian masses. Events seemed to be working in his favor and dashing the hopes of Abbas, Kamil, Ali Yusuf, Abduh, and others. Kitchener had secured the Anglo-Egyptian condominium over the Sudan. Meanwhile, there had been an inconclusive showdown between Kitchener and French officers at Fashoda. The Anglo-French Agreement of 1904, part of a general understanding called the Entente Cordiale, stated that the French accepted the indefinite postponement of British evacuation. Two years later, however, three inflammatory incidents rekindled the nationalist fires, setting the stage for Cromer's retirement.

In January 1906, Ottoman forces landed at Taba, a desert spot near the head of the Gulf of Aqaba, and established a post there. The British protested that Taba was in the territory of Egypt, but the Ottomans disagreed, arguing that Taba was in the Sinai peninsula and that it was a part of Syria. Mustafa Kamil, Ali Yusuf, and other Egyptian editors came out strongly in support of the sultan and bitterly attacked Cromer and the British for trying to humiliate the caliph and Islam. Cromer considered the pro-Ottoman clamor only another anti-British outcry. Istanbul succumbed to a British ultimatum to delimit the frontier in Egypt's favor.

Almost before the Taba affair was concluded the students at the School of Law, ardent followers of Kamil, went out on strike, the first demonstration of its kind in Egypt. In the end Cromer had to arbitrate the matter. By 1908 student strikes and disturbances became ordinary occurrences.

Then, in May 1906, the Dinshaway affair altered irrevocably the course of political life in Egypt. A group of British officers went to Dinshaway, a village near Tanta, to shoot pigeons, a favorite sport of theirs. Without securing permission from the village headman, they greatly antagonized the villagers, who regarded the pigeons as their domesticated birds. A fire broke out, a fracas developed, a gun went off, a village woman was shot, British officers were mauled and one died from heat exhaustion, and a peasant was beaten to death before order was restored. The British judged that stern measures were needed and at Cromer's insistence set up a special tribunal to try the Dinshaway villagers on charges of murder. Composed of Butros Pasha Ghali, the minister of justice, the British judicial adviser, the British vice president of the courts, the Egyptian president of the native courts, and a British army judge, the special tribunal imposed on various villagers sentences of death, public lashings, life imprisonment, or long jail terms. Punishments were carried out immediately, in public view, in the village. The severity of the judgment stunned Egypt and shocked Europe.

For many Egyptians the naked display of power at Dinshaway led to the birth of nationalist feeling and the formation of political parties. Mustafa Kamil set up the Nationalist party; Ali Yusuf founded the Party of Constitutional Reform; and followers of Muhammad Abduh organized the Party of the Nation, Hizb al-Ummah. All these urged the institution of representative government in Egypt, replacement of European officials by Egyptians, and transfer of criminal jurisdiction over foreigners from consular courts to the Mixed Courts. Though Cromer secured the appointment of Saad Zaghlul, a leading member of al-Ummah, as minister of education, Cromer's style of governing Egypt now was unsuccessful and he resigned in 1907. Kamil, on the occasion, wrote in his paper that Cromer had negated the khedive's authority, had seized the Sudan with Egyptian men and money and then stripped Egypt of any influence there, had denied Egyptians any power at home, had insulted Islam, had forced Egyptians to be governed by Englishmen and had converted Egypt into a British colony. Kamil's condemnation was widely accepted in Egypt, and Cromer ultimately came to be seen as epitomizing British imperialism, which was usually viewed by most Egyptians as a negative phenomenon despite a few positive accomplishments.

THE LEGISLATIVE ASSEMBLY AND SAAD ZAGHLUL

Despite the crises of 1906 and financial difficulties in 1907, no popular uprising surfaced. The alliance of nationalists and the khedive against the British was ineffective. Many educated Egyptians, especially among the Coptic Christian minority, supported the Party of the Nation (al-Ummah), a moderate group under the leadership of the scholar and lawyer Ahmad Lutfi al-Sayyid. The leaders of al-Ummah, although wanting a British departure, recognized that Cromer had established financial equilibrium, organized an orderly and tolerably efficient government, and instituted considerable justice in the administration and the courts. For this they were thankful. Life was not bad enough to warrant a revolt.

To replace Cromer, London sent Sir Eldon Gorst, who had been in Egyptian government service from 1886 to 1904. Gorst had instructions to win over Abbas, break the alliance between the palace and the nationalists, and prepare Egypt for self-rule. Gorst began by opening up more administrative positions for Egyptians. He extended the power of the provincial councils but would not consider the nationalists' call for true legislative institutions and a constitution, even though the Ottoman constitution was restored in 1908. Gorst did win over the khedive by concessions on minor matters, but the moderate nationalists and al-Ummah considered the unbridled authority of Abbas to be as dangerous as that of the British.

In 1908, Mustafa Pasha Fahmi bowed to pressure on all sides and finally resigned as prime minister. In his place Gorst installed Butros Pasha Ghali, a leader of the reformist group inside the Coptic Christian community. (His grandson, Boutros Boutros-Ghali, a prominent Egyptian diplomat, became secretary-general of the United Nations in 1992.) For the nationalists a worse choice could not have been found since as a cabinet minister Butros Pasha Ghali had signed the Anglo-Egyptian condominium over the Sudan and as a judge he had sat at the Dinshaway trial. Also, in 1909, the Suez Canal Company, whose concession ran until 1969, offered to pay the Egyptian government a million pounds a year to extend the conces-

sion an additional forty years, but with more profits going to Egypt. Many thought
this to be an attractive proposition and, urged on by al-Ummah leaders and by
Gorst, Butros requested the Legislative Council's approval. The debate over the extension was vehement; Butros was accused of selling Egyptian property and of per-
petrating a dishonorable arrangement; in 1910, before the request was rejected, he
was assassinated.

These events broke Gorst's spirit; overcome by ill health, he returned to England, where he died in 1911. He was replaced by Lord Kitchener, who had served
in Egypt in various capacities from 1883 to 1899. Kitchener's appointment indicated the end of Gorst's policies. International tensions mounted rapidly with the
Italian invasion of Libya, just to the west of Egypt. The resulting Ottoman-Italian
war reinforced Egyptian feeling against European imperialism. The Balkan wars
and diplomatic maneuvers between the Triple Entente (Britain, France, and Russia)
and the Triple Alliance (Germany, Austria, and Italy) made London want serenity
and security in Egypt. Kitchener therefore allowed Abbas to remain as khedive
even though he distrusted him. In 1913 a new Legislative Assembly joined together
the old Legislative Council and General Assembly. Most of the new legislature's
members were elected; by occupation the members were predominantly rich
landowners and lawyers; no seats were reserved for religious minorities; and the
Party of the Nation, al-Ummah, held a majority.

Saad Zaghlul (d. 1927) now became the most prominent Egyptian nationalist
spokesman in the legislature. The son of a village headman, he was educated at
both al-Azhar and the khedivial law school; Zaghlul was a lawyer, judge, and government official with connections to such important figures as Prime Minister
Mustafa Pasha Fahmi, his father-in-law. Zaghlul won a seat in the Legislative Assembly, with a program for attaining justice in the courts, spreading public education, and increasing freedom of the press. Despite opposition from Kitchener,
Zaghlul was popularly designated as the natural leader of the opposition and he became vice president of the assembly. However, the khedive asked Husain Rushdi
and not Zaghlul to form a cabinet, which remained in office until the end of World
War I in 1918. The assembly seemed on the verge of gaining real power over the
cabinet and government administration when it adjourned in June 1914, but the
outbreak of war in Europe stopped this process.

During the summer of 1914, Kitchener became minister of war in London;
Abbas Hilmi, who was in Istanbul, was not permitted to return to Cairo; and martial law was invoked in Egypt. In December Great Britain declared a protectorate
over Egypt and the Sudan. Kitchener's mission as British agent had failed. By 1914
the efficiency of British officials in Egypt could be legitimately questioned, for
their effectiveness was weakened because they were not Egyptians.

Between 1882 and 1914 Britain had succeeded in stabilizing its control over
Egypt and extending its military power into the Sudan as well. This period witnessed substantial economic growth and the development of infrastructure, especially in the production of cotton and the increase of irrigation, while the Suez
Canal had become even more important commercially and strategically. As the
decades passed and Britain gave no sign of leaving, opposition to British personnel,
policies, and power steadily expanded, among both the political elite and the
Egyptian masses. Incidents like that at Dinshaway starkly showed the negative side

of British imperialism; as a result, Egyptian nationalists such as Saad Zaghlul appealed to a wide range of people.

The opportunities and problems the Egyptians were to experience in the post-World War I period were coming quickly to the fore even before 1914. The population was growing very rapidly, and social changes, such as the emergence of the new professionals, the disappearance of the guilds, and debates over gender relations, placed even more pressure on the existing political structure. Only the outbreak of war and subsequent strong military occupation prevented Egyptian nationalists from openly attacking the British position. Such action was reserved for the time following the war.

The British occupation of Egypt and the Sudan was part of a trend throughout the Middle East and North Africa by which European powers gained total control or great influence; this could be seen in France's actions in Tunisia and Morocco, Britain's movement into Cyprus, and the Italian conquest of Libya. Even in the Ottoman central lands and in independent Iran European powers became more and more influential in the decades leading up to World War I.

References

Works cited at the end of Chapters 10, 24, 26, and 27 are also valuable for this chapter.

AMIN, OSMAN: *Muhammad Abduh.* Translated by Charles Wendell. Washington, D.C.: American Council of Learned Societies, 1953.

AMIN, QASIM: *The Liberation of Women: A Document in the History of Egyptian Feminism.* Cairo: American University in Cairo Press, 1992. An important work by a male Egyptian writer, originally published in 1899.

BAER, GABRIEL: *Studies in the Social History of Modern Egypt.* Chicago: University of Chicago Press, 1969. A study of the social background that helps mold political events.

BARON, BETH: *The Women's Awakening in Egypt: Culture, Society, and the Press.* New Haven, Conn.: Yale University Press, 1994. Concentrates on the years 1892–1919 as the author examines public and family issues.

BERQUE, JACQUES: *Egypt: Imperialism and Revolution.* Translated by Jean Stewart. New York: Praeger, 1972. A description of the rise and decline of British power in Egypt, or the interrelated processes of colonization and decolonization, 1882–1952.

BROWN, NATHAN J.: *Peasant Politics in Modern Egypt: The Struggle Against the State.* New Haven, Conn.: Yale University Press, 1990. Examines social structure, images, and actions taken by peasants from 1882 to 1952.

CROMER, EVELYN BARING: *Modern Egypt.* 2 vols. London: Macmillan, 1908. Cromer's account of his rule in Egypt; invaluable.

HOLT, P. M.: *The Mahdist State in the Sudan, 1881–1898: A Study of Its Origins, Development and Overthrow.* 2d ed. Oxford, England: Clarendon Press, 1970.

HOLT, P. M., AND M. W. DALY: *A History of the Sudan from the Coming of Islam to the Present Day.* 4th ed. London: Longman, 1988. A classic discussion of the subject by two authorities on the Sudan.

KEDDIE, NIKKI R.: *Sayyid Jamal ad-Din "Al-Afghani": A Political Biography.* Berkeley: University of California Press, 1972. A definitive biography of the almost legendary political activist and publicist.

LLOYD, GEORGE AMBROSE L.: *Egypt Since Cromer.* 2 vols. London: Macmillan, 1933–1934. Lord Lloyd was an official in Egypt.

MARLOWE, JOHN: *Cromer in Egypt.* New York: Praeger, 1970. Covers Egyptian finances and British negotiations with other European powers as well as the details of Cromer's administration.

MITCHELL, TIMOTHY: *Colonising Egypt.* Cambridge, England: Cambridge University Press, 1988. A subtle examination of European and Egyptian attitudes and language in such fields as education, the effects of which were to foster British control.

REID, DONALD: "Cultural Imperialism and Nationalism: The Struggle to Define and Control the Heritage of Arab Art in Egypt." *International Journal of Middle East Studies* 24 (1992): 57–76. A careful study of how Egyptian culture was influenced by the British.

RICHARDS, ALAN: *Egypt's Agricultural Development, 1800–1980: Technical and Social Change.* Boulder, Colo.: Westview Press, 1981. Excellent treatment of the social impact of agricultural and technical changes; emphasizes importance of drainage and shows the damage caused by its neglect.

AL-SAYYID, AFAF LUTFI: *Egypt and Cromer: A Study in Anglo-Egyptian Relations.* New York: Praeger, 1968. The nationalist movement and the British reaction to it. The author had access to many private papers of nationalist leaders.

SEIKALY, SAMIR: "Coptic Communal Reform, 1860–1914." *Middle Eastern Studies* 6 (1970): 247–275. A fine study of a neglected subject, this article shows that the Christian Copts of Egypt went through many of the same changes as the religious millets in the other parts of the Ottoman Empire in the late nineteenth century.

TIGNOR, ROBERT L.: *Modernization and British Colonial Rule in Egypt, 1882–1914.* Princeton, N.J.: Princeton University Press, 1966. A balanced and fair evaluation written in a clear and orderly fashion; the best general study of this period.

VOLL, JOHN: "The Sudanese Mahdi: Frontier Fundamentalist." *International Journal of Middle East Studies* 10 (1979): 145–166. Valuable for putting the Mahdi into a broad analytical framework and discussing the importance of his life for today's world.

Qajar Iran and Reform

Beginning in the 1790s, the Shiite Qajar dynasty under its first two rulers, Aga Muhammad and Fath Ali, reestablished the political unity of Iran while preserving its independence. As discussed in Chapter 22, the Qajars sought to centralize political and military power in their new capital of Tehran, but they had to deal with the increasingly powerful influences of Russia and Britain as well as internal factors that limited their effectiveness.

During the nineteenth century Iran under the Qajar shahs attempted to modernize its army, civil administration, and economy, but with only limited success. Iran had to watch as Russia and Britain intervened in neighboring territories in central Asia and Afghanistan. Shiite ulama and nationalists came to question the shahs' Europeanizing reforms. The long reign of Nasir al-Din Shah (r. 1848–1896) particularly witnessed many initiatives designed to improve the strength of the country.

MUHAMMAD SHAH AND THE ULAMA

Abbas, the reform-minded crown prince of Iran, died in 1833, and the next year Fath Ali Shah Qajar also died, leaving his grandson Muhammad (r. 1834–1848) as the heir, but some of the numerous Qajar royal family refused to recognize him as shah. The British and Russian ministers in Iran cooperated to fund Muhammad's armed supporters, who assured him the throne. The new shah appointed his tutor, Hajji Mirza Aqasi, as chief minister, a post he held throughout Muhammad's rule. Hajji Mirza had studied under the famous Sufis of the time and had himself been a wandering Sufi. One English observer called him lewd, ignorant, fanatic, and avaricious, while the shah believed he could perform miracles and had direct contact with God.

The legitimacy of the Qajars, including the new Muhammad Shah, rested on the military strength manifested in their founding years and in Iranian cultural-national unity. The Persian language, Shiite Islam, a shared history, and cultural accomplishments helped unite the country under the Qajar dynasty, even though vari-

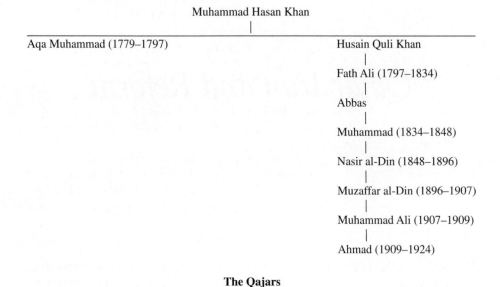

The Qajars

ous linguistic, ethnic, and religious minority groups persisted inside the Iranian realm. Forces working toward potential rebellion and dissolution of the state included tribal groups, foreign imperialism, and the ulama.

Many Shiite Iranians disliked the Qajars and looked to their religious leaders for inspiration and guidance. Ulama held considerable power for several reasons. Shiite theology allowed leeway for them to interpret the Quran and the traditions of the prophet Muhammad and the twelve imams, and gave their rulings on legal and political matters a considerable impact. The ulama frequently mediated confrontations arising between cities and provinces, since the central government could not manage such an arduous task. The ulama also possessed great wealth derived from the taxes that all Shiites were obligated to pay directly to them, as well as from rich endowments (awqaf) scattered across the land. Another factor in the power wielded by the ulama was that the recognized center of Shiite thought lay in shrines in Ottoman Iraq outside of Iran and beyond the reach of Qajar power.

Throughout his reign Muhammad Shah and his minister favored Sufis and Sufism against the established, conservative Shiite ulama, a natural preference, considering the fact that many of the ulama treated the Qajars as usurpers. The shah's subjects found themselves caught between the realities of monarchical power and the religious authority of the ulama, a conflict that was not resolved. By enhancing Sufism Muhammad Shah strengthened the state and the central government. He proceeded to remove many types of cases from religious courts, subjected provincial governors to closer scrutiny from Tehran, continued modest military reforms, issued decrees banning torture as a means of punishment, and abolished the slave trade by sea. An abstainer, he prohibited the sale of alcohol as well.

THE CAUCASUS, CENTRAL ASIA, AND AFGHANISTAN

Another problem facing the new shah was Russian and British expansionism in central Asia and Afghanistan. During the 1826–1828 war initiated by Iran, Russians had captured the Iranian-influenced sections of the Caucasus, and even Tabriz in Iran proper. The Treaty of Turkmanchay of 1828 signaled the definitive loss of the Caucasus to Russia, provided indemnities to the tsar, and, most significant, gave Russians capitulatory commercial and legal rights in Iran, rights that soon were extended to other Europeans.

Russia then embarked on a systematic expansion into central Asia, where in the first half of the nineteenth century three new Uzbeg dynasties in Bukhara, Khiva, and Khokand established central power based on modernizing militaries and increased bureaucracies, while ruling over ethnically and linguistically diverse populations. Eastern Turkish dialects and Persian were the two chief languages used in government and urban life. The Uzbeg rulers undertook conquests and raids into the steppes and against China and Qajar Iran, but the Uzbeg states quarreled with each other and could not fully integrate the various nomadic groups into their political systems, leaving the region open to Russian conquest.

Muhammad Shah's successors saw Russia seeking political control, commercial expansion, and increased leverage against Britain by moving first against the Kazakhs and then the central Asian urban khanates. By the middle 1850s Russia gained control of a large area stretching from northeast of the Caspian Sea to the Aral Sea and beyond to Lake Balkhash. A border agreement with China in 1864 opened the way to successful Russian campaigns in central Asia, leading to the annexation of Tashkent (1865), Samarkand (1868), Khokand (1876), and Merv (1884), and their organization as units of the Russian Empire. The rulers of Bukhara and Khiva became vassals of Russia but maintained some local autonomy. Russia built railways and encouraged cotton production in central Asia, while suppressing the Turkoman tribes that had often raided Iranian Khurasan. And Russia spread its influence toward Afghanistan and northeastern Iran.

The Qajars considered Herat to be the capital of Khurasan and thus a rightful part of their realm, as had often been the case for past dynasties, but this area was contested by independent Afghanistan and by Britain, which feared negative developments near its territories in India. The Sadozai dynasty based on Durrani Pashtun tribal groups had ruled Afghanistan and adjacent areas from its capital at Kabul throughout most of the late eighteenth and early nineteenth centuries, but Dost Muhammad (r. 1819–1863) founded a new Muhammadzai branch of the Durrani dynasty that would rule Afghanistan until 1973. While predominantly Sunnite Afghanistan was sorting out its rulership, peripheral provinces in India, central Asia, and Khurasan (still under the Sadozai Durranis) became independent or were conquered by other groups. British India intervened in the first British-Afghan war to place a Sadozai Durrani ruler on the throne in Kabul from 1839 to 1843, but Dost Muhammad returned triumphant and then set out to establish his central government's authority over all the former provinces of Afghanistan, including Herat.

In 1836–1837 Muhammad Shah Qajar of Iran had attacked Herat. The British tried to dissuade him from the campaign because they felt it would open Afghanistan and the approaches to British India to Russian interference through a pro-Russian Iran. An English artillery officer successfully contrived Herat's defense and the British went to war with Iran, occupying portions of its territory along the Persian Gulf. After a peace was arranged in 1838 the British established a kind of protectorate over Herat.

Iran under Nasir al-Din Shah (r. 1848–1896) attacked and occupied Herat in 1856. The British in India declared war and sent a naval force, cavalry, and artillery into the Persian Gulf, taking Bushire and the island of Kharg. In 1857, at the conclusion of the Crimean War, Nasir al-Din's envoy in Paris negotiated a settlement with the British to end the second Anglo-Iranian war. By the terms of the treaty Iran withdrew from Herat and recognized it as a part of Afghanistan, and the British evacuated the Iranian territories they had occupied in the Persian Gulf. The treaty also assigned special commercial privileges to the British and gave standard capitulatory rights to British nationals in Iran.

Sher Ali (r. 1868–1879) held Herat for Afghanistan while also beginning to modernize the administration of the country. His reforms in tax collection, provincial administration, and education were interrupted by the second British-Afghan war of 1878–1881, which resulted in British control of Afghanistan's foreign policy and the positioning of the country as a buffer state between Russian Central Asia, British India, and Qajar Iran. Sher Ali's nephew Abd al-Rahman (r. 1880–1901) used British subventions to support a policy of harsh centralization inside secure borders. Despite numerous rebellions against him, he succeeded in systemizing tax collections, building a paid army, and establishing some state-run industries. Abd al-Rahman united the mountainous regions occupied by Afghanistan to a greater degree than had been the case before, although local groups still retained a great deal of autonomy.

BABISM AND BAHAISM

Although Muhammad Shah devoted much attention to foreign policy, particularly in central Asia and Afghanistan, the rise of a new religion in Iran also preoccupied him. Babism began in Shiraz with the preaching and teaching of Sayyid Ali Muhammad (b. 1819), a merchant who had spent his youth in religious study. In 1844, one thousand lunar years after the disappearance of the Twelfth Imam of the Shiites, his followers hailed him as the Bab, or "Gate," between the world of the flesh and that of the spirit. Only through him, the Bab, was the Twelfth Imam in touch with the world. He assumed the role of point of manifestation of the divine essence and called for universal peace, improvement of the life of women, destruction of many status distinctions, and a society that followed the spirit rather than the letter of religion.

Iran was witnessing considerable spiritual, social, and intellectual unrest at the time. For more than a generation numerous religious leaders had been preaching about the return of the Twelfth Imam and the coming regeneration of the world. Outbreaks of cholera, military losses to Russia and Britain, economic difficulties, and the brutality and inefficiency of Qajar rule all contributed to an environment where a new religion could flourish. Also, as Shiite theology became more restricted and narrowly defined, theologians with new interpretations and views found it difficult to gain acceptance among the mainstream ulama. Many people hoped the Bab would lead Iran on a spiritual plane to combat the guns, ships, and materialism of the world outside.

At the time of Muhammad Shah's death the Bab was imprisoned in Tabriz and had been interrogated by the crown prince. The Bab now claimed to be the Mahdi-Imam, and he and his followers seceded from Islam. In 1850 the new shah, Nasir al-Din, experiencing serious insurrections by devotees of the Bab, with the approval of three ulama ordered that he be put to death.

Two years after the Bab had been executed, a member of the sect attempted to assassinate the shah. As a consequence, many Babists were massacred throughout Iran. Some leaders of the new religion escaped from Iran to establish two branches of the faith: one became headquartered in the European part of the Ottoman Empire but ultimately died out; the other was centered in Acre and Haifa in Ottoman Palestine. It later spread widely in Europe and the United States under the name of the Baha'i faith and thrives to this day. It renounced the use of force, even when persecuted, as in Iran during the nineteenth century and some parts of the twentieth century.

FIRST YEARS OF NASIR AL-DIN SHAH

When Muhammad Shah died in 1848, Qajar family rivalries were held in check by British and Russian officers. The British legation induced a group of notables to form a regency council for the sixteen-year-old Crown Prince Nasir al-Din while he made his way to Tehran from administering Tabriz. Nasir al-Din Shah appointed his tutor Mirza Taqi Khan Amir-i Kabir as first minister. Taqi was the son of the cook of a high government official, who had given him a fine education. Prior to his elevation to his high post, Taqi had been in Erzurum, where he had learned about the Ottoman reforms of the Tanzimat. He had also participated in a mission to St. Petersburg, the Russian capital, where he saw quite a different world. Taqi became known as a man of stern integrity who possessed great zeal for reform. Naturally, the palace courtiers and the queen mother, who dominated the harem, disliked him. With an empty treasury and a serious revolt in Khurasan, Taqi faced a difficult situation.

Though Taqi's predecessor was superstitious, he was aware of the economic and agricultural changes creeping across the 20 percent of the land that could be farmed. Hajji Mirza recognized that cotton, opium, silk, dried fruits, and nuts had become cash crops for export to foreign markets, tempting the landlords to press their peasants severely in order to garner profits from Russian and British merchants. Land now produced more wealth in addition to the high social status it had previously conferred. Taqi extended this policy and became the merchants' friend. He built the great bazaar in Tehran and encouraged the growth of a mercantile class.

In these years three politically active strata arose beneath the royal court. There was the old elite, landed aristocratic nobles who relied for their power on inherited privileges, extortion, and intrigue. The second stratum consisted of the ulama, who controlled the courts, justice, morals, education, religion, and intellectual life in Iran. The third stratum consisted of the new merchants, many of whom had traveled abroad to the Ottoman lands, Russia, Egypt, India, and even China, and brought home not only wealth but ideas of a wider world.

In suppressing the rebellion in Khurasan, Taqi formed an army of about 20,000 soldiers who were paid on time. Believing that the ulama should not participate in politics, he sent the army to Tabriz in 1850 and carried off the chief religious figure. But Taqi had gone too far, and in 1851 Nasir al-Din was induced by the ulama, the court, and his mother to dismiss the chief minister and to agree to his murder shortly thereafter. Taqi was replaced by Mirza Aqa Khan Nuri, a mediocrity who managed diplomacy and public affairs for his own advantage. Nasir al-Din was never happy with him. Filled with remorse for having executed Taqi, the shah retired to his harem. His rule became based on fear rather than consent, and the ulama and political elite allied against him. Because of Aqa Khan Nuri's failed policies in Afghanistan and the war with Britain, he was dismissed in 1858.

THE AGE OF ATTEMPTED REFORMS

Nasir al-Din ruled for a long time with few rebellions against his authority, and he undertook many reforms while borrowing very little money from abroad, but at the same time most of the reforms turned out to be far less effective than those begun earlier by the Ottomans and Mehmet Ali of Egypt. One factor that ironically promoted both the longevity of his rule and his lack of success in reforms was the competition between the British and the Russians, with each of the two powers fearing that the other might gain an advantage in Iran. Also working against Nasir al-Din's success were his inability to find competent administrators, the primitive state of transportation and infrastructure, the great famine of 1869–1872, which killed hundreds of thousands of people, the nearly autonomous condition of several parts of the country, and the great status of the ulama.

With Iran at peace Nasir al-Din made a trip in 1870 to the Shiite holy places in Ottoman Iraq. He was escorted by Prince Husain Khan, the Iranian ambassador in Istanbul, and met Midhat Pasha, then governor of Baghdad, with whom he discussed Ottoman reforms. Husain accompanied the shah back to Tehran, where he became first minister, attempted some reforms, and dominated much of the government for the next ten years. The journey to Iraq was so pleasant that Nasir al-Din subsequently made three visits to Europe, nearly bankrupting the Iranian treasury. The shah was impressed with the display of vast wealth in Europe, which he believed was a kind of money tree from which power and great comfort were derived. He returned home convinced that foreign money invested in Iran would develop the country into a prosperous state similar to those he saw in Europe.

Modern infrastructure was largely missing: between the urban centers of the central provinces there were vast stretches of mostly barren countryside controlled by nomadic and seminomadic tribes. The central government in Tehran found it impossible to control completely the tribes, even when the sons of tribal leaders were kept as hostages at the shah's court, until the advent of the airplane after World War I finally gave the central authorities more military strength. Outside of Tehran the government could do little beyond collect revenue, and not much of that! However, the building of telegraph lines across Iran, in the main to connect London to India, played an important role in opening Iran to the world. The first line was merely a toy to impress the shah, but within a few years Tehran was connected with several other parts of Iran. The rights to the international lines were sold to English companies beginning in 1862, and a local line, alongside the international ones, carried Iranian messages. No longer was Iran isolated.

The shah and the ministers, always short of funds, soon learned that Europeans would pay handsome sums in ready cash and give enormous bribes for a privilege or concession. In 1872, the shah granted to Baron Julius de Reuter a seventy-year economic concession for the development of Iran's economy and industry. So much clamor against this monopolistic concession was raised in all sectors of society in Iran, and in Russia as well, that obstacles were placed in de Reuter's way to prevent his compliance with the contracts. The money guarantees accrued to the shah, the bribes were kept, and Russia and the populace were satisfied by the concession's termination and appeased by the dismissal of Prince Husain Khan as first minister. But concession hunting continued.

In 1888, Sir Henry Drummond-Wolff arrived in Tehran as the new British minister. He intended to open the Karun River to international steamer traffic to meet possible Russian railway building in the north. Sir Henry gave the shah a written guarantee that England would prevent infringement of the integrity of Iran by any other power. With this guarantee against Russian actions, the shah issued decrees permitting foreigners to operate commercial steamers on the Karun River and to establish the Imperial Bank of Persia, which for sixty years would have the right to issue money in Iran and to engage in financial and commercial transactions.

Russian influence, however, was not completely lost. On the shah's second trip to Europe he was frequently escorted by impressive Russian cossacks. He obtained from the tsar some Russian military instructors, who were to reform and improve the army. By 1879 the shah could see an Iranian Cossack Brigade, with Russian and Iranian officers. For a number of years its leadership was rather poor, but in 1894 it again became a disciplined and effective instrument of Russian pressure in Iran, lasting until 1921. It was the only effective modern unit in the Iranian army, the balance of which consisted for the most part of irregular tribal cavalry and provincial armed forces under the command of local governors. In the early 1900s the infantry numbered only about 13,000 (including the small Cossack Brigade); the regular soldiers were conscripted for life and were poorly armed and paid. Tribal irregular warriors also numbered about 13,000 and were perhaps better armed than the regular army. (Iran had no navy at all until 1885, and thereafter only a very small one.)

Russia also had a letter from Nasir al-Din in 1887 engaging Iran not to give any concession for building a railway without consulting Russia. In 1890 Iran agreed to Russia's demand that no railway would be built for the next ten years; in 1900 the convention was renewed. Thus, by 1914 practically no railways existed in Iran.

Nasir al-Din Shah did accomplish some centralizing and modernizing reforms. Government operations were reorganized several times, and various ministries and advisory councils were created. The shah consolidated in the capital the minting of coins and set up a European-style police force in Tehran, while postage stamps were introduced in 1870. Some factories were built by the government in the 1850s and 1860s but they were failures economically. The shah, largely in response to pressure from the British, took measures against the importation of slaves and the slave trade. A modern government hospital, managed by Germans, was opened in Tehran in 1869. Nasir al-Din Shah also sent students to Europe to study at government expense, although from 1811 to 1911 only about 100 Iranians graduated from European universities. Government officials opened public elementary schools for boys starting in 1873, military high schools in 1882, and a public school for girls in 1897, but most education was still conducted in private primary institutions by the ulama, who opposed government intervention in education.

Culturally, Nasir al-Din Shah's long reign saw the decay of Iranian art in such fields as ceramics, but new art forms, especially photography, and revivals of traditional music and painting lacquer items were supported by the royal court. Old architectural traditions were perpetuated in building palaces, although they were somewhat modified by European influences, and the shah sponsored the building of some new religious structures. Persian writers, including the shah himself, adopted a more comprehensible literary style; the flowery and elaborate forms of earlier days were gradually simplified and clarified. A modern Persian journalistic style of writing came into use. An official newspaper was published; an establishment of higher education, the Dar al-Funun, was founded; a translation bureau was created; French became the chief foreign language studied; and about 160 books were printed in the country during the century.

Many announced reforms were only partially implemented or, after the fall of their sponsors from government office, were abandoned. Nasir al-Din was unable to push through major innovations in government and the military, and the number of reform-minded government leaders was too small to allow them to assume control of the process. Powerful vested interests, including foreign powers, saw the reforms as a threat to their positions, while most Iranians perceived the reforms and the reformers to be too Europeanized. The population of Iran grew somewhat, even though economic, agricultural, and health factors limited natural increase. And many provinces remained in the hands of semihereditary rulers or officials who purchased the right to hold positions; provincial revenues were kept largely in the provinces and not sent on to Tehran. Provincial officials resisted the shah's centralizing, as in the case of attempted judicial reforms, so urban legal procedures remained as before, with criminal cases handled by the police and religious judges dealing with personal law.

THE ECONOMY AND THE TOBACCO CONCESSION

Half of the population of around 10 million lived in villages; perhaps one-quarter of all the people were nomads, and about one-third inhabited cities. The economy depended chiefly on crops, so that when prices for agricultural products and raw materials fell dramatically throughout the world after the mid-1870s, this produced financial crises in many countries, including Iran. The amount of wheat exported in

1894 was eight times what it had been a quarter of a century before, but the price had decreased so much that total receipts for wheat exports remained the same.

It was different for some exported commodities, such as opium, cotton, and rice, whose production and value rose sharply in the 1870s. Agriculture became more diversified and more oriented toward exporting cash crops, as Iran became partially integrated into the world economic system. In response to demand from Europe, knotted pile carpet production became a major industry employing mostly young girls, although European imports nearly destroyed the cotton- and wool-weaving textile industries in southern and central Iran. With the opening up of the country to world trade, imports and exports doubled and then tripled and prices increased markedly. Despite some limited increases in agriculture, year by year the government, the shah, public officials, wealthy merchants, and the lower ranks of the ulama found it more difficult to make ends meet.

Aside from the element of greed, fundamentally the idea behind the granting of most of the concessions to Europeans was to try to consolidate and centralize the economy and to entice foreign capital and expertise to develop the resources of the state. The hope of attracting foreign capital was one motive for the shah's trips to Europe. Unfortunately, the entire process was riddled with corrupt practices and managed by unscrupulous adventurers. Iran was being sold bit by bit to foreigners.

In England in 1889, Drummond-Wolff introduced the shah to a Major Talbot, who asked for the monopoly to buy, sell, and manufacture tobacco in Iran for fifty years. Generous bribes were handed to the shah and others, and the concession was given in 1890. The company to be formed would pay the Iranian treasury £15,000 and 25 percent of its net profits annually; in return the company would control the entire traffic in tobacco—even members of the tobacco sellers' guilds would have to obtain permits from the company to engage in local trade. For many farmers this would mean selling their tobacco to the company and then buying it back.

The Imperial Tobacco Corporation of Persia bought the concession from Talbot and set out to implement the monopoly. By 1891 a nationalist, popular, mass campaign was organized against the government and concentrated on the tobacco issue, for of all the concessions granted to foreign capital this one touched the most people directly. Jamal al-Din al-Afghani, who had returned to Iran in 1889 upon the shah's invitation, was one of the leaders. Jamal al-Din so aroused the shah's ire by preaching openly against the government that he had to take sanctuary in the shrine of Shah Abd al-Azim outside Tehran. From there he continued his attack, scattering leaflets throughout the capital, until Nasir al-Din ordered him removed from the shrine, thus violating sanctuary. He was deposited across the Ottoman frontier.

But the eviction did not end the crisis. Revolt was threatened in Shiraz, Tabriz, Isfahan, Meshhed, and other cities. Merchants rebelled; warnings of violence against those who used tobacco spread across the land; and some merchants burned their entire stock rather than sell it to the company. Ulama petitioned the shah against the monopoly, stating that the Quran prohibited infidels to have control over Muslims. Soldiers dispelled the crowds of protesters in several cities, and some people were killed. Women participated significantly in the protests. A religious decree, promulgated by the leading Shiite theologian at the holy places in Iraq, calling upon all Muslims to abstain from smoking, was observed everywhere in Iran. Even the shah's wives refused to smoke! The shah canceled the concession. This popular victory over the government and the shah by the religious and city leaders made further movements of this nature possible. Moreover, a loan to the government to pay indemnities arising from the cancellation of the tobacco concession opened the door to more such loans in the following decade, leading Iran closer to the brink of bankruptcy.

In the midst of the anti-British tobacco crisis Russian nationals obtained concessions for insurance companies, lumbering, and other endeavors. One of the more important privileges granted Russia was permission to open the Discount and Loan Bank of Persia, which, in fact, was a branch of the Russian ministry of finance. The bank made loans on easy terms to princes, officials, ulama, and merchants; by 1900 it was said that Russia had bought off nearly all the ruling elite. In the middle 1890s there was a standoff between England and Russia in their diplomatic and economic maneuvers in Iran; Russian activity centered in the north, while the British dominated the south.

Pessimism was the paramount mood even in high circles in Iran, as the shah's energy and interest waned. The shah's brother suggested that Iran was like "a lump of sugar in a glass of water" gradually melting away, while the shah's third son, as commander in chief, neglected and robbed the troops. In desperation the first minister, Ali Asghar Khan, even suggested to the British minister that England bribe the shah to reform! Then on May 1, 1896, Nasir al-Din was assassinated by Jamal al-Din al-Afghani's servant and follower at the Shah Abd al-Azim shrine, where his master's sanctuary had been violated.

Iranian reformers, in evaluating the reign of Nasir al-Din Shah and their country's lack of success in Europeanizing reforms as compared with Egypt or the Ottoman Empire, often pointed to the difficult mountainous geography of Iran, its distance from Europe, the lack of infrastructure, an opposition by many religious Iranians to the reform movement, and the frustrating interventions of Russia and Britain. However, unlike central Asia and Egypt, which were conquered by Russia and Britain, Iran was able to keep its independence. And during the reigns of Muhammad Shah and Nasir al-Din Iran did experience some centralization of government and the introduction of new cultural trends, while preserving Shiite Islam against the inroads of a new world religion. Mass opposition to the tobacco concession opened the way in the next decade to a new stage of popular involvement in governmental affairs.

References

Works cited at the end of Chapters 19, 21, and 22 are especially important for this chapter.

ALGAR, HAMID: *Religion and State in Iran, 1785–1906.* Berkeley: University of California Press, 1970. An important volume for understanding the political and religious system of Iran.

AMANAT, ABBAS: *Resurrection and Renewal: The Making of the Babi Movement in Iran, 1844–1850.* Ithaca, N.Y.: Cornell University Press, 1989. A thorough and balanced study of religious and social conditions.

AVERY, PETER: *Modern Iran.* New York: Praeger, 1970. A very substantial, detailed work that begins with the mid-nineteenth century.

BAKHASH, SHAUL: *Iran: Monarchy, Bureaucracy and Reform Under the Qajars: 1858–1896.* London: Ithaca, 1978. A comprehensive treatment of all aspects of the subject.

BALLAND, D.: "Afghanistan: Part X. Political History." *Encyclopaedia Iranica.* Vol. 1, pp. 547–558. London: Routledge, 1982. An excellent review from the eighteenth century to 1979.

BAYAT, MANGOL: *Mysticism and Dissent: Socioreligious Thought in Qajar Iran.* Syracuse, N.Y.: Syracuse University Press, 1982.

BOSWORTH, EDMUND, AND CAROLE HILLENBRAND, EDS.: *Qajar Iran: Political, Social and Cultural Change, 1800–1925.* Edinburgh, Scotland: Edinburgh University Press, 1983. Twenty-one essays dealing with a wide variety of subjects.

BREGEL, YURI: "Central Asia: Part VII. In the 12th–13th/18th–19th Centuries." *Encyclopaedia Iranica.* Vol. 5, pp. 193–205. Costa Mesa, Cal.: Mazda, 1992. The best short treatment of the subject.

FARMAYAN, HAFEZ: "Portrait of a Nineteenth-Century Iranian Statesman: The Life and Times of Grand Vizier Amin ud-Dawlah, 1844–1904." *International Journal of Middle East Studies* 15 (1983): 337–351. A revealing study of the chief rival of Ali Asghar Khan in the 1890s.

GILBAR, GAD: "Demographic Developments in Late Qajar Persia, 1870–1906." *Asian and African Studies* 11 (1976): 125–156. One of a series of thoughtful and judicious analyses of Iran's economic and social history by the author.

ISSAWI, CHARLES, ED.: *The Economic History of Iran, 1800–1914.* Chicago: University of Chicago Press, 1971. Contains some of the documentary material needed for writing a coherent history of the Iranian economy.

KAZEMZADEH, FIRUZ: *Russia and Britain in Persia, 1864–1914: A Study in Imperialism.* New Haven, Conn.: Yale University Press, 1968. A detailed chronicle and interpretation of diplomatic history, using primary sources.

KEDDIE, NIKKI R.: *Religion and Rebellion in Iran: The Iranian Tobacco Protest of 1891–1892.* New York: Humanities Press, 1966. An important work on mass movements against foreign concessions.

MAHDAVI, SHIREEN: "Social Mobility in Qajar Iran: Haj Muhammad Hassan Amin al-Zarb." *Middle Eastern Studies* 26 (1990): 582–595. The biography of a nineteenth-century Iranian merchant and official.

MESKOOB, SHAHROKH: *Iranian Nationality and the Persian Language.* Translated by Michael Hillmann and edited by John R. Perry. Washington, D.C.: Mage, 1992. Essays on how Persian literature, religion, and history influenced national feeling up to the time of the Constitutional Revolution.

NASHAT, GUITY: *The Origins of Modern Reform in Iran, 1870–80.* Urbana: University of Illinois Press, 1982. A thorough discussion of the reforms of Prince Husain Khan and his experiences.

TOUSI, REZA: "The Persian Army, 1880–1907." *Middle Eastern Studies* 24 (1988): 206–229. A useful survey based on British sources.

VOLODARSKY, MIKHAIL: "Persia's Foreign Policy Between the Two Herat Crises, 1831–56." *Middle Eastern Studies* 21 (1985): 111–151. Uses the Russian archives to shed new light on the subject.

Iran's
Constitutional Revolution

Upon the assassination of Nasir al-Din Shah in 1896, the Qajar dynasty and the peoples of Iran had undergone only a very limited degree of modernizing Europeanization. Still, efforts to create a new intellectual climate, the more substantial involvement of Iran in the world economy, reforms in the military and civil government, and the encroachments of Russia and Britain were all leading to a new phase in Iranian history. The popular, religious, and nationalistic opposition to economic concessions to Europeans continued into the reigns of Muzaffar al-Din Shah and his successor, Muhammad Ali Shah, culminating in widespread support for a constitutional revolution. The constitution was preserved despite strong opposition, but civil war and foreign intervention threw the country into great turmoil in the years leading up to World War I.

MUZAFFAR AL-DIN SHAH
AND THE CONSTITUTIONAL REVOLUTION

The Russians and the British recognized Muzaffar al-Din as the new shah in 1896. He ordered Ali Asghar Khan to remain as prime minister, and the new shah's brothers pledged their loyalty and obedience to Muzaffar al-Din. The transfer of power was peaceful and indicative of the long stability in the reigns of the Qajar shahs to this point: in the century from 1797 to 1896 only three shahs had ruled—Fath Ali, Muhammad, and Nasir al-Din.

Muzaffar al-Din (r. 1896–1907) was a sickly, uneducated, good-natured forty-three-year-old prince who was bored and baffled by governmental affairs and preferred the company of his wives, astrologers, and favorites. His first thought after his enthronement was a trip to Europe, supposedly for his health.

Ali Asghar Khan Amin al-Sultan, prime minister for more than a decade of hard times, had collected so many enemies that they were able to prevail upon the weak shah to dismiss him, but he had to be recalled before long because only he could secure the money needed for the shah to travel in Europe. Payments to the troops and the salaries of most officials were at least six months overdue. It was said the minister of taxation "took no bribes, which was thought foolish, and he gave none, which was thought wicked." Ali Asghar Khan's first act was to reorganize the customs offices with Belgian officials in charge, and to take a loan from Russia. After paying Iran's debts, Muzaffar al-Din and his retinue set out for Europe, visiting several health spas for his kidney ailment. By the time he arrived back in Tehran the treasury was again empty. The natural recourse was another loan.

A new commercial agreement with Russia lowered the tariff on many imports from Russia and gave it a powerful grip on Iran's finances and trade. All tariffs on cotton cloth were removed, thereby ruining most Iranian cloth manufacturers. Some of the 1.5 million Iranians who worked at various times in Russia, especially in the Caucasian oil fields around Baku after the petroleum boom began in the 1870s, transferred revolutionary social ideas gained from Russian democrats and leftists back to Iran.

Internally, after the shah ordered a pension of £3000 a year for the court astrologer because he had saved the shah's life when the shah dreamed he was drowning, Ali Asghar Khan lost his temper and said he had "raised large sums to pay for the Shah's tours and toys, but must protest paying for his dreams." A new prime minister was named: Prince Abd al-Majid, Muzaffar al-Din's son-in-law and grandson of Fath Ali Shah. But a change in prime ministers was not a cure for the ills of Iran. Agitation by the ulama against the ministers and the arrogant efficiency of the Belgian customs officials was easily blunted by Abd al-Majid, for the central government was stronger in 1903 than it had been in 1890 at the time of the tobacco affair.

A bad harvest, cholera, the Russo-Japanese War, the high cost of food, and unemployment in the cities helped bring about the important Constitutional Revolution of 1905–1906. The direct cause occurred in December 1905, when several bazaar merchants in Tehran were ordered to be flogged for allegedly raising the price of sugar. Immediately, the merchants closed the bazaar and went on strike. The government ordered them to open the shops or have all their goods confiscated. Thereupon, about 2000 merchants, joined by ulama, fled to the shrine of Shah Abd al-Azim. Supported by Ali Asghar Khan and the crown prince, they insisted upon the removal of Abd al-Majid and other ministers, the ousting of the governor of Tehran, the dismissal of the Belgians from the customs offices, and the convening of a "House of Justice," to be composed of merchants, landowners, and ulama. In January 1906 the shah acceded to their demands and they returned to Tehran.

In the spring, amid further turmoil, the shah had a stroke. Authority was weakened and responsibility diffused. Recognizing that sanctuary was no longer being respected, merchants, guild members, and ulama took sanctuary at the British legation on July 19, 1906. Soon some 14,000 protesters were camping in the legation garden. Giant cauldrons were brought in to prepare food. Russia did not protest, and the British tolerated the invasion. Abd al-Majid was dismissed, and the shah, after being nudged by the British, called for a representative assembly. On September 17, 1906, the shah signed the imperial decree calling for parliamentary elections. It appeared that Iran had taken a step toward limiting the power of the shahs and democracy, pushed not by an armed intervention or a revolution but by passive resistance.

Elections were held early in October. Not waiting for the representatives from the provinces, the successful candidates from Tehran, including many merchants, met to write a constitution and enact basic laws for a legislative body. Tehran was dramatically overrepresented in the parliament, as compared with the more distant provinces. By this time, the shah had recovered sufficiently to return to the capital to open the assembly (majlis). A new prime minister found the treasury empty, tax returns at a low ebb, salaries unpaid for six months, and sentiment in the majlis utterly opposed to any foreign loan. In the end the majlis voted unanimously to float a loan internally.

On December 30, 1906, the constitution was signed by Muzaffar al-Din Shah and Crown Prince Muhammad Ali, who had come to the capital since all knew that the shah was dying. The constitution provided for an elected majlis of 60 representatives from Tehran, and 100 to 140 representatives from the provinces, and a senate of 60 members, half to be elected and half appointed by the shah. The majlis was the dominant body and would control finances and foreign affairs. Equality before the law was guaranteed for all subjects, irrespective of religion, but enactments of the majlis were supposed to be in accordance with the shariah and Shiite Islam was the official religion. (A supplementary fundamental law was added to the constitution in October 1907.)

The British applauded the formation of the constitution; the Russians found it distasteful. The crown prince, who was openly pro-Russian and even spoke Russian, frankly loathed the constitution. Muzaffar al-Din Shah died January 8, 1907, and Muhammad Ali was soon crowned as shah. With an enemy on the throne the constitution's future was in jeopardy.

MUHAMMAD ALI SHAH AND THE COUNTERREVOLUTION

Had the majlis been well organized by skillful and experienced leaders, a patriotic representative government under a constitution might have succeeded in managing Iranian affairs and found a way to avoid bankruptcy. As the members elected in the provinces joined the majlis, however, it became less and less coherent. The members were of varying backgrounds: guildsmen, merchants, ulama, bureaucrats, landowners, and professionals. Most opposed all aspects of the old system of government, yet rival leaders also quarreled over old antagonisms. A member of a prominent Tehran family was elected president of the majlis, while his personal enemy led the opposition. The members from Tabriz were radical in their views as they had been affected by revolutionaries fleeing from Russia. Political societies (anjumans) formed in every locality to influence events; some felt that the majlis was the largest anjuman of all. Within a few months even local anjumans split—in Tabriz between senior and junior clergy and in Meshhed between merchants and shrine officials. The majlis sitting in Tehran could not enforce authority in the provinces, but it prevented local governors from doing so. Local anjumans defied the majlis, the central government, and the local administration. Land taxes went unpaid, and no one collected road tolls. Smuggling prevailed. One force remaining in the provincial cities was the ulama, who claimed they represented justice since they dispensed the holy law while the government with its laws symbolized injustice, an idea that played a decisive role in the thinking of the anjumans; some of the ulama opposed the constitution, while many favored it, at least initially.

Bankruptcy was never admitted, and the total foreign debt remained far below that accumulated by the Ottoman Empire or Egypt. When the finance minister made his report to the majlis, itemizing necessary expenditures, the majlis authorized him to borrow the required funds from the National Bank, which, however, did not exist! It was generally recognized that no government could function without cooperating with the majlis, but it became apparent that the majlis had difficulty functioning at all.

In March 1907, when bankruptcy was near, all agreed that Ali Asghar Khan, the ingenious, detested negotiator of the two Russian loans, should be invited back from exile. He nearly had arranged a loan with Russian, French, German, and British backing when on August 31, 1907, he was assassinated by a radical anjuman member from Tabriz. This blow eventually led to the demise of the majlis.

The constitutionalists suffered a second fatal injury the very same day with the signing of the Anglo-Russian Convention in St. Petersburg. In part, the document set aside the northern portion of Iran, including Tabriz, Tehran, and Meshhed, as a sphere of influence for Russia, and a small, southeastern portion from the Afghanistan border to the Persian Gulf near Bandar Abbas as a British zone; neither power would be paramount in the land between the two zones. London was more concerned with the security of India than with any interests in Iran. Russia obtained a free hand, which the constitutionalists in Tehran feared. Prince Abd al-Qasim Khan, who soon succeeded Ali Asghar Khan, could not comprehend how his British friends could abandon the constitutionalists.

Muhammad Ali Shah, though he swore three times to uphold the constitution, never intended to tolerate it for long. The shah suggested that Russian forces be called in to prevent riots, leading to a split within the royal family itself. The shah left the capital, gathered his forces, and moved on Tehran on June 23, 1908, where the Cossack Brigade bombarded the majlis building, arrested many leaders, and executed three of them. Muhammad Ali Shah, hand in hand with the Russians, was now the absolute ruler of Iran.

MUHAMMAD ALI SHAH ABDICATES

The shah's victory gave him control of the government in Tehran, but it also handed him full responsibility for the country's dire problems. His close friends took over the various ministries and filled their pockets as rapidly as possible to pay personal debts incurred when they had not been in control. Pressed to find a loan, the government received the same message from the Russians and British as before—reform the finances first.

Throughout Iran it was anarchy that reigned, rather than Muhammad Ali. The shah did not have much control or influence outside of Tehran. Religious leaders dominated the local anjumans and city councils. In Tabriz the anjumans and constitutionalists revolted and gradually came to rule the entire city. The shah, with the support of the Russians, besieged Tabriz for nine months without much success until Russian troops surrounded and invaded the city in April 1909. Rebellious forces by this time held Meshhed and Isfahan, and the entire south had slipped away. In Isfahan, power had been seized by Najaf Quli Khan, chief of the Bakhtiyari tribes, whom the shah had tried to remove. In league with the anjumans, Najaf Quli Khan revived the constitutional drive and set out with a small cavalry force for Tehran.

The shah's party in Tehran, along with British and Russian diplomats, failed to grasp the extent of the opposition. Bakhtiyaris from the south joined forces from the north to encircle Tehran, which fell in July 1909. The constitution was restored; Muhammad Ali Shah abdicated and took sanctuary in the Russian legation. Granted a pension, he left Tehran for Russia.

CONSTITUTIONAL GOVERNMENT, 1909–1911

A few days after Muhammad Ali abdicated, his twelve-year-old son took the throne as Ahmad Shah (1909–1924). A trusted Qajar prince was named regent. Weeping when taken from his parents, Ahmad promised that he would be a good shah. In Tehran leaders designated a group to serve until constitutional government could be reestablished, and elections to the second majlis were held in August.

Constitutionalism was supported by Iranian nationalists of all hues and at first even by most of the ulama. As weeks passed the majlis divided into Social Moderates and Democrats. The Democrats believed in the separation of civil and religious power, compulsory conscription, universal education, and land reform; the Social Moderates, the majority, were more conservative in their ideas and supported the ulama, the nobility, and the landowners. Considerable political maneuvering divided the Democrats and Social Moderates, as when Abd al-Qasim Khan was elected the new regent for the young shah.

Russian troops never withdrew from the northern provinces; in 1910 there were still several thousand stationed from Tabriz to Khurasan. Russian demands were greater than any Iranian minister could meet, while Britain accepted the situation. Russia and Britain blocked a new loan; they both evidently intended to limit Tehran until Iran's leaders recognized the overriding position of Russia in every aspect of their affairs. When a somewhat radical cabinet took office in 1910, and even more radical nationalists began to assassinate moderate leaders, the Russians backed attacks on Tehran anjumans, which were driven from the city.

A neutral party, W. Morgan Shuster, an American, was hired in 1911 to be financial adviser to the government. Neither Russia nor England was ever pleased with Shuster's presence in Tehran, and they acted to make his position untenable. Shuster took the view that the Iranian government as dominated by radical members of the majlis was virtuous and that all Iranians and foreigners who opposed reform were bad. Favoring the Democrats and disappointing the Bakhtiyaris, Shuster pressed the majlis to give him the authority to collect and disburse all revenues. Russia opposed reforms that might strengthen the independence of Iran, and the British and Russians openly warned bankers against making loans to Iran. Shuster then began to collect taxes from notables in Tehran who had not paid their taxes in years. Many of these now sided with the foreign legations against the American.

During the summer of 1911 Iran was torn asunder. In the middle of July ex-shah Muhammad Ali, with Russian aid and British agreement, crossed the Caspian Sea and with Turkoman supporters seized control of the province of Mazandaran. Many provinces revolted against Tehran and declared for Muhammad Ali, while in Tehran Najaf Quli Khan and the Bakhtiyaris took control. Government troops loyal to the majlis and financed by Shuster defeated the ex-shah, who returned to Russia in 1912. The Russians invaded Iran after an ultimatum in November 1911, in which they demanded the dismissal of Shuster and stipulated that the Tehran government could not hire foreigners without Russian approval. Najaf Quli Khan was ready to comply, but the majlis voted to reject the ultimatum. Twelve thousand Russian troops captured Tabriz and prepared to take Tehran. The cabinet expelled the majlis from its building on December 24, 1911, not to meet again until World War I, and Shuster was fired the next day.

THE STRANGLING OF IRAN

When Shuster returned to America in 1912, he wrote a book about his experiences in Iran, entitled *The Strangling of Persia,* a phrase used to describe the period extending from Shuster's dismissal to the outbreak of World War I. Shuster's departure was a blow to the Democrats from which they never recovered. Bakhtiyari leaders controlled the government, and their chieftains ruled from behind the scenes. Over the next three years a series of prime ministers proceeded through that office. Many Bakhtiyari khans received lucrative provincial governorships and ministries. The state disintegrated rapidly; local authority soon superseded central rule. Roads were unsafe, and the company that had the concession on the Karun River and overland traffic to Shiraz had to pay local brigands for protection. Trade came to a standstill in many provinces.

In March 1912 the Russian government gave up on Muhammad Ali and attempted to disburse his sympathizers gathered at Meshhed. The city was bombarded, and the sacred Shiite shrine there was looted and shattered, sending a traumatic wave across Iran and destroying any possibility of an understanding or genuine cooperation with Russian officials.

In May 1912 Abd al-Qasim, the regent, left for Switzerland and found excuses for not returning. According to the constitution, his appointment as regent could only be terminated by the majlis and only he could convene it. The Russians and British brought many pressures on the ministers in 1913 and 1914 to grant major concessions for building railways across Iran, but no concession was valid unless approved by the majlis. Abd al-Qasim refused to come home to call it; the two powers were quietly frustrated by a classic Iranian stratagem.

The British discovery of oil in southwestern Iran increased their willingness to grant the Russians a free hand in the north. Among the constant stream of concessions granted at the turn of the century, one signed in 1901 gave to a British subject the exclusive rights to search for and develop natural gas and petroleum in all of Iran except the five northern provinces. Oil was struck in May 1908, and the Anglo-Persian Oil Company was organized the next year. The British bought land on Abadan Island in the Shatt al-Arab to build a refinery and obtained rights-of-way for pipelines. All these negotiations with local groups were carried on without authorization from Tehran. In this area the British were as independent as the Russians in the north and had fewer obstacles and greater success. Britain was deeply concerned about oil and access to it; the British admiralty purchased a majority interest in the company in 1914 as the navy was turning from coal to oil.

During the strife of the Constitutional Revolution, the counterrevolution led by Muhammad Ali Shah, and the "strangling" of Iran by Russia and Britain, little could be done to carry out modernizing reforms in the country. Instead, civil war was followed by foreign invasions, the effects of both being catastrophic for Qajar Iran. Any real constitutional regime and the restoration of peace and economic renewal would have to await the end of the world war that had started in Europe in 1914.

References

Works cited at the end of Chapters 19, 21, and 29 are especially important for this chapter.

ABRAHAMIAN, ERVAND: "The Causes of the Constitutional Revolution in Iran." *International Journal of Middle East Studies* 10 (1979): 381–414. Examines the social causes of the revolution.

BAKHASH, SHAUL: "Iran." *American Historical Review* 96 (1991): 1479–1496. An excellent historiographical review, centering on Shiism, economic growth, and revolutions in the nineteenth and twentieth centuries.

BAYAT, MANGOL: *Iran's First Revolution: Shi'ism and the Constitutional Revolution of 1905–1909.* New York: Oxford University Press, 1991. Emphasizes the roles of dissident ulama, liberals, and social democrats in causing the revolution; should be compared with the book by Martin listed below.

BROWNE, EDWARD G.: *The Persian Revolution of 1905–1909.* New York: Barnes and Noble, 1966. A new impression of the 1910 edition. A full account of the revolution, with eyewitness reports by a keen student of Iranian society.

GARTHWAITE, GENE R.: *Khans and Shahs: A Documentary Analysis of the Bakhtiyari in Iran.* Cambridge, England: Cambridge University Press, 1983. This anthropological and historical treatment is especially valuable for the late nineteenth century.

JAMALZADEH, SAYYED MOHAMMAD ALI: *Isfahan is Half the World: Memories of a Persian Boyhood.* Translated by W. L. Heston. Princeton, N.J.: Princeton University Press, 1983. Lively and beautiful accounts of life and Sufis in Iran before World War I.

KEDDIE, NIKKI R.: *Roots of Revolution: An Interpretive History of Modern Iran.* New Haven, Conn.: Yale University Press, 1981. A brilliant summary and analysis of Iranian history.

MCDANIEL, ROBERT A.: *The Shuster Mission and the Persian Constitutional Revolution.* Minneapolis, Minn.: Bibliotheca Islamica, 1974. A thorough study of the revolution in Iran in 1906 and the failure of the Shuster mission in 1911.

MARTIN, VANESSA: *Islam and Modernism: The Iranian Revolution of 1906.* Syracuse, N.Y.: Syracuse University Press, 1989. An examination of the major ulama in Tehran during the Constitutional Revolution.

SAID, KURBAN: *Ali and Nino.* Translated by Jenia Graman. New York: Pocket Books, 1972. An exciting novel set in Baku and Tehran ca. 1900–1920 which gives a personal view of the impacts of modernization.

SHUSTER, W. MORGAN: *The Strangling of Persia.* Washington, D.C.: Mage, 1987. A reprint of the 1912 book on Iran before World War I.

TAJ AL-SALTANA: *Crowning Anguish: Memoirs of a Persian Princess from the Harem to Modernity, 1884–1914.* Edited by Abbas Amanat. Translated by Anna Vanzan and Amin Neshati. Washington, D.C.: Mage, 1993. This frank autobiography by a daughter of Nasir al-Din Shah says much about court life of the time.

WRIGHT, DENIS: *The English Amongst the Persians During the Qajar Period, 1787–1921.* London: Heinemann, 1977. Colorful and full of anecdotes that illustrate the personal side of the relations of the two peoples.

Impact of World War I upon the Middle East

The history of the modern Middle East is divided into two parts: an early modern period dominated by the Ottoman and Safavid empires (A.D. 1500–1800), and the modern era beginning around 1800, which has been marked by the integration of the Middle East into evolving world systems. Within the last two centuries, World War I marks a definite division between the long nineteenth century and the contemporary age.

Between 1914 and 1918 World War I profoundly affected political, diplomatic, military, economic, and social matters in Iran, Egypt, and the central lands of the Ottoman Empire. For the Ottomans the war had especially important effects, since much of the fighting took place on Ottoman soil. Military casualties were enormous, and millions of civilians were also killed in massacres or by starvation and disease. When the combat stopped in 1918, the ordeal of the Middle East continued, as the victors sought to allocate among themselves the people and lands of occupied countries and regions.

The shot at Sarajevo fired by a Serbian nationalist killed the Archduke Franz Ferdinand of Austria on June 28, 1914, and ricocheted around the world. It proved fatal as well to the Ottoman Empire, while greatly influencing Iran and Egypt. Austria-Hungary and Germany formed the Central Powers, and opposed to them were Serbia, Russia, France, and Great Britain—the Entente group. Many other countries were at least initially neutral, including Italy, Bulgaria, the United States, the Ottoman Empire, and Iran.

IRAN AND EGYPT DURING THE WAR

Ahmad Shah was crowned on July 21, 1914, and ten days later Europe was engulfed in war. In November the shah declared strict neutrality for Iran. When the Ottomans joined the war in November, they said they wished to respect Iranian

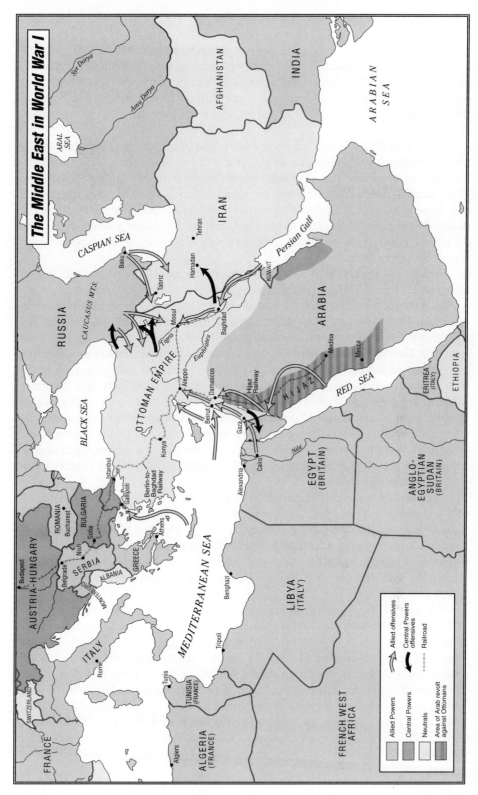

The Middle East in World War I

SWITZERLAND
FRANCE
ITALY
Rome
AUSTRIA-HUNGARY
Budapest
Belgrade
MONTENEGRO
SERBIA
Niš
ALBANIA
GREECE
Athens
Sofia
BULGARIA
Bucharest
ROMANIA
Istanbul
Gallipoli
Berlin-to-Baghdad Railway
Konya

RUSSIA
CAUCASUS MTS.
BLACK SEA
Baku
Tabriz
OTTOMAN EMPIRE
Mosul
Tigris
Euphrates
Aleppo
Damascus
Beirut

CASPIAN SEA
Syr Darya
ARAL SEA
Amu Darya
AFGHANISTAN
IRAN
Tehran
Hamadan
Baghdad
KUWAIT
Persian Gulf

INDIA
ARABIAN SEA

ARABIA
Medina
Mecca
Hijaz Railway
HIJAZ
RED SEA
Gaza
Cairo
Nile
EGYPT (BRITAIN)
Alexandria

MEDITERRANEAN SEA
GREECE
Athens

TUNIS
TUNISIA (FRANCE)
Tripoli
ALGERIA (FRANCE)
Algiers
LIBYA (ITALY)
Benghazi
FRENCH WEST AFRICA

ERITREA (ITALY)
ETHIOPIA
ANGLO-EGYPTIAN SUDAN (BRITAIN)

Allied Powers
Central Powers
Neutrals
Area of Arab revolt against Ottomans

Allied offensives
Central Powers offensives
Railroad

neutrality but could not as long as Russian troops remained in neighboring Azerbaijan. When Iran requested a Russian withdrawal, Russia demanded promises from the Ottomans that they would not attack. Such guarantees were not forthcoming. Ottoman Kurds invaded Iran, and more Russian troops poured into northern Iran. The third majlis opened on January 4, 1915, but Iran was no longer in control of its own affairs.

When World War I burst upon the Middle East, Iran was already experiencing chaotic problems involving internal political and constitutional developments, financial and economic turmoil, and intense imperial rivalry among Russia and Great Britain. After 1911, Iranian nationalists believed that Germany offered the only hope of avoiding an impending partition of Iran by British and Russian imperialists. During the first months of the war Germany concluded a secret treaty with the Iranian government promising arms, ammunition, money, and independence in return for cooperation.

Britain and Russia, aware of these agreements, acted swiftly to hold Iran in their power. Russian troops moved to the outskirts of Tehran. Supporters of the Central Powers then fled to Kermanshah, where an anti-Entente Iranian government lasted into 1916. Ahmad Shah remained in his capital with his cabinet, and technically Iran maintained its neutrality, as the shah received subventions from Britain. A German consul stirred the Qashqai and Bakhtiyari tribes in southern Iran and threatened British oil operations. To counter this danger and protect the wells, whose production increased during the war, the British eventually sent Sir Percy Sykes to organize a military force. In 1917, in cooperation with Russian cossacks from the north, they occupied Kerman, Isfahan, and Shiraz. Russia's collapse, however, left the northern provinces open; for a time German and Ottoman troops held Azerbaijan, but they were recalled at the end of the war and the British remained dominant in Iran. A famine further devastated northern Iran, and the country experienced great difficulties.

On December 18, 1914, Great Britain unilaterally declared the establishment of a protectorate over Egypt, thus ending Egypt's flimsy association with the Ottoman Empire. Although the announcement carried a pledge of ultimate self-government, a protectorate was humiliating to Egyptians. Khedive Abbas Hilmi II, pro-Ottoman and anti-British, had not returned from Istanbul when hostilities broke. He was deposed; his uncle, Husain Kamil, was proclaimed sultan of Egypt.

For nearly four years Egypt served as a military base for hundreds of thousands of British and other Entente forces. Troops requisitioned supplies, taking camels and donkeys from peasants. Starting in 1916 Egyptians were drafted into an army that fought alongside the British, and ultimately many men served in the armed forces. Inflation was rampant, and fortunes were made by illegal practices. The price of cotton more than tripled, and wheat became scarce and costly. As the British military ignored Egyptian sensibilities and the British administrators lost touch with public opinion, the public blamed the British for every ill that befell Egypt. World War I spurred Egyptian nationalism forward in the years between 1914 and 1918.

THE OTTOMAN EMPIRE ENTERS THE WAR

Sentiments in the empire were mixed regarding the war. Influential people desired an alliance with one of the two groups lining up for the war, since the Ottomans had been isolated during the Italian and Balkan wars. In conversations with the Entente for a possible alliance the Ottomans asked about terminating the capitulations. Russia coveted Istanbul and the Straits leading to the Mediterranean Sea, and the Entente powers held the military strength of the Ottomans in low esteem and were not willing to offer the Ottomans the assurances they demanded.

A hard core of army officers, dominant in the Committee of Union and Progress, had come under the spell of German military genius. Guided by Minister of War Enver Pasha, who was confident that Germany would quickly win, key members of the Ottoman cabinet signed with Germany on August 2, 1914, a secret alliance directed against Russia, and the Ottomans then began to mobilize their armies. Pro-German Ottomans feared Russia's desire for Istanbul and hoped to regain effective control of Egypt, while Pan-Turkish leaders wanted to annex the Turks living in Russian Central Asia. The Ottoman-German alliance was reinforced by the surprise entry into the Straits of two German cruisers, which were taken into the Ottoman navy even though they were still staffed by Germans, in place of two powerful Ottoman ships built in England but kept there on the outbreak of war in Europe. The leaders of the Committee of Union and Progress and the government—Enver, Talat, and Jemal—told Germany that if it would shoulder a major share of the burden of war materials, transport, and financing the Ottomans would join the war. By October 16, shipments of the promised German gold reached Istanbul.

On October 29 the Ottoman fleet, including the formerly German ships, shelled Russian Black Sea ports. Russia formally declared war on November 4; England and France soon followed. The sultan pronounced a jihad, or holy war, hoping this might induce Muslims under the French in North Africa, under the British in Egypt, the Sudan, and India, and under Russia in central Asia to rebel, but there were no revolts of any significance. One reason for the failure of the call to jihad was that the Ottoman sultan-caliph was allied with the Christian powers of Germany and Austria-Hungary.

With the formal entry of the Ottoman Empire into the war Germany became very influential. Though transportation, food supplies, finance, and many other highly important wartime problems were frequently left in Ottoman hands, German officials regularly acted as they pleased.

The immediate reaction of Arab subjects to Ottoman entry into the war was threefold. One group looked upon the outbreak of war as an opportunity to obtain a united and independent Arab national state. A second group, consisting largely of some princely Arab families and their clients, regarded the war as a time to rebel against the Ottoman sultan and establish independent Arab kingdoms. Most Arab Ottomans viewed the Ottoman state as the only protection against European imperialism and the preserver of Islamic independence, and thus continued to support the empire until its defeat.

GALLIPOLI CAMPAIGN

The Entente powers assumed the offensive against the Ottomans in 1915. Britain, at the suggestion of Minister of War Lord Kitchener (formerly British representative in Egypt), agreed to send a force to break through the Straits, take Istanbul, drive the Ottomans out of the war, and open a supply route to Russia. After unsuccessful attacks in February and March by British and French naval forces, an Australian and British army began operations on the Gallipoli peninsula in April 1915. The attackers met withering fire and stubborn defense by Ottoman forces led by Mustafa Kemal (Atatürk) and some German officers under the overall command of General Liman von Sanders. Suffering huge losses, the British imperial and French forces, joined by the Italians in August, clung on and nearly succeeded in a breakthrough. Lack of cooperation by the Russians at the Bosphorus end of the Straits, skillful tactics on the part of the Germans and Ottomans, and faulty intelligence work by the offensive forces led first to a stalemate and then to Entente withdrawal from the Straits and defeat in January 1916.

OTTOMAN WAR OPERATIONS

The overall Ottoman war plan called for an attack upon the Russians in the east and an expedition to drive the British from Egypt, while countering the Entente attacks on the Dardanelles and Iraq meant the Ottomans were fighting chiefly on four fronts. In addition, after Bulgaria joined the Central Powers in 1915, Ottoman troops were sent to fight in eastern Europe.

During the last months of 1914 Ottoman forces moved east against Russia, but the strategy was poorly conceived by the rash Enver. The Ottomans had to fall back—nearly 90 percent of the Third Army had been lost to frostbite, disease, and enemy action. Enver relinquished his command and returned to Istanbul. All news of the disaster was censored.

In the campaigns of 1915–1916, with the aid of Armenian revolutionaries and irregular forces, the Russians captured Erzurum, Van, and Trabzon in the east. In 1916 Mustafa Kemal came to that mountainous Caucasus front, but little was accomplished. Transportation was next to impossible; ammunition and supplies of every kind were scarce; and disease was rampant. In February 1917, forty-two Ottoman army surgeons died of spotted typhus alone, and thousands of soldiers died of starvation. The dreadful casualties of Enver's first campaign and the considerable depopulation of the eastern areas as a result of the Armenian massacres and deportations in 1915 created such a weakness on the front facing Russia that it would have been fatal had not Russia been so hard-pressed in the European war theaters from 1915 to 1917.

The revolutions in Russia in 1917, especially the Bolshevik Communist Revolution in the autumn, markedly affected the Caucasus front. All the Russian troops except for the Armenian and Georgian divisions melted away. The Ottomans advanced rapidly to occupy eastern Anatolia, which the March 1918 Treaty of

Brest Litovsk gave to the Ottomans. And by September 1918 the Ottomans captured Baku on the Caspian Sea, killing many Armenians in the process, and occupied Azerbaijan. Germany felt the Ottoman inroads into the Caucasus were going too far and opposed them.

The second ambition of Enver was the conquest of Egypt. Jemal Pasha, Ottoman minister of marine and one of the triumvirate, took command of the Fourth Army and assumed responsibility for Syria, including Palestine. In February 1915, his forces made a surprise attack upon the Suez Canal, but, possessing inadequate strength to hold the eastern bank, they retired. Raids on the Suez Canal compelled the British to maintain a large force; however, the morale of the Ottoman armies was low because they inevitably had to retreat.

When Italy joined the war on the Entente side in May 1915, the Ottomans and Germans sought to attack Italian-controlled Libya; with the assistance of the Sanusi Sufis, an operation was even launched from Libya against Egypt. The British counterattacked, however, and the Ottoman-Libyan forces ultimately could only engage in limited raids on Entente forces.

A massive Ottoman assault against the Suez Canal from Palestine was ordered for February 1916, but poor transport delayed the attack until the hot weather of midsummer. The assault proved a failure, and from that moment until the end of the war the Ottoman armies were on the defensive in this theater of operations. In March and April 1917 at the famous battles of Gaza, Ottoman and German forces withstood heavy British fire and drove the enemy back to a line in Sinai, while the city of Gaza was largely destroyed. Later that year a German-directed operation, including some German combat units as well as Ottoman troops, attempted to gain a favorable decision in Palestine, but again failure of transport, sabotage of supplies, continuing harassment by Arab desert bands, and a buildup of British forces under General Allenby brought disaster.

Another area of major hostilities in the Middle East was Iraq. British contingents from India seized Basrah even before the Ottoman entry into the war, so as to protect nearby Iranian oil operations. A sizable force captured Kut al-Amarah in 1915, but it was defeated just south of Baghdad and fell back to Kut al-Amarah, where the Ottomans forced a humiliating British surrender in 1916. However, the British and Indians reestablished their hold on southern Iraq. A railroad was built, and superior concentrations of men, artillery, and supplies enabled the British to retake Kut al-Amarah and capture Baghdad in 1917. At the time of the armistice in 1918 the British had not yet reached Mosul in the north.

THE ARMENIANS

While World War I was unfolding in the Middle East and shattering the Ottoman Empire, some members of two national groups within the state, the Armenians and the Arabs, openly aided the enemy. Christian Armenians were located in both the Russian and Ottoman empires, caught between the mighty armies that swept back and forth through the Caucasus and eastern Anatolia during the world war.

Some Armenians insisted that their people support the Ottoman government and the war, but other Armenians claimed that the Russian tsar was the protector of all Armenians. In Istanbul and the western cities of the empire Armenians complied with war orders, but in eastern Anatolia some of the Ottoman Armenian population, often following Armenian radical nationalists and remembering persecutions in the recent past, aided Russia by rebelling and, in the region of Van and Erzurum, by open warfare. In April 1915, an Armenian government was proclaimed in Van. In some districts, part of the Muslim population was killed.

These incidents took place before the terrible Armenian deportations ordered in June 1915, which led to the massacres of 1915 and 1916. An estimated 1.5 million Armenians had lived in Ottoman Anatolia at the outbreak of the war. The great preponderance were in the eastern regions. The transfer of all non-Muslims away from points of military concentration was authorized, and non-Muslims in the military forces were relegated to rear service units without weapons. Many of the latter were murdered. Thousands of civilian Armenians also had already died.

During the deportation, disease and inadequate provisions in the Syrian deserts, the general destination, led to the death of tens of thousands from exposure, illness, exhaustion, and starvation. Many were marched off into the desert to die. Everyone suffered. The prosecution of the war on the Caucasus front was hampered from 1915 to 1917 because of the absence of the services normally provided by the Armenian inhabitants of eastern Anatolia. Many Armenians were set upon by marauding bands of Kurds and Turks, who perpetrated numerous atrocities. Representatives of neutral governments protested to Istanbul, and German officials privately lamented the action. Talat, Enver, and the Ottoman government, however, were deaf to all pleas, since influential individuals in the government were actually bent on exterminating the Armenian population in eastern Anatolia. Perhaps 600,000 or more Armenians (about 40 percent of the Ottoman Armenian population) perished, while hundreds of thousands fled elsewhere. Almost no Armenians were left in their ancient homeland in eastern Anatolia. No doubt certain deportations were required, but the total action was entirely beyond the need. Although some Turks did shield and protect Armenian individuals from the Ottoman authorities, the Armenian deportations and massacres were dreadful blots on the record of the Ottoman Empire.

ARAB NATIONALISM

The other pressing ethnic nationalist problem confronting the leaders of the Ottoman government was the loyalty of the Arabs. No open break occurred until June 1916, when Sharif Husain of Mecca proclaimed his revolt in the Hijaz. Even before that, Jemal Pasha found in Syria documents implicating numerous Muslim and Christian Arab leaders in treasonable activities. When Enver called upon Jemal for troops for the Gallipoli campaign, Arab divisions, including many leaders of the al-Ahd secret society of Arab nationalists, were sent in order that more reliable Turkish troops might control Beirut and Damascus. In April 1916, about 200 Arabs were arrested for treason and 22 were hanged; tens of thousands of suspects were deported to Anatolia.

Before further examining the moves for independence made by the Arabs in Syria and the Hijaz, it is important to place British relations with Arabs elsewhere in their proper setting. Arab states existed along the western shore of the Persian Gulf and the southern coasts of Arabia. Almost every one of these protectorates had a treaty of friendship with Great Britain, which exercised power over foreign relations, while a British resident agent advised on all governmental matters and doled out gold sovereigns or Maria Theresa silver dollars to keep everybody happy.

When war became imminent, the British persuaded Abd al-Aziz ibn Abd al-Rahman (known as Ibn Saud) of eastern Arabia to enter into a standard British-Arab agreement: Abd al-Aziz placed his foreign affairs in British hands and accepted a generous subsidy. In return Abd al-Aziz would be at least neutral, and might well engage in actions against the Ottomans in central Arabia.

A rival of Abd al-Aziz was Husain, the Ottoman co-governor of Mecca in western Arabia and a sharif, or lineal descendant of the prophet Muhammad. Since Husain feared Ottoman centralization, the British raised with him and his son Abd Allah the question of an alliance. Thus began the celebrated correspondence between Sharif Husain and the British in Egypt. Husain found himself in a delicate situation with the Ottomans close at hand and not sure about the ultimate intentions of the British or the attitude of the Arab secret societies in Damascus and Beirut. Exchanges of letters between Husain and Sir Henry McMahon, high commissioner for Egypt and the Sudan, brought to a head the issue of Arab independence. Britain promised, upon the successful conclusion of the war, to agree to the creation of an Arab state. The area of the state was to be bounded on the north by a line drawn eastward from Alexandretta to the Iranian frontier and then southward to the Persian Gulf and was to include much of the western Arabian peninsula. Excepted from this were certain areas west of the districts of Damascus, Hims, Hama, and Aleppo; although the meaning of this was often disputed, the exceptions seemed to be the regions where France had interests, thereby implying that perhaps part of Palestine would be included in the area promised to the Arab state.

Husain's son Faisal had conferred clandestinely in Damascus with leaders of the Arab movement, and in 1915 he presented the secret Damascus Protocol to his father. This document defined the Arab state's frontiers as Husain later insisted upon them with McMahon. Although Husain of Mecca was not an Arab nationalist, but rather more like Abd al-Aziz and other Arab princes who feared Ottoman centralization, in a sense he did represent the Arab nationalists of Syria as he dealt with the British. Husain declared a revolt against the Ottomans in the Holy City of Mecca in June 1916 and began a campaign in the Hijaz with the help of the British.

THE SECRET TREATIES

While these negotiations with Husain were in process, the Entente powers were engaged in formulating secret treaties, dividing among themselves the Ottoman Empire. Russia was to obtain Istanbul as well as the Straits, and in return Britain would add to its sphere of influence the neutral zone in Iran. Later the Pact of London was signed to bring Italy into the war. This pact promised Italy sovereignty

The Partition of the Ottoman Empire

To Romania, by 1920

ROMANIA

BULGARIA

BLACK SEA

CAUCASUS

CASPIAN SEA

ARAL SEA

Amu Darya

RUSSIA

Istanbul

Ankara

Trebizond

TURKEY
1923

CRETE

DODECANESE IS.
1923 to Italy

CYPRUS

Aleppo

Mosul

Tigris

Euphrates

Tehran

SYRIA
1920 French Mandates

LEBANON

Damascus

Baghdad

IRAQ
1920 British Mandate

IRAN

MEDITERRANEAN
SEA

Jerusalem

PALESTINE
1920 British Mandate

Basrah

KUWAIT

Persian Gulf

EGYPT
1922 Independent

Medina

BAHRAIN

QATAR

ARABIA

TRUCIAL
OMAN

OMAN

RED SEA

Nile

Mecca

ARABIAN
SEA

ANGLO-EGYPTIAN
SUDAN

ERITREA

YEMEN

ADEN

0   200   400 mi

0   300   600 km

- - - Ottoman Empire, 1914

Proposed Partitions of the Ottoman Empire, 1915, 1916

BLACK
SEA

Istanbul

0   100   200 mi

0   150   300 km

TURKEY

Trebizond

CRETE

CYPRUS

Aleppo

Mosul

IRAQ

Tigris

IRAN

MEDITERRANEAN
SEA

SYRIA

Damascus

Euphrates

Baghdad

PALESTINE

Jerusalem

British

French

Italian

Russian

International

EGYPT

Nile

ARABIA

Basrah

KUWAIT

Persian Gulf

INDIAN

OCEAN

382

over the Dodecanese Islands, the elimination of all rights of the Ottoman caliph yet remaining in Libya, and Antalya in Anatolia.

The most far-reaching of the secret treaties—the Sykes-Picot Agreement of May 16, 1916—allotted to Russia the already promised Straits area and most of eastern Anatolia. France was granted the northern coastal strip of Syria and southeastern Anatolia. Britain obtained an enclave about Haifa and Acre on the Mediterranean, and part of Iraq from Baghdad to the Persian Gulf. Palestine west of the Jordan River was cut from French Syria and promised an international administration because of the holy places. The Arabs of Syria from Damascus and Aleppo eastward through Mosul to the Iranian frontier were consigned to French protection, while the region from Kirkuk to Aqaba became a British sphere.

The secret Sykes-Picot Agreement was signed only a few months after agreements embodied in the Husain-McMahon correspondence were concluded. Husain learned of the Sykes-Picot Agreement and was unhappy with it, but he had little choice but to trust his far more powerful British allies until after the war ended. When Italians learned of the Sykes-Picot arrangements, they insisted upon gaining more land. In 1917 England, France, and Italy agreed that Italy should have the districts around Izmir, Antalya, and Konya, and all of southwestern Anatolia. At the same time, Greece was promised Cyprus and the territory of western Anatolia including Izmir as an inducement to join the war on the Allied side. Conflicting pledges with regard to the future of the Middle East were beginning to mount!

THE BALFOUR DECLARATION AND ZIONISM

Zionist claims had yet to be heard. Zionism was a nationalistic movement that developed among European Jews in the last half of the nineteenth century. Savage attacks in Russia and anti-Jewish prejudice in the nationalistic states of Europe fostered political Zionism and led Theodor Herzl to establish the World Zionist Organization in 1897. The Zionists had repeatedly sought from the Ottomans a Jewish settlement company in Palestine, but Sultan Abdulhamid II refused, believing this would increase his problems of nationalism. The Zionist Congress had declined a British offer in 1903 of a settlement in Uganda, for Zionism without the ancient land of Zion in geographic Palestine would be a paradox. At the outbreak of war in 1914, Zionist activities were centered in Germany. Upon the division of Europe into two camps, however, another center arose in London, led by Dr. Chaim Weizmann (1874–1952). Jewish Zionist volunteers fought as units of the British army in Palestine.

The Zionists lobbied for an Entente commitment to create a Jewish commonwealth in Palestine. Slowly an influential group came to favor the Zionist position, arguing that Palestine, so close to the Suez Canal, would be more closely linked to the British sphere of influence. Success came on November 2, 1917, when Lord Balfour wrote to Lord Rothschild:

> His Majesty's Government view with favour the establishment in Palestine of a national home for the Jewish people and will use their best endeavours to facilitate the

achievement of this object, it being clearly understood that nothing shall be done which may prejudice the civil and religious rights of existing non-Jewish communities in Palestine or the rights and political status enjoyed by Jews in any other country.

The exact meaning of the declaration has been much debated, but it was in all probability contrary both to the Sykes-Picot Agreement and to the Husain-McMahon correspondence. Reasons for its issuance included a British desire to gain support from Jewish circles in the United States and Russia, and a wish to weaken French claims to any part of Palestine. Husain of Mecca was dismayed when the news of the Balfour Declaration reached him.

THE FOURTEEN POINTS

Another Allied promise made during the war took place when Baghdad and Jerusalem fell to British forces in 1917: the victorious generals announced that any future settlement would be made with the consent of local populations. These statements foreshadowed the broad concepts of United States President Woodrow Wilson's Fourteen Points of January 1918. Although the United States was fighting Germany and had not declared war against the Ottoman Empire, Wilson's twelfth point stated that the Turkish parts of the Ottoman Empire should have a "secure sovereignty" and that other nationalities should be given security of life and an opportunity for development. Greeks, Armenians, and Arabs built their hopes upon this point. Some Arabs naively believed that Wilson's declaration recognized their aspirations as proposed by Husain, and that the Fourteen Points nullified the Balfour Declaration and all secret treaties made under the duress of total war.

ENTENTE VICTORY

Failure of an Ottoman campaign in the summer of 1917 opened the way for the British in Egypt to move into Palestine. Jerusalem fell to General Allenby in December 1917. Entente forces proceeded northward along the coast in late 1918, taking Beirut. The Arab revolt of June 1916 shattered the Ottoman regime in the Hijaz, and Arabs under Faisal east of the Jordan River paralleled the actions of Allenby. Under the encouragement of such British liaison officers as Colonel T. E. Lawrence (known as Lawrence of Arabia), and receiving British equipment and gold, the Arabs captured Aqaba and then entered Damascus in October 1918, at about the same time as British imperial forces. The Ottomans under Mustafa Kemal nevertheless held the Entente forces north of Aleppo.

German failures on the western front in Europe during the fall of 1918 and the imminent collapse of Germany, Austria-Hungary, and Bulgaria spelled the end of warfare in the Middle East. Without German assistance the Ottoman Empire could not maintain effective resistance. The British received representatives of a new Ottoman government off Mudros on the island of Lemnos in the Aegean Sea and on October 30, 1918, signed an armistice ending the war. It was nearly an unconditional surrender, since Ottoman forces were to be demobilized, and the Entente were to control the Straits and could occupy any areas they wished. The three leaders of the Committee of Union and Progress government fled the country.

The war, four years long almost to the day, brought many changes to Ottoman society, which disintegrated so fully under the terrible wartime conditions that the British leader Asquith declared, "The Sick Man had really died this time." To describe the miserable conditions in the empire would require many pages. Suffice it to say that the larger cities were disturbed more than the villages, and Istanbul most of all. The Committee of Union and Progress controlled railway transportation and therefore the sale of wheat; the government also encouraged the development of Muslim Turkish merchants and artisans, while prominent individuals made fortunes through war profiteering.

Shortages of every kind developed; foreign goods could not be imported; domestic produce and animals used in agriculture were largely requisitioned by the government; the amount of land under cultivation steadily declined; physical suffering among the masses became widespread; disease and famine were everywhere; and the generally low standard of living deteriorated rapidly, as inflation lifted the prices of everything without much change in wages. About 2.5 million Ottoman Muslims died in Anatolia from 1914 to 1922; hundreds of thousands of the minority communities also died. About one-fifth of the total population of Anatolia died. And starvation, disease, and destruction were widespread in the other parts of the empire as well.

The Ottoman government did enact some desired changes despite these terrible conditions: the capitulations were abolished in 1914; the taxation system was reformed; more women were brought into the workforce; the Ottoman Public Debt Administration was terminated; the powers of the religious communities were limited; and the war-burdened government assumed control over many unaccustomed activities. Despite these and other reforms, the end of the Ottoman state seemed obvious by late 1918.

The war encouraged anti-Ottoman nationalists. As the power of the Ottoman government waned, Arabs, Greeks, Armenians, and other nationalities gave more open expression to their nationalism. For Ottoman Armenians, it led to destruction. To the Greeks, it brought a temporary fulfillment of cherished dreams. And among the Arabs, it created revolt and new Arab states. For the Turks, uncompromising nationalists, such as Mustafa Kemal, now had an opportunity to be heard.

Of the other effects of the war, the presence of many British, French, Italian, and German soldiers meant that thousands of Middle Easterners saw westerners and their manner of living for the first time. The impact of the west upon the Middle East in every facet of its living, from transportation to religion, was more profound and penetrating in these four war years than in earlier contacts through religious, commercial, and intellectual missions from the west. A new age for the Middle East was born.

THE PARIS PEACE CONFERENCE

Less than two weeks after the Mudros armistice halted World War I in the Middle East, Germany signed the armistice with the Entente and war officially ceased.

The fate of the Middle East devolved then upon the several armies of occupation and, perhaps even more importantly, upon "the smoke-filled rooms" of Paris, where diplomats, statesmen, generals, journalists, and representatives of every special interest gathered to make peace. The Middle East, however, was only a small part of the total settlement. Problems with respect to Germany took precedence over all others, and disagreements on European issues delayed the verdict on the Middle East.

The prime conflict concerning the Middle East appeared in the disparities contained in the London Pact of 1915, the Sykes-Picot Agreement, the Balfour Declaration, the Husain-McMahon correspondence, the Fourteen Points, the liberation statements at Baghdad and Jerusalem, and the "make the world safe for democracy" slogan. Britain and France, the dominant military powers, sought to advance their own national and imperial interests rather than the desires of the smaller countries and nationalistic groups that also flocked to Paris. British Prime Minister David Lloyd George and his advisers viewed practically the entire Middle East as a prize. The French leader Georges Clemenceau, on the other hand, stood for a French hold upon Syria and southern Anatolia, hoped to dominate the Straits, and dreamed of having a French adviser at the elbow of the Ottoman sultan. President Wilson discussed plans for peace in the Middle East that would fulfill the pledge made in his Fourteen Points.

The Big Three—Lloyd George, Clemenceau, and Wilson—held major decisions in their hands; many others, however, had greater personal or national interests in the Middle East. Prince Faisal came to Paris to represent his father, Husain of Mecca, and his Kingdom of the Hijaz. Two groups of Armenians presented conflicting claims for their nation. Eleutherios Venizelos (1864–1936), the prime minister of Greece, sought to obtain Allied promises with respect to the Greek "Great Idea," that is, restoration of the Greek empire to include western Anatolia, Constantinople (Istanbul), and the Straits. Prime Minister Orlando of Italy intended to receive the Dodecanese Islands, southwestern Anatolia, and an area in and about Izmir.

Bankers, oil men, merchants, bondholders, missionaries, and humanitarians of sundry types also converged at Paris to lobby for their respective interests. Everyone was there except the Ottomans, although the grand vizir was permitted on one occasion to deliver a statement.

Zionists were able to incorporate a version of the Balfour Declaration in the peace treaties and gain approval of it from the new League of Nations. The Wilsonian policy of the right of national self-determination, however, seemed to block Zionist aims, since Jews constituted not more than 15 percent of the population of Palestine, and a policy of counting heads would have favored the Arab majority, possibly leading to Palestine's inclusion in a larger Arab state. As a result, Wilson proposed to the supreme council that a commission of inquiry go to Syria, Palestine, Iraq, and Armenia to obtain information about national self-determination. At first the French, British, and Italians agreed, but later they refused to cooperate. Therefore, President Henry C. King of Oberlin College and businessman Charles R. Crane, the American appointees, proceeded alone in the spring of 1919 with a staff of experts; their King-Crane report of late 1919 was suppressed because it ran counter to arrangements already dictated between England and France.

SAN REMO AGREEMENT

No permanent decisions regarding the Middle East could be reached in Paris in 1919. The signing of a peace treaty for the area seemed more uncertain than ever because of several factors, including the illness of President Wilson and the opposition of America to accepting a mandate for any territory. Russia was going through a civil war, while Germany and Austria were broken. And Italy was suffering from internal dissension and disillusionment. Questions of the Middle East, therefore, lay squarely between England and France. Meanwhile, armies of occupation governed the Middle East, whose peoples grew restless waiting for their fate to be decided. British forces under Allenby controlled Egypt, Palestine, and Lebanon; Husain and Faisal held sway over the Hijaz and inner Syria, including Damascus; and Britain controlled Iraq.

In the last months of 1919 British contingents in Lebanon were replaced by French units in accord with the Sykes-Picot Agreement. Arab nationalist opposition to this action, anti-Jewish riots in Jerusalem and Jaffa, the election of Faisal as king of Syria and of Abd Allah as king of Iraq by the Arab National Congress in Damascus, growing tension in Baghdad, and insurrection in Egypt—all drove Britain to realize that a treaty for the Middle East was now imperative.

One of the sensitive questions in the settlement between England and France revolved around the division of Mosul oil. The Sykes-Picot Agreement assigned the district of Mosul to France, but Britain pressed the French to allow Mosul to be attached to British-controlled Iraq. In February 1920, an agreement provided that France could buy 25 percent of the crude oil from Iraq. With this in hand the Allied negotiators journeyed to San Remo, Italy, where on April 24, 1920, they reached an agreement on oil, pipelines, mandates, and united action with respect to the Turks and Arabs.

Britain secured mandates for Iraq and Palestine, and France obtained mandates in Syria (and Lebanon); both Britain and France would be supervised by the new League of Nations in the administration of their mandates. Palestine included the lands on each side of the Jordan and extended to the Gulf of Aqaba; the Balfour Declaration was written into the mandate authorization. In addition to the oil understandings, France was given a free hand to deal with Faisal and the Arab Syrian kingdom with force—to crush them if necessary. At San Remo Britain and France also accepted the independence of the Hijaz under Husain of Mecca, although Husain rapidly rejected both the San Remo agreements and the Treaty of Sèvres as well.

THE TREATY OF SÈVRES

The San Remo agreements prepared the way for a peace settlement with the Ottoman Empire, and the Treaty of Sèvres was signed on August 10, 1920. This treaty gave Greece western and eastern Thrace, including Edirne and territory close to Istanbul, and Izmir for at least five years. Armenia was established as an independent state. Kurdistan, east of the Euphrates River, obtained local autonomy. Although Istanbul remained under Ottoman sovereignty, the Straits area was to be controlled by an international commission. The Ottoman Empire would maintain an army of only 50,000. Minority rights were to be respected. New, humiliating articles were added to the reestablished capitulations. And the Ottoman Public Debt Administration was given almost absolute control over economic, financial, and budgetary matters. Equally galling to the Turks was the announcement of the Tripartite Agreement among England, France, and Italy, dividing what remained of Turkey into three spheres of influence almost exactly along the lines marked by wartime secret treaties. The Treaty of Sèvres left Turkey prostrate.

As for the rest of what had been the Ottoman Empire, by this treaty the Ottoman sultan recognized the separation of Syria, Iraq, Arabia, and Egypt. A British protectorate over Egypt was allowed, and the independence of the Arab rulers and their states, subject to treaties of friendship with Britain, was accepted. Provisional independence for Syria and Iraq under a mandatory power was acknowledged.

The Treaty of Sèvres was obsolete before it was drawn, and because of its sections dealing with Turkish portions of the Ottoman Empire it was never fully ratified. Theoretically, then, final arrangements in the Middle East awaited the Treaty of Lausanne in 1923; yet divisions, boundaries, and the disposal of non-Turkish parts of the Ottoman Empire in that final treaty varied only slightly from the transfer of legal authority that was proposed at San Remo and Sèvres. The mandates bargained for at San Remo dictated Arab political and economic life for the next twenty years, and Britain and France immediately took action in their respective spheres.

There was one additional settlement in this era of treaties and engagements. In March 1921, Winston Churchill, who was then colonial secretary, held a lengthy conference in Cairo with most of the British Middle Eastern experts and especially T. E. Lawrence. They put Faisal, ousted by the French from Damascus, on the throne of Iraq and carved from the part of Palestine east of the Jordan the state of Transjordan for his brother Abd Allah, who originally had been promised Iraq. Since the British did not wish to be under any obligation to the French in getting oil out through Syria, a section of the Syrian desert was claimed for Transjordan. This created a British-controlled route from Mosul to the Mediterranean.

ENTENTE OCCUPATION OF TURKEY

The Entente powers took control of Istanbul on November 13, 1918, when a combined fleet dropped anchor in the Golden Horn; soon an Entente army entered the city. British, French, Italian, and American high commissioners assumed responsibility for the four zones established in the city. In this fashion the capital of the 600-year-old Ottoman state, under Muslim control since 1453, fell into the hands of foreign Christians.

Istanbul witnessed drastic inflation, but Greeks and Armenians there welcomed the Allies as liberators, who rolled back time to 1914: the capitulations were restored; the Ottoman Public Debt Administration functioned again; and concession hunting once more became the sport of the day. Tens of thousands of refugees of various nationalities and religions found refuge in Istanbul.

At first Turks were relieved that the fighting had ended, as they were genuinely weary of war. As the occupation proceeded, however, thoughtful Turks grew dismayed at the occupiers' lack of justice, understanding, and political wisdom. It soon became apparent that Sultan Mehmed VI (r. 1918–1922) and his ministers were only puppets. It also became clear that Anatolia would be carved up, if the Allies could agree on partition.

Britain moved northward from Mosul; France claimed southeastern Anatolia as an extension of Syria; and Italian forces landed at Antalya to assure that promises would be fulfilled. One of the tragedies of the time was initiated when Greek troops landed at Izmir to take possession of what the Greeks had been awarded in Paris. Supported by Britain and France, Venizelos began the Greek occupation on May 15, 1919. Organized Turkish resistance occurred almost immediately; Muslim Turkish acceptance of Christian Greek rule in Anatolia was impossible.

TURKISH NATIONALISTS

Following the Greek landing at Izmir, Mustafa Kemal, appointed as inspector general of the Third Army by the sultan, sailed for the Black Sea coast with orders to demobilize troops. Kemal resigned his commission and convened rebellious national congresses at Erzurum and Sivas, calling all patriotic Turks to join the Association for the Defense of Rights in Europe and Anatolia. Many former leaders of the Committee of Union and Progress and other nationalists had already formed local Turkish resistance organizations.

The Greek landing at Izmir produced extensive demonstrations and strikes in Istanbul. As the strength of the nationalists grew in the capital, many members of the Ottoman parliament in Istanbul openly supported the Turkish nationalist movement, so the British in March 1920 occupied the city. Nationalist leaders were sent to Malta. Then, in April 1920, a Grand National Assembly met at Ankara and elected Mustafa Kemal as its president—the Turkish resistance was now fully committed to fight for independence.

Mustafa Kemal and the nationalists in Ankara seemed to be in a hopeless situation. They faced the British in Istanbul and the Straits, the Greeks at Izmir, the Italians at Antalya, the French at Adana, the British in Kurdistan, the Armenians in the northeast, and a hostile Ottoman puppet sultanate in Istanbul. Fortunately for the Turkish nationalists, the enemy never presented a concerted attack, and they were able to meet them one by one.

At Ankara in 1920, Mustafa Kemal defied the victors of World War I. He commanded only the scanty resources of central Anatolia and the veterans of several scattered armies. However, the undefeated Ninth Army, which had operated in the Caucasus and marched to the Caspian Sea, served as his nucleus, and Kemal organized a force about them. Then the Turks under Kazim Karabekir captured Kars, Ardahan, and Mount Ararat from the Armenian republic; the Russian Bolsheviks gained control over the Armenian state, which was incorporated ultimately into the Union of Soviet Socialist Republics. In December 1920 Turkey ceded Batum to Russia in exchange for Russian acknowledgment of Turkish control over the provinces of Kars and Ardahan. A few months later the Treaty of Moscow confirmed this new frontier and pledged Russian aid. In the spring of 1920 the Turks drove the French back to Aleppo and signed an armistice removing them from the combat. In March 1921 Kemal reached an agreement whereby the Italians, in return for economic concessions, evacuated Antalya. Consequently, by the opening of the summer of 1921 Kemal faced only the Greek army and some weak British contingents on the Straits.

TURKISH-GREEK WAR

Since June 1920 the Entente allies, through British insistence, had assigned to the Greeks the task of enforcing the peace terms. Greek armies advanced in Thrace and Anatolia, taking in about a year Edirne in Europe and sections of western Anatolia. The only victories Kemal could show were two battles at Inönü, where Colonel Ismet (1884–1973) won lasting fame in 1921.

Time, however, was on Kemal's side. Britain was undergoing economic and political turbulence and wanted to reduce the size of its armed forces serving in the Middle East and to cut drastically overseas spending. Britain also quarreled with France over problems in Europe. A secret treaty of peace and friendship between France and the Turkish nationalist government was concluded in October 1921, with France hoping to gain economic advantages. Kemal was also aided by political developments in Greece when King Alexander died from the bite of his pet monkey in October 1920 and was succeeded by his father, Constantine, who was recalled from exile. The British distrusted King Constantine, while Turkish nationalists were obtaining war supplies from France, Italy, and Russia.

The Greek advance was checked by the three-week battle of Sakarya, which ended in September 1921. Stubborn Turkish resistance and extended Greek lines of communication decided the issue, although the Turks needed a whole year to regroup their forces for the victorious rush upon Izmir. After a Turkish victory in August 1922, the rout became general: Mustafa Kemal soon entered Izmir, and by September 19 all Greek forces were cleared from Anatolia. Mustafa Kemal won the title of ghazi, warrior for the faith and for the Muslim community, as the Turkish armies became victorious.

The war with Greece had been won, but intense bitterness remained. The Greek army in retreat pursued a scorched-earth policy and committed atrocities against defenseless Turkish villagers in its path. Shortly after the occupation of Izmir, fire broke out and destroyed nearly half of the city.

From Izmir the Turkish nationalists turned to the Straits. An armistice with the government of the Turkish Grand National Assembly was signed in October. Eastern Thrace with Edirne was ceded to the Turks, and the idea of a new peace treaty was accepted. Kemal had won; the British postwar policy for Turkey collapsed, taking David Lloyd George with it.

LAUSANNE CONFERENCE

Invitations to meet at Lausanne were issued both to Kemal and to the sultan's government in Istanbul, compelling the Grand National Assembly to pass a law deposing Mehmed VI. In November, the nationalists took over control of Istanbul, the sultan fled aboard a British cruiser, and the Grand National Assembly chose Mehmed's cousin, Abdulmejid II (r. 1922–1924) as caliph, but without the title of sultan. The Ottoman sultanate had come to its end.

Convening on November 20, 1922, the Lausanne Conference had a stormy course before its final acts were signed on July 24, 1923. England, France, Italy, Russia, Japan, Bulgaria, Romania, Yugoslavia, Greece, and Turkey participated in the deliberations and signed one or more of the several documents that were drawn up. Lord Curzon, the British foreign minister, dominated the conference; his tall figure was a sharp contrast to that of the Turkish delegate, Ismet, an Ottoman army officer and hero of battles against the Greeks, who was only 5 feet 4 inches tall. Ismet proved to be a stubborn yet skillful negotiator who knew that the Turks were willing to fight again if necessary to obtain independence, whereas the British had just sacked their prime minister rather than run the risk of further war. Frequently, when Lord Curzon would arrogantly deliver some advice, he would become infuriated almost to the breaking point when Ismet, who was a trifle deaf, would cup his bad ear and ask him in French to repeat what he said: "Répétez-vous, s'il vous plaît?"

At the Lausanne Conference eastern Thrace with Edirne went with full sovereignty to Turkey. Of the Aegean Islands, Tenedos and Imbros went to Turkey, the Dodecanese to Italy, and the remainder to Greece. The settlement with regard to the Straits gave Turkey sovereignty over the area; however, each shore would be demilitarized for 15 kilometers. The Mosul frontier was left to be negotiated at a later date. In regard to the Armenian and Greek minorities Turkey accepted articles similar to minority clauses inserted in treaties with Austria, Hungary, and Bulgaria, and the Greeks agreed to a compulsory exchange of populations, excluding the Greeks of Istanbul and the Turks of western Thrace. The capitulations were abolished entirely. Financial questions were settled by ending the Ottoman Public Debt Administration and by a proportionate assumption of Ottoman government debts by all successor states. Turkey agreed not to alter her tariff for five years. Ismet went home to Ankara with the knowledge that Turkey was recognized as an independent free nation, except for the demilitarization of the Straits and the undefined border with Iraq.

The exchange of populations between Turkey and Greece, begun in the summer of 1923 under the League of Nations, proceeded over many months. About 1 million Greeks and half as many Turks were moved, at considerable hardship to the individuals involved. The impact upon Greece was most serious. Turkey lost many merchants and businesspeople, but Ismet argued at Lausanne that such a loss would be more than offset by the advantages of a homogeneous and united Turkish nation.

The Treaty of Lausanne was ratified during the summer of 1923. On October 29, 1923, just nine years after the Ottoman Empire entered World War I, the Grand National Assembly in Ankara declared Turkey a republic and elected Mustafa Kemal its president.

IRAN'S POSTWAR PROBLEMS

While the British and their Greek allies were attempting to dominate western Anatolia, London also had dreams of a British zone that would extend from the Mediterranean to India. With Iraq and Palestine already conquered by 1918, Iran was the missing link. An Iranian delegation went to the Paris peace talks, but being anti-British, it was not permitted to attend or to state Iran's case, though Iran did join the League of Nations. A less hostile delegation negotiated and signed, on August 9, 1919, an Anglo-Iranian treaty, which virtually transformed Iran into a dependency of the British Empire. Iranian government departments, finances, and the army would be in British hands. Iran already received a monthly subsidy from Britain and would now gain a loan of £2 million; in return, her tariffs would be controlled by the British as collateral against the loan. The Iranian assembly (majlis) refused to ratify the treaty, and Britain withdrew its forces from Iran.

Communist Russia had denounced the capitulations and tsarist treaties with Iran. Soviet forces conquered formerly Russian Azerbaijan in 1920; while pursuing a tsarist general they also occupied Iranian territory north of the Elburz Mountains and refused to depart until all British military were evacuated. A Soviet Republic of Gilan was established, but Moscow alleged it had no authority over it.

Iran's protests to the League of Nations about Soviet intervention were fruitless, so Iran concluded an agreement with Russia in February 1921. The frontiers and independence of each country were to be respected; Iranian debts to Russia were canceled; all concessions were relinquished, except the Caspian Sea fisheries, since even Communists had to have caviar; and if a third power occupied any part of Iran, Russia might send troops. Russia then withdrew its troops from the Soviet Republic of Gilan, which promptly fell because of internal disputes and an Iranian military expedition.

The independence of Iran was confirmed by the rejection of the Anglo-Iranian treaty of 1919, the withdrawal of British troops, and the Soviet-Iranian treaty of 1921. However, Iran was still torn with strife and economic disorder. Disease, poverty, chaos, and corruption prevailed everywhere. The installations of the Anglo-Persian Oil Company were flourishing, but they were under the thumb of the British government. World War I left Iran in a seemingly hopeless situation.

This devastating war changed not only Iran but the whole of the Middle East in many ways. The rash Ottoman entry into the war sealed its fate, already challenged as it was by competing nationalisms. The Entente distribution of Ottoman lands, the British domination of Egypt and Iran, the continuing French-British-Italian control of North Africa, and renewed Russian Soviet annexation of the Caucasus and central Asia marked what seemed to be the total success of Europe, as the Middle East was incorporated into European-dominated world economic and political systems on terms dictated by the victors in World War I.

From 1919 to 1923, however, some Middle Eastern groups rejected the Entente's terms and brought about revisions in the postwar settlements. Popular uprisings among Arabs, political opposition expressed by the Iranian majlis, and, most remarkably, the vigorous military and diplomatic efforts of Turks succeeded in putting limitations on the dominance of Europe in the Middle East during the two decades following 1918.

References

Volumes cited in Chapters 21, 23, 26, 27, 28, and 30 are pertinent to this chapter.

AHMAD, FEROZ: "War and Society Under the Young Turks, 1908–18." *Review* 11 (1988): 265–286. An outstanding discussion by a leading authority on the topic.

BUSCH, BRITON COOPER: *Britain, India and the Arabs, 1914–1921.* Berkeley: University of California Press, 1971. A detailed account of World War I in the Middle East from the viewpoint of the British in India, using Indian archives.

————: *Mudros to Lausanne: Britain's Frontier in West Asia, 1918–1923.* Albany: State University of New York Press, 1976. A study of British policy in the area between the Straits and central Asia after the breakup of the Ottoman and Russian empires and the emergence of a new balance of power.

DADRIAN, VAHAKN N.: "The Documentation of the World War I Armenian Massacres in the Proceedings of the Turkish Military Tribunal." *International Journal of Middle East Studies* 23 (1991): 549–576. In this and other works the author carefully examines records establishing the involvement of the Committee of Union and Progress in the Armenian massacres.

DENOVO, JOHN A.: *American Interests and Policies in the Middle East, 1900–1939.* Minneapolis, Minn.: University of Minnesota Press, 1963. A thorough work that includes all aspects of American interests.

DJEMAL PASHA, AHMED: *Memories of a Turkish Statesman, 1913–1919.* New York: Doran, 1922. The autobiography of one of the Ottoman triumvirate during the war.

DYER, GWYNNE: "Turkish 'Falsifiers' and Armenian 'Deceivers': Historiography and the Armenian Massacres." *Middle Eastern Studies* 12 (1976): 99–107. An excellent sketch of some books on the Armenian massacres; shows the highly partisan nature of much written on both sides of the issue.

EDIB (ADIVAR), HALIDÉ: *The Turkish Ordeal.* New York: Century, 1928. Written by a woman who participated in the Turkish struggle for independence.

EMIN, AHMED: *Turkey in the World War.* New Haven, Conn.: Yale University Press, 1930. A basic study of the political, economic, and social forces in the Ottoman Empire during the war years.

FROMKIN, DAVID: *A Peace to End All Peace: The Fall of the Ottoman Empire and the Creation of the Modern Middle East.* New York: Avon, 1989. A popular account of wartime diplomacy, centering around British activities.

HELMREICH, PAUL C.: *From Paris to Sèvres: The Partition of the Ottoman Empire at the Peace Conference of 1919–1920.* Columbus: Ohio State University Press, 1974. Objective and very well organized topically and chronologically.

HOVANNISIAN, RICHARD G.: "The Historical Dimensions of the Armenian Question, 1878–1923." In Richard G. Hovannisian, ed., *The Armenian Genocide in Perspective,* pp. 19–41. New Brunswick, N.J.: Transaction Books, 1986. An able summary of evidence supporting Armenian claims of Ottoman guilt in the massacres as well as a general discussion of Ottoman-Armenian relations.

HUREWITZ, J. C., COMPILER, TRANS., ED.: *The Middle East and North Africa in World Politics: A Documentary Record.* Vol. 2: *British-French Supremacy, 1914–1945.* 2d ed. New Haven, Conn.: Yale University Press, 1979. This volume contains significant documents for this crucial period.

KEDOURIE, ELIE: *In the Anglo-Arab Labyrinth: The McMahon-Husayn Correspondence and Its Interpretations, 1914–1939.* Cambridge, England: Cambridge University Press, 1976. A thorough examination of the correspondence and the conversations, followed by a full analysis of the various interpretations and historical reports of them.

KENT, MARIAN, ED.: *The Great Powers and the End of the Ottoman Empire.* London: George Allen and Unwin, 1984. Seven authors evaluate the diplomatic history of the Ottoman Empire, Austria, Italy, Russia, Germany, France, and Great Britain from around 1900 to 1923.

KLIEMAN, AARON S.: *Foundations of British Policy in the Arab World: The Cairo Conference of 1921.* Baltimore: Johns Hopkins University Press, 1970. A first-rate account of this prestigious meeting, drawn from official sources.

LAWRENCE, T. E.: *Seven Pillars of Wisdom.* London: Jonathan Cape, 1935. The full story of Lawrence of Arabia's activities among the Arabs during the war; a literary masterpiece whose historical accuracy has been much debated.

MACFIE, A. L.: "The Straits Question in the First World War, 1914–18." *Middle Eastern Studies* 19 (1983): 43–74. In this and other studies, the author has carefully evaluated relationships between Britain, France, and Russia.

MONROE, ELIZABETH: *Britain's Moment in the Middle East, 1914–1971.* 2d ed. Baltimore: Johns Hopkins University Press, 1981. A comprehensive and classic survey.

MOOREHEAD, ALAN: *Gallipoli.* New York: Harper, 1956. The story of the famous campaign.

NICOLLE, DAVID: *The Ottoman Army, 1914–18.* London: Osprey, 1994. The illustrations and drawings in this short booklet are excellent.

OLSON, WILLIAM J.: *Anglo-Iranian Relations During World War I.* London: Frank Cass, 1984. An excellent treatment of British policy and Iranian governments up to 1920.

SACHAR, HOWARD M.: *The Emergence of the Middle East: 1914–1924.* New York: Knopf, 1969. A well-documented account of the area from a European rather than a Middle Eastern view.

SIMON, RACHEL: *Libya Between Ottomanism and Nationalism: The Ottoman Involvement in Libya During the War with Italy (1911–1919).* Berlin: Klaus Schwarz, 1987. A detailed examination based on Ottoman archival sources.

SONYEL, SALAHI RAMSDAN: *Turkish Diplomacy, 1918–1923: Mustafa Kemal and the Turkish National Movement.* London: Sage, 1975. A clear study of international diplomacy centering around the diplomacy of the nationalists. Based on primary sources in Turkish and western languages.

STIVERS, WILLIAM: *Supremacy and Oil: Iraq, Turkey, and the Anglo-American World Order, 1918–1930.* Ithaca, N.Y.: Cornell University Press, 1982.

STORRS, RONALD: *Orientations.* London: Nicholson and Watson, 1937. Storrs was the Oriental secretary to the British high commissioner in Egypt during the war.

SWIETOCHOWSKI, TADEUSZ: *Russian Azerbaijan, 1905–1920: The Shaping of National Identity in a Muslim Community.* New York: Cambridge University Press, 1985. An excellent account of political, military, and national history that includes the World War I period.

TAUBER, ELIEZER: *The Arab Movements in World War I.* London: Frank Cass, 1993. A thorough discussion of Arab nationalists and their connections with the Arab Revolt.

TOYNBEE, ARNOLD J.: *Survey of International Affairs, 1925.* Vol. 1: *The Islamic World Since the Peace Settlement.* London: Oxford University Press, 1927. By the renowned historian who wrote world historical studies, as well as works dealing with the Middle East.

TRUMPENER, ULRICH: *Germany and the Ottoman Empire, 1914–1918.* Princeton, N.J.: Princeton University Press, 1968. Largely based on German sources, this outstanding book discusses the alliance of 1914, the conduct of the war, financing, Armenian persecutions, German economic efforts, and political evolution of the alliance.

VITAL, DAVID: *Zionism: The Crucial Phase.* Oxford, England: Clarendon Press, 1987. An excellent account of Zionist internal organization and relationships with Britain and France from 1907 to 1919.

VON SANDERS, LIMAN: *Five Years in Turkey.* Baltimore: Williams and Wilkins, 1928. The record of a German commanding general stationed in the Ottoman Empire during the war.

WILSON, ARNOLD T.: *Loyalties: Mesopotamia, 1914–1917.* London: Oxford University Press, 1930. A record of the military occupation of Iraq by a British participant long active in that part of the world.

WILSON, JEREMY: *Lawrence of Arabia: The Authorized Biography of T. E. Lawrence.* New York: Atheneum, 1990. This lengthy work shows careful consideration of the controversial life of its subject.

Glossary

Some concepts, terms, and abbreviations are briefly defined here; for place-names and persons, see the Index.

abu   father of

adet   customary law and taxes, as opposed to shariah

aga, agha, aqa   generally a high-ranking officer; title of respect

Alids   descendants of Ali, the cousin of the prophet Muhammad, and their adherents

alim (plural is ulama)   a religious scholar, official, theologian

Allah   God

amir   prince, military commander, governor

amir al-umara   commander of commanders, supreme commander

anjuman   a society of Muslims, especially used in Iran

Aramco   the Arabian American Oil Company, in Saudi Arabia

ayatollah   a high-ranking Twelver Shiite religious scholar

b.   born; in the middle of a name this means son of, as in Ahmad b. Mustafa, or Ahmad the son of Mustafa

Bedouin   a pastoral nomad

bey   army officer, ruler, official; a title of respect

beylerbey   a high-ranking Ottoman soldier or governor

ca.   circa, about

caliph   a successor of Muhammad, the messenger of God, as leader of the Muslim community

capitulations   legal and tax privileges granted to foreigners

C.E.N.T.O.   Central Treaty Organization

chador   a woman's robe or dress, covering most parts of the body

d.   died

derebey   a valley lord, an Ottoman local leader

devshirmeh an Ottoman conscription system for Christian youths

dhimmi a protected non-Muslim

diwan (divan) a poetry collection; register for tax purposes; council

E.E.C., E.U., European Economic Community, European Union

fatwa a religious opinion issued by a mufti

futuwwa associations of youths and the ideals associated with them

ghazi a raider, a warrior for the faith of Islam

ghulam a male slave soldier and administrator, especially in Safavid Iran

hadith a saying or action of the prophet Muhammad

hajj pilgrimage to Mecca

Hamas an abbreviation for the Palestinian group, the Islamic Resistance Movement

hijrah the movement of Muslims and especially the prophet Muhammad from Mecca to Medina in the year 622

ijma consensus of the Muslim scholars

ikhwan a brotherhood, an organization of fellow believers, especially in Saudi Arabia and Egypt

imam leader in prayer; leader of the Muslims, especially used by Shiites

intifada shaking off, an Arab insurrection in Palestine

janissary an Ottoman infantry soldier

jihad inner struggle for religious improvement; holy war

jizyah a tax on non-Muslims

kanun (qanun) a law or regulation issued by a government and based on the opinion of a ruler

khan Turkish or Mongol chieftain, prince, ruler

khedive prince, especially used in nineteenth-century Egypt

khutbah sermon

kibbutz (plural is kibbutzim) a Jewish collective settlement, village

madrasah an upper-level Muslim school specializing in religion and law

Mahdi the rightly guided one, the Messiah

majlis political assembly, parliament, council

majlis al-shura consultative council

Mamluk a military slave soldier; a ruling system based on freed military slaves, especially in Egypt

mawla (plural is mawali) a client; a person brought into a tribe or group

mihrab niche indicating direction for prayer in a mosque

millet semiautonomous religious community in the Ottoman Empire

minbar a pulpit in a mosque

mufti a Muslim legal consultant who issues fatwas

mujtahid an interpreter of Islamic law

mullah (molla) religious teacher and leader; alim

N.A.T.O. the North Atlantic Treaty Organization

O.P.E.C. the Organization of Petroleum Exporting Countries

Orientalists western scholars of Islam and the Middle East

P.L.O. the Palestine Liberation Organization

Pan-Arabism an approach to Arab nationalism that argues for a large, inclusive Arab state to include all Arabs

Pan-Turkism an approach to Turkish and Turkic nationalism that argues for a large, inclusive Turkish state to include all Turks

pasha an Ottoman title, originally military

Phanariote a Greek Ottoman official

qadi judge

qizilbash pro-Safavid tribal and Sufi groups

r. reigned

ray personal opinion in Islamic law

reaya taxpaying subjects of the Ottoman Empire

rentier state a government that controls and distributes large sums of money derived from the foreign sale of oil

riddah apostacy or breaking away from Islam

sabra a native-born Israeli Jew

sadr a Safavid religious official

sayyid a descendant of Husain, the son of Ali and grandson of the prophet Muhammad; also a title of respect

shah king, emperor

shaikh a chief; a Sufi leader; an elder; also a title of respect

shaikh al-Islam the leading Muslim religious official; the chief Ottoman mufti

shariah the holy law of Islam; also the right path

sharif a descendant of Hasan, son of Ali and grandson of the prophet Muhammad

Shiite a Muslim who believes Ali and his descendants to be the rightful leaders of the Islamic community

sipahi an Ottoman cavalryman

Sufi a Muslim mystic; a mystical approach to religion

sultan the holder of power

Sunnite a follower of the sunnah—the custom, usual procedure, and behavior of the prophet Muhammad and his companions

surah a chapter of the Quran

tanzimat reforms, in particular those in the Ottoman Empire during the nineteenth century
themes Byzantine military districts

ulama plural of alim
ummah the community of Muslim believers
U.N. United Nations
U.S. United States

valide sultan mother of the sultan
vilayet an Ottoman province
vizir (wazir, vezir, vizier) a high-ranking deputy to the ruler

wafd a delegation; especially refers to an Egyptian political movement in the twentieth century
waqf (vakif; plural is awqaf or evkaf) an endowed charitable or religious trust

zakat a tax imposed upon Muslims for charity
Zionism Jewish nationalism

Index